Lecture Notes in Computer Science　　8837

Commenced Publication in 1973
Founding and Former Series Editors:
Gerhard Goos, Juris Hartmanis, and Jan van Leeuwen

Franck Cassez   Jean-François Raskin (Eds.)

Automated Technology for Verification and Analysis

12th International Symposium, ATVA 2014
Sydney, NSW, Australia, November 3-7, 2014
Proceedings

 Springer

Volume Editors

Franck Cassez
NICTA
Kensington, NSW, Australia
E-mail: franck.cassez@nicta.com.au

Jean-François Raskin
Université Libre de Bruxelles
Brussels, Belgium
E-mail: jraskin@ulb.ac.be

ISSN 0302-9743   e-ISSN 1611-3349
ISBN 978-3-319-11935-9   e-ISBN 978-3-319-11936-6
DOI 10.1007/978-3-319-11936-6
Springer Cham Heidelberg New York Dordrecht London

Library of Congress Control Number: 2014950907

LNCS Sublibrary: SL 2 – Programming and Software Engineering

Typesetting: Camera-ready by author, data conversion by Scientific Publishing Services, Chennai, India

Printed on acid-free paper

Springer is part of Springer Science+Business Media (www.springer.com)

Preface

ATVA 2014 was the 12th edition of the ATVA conference series. The purpose of ATVA is to promote research on theoretical and practical aspects of automated analysis, verification, and synthesis by providing an international forum for interaction among the researchers in academia and industry.

This year, 70 regular papers and six tool papers were submitted to the conference. The Program Committee decided to accept 29 papers. The program also included three invited talks and three invited tutorials given by Prof. Roderick Bloem (TU Graz), Prof. Ahmed Bouajjani (University of Paris 7), and Prof. Krishnendu Chatterjee (IST Austria).

Many worked hard and offered their valuable time generously to make ATVA 2014 successful. First of all, the conference organizers thank the 129 researchers who worked hard to complete and submit papers to the conference. No less than 279 reviews (four for each submission on average) were written by Program Committee (PC) members and their sub-reviewers in order to select the papers to be presented at the conference. Steering Committee members also deserve special recognition. Without them, a competitive and peer-reviewed international symposium like ATVA simply cannot take place.

Many organizations sponsored the symposium. They include: The New South Wales Government (Trade & Investment), NICTA, Red Lizard Software, and the University of New South Wales (UNSW).

Finally, we thank EasyChair for providing us with the infrastructure to manage the submissions, the reviewing process, the PC discussion and the preparation of the proceedings.

July 2014   Jean-François Raskin
                                                                      Franck Cassez

Organization

Program Committee

Ahmed Bouajjani	LIAFA, University of Paris Diderot, France
Franck Cassez	NICTA Sydney (PC Co-chair), Australia
Supratik Chakraborty	IIT Bombay, India
Alessandro Cimatti	FBK-irst, Italy
Deepak D'Souza	Indian Institute of Science, Bangalore, India
Hung Dang Van	UET, Vietnam National University, Hanoi
Giorgio Delzanno	DIBRIS, Università di Genova, Italy
E. Allen Emerson	The University of Texas at Austin, USA
Pierre Ganty	IMDEA Software Institute, Spain
Patrice Godefroid	Microsoft Research
Kim Guldstrand Larsen	Aalborg University, Denmark
Teruo Higashino	Osaka University, Japan
Alan Hu	University of British Columbia, Canada
Ralf Huuck	NICTA Sydney (General Chair), Australia
Joost-Pieter Katoen	RWTH Aachen University, Germany
Moonzoo Kim	KAIST, South Korea
Gerwin Klein	NICTA Sydney and UNSW, Australia
Orna Kupferman	Hebrew University, Israel
Marta Kwiatkowska	University of Oxford, UK
Insup Lee	University of Pennsylvania, USA
Oded Maler	CNRS-VERIMAG, France
Annabelle McIver	Macquarie University, Australia
Madhavan Mukund	Chennai Mathematical Institute, India
Mizuhito Ogawa	Japan Advanced Institute of Science and Technology
Sungwoo Park	Pohang University of Science and Technology, South Korea
Doron Peled	Bar-Ilan University, Israel
Andreas Podelski	University of Freiburg, Germany
Jean-Francois Raskin	Université Libre de Bruxelles (PC Co-chair), Belgium
Pierre-Alain Reynier	Aix-Marseille Université, France
Jie-Hong Rolland-Jiang	National Taiwan University
Jing Sun	The University of Auckland, Australia
P.S. Thiagarajan	National University of Singapore
Ron Van Der Meyden	UNSW, Australia
Rob Van Glabbeek	NICTA Sydney, Australia
Bow-Yaw Wang	Academia Sinica, Taiwan

Chao Wang   Virginia Tech, USA
Farn Wang   National Taiwan University
Karsten Wolf   Universität Rostock, Germany
Hsu-Chun Yen   National Taiwan University
Wang Yi   Uppsala University, Sweden
Wenhui Zhang   Institute of Software, Chinese Academy
                                     of Sciences

Additional Reviewers

Abate, Alessandro   Forejt, Vojtech
Abbas, Houssam   Fränzle, Martin
Akshay, S.   Fu, Hongfei
Almagor, Shaull   Gario, Marco
Asarin, Eugene   Greenaway, David
Atig, Mohamed Faouzi   Griggio, Alberto
Avni, Guy   Habermehl, Peter
Basset, Nicolas   Hashimoto, Kenji
Baudru, Nicolas   Heizmann, Matthias
Bayless, Sam   Hoenicke, Jochen
Ben-Amram, Amir   Hsu, Zeu-Chen
Bingham, Brad   Huang, Xiaowei
Bouyer, Patricia   Iosif, Radu
Bozga, Marius   Ivanov, Radoslav
Bozzano, Marco   Jansen, Christina
Bruintjes, Harold   Jovanovic, Aleksandra
Cai, Xiaojuan   K.R., Raghavendra
Chatterjee, Krishnendu   Kiefer, Stefan
Chen, Chien-An   Kim, Baekgyu
Chen, Sanjian   Kim, Yunho
Chen, Yu-Fang   King, Andrew
Chiang, Ting-Wei   Kwak, Taehoon
Cranen, Sjoerd   Köpf, Boris
Cuijpers, Pieter   Lee, Nian-Ze
Dalsgaard, Andreas Engelbredt   Li, Guiqiang
Decker, Normann   Mai Phuong, Nam
Degorre, Aldric   Maneth, Sebastian
Dehnert, Christian   Matichuk, Daniel
Deng, Yuxin   Mattarei, Cristian
Divakaran, Sumesh   Matteplackel, Raj Mohan
Do, Thi Bich Ngoc   Mereacre, Alexandru
Enea, Constantin   Mikučionis, Marius
Feng, Lu   Mover, Sergio
Fernandez, Matthew   Murray, Toby

Nguyen, Tang
Niebert, Peter
Noll, Thomas
Ogata, Kazuhiro
Park, Yongbae
Parker, David
Peyronnet, Sylvain
Pham-Ngoc, Hung
Prabhakar, Pavithra
Randour, Mickael
Roederer, Alex
Sangnier, Arnaud
Schanda, Florian
Sewell, Thomas
Shah, Simoni
Sighireanu, Mihaela
Song, Jiyoung

Srivathsan, B.
Talbot, Jean-Marc
Tonetta, Stefano
Truong, Hoang
Tsai, Ming-Hsien
Ujma, Mateusz
Wang, Shaohui
Wang, Yan
Wang, Yu-Chan
Wijs, Anton
Wu, Peng
Wu, Zhilin
Xue, Bingtian
Yi, Qiuping
Yuen, Shoji
Zucca, Elena

Abstracts of the
Invited Talks
and
Tutorials

Verification of Concurrent Programs: Decidability, Complexity, Reductions (Tutorial)

Ahmed Bouajjani

LIAFA, Université Paris Diderot (Paris 7) & Institut Universitaire de France
abou@liafa.univ-paris-diderot.fr

Concurrency is omnipresent in computer systems, at all levels, from applications relying on high level synchronization mechanisms and using abstract data structures, to low level code implementing concurrent/distributed data structures and system services over multi-core architectures/large-scale networks. The automated verification of concurrent programs is a challenging problem due to their highly complex behaviours.

We will address the problem of verifying automatically concurrent programs, from the point of view of decidability and complexity. We will show the difficulties that raise in addressing this problem in different contexts: shared-memory, message passing, dynamic creation of tasks, recursion, relaxed memory models, etc. We will overview existing approaches for handling these issues, and we will show in particular how verification problems for concurrent programs can be reduced to "simpler" problems (stated as reachability queries either on sequential programs, or on concurrent but sequentially consistent programs) for which there are already know verification algorithms and tools.

Automatic Correctness Checking of Implementations of Concurrent Objects (Invited Talk)

Ahmed Bouajjani[1,2], Michael Emmi[3], Constantin Enea[1], and Jad Hamza[1]

[1] LIAFA, Université Paris Diderot
[2] Institut Universitaire de France
[3] IMDEA Software Institute

Efficient implementations of concurrent objects such as semaphores, locks, and data structures (like sets, stacks, and queues), are essential to modern computing. Clients of these libraries assume that the latter are conform to reference implementations where typically operations are atomic, as it helps apprehending the library behaviors. However, in order to minimize synchronization overhead between concurrent object invocations, implementors of concurrent objects avoid blocking operations such as lock acquisition, allowing operations to be concurrently intertwined. Still, they must ensure that this relaxation is fully transparent to the client, that is, the interactions of the library with the client should be conform to his expectations. This is a notoriously hard and error prune task. Therefore, algorithmic methods for checking conformance between implementations of concurrent objets is in high demand.

Conformance is formally captured by the concept of *observational refinement*: Given two libraries L_1 and L_2, each of them implementing the operations of some concurrent object, L_1 refines L_2 if and only if for every (library-client) program P, every execution of P invoking L_1 is also possible when P invokes L_2 instead.

We address in this talk the problem of observational refinement checking. We investigate semantical and algorithmic aspects related to this problem, especially, we show the links between observational refinement and the linearizability correctness criterion, we examine the decidability and the complexity of this problem, and we present a new approach for efficient detection of refinement violations.

The Complexity Landscape of Partial-Observation Stochastic Games (Invited Talk)*

Krishnendu Chatterjee

IST Austria (Institute of Science and Technology Austria)

Two-player games on graphs are central in many problems in computer science, specially in analysis of reactive systems. Partial-observation games on graphs naturally arise when not every aspect of the reactive system can be observed (such as due to imprecision in sensors that monitor the system, or certain variables of the system are hidden). We study partial-observation stochastic games on graphs, where the objectives of the players are complementary (i.e., the game is zero-sum). Partial-observation games can be classified based on the information available to the players as follows: (a) general (or two-sided) partial-observation (both players have partial knowledge about the game); (b) one-sided partial-observation (one player has partial-observation and the opponent player has complete-observation); and (c) perfect-observation (both players have complete knowledge of the game). The one-sided partial-observation stochastic games subsume several important special cases such as one-player partial-observation stochastic games (or partial-observation Markov decision processes (POMDPs)) and probabilistic automata (or blind POMDPs). The classification of strategies based on the randomization available is as follows: (a) the players may not be allowed to use randomization (deterministic or pure strategies), or (b) they may choose a probability distribution over actions but the actual random choice is external and not visible to the player (actions invisible), or (c) they may use full randomization. We consider all these classes of games with reachability, and parity objectives that can express all ω-regular objectives. The analysis problems are classified as follows: (a) the *qualitative* analysis that asks whether there exists a strategy that ensures that the objective is satisfied with probability 1; and (b) the more general *quantitative* analysis that asks whether there exists a strategy that ensures that the objective is satisfied with probability at least $\lambda \in (0, 1]$.

In this talk we will cover a wide range of results that describes the complexity landscape for partial-observation stochastic games: for perfect-observation games [3, 13, 14]; for POMDPs [18, 1, 9, 15, 4, 8]; for one-sided partial-observation

---

* The research was partly supported by Austrian Science Fund (FWF) Grant No P 23499- N23, FWF NFN Grant No S11407-N23 (RiSE), ERC Start grant (279307: Graph Games), and Microsoft faculty fellows award.

games [11, 6, 17, 12]; and for general partial-observation games [2, 6, 7]. Recent surveys [3, 10] cover many of these results.

Acknowledgements. The talk is based on joint work with several collaborators, namely, Martin Chmelik, Laurent Doyen, Hugo Gimbert, Thomas A. Henzinger, Marcin Jurdzinski, Sumit Nain, Jean-Francois Raskin, Mathieu Tracol, and Moshe Y. Vardi.

References

1. Baier, C., Bertrand, N., Größer, M.: On decision problems for probabilistic büchi automata. In: Amadio, R.M. (ed.) FOSSACS 2008. LNCS, vol. 4962, pp. 287–301. Springer, Heidelberg (2008)
2. Bertrand, N., Genest, B., Gimbert, H.: Qualitative determinacy and decidability of stochastic games with signals. In: LICS, pp. 319–328. IEEE Computer Society (2009)
3. Chatterjee, K.: Stochastic ω-Regular Games. PhD thesis, UC Berkeley (2007)
4. Chatterjee, K., Chmelik, M., Tracol, M.: What is decidable about partially observable Markov decision processes with omega-regular objectives. In: Proceedings of CSL 2013: Computer Science Logic (2013)
5. Chatterjee, K., Doyen, L.: The complexity of partial-observation parity games. In: Fermüller, C.G., Voronkov, A. (eds.) LPAR-17. LNCS, vol. 6397, pp. 1–14. Springer, Heidelberg (2010)
6. Chatterjee, K., Doyen, L.: Partial-observation stochastic games: How to win when belief fails. In: Proceedings of LICS 2012: Logic in Computer Science, pp. 175–184. IEEE Computer Society Press (2012)
7. Chatterjee, K., Doyen, L.: Games with a weak adversary. In: Esparza, J., Fraigniaud, P., Husfeldt, T., Koutsoupias, E. (eds.) ICALP 2014, Part II. LNCS, vol. 8573, pp. 110–121. Springer, Heidelberg (2014)
8. Chatterjee, K., Doyen, L., Gimbert, H., Henzinger, T.A.: Randomness for free. In: Hliněný, P., Kučera, A. (eds.) MFCS 2010. LNCS, vol. 6281, pp. 246–257. Springer, Heidelberg (2010)
9. Chatterjee, K., Doyen, L., Henzinger, T.A.: Qualitative analysis of partially-observable markov decision processes. In: Hliněný, P., Kučera, A. (eds.) MFCS 2010. LNCS, vol. 6281, pp. 258–269. Springer, Heidelberg (2010)
10. Chatterjee, K., Doyen, L., Henzinger, T.A.: A survey of partial-observation stochastic parity games. Formal Methods in System Design 43(2), 268–284 (2013)
11. Chatterjee, K., Doyen, L., Henzinger, T.A., Raskin, J.-F.: Algorithms for omega-regular games of incomplete information. Logical Methods in Computer Science 3(3:4) (2007)
12. Chatterjee, K., Doyen, L., Nain, S., Vardi, M.Y.: The complexity of partial-observation stochastic parity games with finite-memory strategies. In: Muscholl, A. (ed.) FOSSACS 2014 (ETAPS). LNCS, vol. 8412, pp. 242–257. Springer, Heidelberg (2014)
13. Chatterjee, K., Jurdziński, M., Henzinger, T.: Simple stochastic parity games. In: Baaz, M., Makowsky, J.A. (eds.) CSL 2003. LNCS, vol. 2803, pp. 100–113. Springer, Heidelberg (2003)

14. Chatterjee, K., Jurdziński, M., Henzinger, T.: Quantitative stochastic parity games. In: SODA 2004, pp. 121–130. SIAM (2004)
15. Chatterjee, K., Tracol, M.: Decidable problems for probabilistic automata on infinite words. In: LICS, pp. 185–194 (2012)
16. Condon, A.: The complexity of stochastic games. I&C 96(2), 203–224 (1992)
17. Nain, S., Vardi, M.Y.: Solving partial-information stochastic parity games. In: LICS, pp. 341–348 (2013)
18. Paz, A.: Introduction to probabilistic automata (Computer science and applied mathematics). Academic Press (1971)

Multidimensional Quantitative Games and Markov Decision Processes (Invited Tutorial)*

Krishnendu Chatterjee

IST Austria (Institute of Science and Technology Austria)

Traditionally analysis problems for reactive systems have been studied with respect to Boolean properties (to specify correctness of systems). Recent trends in analysis of embedded systems require to analyse quantitative properties such as average success rate. We will present different reactive system models (such as game graphs, or Markov decision processes) with several classical quantitative (such as mean-payoff) objectives, as well as combination of quantitative and Boolean objectives. We will survey many recent results of game graphs [7, 14, 12, 13, 8, 10, 3] and Markov decision processes [11, 2, 5, 4, 6, 9, 1] with respect to the above mentioned objectives.

Acknowledgements. The talk is based on joint work with several collaborators, namely, Tomas Brazdil, Vaclav Brozek, Laurent Doyen, Vojtech Forejt, Hugo Gimbert, Thomas A. Henzinger, Marcin Jurdzinski, Antonin Kucera, Rupak Majumdar, Youssouf Oualhadj, Alexander Rabinovich, Mickael Randour, Jean-Francois Raskin, Yaron Velner, and Dominik Wojtczak.

References

1. Brázdil, T., Brozek, V., Chatterjee, K., Forejt, V., Kucera, A.: Two views on multiple mean-payoff objectives in markov decision processes. In: LICS, pp. 33–42 (2011)
2. Chatterjee, K.: Markov decision processes with multiple long-run average objectives. In: Arvind, V., Prasad, S. (eds.) FSTTCS 2007. LNCS, vol. 4855, pp. 473–484. Springer, Heidelberg (2007)
3. Chatterjee, K., Doyen, L.: Energy parity games. In: Abramsky, S., Gavoille, C., Kirchner, C., Meyer auf der Heide, F., Spirakis, P.G. (eds.) ICALP 2010. LNCS, vol. 6199, pp. 599–610. Springer, Heidelberg (2010)
4. Chatterjee, K., Doyen, L.: Energy and mean-payoff parity markov decision processes. In: Murlak, F., Sankowski, P. (eds.) MFCS 2011. LNCS, vol. 6907, pp. 206–218. Springer, Heidelberg (2011)

* The research was partly supported by Austrian Science Fund (FWF) Grant No P 23499- N23, FWF NFN Grant No S11407-N23 (RiSE), ERC Start grant (279307: Graph Games), and Microsoft faculty fellows award.

5. Chatterjee, K., Doyen, L.: Games and markov decision processes with mean-payoff parity and energy parity objectives. In: Kotásek, Z., Bouda, J., Černá, I., Sekanina, L., Vojnar, T., Antoš, D. (eds.) MEMICS 2011. LNCS, vol. 7119, pp. 37–46. Springer, Heidelberg (2012)
6. Chatterjee, K., Doyen, L., Gimbert, H., Oualhadj, Y.: Perfect-information stochastic mean-payoff parity games. In: Muscholl, A. (ed.) FOSSACS 2014 (ETAPS). LNCS, vol. 8412, pp. 210–225. Springer, Heidelberg (2014)
7. Chatterjee, K., Doyen, L., Henzinger, T.A., Raskin, J.-F.: Generalized mean-payoff and energy games. In: FSTTCS, pp. 505–516 (2010)
8. Chatterjee, K., Doyen, L., Randour, M., Raskin, J.-F.: Looking at mean-payoff and total-payoff through windows. In: Van Hung, D., Ogawa, M. (eds.) ATVA 2013. LNCS, vol. 8172, pp. 118–132. Springer, Heidelberg (2013)
9. Chatterjee, K., Forejt, V., Wojtczak, D.: Multi-objective discounted reward verification in graphs and mDPs. In: McMillan, K., Middeldorp, A., Voronkov, A. (eds.) LPAR-19 2013. LNCS, vol. 8312, pp. 228–242. Springer, Heidelberg (2013)
10. Chatterjee, K., Henzinger, T.A., Jurdzinski, M.: Mean-payoff parity games. In: LICS, pp. 178–187 (2005)
11. Chatterjee, K., Majumdar, R., Henzinger, T.A.: Markov decision processes with multiple objectives. In: Durand, B., Thomas, W. (eds.) STACS 2006. LNCS, vol. 3884, pp. 325–336. Springer, Heidelberg (2006)
12. Chatterjee, K., Randour, M., Raskin, J.-F.: Strategy synthesis for multi-dimensional quantitative objectives. In: Koutny, M., Ulidowski, I. (eds.) CONCUR 2012. LNCS, vol. 7454, pp. 115–131. Springer, Heidelberg (2012)
13. Chatterjee, K., Velner, Y.: Hyperplane separation technique for multidimensional mean-payoff games. In: D'Argenio, P.R., Melgratti, H. (eds.) CONCUR 2013 – Concurrency Theory. LNCS, vol. 8052, pp. 500–515. Springer, Heidelberg (2013)
14. Velner, Y., Chatterjee, K., Doyen, L., Henzinger, T.A., Rabinovich, A., Raskin, J.-F.: The complexity of multi-mean-payoff and multi-energy games. CoRR, abs/1209.3234 (2012)

Table of Contents

Verifying Communicating Multi-pushdown Systems via Split-Width 1
C. Aiswarya, Paul Gastin, and K. Narayan Kumar

Booster: An Acceleration-Based Verification Framework for Array
Programs 18
Francesco Alberti, Silvio Ghilardi, and Natasha Sharygina

A Bounded Model Checker for SPARK Programs 24
Cláudio Belo Lourenço, Maria João Frade, and Jorge Sousa Pinto

Acceleration of Affine Hybrid Transformations 31
Bernard Boigelot, Frédéric Herbreteau, and Isabelle Mainz

A Mechanized Proof of Loop Freedom of the (Untimed) AODV Routing
Protocol 47
Timothy Bourke, Rob van Glabbeek, and Peter Höfner

Quantitative Verification of Weighted Kripke Structures 64
Patricia Bouyer, Patrick Gardy, and Nicolas Markey

Formal Safety Assessment via Contract-Based Design 81
*Marco Bozzano, Alessandro Cimatti, Cristian Mattarei, and
Stefano Tonetta*

Verification of Markov Decision Processes Using Learning Algorithms ... 98
*Tomáš Brázdil, Krishnendu Chatterjee, Martin Chmelík,
Vojtěch Forejt, Jan Křetínský, Marta Kwiatkowska,
David Parker, and Mateusz Ujma*

Test Coverage Estimation Using Threshold Accepting 115
Thao Dang and Noa Shalev

On Time with Minimal Expected Cost! 129
*Alexandre David, Peter G. Jensen, Kim Guldstrand Larsen,
Axel Legay, Didier Lime, Mathias Grund Sørensen, and
Jakob H. Taankvist*

Fast Debugging of PRISM Models 146
*Christian Dehnert, Nils Jansen, Ralf Wimmer, Erika Ábrahám, and
Joost-Pieter Katoen*

ACME: Automata with Counters, Monoids and Equivalence (Tool Paper)   163
Nathanaël Fijalkow and Denis Kuperberg

Modelling and Analysis of Markov Reward Automata................   168
*Dennis Guck, Mark Timmer, Hassan Hatefi, Enno Ruijters, and
Mariëlle Stoelinga*

Extensional Crisis and Proving Identity...........................   185
*Ashutosh Gupta, Laura Kovács, Bernhard Kragl, and
Andrei Voronkov*

Deciding Entailments in Inductive Separation Logic with Tree
Automata..   201
Radu Iosif, Adam Rogalewicz, and Tomáš Vojnar

Liveness Analysis for Parameterised Boolean Equation Systems........   219
Jeroen J.A. Keiren, Wieger Wesselink, and Tim A.C. Willemse

Rabinizer 3: Safraless Translation of LTL to Small Deterministic
Automata..   235
Zuzana Komárková and Jan Křetínský

PeCAn: Compositional Verification of Petri Nets Made Easy   242
*Dinh-Thuan Le, Huu-Vu Nguyen, Van-Tinh Nguyen,
Phuong-Nam Mai, Bao-Trung Pham-Duy, Thanh-Tho Quan,
Étienne André, Laure Petrucci, and Yang Liu*

The Context-Freeness Problem Is coNP-Complete for Flat Counter
Systems   248
Jérôme Leroux, Vincent Penelle, and Grégoire Sutre

Efficiently and Completely Verifying Synchronized Consistency
Models   264
Yi Lv, Luming Sun, Xiaochun Ye, Dongrui Fan, and Peng Wu

Symmetry Reduction in Infinite Games with Finite Branching   281
Nicolas Markey and Steen Vester

Incremental Encoding and Solving of Cardinality Constraints   297
Sven Reimer, Matthias Sauer, Tobias Schubert, and Bernd Becker

Formal Verification of Skiplists with Arbitrary Many Levels   314
Alejandro Sánchez and César Sánchez

Using Flow Specifications of Parameterized Cache Coherence Protocols
for Verifying Deadlock Freedom....................................   330
Divjyot Sethi, Muralidhar Talupur, and Sharad Malik

A Game-Theoretic Approach to Simulation of Data-Parameterized
Systems   348
Orna Grumberg, Orna Kupferman, and Sarai Sheinvald

Nested Reachability Approximation for Discrete-Time Markov Chains
with Univariate Parameters 364
    Guoxin Su and David S. Rosenblum

Symbolic Memory with Pointers 380
    Marek Trtík and Jan Strejček

Trace Abstraction Refinement for Timed Automata 396
    Weifeng Wang and Li Jiao

Statistically Sound Verification and Optimization for Complex
Systems 411
    Yan Zhang, Sriram Sankaranarayanan, and Fabio Somenzi

Author Index 429

Verifying Communicating Multi-pushdown Systems via Split-Width[*]

C. Aiswarya[1], Paul Gastin[2], and K. Narayan Kumar[3]

[1] Uppsala University, Sweden
aiswarya.cyriac@it.uu.se
[2] LSV, ENS Cachan, CNRS & INRIA, France
gastin@lsv.ens-cachan.fr
[3] Chennai Mathematical Institute, India
kumar@cmi.ac.in

Abstract. Communicating multi-pushdown systems model networks of multi-threaded recursive programs communicating via reliable FIFO channels. We extend the notion of split-width [8] to this setting, improving and simplifying the earlier definition. Split-width, while having the same power of clique-/tree-width, gives a divide-and-conquer technique to prove the bound of a class, thanks to the two basic operations, shuffle and merge, of the split-width algebra. We illustrate this technique on examples. We also obtain simple, uniform and optimal decision procedures for various verification problems parametrised by split-width.

1 Introduction

This paper is about the formal verification of multi-threaded recursive programs communicating via reliable FIFO channels. This is an important but highly challenging problem. Recent researches have developed several approximation techniques for the verification of multi-threaded recursive programs (abstracted as multi-pushdown systems) and communicating machines. We continue this line of research. We propose a generic under-approximation class, and give uniform decision procedures for a variety of verification problems including reachability and model-checking against logical specifications.

We model the system as a collection of finite state machines, equipped with unbounded stack and queue data-structures. Thus, we get a faithful modelling of programs using such data-structures. They can also be used to model implicit features in a distributed setting, e.g., stack models recursion and queues model communication channels. Such systems are called stack-queue distributed system (SQDS) in this paper. The behaviour of an SQDS, called a stack-queue MSC (SQMSC), is a tuple of sequences of events (one per program/process). In addition a binary matching relation links corresponding writes (push/send) and reads (pop/receive). These were called stack-queue graphs in [20], run graphs in [15] and they jointly generalise nested words [1], multiply nested words [17] and Message Sequence Charts (MSC) [16]. An example is given is Fig. 1.

---

[*] This work is partially supported by LIA InForMel.

F. Cassez and J.-F. Raskin (Eds.): ATVA 2014, LNCS 8837, pp. 1–17, 2014.
© Springer International Publishing Switzerland 2014

These systems are Turing powerful, and hence their verification is undecidable. Several under-approximations [11,13,10,21,17,19,2,5] have been studied in the literature. SQMSCs form a class of graphs, and hence bounds on clique-/tree-width can also be used as an under-approximation, as they give decidability for model-checking against powerful MSO logic. Since SQMSCs have bounded degree, it follows from Courcelle's result that a bound on tree-width is necessary for obtaining decidability against MSO model-checking. In fact, a bound on tree-width is established in [20] for many of the known decidable classes. Thus [20] gives the first unified proof of decidability of reachability of these classes. In [15], a bound on the tree-width of the run graphs of restricted communicating pushdown systems is shown via hyper-edge replacement grammars.

We propose another measure called split-width, which is specific to SQMSCs (as opposed to generic graphs) and hence simpler. It is based on a divide-and-conquer decomposition mechanism[1] (or dually an algebra[2]) for SQMSCs, and provide a natural tree-embedding of SQMSCs. This way, every verification problem can be stated equivalently over trees, and hence can be solved efficiently.

Furthermore, split-width is as powerful as tree-width (see [7]), and the respective bounds lie in a linear factor of each other. Thus bounding split-width can also be seen as a way to bound tree-width, which is often a difficult task. A bound on split-width has been established for many known decidable classes in [8,7]. The systematic way of bounding the split-width helped in generalising these classes and in discovering new decidable classes.

As said before, split-width is a measure based on decomposing an SQMSC into atomic pieces. The atomic pieces are single events and edges linking writes and reads. The idea is to decompose an SQMSC by the repeated application of two operations: split and divide. *Split* chops the edge between neighbouring events and *divide* separates such split-SQMSCs into independent parts. We may need several splits before it can be divided, and the maximum number of such splits on a decomposition is its width. The split-width is the width of an optimal decomposition – one that minimises the maximum number of splits.

The above decomposition procedure can be abstracted as a term in an algebra. This gives a natural embedding of SQMSCs into trees, similar to how parse trees give a tree-representation for a word in a context-free language. The valid tree-embeddings of SQMSC with split-width at most k form a regular tree-language. Thus we can translate every problem (see below) on SQDS/SQMSC to an equivalent one on tree-domains.

We consider several verification problems starting from reachability. We use Monadic Second Order logic (MSO), Propositional Dynamic Logic with and without intersection (IPDL/PDL) and Temporal Logics (TL) as specification

---

[1] k-decompositions are a divide and conquer technique for bounding tree-width. The role played by edges in split-width is played by vertices there. Further, split-width decompositions are duplication free allowing us to reason about SQMSCs easily.

[2] Split-width algebra is in some sense a restriction of special tree-width algebra [6] resulting in decomposition trees where the matching edges occur at the lowest level.

languages. Satisfiability checking, and model-checking of SQDS against specifications given in these formalisms are also addressed.

With split-width as a parameter, we get *uniform* decision procedures with *optimal complexities* for *all* verification problems on SQDS/SQMSC. The complexities range from non-elementary for MSO to 2EXPTIME for IPDL to EXP-TIME for PDL/TL and reachability. However, the complexity is only *polynomial* in the number of states of the SQDS. Thus, if the bound on split-width is fixed a priori, then reachability is in PTIME.

Split-width was originally introduced in [8] as a technique to prove decidability of MSO model checking of multi-pushdown systems. In this paper, we generalise this notion to more complex behaviours involving multiple processes with several local stacks and queues and multiple channels between the processes for communication. In another dimension, we address more verification problems, for example model checking an SQDS against PDL. Finally, we describe a uniform approach to address these variety of problems simplifying the original proofs and constructions in [8].

2 Preliminaries: Systems and Behaviours

In this section we describe our formal model called *Stack-Queue Distributed Systems* (SQDS). Such a system consists of a finite collection of *processes* each of which having finitely many control locations. Further the collection has access to a set of stacks and queues. Each data-structure (stack/queue) is written to by a unique process (called its *writer*) and read from by a unique process (called its *reader*). For stacks we additionally require that the reader and writer are the same process. Such a system is a formal model of distributed multi-threaded programs communicating via reliable FIFO channels. The call-stack of one thread is modelled with a stack, while the reliable FIFO channels connecting the processes are modelled with queues. In addition, processes may use stacks and queues as local data structures, e.g. in task schedulers, in resource request managers etc. They can also arise when a process represents the global behaviour of a collection of distributed processes along with the channels interconnecting them.

An Architecture $\mathfrak{A}$ is a tuple (**Procs**, **Stacks**, **Queues**, Writer, Reader) consisting of a fintie set **Procs** of processes, a finite set of **Stacks**, a finite set of **Queues** and functions Writer and Reader which assign to each stack/queue the process that will write (push/send) into it and the process that will read (pop/receive) from it respectively. We write **DS** for **Stacks** $\uplus$ **Queues**.

A stack d must be local to its process, so Writer(d) = Reader(d). On the other hand, a queue d may be local to a process p if Writer$(d) = p =$ Reader(d), otherwise it provides a FIFO channel from Writer(d) to Reader(d).

A Stack-Queue Distributed System (SQDS) over an architecture $\mathfrak{A}$ and an alphabet Σ is a tuple $\mathcal{S} = ($Locs, Val, $($Trans$_p)_{p \in \mathbf{Procs}}, \ell_{\mathrm{in}},$ Fin$)$ where Locs is a finite set of locations, Val is a finite set of values that can be stored in the data-structures, $\ell_{\mathrm{in}} \in$ Locs is the initial location, Fin $\subseteq$ Locs$^{\mathbf{Procs}}$ is the set of global final locations, and Trans$_p$ is the set of transitions of process p. Trans$_p$

may have write (resp. read) transitions on data-structure d only if $\mathsf{Writer}(d) = p$ (resp. $\mathsf{Reader}(p) = d$). For $\ell, \ell' \in \mathsf{Locs}$, $a \in \Sigma$, $d \in \mathbf{DS}$ and $v \in \mathsf{Val}$, Trans_p has

- internal transitions of the form $\ell \xrightarrow{a} \ell'$,
- write transitions of the form $\ell \xrightarrow{a,d!v} \ell'$ with $\mathsf{Writer}(d) = p$, and
- read transitions of the form $\ell \xrightarrow{a,d?v} \ell'$ with $\mathsf{Reader}(d) = p$.

For an SQDS $\mathcal{S}$, by $\mathsf{sizeof}(\mathcal{S})$ we denote its number of states ($|\mathsf{Locs}|$).

Intuitively, an SQDS consists of a collection of finite state automata equipped with a collection of stacks and queues. In each step, a process uses an internal transition to simply change its state, or uses a write transition to append a value to the tail of a particular queue or stack, or uses a read transition to remove a value from the head (or tail) of a queue (resp. of a stack). The transition relation makes explicit the identity of the data-structure being accessed and the type of the operation. As observed in [1,17,8,20] it is often convenient to describe the semantics of such systems as a labeling of words decorated with a matching relation per data-structure instead of using configurations and moves.

This is also consistent with the usual semantics of distributed systems given as labelings of appropriate partial orders [23,13,11]. We now describe formally the structures that represent behaviours of such SQDS.

A Stack-Queue MSC (SQMSC) over architecture $\mathfrak{A}$ and alphabet Σ is a tuple $\mathcal{M} = ((\mathcal{E}_p)_{p \in \mathbf{Procs}}, \to, \lambda, (\rhd^d)_{d \in \mathbf{DS}})$ where $\mathcal{E}_p$ is the finite set of events on process p, $\to$ relates only events within a process, i.e., $\to = \uplus \to_p$ where $\to_p = \to \cap (\mathcal{E}_p \times \mathcal{E}_p)$, $\to_p$ is the covering relation of a linear order on $\mathcal{E}_p$, $\rhd^d$ is the relation matching write events on data-structure d with their corresponding read events and $\lambda(e) \in \Sigma$ is the letter labeling event e. We set $\mathsf{pid}(e) = p$ if $e \in \mathcal{E}_p$, and $\mathcal{E} = \uplus_p \mathcal{E}_p$. We also let $\rhd = \bigcup_{d \in \mathbf{DS}} \rhd^d$ be the set of all matching edges. We require the relation $< = (\to \cup \rhd)^+$ to be a strict partial order on the set of events. Finally, the matching relations should comply with the architecture: $\rhd^d \subseteq \mathcal{E}_{\mathsf{Writer}(d)} \times \mathcal{E}_{\mathsf{Reader}(d)}$.

- data-structure accesses are disjoint: if $e_1 \rhd^d e_2$ and $e_3 \rhd^{d'} e_4$ are distinct edges ($d \neq d'$ or $(e_1, e_2) \neq (e_3, e_4)$) then they are disjoint ($|\{e_1, e_2, e_3, e_4\}| = 4$),
- $\forall d \in \mathbf{Stacks}$, $\rhd^d$ conforms to LIFO: if $e_1 \rhd^d f_1$ and $e_2 \rhd^d f_2$ are different edges then we do not have $e_1 < e_2 < f_1 < f_2$.
- $\forall d \in \mathbf{Queues}$, $\rhd^d$ conforms to FIFO: if $e_1 \rhd^d f_1$ and $e_2 \rhd^d f_2$ are different edges then we do not have $e_1 < e_2$ and $f_2 < f_1$.

We denote by $\mathbb{SQMSC}(\mathfrak{A}, \Sigma)$ the set of SQMSCs over $\mathfrak{A}$ and Σ. An SQMSC over an architecture with one process and one stack is a nested word [1]. An SQMSC over an architecture with no stacks and at most one queue between every pair of processes is a Message Sequence Chart [16]. An SQMSC is depicted in Figure 1.

An event e is a *read event* (on data-strucutre d) if there is an f such that $f \rhd^d e$. We define *write events* similarly and an event is *internal* if it is neither a read nor a write. To define the run of an SQDS over an SQMSC $\mathcal{M}$, we introduce two notations. For $p \in \mathbf{Procs}$ and $e \in \mathcal{E}_p$, we denote by e^- the unique event such that $e^- \to e$ if it exists, and we let $e^- = \perp_p \notin \mathcal{E}$ otherwise. We let $\max_p(\mathcal{M})$ be the maximal event of $\mathcal{E}_p$ if it exists and $\max_p(\mathcal{M}) = \perp_p$ otherwise.

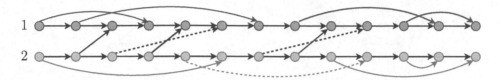

Fig. 1. An SQMSC over 2 processes, 3 queues and 2 stacks. Two queues form channels from Proc. 2 to Proc. 1, while the 3rd queue is a self-queue on Proc. 1.

A Run of an SQDS $\mathcal{S}$ over an SQMSC $\mathcal{M}$ is a mapping $\rho\colon \mathcal{E} \to$ Locs satisfying the following consistency conditions (with $\rho(\bot_p) = \ell_{in}$):

- if e is an internal event then $\rho(e^-) \xrightarrow{\lambda(e)} \rho(e) \in \text{Trans}_{\text{pid}(e)}$,
- if $e \rhd^d f$ for some data-structure $d \in \mathbf{DS}$ then for some $v \in$ Val we have both
$$\rho(e^-) \xrightarrow{\lambda(e),d!v} \rho(e) \in \text{Trans}_{\text{pid}(e)} \text{ and } \rho(f^-) \xrightarrow{\lambda(f),d?v} \rho(f) \in \text{Trans}_{\text{pid}(f)}.$$
The run is accepting if $(\rho(\max_p(\mathcal{M})))_{p \in \mathbf{Procs}} \in$ Fin. The *language* $\mathscr{L}(\mathcal{S})$ accepted by an SQDS $\mathcal{S}$ is the set of SQMSCs on which it has an accepting run.

The reachability problem asks, given an SQDS $\mathcal{S}$, whether some global final locations from Fin is reachable in $\mathcal{S}$? This is equivalent to the language emptiness problem for SQDS and is undecidable. We get decidability (cf. Theorem 9) for the bounded split-width reachability problem: given a parameter k, does $\mathscr{L}(\mathcal{S})$ contain at least one SQMSC with split-width at most k? The complexity of our decision procedure is only polynomial in sizeof($\mathcal{S}$) though exponential in k and $|\mathfrak{A}|$. We also obtain optimal decision procedures (cf. Theorem 16) for the bounded split-width model-checking problems wrt. MSO (non-elementary) and PDL (polynomial in sizeof($\mathcal{S}$), and exponential in k, $|\mathfrak{A}|$ and the formula).

3 The Split-Width Algebra for SQMSCs

The idea is to decompose each SQMSC into *atomic pieces*. We begin by removing some of the $\to$ edges to create holes which we call *elastic edges*. This operation is called *split*. We call an SQMSC with elastic edges a *split-SQMSC*.

After removing some $\to$ edges it is possible that the entire split-SQMSC consists of two disjoint parts with only elastic edges connecting them. At this point we may break-up this split-SQMSC into these two parts and then continue decomposing them separately. This operation is called *divide*. Our aim is to use split and divide repeatedly until we are left with the atomic parts, which are either internal events or an edge of the form $e \rhd^d f$. Figure 2a describes this decomposition on an SQMSC where the elastic edges are dashed ($\text{---}\!\!\rightarrow$).

For any such complete break up of an SQMSC, its width is the maximum number of elastic edges of all the split-SQMSCs produced. The break-up described in Figure 2a has width 2. There may be several ways of starting with an SQMSC and breaking it down into its atomic components. A different and somewhat more trivial decomposition with width 5 is described in Figure 2b.

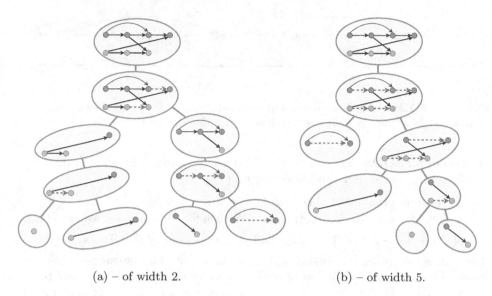

(a) – of width 2.   (b) – of width 5.

Fig. 2. Two decompositions of an SQMSC (consecutive splits are contracted)

The *split-width* of an SQMSC is the minimum width among all possible ways of breaking it up into its atomic parts using split and divide. A class C of SQMSCs has split-width k if each of its members has split-width at most k.

We begin by formalizing the idea of SQMSCs with holes. As explained above, it is done by identifying a subset of the $\rightarrow$ edges as *elastic edges* standing for holes which may be filled later (or dually for a part that has been removed). Then we describe the split-width algebra.

A Split-SQMSC is an SQMSC in which $\rightarrow$ edges are partitioned into *rigid* edges (denoted $\xrightarrow{r}$) and *elastic* edges (denoted $\xrightarrow{e}$). It is a pair $\mathcal{A\!\!4} = (\mathcal{M}, \xrightarrow{e})$ where $\mathcal{M} = ((\mathcal{E}_p)_{p\in\mathbf{Procs}}, \rightarrow, \lambda, (\rhd^d)_{d\in\mathbf{DS}})$ is an SQMSC and $\xrightarrow{e} \subseteq \rightarrow$. We let $\xrightarrow{r} = \rightarrow \setminus \xrightarrow{e}$ be the rigid edges of $\mathcal{A\!\!4}$.

The *elasticity* of a split-SQMSC is the number of elastic edges it has. A emphcomponent is a maximal connected component of the graph when restricted to only rigid edges ($\xrightarrow{r}$). For instance, the split-SQMSC on right has elasticity one, and three components.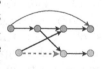

The Split-Width Algebra over $\mathfrak{A}$ and Σ is given by the following syntax:

$$s ::= (a, p) \mid (a, \mathsf{Writer}(d)) \rhd^d (a', \mathsf{Reader}(d)) \mid \mathsf{merge}(s) \mid s \sqcup\!\!\sqcup s$$

where $a, a' \in \Sigma$, $p \in \mathbf{Procs}$ and $d \in \mathbf{DS}$. We use *split-terms* to refer to the terms of this algebra. Note that, the binary operators $\rhd^d$ may only be applied to atomic terms. The operator merge denotes the dual of the split operation while $\sqcup\!\!\sqcup$ represents the dual of the divide operation. The terms of this algebra represent sets of split-SQMSCs (rather than SQMSCs) as there are many ways of shuffling together two split-SQMSCs (and also many choices for converting some elastic edge into a rigid one).

- $[\![(a,p)]\!]$ is the SQMSC consisting of a single event labeled a on process p.
- $[\![(a,p) \rhd^d (a',p')]\!]$ is the split-SQMSC consisting of two events, e labeled a on process p, and e' labeled a' on process p'. These events are connected by a matching edge: $e \rhd^d e'$. Moreover, if $p = p'$, these two events are also linked by an elastic edge: $e \overset{\circ}{\to} e'$.

The merge operator when applied to a split-SQMSC $\mathcal{M}$ returns the set of split-SQMSCs obtained by replacing one elastic edge by a rigid edge and is extended naturally to sets of split-SQMSCs. The $\sqcup\!\sqcup$ operator applied to two split-SQMSCs $\mathcal{M}_1$ and $\mathcal{M}_2$ returns the set of split-SQMSCs that can be divided into $\mathcal{M}_1$ and $\mathcal{M}_2$ and is once again extended naturally to an operation on sets.

Formally, $[\![\mathsf{merge}((\mathcal{M}, \overset{\circ}{\to}))]\!]$ contains any split-SQMSC $(\mathcal{M}, \overset{\circ}{\to}')$ such that $\overset{\circ}{\to}' \subseteq \overset{\circ}{\to}$ and $|\overset{\circ}{\to}'| = |\overset{\circ}{\to}| - 1$. The number of components and the elasticity decrease by 1 as the result of a merge. Further, $|\mathsf{merge}(\mathcal{M})| = \mathsf{elasticity}(\mathcal{M})$.

Let $\mathcal{M}_i = (\mathcal{M}_i, \overset{\circ}{\to}_i)$ with $\mathcal{M}_i = ((\mathcal{E}^i_p)_{p \in \mathbf{Procs}}, \to_i, \lambda_i, (\rhd^d_i)_{d \in \mathbf{DS}})$ for $i \in \{1,2\}$ be two split-SQMSCs with disjoint sets of events. Then, $\mathcal{M}_1 \sqcup\!\sqcup \mathcal{M}_2$ is the set of split-SQMSCs $\mathcal{M} = (\mathcal{M}, \overset{\circ}{\to})$ with $\mathcal{M} = ((\mathcal{E}_p)_{p \in \mathbf{Procs}}, \to, \lambda, (\rhd)_{d \in \mathbf{DS}})$ such that
- apart from the elastic edges, $\mathcal{M}$ is the disjoint union of $\mathcal{M}_1$ and $\mathcal{M}_2$, i.e., $\mathcal{E}_p = \mathcal{E}^1_p \uplus \mathcal{E}^2_p$, $\lambda = \lambda_1 \uplus \lambda_2$, $\mathsf{pid} = \mathsf{pid}_1 \uplus \mathsf{pid}_2$, $\rhd^d = \rhd^d_1 \uplus \rhd^d_2$ and $\overset{r}{\to} = \overset{r}{\to}_1 \uplus \overset{r}{\to}_2$,
- for each i, the order of the components of $\mathcal{M}_i$, as prescribed by the elastic edges $\overset{\circ}{\to}_i$, is preserved in $\mathcal{M}$: $\overset{\circ}{\to}_1 \cup \overset{\circ}{\to}_2 \subseteq \to^*$.

Note that, the number of components of any split-SQMSC $\mathcal{M} \in (\mathcal{M}_1 \sqcup\!\sqcup \mathcal{M}_2)$ is the sum of the number of components in $\mathcal{M}_1$ and $\mathcal{M}_2$.

Example 1. The tree on right depicts the split-term
$s = \mathsf{merge}(((a,1) \rhd^s (b,1)) \sqcup\!\sqcup (((b,2) \rhd^q (a,1)) \sqcup\!\sqcup (a,2)))$.
$[\![s]\!]$ has 18 split-SQMSCs , of which two are shown below:

We can easily check that all the split-SQMSC in the semantics $[\![s]\!]$ of any split-term s have the same set of non-empty processes, denoted $\mathsf{Procs}(s)$, the same number of components, hence also the same elasticity, donoted $\mathsf{elasticity}(s)$.

The *width* of a split-term s, denoted $\mathsf{swd}(s)$, is the maximum elasticity of all its sub-terms. For instance, the elasticity of the split-term s of Ex. 1 is two and its width is three. The *split-width* of a split-SQMSC $\mathcal{M}$, denoted $\mathsf{swd}(\mathcal{M})$, is the minimum width of all split-terms s such that $\mathcal{M} \in [\![s]\!]$. For instance, $\mathcal{M}_1$ and $\mathcal{M}_2$ of Ex. 1 have split-width two since they are respectively in the semantics of
$$s_1 = (\mathsf{merge}(((a,1) \rhd^s (b,1)) \sqcup\!\sqcup ((b,2) \rhd^q (a,1)))) \sqcup\!\sqcup (a,2)$$
$$s_2 = ((a,1) \rhd^s (b,1)) \sqcup\!\sqcup \mathsf{merge}(((b,2) \rhd^q (a,1)) \sqcup\!\sqcup (a,2)).$$

Remark 2. The split-width algebra over $\mathfrak{A}$ can generate any SQMSC $\mathcal{M} = ((\mathcal{E}_p)_{p \in \mathbf{Procs}}, \to, \lambda, (\rhd)_{d \in \mathbf{DS}})$ over $\mathfrak{A}$. In fact a sequence of shuffles of basic split-terms will generate a split-SQMSC $\mathcal{M}_1 = (\mathcal{M}, \overset{\circ}{\dashrightarrow}_1 = \rightarrow)$. This will then be followed by a sequence of merges to get the split-SQMSC $\mathcal{M}_2 = (\mathcal{M}, \overset{\circ}{\dashrightarrow}_2 = \emptyset)$.

Some classes of bounded split-width are given below. (See [8,7] for more involved classes).

Nested Words have split-width bounded by 2. This follows easily since a nested word is either the concatenation of two nested words, or of the form $a\overset{\frown}{\rightarrow}w_1\overset{\frown}{\rightarrow}b$ where w_1 is a nested word, or a basic nested word of the form a or $a\overset{\frown}{\rightarrow}b$.

Message Sequence Graphs are graphs in which the edges are labelled by MSCs from a finite set Γ. A path in an MSG generates an MSC $\mathcal{M} \in \Gamma^*$ by concatentation of the edge labels along the path. It is easy to see that all MSCs in Γ^* have split-width bounded by $|\mathbf{Procs}| + m$ where m the maximum size of an MSC from Γ. Indeed, let $\mathcal{M} = \mathcal{M}_1 \cdot \mathcal{M}_2 \cdot \ldots \cdot \mathcal{M}_n = \mathcal{M}' \cdot \mathcal{M}_n \in \Gamma^+$. We decompose this MSC recursively as follows: If $\mathcal{M}'$ is nonempty, then remove the $\rightarrow$ edges added at the last concatenation by splits, and then divide into $\mathcal{M}'$ and $\mathcal{M}_n$; recursively decompose each of them. If $\mathcal{M} \in \Gamma$, then it can be decomposed naively, with split-width bounded by its size.

Proposition 3. *Let G be an MSG over Γ and let $m = \max\{|M| : M \in \Gamma\}$. Then the split-width of any MSC generated by G is bounded by $|\mathbf{Procs}| + m$.*

In fact, MSCs generated from a finite set Γ are existentially bounded. This larger class also has bounded split-width as demonstrated below.

Existentially k-Bounded MSCs are those in which the events can be linearly ordered (extending the partial order $\leq$) such that the number of unmatched writes at any point is bounded by k. Let this linear order be denoted $\preceq$. We decompose an existentially k bounded MSC as follows. We split the $\rightarrow$ edge originating from the first $k + 1$ events in the $\preceq$ order. Let us call these events *detached* events. Among the detached events, we divide 1) all read events along with their partners (since the partner write event precedes the read, it is also detached), and 2) all internal events, as atomic pieces from the rest of the split-MSC. At this point, all detached events are writes. Since there cannot be more than k unmatched writes at any point, the number of detached events is strictly less than $k + 1$. Hence, we proceed by splitting more $\rightarrow$ edges in the $\preceq$ order until there are $k + 1$ detached events. Then we follow with the divide operation as before, and repeat until the whole MSC is decomposed. Thus,

Proposition 4. *Existentially k-bounded MSCs have split-width at most $k + 1$.*

4   Split-SQMSC to Trees

One key interest in defining the split-width algebra is that the class of k split-width SQMSCs can be seen as a regular tree language and that model-checking problems of this class can be reduced to problems on tree automata. As a first step we show how to encode SQMSC of bounded split-width as binary trees.

As it stands, each split-term s defines a set of split-SQMSCs $[\![s]\!]$. In order to reason about each split-SQMSC we decorate split-terms with additional labels so that each such labeled term denotes a unique split-SQMSC. The reason $[\![s]\!]$ is a set is that the operations merge and $⊔$ are *ambiguous*. For instance, the merge operation replaces one elastic edge by a rigid edge, but does not specify which. By decorating each merge operation with the identity of this edge we resolve this ambiguity. The shuffle operation permits the interleaving of the components coming from its two operands in multiple ways and we disambiguate it by decorating each shuffle operation with the precise ordering of these components. The key observation is that we only need a finite set of labels to disambiguate every split-term of width at most k. Our labels consist of a word per process, containing one letter per component indicating the origin of that component. At merge nodes we use letters m to denote that it is the result of a merge and i to indicate that it is inherited as it is from the operand. At a shuffle node we use letters ℓ to indicate it comes from the left operand and r to indicate it comes from the right. For instance, the figure on the right dismabiguates the split-term s of Ex. 1 to represent $\mathcal{M}_1$.

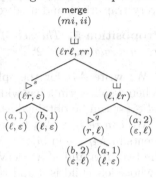

Fig. 3. A 3-DST

Consider the set of labels $L_k = (\{i, m\}^{\leq k+1})^{\mathbf{Procs}} \cup (\{\ell, r\}^{\leq k+1})^{\mathbf{Procs}}$. A k-*disambiguated split-tree* or k-DST is a split-term s of width at most k, treated as a binary tree, labeled by L_k, and satisfying some validity conditions. Hence, each node n of t corresponds to a subterm s_n of s, and we denote its labeling by $(W_p(n))_{p \in \mathbf{Procs}}$. We define simultaneously, the validity condition for the labeling at each node n, and the split-SQMSC $\mathcal{M}_n$ identified by this labeling.

1. If n is a leaf with associated split-term $s_n = (a, p)$, then $\mathcal{M}_n$ is the unique split-SQMSC in $[\![s_n]\!]$. We set $W_p(n) = \ell$ as a convention and $W_{p'}(n) = \varepsilon$ for all $p' \neq p$.
2. If n is a $\rhd^d$ node, then its children must be leaves n' and n'' and $s_n = s_{n'} \rhd^d s_{n''}$. Again, $\mathcal{M}_n$ is the unique split-SQMSC in $[\![s_n]\!]$. Let p' and p'' be the processes of the children. We let $W_p(n) = \varepsilon$ for all $p \notin \{p', p''\}$. If $p' = p''$ then we let $W_{p'}(n) = \ell r$, and otherwise we let $W_{p'}(n) = \ell$ and $W_{p''}(n) = r$.
3. If n is a merge node, then it has a single child n' and $s_n = \mathsf{merge}(s_{n'})$. In this case, there must be exactly one process p such that $W_p(n) \in i^* m i^*$ and $|W_p(n)| = |W_p(n')| - 1$ and for all other $p' \neq p$, we have $W_{p'}(n) \in i^*$ and $|W_{p'}(n)| = |W_{p'}(n')|$. Further, $\mathcal{M}_n$ is the split-SQMSC obtained from $\mathcal{M}_{n'}$ by merging on process p the component indicated by m in $W_p(n)$ with the next component. Clearly $\mathcal{M}_n \in [\![s_n]\!]$.
4. If n is a shuffle node, it has two children n' and n'' and $s_n = s_{n'} ⊔ s_{n''}$. Then, for each process $p \in \mathbf{Procs}$, we have $W_p(n) \in \{\ell, r\}^{\leq k+1}$ and $\#_\ell(W_p(n)) = |W_p(n')|$ and $\#_r(W_p(n)) = |W_p(n'')|$. Moreover, $\mathcal{M}_n$ is the unique split-SQMSC (if it exists) obtained by shuffling the components of $\mathcal{M}_{n'}$ and $\mathcal{M}_{n''}$ as indicated by $(W_p(n))_{p \in \mathbf{Procs}}$ and once again $\mathcal{M}_n \in [\![s_n]\!]$.

Clearly, the validity conditions above for k-DSTs can be checked with a deterministic bottom-up tree automaton. However, the above validity conditions are not sufficient, as the LIFO/FIFO policies on the data-structure may be violated at a shuffle, and hence its semantics could be empty. But we can modify this bottom-up automaton to check whether the shuffles respect the LIFO/FIFO policies. To this end, the automaton keeps a subset of $\mathbf{DS} \times \{1, \ldots, k\} \times \{1, \ldots, k\}$ in its state. If a tuple (d, i, j) is in the state labelling a node n, then it means that there is some $\triangleright^d$ edge from the ith component of $\mathsf{Writer}(d)$ to the jth component of $\mathsf{Reader}(d)$ in $[\![s_n]\!]$. This information can be consistently updated at every transition, and used to forbid invalid shuffles. Thus,

Proposition 5. *The set of k-DSTs is a regular tree language recognized by a tree automaton with $2^{\mathcal{O}(k|\mathfrak{A}|)}$ many states.*

We write $\mathcal{M}_t$ for the split-SQMSC described by the root of some DST t. When a split-term s has width k, it is not difficult to see that, any split-SQMSC $\mathcal{M} \in [\![s]\!]$ can be obtained as $\mathcal{M}_t$ for some k-DST t with associated split-term s.

We can recover $\mathcal{M}_t$ from t and hence *reason* about $\mathcal{M}_t$ using t. Clearly the events in $\mathcal{M}_t$ are in bijective correspondence with the leaves of t and we identify the two. If n and n' are leaves of t then $n \triangleright^d n'$ in $\mathcal{M}_t$ iff there is a $\triangleright^d$ node in t whose left child is n and right child is n'.

When is $n \xrightarrow{\mathsf{r}} n'$ in $\mathcal{M}_t$? The $\xrightarrow{\mathsf{r}}$ edge connecting them is to be found in some merge common ancestor of n and n'. We walk up the tree starting at leaf n tracking the identity of the component whose last event is n (this component may grow in size as previous components are merged with it), till a merge node x merging this component with the next is encountered. We also walk up the tree starting at the leaf n' tracking the identity of its component till a merge node x' merging this component with the previous one is encountered. These routes from n and n' are marked in red and blue in Fig. 3.

Clearly, $n \xrightarrow{\mathsf{r}} n'$ iff $x = x'$. It is easy to build a bottom-up tree automaton to carry out this tracking and to check if $x = x'$. This gives us the first part of the following Proposition. The second part follows from the observation that having found x one may walk down from there to the leaf n'.

Proposition 6.   – *There is a deterministic bottom-up tree automaton with at most $3k|\mathbf{Procs}| + 2$ states which accepts the set of k-DSTs t having exactly two marked leaves n and n' such that $n \xrightarrow{\mathsf{r}} n'$ in the split-SQMSC $\mathcal{M}_t$.*
   – *There is a deterministic tree-walking automaton with at most $2k|\mathbf{Procs}|$ states which has an accepting run on a k-DST t from leaf n to leaf n' iff $n \xrightarrow{\mathsf{r}} n'$ in the split-SQMSC $\mathcal{M}_t$.*

Remark 7. It is also possible to restrict Prop. 5 and Prop. 6 to k-DSTs that identify SQMSCs (as opposed to split-SQMSCs). An analogue of Prop. 6 can also be established for the relation $\xrightarrow{\mathsf{r}}^{-1}$ as well as $\xrightarrow{\mathsf{e}}$ and $\xrightarrow{\mathsf{e}}^{-1}$.

Reachability and Other Problems on SQDS We now use the above results to show decidability of reachability of SQDS parametrized by a bound on split-width. Our decision procedure is only polynomial in the number of states of the SQDS, while it is exponential in the number of processes, number of data-structures and split-width.

Proposition 8. *Given an SQDS S over $(\mathfrak{A}, \Sigma)$ and any integer $k > 0$, one can effectively construct a tree automaton $\mathcal{A}_S^k$ with $|\mathsf{Locs}|^{O(k|\mathfrak{A}|)}$ many states such that $L(\mathcal{A}_S^k) = \{t \mid t$ is a k-DST, $\mathcal{M}_t \in \mathscr{L}(S)\}$.*

Recall, from Sec. 2, that a run of an SQDS is just a labeling ρ of the events by locations. Our aim is to construct a bottom-up tree automaton that simulates such runs on any k-DST.

Let t be a k-DST. The events of $\mathcal{M}_t$ are the leaves of t. The bottom-up tree automaton guesses a possible labeling of the events (the leaves) and verifies that it defines a run as it walks up the DST. Actually, at each leaf e, the automaton guesses the location labels assigned to e as well as to e^-. Due to this double labeling, if e is an internal event then consistency can be checked immediately. Similarly, if $e \vartriangleright^d f$ then, by nondeterministically guessing the value that is placed and removed from the data-structure by transitions at these two events, the automaton checks for consistency. This is done as it visits the parent of these two nodes (labeled $\vartriangleright^d$). It remains to verify the correctness of the guess about the labeling of e^- at each e.

The correctness of the guess at leaf e is verified at the unique merge node m_e in the tree that adds the $\xrightarrow{r}$ (or equivalently $\rightarrow$) edge connecting e^- and e. Thus, the guessed location labels of e^- and e need to be carried in the state of the automaton till this node is reached. The key observation is that at every node in the path from e to m_e, e is the left-most event in its component and similarly, e^- is the right-most event in its component along the path from e^- to m_e. In other words, as the automaton walks up the tree, it only needs to keep the guesses for the first and last events in each component (in each process). The number of such events is bounded by $|\mathbf{Procs}|(k + 1)$, explaining the complexity stated in Prop. 8.

It is easy to maintain this information. At a merge node, apart from checking the correctness as explained above, the unnecessary labels (e/e^- if they are not the first or last events of the merged component) are dropped and other labels are inherited. At a shuffle node, the labels for each component are simply inherited. Finally, when the automaton reaches the root, there is only one component per process. The entire run accepts if in each process the location labeling e^- of the first event is ℓ_{in} and the tuple of locations labeling the last events of each process is a final state in Fin. In all this we have assumed that the automaton reads a k-DST, but that can be arranged using Prop. 5, completing the proof. As an immediate application we have the following theorem.

Theorem 9. *The bounded split-width reachability problem for SQDS over $(\mathfrak{A}, \Sigma)$ is* EXPTIME-*complete. The complexity is, however, only polynomial in the size of the SQDS.*

Reachability problem for S reduces to the emptiness problem for $\mathcal{A}_S^k$. Notice that an SQMSC $\mathcal{M}$ of split-width at most k is accepted by S iff *all* k-DSTs representing $\mathcal{M}$ are accepted by $\mathcal{A}_S^k$. Hence, the universality problem reduces to checking whether $\mathcal{A}_S^k$ accepts *all* k-DSTs representing SQMSCs, which is just the equivalence problem of tree automata. Finally, the containment problem reduces to the containment problem for associated tree automata.

Corollary 10. *The universality problem for SQDS and inclusion problem for SQDSs wrt. k-split-width SQMSCs are decidable in* 2-EXPTIME.

5   Further Results

We now describe logical formalisms for specifying properties of SQMSCs and we give optimal decision procedures for the satisfiability problem of these logics as well as for model-checking SQDSs against specifications in these logics, when the problems are parametrised by split-width.

Monadic Second Order Logic over $\mathsf{SQMSC}(\mathfrak{A}, \Sigma)$ is denoted $\mathsf{MSO}(\mathfrak{A}, \Sigma)$. Its syntax is given below, where $p \in \mathbf{Procs}$, $d \in \mathbf{DS}$ and $a \in \Sigma$.
$$\varphi ::= a(x) \mid p(x) \mid x \leq y \mid x \in X \mid x \to y \mid x \rhd^d y \mid \varphi \vee \varphi \mid \neg\varphi \mid \exists x\,\varphi \mid \exists X\,\varphi$$
Every sentence in MSO defines a language of SQMSCs consisting of all those that satisfy that sentence. Note that, for an SQDS $\mathcal{S}$ over $\mathfrak{A}$ and Σ, $\mathscr{L}(\mathcal{S})$ can be described in $\mathsf{MSO}(\mathfrak{A}, \Sigma)$. While the satisfiability and model-checking are undecidable for MSO, it becomes decidable when parametrised by split-width.

Theorem 11. *From any* $\mathsf{MSO}(\mathfrak{A}, \Sigma)$ *sentence ψ one can effectively construct a tree automaton $\mathcal{A}_\psi^k$ such that $L(\mathcal{A}_\psi^k) = \{t \mid t$ is a k-DST, $\mathcal{M}_t \models \psi\}$.*

By Prop. 5 and Remark 7 we may assume that the input is a k-DST representing an SQMSC. The argument is quite standard: construct the automaton inductively, using closure under union, intersection, complement and projection to handle the boolean operators and quantifiers. This leaves the atomic formulas. The formula $a(x)$ is translated to a tree automaton that verifies that x is a leaf and that it is labeled a and similarly for $p(x)$. The formula $x \in X$ is translated to a tree automaton that verifies that x is a leaf and belongs to the set of leaves labeled by X. $x \rhd^d y$ just requires us to verify that the leaves labeled x and y have a parent labeled $\rhd^d$. Finally, $x \to y$ is handled using Prop. 6.

As always, the combination of projection and complementation means that the size of the constructed automaton grows as a non-elementary function wrt. the size of the formula. Now, we examine other logics having decision procedures with reasonable complexity.

Propositional Dynamic Logic (PDL) is a well-studied logical formalism for describing properties of programs. As in a modal logic, formulas in PDL assert properties of nodes in a graph, in our case events in an SQMSC. Unlike a modal logic where modal operators only refer to neighbours of the current node, PDL uses *path modalities* to assert properties on nodes reachable via paths conforming to some regular expressions. Traditionally, PDL is used to express *branching-time* properties of *transition systems* (or *Kripke structures*). However, in the study of concurrent systems where each behaviour has a graph-like structure, PDL may be used to express properties of behaviours (i.e., linear-time properties of the system under consideration) as illustrated in [14,3,4]. PDL and its extensions with *converse* and *intersection* are studied in this sense here. The syntax of state formulas (σ) and path formulas (π) of $\mathsf{ICPDL}(\mathfrak{A}, \Sigma)$ are given by

$$\sigma ::= \top \mid p \mid a \mid \sigma \vee \sigma \mid \neg \sigma \mid \langle \pi \rangle \sigma$$

$$\pi ::= \underline{\sigma} \mid \to \mid \rhd^d \mid \to^{-1} \mid (\rhd^d)^{-1} \mid \pi + \pi \mid \pi \cap \pi \mid \pi \cdot \pi \mid \pi^*$$

where $p \in \mathbf{Procs}$, $d \in \mathbf{DS}$ and $a \in \Sigma$. If backward edges $\to^{-1}$ and $(\rhd^d)^{-1}$ are not allowed the fragment is called PDL with intersection (IPDL). If intersection $\pi \cap \pi$ is not allowed, the fragment is PDL with converse (CPDL). In simple PDL neither backwards edges nor intersection are allowed.

The formula p asserts that current event belongs to process p, and a asserts that it is labeled by a. The formula $\langle \pi \rangle \sigma$ at e asserts the existence of an e' satisfying σ and a path $e = e_1, e_2, \ldots, e_k = e'$ that conforms to π. The only paths that conform to $\underline{\sigma}$ are the trivial paths from e to e for any e that satisfies σ. Similarly $\to$ and $\rhd^d$ identify pairs related by the corresponding edge relation in the SQMSC. Finally $\cdot$, $+$ and $*$ correspond to composition, union and iteration of paths as in regular expressions.

The formula $\langle \to^* \rangle \alpha$ asserts that α holds at a future event on the same process while the formula $\langle (\beta \cdot \to^{-1})^* \rangle \alpha$ asserts that, β has been true at all the events in the current process since the last event (on this process) that satisfied α.

The formula $\langle \pi_1 \cap \pi_2 \rangle \alpha$ at an event e asserts the existence of an e' satisfying α, a path from e to e' conforming to π_1 and a path from e to e' conforming to π_2. For instance, the formula $\langle \rhd^d \cap (\to^* \cdot \underline{b} \cdot \to^*) \rangle \top$ holds at event e only if there is an e' with $e \rhd^d e'$ and b holds somewhere between e and e', all 3 events being on the same process.

Observe that PDL formulas have implicit free variables. To define languages of SQMSC with PDL we introduce sentences with the following syntax: $\phi = \top \mid \mathsf{E}\sigma \mid \phi \vee \phi \mid \neg \phi$ where σ is an $\mathsf{ICPDL}(\mathfrak{A}, \Sigma)$ state formula. The sentence $\mathsf{E}\sigma$ is true on SQMSC $\mathcal{M}$ if $\mathcal{M}, e \models \sigma$ for some event e of $\mathcal{M}$.

Decidability for MSO implies decidability for all the variants of PDL. However, we get more efficient decision procedures by working directly on it.

Theorem 12. *From any CPDL sentence ϕ one can effectively construct a tree automaton $\mathcal{A}_\phi^k$ whose size is $2^{O(|\mathfrak{A}|^2 \cdot k^2 \cdot |\phi|^2)}$ such that*

$$L(\mathcal{A}_\phi^k) = \{t \mid t \text{ is a } k\text{-DST}, \mathcal{M}_t \models \phi\}.$$

The idea here is to use alternating 2-way tree automata (A2A). For a PDL sentence $\mathsf{E}\sigma$ the A2A walks down to a leaf and starts a single copy of the A2A that will verify the formula σ. For each σ we construct an automaton $\mathcal{A}_\sigma$ such that $\mathcal{A}_\sigma$ has an accepting run from a leaf n if and only if the event n in the associated SQMSC satisfies σ. The automata for the atomic formulas $\top$, p and a are self-evident. For $\vee$ and $\neg$ we use the constructions for union and complementation for A2A. The case where $\sigma = \langle \pi \rangle \sigma'$ needs a little bit of work. Suppose π does not use any state formulas then we construct a finite automaton $\mathcal{B}_\pi$ equivalent to the regular expression π (over the alphabet $D = \{\to, \to^{-1},$

$\triangleright^d, (\triangleright^d)^{-1} \mid d \in \mathbf{DS}\})$. We non-deterministically guess an accepting run of $\mathcal{B}_\pi$, simulating each move labeling this run using the tree-walking automata given by Prop. 6 and Remark 7. Notice that each such simulation of a move from D begins and ends at a leaf. Finally, when reaching a final state of $\mathcal{B}_\pi$, we start a copy of the automaton $\mathcal{A}_{\sigma'}$. Checking state formulas in π adds no complication due to the power of alternation. To verify the formula $\underline{\alpha}$ we simply propagate a copy of the automaton $\mathcal{A}_\alpha$ at the current node (leaf). All this can be formalized to get an A2A $\mathcal{A}_\sigma$ of size $\mathcal{O}(k \cdot |\mathbf{Procs}| \cdot |\sigma|)$. We then use Vardi's result [22] to convert this into an ordinary tree automaton of size $2^{\mathcal{O}(k^2 \cdot |\mathbf{Procs}|^2 \cdot |\sigma|^2)}$.

The intersection operator in IPDL adds an additional level of complexity, since the path expression $\pi_1 \cap \pi_2$ requires that the tree walking automata propagated to handle π_1 and π_2 have to end up at the same leaf. However, the technique of [12] to decide IPDL over trees can be adapted to our setting as well. As in [12] this results in an additional exponential increase in size. The details of this construction is provided in a preliminary version of this paper [9].

Theorem 13. *From any ICPDL sentence ϕ one can effectively construct a tree automaton $\mathcal{A}_\phi^k$ of doubly exponential size such that*
$$L(\mathcal{A}_\phi^k) = \{t \mid t \text{ is a } k\text{-DST}, \ \mathcal{M}_t \models \phi\}.$$

Theorem 14. *The satisfiability problem for* $\mathsf{CPDL}(\mathfrak{A}, \Sigma)$ *over k-split-width SQMSCs is* EXPTIME-*complete. The satisfiability problem for* $\mathsf{ICPDL}(\mathfrak{A}, \Sigma)$ *over k-split-width SQMSCs is* 2-EXPTIME-*complete.*

Temporal Logics. Another reason to study PDL over SQMSCs is that it naturally subsumes an entire family of temporal logics. The classical linear time temporal logic (LTL) is interpreted over discrete linear orders and comes with two basic temporal operators: the *next state* ($\mathsf{X}\varphi$) which asserts the truth of φ at the next position and the *until* ($\varphi_1 \, \mathsf{U} \, \varphi_2$) which asserts the existence of some future position where φ_2 holds such that φ_1 holds everywhere in between. In the setting of SQMSCs, following [14], it is profitable to extend this to a whole family of temporal operators by parametrizing the steps used by *next* and *until* with path expressions.

The syntax of local temporal logics $\mathsf{TL}(\mathfrak{A}, \Sigma)$ is as follows, where $a \in \Sigma$, $p \in \mathbf{Procs}$ and π is a path expression:
$$\varphi = a \mid p \mid \neg\varphi \mid \varphi \vee \varphi \mid \mathsf{X}_\pi \varphi \mid \varphi \, \mathsf{U}_\pi \, \varphi$$
For example, $\varphi \, \mathsf{U}_\pi \, \psi$ asks for the existence of a sequence of events related by π-steps and such that ψ holds at the last event of the sequence and φ holds at intervening events in the sequence. The translation in PDL gives $\langle (\varPhi \cdot \pi)^* \rangle \varPsi$, where $\varPhi$ and $\varPsi$ are the PDL translations of φ and ψ respectively. When π is $\rightarrow$ it corresponds to the classical until along a process, and when π is $\rightarrow + \triangleright$ it corresponds to an *existential until* in the partial order of the SQMSC. We may also use backward steps such as $\rightarrow^{-1}$ or $\rightarrow^{-1} + \triangleright^{-1}$ and thus $\mathsf{TL}(\mathfrak{A}, \Sigma)$ has both future and past modalities. Hence, from Theorem 12 we obtain

Corollary 15. *The satisfiability problem for* $\mathsf{TL}(\mathfrak{A}, \Sigma)$ *over k-split-width SQM-SCs is* EXPTIME-*complete.*

Model-Checking. The k-split-width model-checking problem for a logic $\mathcal{L}$ determines, given an SQDS and a formula φ in $\mathcal{L}$, whether some SQMSC of split-width at most k accepted by the SQDS satisfies φ.

Theorem 16. *The k-split-width model-checking problem for MSO can be solved with non-elementary complexity. The k-split-width model-checking problem for CPDL and Temporal Logics are* EXPTIME-*complete. The k-split-width model-checking problem for ICPDL is* 2-EXPTIME-*complete. The complexities of these three problems are only polynomial in the size of the SQDS.*

We use Prop. 8 to construct $\mathcal{A}_\mathcal{S}^k$ from $\mathcal{S}$, and Theorems 11, 12 and 13 to construct from the formula φ a tree automaton $\mathcal{A}_\varphi^k$ that recognizes all k-DSTs representing SQMSCs that satisfy φ. The model-checking problem then reduces to the emptiness of the intersection of the tree automata $\mathcal{A}_\varphi^k$ and $\mathcal{A}_\mathcal{S}^k$.

6 Discussions

Optimal Complexities of the Decision Procedures. The PTIME hardness on the size of the SQDS follows from the PTIME hardness of the emptiness checking of nested-word automata, since nested-words have split-width bounded by 2. The hardness wrt. size of the (ϵ,C,IC)PDL formula follows from the corresponding case of nested words [3] (or equivalently trees [12]). The hardness wrt. the bound on split-width is a consequence of the following facts. 1. Reachability problem can be reduced to both satisfiability problem and model-checking problem of temporal logics. 2. Satisfiability and model-checking problems of temporal logics reduce to the corresponding problems of PDL and MSO. 3. Split-width of m-phase bounded multi-pushdown systems is bounded by 2^m [8]. 4. Reachability of bounded phase multi-pushdown systems is 2ETIME-hard [18].

Further Optimisations. A split-term is almost a path if one operand of any shuffle node is an atomic piece (or a subterm whose size is bounded by an a priori fixed constant). Such split-terms are said to be *word-like*. If a class admits bounded split-width via word-like decompositions, then we can obtain a better space complexity for our procedures by using finite state word-automata instead of tree-automata. Thus, the complexity for reachability in this case would be only NLOGSPACE in the number of states of the SQDS though PSPACE in $\mathfrak{A}$ and the bound on split-width. It would be PSPACE in the size of the PDL and temporal logic formula for model-checking, matching the lower bounds for the case of words. The class of SQMSCs having split-width bounded via word-like split-terms subsume interesting classes, like existentially k-bounded MSCs since the decomposition given on page 8 yields word like split-terms.

Bag Data-Structure. We could have added bags as a possible data-structure and extended our definition of systems and behaviours accordingly. For a discussion of such systems and associated results, the reader is referred to a preliminary version of this paper [9].

Acknowledgement. We thank Benedikt Bollig for many helpful comments.

References

1. Alur, R., Madhusudan, P.: Adding nesting structure to words. Journal of the ACM 56(3), 1–43 (2009)
2. Atig, M.F., Bollig, B., Habermehl, P.: Emptiness of multi-pushdown automata is 2ETIME-Complete. In: Ito, M., Toyama, M. (eds.) DLT 2008. LNCS, vol. 5257, pp. 121–133. Springer, Heidelberg (2008)
3. Bollig, B., Cyriac, A., Gastin, P., Zeitoun, M.: Temporal logics for concurrent recursive programs: Satisfiability and model checking. In: Murlak, F., Sankowski, P. (eds.) MFCS 2011. LNCS, vol. 6907, pp. 132–144. Springer, Heidelberg (2011)
4. Bollig, B., Kuske, D., Meinecke, I.: Propositional dynamic logic for message-passing systems. Logical Methods in Computer Science 6(3:16) (2010)
5. Breveglieri, L., Cherubini, A., Citrini, C., Crespi-Reghizzi, S.: Multi-pushdown languages and grammars. Int. J. Found. Comput. Sci. 7(3), 253–292 (1996)
6. Courcelle, B.: Special tree-width and the verification of monadic second-order graph properties. In: FSTTCS. LIPIcs, vol. 8, pp. 13–29 (2010)
7. Cyriac, A.: Verification of Communicating Recursive Programs via Split-width. PhD thesis, ENS Cachan (2014),
   http://www.lsv.ens-cachan.fr/~cyriac/download/
   Thesis_Aiswarya_Cyriac.pdf
8. Cyriac, A., Gastin, P., Narayan Kumar, K.: MSO decidability of multi-pushdown systems via split-width. In: Koutny, M., Ulidowski, I. (eds.) CONCUR 2012. LNCS, vol. 7454, pp. 547–561. Springer, Heidelberg (2012)
9. Cyriac, A., Gastin, P., Narayan Kumar, K.: Verifying Communicating Multi-pushdown Systems. Technical report (January 2014),
   http://hal.archives-ouvertes.fr/hal-00943690
10. Ganty, P., Majumdar, R., Monmege, B.: Bounded underapproximations. Formal Methods in System Design 40(2), 206–231 (2012)
11. Genest, B., Kuske, D., Muscholl, A.: A Kleene theorem and model checking algorithms for existentially bounded communicating automata. Inf. Comput. 204(6), 920–956 (2006)
12. Göller, S., Lohrey, M., Lutz, C.: PDL with intersection and converse: satisfiability and infinite-state model checking. J. Symb. Log. 74(1), 279–314 (2009)
13. Henriksen, J.G., Mukund, M., Narayan Kumar, K., Sohoni, M.A., Thiagarajan, P.S.: A theory of regular MSC languages. Inf. Comput. 202(1), 1–38 (2005)
14. Henriksen, J.G., Thiagarajan, P.S.: Dynamic linear time temporal logic. Ann. Pure Appl. Logic 96(1-3), 187–207 (1999)
15. Heußner, A.: Model checking communicating processes: Run graphs, graph grammars, and MSO. ECEASST 47 (2012)
16. ITU-TS. ITU-TS Recommendation Z.120: Message Sequence Chart (MSC). ITU-TS, Geneva (February 2011)
17. La Torre, S., Madhusudan, P., Parlato, G.: A robust class of context-sensitive languages. In: LICS, pp. 161–170. IEEE Computer Society (2007)
18. La Torre, S., Madhusudan, P., Parlato, G.: An infinite automaton characterization of double exponential time. In: Kaminski, M., Martini, S. (eds.) CSL 2008. LNCS, vol. 5213, pp. 33–48. Springer, Heidelberg (2008)

19. La Torre, S., Napoli, M.: Reachability of multistack pushdown systems with scope-bounded matching relations. In: Katoen, J.-P., König, B. (eds.) CONCUR 2011. LNCS, vol. 6901, pp. 203–218. Springer, Heidelberg (2011)
20. Madhusudan, P., Parlato, G.: The tree width of auxiliary storage. In: Ball, T., Sagiv, M. (eds.) POPL, pp. 283–294. ACM (2011)
21. Qadeer, S., Rehof, J.: Context-bounded model checking of concurrent software. In: Halbwachs, N., Zuck, L.D. (eds.) TACAS 2005. LNCS, vol. 3440, pp. 93–107. Springer, Heidelberg (2005)
22. Vardi, M.Y.: The taming of converse: Reasoning about two-way computations. In: Parikh, R. (ed.) Logics of Programs. LNCS, vol. 193, pp. 413–423. Springer, Heidelberg (1985)
23. Zielonka, W.: Notes on finite asynchronous automata. R.A.I.R.O. — Informatique Théorique et Applications 21, 99–135 (1987)

Booster: An Acceleration-Based Verification Framework for Array Programs[*]

Francesco Alberti[1,3], Silvio Ghilardi[2], and Natasha Sharygina[1]

[1] University of Lugano, Lugano, Switzerland
[2] Università degli Studi di Milano, Milan, Italy
[3] VERIMAG, Grenoble, France

Abstract. We present BOOSTER, a new framework developed for verifying programs handling arrays. BOOSTER integrates new acceleration features with standard verification techniques, like Lazy Abstraction with Interpolants (extended to arrays). The new acceleration features are the key for scaling-up in the verification of programs with arrays, allowing BOOSTER to efficiently generate required quantified safe inductive invariants attesting the safety of the input code.

1 Introduction

In this paper we present BOOSTER, a tool for the verification of software systems handling arrays. The novelty of BOOSTER with respect to other tools supporting array analysis [7, 10, 11, 13, 14, 17] is its being based on *acceleration* procedures.

Acceleration procedures target the generation of the transitive closure of relations encoding system evolution. In our case, acceleration is applied to relations encoding loops of the analyzed program. With respect to abstraction-based procedures, acceleration offers a *precise* solution (not involving over-approximations) to the problem of computing the reachable state-space of a transition system, but on the other side has syntactic restrictions preventing its general application. On the other side, abstraction-based solutions are usually a very general framework, but they also require heuristics (and in some cases even user guidance) in order to increase their practical effectiveness. As an example, the *Lazy Abstraction with Interpolants* one (LAWI [3, 18]), which has been shown to be one of the most effective abstraction-based framework in verification [8], relies on Craig interpolants for refining the level of abstraction. Craig interpolants, however, are not unique, and it has been shown that different interpolants might seriously affects the performance of the verification task [19].

BOOSTER exploits acceleration in two different ways. Accelerations of loops falling in decidable fragments are handled precisely, following the schema presented in [6]. Those requiring over-approximations and suitable refinement procedures (as discussed in [5]) are handled by an improved version of the MCMT model-checker [15], the fixpoint engine integrated in BOOSTER.

[*] The work of the first author was supported by Swiss National Science Foundation under grant no. P1TIP2_152261.

F. Cassez and J.-F. Raskin (Eds.): ATVA 2014, LNCS 8837, pp. 18–23, 2014.
© Springer International Publishing Switzerland 2014

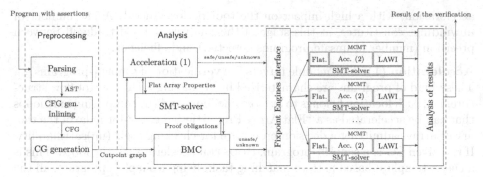

Fig. 1. The architecture of BOOSTER

The architecture of BOOSTER, detailed in the next section, is structured according to the standard compilers architecture, where the initial parsing phase generates an intermediate representation of the code which is subject to several optimizations before being fed to an engine for checking its safety. From this point of view, acceleration can be viewed as the most important and distinguishing optimization of our approach, while an abstraction-based module acts as the engine performing the analysis.

Our experimental evaluation, performed on a benchmark suite comprising programs with arrays selected from heterogeneous sources, attests the effectiveness of our new tool and the impressive benefits brought by acceleration procedures.

2   The Tool

BOOSTER is written in C++, and it is available at http://www.inf.usi.ch/phd/alberti/prj/booster/. Fig. 1 depicts its architecture. In this section we describe the features implemented in BOOSTER.

Preprocessing. Given a program, BOOSTER generates its control-flow graph (CFG) and inlines procedure calls. From the CFG, BOOSTER builds the *cutpoint graph* (CG) of the input program [16]. A cutpoint graph is a graph-representation of the input code where each vertex represents either the entry/exit block of the program or a loop-head, and the edges are labeled with sequences of assumptions or assignments. The representation of the input code as a cutpoint graph is extremely beneficial for applying acceleration techniques, and it is adopted to maximize the application of acceleration procedures. Indeed, acceleration techniques for code handling arrays can be applied only to transitions representing self-loops (and matching some other syntactic patterns [5,6]).

BMC. This module has been devised as a preliminary rather rough analysis: BOOSTER adopts a Bounded Model Checking approach [9] at the very beginning of the analysis in order to detect unsafe programs *before* enabling analysis (like acceleration) with a high impact on the tool performances[1]. A low number of unwindings constitutes, at this stage of the analysis, a good trade-off between precision (number of unsafe programs detected) and efficiency.

Acceleration (1). This module targets the verification of simple_A^0-programs [6]. These kind of programs are characterized by (i) having a flat control-flow structure, i.e., each location belongs to at most one loop, and (ii) comprising only loops that can be accelerated as a "Flat Array Properties", i.e., $\exists\forall$-formulæ of the theory of arrays admitting a decision procedure for checking their (un)satisfiability. If the given CG is a simple_A^0-program, BOOSTER accelerates all the loops. This is a cheap template-based pattern matching task: being a simple_A^0-program, all the loops of the program match the pattern given in [6]. The loops are substituted with their accelerated counterparts; subsequently BOOSTER generates the proof-obligations, which are Flat Array Properties, required to check the (un)safety of the program. Unfortunately, this fragment is not entirely covered by decision procedures implemented in available SMT-solvers. In practice, BOOSTER relies on the Z3 SMT-solver [12] for solving such queries. The SMT-solver is usually very efficient on unsatisfiable proof obligations, but might struggle on satisfiable ones. The BMC analysis executed before this module, however, is generally able to find the corresponding traces, reporting the unsafety of the code before starting this acceleration procedure. It is also important to notice that, at this stage of the analysis, BOOSTER exploits the *full power* of acceleration on a well-defined class of transitions, i.e., the loops of simple_A^0-programs.

Transition System Generation. If the program is not a simple_A^0-program or the SMT-solver exploited by the "Acceleration (1)" module times out, the CG of the program is translated into a transition system and then fed into MCMT.

MCMTv2.5 MCMT is a model-checker based on a backward reachability analysis approach for array-based transition systems, formal models suitable for the representation of many classes of real systems, including programs with arrays. MCMT is written in C and available at http://users.mat.unimi.it/users/ghilardi/mcmt/. The version of MCMT included in BOOSTER extends the previous version [15] implementing (i) the new Lazy Abstraction with Interpolants (LAWI) for Arrays approach [1] and (ii) acceleration procedures for array relations [5] (this also differentiates MCMT from SAFARI [2]).

Flattening. Flattening is a preprocessing technique exploited inside MCMT to reduce the transition formulæ and state formulæ to a format where array variables are indexed only by existentially quantified variables. It is based on the rewriting rule $\phi(a[t], ...) \rightsquigarrow \exists x(x = t \wedge \phi(a[x], ...))$. This format is particularly indicated for inferring *quantified* predicates within the LAWI framework and it is exploited by the *term abstraction* heuristic [2].

---

[1] Formulæ generated by the "Acceleration (1)" module contain alternation of quantifiers and it has been proven that checking their satisfiability may be a NExpTime-complete problem [6].

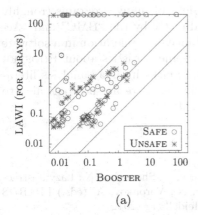

BENCHMARK	STATUS	TIME (s)
set property	SAFE	1.60
set property (bug)	UNSAFE	1.95
bubble sort	SAFE	0.23
bubble sort (bug)	UNSAFE	0.09
palindrome	SAFE	0.02
sentinel	SAFE	0.01
strcpy	SAFE	0.01
strcmp	SAFE	0.02
init even	SAFE	0.02
double swap	SAFE	0.16
merge interleave	SAFE	0.09
merge interleave (bug)	UNSAFE	0.11

(a)   (b)

Fig. 2. BOOSTER performances

Acceleration (2). MCMT adopts acceleration as a preprocessing step, following the approach described in [5]. In contrast with the "Acceleration (1)" module discussed previously, acceleration here is applied to a wider class of transitions, but preimages along accelerated formulæ are not kept precise given their intractable format[2], but are over-approximated with their *monotonic abstraction* [4].

LAWI. MCMT implements the Lazy Abstraction with Interpolants for Array framework (following the description given in [2]) enhanced with a suitable refinement procedure for handling the over-approximations introduced to exploit accelerated relations [5].

Portfolio Approach. The "term abstraction" heuristic has a great impact on the performances of the LAWI framework for arrays [2]. It leverages the flat encoding of formulæ manipulated by the model-checker in order to generate quantified predicates for a successful array analysis. BOOSTER nullifies the required user ingenuity for defining a proper term abstraction list. Internal heuristics, inherited from [2], generate some suitable term abstraction lists. The fixpoint engine is subsequently executed adopting a portfolio approach, according to which BOOSTER generates several parallel instances of MCMT, each with different settings (including different term abstraction lists).

3   Experimental Evaluation and Conclusion

We evaluated BOOSTER on a large set of programs (both safe and unsafe) with arrays taken from several heterogeneous sources. Fig. 2a compares BOOSTER running time with and without acceleration procedures[3]. This figure clearly shows that acceleration is a key feature in the BOOSTER framework: it significantly reduces the divergence cases and allows to achieve a speed-up up to two orders

---

[2] These ∃∀-formulæ might produce proof obligations falling outside known decidable fragments of array theories and may invalidate the internal heuristics of MCMT.
[3] Without acceleration the verification is performed entirely by the LAWI module.

of magnitude. We also report that the (un)safety of many programs (roughly the 50% of our benchmark suite) is detected directly by the "BMC" and "Acceleration (1)" modules, remarking the importance of acceleration in a software verification framework. We report in Table 2b some statistics about BOOSTER running times for challenging well-known benchmarks in array-analysis literature, observing that, to the best of our knowledge, there are no tools able to deal with all the programs in our benchmark suite.

References

1. Alberti, F., Bruttomesso, R., Ghilardi, S., Ranise, S., Sharygina, N.: Lazy abstraction with interpolants for arrays. In: Bjørner, N., Voronkov, A. (eds.) LPAR-18 2012. LNCS, vol. 7180, pp. 46–61. Springer, Heidelberg (2012)
2. Alberti, F., Bruttomesso, R., Ghilardi, S., Ranise, S., Sharygina, N.: SAFARI: SMT-Based Abstraction for Arrays with Interpolants. In: Madhusudan, P., Seshia, S.A. (eds.) CAV 2012. LNCS, vol. 7358, pp. 679–685. Springer, Heidelberg (2012)
3. Alberti, F., Bruttomesso, R., Ghilardi, S., Ranise, S., Sharygina, N.: An extension of lazy abstraction with interpolation for programs with arrays. FMSD 45(1), 63–109 (2014)
4. Alberti, F., Ghilardi, S., Pagani, E., Ranise, S., Rossi, G.P.: Universal guards, relativization of quantifiers, and failure models in model checking modulo theories. JSAT 8(1/2), 29–61 (2012)
5. Alberti, F., Ghilardi, S., Sharygina, N.: Definability of accelerated relations in a theory of arrays and its applications. In: Fontaine, P., Ringeissen, C., Schmidt, R.A. (eds.) FroCoS 2013. LNCS, vol. 8152, pp. 23–39. Springer, Heidelberg (2013)
6. Alberti, F., Ghilardi, S., Sharygina, N.: Decision procedures for flat array properties. In: Ábrahám, E., Havelund, K. (eds.) TACAS 2014. LNCS, vol. 8413, pp. 15–30. Springer, Heidelberg (2014)
7. De Angelis, E., Fioravanti, F., Pettorossi, A., Proietti, M.: VeriMAP: A tool for verifying programs through transformations. In: Ábrahám, E., Havelund, K. (eds.) TACAS 2014. LNCS, vol. 8413, pp. 568–574. Springer, Heidelberg (2014)
8. Beyer, D.: Status report on software verification. In: Ábrahám, E., Havelund, K. (eds.) TACAS 2014. LNCS, vol. 8413, pp. 373–388. Springer, Heidelberg (2014)
9. Biere, A., Cimatti, A., Clarke, E.M., Zhu, Y.: Symbolic model checking without bdds. In: Cleaveland, W.R. (ed.) TACAS 1999. LNCS, vol. 1579, pp. 193–207. Springer, Heidelberg (1999)
10. Bjørner, N., McMillan, K., Rybalchenko, A.: On solving universally quantified Horn clauses. In: Logozzo, F., Fähndrich, M. (eds.) Static Analysis. LNCS, vol. 7935, pp. 105–125. Springer, Heidelberg (2013)
11. Cousot, P., Cousot, R., Logozzo, F.: A parametric segmentation functor for fully automatic and scalable array content analysis. In: POPL, pp. 105–118 (2011)
12. de Moura, L., Bjørner, N.: Z3: An efficient SMT solver. In: Ramakrishnan, C.R., Rehof, J. (eds.) TACAS 2008. LNCS, vol. 4963, pp. 337–340. Springer, Heidelberg (2008)
13. Dragan, I., Kovács, L.: LINGVA: Generating and proving program properties using symbol elimination. In: PSI (to appear, 2014)
14. Garg, P., Löding, C., Madhusudan, P., Neider, D.: ICE: A robust framework for learning invariants. In: Biere, A., Bloem, R. (eds.) CAV 2014. LNCS, vol. 8559, pp. 69–87. Springer, Heidelberg (2014)

15. Ghilardi, S., Ranise, S.: MCMT: A Model Checker Modulo Theories. In: Giesl, J., Hähnle, R. (eds.) IJCAR 2010. LNCS, vol. 6173, pp. 22–29. Springer, Heidelberg (2010)
16. Gurfinkel, A., Chaki, S., Sapra, S.: Efficient predicate abstraction of program summaries. In: Bobaru, M., Havelund, K., Holzmann, G.J., Joshi, R. (eds.) NFM 2011. LNCS, vol. 6617, pp. 131–145. Springer, Heidelberg (2011)
17. Hoder, K., Kovács, L., Voronkov, A.: Invariant Generation in Vampire. In: Abdulla, P.A., Leino, K.R.M. (eds.) TACAS 2011. LNCS, vol. 6605, pp. 60–64. Springer, Heidelberg (2011)
18. McMillan, K.L.: Lazy abstraction with interpolants. In: Ball, T., Jones, R.B. (eds.) CAV 2006. LNCS, vol. 4144, pp. 123–136. Springer, Heidelberg (2006)
19. Rollini, S.F., Alt, L., Fedyukovich, G., Hyvärinen, A.E.J., Sharygina, N.: PeRIPLO: A framework for producing effective interpolants in sat-based software verification. In: McMillan, K., Middeldorp, A., Voronkov, A. (eds.) LPAR-19 2013. LNCS, vol. 8312, pp. 683–693. Springer, Heidelberg (2013)

A Bounded Model Checker for SPARK Programs

Cláudio Belo Lourenço, Maria João Frade, and Jorge Sousa Pinto

HASLab/INESC TEC & Universidade do Minho, Portugal

Abstract. This paper discusses the design and implementation of a bounded model checker for SPARK code, and provides a proof of concept of the utility and practicality of bounded verification for SPARK.

Introduction. SPARK is a programming language and toolset designed for the development of high-assurance software [4]. The language is based on a restricted subset of Ada (see [1] for a full description), complemented by an expressive system of contracts, to describe the specification and design of programs. The SPARK platform provides a set of tools that allow users to reason about the correctness of the source code, making possible the detection of problems early in the software lifecycle. The tools are based on deductive verification and as such give full guarantees, but they require the user to provide *contracts* and *loop invariants*, which are often difficult to write.

We believe that *Bounded Model Checking* (BMC) of software can be helpful as a complement to the existing tools, particularly for finding errors and/or validating annotations, or in assisting with the conversion of existing Ada code to SPARK. The key idea of BMC of software, as implemented by the flagship CBMC tool [6] for ANSI-C code, is to encode *bounded behaviors* of the program as logical formulas whose models describe executions leading to violations of some given property. The use of *assert* and *assume* annotations provide a convenient property specification mechanism. An `assert` ϕ statement signifies that the property ϕ should hold at that point of the program. If ϕ does not hold, that violation is reported and a counter-example is given. Asserts can be used, for instance, to automatically instrument the code regarding safety properties. On the other hand, an `assume` ψ annotation states that one can rely on the fact that ψ is true at that point of the program.

This paper presents the design of a BMC tool for SPARK 2005 programs. Rather than producing the definitive BMC tool for SPARK, which would not make sense at the present moment of development of the language (SPARK 2014 had not been launched when our development began), the main goal of the present paper is to provide a proof of concept of the utility and practicality of BMC of SPARK software, as a complement to deductive verification. A bounded model checker may also serve other purposes in addition to formal verification: in [2] it is reported how CBMC has been used for *coverage analysis* of safety-critical code, in precisely the same context in which SPARK is widely used. Other applications of BMC of software include *automated fault localization* [9].

F. Cassez and J.-F. Raskin (Eds.): ATVA 2014, LNCS 8837, pp. 24–30, 2014.

```
package Marray is
  Array_Size: constant:=10;
  subtype Ind is Integer range 1 .. Array_Size;
  type VArray is array (Ind) of Integer;
  procedure MaxArray(V: in VArray; M: out Ind);
  --# derives M from V;
  --# post (for all I in Ind => (V(I) <= V(M)));
end Marray;

package body Marray is
  procedure MaxArray(V: in VArray; M: out Ind) is
    I: Integer;
    Max: Ind;
  begin
    Max := Ind'First;
    --% notOverflow(+,Integer ,INDICES'FIRST,1);
    I := Ind'First+1;
    loop
      --# assert(for all J in Ind range Ind'First..(I-1) => (V(J) <= V(Max)));
      --# assert(I >= Ind'First) and (I <= Ind'Last + 1);
      exit when I > Ind'Last;
      --% assert (I >= VARRAY'FIRST) and (I <= VARRAY'LAST);
      --% assert (MAX >= VARRAY'FIRST) and (MAX <= VARRAY'LAST);
      if V(I) > V(Max) then
        Max := I;
      end if;
      --% notOverflow(+,Integer ,I ,1);
      I := I + 1;
    end loop;
    M := Max;
  end MaxArray;
end MArray;
```

SPARK-BMC. SPARK-BMC[1] is an open source prototype bounded model checker for SPARK programs. It is developed in Haskell and uses as backend the SMT solver Z3 [8]. The tool checks SPARK programs for violations of properties annotated in the code. Annotations are inserted as comments beginning with a user predefined character, assumed distinct from SPARK annotations (--% in this paper). The annotations that may be used are assert C; assume C; and notOverflow(op,type,e1,e2), used to check if an overflow is originated. These can be inserted to express useful properties for debugging, and in particular safety properties corresponding to the absence of runtime exceptions (such as overflow, array out-of-bounds accesses and division by zero), which can be checked without requiring invariants. The figure shows a SPARK program (including loop invariants) containing a procedure that finds the maximum element in an array. The annotations corresponding to overflow and array out of bounds, to be checked by SPARK-BMC, are also included.

The reader is referred to [13] for a complete description of the implementation details that will now be outlined. The algorithm begins with a normalization into a subset of SPARK (e.g. transforming type attributes and enumerations into integer expressions) and inlining of routine calls. SPARK does not allow for any form of recursion, so no bound is applied on the length of this expansion. Loops are then unwound a fixed number of times (which reduces them to sequences of nested if statements), and the program is thus transformed into a monolithic iteration-free program. To enforce soundness, an unwinding assertion can be optionally inserted, to ensure that the loop has been sufficiently unwound.

In order to extract a logical formula from the iteration-free program one has to first transform it into a *single assignment* form, in which the values of the variables do not change once they have been used (so that assignments can be

---

[1] Available from the repository https://bitbucket.org/vhaslab/spark-src

seen as logical equalities). The program is then subject to Conditional Normal Form (CNF) normalization, which transforms it into a sequence of statements of the form if b then S, where S is an assignment, assert or assume statement, and the guard b encodes the path condition leading to that command. Two sets of formulas $\mathcal{C}$ and $\mathcal{P}$ are then extracted. $\mathcal{C}$ describes logically the operational contents of the program, and includes a formula $b \to x = e$ for every statement if b then $x := e$. $\mathcal{P}$ on the other hand contains the properties to be established, extracted from the guarded assert and assume statements of the CNF. If no assert fails in any execution of the program one has that $\bigwedge \mathcal{P}$ is a logical consequence of $\mathcal{C}$. Any model found for the set of formulas $\mathcal{C} \cup \{\neg \bigwedge \mathcal{P}\}$ corresponds to a counter-example: an execution leading to a violation of some assertion in $\mathcal{P}$.

Experiences with implementing SMT-based bounded model checkers [3,7] have produced quite positive results, which justifies our choice of this class of solvers. SPARK-BMC employs a bit-vector rather than an unbounded integers theory, which has the advantage of capturing precisely the low-level fixed-width machine semantics of program data types. The SPARK programming language includes modular types, whose modular semantics are directly captured by fixed-size bit-vectors. Signed integers are also conveniently encoded as bit-vectors. Finally, arrays are modeled by a theory of arrays.

Evaluation. At the present stage of development of SPARK-BMC we can successfully check multi-procedure programs manipulating arrays and discrete types, and as such we are able to run SPARK-BMC on a great variety of programs. Our preliminary results clearly illustrate the positive aspects of automated verification for SPARK code. The tool scales well for certain classes of programs, and even for other, algorithmically more complicated programs, it is able to check for property violations in the first few iterations of loops. Let us turn back to the MaxArray example to show how the tool can discover subtle bugs without the need for user annotations. One common error would be to write the exit condition as exit when I>Ind'Last+1, which would cause an array out of bounds exception in the array access contained in the expression V(I)>V(MAX) that could easily be missed. The SPARK tools (based on deductive verification) would generate a Verification Condition (VC) stating that the loop invariant is preserved by iterations of the loop, and another VC to enforce that whenever V(I)>V(MAX) is evaluated the value of I lies within the range of the array. For the MaxArray code both VCs are successfully discharged, but if the exit condition is modified to the above, then the invariant preservation condition can no longer be proved (it fails in the last iteration). If the invariant is corrected to I<=Ind'Last+2, then the invariant preservation VC is discharged, but not the other VC: the invariant is now correct, but does not prevent the out-of-bounds access. This illustrates that with deductive verification it can be hard to detect exactly what went wrong – is the program unsafe, or is the user-provided invariant wrong? To use SPARK-BMC on this program, it must first be annotated as discussed before. Depending on the user-provided bound K, SPARK-BMC will either indicate that the unwinding assertion fails, or else (for $K > 10$) that an assert violation occurs. In this case the tool displays the violated assertion, as well as the current values of the relevant variables.

We have assessed the behaviour of SPARK-BMC with a number of example programs, taken both from academic papers and from problem sets proposed in the context of program verification competitions. We have either transcribed to SPARK an algorithm implemented in C, or, when this was not available, coded it from scratch. All the code can be found in the project's repository.

Experimental Results: Problem Set I. We use a first set of example programs to illustrate that BMC can be used in practice on programs that have been designed to be verified with deductive verification tools. Although these are all relatively simple problems, they are algorithmically complicated, which creates difficulties for a BMC approach. Our purpose here is to investigate the viability of the approach for small problem sizes (bounded loops requiring up to 100 iterations). Specifically, we have applied SPARK-BMC to an implementation of the *inverting an injection* problem taken from [12], which we have ported to SPARK:

```
MAXLEN: constant := 20;

subtype Index
    is Integer range 0..MAXLEN;
type ArrayType
    is array (Index) of Integer;

procedure Invert(A: in ArrayType;
                 N: in Integer;
                 B: out ArrayType)is
begin
  for I in Index range 0 .. N - 1
  loop
    B(A(I)) := I;
  end loop;
end Invert;
```

```
procedure PropertyCheck is
  A,B: ArrayType;
  N: Integer;
begin
  --% assume (N > 0 and N <= MAXLEN);
  for I in Index range 0 .. N - 1 loop
    --% assume (A(I) >= 0 and A(I) < N);
    for J in Index range I + 1 .. N - 1 loop
      --% assume (A(I) /= A(J));
    end loop;
  end loop;
  Invert(A,N,B);
  for I in Index range 0 .. N - 1 loop
    for J in Index range I + 1 .. N - 1 loop
      --% assert (A(I) /= A(J));
    end loop;
  end loop;
  for I in Index range 0 .. N - 1 loop
    --% assert (B(A(I)) = I);
  end loop;
end PropertyCheck;
```

The problem is described as follows: *Invert an injective (and thus surjective) array A of N elements in the subrange from 0 to N-1.* The verification tasks are to prove that the output array B is injective and that B(A(I)) = I for 0 <= I < N. SPARK-BMC succeeds in both tasks for the given bound, with no further annotations in addition to the assumes and asserts shown in the PropertyCheck procedure, which state that the properties described above hold after calls to Invert, for executions corresponding to an injective array A.

We additionally tested the tool with the following: *SUM&MAX* from [12]; *finding the maximum in an array* and *finding two duplets in an array* from [5]; and finally *binary search in an array* from [14]. The table below shows the verification time (in seconds) vs. the number of iterations unwound, as required by the problem size. While in all cases, for a sufficiently small number of iterations, SPARK-BMC succeeds in the verification task in a completely automatic way, it easily becomes impractical to reach even a modest number of iterations.

	5	10	15	20
SUM&MAX	11.13	2013.58	14678.57	
Inverting an Injection - Property 1	0.79	16.89	129.84	1659.15
Inverting an Injection - Property 2	0.81	317.51	100370.81	
Finding the maximum in an array	3.70	7930.35		
Finding two duplets in an array	2.35	425.23		
Binary search in array	2.39	12.77	51.01	227.02

Experimental Results: Problem Set II. We use both SPARK-BMC and CBMC on a second set of example programs (running on the SPARK and C versions of the same algorithm). In order to compare both tools at a purely logical level, the times registered for CBMC were measured with the *constant propagation and simplification* option switched off. We stress that our goal with these comparisons is not to present SPARK-BMC as competing with CBMC – we aim merely to validate the algorithm underlying SPARK-BMC, and demonstrate the practicality of bounded verification with a diverse set of problems.

The programs in this second set have been used to illustrate the performance of various software model checking and symbolic execution tools [10,11][2]. Although we do not present results obtained with these tools, they would surely outperform BMC tools, since the example programs are designed to illustrate situations that are advantageous to them. The programs are algorithmically simpler than in the previous set, and would be straightforward to verify deductively. Bounded verification scales quite well for these programs, with reasonable verification times for up to 1000 iterations. The graphs below show that in all programs CBMC (even with constant propagation switched off) performs better than SPARK-BMC. However, it can be seen that in a log-lin scale the shapes of the SPARK-BMC curves are relatively close to the CBMC curves.

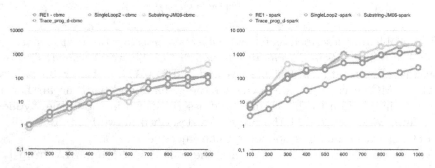

In fact, when we run CBMC on the examples from the first problem set (times not shown in the graph), SPARK-BMC behaves marginally better than CBMC with *binary search in array*, and much better than CBMC with *inverting an injection* (CBMC becomes impractical to use with just 15 iterations). It seems that for algorithmically more complicated code the size of the propositional formulas generated by CBMC increases very significantly.

---

[2] The C code can be found online at http://map.uniroma2.it/smc/simp/ and http://www.cfdvs.iitb.ac.in/~bhargav/dagger.php

Conclusion. We have demonstrated the advantages of bounded SMT-based automated verification for SPARK code, and shown that it is practical to check for property violations with no loop invariant annotations required. In the near future our work will focus on adapting SPARK-BMC to work with the SPARK 2014 language definition, as well as on including support for other SMT solvers. An interesting challenge, which will certainly increase the usefulness of SPARK-BMC as a complement to the SPARK tools, is to extend it in order to validate and debug SPARK contracts.

Acknowledgment. This work is funded by ERDF - European Regional Development Fund through the COMPETE Programme (operational programme for competitiveness) and by National Funds through the FCT - Fundação para a Ciência e a Tecnologia (Portuguese Foundation for Science and Technology) within project **FCOMP-01-0124-FEDER-020486**.

References

1. Altran Praxis. SPARK - The SPADE Ada Kernel (including RavenSPARK), Edition 7.2 (December 2011)
2. Angeletti, D., Giunchiglia, E., Narizzano, M., Puddu, A., Sabina, S.: Using bounded model checking for coverage analysis of safety-critical software in an industrial setting. J. Autom. Reason. 45(4), 397–414 (2010)
3. Armando, A., Mantovani, J., Platania, L.: Bounded model checking of software using SMT solvers instead of SAT solvers. Int. J. Softw. Tools Technol. Transf. 11(1), 69–83 (2009)
4. Barnes, J.: High Integrity Software: The SPARK Approach to Safety and Security. Addison-Wesley Longman Publishing Co., Inc., Boston (2003)
5. Bormer, T., et al.: The COST IC0701 verification competition 2011. In: Beckert, B., Damiani, F., Gurov, D. (eds.) FoVeOOS 2011. LNCS, vol. 7421, pp. 3–21. Springer, Heidelberg (2012)
6. Clarke, E., Kroning, D., Lerda, F.: A Tool for Checking ANSI-C Programs. In: Jensen, K., Podelski, A. (eds.) TACAS 2004. LNCS, vol. 2988, pp. 168–176. Springer, Heidelberg (2004)
7. Cordeiro, L., Fischer, B., Marques-Silva, J.: SMT-based bounded model checking for embedded ANSI-C software. In: ASE 2009. IEEE Computer Society (2009)
8. de Moura, L., Bjørner, N.S.: Z3: An efficient SMT solver. In: Ramakrishnan, C.R., Rehof, J. (eds.) TACAS 2008. LNCS, vol. 4963, pp. 337–340. Springer, Heidelberg (2008)
9. Griesmayer, A., Staber, S., Bloem, R.: Automated fault localization for C programs. Electronic Notes in Theoretical Computer Science 174(4), 95–111 (2007)
10. Jaffar, J., Navas, J.A., Santosa, A.E.: Unbounded symbolic execution for program verification. In: Khurshid, S., Sen, K. (eds.) RV 2011. LNCS, vol. 7186, pp. 396–411. Springer, Heidelberg (2012)
11. Jhala, R., McMillan, K.L.: A practical and complete approach to predicate refinement. In: Hermanns, H., Palsberg, J. (eds.) TACAS 2006. LNCS, vol. 3920, pp. 459–473. Springer, Heidelberg (2006)

12. Klebanov, V., et al.: The 1st verified software competition: Experience report. In: Butler, M., Schulte, W. (eds.) FM 2011. LNCS, vol. 6664, pp. 154–168. Springer, Heidelberg (2011)
13. Lourenço, C.B.: A Bounded Model Checker for SPARK Programs. Master's thesis, University of Minho (2013)
14. Weide, B.W., et al.: Incremental benchmarks for software verification tools and techniques. In: Shankar, N., Woodcock, J. (eds.) VSTTE 2008. LNCS, vol. 5295, pp. 84–98. Springer, Heidelberg (2008)

Acceleration of Affine Hybrid Transformations*

Bernard Boigelot[1], Frédéric Herbreteau[2], and Isabelle Mainz[1]

[1] Institut Montefiore, B28, Univ. Liège, Belgium
{boigelot,mainz}@montefiore.ulg.ac.be
[2] Univ. Bordeaux & CNRS, LaBRI, UMR 5800, Talence, France
fh@labri.fr

Abstract. This work addresses the computation of the set of reachable configurations of linear hybrid automata. The approach relies on symbolic state-space exploration, using acceleration in order to speed up the computation and to make it terminate for a broad class of systems. Our contribution is an original method for accelerating the control cycles of linear hybrid automata, i.e., to compute their unbounded repeated effect. The idea consists in analyzing the data transformations that label these cycles, by reasoning about the geometrical features of the corresponding system of linear constraints. This approach is complete over Multiple Counters Systems (MCS), and is able to accelerate hybrid transformations that are out of scope of existing techniques.

1 Introduction

Hybrid automata [14] are a powerful formalism for modeling systems that combine discrete and continuous features, in particular those depending on physical processes that involve undiscretized time. Linear hybrid automata are a restricted form of hybrid automata that are amenable to automated analysis of some of their properties, while not sacrificing too much expressive power, which remains sufficient for modeling precisely enough a large range of systems.

This work addresses the general problem of analyzing reachability properties of linear hybrid automata, by computing an exact representation of their set of reachable configurations. Since this set is generally infinite, both because variables of hybrid automata are unbounded and take their value over a dense domain, this computation has to be performed symbolically, representing the manipulated sets with the help of dedicated data structures. Moreover, since linear hybrid automata are Turing complete, the computation of their reachability set cannot be guaranteed to terminate in all cases. A possible workaround would be to introduce approximations, such as widening operators [12], in order to force termination. We make a different choice and aim at an exact computation algorithm without guarantee of termination, trying to make it powerful enough for handling a relevant subclass of systems.

---

* This work is supported in part by the grant 2.4545.11 of the Belgian Fund for Scientific Research (F.R.S.-FNRS).

F. Cassez and J.-F. Raskin (Eds.): ATVA 2014, LNCS 8837, pp. 31–46, 2014.

Computing the reachability set of a system can be achieved by forward symbolic state-space exploration: At each step, one propagates reachability information from the current set of reachable configurations in order to make it bigger. The procedure terminates upon reaching a fixed point. For hybrid automata, an exploration step corresponds to letting time elapse in the current control location, or to following a transition from one location to another.

This approach is not sufficient for analyzing all interesting case studies. One reason is that some linear hybrid automata have configurations that are only reached after an unbounded number of exploration steps; a typical example is the *leaking gas burner* studied in [15]. This problem is tackled by *acceleration* techniques, aimed at computing in finite time sets of configurations that are reached after following arbitrarily long control paths. For instance, accelerating a cyclic path, which corresponds to a loop in a program, amounts to computing in one step all the configurations that can be reached by iterating this cycle arbitrarily many times [2].

In order to be able to perform cycle acceleration with linear hybrid automata, one first needs a symbolic representation system that is expressive enough for the sets of values produced by unbounded loop iterations, as well as a formalism for describing the data transformations labeling control paths. The main problems are then to decide whether the effect of unbounded iterations of such a path can be computed over symbolically represented sets, and to carry out this computation.

Solutions to these problems have been proposed in earlier work: Sets of reachable data values can be expressed in the first-order logic $\langle \mathbb{R}, \mathbb{Z}, +, \leq \rangle$, which generalizes Presburger arithmetic to mixed integer and real variables, and for which usable data structures have been developed [7]. The transformations undergone by variables along control paths of linear hybrid automata[1] correspond to *Linear Hybrid Relations (LHR)*, the acceleration of which is studied in [5,6].

The cycle acceleration method proposed in [5] is able to handle a broad class of LHR, in particular all *Multiple Counters Systems (MCS)* [11]. This subclass of LHR is relevant in practice since it has been established that accelerating arbitrary control paths of *timed automata* [1], reduces to the same problem over MCS. It is actually proved in [5] that acceleration of MCS makes it possible to compute symbolically the reachability set of timed automata with a guarantee of termination.

The results of [5] nevertheless suffer from two weaknesses. First, when this acceleration method is applied to purely integer transformations, which can be seen as a particular case of LHR, it is not able to handle all instances covered by an acceleration procedure that has been specifically developed for such transformations [2,3]. Second, the method is sensitive to the coordinate system used for expressing data values. For instance, even though all MCS can be accelerated, the same property does not hold for LHR obtained after applying linear variable change operations to MCS.

---

[1] The results of [5,6] actually consider the slightly smaller class of *strongly linear* hybrid automata but their extension to linear hybrid automata is immediate.

The goal of this work is to broaden substantially the scope of cycle acceleration of linear hybrid relations, by developing a new approach that does not have
these weaknesses. For purely integer transformations, an obvious solution would
be to detect whether the considered LHR belongs to this class, and then branch
to a specific acceleration algorithm. This approach would not improve the state
of the art, and we propose instead a solution that is not only able to handle
all integer transformations that can be accelerated by the specialized algorithm
of [3], but also combinations of such discrete transformations with simple continuous ones. After studying the properties of this solution, we then generalize
it into a method that becomes powerful enough for handling all transformations
extracted from MCS, as well as their transformations by arbitrary linear variable
change operations.

2   Preliminaries

2.1   Algebra Basics

A *linear constraint* over variables $x \in \mathbb{R}^n$, with $n \geq 0$, is a constraint of the
form $a.x \# b$, with $a \in \mathbb{Q}^n$, $b \in \mathbb{Q}$ and $\# \in \{<, \leq, =, \geq, >\}$. This constraint is
strict if $\# \in \{<, >\}$, and *non-strict* otherwise. It is an *inequality* constraint if
$\# \in \{<, \leq, \geq, >\}$, and an *equality* constraint otherwise. A constraint $a.x \# b$ is
said to be *saturated* by a value $v \in \mathbb{R}^n$ if this value satisfies $a.v = b$.

The set of points $x \in \mathbb{R}^n$ that satisfy a given finite conjunction of equality
constraints forms an *affine space*. An affine space $S \subseteq \mathbb{R}^n$ can be expressed in
the form $S = A\mathbb{R}^m + b$, where $0 \leq m \leq n$, $A \in \mathbb{Q}^{n \times m}$ is a matrix with rank m,
and $b \in \mathbb{Q}^n$. The value m then corresponds to the *dimension* of S. The affine
space of smallest dimension that contains a given set is unique, and known as
the *affine hull* of this set.

The set of solutions of a finite conjunction of linear constraints forms a *convex
polyhedron*, the dimension of which is defined as the dimension of its affine hull.
Within $\mathbb{R}^n$, a convex polyhedron of dimension n can be represented by a finite
canonical conjunction of constraints, i.e., a set of constraints that is uniquely
determined by the polyhedron. For each constraint in this set, there exists at
least one point that saturates this constraint, and that satisfies all the other
ones without saturating them. Convex polyhedra of dimension $m < n$ can be
expressed as $A\Pi + b$, where $A \in \mathbb{Q}^{n \times m}$, $b \in \mathbb{Q}^n$, and $\Pi \subseteq \mathbb{R}^m$ is a polyhedron
of dimension m that is represented canonically. In order to simplify notations,
we sometimes denote a set $\{v\}$ as v, and write $S_1 + S_2$ to mean $\{v_1 + v_2 \mid v_1 \in S_1 \wedge v_2 \in S_2\}$.

2.2   Linear Hybrid Relations

A *Linear Hybrid Automaton (LHA)* is composed of a finite control graph extended with a given number n of variables $x_1, x_2, \ldots, x_n$ that take their values
in $\mathbb{R}$. These variables can be grouped into a vector x whose domain is $\mathbb{R}^n$. We

refer the reader to [5,6,14] for further details and formal definitions. An example is given in Figure 2.

A *configuration* of a LHA is a pair $(\ell, \boldsymbol{v})$ where ℓ is a control location and $\boldsymbol{v}$ assigns a value to each variable. The current configuration can change in two ways. The first one *(time step)* is to let time elapse, in which case the control location remains constant, and the variable values evolve according to the *invariant* and *evolution law* of this location. Those are expressed as linear constraints over respectively the variable values, and their first time derivative. The second mechanism *(transition step)* is to follow a transition, which moves the control location and applies a discrete transformation to the variable values. This transformation is defined by linear constraints involving the initial and final values of the variables, taken across the transition.

The semantics of LHA is defined as follows. A configuration c_2 is reachable from a configuration c_1 if there exists a finite sequence of time and transition steps that leads from c_1 to c_2. A reachable configuration is one that is reachable from a designated initial set.

It has been shown in [6] that every finite control path of a LHA induces a transformation over its variables that can be characterized as follows.

Definition 1. *A Linear Hybrid Relation (LHR)* is a relation

$$\theta = \left\{ (\boldsymbol{x}, \boldsymbol{x}') \in \mathbb{R}^n \times \mathbb{R}^n \;\middle|\; P \begin{bmatrix} \boldsymbol{x} \\ \boldsymbol{x}' \end{bmatrix} \preceq \boldsymbol{q} \right\},$$

where $P \in \mathbb{Z}^{m \times 2n}$, $\boldsymbol{q} \in \mathbb{Z}^m$, $\preceq \, \in \{<, \leq\}^m$, *and* $m \geq 0$.

We write $\theta = (P, \boldsymbol{q}, \preceq)$ to denote a relation of this form. Given a path in a LHA moving from a location ℓ to a location ℓ', one can compute P and $\boldsymbol{q}$ such that two values $\boldsymbol{v}, \boldsymbol{v}' \in \mathbb{R}^n$ satisfy the LHR $(P, \boldsymbol{q}, \preceq)$ iff $(\ell', \boldsymbol{v}')$ is reachable from $(\ell, \boldsymbol{v})$ by following the time and transition steps corresponding to this path.

In this work, for the sake of simplicity, we assume that all inequality constraints that appear in LHR are non-strict, i.e., that $\preceq$ stands for $\leq^m$, and that LHR are characterized by their pair $(P, \boldsymbol{q})$. All results in this paper can straightforwardly be extended to the more general setting of mixed strict and non-strict constraints.

Let θ be a LHR. Following [5], we call a constraint of this LHR *static* if it involves only either $\boldsymbol{x}$ or $\boldsymbol{x}'$. For a set $S \subseteq \mathbb{R}^n$, its *image* $\theta(S)$ by θ is given by $\{\boldsymbol{x}' \in \mathbb{R}^n \mid \exists \boldsymbol{x} \in S : (\boldsymbol{x}, \boldsymbol{x}') \in \theta\}$. This can alternatively be expressed as $\theta(S) = (\theta \cap (S \times \mathbb{R}^n))|_{[n+1,2n]}$, where $U|_I$ denotes the *projection* of the elements of U onto the vector components belonging to I. Given two LHR θ_1 and θ_2, their *composition* $\theta_2 \circ \theta_1$ is the LHR θ such that $\theta(S) = \theta_2(\theta_1(S))$ for all sets S. Note that we have $\theta_2 \circ \theta_1 = ((\theta_1 \times \mathbb{R}^n) \cap (\mathbb{R}^n \times \theta_2))|_{[1,n]\cup[2n+1,3n]}$. Finally, for every k, the result of composing $k - 1$ times a LHR θ with itself is denoted θ^k, with θ^0 corresponding to the identity relation.

2.3   Representation of Convex Polyhedra

In the following sections, we study the effect and repeated effect of LHR on sets. The image $\theta(v)$ of a point $v \in \mathbb{R}^n$ by a LHR θ is the set of points v' such that (v, v') satisfies the linear constraints of θ, that is, a convex polyhedron. We now study some topological properties of such polyhedra.

Following the discussion in Section 2.1, we consider w.l.o.g. a convex polyhedron $\Pi \subseteq \mathbb{R}^n$ of dimension n, defined by its canonical set of inequality constraints. As explained in [4,13], such a polyhedron induces a finite equivalence relation $\sim_\Pi$ on the points of $\mathbb{R}^n$: One has $v \sim_\Pi v'$ iff these two points saturate identical subsets of constraints of Π. The equivalence classes of $\sim_\Pi$ correspond to the *geometrical components* of Π. For each geometrical component C, its affine hull aff(C) matches the constraints of Π saturated by C, and its *dimension* is defined as the one of this affine hull. The geometrical components of Π are linked together by an *incidence* partial order $\prec_\Pi$: One has $C_1 \prec_\Pi C_2$ iff aff(C_1) $\subset$ aff(C_2), i.e., iff the constraints saturated in C_1 are a superset of those saturated in C_2.

Those properties lead to a data structure for representing symbolically convex polyhedra: A *Convex Polyhedron Decision Diagram (CPDD)* representing a polyhedron Π is a directed acyclic graph in which:

- The nodes correspond to the geometrical components of Π, and are labeled by the constraints of Π that they saturate, written as equalities (in other words, by the affine hull of their geometrical component).
- If Π admits a unique minimal component with respect to the incidence order $\prec_\Pi$, then the node q_0 associated to this component is marked as initial. Otherwise, the initial node q_0 is an additional special node in which all constraints are considered to be saturated (yielding an empty affine hull).
- The edges follow the incidence relation, removing those that are redundant by transitivity. An edge from q_1 to q_2 is labeled by the constraints that are saturated in q_1 and not in q_2, written as strict inequalities.

An example of CPDD is given in Figure 1. This data structure actually provides a simple procedure for locating the geometrical component of Π to which a given point $v \in \mathbb{R}^n$ belongs: Starting from the initial node, one follows edges labeled by inequality constraints that are satisfied by v. The procedure ends upon reaching a node labeled by equality constraints satisfied by v, which then represents the component to which v belongs. If several paths can be followed from a given node, one of them can be chosen arbitrarily without the need for backtracking.

This procedure illustrates an essential property of convex polyhedra: The points contained in a geometrical component are exactly those that saturate the constraints associated to this component, and that do not saturate the other constraints. This property will be exploited in order to establish a key result in Section 4.

It is worth mentioning that CPDD nodes do not correspond to all possible combinations of saturated linear constraints, but only to those that are associated to geometrical components. For instance, the CPDD depicted in Figure 1

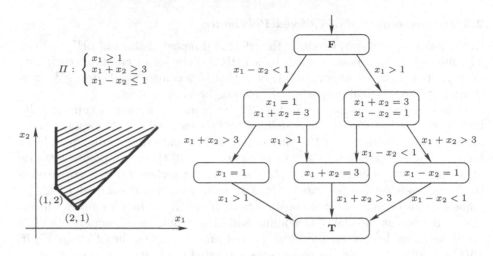

Fig. 1. Example of Convex Polyhedron Decision Diagram

does not have a node corresponding to the set of constraints $\{x_1 \geq 1, x_1 - x_2 \leq 1\}$, since these constraints cannot be saturated while simultaneously satisfying $x_1 + x_2 \geq 3$.

Algorithms are available for building and manipulating polyhedra represented by CPDD, in particular for computing their canonical form (which is unique up to isomorphism), as well as their intersection and projection. This data structure has been generalized to non-convex polyhedra in [4,13].

2.4 Cycle Acceleration

The *cycle acceleration* problem consists in checking, within a symbolic representation system, whether the image of any representable set by unbounded iterations of a given data transformation is representable as well. In such a case, this transformation is said to be *iterable* [2]. One also needs an algorithm for computing symbolically the image of represented sets by iterable transformations. This decision does not have to be precise: a sufficient criterion can be used provided that it handles practically relevant transformations.

In the next section, we recall two iterability criteria, one developed for linear transformations over integer variables and one for linear hybrid relations, and show that they can be combined into a criterion that has a broader scope.

3 Affine Hybrid Transformations

3.1 Discrete and Hybrid Periodic Transformations

Over the domain $\mathbb{Z}^n$, it has been established that transformations of the form $x \mapsto Ax + b$, with $A \in \mathbb{Z}^{n \times n}$ and $b \in \mathbb{Z}^n$, are iterable within Presburger arithmetic, i.e., the first-order theory $\langle \mathbb{Z}, +, < \rangle$, iff there exists $p \in \mathbb{N}_{>0}$ such that $A^{2p} = A^p$. This criterion can be decided using only integer arithmetic, and a suitable value of p can be computed whenever one exists [2,3].

Transformations θ that satisfy this criterion have an *ultimately periodic* behavior: For every $v \in \mathbb{Z}^n$, the sequence $\theta^p(v)$, $\theta^{2p}(v)$, $\theta^{3p}(v)$, ... is such that $\theta^{(k+1)p}(v) = \theta^{kp}(v) + \delta$ for all $k > 0$, where $\delta \in \mathbb{Z}^n$ is a constant increment vector. It is also known that adding a linear guard $Px \leq q$, with $P \in \mathbb{Z}^{m \times n}$, $q \in \mathbb{Z}^m$ and $m \geq 0$, to an iterable transformation produces one that is iterable as well.

Hybrid transformations can also show a periodic behavior. It has been proved in [6] that LHR θ over $\mathbb{R}^n$ in which all constraints have the form $p.(x' - x) \leq q$, with $p \in \mathbb{Z}^n$ and $q \in \mathbb{Z}$ have this property: For every $v \in \mathbb{R}^n$, the sequence $\theta(v)$, $\theta^2(v)$, $\theta^3(v)$, ... is such that $\theta^{k+1}(v) = \theta^k(v) + \Delta$ for all $k > 0$, where $\Delta \subseteq \mathbb{R}^n$ is an increment that now takes the form of a constant convex polyhedron.

A natural idea is therefore to study hybrid transformations that have a periodic behavior, but with a period that may be greater than one. The following definition generalizes linear integer transformations to the hybrid case.

Definition 2. *An Affine Hybrid Transformation (AHT) is a LHR $\theta \subseteq \mathbb{R}^n \times \mathbb{R}^n$ such that for every $x \in \mathbb{R}^n$,*

$$\theta(x) = Ax + \Pi,$$

where $A \in \mathbb{Q}^{n \times n}$, and $\Pi \subseteq \mathbb{R}^n$ is a convex polyhedron.

The iterability criterion obtained for linear integer transformations straightforwardly extends to AHT.

Theorem 3. *Let θ be an AHT $x \mapsto Ax + \Pi$, with $A \in \mathbb{Q}^{n \times n}$. If A is such that $A^{2p} = A^p$ for some $p \in \mathbb{N}_{>0}$, then θ is iterable within $\langle \mathbb{R}, \mathbb{Z}, +, \leq \rangle$. Moreover, adding static constraints to an iterable AHT that satisfies this property produces a LHR that is iterable as well.*

Proof sketch. For every $v \in \mathbb{R}^n$ and $k > 1$, one has $\theta^{kp}(v) = A^{kp}v + \sum_{i=0}^{kp-1} A^i \Pi$. If $A^{2p} = A^p$, this simplifies into $\theta^{kp}(v) = A^p v + \sum_{i=0}^{2p-1} A^i \Pi + (k-2) \sum_{i=p}^{2p-1} A^i \Pi$. Using the mechanisms introduced in [6], this leads to a formula of $\langle \mathbb{R}, \mathbb{Z}, +, \leq \rangle$ defining $\theta^k(v)$ for all $k \geq 0$ in terms of v and k.   □

In order to be able to exploit the acceleration of AHT during symbolic state-space exploration of linear hybrid automata, two problems need to be solved:

- Given a LHR expressed as a conjunction of linear constraints, deciding whether it is equivalent to an AHT and, in the positive case, computing the corresponding matrix A.
- Deciding whether a matrix $A \in \mathbb{Q}^{n \times n}$ is such that $A^{2p} = A^p$ for some $p \in \mathbb{N}_{>0}$, and computing such a value p.

The former problem is addressed in Section 3.2. The latter can be solved by adapting a result from [2,3]:

Theorem 4. *A matrix $A \in \mathbb{Q}^{n \times n}$ is such that $A^{2p} = A^p$ for some $p \in \mathbb{N}_{>0}$ if and only if A^p is diagonalizable and has eigenvalues that belong to $\{0, 1\}$. There exists an algorithm for deciding this criterion and computing a suitable value of p, using only integer arithmetic.*

Proof sketch. This result is established in [2,3] for matrices with integer components, the idea being to check whether they admit a characteristic polynomial that can be decomposed into a product of cyclotomic polynomials. The method proposed in [2,3] for performing this operation also applies to rational matrices. □

3.2   Detecting Affine Hybrid Transformations

We now address the problems of deciding whether a LHR is affine, that is, whether $\theta = (P, q)$ is equivalent to some AHT $x \mapsto Ax + \Pi$, and of computing the corresponding matrix A and convex polyhedron Π.

When θ is affine, the image of a set $S \subseteq \mathbb{R}^n$ is obtained by first applying to each point in S a transformation $x \mapsto Ax$, where $A \in \mathbb{Q}^{n \times n}$ is identical for each point, and then adding a constant convex polyhedron Π to the result.

Let us assume that this polyhedron has at least one vertex, i.e., a geometrical component of dimension 0. We can actually make this assumption without loss of generality, since it follows from [5] that if an affine transformation θ does not satisfy this property, then its acceleration can be reduced to that of a LHR of smaller dimension.

The image by θ of an arbitrary point $x \in \mathbb{R}^n$ is the polyhedron $Ax + \Pi$, which corresponds to Π translated by the vector Ax. Consider a particular vertex v_i of this polyhedron, in other words, a point that is the only one to saturate some given subset of its constraints. The vertex v_i is the translation of a vertex b_i of Π by the vector Ax, that is, $v_i = Ax + b_i$. The same reasoning applied to other vertices will yield the same matrix A.

Recall that the constraints defining θ are expressed over the variables x and x', the value of which is respectively considered before and after applying the transformation. A transformation of the form $x \mapsto Ax + b_i$ thus corresponds to the saturated form $x' = Ax + b_i$ of some constraints of θ. Since this set of saturated constraints is satisfiable, an important observation is that it must correspond to a geometrical component of the convex polyhedron $\Theta \subseteq \mathbb{R}^{2n}$ defined by the constraints of θ. In other words, there must exist in this polyhedron a geometrical component C_i that has an affine hull equal to $x' = Ax + b_i$.

Since we have considered the vertices of Π, which are its geometrical components of smallest dimension, the components C_i with this property must correspond to the minimal non-empty components of Θ. We thus have the following result.

Theorem 5. *There exists a procedure for deciding whether a LHR $\theta \subseteq \mathbb{R}^n \times \mathbb{R}^n$ is an Affine Hybrid Transformation.*

Proof sketch. A simple strategy for deciding whether θ is affine consists in inspecting the minimal non-empty geometrical components in a symbolic representation of Θ. The following procedure can be used:

1. Build a CPDD representing Θ.
2. Select one of its minimal non-empty components.
3. Extract a matrix A from the affine hull of this component.
4. Compute $\Pi = \theta(\mathbf{0})$.
5. Check whether θ is equivalent to $\boldsymbol{x} \mapsto A\boldsymbol{x} + \Pi$, by comparing Θ with the polyhedra induced by the corresponding sets of constraints.

If the polyhedron Π satisfies our initial hypothesis of having at least one vertex, then performing Step 3 simply amounts to checking that the considered affine hull is defined by constraints of the form $\boldsymbol{x}' = A\boldsymbol{x} + \boldsymbol{b}_i$, and then syntactically extracting A from these constraints. Otherwise, if Π does not have vertices, this operation can still be performed but after first applying to the affine hull constraints the *rank* and *subspace* reductions of [5]. Those correspond intuitively to applying a linear coordinate transformation that results in constraints expressed in terms of the smallest possible number of independent variables. More precisely, the rank reductions amount to performing the following operations. First, the set of constraints is rewritten in the form $P_2\boldsymbol{x}' = P_1\boldsymbol{x} + \boldsymbol{q}$, where $P_1, P_2 \in \mathbb{Z}^{m \times n}$, $\boldsymbol{q} \in \mathbb{Z}^m$ and $m \geq 0$. If the rank r of P_1 is less than n, then a linear variable change operation is applied in order to express the transformation in terms of only r distinct variables. The same procedure is also carried out if the rank of P_2 is less than n. In addition, subspace reductions are applied when the set of constraints $P_2\boldsymbol{x}' = P_1\boldsymbol{x} + \boldsymbol{q}$ implies static constraints on either $\boldsymbol{x}$ or $\boldsymbol{x}'$. The reduction consists in performing a linear variable change operation onto the largest number of distinct variables that are not statically constrained.   □

This procedure is illustrated in Section 5.1. In practice, since it follows from Theorem 3 that static constraints do not hamper iterability, a good strategy is to remove them before checking whether a LHR is affine. Finally, note that the acceleration method for AHT discussed in this section is able to successfully process all linear integer transformations that are handled by [2,3].

4   Generalized Affine Transformations

4.1   Principles

Affine hybrid transformations θ have the property that we can compute from their set of constraints a value $p \in \mathbb{N}_{>0}$ such that θ^p has an ultimately periodic behavior. In other words, iterating θ reduces to iterating θ^p, which is feasible within additive arithmetic. We call such a value p a *period* of θ.

In Section 3, we have shown that such a period p can be obtained by inspecting matrices extracted from the minimal geometrical components of the polyhedron $\Theta \subseteq \mathbb{R}^{2n}$ induced by the constraints of θ. If θ is affine, then these matrices happen to be identical for all components, which represents the fact that they are similarly affected by θ^p, in the sense that they share the same periodic behavior.

This sufficient condition for iterability is not at all necessary: If the geometrical components of Θ correspond to matrices $A_1, A_2, \ldots$ that are not identical, but yield values $p_1, p_2, \ldots$ such that $A_i^{2p_i} = A_i^{p_i}$ for all i, then all those components share an ultimately periodic behavior of period $p = \text{lcm}(p_1, p_2, \ldots)$. A possible acceleration procedure thus consists in computing such a value p by inspecting the geometrical components of Θ, computing p as the least common multiple of their detected periodicities p_i, and then checking whether θ^p reduces to a periodic transformation that is iterable within $\langle \mathbb{R}, \mathbb{Z}, +, \leq \rangle$. This inspection does not necessarily have to be carried out for all geometrical components: The iterability of θ^p can be checked whenever a candidate value for p has been obtained. If the analysis of a geometrical component fails to produce a periodicity p_i, the procedure can nevertheless continue with the other components.

This approach shares similarities with the solution proposed in [5] for accelerating *Multiple Counters Systems (MCS)* [11], which are a subclass of LHR in which all constraints are of the form $z_i \# z_j + c$, with $z_i, z_j \in \{x_1, \ldots, x_n, x'_1, \ldots, x'_n\}$, $\# \in \{<, \leq, =, \geq, >\}$, and $c \in \mathbb{Z}$. This solution proceeds by building directed weighted graphs that represent the set of constraints of a MCS θ, and then measuring the weights $p_1, p_2, \ldots$ of the simple cycles in these graphs. The value $p = \text{lcm}(p_1, p_2, \ldots)$ provides a (non necessarily optimal) candidate for the periodicity of θ. It is shown in [5] that this technique is able to accelerate every MCS.

In Section 4.2, we establish a connection between the acceleration technique presented in this paper and the one proposed for MCS in [5], by showing that the periodicities that are captured by the graph analysis method can also be detected by the inspection of geometrical components. As a consequence, our technique is complete over MCS. Compared with the method of [5], it has the important advantage of being closed under linear variable change operations, since those do not affect the properties of geometrical components of polyhedra. Furthermore, our approach is not limited to handling MCS, unlike the acceleration method developed in [11].

After a candidate periodicity value p has been obtained by inspecting the geometrical components of Θ, it remains to check whether the transformation θ^p has a periodic behavior that can be captured within $\langle \mathbb{R}, \mathbb{Z}, +, \leq \rangle$. This problem is addressed in Section 4.3.

4.2   Multiple Counters Systems

Let us briefly describe the method introduced in [5] for computing the periodicity of a MCS θ. As discussed in Section 2.2, for the sake of clarity, we consider that all inequality constraints are non-strict.

The first step is to build a finite directed graph G_θ, in which the nodes correspond to the variables $x_1, x_2, \ldots, x_n$, and the edges $(x_i, (c, d), x_j)$ are labeled with a *cost* $c \in \mathbb{Z}$ and a *depth* $d \in \{-1, 0, 1\}$. This graph represents the constraints of θ:

- A constraint $x_j \leq x_i + c$ or $x'_j \leq x'_i + c$ is represented by an edge $(x_i, (c, 0), x_j)$.
- A constraint $x'_j \leq x_i + c$ is represented by an edge $(x_i, (c, 1), x_j)$.
- A constraint $x'_j \geq x_i + c$ is represented by an edge $(x_j, (-c, -1), x_i)$.

The paths of G_θ correspond to combinations of constraints of θ. The cost and depth of such a path σ are defined as the sum of the individual cost and depth of the edges that compose it. For every $k > 0$, a path σ of depth k in G_θ represents a constraint $x'_j \leq x_i + c$ of the transformation θ^k, where x_i and x_j are respectively the origin and destination nodes of σ, c is the cost of σ, and the intermediate depths reached at each node visited by σ remain in the interval $[0, k]$. In the same way, the paths of G_θ of depth $-k$ or 0 also correspond to constraints of θ^k.

The main result of [5] is to show that, in order to obtain all constraints of θ^k, it is sufficient to consider the paths of G_θ of suitable depth that contain only unbounded occurrences of a single simple cycle. A periodicity p of θ, i.e., a value such that θ^p reduces to a periodic transformation, is then obtained by computing the least common multiple of the depths of the simple cycles of G_θ. This periodicity may not be the smallest one for θ, but this is not problematic.

We are now going to establish that such a periodicity p can also be computed by the procedure outlined in Section 4.1. This property is a consequence of the following result.

Theorem 6. *Let $k > 0$, and σ be a simple cycle of G_θ of depth $\pm k$ and cost c, representing a constraint $x'_i \leq x_i + c$ or $x'_i \geq x_i - c$ of θ^k. If this constraint can be saturated[2] by values of x and x' that satisfy $(x, x') \in \theta^k$, then there exists a geometrical component of Θ producing a matrix $A \in \mathbb{Q}^{n \times n}$ such that $A^{2k} = A^k$.*

Proof sketch. Let S be the set of constraints of θ that are represented by the edges of G_θ composing σ. Since the constraint represented by σ can be saturated, there exist values $v, v' \in \mathbb{R}^n$ that can respectively be assigned to x and x' in order to saturate all constraints in S.

The values v and v' may also saturate other constraints of θ. Let S' denote the set of constraints of θ that are necessarily saturated when S is saturated, i.e., that are saturated by every v and v' that saturate S. The set S' contains only constraints that are either saturated for all $v, v' \in \mathbb{R}^n$, or correspond to one or several simple cycles of G_θ. In the latter case, it can be established that each of these cycles shares the same depth $\pm k$ as σ.

One can thus find values v and v' that saturate all constraints in $S \cup S'$, and do not saturate the other constraints of θ. From the discussion in Section 2.3, it follows that the point $(v, v') \in \mathbb{R}^{2n}$ belongs to a geometrical component of Θ with an affine hull that exactly corresponds to the solutions of $S \cup S'$.

The matrix A produced by this component using the procedure described in Section 3.2 has the following property. Let $X \subseteq \{x_1, \ldots, x_n\}$ denote the set of all variables visited by the simple cycles of G_θ that correspond to the constraints

---

[2] This saturation requirement intuitively expresses the property that the constraint is essential, i.e., that it is not implied by other constraints of θ^k.

in $S \cup S'$. Recall that these simple cycles are all of depth $\pm k$. It follows that the transformation $\boldsymbol{x} \mapsto A^k \boldsymbol{x}$ preserves the values of the variables in X and assigns the value $\boldsymbol{0}$ to the other variables. One thus has $A^{2k} = A^k$. $\qquad \square$

In [5], a candidate value for the periodicity p of θ is obtained by computing the least common multiple of the depths p_i of all simple cycles in G_θ. Theorem 6 shows that each such value p_i will also be computed by the procedure discussed in Section 4.1, provided that the underlying cycle represents a constraint that is not redundant. The reciprocal property does not hold: Some geometrical components of Θ may correspond to a set of saturated constraints of θ that does not form a cycle. The inspection of such components may produce matrices A that do not yield a periodicity p_i, or yield a spurious one. This is not problematic, since a transformation θ such that θ^p has a periodic behavior is also periodic when it is raised to a power equal to an integer multiple of p.

4.3   Checking Periodicity

We now investigate the possibility of validating a candidate periodicity $p \in \mathbb{N}_{>0}$ for a LHR θ, i.e., checking whether θ^p has a periodic behavior that can be accelerated. Note that, for every $j \in [0, p-1]$ and $k \geq 0$, one has $\theta^{j+kp} = (\theta^p)^k \circ \theta^j$, hence accelerating θ reduces to accelerating θ^p.

Let θ' be the LHR defined by the *periodic* constraints of θ^p, i.e., those of the form $\boldsymbol{p}.(\boldsymbol{x}' - \boldsymbol{x}) \# q$, with $\boldsymbol{p} \in \mathbb{Z}^n$, $q \in \mathbb{Z}$, and $\# \in \{\leq, =, \geq\}$. Following [6], one can obtain a formula of $\langle \mathbb{R}, \mathbb{Z}, +, \leq \rangle$ representing the relation $\boldsymbol{x}' \in (\theta')^k(\boldsymbol{x})$ for all $k \geq 0$ in terms of the variables $\boldsymbol{x}$, $\boldsymbol{x}'$, and k. The problem is thus to check whether the acceleration of θ (or, equivalently, θ^p) can be reduced to the acceleration of θ'.

We first consider the case of a MCS θ for which we have obtained a period p by applying either the method introduced in Section 4.1, or the one given in [5]. For any $k \geq 0$, we know that the constraints of θ^{kp} are represented by paths of depth 0, k or $-k$ in the graph G_{θ^p}. It has been shown in [5] that it is sufficient to consider the paths of this graph that are either acyclic, or contain repetitions of only a single cycle of length 1. Such cycles correspond to periodic constraints, which are captured in θ'.

The transformation θ^p therefore satisfies two properties. The first one states that there exists $m > 0$ such that $m \leq n$, and every composition of m constraints of θ^p that results in a constraint of θ^{mp} necessarily includes at least one periodic constraint from θ'. Formally, this condition can be expressed as

$$\theta^{mp} = \bigcap_{i+j=m-1} \left[\theta^{ip} \circ \theta' \circ \theta^{jp} \right]. \tag{1}$$

The second property states that, in compositions of constraints of θ^p, periodic constraints do not need to be repeated at more than one place. Formally, we have

$$\forall i < m : \left[\theta' \circ \theta^{ip} \circ \theta' \right] \supseteq \left[(\theta')^2 \circ \theta^{ip} \right] \cap \left[\theta^{ip} \circ (\theta')^2 \right]. \tag{2}$$

In the case of MCS, Conditions 1 and 2 are always satisfied. For more general LHR θ, they can be used as a sufficient criterion for validating a candidate value p for the periodicity of θ. This is illustrated in Section 5.1 below. In practical applications, these conditions can be decided by operations over CPDD representations of the transformations, as discussed in Section 2.3.

The last step is to show that a LHR θ that satisfies Conditions 1 and 2 can be accelerated. These conditions imply that for all $k \geq m$, we have

$$\theta^{kp} = \bigcap_{i+j=m-1} \left[\theta^{ip} \circ (\theta')^{k-i-j} \circ \theta^{jp} \right].$$

Since θ' can be accelerated, this expression can be turned into a formula of $\langle \mathbb{R}, \mathbb{Z}, +, \leq \rangle$ representing the relation $\boldsymbol{x}' \in (\theta')^k(\boldsymbol{x})$ in terms of $\boldsymbol{x}$, $\boldsymbol{x}'$, and k.

5   Examples

5.1   Periodic LHR

Let us illustrate the approach proposed in this paper on the LHR $\theta \subseteq \mathbb{R}^2 \times \mathbb{R}^2$ defined by the set of constraints

$$\theta : \begin{cases} x_2' + x_1 \leq -1 \\ x_2' - x_1' + x_2 \leq -1 \\ 2x_2' - x_1' + x_1 + x_2 \geq -4. \end{cases}$$

First Step: Extracting a Candidate Periodic Matrix A from θ. The convex polyhedron $\Theta \subseteq \mathbb{R}^4$ induced by these constraints admits three minimal non-empty geometrical components, with the corresponding affine hulls

$$\alpha_1 : \begin{cases} x_2' + x_1 = -1 \\ x_2' - x_1' + x_2 = -1, \end{cases}$$

$$\alpha_2 : \begin{cases} x_2' + x_1 = -1 \\ 2x_2' - x_1' + x_1 + x_2 = -4, \end{cases}$$

and

$$\alpha_3 : \begin{cases} x_2' - x_1' + x_2 = -1 \\ 2x_2' - x_1' + x_1 + x_2 = -4. \end{cases}$$

The affine hull α_1 can equivalently be represented by the following constraints, from which we deduce the matrix A below:

$$\begin{cases} x_1' = -x_1 + x_2 \\ x_2' = -x_1 - 1 \end{cases} \qquad A = \begin{bmatrix} -1 & 1 \\ -1 & 0 \end{bmatrix}$$

Note that the affine hulls α_2 and α_3 produce the same matrix A, which hints at the property that θ is affine.

Using the algorithm mentioned in Theorem 4, one obtains that this matrix is such that $A^6 = A^3$ (actually, it satisfies the stronger property $A^3 = I_2$, where I_2 denotes the identity matrix of size 2), which gives a candidate periodicity $p = 3$.

Second Step: Checking Whether θ Is Affine. Following the procedure given in Section 3.2, we can compute a polyhedron Π such that θ is equivalent to $x \mapsto Ax + \Pi$. This yields:

$$\Pi : \begin{cases} x_2' \leq -1 \\ x_2' - x_1' \leq -1 \\ 2x_2' - x_1' \geq -4. \end{cases}$$

From Theorem 3, we deduce that θ is iterable within $\langle \mathbb{R}, \mathbb{Z}, +, \leq \rangle$.

Alternative Second Step: Checking the Candidate Period. Alternatively, we may avoid computing Π and directly use the technique of Section 4.3 for checking that the candidate periodicity $p = 3$ is valid. We obtain that θ^3 is of the form:

$$\begin{cases} -4 \leq x_1' - x_1 \leq 4 \\ -4 \leq x_2' - x_2 \leq 4 \\ -4 \leq x_1' - x_2' - x_1 + x_2 \leq 4 \\ x_1' + x_2' - x_1 - x_2 \leq 6 \\ x_1' - 2x_2' - x_1 + 2x_2 \leq 6 \\ 2x_1' - x_2' - 2x_1 + x_2 \geq -6, \end{cases}$$

which is periodic since all its constraints are expressed over $x_1' - x_1$ and $x_2' - x_2$. For all $k > 1$, one thus has:

$$\theta^{3k} : \begin{cases} -4k \leq x_1' - x_1 \leq 4k \\ -4k \leq x_2' - x_2 \leq 4k \\ -4k \leq x_1' - x_2' - x_1 + x_2 \leq 4k \\ x_1' + x_2' - x_1 - x_2 \leq 6k \\ x_1' - 2x_2' - x_1 + 2x_2 \leq 6k \\ 2x_1' - x_2' - 2x_1 + x_2 \geq -6k. \end{cases}$$

The reflexive and transitive closure of θ^{3k} can be obtained by quantification over k. As a result, θ is iterable within $\langle \mathbb{R}, \mathbb{Z}, +, \leq \rangle$.

5.2   Linear Hybrid Automaton

As a second example, consider the linear hybrid automaton H in Figure 2. The effect of the cycle in H, starting from the leftmost location and preceding each transition by the passage of time, is described by the LHR θ_H below. The variable x has been eliminated using the reductions of [5] since, after the first iteration, the cycle starts and ends with $x = 0$.

$$\theta_H = \begin{cases} y + t - y' + t' \leq 1 \\ -2y + z - t + 2y' - z' - t' \leq -1 \\ y - y' \leq -10 \end{cases}$$

The convex polyhedron $\Theta_H \subseteq \mathbb{R}^6$ induced by θ_H has one minimal non-empty geometrical component, obtained by saturating all the constraints of θ_H. Its

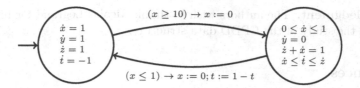

Fig. 2. Linear Hybrid Automaton H

affine hull is described by the following constraints, from which we derive the matrix A_H.

$$\begin{cases} y' = y + 10 \\ z' = z + 10 \\ t' = -t + 11 \end{cases} \qquad\qquad A_H = \begin{bmatrix} 1 & 0 & 0 \\ 0 & 1 & 0 \\ 0 & 0 & -1 \end{bmatrix}$$

Using the algorithm mentioned in Theorem 4, we get a candidate period $p = 2$ since $A_H^2 = I_3$ (the identity matrix of dimension 3). Following the approach of Section 4.3 confirms that θ_H^2 is periodic. Hence, $(\theta_H^2)^*$ can be computed using the techniques of [6]. One then obtains $\theta_H^* = (\theta_H^2)^* \circ (\theta_H \cup Id)$. Note that the computation of θ_H^* was out of scope of the techniques of [5,6], which cannot handle periodicities greater than one.

6   Conclusions

This paper introduces an original method for accelerating the data transformations that label control cycles of linear hybrid automata. Given such a transformation θ, the idea consists in constructing a convex polyhedron from its linear constraints, and then inspecting the geometrical components of this polyhedron in order to compute a value p such that θ^p is periodic.

This method is able to accelerate all transformations that can be handled by the specialized algorithms developed in [3,5,6,11], in particular *Multiple Counters Systems*, to which the reachability analysis of timed automata can be reduced. Compared with those solutions, our method has the advantage of being closed under linear changes of coordinates, which naturally do not affect the geometrical features of polyhedra. Our acceleration algorithm can also potentially be applied to the *octagonal* transformations studied in [8,9,10], and an open question is to establish whether it provides full coverage of such transformations.

We did not analyze the practical cost of our acceleration procedure, which actually depends on the implementation details of the symbolic data structure used for manipulating polyhedra, and on the heuristics employed for selecting the geometrical components to be inspected. In all our case studies, considering the minimal non-empty components for which a non-trivial matrix A can be extracted turned out to be sufficient, but we do not know whether this property holds in all cases.

Acknowledgment. The authors wish to thank Nicolas Legrand for his contribution to the study of the CPDD data structure.

References

1. Alur, R., Dill, D.L.: A theory of timed automata. Theoretical Computer Science 126(2), 183–235 (1994)
2. Boigelot, B.: Symbolic Methods for Exploring Infinite State Spaces. Ph.D. thesis, Université de Liège (1998)
3. Boigelot, B.: On iterating linear transformations over recognizable sets of integers. Theoretical Computer Science 309(1-3), 413–468 (2003)
4. Boigelot, B., Brusten, J., Degbomont, J.F.: Automata-based symbolic representations of polyhedra. In: Dediu, A.-H., Martín-Vide, C. (eds.) LATA 2012. LNCS, vol. 7183, pp. 3–20. Springer, Heidelberg (2012)
5. Boigelot, B., Herbreteau, F.: The power of hybrid acceleration. In: Ball, T., Jones, R.B. (eds.) CAV 2006. LNCS, vol. 4144, pp. 438–451. Springer, Heidelberg (2006)
6. Boigelot, B., Herbreteau, F., Jodogne, S.: Hybrid acceleration using real vector automata. In: Hunt Jr., W.A., Somenzi, F. (eds.) CAV 2003. LNCS, vol. 2725, pp. 193–205. Springer, Heidelberg (2003)
7. Boigelot, B., Jodogne, S., Wolper, P.: An effective decision procedure for linear arithmetic over the integers and reals. ACM Transactions on Computational Logic 6(3), 614–633 (2005)
8. Bozga, M., Gîrlea, C., Iosif, R.: Iterating octagons. In: Kowalewski, S., Philippou, A. (eds.) TACAS 2009. LNCS, vol. 5505, pp. 337–351. Springer, Heidelberg (2009)
9. Bozga, M., Iosif, R., Konečný, F.: Fast acceleration of ultimately periodic relations. In: Touili, T., Cook, B., Jackson, P. (eds.) CAV 2010. LNCS, vol. 6174, pp. 227–242. Springer, Heidelberg (2010)
10. Bozga, M., Iosif, R., Konečný, F.: Safety problems are NP-complete for flat integer programs with octagonal loops. In: McMillan, K.L., Rival, X. (eds.) VMCAI 2014. LNCS, vol. 8318, pp. 242–261. Springer, Heidelberg (2014)
11. Comon, H., Jurski, Y.: Multiple counters automata, safety analysis and Presburger arithmetic. In: Vardi, M.Y. (ed.) CAV 1998. LNCS, vol. 1427, pp. 268–279. Springer, Heidelberg (1998)
12. Cousot, P., Cousot, R.: Abstract interpretation: A unified lattice model for static analysis of programs by construction or approximation of fixpoints. In: Proc. POPL 1977, pp. 238–252. ACM Press (1977)
13. Degbomont, J.F.: Implicit Real-Vector Automata. Ph.D. thesis, Université de Liège (2013)
14. Henzinger, T.A.: The theory of hybrid automata. In: Proc. LICS 1996, pp. 278–292. IEEE Computer Society Press (1996)
15. Zhou, C., Hoare, C.A.R., Ravn, A.P.: A calculus of durations. Information Processing Letters 40(5), 269–276 (1991)

A Mechanized Proof of Loop Freedom of the (Untimed) AODV Routing Protocol

Timothy Bourke[1,2], Rob van Glabbeek[3,4], and Peter Höfner[3,4]

[1] INRIA Paris-Rocquencourt, France
[2] Ecole normale supérieure, Paris, France
[3] NICTA, Australia
[4] Computer Science and Engineering, UNSW, Australia

Abstract. The Ad hoc On-demand Distance Vector (AODV) routing protocol allows the nodes in a Mobile Ad hoc Network (MANET) or a Wireless Mesh Network (WMN) to know where to forward data packets. Such a protocol is 'loop free' if it never leads to routing decisions that forward packets in circles. This paper describes the mechanization of an existing pen-and-paper proof of loop freedom of AODV in the interactive theorem prover Isabelle/HOL. The mechanization relies on a novel compositional approach for lifting invariants to networks of nodes. We exploit the mechanization to analyse several improvements of AODV and show that Isabelle/HOL can re-establish most proof obligations automatically and identify exactly the steps that are no longer valid.

1 Introduction

Mobile Ad hoc Networks (MANETs) and Wireless Mesh Networks (WMNs) are self-configuring wireless networks for mobile devices. Their nodes are reactive systems that cooperate to pass data packets from one node to another towards each packet's ultimate destination. This global service must satisfy certain correctness properties—for example, that data packets are never sent in circles. Proofs of such properties tend to be long and complicated, often involving many case distinctions over possible messages sent and combinations of Boolean predicates over internal data structures. For example, the only prior existing proof[1] of loop freedom of the Ad hoc On-demand Distance Vector (AODV) routing protocol—one of the four protocols currently standardized by the IETF MANET working group, and the basis of new WMN routing protocols such as HWMP in the IEEE 802.11s wireless mesh network standard [14]—is about 18 pages long and requires around 40 lemmas to prove the final statement [8]. This proof is based on a process-algebraic model.

Mechanizing process calculi and process-algebraic models in an Interactive Theorem Prover (ITP) like Isabelle/HOL [20] can now almost be considered routine [1, 9, 11, 13]. However, a lot of this work focuses on process calculi

---

[1] Earlier, and simpler, proofs appear in [2,22] and [26], but none of them is complete and valid for AODV as standardized in [23]. We justify this statement in Section 9.

F. Cassez and J.-F. Raskin (Eds.): ATVA 2014, LNCS 8837, pp. 47–63, 2014.

themselves—for example, by treating variable binding [1] or proving that bisimulation is a congruence [11,13]. While the study of security protocols has received some attention [7], comparatively little work has been done on mechanizing the application of such calculi to the practical verification of network protocols. In this paper, however, we focus on an application and mechanize the proof of loop freedom of AODV, a crucial correctness property. Our proof uses standard transition-system based techniques for showing safety properties [15,16], as well as a novel compositional technique for lifting properties from individual nodes to networks of nodes [4]. We demonstrate these techniques on an example of significant size and practical interest.

The development described in this paper builds directly on the aforementioned model and pen-and-paper proof of loop freedom of AODV [8]. While the process algebra model and the fine details of the original proof are already very formal, the implication that transfers statements about nodes to statements about networks involves coarser reasoning over execution sequences. Our mechanization simplifies and clarifies this aspect by explicitly stating the assumptions made of other nodes and by reformulating the original reasoning into an invariant form, that is, by reasoning over pairs of states rather than sequences of states.

Given that a proof already exists and that mechanization can be so time-consuming, why do we bother? Besides the added confidence and credibility that come with having even the smallest details fastidiously checked, the real advantage in encoding model, proof, and framework in the logic of an ITP is that they can then be analysed and manipulated (semi-)automatically. Section 8 describes how we exploited this fact to verify variations to the basic protocol, and Section 9 argues that such models aid review and repeatability. We expect that the work described will serve as a convenient and solid base for showing other properties of the AODV protocol and studying other protocols, and, eventually, to serve as a specification for refinement proofs. Finally, although any such work benefits from the accumulation of technical advances and engineering improvements to ITPs, we argue that it cannot yet be considered routine.

The paper is structured as follows. In Section 2 we informally describe the AODV protocol. Section 3 briefly states the theorem of loop freedom of AODV in the form given to Isabelle/HOL. The following three sections explain the meaning of this statement: Section 4 describes how the model of AODV in the process algebra AWN (Algebra for Wireless Networks) [8] is translated into Isabelle/HOL; Section 5 describes the formalization of network properties such as loop freedom; and, Section 6 explains our formalization of invariance of network properties. Section 7 summarizes how we proved the theorem in Isabelle/HOL. Section 8 describes several improvements of AODV, proposed in [8], and illustrates the use of Isabelle/HOL in proving loop freedom of these variants. Once the original proof has been mechanized, Isabelle/HOL can re-establish most proof obligations for these improvements automatically, and identify exactly the steps that are no longer valid and that need to be adjusted. A detailed discussion of related work follows in Section 9, followed by concluding remarks.

There is only space to show the most important parts of our mechanization of the process algebra AWN and of the model of AODV. Comparing these parts

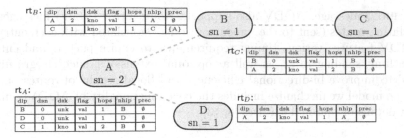

Fig. 1. Example AODV instance

before [8, §§4–6] and after mechanization in Isabelle/HOL, should give sufficient clues about the remaining parts. By focusing mainly on the application (loop freedom of AODV), we only show a glimpse of our proof method. A companion paper [4] presents the technical details of the mechanization of AWN and the associated framework for compositional proof. Source files of the complete mechanization in Isabelle/HOL are available online [5].

2 The AODV Routing Protocol

The purpose of AODV [23] is to route data packets between nodes. Figure 1 shows an example network with four nodes addressed A, B, C, and D. Each node maintains a local *sequence number* (sn) and a *routing table* (rt). Imagine that the former are all set to 1, that the latter are all empty, and that A wants to send data to C. No route is known, so A increments its sn to 2 and broadcasts a Route Request (RREQ) message to its neighbours B and D. Both neighbours immediately add a routing table entry with the *destination address* (dip) as A, the *destination sequence number* (dsn) as 2, as sent by A, the *destination-sequence-number status* (dsk) as 'known' (kno), the *route status* (flag) as 'valid' (val), the *number of hops to the destination* (hops) as 1, the *next hop address* (nhip) as A, and an empty set of *precursors* (nodes known to be interested in this route).

Since neither B nor D has a routing table entry for C, they both in turn forward the RREQ message to their neighbours, which causes A to add entries for B and D, and C to add an entry for B. Since (forwarded) RREQs only include the sn of the originating node—A in this case—the dsn and dsk fields of these new entries are set to 0 and 'unknown' (unk), respectively. Node C also adds an entry for A to its routing table, with hop count 2 and next hop B. Since C is the destination, it replies to the request with a Route Reply (RREP) message, which is destined for A and unicast to B. On receipt, B updates its rt with a route to C (adding A as precursor) and forwards the message to A. When A receives this message it updates its rt and starts forwarding data packets to C via B. All established routing table entries are summarized in Figure 1.

Besides this basic scenario, AODV also supports early generation of RREP messages by 'intermediate nodes' [23, §6.6.2]: whenever an intermediate node has information about a route to the destination, rather than forwarding the RREQ message, it generates an RREP message and sends it back to the originator of the RREQ message. AODV also supports Route Error (RERR) messages for invalidating routes (sent to the 'precursor nodes' associated with each entry).

AODV features various timing requirements to expire packets and entries, and to limit sending rates, as well as optional extensions, such as 'gratuitous RREPs' to improve bi-directional efficiency, and 'local repair' of routes on link loss. The model we mechanize includes the core functionality of AODV, but not timing details or optional features [8, §3].

3 Loop Freedom

Routing protocols must continue to correctly route data even as nodes appear, disappear, and move. It is essential that they maintain *loop freedom*: the absence of cycles across different routing tables. For instance, the example network would have a cycle if D came into range of B, B updated its route for C to pass via D, and D added a route for C via A. Proofs of loop freedom when route replies are only generated by destination nodes are relatively subtle, but they become really delicate when intermediate nodes may also generate RREP messages.

The main result shown in our mechanization is:

Theorem 1 (AODV loop freedom). *For any well-formed network term* n, closed (pnet (λi. paodv i ⟨⟨ qmsg) n) ⊨ netglobal (λσ. ∀ dip. irrefl ((rt-graph σ dip)$^+$)).

Most of this paper is concerned with explaining the various elements of this statement and its proof in Isabelle/HOL. In sum, the variable n represents any well formed term describing a network instance—a term is well formed iff all nodes therein have distinct addresses. It is mapped to an automaton by the functions pnet and closed. A node with address i comprises an instance of the protocol, paodv i, reading messages from a queue process, qmsg. All reachable states of this model are shown to satisfy the formula at right of the '⊨', which (1) maps a state structured like the network term into a function from each node address to that node's local state (netglobal), (2) abstracts this map into a directed graph with an arc from one node to another when the former has a valid routing table entry for a given dip to the latter (rt-graph), and finally, (3) claims that the transitive closure of each such graph is irreflexive.

4 Modelling AODV

In Isabelle/HOL we formalize AODV following the model from [8], which is expressed in a process algebra called AWN [8, §4]. In AWN, a network instance running a protocol is modelled in five layers, from the bottom up: (1) sequential processes, (2) local parallel composition at a single network node, (3) nodes of the form *ip*:*P*:*R* with *ip* the node's address, *R* the set of reachable neighbours, and *P* the process running on the node, (4) partial networks of nodes, and, (5) networks closed to further interaction. The behaviour of each layer is defined by Structural Operational Semantics (SOS) rules over either process terms or lower layers. By including initial states, the first layer defines an automaton and the others become functions over automata.

$p_1 \oplus p_2$ call(pn) $\{l\}[\![u]\!]$ p $\{l\}\langle g \rangle$ p $\{l\}$unicast(s_{ip}, s_{msg}).p $\triangleright$ q $\{l\}$broadcast(s_{msg}).p

$\{l\}$groupcast(s_{ips}, s_{msg}).p $\{l\}$send(s_{msg}).p $\{l\}$receive(u_{msg}).p $\{l\}$deliver(s_{data}).p

(a) Term constructors for ('s, 'p, 'l) seqp.

$$\frac{\xi' = u\, \xi}{((\xi,\ \{l\}[\![u]\!]\ p),\ \tau,\ (\xi',\ p)) \in \text{seqp-sos}\ \Gamma} \qquad \frac{((\xi,\ p),\ a,\ (\xi',\ p')) \in \text{seqp-sos}\ \Gamma}{((\xi,\ p \oplus q),\ a,\ (\xi',\ p')) \in \text{seqp-sos}\ \Gamma}$$

$$\frac{((\xi,\ \Gamma\ pn),\ a,\ (\xi',\ p')) \in \text{seqp-sos}\ \Gamma}{((\xi,\ \text{call(pn)}),\ a,\ (\xi',\ p')) \in \text{seqp-sos}\ \Gamma} \qquad \frac{((\xi,\ q),\ a,\ (\xi',\ q')) \in \text{seqp-sos}\ \Gamma}{((\xi,\ p \oplus q),\ a,\ (\xi',\ q')) \in \text{seqp-sos}\ \Gamma}$$

$$((\xi,\ \{l\}\text{broadcast}(s_{msg}).p),\ \text{broadcast}\ (s_{msg}\ \xi),\ (\xi,\ p)) \in \text{seqp-sos}\ \Gamma$$

(b) SOS rules for sequential processes: subset of seqp-sos.

Fig. 2. Sequential processes: terms and semantics

The four node network of Figure 1 is, for example, modelled as
closed (pnet (λi. paodv i $\langle\langle$ qmsg) (($\langle$A; {B, D}$\rangle$ $\|$ ($\langle$B; {A, C}$\rangle$ $\|$ (($\langle$C; {B}$\rangle$ $\|$ $\langle$D; {A}$\rangle$)))))),
where the function closed models layer 5, closing a network, and pnet fabricates
a partial network from a function mapping addresses to node processes and an
expression describing the initial topology. For example, $\langle$A; {B, D}$\rangle$ becomes the
node $\langle$A : paodv A $\langle\langle$ qmsg : {B, D}$\rangle$ with address A, initial neighbours B and D,
and running a local composition of the protocol process paodv (initialized with its
address) fed by a queue qmsg of incoming messages. The communication ranges
of nodes are independent of the structure of their composition and may change
during an execution. We now briefly describe each layer in more detail. Full
details of AWN, with all SOS rules, can be found in [8] and the source files [5].

(1) Sequential processes. Both the AODV protocol logic and the behaviour
of message queues are specified by process terms of type ('s, 'p, 'l) seqp, parameterized by 's, the type of the data state manipulated by the term, 'p, the type of
process names, and 'l, the type of labels. We write ξ or ξ' for variables of type
's, and p, p', q, or q' for those of type ('s, 'p, 'l) seqp. Labels are used to refer to
particular control locations.

The term constructors are summarized in Figure 2a: *assignment,* $\{l\}[\![u]\!]$ p,
which transforms the data state deterministically (u has type 's $\Rightarrow$'s) and then
acts as p; *guard/bind,* $\{l\}\langle g \rangle$ p, which returns the set of states where the guard
evaluates to true, one of which is chosen nondeterministically; *network synchronizations,* receive/unicast/broadcast/groupcast, whose destinations and contents depend on the data state; *internal communications,* send/receive/deliver, which do
not need specified destinations and whose contents depend on the data state;
choice ($\oplus$), combining the possibilities of two subterms; and *call* (call), which
jumps to a named process. The argument s_{msg} of broadcast is a data expression
with variables, which evaluates to a message. It thus has type 's $\Rightarrow$ msg. The
argument u_{msg} of receive, on the other hand, is a variable that upon receipt of

a message is evaluated to the message received. It has the type of a message-dependent state change (msg ⇒ 's ⇒ 's). A guard is of type 's ⇒ 's set. It can express both a construct that nondeterministically binds variables, giving a set of possible successor states, and one that returns a singleton set containing the current state provided it satisfies a given condition and the empty set otherwise.

The SOS rules for sequential processes, seqp-sos, define a set of transitions. A transition is a triple relating a source state, an action, and a destination state. The states of sequential processes pair data components of type 's with control terms of type ('s, 'p, 'l) seqp. A set of transitions is defined relative to a *(recursive) specification* Γ of type 'p ⇒ ('s, 'p, 'l) seqp, which maps process names to terms. Some of the rules are shown in Figure 2b.

These elements suffice to express the control logic of the AODV protocol. We introduce six mutually recursive processes whose names are shown in Figure 3. This figure shows the control structure of the specification Γ_{aodv}, which maps each name to a term. The main process is called PAodv. It can broadcast control packets or send data packets—the two descending subtrees at the very left—or on receiving a message descend into one of the other terms depending on the message content the five-pronged choice leading to the other labels. All paths loop back to PAodv. The smallest subprocess, at bottom right, is defined as

$$\Gamma_{aodv} \text{ PNewPkt} = \text{labelled PNewPkt (}$$
$$\langle \lambda \xi. \text{ if dip } \xi = \text{ip } \xi \text{ then } \{\xi\} \text{ else } \emptyset \rangle$$
$$\text{deliver(data)} . \ [\![\text{clear-locals}]\!] \ \text{call(PAodv)}$$
$$\oplus \langle \lambda \xi. \text{ if dip } \xi \neq \text{ip } \xi \text{ then } \{\xi\} \text{ else } \emptyset \rangle$$
$$[\![\lambda \xi. \ \xi (\![\text{store} := \text{add (data } \xi) \text{ (dip } \xi) \text{ (store } \xi))]\!)]\!]$$
$$[\![\text{clear-locals}]\!] \ \text{call(PAodv))}.$$

It branches on whether or not the dip and ip variables have the same value in the current state, and then either delivers a message or updates the variable store. Each branch then loops back to the main process. The labelled function recursively labels the control states from PNewPkt-:0 through PNewPkt-:4.

The graph of Figure 3 summarizes the just over 100 control locations and shows that the model contains both significant branching and sequencing, some of which is exploited in the verification. The thicker, solid lines are synchronizing actions. The dashed lines are assignments or guards. Each straight sequence of dashed lines, which correspond to a sequence of assignments, could in fact be replaced by a single dashed line, by nesting state transformations. However,

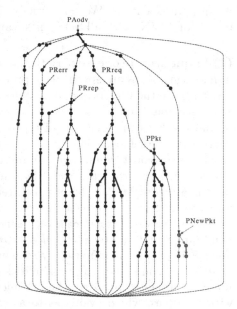

Fig. 3. Process term graph of Γ_{aodv}

this would make the model easier to get wrong, harder to read, and less like implementations in programming languages. Moreover, it is easier to verify many small steps, especially since typically most are dispatched automatically.

The AODV data state is modelled in a standard way using records [25, §3.3]. There are five global variables:[2] ip, the local address of type nat; sn, the current sequence number, also a nat; rreqs, a set of pairs of addresses and request identifiers that tracks already handled route requests; store, a partial map from addresses to a status and queue of pending data packets; and rt, the routing table, a partial map from addresses to entries of type sqn × k × f × nat × ip × ip set, where sqn and ip are synonyms for nat. Each subprocess also has its own local variables, which in the original process algebra [8] are often initialized from expressions during subprocess invocation. While it may seem 'tidy' to explicitly model variable locality, it complicates syntactic details and the aim of working ultimately on transition systems where there is no notion of a subprocess. Furthermore, the recursion through Γ_{aodv} induced by call already entails one or two technical details, as we discuss in [4], even before variable assignment is considered. So, rather than stay faithful to these details in the mechanization, we simply include the union of 12 local variables in the state record. When invoking a subprocess, these variables are set to arbitrary values,[3] by clear-locals, before combining assignment and call. This pragmatic solution works well in our setting.

The routing table, rt, is central to AODV and thus to this verification. Several functions are defined to access, add, update, and invalidate its entries. For example, the function nhop of type rt ⇒ ip ⇀ ip gives the next hop for an address if defined; update of type rt ⇒ ip ⇒ r ⇒ rt encodes the rules determining if and how an entry is modified, invalidate of type rt ⇒ (ip ⇀ sqn) ⇒ rt marks a set of routes as invalid (possibly individually setting sequence numbers), and addpreRT of type rt ⇒ ip ⇒ ip set ⇀ rt adds precursors to an entry. These (partial) functions are defined in the λ-calculus of Isabelle/HOL.

The process state is a pair of a data record and a process term. The (singleton) set of initial states is given by a function, σ_{aodv} i = {(aodv-init i, Γ_{aodv} PAodv)} where i is the initial value of ip. The process term represents the control state: a sort of a symbolic program counter. As the rules in Figure 2 indicate, process labels have no influence on the flow of control (unlike in [16]). They exist only to aid verification. The sets of initial states and transitions are bundled into a generic automaton structure with two fields to model an AODV process:

paodv i = (|init = {(aodv-init i, Γ_{aodv} PAodv)}, trans = seqp-sos Γ_{aodv} |).

The states of this automaton (an overapproximation of the set of reachable states) are determined by the type of the sources and targets of the transitions.

Having considered sequential processes, we now consider the other four layers.

(2) Local parallel composition. An instance of AODV must always be willing to accept a message from its environment. To achieve this, and to model

---

[2] These variables are global in that their values are maintained indefinitely; however, they are local to each specific process running on a specific node.

[3] Almost: as sip may not equal ip, we use ξ(|sip := SOME x. x ≠ ip ξ|).

asynchronous message transmission, the protocol process is combined with a simple FIFO-queue model (modelled as a sequential process): paodv i $\langle\!\langle$ qmsg. The composition operator applies to automata:

$$s \langle\!\langle t = (\!|\text{init} = \text{init } s \times \text{init } t, \text{trans} = \text{parp-sos } (\text{trans } s) (\text{trans } t)|\!).$$

The rules for parp-sos can be found in [5, 8].

(3–4) Nodes and partial networks. Networks of AODV instances are specified as values of an inductive type: a net-tree is either a node $\langle i; R_i \rangle$ with address i and a set of neighbour addresses R_i, or a composition of two net-trees $p_1 \| p_2$. The function pnet maps each such value to an automaton:

$$\text{pnet np } \langle i; R_i \rangle = \langle i : \text{np } i : R_i \rangle$$
$$\text{pnet np } (p_1 \| p_2) = (\!|\text{init} = \{s_1\|s_2 \mid s_1 \in \text{init } (\text{pnet np } p_1) \wedge s_2 \in \text{init } (\text{pnet np } p_2)\},$$
$$\text{trans} = \text{pnet-sos } (\text{trans } (\text{pnet np } p_1)) (\text{trans } (\text{pnet np } p_2))|\!),$$

where np is a function from addresses i to parallel process expressions, such as $\lambda i.$ paodv i $\langle\!\langle$ qmsg, and where

$$\langle i : \text{np} : R_i \rangle = (\!|\text{init} = \{s^i_{R_i} \mid s \in \text{init np}\}, \text{trans} = \text{node-sos } (\text{trans np})|\!).$$

The states of such automata mirror the structure of the original network term. Node states are denoted s^i_R and composed states are denoted $s_1\|s_2$. During an execution of a network, the tree structure and addresses remain constant, but the neighbours, control states, and data states of nodes may evolve.

(5) Complete networks. Such a network is closed to new node interactions:

$$\text{closed } A = A(\!|\text{trans} := \text{cnet-sos } (\text{trans } A)|\!).$$

In sum, this section has presented the part of Theorem 1 to the left of the '$\models$'.

5   Stating Network Properties

Our verification exploits the inductive structure of net-trees and states. Experience taught us to keep this structure for as long as possible and only later to transform it into a partial mapping from addresses to data records, using:

$$\text{netlift sr } (s^i_R) = [i \mapsto \text{fst } (\text{sr } s)]$$
$$\text{netlift sr } (s\|t) = \text{netlift sr } s + \text{netlift sr } t,$$

where sr divides the state into 'exposed' parts (the poadv data state) and 'masked' parts (the paodv control term and the states of qmsg). The fst then elides the latter. The result of netlift is a partial function from addresses to the exposed part of the state of the corresponding node. It is made total by mapping missing elements to the initial (data) state before being passed to a property P:

$$\text{netglobal } P = \lambda s. P \text{ (default aodv-init } (\text{netlift fst } s)),$$

where default df f = $(\lambda i.$ case f i of None $\Rightarrow$ df i | Some s $\Rightarrow$ s). P is a property over a function, written σ, from addresses i to data records. It can thus speak, for instance, of the routing table maintained by node i. The function netglobal turns such a property into a property of network states s.

An example of P occurs in Theorem 1: $\lambda\sigma.$ $\forall$dip. irrefl$((\text{rt-graph}\ \sigma\ \text{dip})^+)$. Here rt-graph is a function that, given an address dip and a function σ from addresses to data states, generates a routing graph: its vertices are all possible addresses i and there is an arc (ip, ip$'$) iff ip $\neq$ dip and the entry for dip in the routing table at node ip has the form $(*, *, \text{val}, *, \text{ip}', *)$. An arc in this routing graph indicates that ip$'$ is the next hop on a valid route to dip known by ip; a path in a routing graph describes a route towards dip discovered by AODV. We say σ is *loop free* if the routing graphs rt-graph σ dip are acyclic, for all destinations dip, i.e. if $P\sigma$ holds. A network state s is *loop free* iff the function netmap s from addresses to data records is loop free, i.e. if netglobal P s. Finally, a routing protocol, such as AODV, is *loop free* iff all reachable network expressions are loop free. This quantification over reachable network expressions is encoded in the symbol $\models$.

In sum, this section has presented the part of Theorem 1 to the right of the '$\models$'.

6 Stating Invariance of Network Properties

As Theorem 1 is a safety property, we need only consider questions of invariance, that is, properties of reachable states. The meta theory is classic [19, Part III].

Definition 1 (reachability). *For an automaton A and an assumption I over actions,* reachable A I *is the smallest set defined by the rules:*

$$\frac{s \in \text{init } A}{s \in \text{reachable } A\ I} \qquad \frac{s \in \text{reachable } A\ I \quad (s,\ a,\ s') \in \text{trans } A \quad I\ a}{s' \in \text{reachable } A\ I}$$

Definition 2 (invariance). *For an automaton A and an assumption I over actions, a predicate P is* invariant, *written $A \models (I \rightarrow) P$, iff $\forall s \in$ reachable A I. P s.*

Definition 3 (transition invariance). *For an automaton A and an assumption I over actions, a predicate P is* transition invariant, *written $A \models (I \rightarrow) P$, iff $\forall a.\ I\ a \longrightarrow (\forall s \in$ reachable A I. $\forall s'.\ (s,\ a,\ s') \in$ trans A $\longrightarrow P\ (s,\ a,\ s'))$.*

We recover the standard definition when I is λ-. True and write simply $A \models P$.

In sum, this finishes the presentation of Theorem 1.

7 Our Proof

To show invariance, we follow the compositional strategy elucidated in [24, §1.6.2]. That is, we take as a basic element automata with seqp-sos Γ_{aodv} as the set of transitions, show invariance using induction, and then develop proof rules for each of the operators defined in the previous section to lift the results to complete networks. The inductive assertion method is also classic, see, for example, Manna & Pnueli [16, Rule INV-B]. Its core, in Isabelle, is the induction principle associated with Definition 1.

Both the original and mechanized proofs of Theorem 1 involve a succession of invariants and transition invariants leading to the ultimate result. As an example,

$$\mathsf{paodv}\ i \models \mathsf{onl}\ \varGamma_{\mathsf{aodv}}\ (\lambda(\xi, \text{-}).\ \forall\mathsf{ip} \in \mathsf{kD}\ (\mathsf{rt}\ \xi).\ 1 \le \mathsf{the}\ (\mathsf{dhops}\ (\mathsf{rt}\ \xi)\ \mathsf{ip})) \qquad (1)$$

states that 'all routing table entries have a hop count greater than or equal to one' (kD gives the domain of a routing table; the the adds an obligation to show that ip is in the domain of dhops (rt ξ)). This particular predicate only ranges over the data state, ξ, but others also range over labels, for example,

$$\mathsf{paodv}\ i \models (\mathsf{recvmsg}\ \mathsf{P} \to) \ \mathsf{onl}\ \varGamma_{\mathsf{aodv}}\ (\lambda(\xi, \mathsf{l}).\ \mathsf{l} \in \{\mathsf{PAodv\text{-}:1}\} \longrightarrow \mathsf{P}\ (\mathsf{msg}\ \xi)) \qquad (2)$$

states that 'if for every receive m, m satisfies P, then the msg variable also satisfies P at location PAodv-:1'. The map onl $\varGamma$ P, defined by $\lambda(\xi, \mathsf{p}).\ \forall\mathsf{l} \in \mathsf{labels}\ \varGamma\ \mathsf{p}.\ \mathsf{P}\ (\xi, \mathsf{l})$, extracts labels from control states, which obviates the need to include and maintain process terms in invariants.[4]

Invariants like these are solved by establishing them for all possible initial states, and showing that they are preserved by all transitions. The soundness of this method is also formally justified in Isabelle/HOL [4].

This approach suffices for showing nearly all intermediate invariants, but not for expressing the final invariant from which Theorem 1 follows. The authors of the original proof [8, Theorem 7.30] introduce a notion of 'quality' of routing table entries, and show that it strictly increases along any valid route to a destination dip. They formalize this as

$$``dip \in \mathsf{vD}_N^{ip} \cap \mathsf{vD}_N^{nhip}\ \wedge\ nhip \ne dip\ \Rightarrow\ \xi_N^{ip}(\mathsf{rt}) \sqsubseteq_{dip} \xi_N^{nhip}(\mathsf{rt})",$$

where N is a "reachable network state", vD_N^{ip} are the addresses for which ip has valid routing entries, and $nhip$ is the address of the next hop toward dip at ip. But our basic invariants, like (1) or (2), can only refer to the local model's state (ξ). How can we compare the states at two nodes (ξ^{ip} and ξ^{nhip}) without immediately introducing the whole model before the '$\models$'?

Our solution is to introduce 'open' versions of the SOS rules and operators, and of reachability and (transition) invariance.

The *open* SOS of AWN differs from the default (*closed*) version by modelling data states as (total) functions from node addresses to data records. That is, rather than define rules over a variable ξ of type state, they are defined over a variable σ of type ip $\Rightarrow$ state. At the level of sequential processes, the open equivalent of seqp-sos (oseqp-sos) is additionally parameterized by an address i, and the SOS rules only constrain this ith component. At the level of local parallel compositions within a node, we simply inherit the data state from the left argument (the process aodv).[5] The lifting to node expressions is unproblematic. The composition of two partial networks effectively synchronizes the state mappings: the only transitions that can occur are those where, given a source state (σ), both components agree on a destination state (σ').

---

[4] Using labels is standard, see, for instance, [16, Chap. 1], or the 'assertion networks' of [24, §2.5.1]. Isabelle rapidly dispatches uninteresting cases.

[5] This suffices for our work, but a symmetric solution may be preferable.

We developed a framework for stating invariants over automata with open transitions. These invariants differ from those like (1) and (2) in that assumptions are not stated over incoming messages but rather over synchronized and interleaved transitions—that is, over communications with an environment and over the independent actions of the environment—and properties are stated over the entire state of the network. We show invariants at the level of a single process (paodv i), with the additional obligation of showing their preservation under all interleaving transitions that satisfy the stated assumption, and then 'lift' them to arbitrary closed networks by applying a succession of generic lemmas, one for each layer of AWN. The additional obligation is exploited as a hypothesis in the induction that lifts results over partial networks (that is, when only one side acts, the property remains invariant). The lifting rules require showing that a process satisfies the assumptions on synchronizations and interleavings made in the invariant statement. These assumptions must also be lifted for each layer; care is required to avoid circularity in such assumption-guarantee invariants.

The framework includes a generic 'transfer' lemma that infers from an invariant over an open model, a similar invariant over the corresponding closed model—in our case, the very model presented in Section 4. One need only show a relation between the np given to pnet (see page 54) and a corresponding onp and opnet of the open model. This transfer of results means that all of the definitions and lemmas associated with the open model are but a proof strategy: they are not needed to understand the statement of Theorem 1 and their soundness is guaranteed by Isabelle/HOL. The details of this proof strategy are given in [4].

Route quality. For completeness, we include the definition used for route quality. We write $(rt_1 \sqsubset_i rt_2) = (rt_1 \sqsubseteq_i rt_2 \wedge \neg\, rt_2 \sqsubseteq_i rt_1)$, to mean that the quality of the route to address i in route table rt_2 is strictly better than that in rt_1, where,

$$(rt_1 \sqsubseteq_i rt_2) = (\mathsf{nsqn}\ rt_1\ i < \mathsf{nsqn}\ rt_2\ i$$
$$\vee\ (\mathsf{nsqn}\ rt_1\ i = \mathsf{nsqn}\ rt_2\ i \wedge \mathsf{the}\ (\mathsf{dhops}\ rt_2\ i) \leq \mathsf{the}\ (\mathsf{dhops}\ rt_1\ i))),$$

provided $i \in \mathsf{kD}\ rt_1$ and $i \in \mathsf{kD}\ rt_2$. The function dhops rt i yields the number of hops to i according to rt. We encode the notion of *net sequence numbers* from [8, §7.5]:

$$\mathsf{nsqn}\ rt\ i = (\text{if flag } rt\ i = \mathsf{Some}\ \mathsf{val} \vee \mathsf{sqn}\ rt\ i = 0 \text{ then } \mathsf{sqn}\ rt\ i \text{ else } \mathsf{sqn}\ rt\ i\ \text{-}\ 1),$$

where flag states whether a route is valid (val) or invalid (inv) and sqn gives the stored sequence number.

Results. Our mechanization of the AODV model and the proof of loop freedom (not including the framework of [4]) involves 360 lemmas, of which 40 are invariants, with a proof text spanning 80 printed pages. The pen-and-paper proof [8] involves 40 lemmas over 18 pages. Many of the mechanized lemmas are of course trivial, for example, simplification rules for projections from routing tables.

The pen-and-paper proof is fastidious and we did not find any major errors: (1) type checking found a minor typo in the model, (2) one proof invoked an incorrect invariant requiring the addition and proof of a new invariant based on an existing one, (3) a minor flaw in another proof required the addition of a new invariant. Of course, this was not known beforehand! Nevertheless, our mechanized proof provides supplementary evidence for the stated property.

8   Analysing Variants of AODV

A mechanized model and proof greatly facilitates the analysis of protocol variants, such as different interpretations of the informal text of a standard, or proposed improvements for future versions of a standard. Since such variants often only differ in minor details, most proofs stay the same or are adapted automatically. An ITP tries to 'replay' the original proof and, in case of a failure, it indicates those proof steps that are no longer valid. One can thus concentrate on important changes in the proof. This avoids the tedious, time-consuming, and error-prone manual chore of establishing which steps remain valid for each invariant, especially for long proofs. We support our claim by proving the loop freedom property of four variants of AODV.

(1) Skipping route request identifiers. AODV uses route request identifiers to uniquely identify RREQ messages. Since it has been shown [8, §10.1] that a combination of IP addresses and sequence numbers adequately serves the same purpose, the identifier can be dropped and the size of the RREQ messages reduced. This very minor modification only requires a change in the type of RREQ, and related propositions and lemmas. Implementing these changes in Isabelle/HOL only took several minutes—the invariant lemmas were re-proved automatically.

(2) Forwarding route replies. During route discovery, an RREP message is unicast back towards the originator of the triggering RREQ message. Every intermediate node on the selected route processes the RREP message and, in most cases, forwards it towards the originator. However, intermediate nodes must discard RREP messages from which they cannot distil any new routing information. As a consequence, the originator node will not receive a reply.[6]

An alternative is to require intermediate nodes to forward *all* RREP messages. This behaviour is modelled by deleting three lines of the original specification; including one choice operator ($\oplus$) and two guards, potentially invalidating the proofs of many invariants. To avoid the forwarding of outdated information, we change three lines in the specification (including two guards) to ensure that the best available information is always sent; see [8, §10.2] for details.

Of the 360 lemmas in the original proof, only 7 are no longer valid. Four of these are easily repaired: since some lines of the specification are deleted, the automatically generated labels change and references in the proofs must be adapted—a tedious, but routine find-and-replace chore. So, in fact only three invariants require non-trivial user interaction and a new proof—around three hours of manual effort. This corresponds with the pen-and-paper proof, which requires a single page [8, pp. 106–107] and a new invariant [8, Prop. 7.38].

(3) From groupcast to broadcast. Each routing table entry contains a set of precursors (Section 2), a set of the IP addresses of all nodes that are currently known to be potential users of the route, and that are located one hop further

---

[6] See http://www.ietf.org/mail-archive/web/manet/current/msg05702.html

away from the destination. This information is recorded so that these nodes can be informed via RERR message if the route becomes invalid. However, precursor lists are incomplete: nodes not handling a route reply have no information about precursors for routes established while handling RREQ messages—see [8, §10.4] for examples. As a consequence, some nodes cannot be informed of a link break and will use a broken route, and data packets can be lost.

One solution is to abandon precursors and to replace groupcasts by broadcasts. The AODV specification is updated by dropping the precursor field of routing table entries, and making minor changes to related functions and function calls. All 7 occurrences of groupcast must also be replaced by an appropriate broadcast-statement; in one case this necessitates the introduction of a new guard. 16 assignments dealing with the generation and maintenance of precursor lists, and the calculation of groupcast destinations, are deleted.

Several changes ensued. (1) Around 30 definitions and lemmas about precursor lists are no longer needed. (2) About 75 lemmas and proofs then require adjustments for typing errors and references to deleted lemmas. (3) The labels in 6 invariants must be updated. (4) One invariant requires a careful adjustment: the removal of one case of a case distinction.

In sum, the specification changes broke many invariant proofs, but these were easily fixed in around three hours.

(4) Forwarding route requests. During route discovery, an RREQ message is dropped if a node (destination or intermediate) replies to the sender with an RREP message. This dropping of the RREQ message may inadvertently lead to non-optimal routes to the originator at nodes laying 'downstream' of the node that sent the reply [17].

One possible solution is to make nodes forward *all* RREQs that they have not handled earlier. The forwarded RREQ messages must be augmented with a Boolean flag to indicate that a reply has already been generated and sent. The specification of this variant differs in only eight lines from the original [8, §10.5].

As before, the proof is adapted in response to feedback from Isabelle/HOL. (1) 17 lemmas must now include the newly introduced flag. (2) The labels in 4 invariants must be updated. (3) Only one invariant proof required major changes.

9   Related Work

Bhargavan et al. [2]. Bhargavan, Obradovic, and Gunter apply a mix of manual reasoning, interactive theorem proving, and model checking to a preliminary draft (version 2) of AODV and show that this early draft is not loop free. They also suggest three improvements, of which one has been incorporated into the standard [23], and present a proof of loop freedom for the modified version. A central role in this proof is played by an invariant stating that along a route either sequence numbers increase, or, when they stay constant, that the hop count decreases [2, Theorem 17]. However, this is only true for valid routes—an assumption that is not stated. Even were the assumption adopted, it is not clear how the property can be shown using step-by-step reasoning which must treat the case of invalid routes that become valid again. Looking at the proofs in [2], it turns out that Lemma 20(1) of [2] is invalid. This failure is surprising, given that according to [2] Lemma 20 is automatically verified by SPIN. A possible explanation might be that this lemma is obviously valid for the version of AODV prior to the recommendations of [2].

Bhargavan et al. concede that they do not formally prove the abstractions they use for model checking [2, p.565], and it is not otherwise clear whether or how they ensure consistency with their ITP models. Besides the obvious question of soundness, these manual steps make it harder to reproduce the stated results. If any part of the model is changed, the automatic components can be rerun, but both the relations between them and any other manual reasoning must be carefully re-evaluated. In contrast, our development is a complete mechanization that is automatically validated by Isabelle/HOL in less than 15 minutes.

Zhou et al. [26]. Zhou, Yang, Zhang, and Wang model AODV as a set of finite traces—lists of events—defined inductively using a technique expounded by Paulson [21]. The model features 15 cases for adding a new event to an existing trace τ; most involve conditions on 'observation functions' that recurse over τ to 'recreate' the system state. Zhou et al. show the invariant proposed by Bhargavan et al. but with an explicit assumption on route activity. They do so using an ingenious but intricate lemma ('165') that exploits the identification of states and histories to reason across periods of route invalidity.

Both our mechanization and the original pen-and-paper proof [8] were completed without access to the details of Zhou et al.'s work. When we were able to examine their model in detail, we were reassured to see that the two models largely agree on the reading of the standard. But there are two crucial differences. First, we model route replies by intermediate nodes and Zhou et al. do not. This feature is a core part of the AODV standard [23, §6.6.2] and quite subtle—even small deviations, such as a different reading of the standard, risk introducing loops [10]. While we think it would be possible to add such replies to their model without introducing loops, extending the proof would not be trivial and would likely require new invariants similar to those that we use. Second, Zhou et al. model some timing details and we do not. But they sidestep central issues. For example, according to the standard a route is expired in two steps: "the Lifetime field in the routing table plays [a] dual role—for a valid route it is the expiry time, and for an invalid route it is the deletion time" [23, §6.11]. Zhou et al. model the first step but not the second. Route deletion, however, is fundamental to a timed model since all route information is lost; it complicates even the basic lemma that local sequence numbers never decrease (their '163').

Apart from content, the two models also differ in style. While the model of Zhou et al. is event-based and declarative, ours is more operational—it states what an abstract implementation of the protocol does step-by-step. The difference is important for two reasons: validation against the standard [23] and refinement to an implementation. Arguably, such standards are often quite operational, perhaps because they are written by and for implementers. We expect it to be easier to state and show some kind of simulation relation between the states and transitions of our model and those of an implementation (model).

As this discussion shows, in addition to guaranteeing soundness and facilitating repeatability and reuse, mechanized proofs aid detailed comparisons with related work (provided the proof scripts are available for study). Since an ITP checks the proofs, one can focus on comparing models and properties. Furthermore, rather than puzzle over details omitted or unclear from published accounts, one can look for answers in the mechanization. AODV is an interesting case study since at least two mechanical models exist, and the protocol is of industrial relevance, complicated enough to be interesting, but not so large as to pose too many engineering problems.

Mechanically verifying reactive systems. Apart from the process-algebraic work described in the introduction, several other approaches for verifying reactive systems have been mechanized, namely UNITY [12], I/O Automata [18], and TLA$^+$ [6]. The main difference with our approach is that they typically do not distinguish control and data states—specifications are essentially flat sets of transitions. The last two frameworks, in particular, have focused on the verification of practical protocols but not, to our knowledge, on the kind of routing protocol exemplified by AODV.

10   Conclusion

We have presented a mechanical proof of a model that corresponds to an interpretation of the current version of the AODV standard [23]; the fidelity of this model is argued in [8]. It includes route replies from intermediate nodes but not timing features. Such a mechanization does more than confirm the correctness of the existing pen-and-paper proof, it provides a computerized object that can be examined by others and serve as a foundation for analyses of variants and extensions to, and other properties of AODV. We believe that our mechanization of the process algebra AWN, and the general framework for compositionally proving safety properties is also applicable to the study of other protocols.

A number of interesting questions remain. (1) What is the best way to manage variant models in a proof assistant? (2) How suitable is such a model for showing refinements to more detailed implementation models? (3) Can we validate our model against a real AODV implementation as has been done for the Transmission Control Protocol [3]? (4) We have not modelled timing details, which is not just a question of modelling, but also one of which invariants are needed to show loop freedom when routes can be spontaneously deleted. Ideally, timing details could also be incorporated into refinement proofs.

Acknowledgements. The authors thank G. Klein and M. Pouzet for their support and complaisance, M. Daum for his participation in early work, and L. Mandel and anonymous reviewers for their comments on a previous version.

NICTA is funded by the Australian Government through the Department of Communications and the Australian Research Council through the ICT Centre of Excellence Program.

References

1. Bengtson, J., Parrow, J.: Psi-calculi in Isabelle. In: Berghofer, S., Nipkow, T., Urban, C., Wenzel, M. (eds.) TPHOLs 2009. LNCS, vol. 5674, pp. 99–114. Springer, Heidelberg (2009)
2. Bhargavan, K., Obradovic, D., Gunter, C.A.: Formal verification of standards for distance vector routing protocols. J. ACM 49(4), 538–576 (2002)
3. Bishop, S., Fairbairn, M., Norrish, M., Sewell, P., Smith, M., Wansbrough, K.: Engineering with logic: HOL specification and symbolic-evaluation testing for TCP implementations. In: POPL 2006, pp. 55–66. ACM (2006)
4. Bourke, T., van Glabbeek, R.J., Höfner, P.: Showing invariance compositionally for a process algebra for network protocols. In: Klein, G., Gamboa, R. (eds.) ITP 2014. LNCS, vol. 8558, pp. 144–159. Springer, Heidelberg (2014)
5. Bourke, T., Höfner, P.: Loop freedom of the (untimed) AODV routing protocol. Archive of Formal Proofs (2014), http://afp.sf.net/entries/AODV.shtml
6. Chaudhuri, K., Doligez, D., Lamport, L., Merz, S.: Verifying safety properties with the TLA+ proof system. In: Giesl, J., Hähnle, R. (eds.) IJCAR 2010. LNCS, vol. 6173, pp. 142–148. Springer, Heidelberg (2010)
7. Dutertre, B., Schneider, S.: Using a PVS embedding of CSP to verify authentication protocols. In: Gunter, E.L., Felty, A.P. (eds.) TPHOLs 1997. LNCS, vol. 1275, pp. 121–136. Springer, Heidelberg (1997)
8. Fehnker, A., van Glabbeek, R.J., Höfner, P., McIver, A., Portmann, M., Tan, W.L.: A process algebra for wireless mesh networks used for modelling, verifying and analysing AODV. Technical Report 5513, NICTA (2013), http://arxiv.org/abs/1312.7645
9. Feliachi, A., Gaudel, M.-C., Wolff, B.: Isabelle/Circus: A process specification and verification environment. In: Joshi, R., Müller, P., Podelski, A. (eds.) VSTTE 2012. LNCS, vol. 7152, pp. 243–260. Springer, Heidelberg (2012)
10. van Glabbeek, R.J., Höfner, P., Tan, W.L., Portmann, M.: Sequence numbers do not guarantee loop freedom —AODV can yield routing loops—. In: MSWiM 2013, pp. 91–100. ACM (2013)
11. Göthel, T., Glesner, S.: An approach for machine-assisted verification of Timed CSP specifications. Innovations in Systems and Software Engineering 6(3), 181–193 (2010)
12. Heyd, B., Crégut, P.: A modular coding of UNITY in COQ. In: Goos, G., Hartmanis, J., van Leeuwen, J., von Wright, J., Grundy, J., Harrison, J. (eds.) TPHOLs 1996. LNCS, vol. 1125, pp. 251–266. Springer, Heidelberg (1996)
13. Hirschkoff, D.: A full formalisation of π-calculus theory in the Calculus of Constructions. In: Gunter, E.L., Felty, A.P. (eds.) TPHOLs 1997. LNCS, vol. 1275, pp. 153–169. Springer, Heidelberg (1997)
14. IEEE: IEEE standard for information technology—telecommunications and information exchange between systems—local and metropolitan area networks—specific requirements part 11: Wireless LAN medium access control (MAC) and physical layer (PHY) specifications amendment 10: Mesh networking (2011)
15. Lynch, N.A.: Distributed Algorithms. Morgan Kaufmann (1996)
16. Manna, Z., Pnueli, A.: Temporal Verification of Reactive Systems: Safety. Springer (1995)
17. Miskovic, S., Knightly, E.W.: Routing primitives for wireless mesh networks: Design, analysis and experiments. In: INFOCOM 2010, pp. 2793–2801. IEEE (2010)

18. Müller, O.: I/O automata and beyond: Temporal logic and abstraction in Isabelle. In: Grundy, J., Newey, M. (eds.) TPHOLs 1998. LNCS, vol. 1479, pp. 331–348. Springer, Heidelberg (1998)

19. Müller, O.: A Verification Environment for I/O Automata Based on Formalized Meta-Theory. Ph.D. thesis, TU München (1998)

20. Nipkow, T., Paulson, L.C., Wenzel, M.: Isabelle/HOL. LNCS, vol. 2283. Springer, Heidelberg (2002)

21. Paulson, L.C.: The inductive approach to verifying cryptographic protocols. J. Computer Security 6(1-2), 85–128 (1998)

22. Perkins, C.E., Royer, E.M.: Ad-hoc On-Demand Distance Vector Routing. In: Mobile Computing Systems and Applications (WMCSA 1999), pp. 90–100. IEEE (1999)

23. Perkins, C.E., Belding-Royer, E.M., Das, S.R.: Ad hoc on-demand distance vector (AODV) routing. RFC 3561 (Experimental), Network Working Group (2003), http://www.ietf.org/rfc/rfc3561.txt

24. de Roever, W.P., de Boer, F., Hannemann, U., Hooman, J., Lakhnech, Y., Poel, M., Zwiers, J.: Concurrency Verification: Introduction to Compositional and Noncompositional Methods. Cambridge Tracts in Theoretical Computer Science, vol. 54. Cambridge University Press (2001)

25. Schirmer, N., Wenzel, M.: State spaces—the locale way. In: Huuck, R., Klein, G., Schlich, B. (eds.) SSV 2009. ENTCS, vol. 254, pp. 161–179. Elsevier (2009)

26. Zhou, M., Yang, H., Zhang, X., Wang, J.: The proof of AODV loop freedom. In: WCSP 2009. IEEE (2009)

Quantitative Verification
of Weighted Kripke Structures*

Patricia Bouyer, Patrick Gardy, and Nicolas Markey

LSV, CNRS & ENS Cachan, France

Abstract. Extending formal verification techniques to handle quantitative aspects, both for the models and for the properties to be checked, has become a central research topic over the last twenty years. Following several recent works, we study model checking for (one-dimensional) weighted Kripke structures with positive and negative weights, and temporal logics constraining the total and/or average weight. We prove decidability when only accumulated weight is constrained, while allowing average-weight constraints alone already is undecidable.

1 Introduction

Quantitative Verification. Model checking [CGP00] has been developed for almost 40 years as a formal method for verifying correctness flushing out bugs of computerized systems: this technique first consists in representing the system under study as a mathematical model (a finite-state transition system, in the most basic setting), expressing the correctness property in some logical formalism, and running an algorithm that exhaustively explores the set of behaviours of the model for proving or disproving the property. Model checking has been successfully applied on various real-life case studies.

Though model checking has primarily concentrated on pure qualitative analysis via the development of various temporal logics [Pnu77,CE82,QS82], rich models and logics have also been developed in order to take into account quantitative aspects of reactive systems and of their correctness properties.

In particular, there has been quite a lot of efforts invested in the study of *weighted* discrete transition systems, like weighted Kripke structures [CC95] or counter automata (or VASS) [EN94]. In these models, the weight gives some quantitative information on the system, which might be timing information and constraints, or energy consumption, or value of a discrete variable, etc. This weight can either be some information that we observe on the system (like in weighted Kripke structures) or its value can constrain the further behaviour of the system (like in counter automata).

On such models, there are many interesting verification questions that can be asked. First one can be interested in qualitative structural and logical properties of the system, that can for instance be expressed using some logical formalism.

---

* Partly supported by ERC Starting Grant EQualIS and EU FP7 project Cassting.

F. Cassez and J.-F. Raskin (Eds.): ATVA 2014, LNCS 8837, pp. 64–80, 2014.

Then one can be more interested in quantitative properties of the system, like (among others) mean-payoff constraints [ZP96] (the limit-average of the weight along an execution satisfies some constraint), or energy constraints [BFL+08] (all along the execution, the weight satisfies some constraint). More interestingly, one might be interested in properties that might mix qualitative logical properties and quantitative constraints. For instance, in a robot-planning system, one would like to verify that an autonomous robot can always go back to its home base without running out-of-energy.

In this setting, weights in weighted transition systems have been most often restricted to range over the *nonnegative integers* (mostly for representing timing information), and temporal logics have been augmented either with constrained modalities [Koy90,EMSS92] or with explicit variables [AH94], and efficient algorithms have been developed and implemented [BLN03,JLSØ13]. Models with both positive and negative weights have also been studied, but mostly qualitative behaviours alone have been analyzed (this is the case in counter automata—see [HKOW09,GHOW10,Haa12] for recent references), or quantitative constraints have been analyzed (in weighted Kripke structures or games [CDHR10,CRR12]). Mixing qualitative logical properties and quantitative constraints has only poorly been addressed so far, and many works only consider specifications given as a conjunction of a qualitative logical property and a quantitative constraint: this is for instance the case of optimal reachability, mean-payoff parity games [BMOU11], energy parity games [CD12], mean-payoff LTL synthesis [BBFR13].

In that direction, the most relevant and advanced propositions are those of [DG09] and of [BCHK11]. In [DG09], LTL is (roughly) extended with Presburger constraints over weights and interpreted over one-counter automata (and an extension thereof). The satisfiability and model checking problems are addressed, and it is shown that only a restriction to a single weight leads to decidability. In [BCHK11], CTL and LTL are extended with (prefix) accumulative values over finitely many variables: these logics embed numerical assertions such as $\mathsf{Sum}(x) \sim c$ (*e.g.* to compare the accumulated amount of some resource x against some value c) and $\mathsf{Avg}(x) \sim c$ (*e.g.* to constrain the average consumption of some resource x). In this context, the authors of [BCHK11] show undecidability of the logics in general, and propose several fragments for which model checking is decidable: (*i*) LTL with limit-average, where (roughly) a property can be rewritten as a conjunction of a qualitative logical property and a quantitative constraint; and (*ii*) CTL restricted to **EF** and **EX** modalities, with all kinds of numerical assertions, but where the qualitative logical part of the formula is rather poor. Notice that this decidability result is rather surprising, since reachability in two-counter machines is undecidable. The difference is that here counters can go negative, and taking the Parikh image of a path is enough for checking properties expressed in the **EF**-fragment. Designing logical languages that can express intricate properties mixing qualitative logical features and quantitative constraints, and for which model checking remains decidable, seems therefore to be a real challenge!

Our Contribution. We investigate further the temporal logics with prefix accumulation that has been proposed in [BCHK11], and we study the impact of restricting the logic to a single weight. The logics we consider are therefore based on CTL and LTL, and they extend the standard logics with two kinds of numerical assertions: Sum $\sim c$ expresses that the accumulated weight satisfies the constraint $\sim c$, and Avg $\sim c$ expresses that the current average of the weight satisfies the constraint $\sim c$. The extension of CTL is called WCTL and the extension of LTL is called WLTL. Those two logics will be interpreted on weighted Kripke structures, and we will be interested in the model checking problem.

We prove in this paper that when using only Sum constraints, model checking for both CTL and LTL extensions is decidable. On the contrary, allowing Avg constraints leads to undecidability for both branching and linear time. This undecidability result for our logic WLTL$_{Avg}$ is to be compared with the decidability of LTL with limit-average modalities of [BCHK11]: limit-average constraints can be made disjoint from the logical property expressed by the formula of LTL, whereas average modalities are really mixed with the logical property. Finally, we define a *flat* fragment of WLTL allowing both Sum and Avg constraints, but restricting the way they can be nested in the formula; we prove that this fragment has decidable model checking.

2   Definitions

2.1   Weighted Kripke Structures

Definition 1. *Let* AP *be a finite set of atomic propositions. A weighted Kripke structure over* AP *is a tuple* $\mathcal{K} = \langle S, R, \ell \rangle$ *where* S *is a finite set of states,* $R \subseteq S \times W \times S$ *(where* $W \subseteq \mathbb{Z}$ *is the set of weights[1] of* $\mathcal{K}$, *which we assume are given in binary notation) is a weighted transition relation (which we assume total, meaning that for all* $s \in S$, *there exists* $w \in \mathbb{Z}$ *and* $s' \in S$ *s.t.* $(s, w, s') \in R$*), and* $\ell: S \to 2^{\mathsf{AP}}$ *is a function labelling the states with atomic propositions.*

A weighted Kripke structure with zero-tests is a weighted Kripke structure with extra zero-test transitions, that is, $R \subseteq S \times (W \cup \{= 0\}) \times S$.

A weighted Kripke structure (with zero-tests) is unitary *if its set of weights* W *is included in* $\{-1, 0, +1\}$.

Let $\mathcal{K} = \langle S, R, \ell \rangle$ be a weighted Kripke structure, $s_0 \in S$ be a state of $\mathcal{K}$, and $w_0 \in \mathbb{Z}$. A *run* in $\mathcal{K}$ from (s_0, w_0) is a (finite or infinite) sequence $\pi = (q_i, w_i)_{i \in I}$ such that $q_0 = s_0$, I is an interval of $\mathbb{N}$ containing 0, and for all $i \in I \setminus \{0\}$, $(q_{i-1}, w_i - w_{i-1}, q_i) \in R$. When I is finite, we write $|\pi|$ for the length of π (the cardinal of I), and we write $\mathsf{last}(\pi)$ (resp. $\mathsf{last}_q(\pi)$, $\mathsf{last}_w(\pi)$) for the configuration $(q_{\max(I)}, w_{\max(I)})$ (resp. the state $q_{\max(I)}$, the weight $w_{\max(I)}$). Given a path $\pi = (q_i, w_i)_{i \in I}$ and $k \in I$, the prefix of π up to k is the path $\pi_{\le k} = (q_i, w_i)_{i \in [0,k]}$; the suffix of π from k is the path $\pi_{\ge k} = (q_{k+i}, w_{k+i})_{i \in \mathbb{N} \cap (I-k)}$. When $\mathcal{K}$ has

---

[1] Rational weights would easily be handled, after scaling the values by the least common multiple of their denominators.

zero-tests, a run in $\mathcal{K}$ is a sequence $\pi = (q_i, w_i)_{i \in I}$ where for all $i \in I \setminus \{0\}$, either $(q_{i-1}, w_i - w_{i-1}, q_i) \in R$, or $w_i = w_{i-1} = 0$ and $(q, = 0, q') \in R$.

Weighted Kripke structures (with or without zero-tests) are related to counter automata [Min61]. A *one-counter automaton*[2] is a weighted Kripke structure with zero-tests in which runs are restricted to only visit configurations with nonnegative weight: the state space is $S \times \mathbb{N}$, and it is not possible to take a transition that would make the counter (or weight) negative. It is also usual to have branching zero-tests in one-counter automata, instead of our simple "guarded transitions" (zero-tests transitions). However, branching tests in one-counter automata can easily be implemented in weighted Kripke structures with zero-tests (for instance, to test whether the value of the counter is positive, we put in sequence a decrementation of -1 followed by an incrementation of $+1$).

The execution tree of a weighted Kripke structure $\mathcal{K}$ from some configuration (s_0, w_0) is the $(S \times \mathbb{Z})$-tree

$$\mathcal{T} = \{\pi \in (S \times \mathbb{Z})^* \mid \pi \text{ is a run from } (s_0, w_0) \text{ in } \mathcal{K}\}$$

For convenience, we label each node π of $\mathcal{T}$ with $\mathsf{last}(\pi)$, which then relates each node of $\mathcal{T}$ with its corresponding state of $\mathcal{K}$. A *branch* of $\mathcal{T}$ is an infinite run π from (s_0, w_0) in $\mathcal{K}$: every prefix $\pi_{\leq i}$ ($i \in \mathbb{N}$) is then an element of $\mathcal{T}$. We write $B(\mathcal{T})$ for the set of branches of $\mathcal{T}$.

2.2   Weighted Temporal Logics

We extend both branching-time temporal logic CTL [CE82,QS82] and linear-time temporal logic LTL [Pnu77] with numerical constraints on weights:

Definition 2. *A numerical assertion is built on the following grammar:*

$$\alpha ::= \mathsf{Sum} \sim c \mid \mathsf{Avg} \sim c$$

where $\sim$ ranges over $\{<, \leq, =, \geq, >\}$ and c ranges over $\mathbb{Q}$.
Fix a set AP *of atomic propositions. The syntax of* WCTL *over* AP *is given as*

$$\phi ::= p \mid \alpha \mid \neg\phi \mid \phi \wedge \phi \mid \mathbf{EX}\,\phi \mid \mathbf{AX}\,\phi \mid \mathbf{E}\phi\,\mathbf{U}\,\phi \mid \mathbf{A}\phi\,\mathbf{U}\,\phi \mid w \cdot \phi$$

where p ranges over AP *and α ranges over numerical assertions.*
The syntax of WLTL *over* AP *is given as*

$$\phi ::= p \mid \alpha \mid \neg\phi \mid \phi \wedge \phi \mid \mathbf{X}\,\phi \mid \phi\,\mathbf{U}\,\phi \mid w \cdot \phi$$

where p ranges over AP *and α ranges over numerical assertions.*
The operation $w \cdot \phi$ in both logics is called the reset *operation.*

---

[2] Counter automata are often required to have set of weights included in $\{-1, 0, +1\}$, which we call *unitary* counter automata in the sequel. The counter automata we consider here correspond to *succinct* counter automata of [HKOW09,GHOW10].

In the sequel, we write $\mathsf{WCTL_{Sum}}$ (resp. $\mathsf{WCTL_{Avg}}$) for the fragments of WCTL using only Sum (resp. Avg) in numerical assertions. We also write $\mathsf{WCTL^{rf}}$, $\mathsf{WCTL^{rf}_{Sum}}$ and $\mathsf{WCTL^{rf}_{Avg}}$ for the respective fragments with no reset operations. Also, we write $\mathsf{WLTL_{Sum}}$ (resp. $\mathsf{WLTL_{Avg}}$) for the fragments of WLTL using only Sum (resp. Avg) in numerical assertions. We also write $\mathsf{WLTL^{rf}}$, $\mathsf{WLTL^{rf}_{Sum}}$ and $\mathsf{WLTL^{rf}_{Avg}}$ for the respective fragments with no reset operations.

The semantics of numerical assertions is defined on finite runs π of a weighted Kripke structure $\mathcal{K}$ as follows (boolean combinations omitted):

$$\pi \models \mathsf{Sum} \sim c \quad \text{iff} \quad \mathsf{last}_w(\pi) \sim c$$
$$\pi \models \mathsf{Avg} \sim c \quad \text{iff} \quad \mathsf{last}_w(\pi) \sim c \cdot |\pi|$$

Such constraints can for instance be used to express the so-called *energy constraints* [BFL$^+$08,CDHR10], requiring that $\mathsf{Sum} \geq 0$ all along a run. We can also reinforce this condition by additionally requiring that, at the end of the run, the average energy level (over the prefix) has remained within a given range.

Semantics of WCTL. The semantics of WCTL is defined inductively, on the execution tree of a weighted Kripke structure. Let $\mathcal{K}$ be a weighted Kripke structure and (s_0, w_0) be an initial configuration. Let $\mathcal{T}$ be the execution tree of $\mathcal{K}$ from (s_0, w_0); fix a branch π of $\mathcal{T}$, a position $i \in \mathbb{N}$ along π (with the intended meaning that i corresponds to the node $\pi_{\leq i}$ of $\mathcal{T}$; in particular, the node at position 0 corresponds to (s_0, w_0)). The semantics of WCTL is defined as follows (atomic propositions and boolean operators omitted):

$$
\begin{aligned}
\mathcal{T}, \pi, i \models \alpha \quad &\text{iff} \quad \pi_{\leq i} \models \alpha \\
\mathcal{T}, \pi, i \models \mathbf{EX}\,\phi \quad &\text{iff} \quad \exists \pi' \in B(\mathcal{T}).\,(\pi_{\leq i} = \pi'_{\leq i} \text{ and } \mathcal{T}, \pi', i+1 \models \phi) \\
\mathcal{T}, \pi, i \models \mathbf{AX}\,\phi \quad &\text{iff} \quad \forall \pi' \in B(\mathcal{T}).\,(\pi_{\leq i} = \pi'_{\leq i} \Rightarrow \mathcal{T}, \pi', i+1 \models \phi) \\
\mathcal{T}, \pi, i \models \mathbf{E}\phi_1 \,\mathbf{U}\,\phi_2 \quad &\text{iff} \quad \exists \pi' \in B(\mathcal{T}).\exists j \geq i.\,(\pi_{\leq i} = \pi'_{\leq i} \text{ and } \\
&\qquad \mathcal{T}, \pi', j \models \phi_2 \text{ and } \forall i \leq k < j.\, \mathcal{T}, \pi', k \models \phi_1) \\
\mathcal{T}, \pi, i \models \mathbf{A}\phi_1 \,\mathbf{U}\,\phi_2 \quad &\text{iff} \quad \forall \pi' \in B(\mathcal{T}).\exists j \geq i.\,(\pi_{\leq i} = \pi'_{\leq i} \Rightarrow \\
&\qquad \mathcal{T}, \pi', j \models \phi_2 \text{ and } \forall i \leq k < j.\, \mathcal{T}, \pi', k \models \phi_1) \\
\mathcal{T}, \pi, i \models w \cdot \phi \quad &\text{iff} \quad \mathcal{T}', \pi', 0 \models \phi \text{ where } \mathcal{T}' \text{ is the execution tree of } \mathcal{K} \\
&\qquad \text{from } (\mathsf{last}_q(\pi_{\leq i}), 0) \text{ and } \pi' \in B(\mathcal{T}')
\end{aligned}
$$

Notice that the value of $\mathcal{T}', \pi', 0 \models \phi$ in the semantics of $w \cdot \phi$ does not depend on the choice of the branch π', so the semantics is well-defined. We can generalize that remark:

Lemma 3. *Pick $\pi, \pi' \in B(\mathcal{T})$.*

- *If $\pi_{\leq i} = \pi'_{\leq i}$ for some position $i \in \mathbb{N}$, then for every formula $\phi \in \mathsf{WCTL}$,*

$$\mathcal{T}, \pi, i \models \phi \quad \text{iff} \quad \mathcal{T}, \pi', i \models \phi.$$

– If $last(\pi_{\leq i}) = last(\pi'_{\leq j})$ for some $i, j \in \mathbb{N}$, then for all $\phi \in \mathsf{WCTL}_{Sum}$,

$$\mathcal{T}, \pi, i \models \phi \quad \textit{iff} \quad \mathcal{T}, \pi', j \models \phi.$$

The value of $\mathcal{T}, \pi, 0 \models \phi$ does not depend on the choice of the branch $\pi \in B(\mathcal{T})$; we then define the truth value of $\mathcal{K}, (s_0, w_0) \models \phi$ as that of $\mathcal{T}, \pi, 0 \models \phi$, where $\mathcal{T}$ is the execution tree of $\mathcal{K}$ from (s_0, w_0) and π is any branch of $\mathcal{T}$.

Definition 4 (WCTL model-checking problem). *Let ϕ be a WCTL formula, let $\mathcal{K}$ be a weighted Kripke structure and s_0 be an initial state. The model-checking problem with fixed initial credit asks, for a given $w_0 \in \mathbb{Z}$, whether $\mathcal{K}, (s_0, w_0) \models \phi$. The model-checking problem with unknown initial credit asks whether there exists $w_0 \in \mathbb{Z}$ such that $\mathcal{K}, (s_0, w_0) \models \phi$.*

Semantics of WLTL. The semantics of WLTL is defined inductively over infinite runs of a weighted Kripke structure. Let $\mathcal{K}$ be a weighted Kripke structure, π be an infinite run in $\mathcal{K}$ from some configuration (s_0, w_0), and $i \in \mathbb{N}$ be a position along π. The semantics of WLTL is defined as follows (simple cases omitted):

$$\pi, i \models \alpha \qquad \text{iff} \qquad \pi_{\leq i} \models \alpha$$
$$\pi, i \models \mathbf{X}\,\phi \qquad \text{iff} \qquad \pi, i+1 \models \phi$$
$$\pi, i \models \phi_1 \,\mathbf{U}\, \phi_2 \quad \text{iff} \quad \exists j \geq i.\ (\pi, j \models \phi_2 \text{ and } \forall i \leq k < j.\ \pi, k \models \phi_1)$$
$$\pi, i \models w \cdot \phi \qquad \text{iff} \qquad \pi', 0 \models \phi \text{ where } \pi' \text{ is the run of } \mathcal{K} \text{ from } (\mathsf{last}_q(\pi_{\leq i}), 0)$$
$$\text{that follows the same transitions as } \pi_{\geq i}.$$

As for WCTL, the reset operator imposes that further numerical assertions will count from the current position only, this is why the position is reset to 0.

We write $\mathcal{K}, (s_0, w_0) \models \phi$ whenever there exists an infinite run π from (s_0, w_0) in $\mathcal{K}$ such that $\pi, 0 \models \phi$. Note that the choice of an existential semantics is arbitrary and harmless, given that the logic is closed under negation.

Definition 5 (WLTL model-checking problem). *Let ϕ be a WLTL formula, let $\mathcal{K}$ be a weighted Kripke structure and s_0 be an initial state. The model-checking problem with fixed initial credit asks, for a given $w_0 \in \mathbb{Z}$, whether $\mathcal{K}, (s_0, w_0) \models \phi$. The model-checking problem with unknown initial credit asks whether there exists $w_0 \in \mathbb{Z}$ such that $\mathcal{K}, (s_0, w_0) \models \phi$.*

Remark 6. Note that the reset operator which is used in both logics is a powerful operator, which can be used to express multiple numerical constraints on various portions of a run. This is a rather standard operator in temporal logics, which is for instance in the core of linear-time timed temporal logic TPTL [AH94]. Note nevertheless that the logics WCTL and WLTL above only allow for one weight variable in a given formula. We will see that the reset operator does not impact much on the model checking of WCTL, but has a strong impact on WLTL model checking.

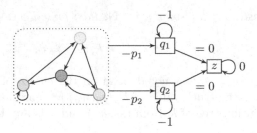

Fig. 1. From $\mathsf{WCTL}^{\mathsf{rf}}_{\mathsf{Sum}}$ to CTL (there is one transition from each state in the dotted box (which is the original weighted Kripke structure) to each state q_i)

3 Algorithm for Model Checking $\mathsf{WCTL}_{\mathsf{Sum}}$

In this section we prove the decidability of the model-checking of $\mathsf{WCTL}_{\mathsf{Sum}}$ over weighted Kripke structures by reducing it to the model-checking of CTL over one-counter automata. We proceed by first removing numerical assertions from the formulas (which requires to modify also the Kripke structure), and then by building a one-counter automaton and a CTL formula. We then apply the results of [Haa12,Ser06], and carefully analyze the complexity of the algorithm.

We first focus on logic $\mathsf{WCTL}^{\mathsf{rf}}_{\mathsf{Sum}}$, and will explain at the end of the section how we can extend the result to $\mathsf{WCTL}_{\mathsf{Sum}}$.

3.1 Moving Quantitative Constraints into the Model

We prove that model checking $\mathsf{WCTL}^{\mathsf{rf}}_{\mathsf{Sum}}$ is logspace-reducible to model checking CTL on structures allowing zero-tests. This is achieved by adding "tests modules" in the model, and replacing Sum constraints with a CTL condition in the corresponding test modules.

Let $\mathcal{K} = \langle S, R, \ell \rangle$ be a weighted Kripke structure, and ϕ be a $\mathsf{WCTL}^{\mathsf{rf}}_{\mathsf{Sum}}$ formula involving integer constants $\mathcal{P} = \{p_1, ..., p_k\}$. We define a new weighted Kripke structure *with zero tests* $\mathcal{K}'_{\mathcal{P}} = \langle S', R', \ell' \rangle$ as follows:

- $S' = S \cup \{q_i \mid 1 \le i \le k\} \cup \{z\}$,
- $R' = R \cup \{(s, -p_i, q_i), (q_i, -1, q_i), (q_i, = 0, z), (z, 0, z) \mid s \in S,\ 1 \le i \le k\}$,
- $\ell' : \begin{cases} s \in S \mapsto \ell(s) \\ s = q_i \mapsto a_i \\ s = z \mapsto \mathsf{zero} \end{cases}$

The a_i are fresh atomic propositions. The construction is depicted on Fig. 1 for two constants p_1 and p_2. The intuition is as follows: whenever the formula requires comparing the current weight with p_i in a state s of $\mathcal{K}$, the new formula will query the existence of a transition to q_i, and check that the value of the weight when reaching q_i is nonnegative (by testing whether state z is reachable).

Now, after an easy transformation of ϕ into $\widehat{\phi}$ in order not to evaluate subformulas in newly-added states, we get:

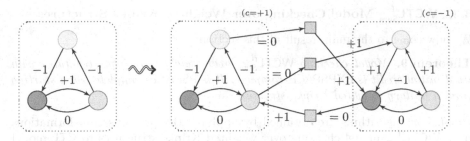

Fig. 2. From weighted Kripke structures to one-counter automata

Proposition 7. *Let* $\mathcal{K} = \langle S, R, \ell \rangle$ *be a weighted Kripke structure. Let* ϕ *be a* WCTL$_{Sum}^{rf}$ *formula with integer constants in* $\mathcal{P}$, *and* $s_0 \in S$ *and* $v \in \mathbb{Z}$. *Let* $\mathcal{K}'_{\mathcal{P}}$ *be the weighted Kripke structure with zero test as defined above, and* $\widehat{\phi}$ *be the formula obtained from* ϕ *by the transformation above. Then*

$$\mathcal{K}, (s_0, v) \models \phi \quad \textit{iff} \quad \mathcal{K}'_{\mathcal{P}}, (s_0, v) \models \widehat{\phi}.$$

Note that the size of $\mathcal{K}'_{\mathcal{P}}$ is polynomial in $\mathcal{K}$ and ϕ, and so is $\widehat{\phi}$.

3.2 From Weighted Kripke Structures to One-Counter Automata

We now reduce the model checking problem for CTL on weighted Kripke structures with zero tests to the same problem on unitary one-counter automata, in order to invoke the algorithms for CTL model-checking of [Haa12,Ser06]. The one-counter automaton will be made of two copies of the weighted Kripke structure: one to be used when the accumulated weight is nonnegative, and one when it is nonpositive. We will have zero-tests between both copies. Prior to this transformation, we first make the Kripke structure unitary, so that no transition will jump from positive to negative weights, or vice-versa, without hitting zero.

We now come to the transformation of this unitary weighted Kripke structure into a unitary one-counter automaton $\mathcal{C}$. The natural idea is to consider two copies of each state: one is used when the accumulated weight is nonnegative, and one when the total weight is nonpositive. By considering the opposite value of the weight in the second copy, we end up with a unitary one-counter automaton. Fig. 2 illustrates this construction on a simple example.

Again rewriting the formula as $\widehat{\phi}$ to "hide" newly added states, we get:

Proposition 8. *Let* $\mathcal{K} = \langle S, R, \ell \rangle$ *be a weighted Kripke structure with zero-tests,* ϕ *be a* CTL *formula,* $s_0 \in S$ *and* $w_0 \in \mathbb{Z}$. *Let* $\mathcal{C}$ *be the one-counter automaton obtained above, and* $\widehat{\phi}$ *be the formula obtained from* ϕ. *Then*

$$\mathcal{K}, (s_0, w_0) \models \phi \quad \textit{iff} \quad \mathcal{C}, ((s_0, sign(w_0)), |w_0|) \models \widehat{\phi}$$

where $sign(0)$ *can be taken as either* $+1$ *or* -1.

3.3 WCTL$_{Sum}^{rf}$ Model Checking over Weighted Kripke Structures

We now come to the main result of this section:

Theorem 9. *Model checking* WCTL$_{Sum}^{rf}$ *over weighted Kripke structures with fixed initial credit is* EXPSPACE-*complete. It is* PSPACE-*complete when starting from a unitary weighted Kripke structure.*

Proof. The algorithms are obtained by applying the previous transformations from WCTL$_{Sum}^{rf}$ model checking over weighted Kripke structures to CTL model checking over unitary one-counter automata, and then relying on the PSPACE algorithm of [Haa12,Ser06] for model checking unitary one-counter automata.

Hardness is easily proved by reducing the model-checking problem of CTL over one-counter automata to that for WCTL$_{Sum}^{rf}$ over weighted Kripke structures. The former problem was proved EXPSPACE-complete in [GHOW10], and PSPACE-complete over unitary one-counter automata in [GL10]. The reduction is rather straightforward, by reinforcing the CTL formula in order to enforce nonnegative value of the accumulated weight all along the paths.   □

We can now extend the above algorithm to handle the reset operator: when a formula ϕ contains $w \cdot \psi$ as a subformula, we first evaluate ψ in all the states of the Kripke structure, assuming initial weight zero, and apply a classical labelling algorithm. In the end:

Theorem 10. *Model checking* WCTL$_{Sum}$ *over weighted Kripke structures with fixed initial credit is* EXPSPACE-*complete; it is* PSPACE-*complete when starting from a unitary weighted Kripke structure.*

3.4 Model Checking WCTL$_{Sum}$ with Unknown Initial Credit

The model checking of WCTL$_{Sum}$ with unknown initial credit can be reduced to the fixed initial credit case by adding an initial module which allows to set the weight to any value. We can state the following result:

Theorem 11. *Model checking* WCTL$_{Sum}$ *over weighted Kripke structures with unknown initial credit is* EXPSPACE-*complete; it is* PSPACE-*complete when starting from a unitary weighted Kripke structure.*

This result has to be compared with the lower-bound problems in weighted timed automata which is PSPACE-complete with unknown initial credit, but becomes undecidable with fixed initial credit [BLM14].

4 Model Checking WCTL$_{Avg}$ Is Undecidable

In this section, we prove that constraining the average of the weight value leads to undecidability:

Theorem 12. *Model checking* WCTL$_{Avg}^{rf}$ *(and therefore* WCTL$_{Avg}$*) over weighted Kripke structures is undecidable.*

Proof. We encode the halting problem for (deterministic) two-counter machines into our model-checking problem with fixed initial value. The values c_1 and c_2 of the counters at a given position along an execution is encoded by the length of the path being of the form $2^{c_1} \cdot 3^{c_2} \cdot 5^a$, where a is a nonnegative integer. Decrementing counter c_1 will then amount to multiplying the length of the path by $5/2$, which will be achieved by taking a self-loop on a state until the total average value of the weight reaches a given value.

We illustrate the construction on an example. Figure 3 depicts a *module* from (q, A_k) to $(q', A_{k'})$. This module will be used to modify (increment or decrement) the counters. The $\mathsf{WCTL}^{\mathrm{rf}}_{\mathsf{Avg}}$ formula will enforce that the average weight value of a path ending in a state labelled A_k be exactly k, for all $0 \le k \le 2$. Consider such a path, of length n, ending in state (q, A_k) of Figure 3 (so that the accumulated weight is $k \cdot n$). With j taking values 2, 3, 5/2 or 5/3 will implement all four instructions modifying the counters. Now, we extend this path following the depicted module, until reaching $(q', A_{k'})$. Write $x - 2$ for the number of times we take the self-loop on state (r, k, k'). Then the length of the path when reaching $(q', A_{k'})$ is $n + x$, and its total accumulated weight is $k \cdot n + \frac{(jk' - k) \cdot x}{j - 1}$. The requirement that the average be k' in $(q', A_{k'})$ entails

$$k \cdot n + \frac{(jk' - k) \cdot x}{j - 1} = k' \cdot (n + x).$$

One easily checks that, provided $k \ne k'$, this implies $x = (j - 1) \cdot n$, so that the length of the whole path when reaching $(q', A_{k'})$ is $j \cdot n$ (assuming $j > 1$), and the average is indeed k'.

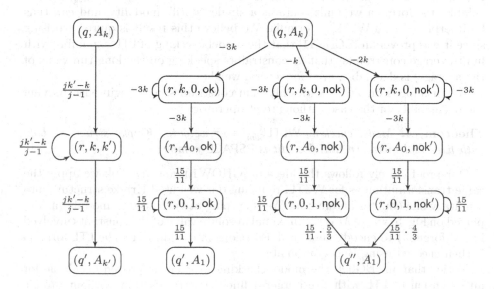

Fig. 3. Updating counters   **Fig. 4.** Testing counters (here c_2)

Similarly, Figure 4 is a module testing whether counter c_2 equals zero. Starting in state (q, A_k) with a path of length n, and total accumulated weight $k \cdot n$, it is rather clear that we can reach state (r, A_0, ok) if, and only if, n is an integer multiple of 3 (which means that $c_2 > 0$). State (r, A_0, ok) is then reached by a path of total length $4n/3$, and accumulated weight zero. Then the path goes to $(r, 0, 1, \mathsf{ok})$, and takes the loop $x - 2$ times, and reaches (q', A_1). The accumulated weight then is $15x/11$, and the length of the path is $4n/3 + x$. The average is 1 exactly when $x = 11n/3$, for which the total length of the path is $5n$; this way, the counters are back to their original value when reaching (q', A_1).

If we follow the middle branch of the module, we reach (r, A_0, nok) with average zero if, and only if, $n - 1$ is an integer multiple of 3, which implies that n is not, so that $c_2 = 0$. The length of the path when reaching (r, A_0, nok) is $n + 1 + (n-1)/3$. We then reach (q'', A_1) after looping $x - 2$ times on $(r, 0, 1, \mathsf{nok})$; then the length of the path is $(4n+2)/3 + x$, and the total weight is $(x + 2/3) \cdot 15/11$. Since we require the average weight to equal 1, we get $x = (11n - 2)/3$, which yields a total final length of $5n$, as expected. A similar computation can be conducted for the rightmost branch.   □

Remark 13. Notice that this can be made to work with only nonnegative and/or integer weights, by shifting and/or multiplying all weights and average constraints by some constant.

5   Algorithms for Model Checking Fragments of WLTL

5.1   Decidability of WLTL$^{\mathsf{rf}}_{\mathsf{Sum}}$ Model Checking

It follows from the proof of Theorem 12 that model checking WLTL$^{\mathsf{rf}}_{\mathsf{Avg}}$ is undecidable: the formula we built contains a single "until" modality, and can thus be interpreted as a WLTL$^{\mathsf{rf}}_{\mathsf{Avg}}$ formula. We believe this result is quite surprising since it was proven in [BCHK11] that the model checking of LTL extending with limit-average constraints (that is, constraints speaking on the long-run value of the average) is decidable, even for several weights.

We thus focus on WLTL with only Sum constraints, and begin with proving the decidability of the case without reset operator:

Theorem 14. *Model checking* WLTL$^{\mathsf{rf}}_{\mathsf{Sum}}$ *over weighted Kripke structures both with fixed and unknown initial credit is* PSPACE-*complete.*

Our proof closely follows the ideas of [GHOW10] and [DG09]: we apply the same transformation as for WCTL, reducing our weighted Kripke structure into a unitary one-counter automaton. We then plug at each state a module (as displayed on Fig. 5, where M is the maximal absolute value of the constants involved in the formula) to encode numerical assertions into plain LTL. The LTL formula is then checked using Büchi automata.

Notice that in [DG09], the model-checking problem is proven decidable for an extension of LTL with Presburger-defined constraints (but without atomic propositions) over one-dimensional weighted Kripke structures with zero tests.

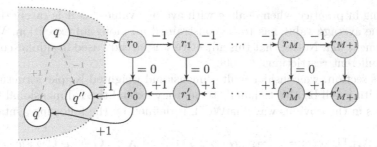

Fig. 5. From $\mathsf{WLTL}^{\mathrm{rf}}_{\mathsf{Sum}}$ to LTL (notice that q' and q'' also have their corresponding test modules, which we omitted to draw for the sake of readability)

How to handle atomic propositions for that problem is not addressed in [DG09]. The extension to unknown initial credit is similar to the case of $\mathsf{WCTL}_{\mathsf{Sum}}$.

5.2 $\mathsf{WLTL}_{\mathsf{Sum}}$ Model Checking Is Undecidable

In this section, we prove that contrary to the case of $\mathsf{WCTL}_{\mathsf{Sum}}$, the reset operator makes model checking undecidable. This is not so surprising, and is actually a corollary of a similar result for LTL with one register over one-counter automata [DLS10, Thm. 17].

LTL with registers extends LTL with a way of *storing* the current value of a counter (or other data, depending on the underlying model), and compare the stored value later on during the execution. For instance, $\downarrow \phi$ stores the current value of the counter before evaluating ϕ. Then $\uparrow$ evaluates to true at positions where the value of the counter equals the value stored in the register. For instance, $\downarrow \neg \mathbf{X}\mathbf{F} \uparrow$, means that it must never be the case that the value of the counter equals its initial value.

The translation of LTL with *one* register into $\mathsf{WLTL}_{\mathsf{Sum}}$ is then straightforward: $\downarrow$ corresponds to setting the weight to zero, and $\uparrow$ simply means $\mathsf{Sum} = 0$. In order to encode the behaviours of a one-counter automaton as a weighted Kripke structure, we have to additionally require that the accumulated weight remains nonnegative, by adding $\mathbf{G}\,(\mathsf{Sum} \geq 0)$ as a global conjunct. The following theorem directly follows:

Theorem 15. *Model checking $\mathsf{WLTL}_{\mathsf{Sum}}$ over weighted Kripke structures is undecidable.*

5.3 Model Checking a *Flat* Fragment of WLTL

We conclude this part with a fragment of WLTL which forbids numerical assertions on the left-hand-side of an "until" formula. As we prove below, model checking our fragment is decidable, so that it offers an alternative to the fragments $\mathbf{EF}^{\Sigma}$ and $\mathsf{LTL}^{\mathrm{lim}}$ of [BCHK11], with a lower complexity. Also, our fragment allows us to use multiple variables, as well as average assertions. The syntactic restriction is the price to pay for this, but we believe that the fragment remains interesting in practice when dealing with average values, as it is rarely the case that some average value has to be constrained all along an execution. We call this fragment *flat*. Notice that this adjective was already used in similar contexts, but for different restrictions [CC00].

In this section, we consider multi-dimensional weighted Kripke structures, as our algorithm will be able to handle them; they extend the 1-dimensional Kripke structures in the obvious way. FlatWLTL is defined by the following syntax:

$$\mathsf{FlatWLTL} \ni \phi ::= p \mid \neg p \mid \alpha \mid \phi \vee \phi \mid \phi \wedge \phi \mid \mathbf{X}\,\phi \mid \mathbf{G}\,\psi \mid \psi\,\mathbf{U}\,\phi \mid w \cdot \phi$$

where α ranges over numerical assertions, ψ ranges over LTL and, and w ranges over the set of variables. The semantics follows that of WLTL.

Notice that our fragment allows both Sum and Avg constraints, as well as the reset operator. Also notice that our logic includes a restricted version of the release modality, namely $\phi\,\mathbf{R}\,\psi$, which can be expressed as $\mathbf{G}\,\psi \vee \psi\,\mathbf{U}\,(\phi \wedge \psi)$.

Additionally, using the techniques in [BCHK11], this allows us to transform Avg-assertions into Sum-assertions (if we have to check $\mathsf{Avg}(x) \leq c$, we introduce a new variable x_c whose updates are shifted by $-c$ compared to the updates of x, and then check $\mathsf{Sum}(x_c) \leq 0$). Hence we can assume that our formula does not contain Avg assertions.

We first prove that a path satisfying a formula in FlatWLTL can be decomposed into finitely many segments, delimited with positions where some numerical assertions have to be checked.

Pick $\phi \in \mathsf{FlatWLTL}$, and a path π in a weighted Kripke structure $\mathcal{K}$ such that $\pi, 0 \models \phi$. We inductively build a finite set of positions along π at which we may have to evaluate numerical assertions; at all other positions, only pure-LTL formulas will need to be evaluated. For this, we consider the tree of ϕ, and we proceed inductively. We first decorate the root of the tree of ϕ with 0 (to indicate that ϕ holds true at position 0). If ϕ is pure LTL, then we end the labelling. Then, from a node representing subformula ψ that has been decorated with integer i, we distinguish between the different types of nodes:

- if the node corresponds to an atomic proposition, the negation thereof, or a numerical assertion, we are done;
- if the node corresponds a reset operator (that is, $\psi = w \cdot \psi'$), we label its successor node, which corresponds to subformula ψ', with i;
- if the node is a conjunction of subformulas (that is, $\psi = \psi_1 \wedge \psi_2$), we mark all successors of this node with i. Notice that indeed all subformulas have to hold true at position i of π;
- if the node is a disjunction of subformulas, then one of the disjunct has to hold true at position i of π. We label this successor with i;
- if the node is a **X**-modality, we label its successor node with $i + 1$;
- if the node if a **G**-modality, we decorate its successor node with the interval $[i, +\infty)$ (hence the inductive labelling ends here for this branch, since the formula is flat);

– if the node is an **U**-modality, then there must be a position $j \geq i$ along π at which the right-hand-side subformula of this **U**-formula holds true. We decorate the right-hand-side successor node of the present node with j, and the left-hand-side node with $[i, j - 1]$. The inductive labelling ends here for the left-hand-side branch since the formula is flat.

The following trivially holds: for every node that has been labelled by an integer i, if that node corresponds to subformula ψ, then $\pi, i \models \psi$. Conversely, if for some run π we can label consistently the tree representation of ϕ with integers (or intervals on pure LTL formulas) such that the root is labelled with 0, then $\pi, 0 \models \phi$.

This way, we have identified sufficiently many witnessing positions where some numerical assertions may have to be checked. Let $\mathcal{P} = \{i_0 = 0, i_1, ..., i_k\}$ be the set of integers (named *breakpoints* hereafter) labelling the tree of ϕ, assuming $i_l < i_m$ whenever $l < m$. By construction, we have that $k \leq |\phi|$. Between any two such consecutive positions, the decorated tree gives us (conjunctions of) LTL subformulas to be checked at every intermediary position (the above labelling tells us that all positions between two checkpoints have to satisfy the same LTL subformulas of ϕ). The tree also indicates those breakpoints where we reset some of the weight variables. Note that given two labellings of the formula tree yielding the same order on breakpoints and making the same choices in the disjunctions, the very same formulas have to be verified between two breakpoints.

As a first step of our (non-deterministic) algorithm, we pick a number $k + 1$ of (at most $|\phi|$) breakpoints, and guess a labelling of the formula tree with the indices of the breakpoints (or intervals) that respects the rules defined earlier. Then we uniquely associate with each $h \in [0, k]$ an LTL "right-hand-side" subformula ξ_h and a numerical assertion α_h to be checked at breakpoint i_h, and an LTL formula ζ_h that has to be checked at intermediary positions before the next breakpoint (with ζ_k being enforced at all positions after the last breakpoint). As noted above, those formulas are uniquely fixed by the order of breakpoints and the labelling of the formula tree; moreover ξ_h and ζ_h are conjunctions of pure LTL subformulas of ϕ whereas α_h are conjunctions of numerical assertions appearing as subformulas of ϕ or negations of such subformulas. See Fig. 6 for an example of a formula tree labelled with breakpoints.

With each formula ξ_h selected above, we associate a Büchi automaton $\mathcal{A}_{\xi_h'}$ where ξ_h' is the formula $\mathbf{G}(b_h \Rightarrow \xi_h)$ and b_h is a fresh atomic proposition that only holds true at breakpoint i_h (note that the value of i_h is not known). Similarly, with formulas ζ_h, we associate an automaton $\mathcal{A}_{\zeta_h'}$ enforcing formula $\zeta_h' = \mathbf{G}(c_h \Rightarrow \zeta_h)$, where atomic proposition c_h only holds true between i_h and i_{h+1}.

Our algorithm will check the existence of segments between two breakpoints that satisfy the required properties. Each segment corresponds to a finite path in the product $\mathcal{L}$ of the weighted Kripke structure $\mathcal{K}$ and all the Büchi automata built above. When working with the j-th segment, proposition b_j is set to true at the first step, and c_j holds true all along this segment. This way, the automata $\mathcal{A}_{\xi_j'}$ and $\mathcal{A}_{\zeta_j'}$ play their roles of checking ξ_j at the beginning of the segment, and ζ_j at every position in the segment. The automata that have already

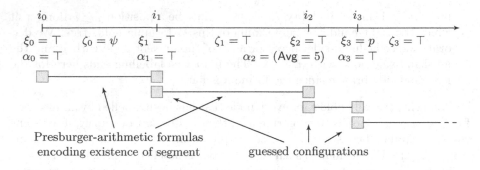

Fig. 7. Schematics representation of our algorithm

been "activated" (at previous break-points) keep on running, finishing their computations, while the automata corresponding to later breakpoints remain "idle".

One configuration of $\mathcal{L}$ (i.e. a state of $\mathcal{K}$ and a state per Büchi automaton constructed above) can be stored using polynomial space. However, we do not have a bound on the length of the segments, which prevents us from guessing the path on-the-fly. Instead, we guess the configurations of $\mathcal{L}$ at each breakpoint (there are at most $|\phi|$ breakpoints). It remains to decide the existence of a path in $\mathcal{L}$ from the configuration in one breakpoint to the configuration in the next one, and checking that the numerical assertions at each breakpoint are satisfied. Following the ideas of [BCHK11], we can encode the existence of each segment by assigning one variable with each transition of $\mathcal{L}$: each variable represents the number of times this transition will be taken along the segment, and one can

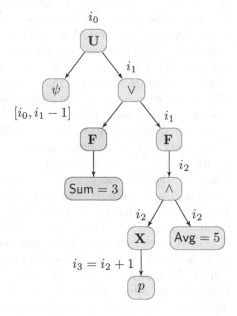

Fig. 6. Labelling of the tree of formula $\psi \, \mathbf{U} \, \big[\mathbf{F}\,(\mathsf{Sum} = 3) \vee \mathbf{F}\,(\mathbf{X}\,(p) \wedge \mathsf{Avg} = 5)\big]$ (assuming $\psi \in \mathsf{LTL}$) with breakpoints

easily write a Presburger-arithmetic formula expressing that a valuation for those variables corresponds to a path and that the numerical assertions are fulfilled. Notice that we can easily handle reset operators in those equations. In the end, our formula is in the existential fragment of Presburger arithmetic, and has size exponential, so that our procedure runs in NEXPTIME.

Theorem 16. *Model checking* FlatWLTL *over weighted Kripke structures is decidable in* NEXPTIME.

References

[AH94]   Alur, R., Henzinger, T.A.: A really temporal logic. Journal of the
            ACM 41(1), 181–203 (1994)
[BBFR13]   Bohy, A., Bruyère, V., Filiot, E., Raskin, J.-F.: Synthesis from ltl specifica-
            tions with mean-payoff objectives. In: Piterman, N., Smolka, S.A. (eds.)
            TACAS 2013 (ETAPS 2013). LNCS, vol. 7795, pp. 169–184. Springer,
            Heidelberg (2013)
[BCHK11]   Boker, U., Chatterjee, K., Henzinger, T.A., Kupferman, O.: Temporal
            specifications with accumulative values. In: LICS 2011, pp. 43–52. IEEE
            Comp. Soc. Press (2011)
[BFL+08]   Bouyer, P., Fahrenberg, U., Larsen, K.G., Markey, N., Srba, J.: Infinite
            runs in weighted timed automata with energy constraints. In: Cassez, F.,
            Jard, C. (eds.) FORMATS 2008. LNCS, vol. 5215, pp. 33–47. Springer,
            Heidelberg (2008)
[BLM14]   Bouyer, P., Larsen, K.G., Markey, N.: Lower-bound constrained runs in
            weighted timed automata. Performance Evaluation 73, 91–109 (2014)
[BLN03]   Beyer, D., Lewerentz, C., Noack, A.: Rabbit: A tool for BDD-based veri-
            fication of real-time systems. In: Hunt Jr., W.A., Somenzi, F. (eds.) CAV
            2003. LNCS, vol. 2725, pp. 122–125. Springer, Heidelberg (2003)
[BMOU11]   Bouyer, P., Markey, N., Olschewski, J., Ummels, M.: Measuring permis-
            siveness in parity games: Mean-payoff parity games revisited. In: Bul-
            tan, T., Hsiung, P.-A. (eds.) ATVA 2011. LNCS, vol. 6996, pp. 135–149.
            Springer, Heidelberg (2011)
[CC95]   Campos, S.V.A., Clarke, E.M.: Real-time symbolic model checking for
            discrete time models. In: Real-Time Symbolic Model Checking for Dis-
            crete Time Models. AMAST Series in Computing, vol. 2, pp. 129–145.
            World Scientific (1995)
[CC00]   Comon, H., Cortier, V.: Flatness is not a weakness. In: Clote, P.G.,
            Schwichtenberg, H. (eds.) CSL 2000. LNCS, vol. 1862, pp. 262–276.
            Springer, Heidelberg (2000)
[CD12]   Chatterjee, K., Doyen, L.: Energy parity games. Theoretical Computer
            Science 458, 49–60 (2012)
[CDHR10]   Chatterjee, K., Doyen, L., Henzinger, T.A., Raskin, J.-F.: Generalized
            mean-payoff and energy games. In: FSTTCS 2010. Leibniz International
            Proceedings in Informatics, vol. 8, Leibniz-Zentrum für Informatik (2010)
[CE82]   Clarke, E.M., Emerson, E.A.: Design and synthesis of synchronization
            skeletons using branching-time temporal logic. In: Kozen, D. (ed.) Logic
            of Programs 1981. LNCS, vol. 131, pp. 52–71. Springer, Heidelberg (1982)
[CGP00]   Clarke, E.M., Grumberg, O., Peled, D.A.: Model checking. MIT Press
            (2000)
[CRR12]   Chatterjee, K., Randour, M., Raskin, J.-F.: Strategy synthesis for multi-
            dimensional quantitative objectives. In: Koutny, M., Ulidowski, I. (eds.)
            CONCUR 2012. LNCS, vol. 7454, pp. 115–131. Springer, Heidelberg
            (2012)
[DG09]   Demri, S., Gascon, R.: The effects of bounding syntactic resources on
            Presburger LTL. Journal of Logic and Computation 19(6), 1541–1575
            (2009)
[DLS10]   Demri, S., Lazić, R., Sangnier, A.: Model checking memoryful linear-time
            logics over one-counter automata. Theoretical Computer Science 411(22-
            24), 2298–2316 (2010)

[EMSS92]   Emerson, E.A., Mok, A.K.-L., Sistla, A.P., Srinivasan, J.: Quantitative temporal reasoning. Real-Time Systems 4, 331–352 (1992)

[EN94]   Esparza, J., Nielsen, M.: Decidability issues for petri nets - a survey. Bulletin of the EATCS 52, 244–262 (1994)

[GHOW10]   Göller, S., Haase, C., Ouaknine, J., Worrell, J.: Model checking succinct and parametric one-counter automata. In: Abramsky, S., Gavoille, C., Kirchner, C., Meyer auf der Heide, F., Spirakis, P.G. (eds.) ICALP 2010. LNCS, vol. 6199, pp. 575–586. Springer, Heidelberg (2010)

[GL10]   Göller, S., Lohrey, M.: Branching-time model checking of one-counter processes. In: STACS 2010. Leibniz International Proceedings in Informatics, vol. 20, pp. 405–416. Leibniz-Zentrum für Informatik (2010)

[Haa12]   Haase, C.: On the Complexity of Model Checking Counter Automata. PhD thesis, University of Oxford, UK (2012)

[HKOW09]   Haase, C., Kreutzer, S., Ouaknine, J., Worrell, J.: Reachability in succinct and parametric one-counter automata. In: Bravetti, M., Zavattaro, G. (eds.) CONCUR 2009. LNCS, vol. 5710, pp. 369–383. Springer, Heidelberg (2009)

[JLSØ13]   Jensen, J.F., Larsen, K.G., Srba, J., Oestergaard, L.K.: Local model checking of weighted CTL with upper-bound constraints. In: Bartocci, E., Ramakrishnan, C.R. (eds.) SPIN 2013. LNCS, vol. 7976, pp. 178–195. Springer, Heidelberg (2013)

[Koy90]   Koymans, R.: Specifying real-time properties with metric temporal logic. Real-Time Systems 2(4), 255–299 (1990)

[Min61]   Minsky, M.L.: Recursive unsolvability of Post's problem of "tag" and other topics in theory of Turing machines. Annals of Mathematics 74(3), 437–455 (1961)

[Pnu77]   Pnueli, A.: The temporal logic of programs. In: FOCS 1977, pp. 46–57. IEEE Comp. Soc. Press (1977)

[QS82]   Queille, J.-P., Sifakis, J.: Specification and verification of concurrent systems in CESAR. In: Dezani-Ciancaglini, M., Montanari, U. (eds.) Programming 1982. LNCS, vol. 137, pp. 337–351. Springer, Heidelberg (1982)

[Ser06]   Serre, O.: Parity games played on transition graphs of one-counter processes. In: Aceto, L., Ingólfsdóttir, A. (eds.) FOSSACS 2006. LNCS, vol. 3921, pp. 337–351. Springer, Heidelberg (2006)

[ZP96]   Zwick, U., Paterson, M.: The complexity of mean payoff games on graphs. Theoretical Computer Science 158(1-2), 343–359 (1996)

Formal Safety Assessment
via Contract-Based Design*

Marco Bozzano, Alessandro Cimatti, Cristian Mattarei, and Stefano Tonetta

Fondazione Bruno Kessler, Trento, Italy
{bozzano,cimatti,mattarei,tonettas}@fbk.eu

Abstract. Safety Assessment (SA) is an engineering discipline aiming at the analysis of systems under faults. According to industrial practice and standards, SA is based on the construction of complex artifacts such as Fault Trees, which describe how certain faults may cause some top-level events. SA is intended to mirror the hierarchical design of the system focusing on the safety aspects.

In this paper, we propose a formal approach where the nominal specification of a hierarchically decomposed system is automatically extended to encompass faults. The approach is based on a contract-based design paradigm, where components at different levels of abstraction are characterized in terms of the properties that they have to guarantee and the assumptions that must be satisfied by their environment. The framework has several distinguishing features. First, the extension is fully automated, and requires no human intervention, based on the idea that intermediate events are failures to fulfill the contracts. Second, it can be applied stepwise, and provides feedback in the early phases of the design process. Finally, it efficiently produces hierarchically organized fault trees.

1 Introduction

Complex systems are often the result of two complementary processes. On the one side, *hierarchical design* refines a set of requirements into increasingly detailed levels, decomposing a system into subsystems, down to basic components. On the other side, the process of *safety assessment* (SA) analyzes the impact of faults. This process is intended to pinpoint the consequences of faults (e.g., a valve failing to operate) on high-level functions (e.g., loss of thrust to engines).

In architectural design, the failure of components is typically not modeled explicitly. Failures are typically artificially introduced in the model for safety assessment. However, the design that is later implemented in real software and hardware components contains only the nominal interfaces and behaviors. It may contain redundancy mechanism or failure monitoring, but not the failure themselves. We call such architectural design the *nominal architecture*. Modeling and analysis of faults is the objective of SA. Unfortunately, there is often a gap between the design of the nominal architecture and SA, which are carried out by different teams, possibly on out-of-sync components. This requires substantial effort, and it is often based on unclear semantics.

---

* The research leading to these results has received funding from the ARTEMIS JU under grant agreement n° 295373 and from National funding.

F. Cassez and J.-F. Raskin (Eds.): ATVA 2014, LNCS 8837, pp. 81–97, 2014.

In this paper, we conceived a new formal methodology to support a tight integration between the architectural design and the SA process. Our approach builds on two main ingredients. First, we use Contract-Based Design (CBD) - a hierarchical technique that provides formal support to the architectural decomposition of a system into subsystems and subcomponents. Components at different levels of abstraction are characterized by contracts (assumptions/guarantees). CBD can provide feedback in the early stages of the process, by specifying blocks in abstract terms (e.g., in terms of temporal logic [17]), without the need for a behavioral model (e.g., in terms of finite-state machines). Second, we use the idea of fault injection (a.k.a. model extension), which enables the transformation of a nominal model into one encompassing faults. This is done by introducing additional variables controlling the activation of faults, hence controlling whether the system is behaving according to the nominal or the faulty specification. Within this setting, it is possible to automatically generate Fault Trees (FTs) using model checking techniques. This approach focused in the past on behavioral models [21,13], and is flat, i.e., it generates two-level FTs corresponding to the DNF of their minimal cut sets (MCSs) [11]; as such, it is unable to exploit system hierarchy.

The novel contribution of our approach is the extension of CBD for SA (CBSA): given a nominal contract-based system decomposition, we automatically obtain a decomposition with fault injections. The insight is that the failure mode variables are directly extracted from the structure of the nominal description, in that they model the failure of a component to satisfy its contract. The approach is proved to preserve the correctness of refinement: the extension of a correct refinement of nominal contracts yields an extended model where the refinements are still correct. Once the contracts are extended, it is possible to automatically construct FTs that mimic the structure of the architecture, and formally characterize how lower-level or environmental failures may cause failures at higher levels. This approach has several important features. First, it is fully automated, since SA models are directly obtained from the design models, without further human intervention. Second, it can be applied early in the development process and stepwise along the refinement of the design, providing a tight connection between design and SA. Third, it allows for the generation of artifacts that are fundamental in SA, namely FTs that follow the hierarchical decomposition of the system architecture.

The framework has been implemented extending the OCRA tool [15], which supports CBD. We show experimentally that our approach is able to produce hierarchically organized FTs automatically and efficiently. Furthermore, when applied to behavioral descriptions, the partitioning provided by CBD demonstrates a much better scalability than the monolithic approach provided by previous techniques for Model-Based Safety Assessment (MBSA) [13], which generate flat FTs.

This paper is structured as follows. In Sect. 2, we discuss some related work. In Sect. 3, we present the state of the practice in SA. In Sect. 4, we present some background on formal verification and CBD. In Sect. 5, we discuss contract-based fault injection, and in Sect. 6, we discuss how to generate FTs. In Sect. 7, we present the experimental evaluation. In Sect. 8, we conclude and discuss future work.

2   Related Work

In recent years, there has been a growing industrial interest in MBSA, see e.g., [13]. These methods are based on a single safety model of a system. Formal verification tools based on model checking have been extended to automate the generation of artifacts such as FTs and FMEA tables [13,12,9,11,10], and used for certification of safety critical systems, see e.g., the Cecilia OCAS platform by Dassault Aviation. However, the scope of such methods is limited to the generation of the MCSs, represented as a two-level FT. This limitation has an impact in terms of scalability, and readability of the FTs. Our approach overcomes the previous limitations – both in terms of scalability (compare Section 7) and significance of the generated FTs (we produce hierarchically organized FTs, as per [4]). Moreover, as a difference with traditional MBSA, we follow a fully top-down development approach, which closely resembles the SA process as described, e.g., in [4], providing feedback in much earlier stages of the design.

An alternative approach for the generation of more structured FTs is based on actors-oriented design [23,20], however these techniques do not account for a stepwise refinement of SA, as outlined in [4]. Specifically, even in presence of minor changes, this approach does not provide the possibility to refine, extend or reuse previous FTA.

Our work is similar in spirit to [5], which presents a methodology based on retrenchment (an extension of classical refinement), to generate hierarchical FTs from systems represented as circuits, exploiting the system dataflow. A major difference is that retrenchment does not focus on top-down development, but rather on the relation between nominal and faulty behaviors. It takes as input the system hierarchy and the behavioral models, hence it does not support the FT generation along the stepwise refinement. Moreover, the framework is theoretical and, although an algorithm for generation of FTs is provided, implementation issues for its realization are not discussed.

In [6], contracts are (manually) generated after a safety and design process. The FT is manually constructed starting from some diagrams describing the system behavior. State machines are extended with faulty behavior to analyze the hazards. Differently from our work, FTA and hazards analysis are used to collect information to specify the contracts. We instead start from the contracts to derive automatically the FT.

In this paper, we based the fault-tree generation on the contract-based refinement. There are other more mature refinement techniques such as the B Method [2], but we are not aware of approaches to FT generation based on these refinements.

Finally, in the context of fault diagnosis, the work described in [25] constructs diagnoses by exploiting the hierarchy of a circuit; the health variable associated with a region of the circuit, called cone, resembles the idea of intermediate event in a FT. However, this work does not focus on architectural design and stepwise refinement.

3   Safety Assessment: State of the Practice

Safety assessment is an integral part of the system development of complex systems. As an example, [3] describes the typical development process for civil aircraft as being constituted of different activities, including: a conceptual design, whereby intended aircraft functions are identified; the system architecture design, which is responsible for designing the architecture down to the item level, and allocating aircraft functions to the appropriate items; the allocation of system requirements to items; finally, the implementation of individual items (in software and/or in hardware) and the items/system integration activity. In practice, development may involve multiple iterative cycles, whereby the system architecture and allocated requirements are progressively refined.

In this context, safety assessment has the goal to show that the implemented system meets the identified safety requirements and complies with certification requirements. Safety assessment is strictly intertwined with, and carried out across all phases of development. For example, [4] distinguishes a preliminary aircraft- or system-level safety assessment (PASA/PSSA), which aims at validating the proposed architecture in terms of safety and allocating safety requirements to items, and an aircraft- or system-level safety assessment (ASA/SSA), which systematically evaluates the implemented aircraft and systems in order to show that they meet the safety requirements.

Fault Tree Analysis (FTA) [4,26] is a traditional safety assessment method, which can be applied across different phases. It is as a deductive technique, whereby an undesired state (the so called *top level event*) is specified, and the system is analyzed for the possible chains of *basic events* (e.g., system faults) that may cause the top event to occur. A FT makes use of logical gates to depict the logical interrelationships linking such events, and it can be evaluated quantitatively, e.g., to determine the probability of a safety hazard. FTs are developed starting from the top event; causes which are considered to be elementary faults are developed as basic events, and the remaining causes as *intermediate events*. This rule applies recursively to the intermediate events, which must in turn be traced back to their causes, until the tree is fully developed [26].

Example 1 (WBS). The Wheel Braking System (WBS) case study was introduced in [4], and later used to describe a formal specification ([19]) and refinement ([17]) of contracts along a system architecture – it is therefore an ideal case study to evaluate our approach. Fig. 1 shows the WBS architecture. The WBS controls the braking of the main gear wheels for taxiing and landing phases of an aircraft. Braking is commanded either via brake pedals or automatically. The brake is operated by two independent sets of hydraulic pistons, supplied by independent power lines: the "green power supply" (GP), used in normal mode, and the "blue power supply" (BP), used in alternate mode. The alternate system (AWBS) is in stand by and is selected automatically when the normal one (NWBS) fails. An emergency brake system (EWBS) is activated when both NWBS and AWBS fail. In normal mode, the brake is controlled by the Braking System Control Unit (BSCU), implemented with two redundant control units. Each sub-unit (SB1 and SB2) receives an independent pedal-position signal. Monitors detect the failure of the sub-units, producing the "Valid" signals, and of the whole BSCU. The Braking System Annunciation (BSA) monitors the output of the WBS, and it raises a signal in case of every braking systems fail to operate. [4] also describes a PSSA of the WBS, using FTA to analyze the "Unannunciated loss of all wheel braking" top event. The resulting FT (Fig. 2) reflects how the top event depends on the unannounciated loss of the three braking systems and develops the tree downwards, identifying the failures contributing to the unannounciated loss of normal braking. An example of intermediate event is "Normal Brake System does not operate", whereas "Switch failed stuck in intermediate position" is a basic event.

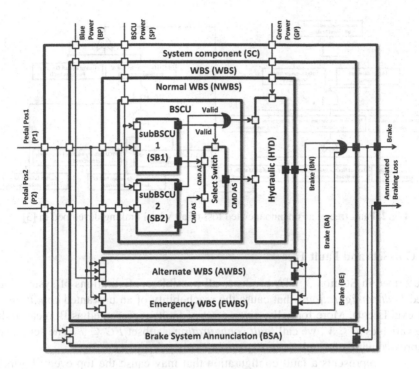

Fig. 1. WBS architecture (the names in parenthesis define the abbreviations)

4 Background Notions of Formal Methods

4.1 LTL Model Checking

States and traces are defined over a set V of state variables. A state is an assignment to V of values in a given domain, while a trace is an infinite sequence $\sigma = s_0, s_1, s_2, \ldots$ of states. We denote with $Tr(V)$ the set of all traces over V. We define a *language* as a set of traces. We denote with $\sigma[i]$ the i-th state of σ. We use Linear-time Temporal Logic (LTL) [24] to represent sets of traces. We assume that the reader is familiar with LTL. Given an LTL formula ϕ and a trace σ, we write $\sigma \models \phi$ if the trace σ satisfies the formula ϕ. We define the language $\mathcal{L}(\phi)$ as the set of traces σ such that $\sigma \models \phi$.

A transition system is a tuple $\langle V, \iota, \tau \rangle$, where V is a set of state variables, ι is the initial formula over V, τ is the transition formula over V and V' (V' is the set of next versions of the variables in V). A path of a transition system $M = \langle V, \iota, \tau \rangle$ is a sequence $s_0, s_1, \ldots$ of assignments to V such that s_0 satisfies ι and for each $k \geq 0$, $\langle s_k, s_{k+1} \rangle$ satisfies τ. We denote with $\mathcal{L}(M)$ the set of paths of M. Given a transition system M and an LTL formula ϕ, the model checking problem is the problem of checking if every trace accepted by M satisfies ϕ, i.e., if $\mathcal{L}(M) \subseteq \mathcal{L}(\phi)$.

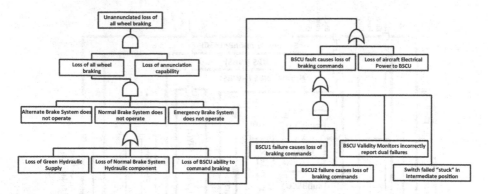

Fig. 2. Fault tree of an unannounciated loss of all wheel braking developed in [3]

4.2 Cut-Sets and Fault Tree

As described in Section 3, FTA produces all possible configurations of system faults (called *fault configurations*) that cause the reachability of an unwanted condition (the Top Level Event). More formally, given a set of faults represented as Boolean failure mode variables $\mathcal{F} \subseteq V$, we call *fault configuration* a subset $FC \subseteq \mathcal{F}$. The set FC can be expressed with a formula over $\mathcal{F}$, namely $FC^{\top} = \bigwedge_{f \in FC}(f = \top)$.

A *cut set* represents a fault configuration that may cause the top event. Formally, we generalize the definition in [11] to infinite traces and LTL, as follows. Let L be a language of traces over the variables V and let TLE an LTL formula over V. We say that FC is a cut set of TLE in L, written $FC \in CS(L, TLE, \mathcal{F})$, iff there exists a trace σ in L such that: i) $\sigma \models TLE$; ii) $FC \subseteq \mathcal{F}$ and $\forall f \in FC \; \exists \, i, \, (\sigma[i] \models f = \top)$.

Intuitively, a cut set corresponds to the set of failure mode variables that are active along a trace witnessing the occurrence of TLE. *Minimal cut sets* (MCSs), written $MCS(L, TLE, \mathcal{F})$, are those that are minimal in terms of failure mode variables: $MCS(L, TLE, \mathcal{F}) = \{cs \in CS(L, TLE, \mathcal{F}) \mid \forall cs' \in CS(L, TLE, \mathcal{F}) \, (cs' \subseteq cs \rightarrow cs' = cs)\}$. Moreover, the set $MCS(L, TLE, \mathcal{F})$ can be expressed with a formula over $\mathcal{F}$ in disjunctive normal form, namely $MCS^{\top}(L, TLE, \mathcal{F}) = \bigvee_{FC \in MCS(L, TLE, \mathcal{F})} FC^{\top}$.

A Fault Tree (FT) [26] can be represented as a set of Boolean formulae over Basic Events (BE) and Intermediate Events (IE). This representation defines a tree where leaves are BE, and nodes are IE. More specifically, the Backus-Naur Form of a Fault Tree FT is as follows: $FT ::= IE \mapsto FT | FT \wedge FT | FT \vee FT | BE$. According to this definition, the first level of the FT represented in Figure 2 can be then expressed as "Unannuciated loss of all wheel braking" (the TLE) $\mapsto$ "Loss of all wheel braking" (an Intermediate Event) $\wedge$ "Loss of annunciation capability" (a Basic Event). The second level extends the IEs of the first one, and in this example it is as: "Loss of all wheel braking" $\mapsto$ "Alternate Brake System does not operate" $\wedge$ "Normal Brake System does not operate" $\wedge$ "Emergency Brake System does not operate". The successor levels recursively define the IEs, while the Basic Events are treated as terminals, as defined by the BNF representation of a FT.

4.3 Contract-Based Design

Components and System Architectures. A component interface consists of a set of ports, which are divided into input and output ports[1]. Input ports are those controlled by the environment and fed to the component. The output ports are those controlled by the component and communicated to the environment. Formally, each component S has interface $\langle I_S, O_S \rangle$ of input and output ports. We denote with V_S the set of ports related to the component interface S given by the union of I_S and O_S.

In order to formalize decomposition, we need to specify the interconnections between the ports, i.e. how the information is propagated around. Intuitively, the input ports of a component are driven by other ports, possibly combined by means of generalized (e.g., arithmetic) gates. These combinations, in the following referred to as *drivers*, depend on the type of the port. Without loss of generality, we assume that ports are either Boolean- or real-valued. The driver for a Boolean port is a Boolean formula; for a real-valued port it is a real arithmetic expression. Therefore, we define a *decomposition* of a component S as a pair $\rho = \langle Sub, \gamma \rangle$ where Sub is a non-empty set of (sub)components such that $S \notin Sub$, and the connection γ is a function that:

– maps each port in O_S into a driver over the ports in $I_S \cup \bigcup_{S' \in Sub} O_{S'}$, and
– for each $U \in Sub$, maps each port in I_U into a driver over the ports in $I_S \cup \bigcup_{S' \in Sub} O_{S'}$.

We extend γ to Boolean and temporal formulas so that $\gamma(\phi)$ is the formula obtained by substituting each symbol s in O_S and I_U for all $U \in Sub$ with $\gamma(s)$. Note that, since ϕ is a Boolean or temporal formula over the ports of a single component, $\gamma(s)$ does not contain s and therefore $\gamma(\phi)$ is well defined (there is no circularity in the substitution).

A system architecture is a tree of components where for each non-leaf component S a decomposition $\langle Sub_S, \gamma_S \rangle$ is defined such that Sub_S are the children of S in the tree. Let Sub^* be the set of components in the architecture tree. Let γ be the union of γ_S with $S \in Sub^*$, i.e., γ takes an expression over $\bigcup_{S \in Sub^*} V_S$ and substitute s with γ_S for every $s \in O_S \cup \bigcup_{S' \in Sub_S} I_{S'}$ (we are assuming that the sets of ports of different components are disjoint). We denote with γ^* the iterative application of γ until reaching a fixpoint. Thus, γ^* takes an expression over $\bigcup_{S \in Sub^*} V_S$ and applies γ until the expression contains only input ports of the root and output ports of the leaf components.

Note that, for simplicity, we are considering only synchronous decompositions for which we need only a mapping of symbols. The framework can be extended to the asynchronous case by considering also further constraints to correlate the ports. In the following, we also assume that we have only one instance for each component so that we can identify the instance with its type to simplify the presentation. In practice, we deal with multiple instances by renaming the ports adding the instance name as prefix.

Example 2. The WBS architecture, informally introduced in Examples 1, can be formalized with the notion of decomposition defined above. For example, the top-level system component SC has two subcomponents, namely WBS and BSA. Therefore $Sub(SC) = \{WBS, BSA\}$. The mapping γ is in most of cases just a renaming. For

---

[1] For simplicity, we ignore here the distinction between data and event ports.

example, the input port P1 of WBS is driven by the input port P1 of SC. Formally $\gamma(WBS.P1) = SC.P1$ (since we avoided the distinction between component types and instances to simplify the notation, we here use the dot notation to have a unique name for each port). In few cases, the driver is not atomic. For example, the output port Valid of BSCU is driven by the disjunction of the homonyms of SB1 and SB2. Formally, $\gamma(BSCU.Valid) = SB1.Valid \vee SB2.Valid$.

Trace-Based Components Implementation and Environment. A component S encapsulates a state which is hidden to the environment. It interacts with the environment only through the ports. This interaction is represented by a trace in $Tr(V_S)$.

An input trace is a trace restricted to assignments to the input ports. Similarly, an output trace is a trace restricted to assignments to the output ports. Given an input trace $\sigma^I \in Tr(I_S)$ and an output trace $\sigma^O \in Tr(O_S)$, we denote with $\sigma^I \times \sigma^O$ the trace σ such that for all i, $\sigma[i](x) = \sigma^I[i](x)$ if $x \in I_S$ and $\sigma[i](x) = \sigma^O[i](x)$ if $x \in O_S$.

For simplicity, we do not distinguish between a language (set of traces) and the behavioral model that generates it. Therefore, both implementations and environments of a component S are seen as subsets of $Tr(V_S)$ (note that we are considering also the output ports for the language of the environment because this can be affected by the component implementation).

A decomposition of S generates a composite implementation given by the composition of the implementation of the subcomponents, as well as a composite environment for each subcomponent given by the environment of S and the implementations of the other subcomponents. In order to define formally these notions, we extend γ to states seen as conjunctions of equalities (assignments). Note that, if s is a state, then $\gamma(s)$ represents a set of states. Considering the example of γ introduced in Example 2, if $BSCU.Valid = \top$, then $\gamma(BSCU.Valid = \top)$ is equal to $(SB1.Valid \vee SB2.Valid) = \top$. Finally, we extend γ to traces seen as sequence of states.

Given a decomposition $\langle Sub, \gamma \rangle$ of S with $Sub = \{S_1, \ldots, S_n\}$ and an implementation M_j for each subcomponent interface $S_j \in Sub$, we define the composite implementation $CI_\gamma(\{M_j\}_{S_j \in Sub})$ of S taking the product of the traces of the subcomponents and projecting on the ports of the component S:

$$CI_\gamma(\{M_j\}_{S_j \in Sub}) := \{\sigma^I \times \sigma^O \in Tr(V_S) \mid \exists \sigma_1^O \in Tr(O_{S_1}), \ldots, \sigma_n^O \in Tr(O_{S_n}) \text{ s.t.}$$
$$\sigma^I \times \sigma_1^O \times \ldots \times \sigma_n^O \in \gamma(M_1) \cap \ldots \cap \gamma(M_n) \cap \gamma(\sigma^O)\}$$

Similarly, given a subcomponent $S_h \in Sub$, an implementation M_j for each subcomponent $S_j \in Sub\setminus$ with $j \neq h$, and an environment E for S, we define the composite environment $CE_\gamma(E, \{M_j\}_{S_j \in Sub, j \leq h})$ of S_h taking the product of the traces of E and the other subcomponents and projecting on the ports of $\S_h$:

$$CI_\gamma(\{M_j\}_{S_j \in Sub, j \neq h}) := \{\sigma_h^I \times \sigma_h^O \in Tr(V_{S_h}) \mid \exists \sigma^I \in Tr(I_S), \sigma_1^O \in Tr(O_{S_1}), \ldots$$
$$\ldots, \sigma_n^O \in Tr(O_{S_n}) \text{ s.t. } \sigma^I \times \sigma_1^O \times \ldots \times \sigma_n^O \in \gamma(M_1) \cap \ldots \cap \gamma(M_n) \cap \gamma(\sigma_h^I)\}$$

Contracts. A component contract is a pair of properties, called the *assumption*, which must be satisfied by the component environment, and the *guarantee*, which must be satisfied by the component implementation when the assumption holds. We assume as given an assertion language for which every assertion $\mathcal{A}$ has associated a set of variables $V_{\mathcal{A}}$ and a semantics $L(\mathcal{A})$ as a subset of $Tr(V_{\mathcal{A}})$. In practice, we will use LTL to specify such assertions, but the approach can be applied to any linear-time temporal logic.

Given a component S, a contract for S is a pair $C = \langle \mathcal{A}, \mathcal{G} \rangle$ of assertions over V_S representing respectively an *assumption* and a *guarantee* for the component. Let M and E be respectively an implementation and an environment of S. We say that M is an implementation satisfying C iff $M \cap L(\mathcal{A}) \subseteq L(\mathcal{G})$. We say that E is an environment satisfying C iff $E \subseteq L(\mathcal{A})$. We denote with $\mathcal{M}(C)$ and with $\mathcal{E}(C)$, respectively, the implementations and the environments satisfying the contract C.

Two contracts C and C' are *equivalent* (denoted with $C \equiv C'$) iff they have the same implementations and environments, i.e., iff $\mathcal{M}(C) = \mathcal{M}(C')$ and $\mathcal{E}(C) = \mathcal{E}(C')$. A contract $C = \langle \mathcal{A}, \mathcal{G} \rangle$ is in normal form iff the complement $\overline{L(\mathcal{A})}$ is contained in $L(\mathcal{G})$. We denote with $nf(C)$ the assertion $\neg \mathcal{A} \vee \mathcal{G}$. The contract $\langle \mathcal{A}, nf(C) \rangle$ is in normal form and is equivalent to (i.e., has the same implementations and environments of) C [7].

Example 3 (WBS contract). We are interested in defining the contract related to the requirement of the WBS that, given the application of the braking pedals, must activate the brakes. This is formalized with the LTL formula $\mathcal{G} = \mathbf{G}((P1 \vee P2) \rightarrow \mathbf{F}(Brake))$. The WBS component requires an environment that provides the same signal on the pedal application and such that power is always supplied to the BSCU and hydraulic pumps. This is formalized in the LTL formula $\mathcal{A} = \mathbf{G}((P1 = P2) \wedge GP \wedge BP \wedge SP)$.

Contract Refinement. Since the decomposition of a component S into subcomponents induces a composite implementation of S and composite environment for the subcomponents, it is necessary to prove that the decomposition is correct with respect to the contracts. In particular, it is necessary to prove that the composite implementation of S satisfies the guarantee of S's contracts and that the composite environment of each subcomponent U satisfies the assumptions of U's contracts. We perform this verification compositionally only reasoning with the contracts of the subcomponent independently from the specific implementation of the subcomponents or the specific environment.

In the following, for simplicity, we assume that each component S has only one contract denoted with C_S and is refined by the contracts of all subcomponents (the approach can be easily extended to the general case [17]). Given a component S and a decomposition $\rho = \langle Sub, \gamma \rangle$, the set of contracts $\mathcal{C} = \bigcup_{S' \in Sub(S)} C_{S'}$ is a refinement of C_S, written $\mathcal{C} \leq_\rho C_S$, iff the following conditions hold:

1. given an implementation $M_{S'}$ for each subcomponent $S' \in Sub(S)$ such that $M_{S'}$ satisfies the contract $C_{S'}$, then $CI_\gamma(\{M_{S'}\}_{S \in Sub(S)})$ satisfies C_S (i.e., the correct implementations of the sub-contracts form a correct implementation of C_S);
2. for every subcomponent S'' of S, given an environment E of S satisfying C_S and an implementation $M_{S'}$ for each subcomponent $S' \in Sub(S)$ such that $M_{S'}$ satisfies the contract $C_{S'}$, then $CE_\gamma(E, \{M_{S'}\}_{S' \in Sub(S)})$ satisfies $C_{S''}$ (i.e., the correct implementation of the other subcomponents and a correct environment of C_S form a correct environment of $C_{S''}$).

Example 4 (WBS contract refinement). As shown in Fig. 1, the WBS component is decomposed into NWBS, AWBS and EWBS. The contracts of these subcomponents are $C_{nwbs} = \langle \mathbf{G}((P1 = P2) \wedge SP \wedge GP), \mathbf{G}((P1 \vee P2) \rightarrow \mathbf{F}(BN)) \rangle$, $C_{awbs} = \langle \mathbf{G}(BP), \mathbf{G}(((P1 \vee P2) \wedge \neg \mathbf{F}(BN)) \rightarrow \mathbf{F}(BA)) \rangle$, $C_{ewbs} = \langle \top, \mathbf{G}(((P1 \vee P2) \wedge \neg \mathbf{F}(BN) \wedge \neg \mathbf{F}(BA)) \rightarrow \mathbf{F}(BE)) \rangle$. The connection are defined in a straightforward way. It is easy to see that the these contracts correctly refine the contract of the WBS component. We remark that the implementation of the NWBS would be sufficient to ensure the guarantee of the parent component i.e., AWBS and EWBS systems are redundant and play a role only in case of failures.

5 Contract-Based Fault Injection

The goal of our approach is to take as input an architecture enriched with a correct contract refinement and automatically generate a hierarchically organized FT. The idea is to introduce, for each component and for each contract, two failure ports: one representing the failure of the component implementation to satisfy the guarantee, the other representing the failure of the component environment to satisfy the assumption. This step is represented by the arrow labeled 1.1 in Fig. 3. The connections among such failures are automatically generated and they are later used to produce the FT, as illustrated by label 1.2 in Fig. 3. The successive refinement of components (i.e., layers 2 and 3 in Fig. 3) allows us to extend the analysis and generate a more detailed FT. These characteristics of the CBSA approach mimic the recommended practices outlined in [4].

5.1 Extension of Components and Contracts

Given a component interface $\langle I_S, O_S \rangle$ of the component S, we define the extended interface $\langle I_S^X, O_S^X \rangle$ as the interface in which the inputs has been extended with the new Boolean port f_S^I and the output has been extended with the new Boolean port f_S^O. Namely, $\langle I_S^X, O_S^X \rangle$ is defined as $\langle I_S \cup \{f_S^I\}, O_S \cup \{f_S^O\} \rangle$. Intuitively, f_S^O represents the failure of the component implementation to meet its requirements, while f_S^I represents the failure of the component environment to fulfill the component's assumptions.

The "nominal" contract of a component is extended to weaken both assumption and guarantee, in order to take into account the possible failure of the environment and of the implementation. Given the contract $\langle A_S, G_S \rangle$ of S, we define the extended contract $\langle A_S^X, G_S^X \rangle$ as follows $A_S^X = (\neg f_S^I) \rightarrow A_S$ and $G_S^X = (\neg f_S^O) \rightarrow G_S$.

Note that in this simple contract extension the failure is timeless in the sense that either there are no failures and the nominal contract holds, or nothing is assumed or guaranteed. By convention, the failure ports are evaluated initially and the future values are don't cares. More complex contract extensions will be developed in the future.

5.2 Contract-Based Synthesis of Extended System Architecture

We now describe how we generate an extended system architecture given a nominal one with a correct contract refinement. In the extended architecture, components' interfaces and contracts are extended as described in the previous section, while we automatically synthesize the connections among the extended components. The synthesis ensures that the refinement of contracts in the extended architecture is correct by construction.

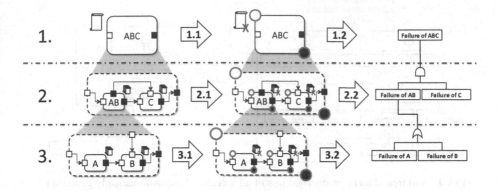

Fig. 3. Contract-based Safety Assessment Process

For each component S, we define the extended connection mapping γ^X so that $\gamma^X(p) = \gamma(p)$ for all original ports, i.e., for $p \in I_S \cup O_S$, while for the new failure ports γ^X is defined as follows:

- $\gamma^X(f_S^O) := MCS^\top(\gamma((\bigwedge_{S' \in Sub(S)}(\mathcal{A}_{S'}^X \to \mathcal{G}_{S'}^X)) \wedge \mathcal{A}_S^X), \neg\gamma(\mathcal{G}_S), \{f_S^I\} \cup \{f_{S'}^O\}_{S' \in Sub(S)})$. Intuitively, the driver of the failure of S's guarantee is given by all combinations of the failures of the subcomponents and the environment that are compatible with the violation of the guarantee of S.

- for all $U \in Sub(S)$, $\gamma^X(f_U^I) := MCS^\top(\gamma(\bigwedge_{S' \in Sub(S) \setminus \{U\}}(\mathcal{A}_{S'}^X \to \mathcal{G}_{S'}^X) \wedge \mathcal{A}_S^X), \neg\gamma(\mathcal{A}_U), \{f_S^I\} \cup \{f_{S'}^O\}_{S' \in Sub(S) \setminus \{U\}})$. Intuitively, the driver of the failure of U's assumption is given by all combinations of the failures of the other subcomponents and the environment of S that are compatible with the violation of the assumption of U.

The resulting extended contract refinement is correct:

Theorem 1. *If $\{C_{S'}\}_{S' \in Sub(S)} \preceq_\gamma C_S$, then $\{C_{S'}^X\}_{S' \in Sub(S)} \preceq_{\gamma^X} C_S^X$.*

Example 5 (Synthesis of faults dependencies for WBS component). Given the extended contract C_{wbs}^X, the safety analysis will produce the dependencies formulae for each fault port f_{wbs}^O, f_{nwbs}^I, f_{awbs}^I and f_{ewbs}^I. Specifically, the resulting faults dependency for $f_{wbs}^O := (f_{awbs}^O \wedge f_{nwbs}^O \wedge f_{ewbs}^O) \vee (f_{wbs}^I \wedge f_{ewbs}^O)$, which means that every assignment of such formula will cause the failure of f_{wbs}^O. This result confirms that the braking ability of the WBS is guarantee if at least one of NWBS, AWBS and EWBS is working, but in case of loss of the power sources (f_{wbs}^I) the EWBS is necessary in order to guarantee the right behaviour. The following analysis for f_{nwbs}^I and f_{awbs}^I will produce respectively $f_{nwbs}^I := f_{wbs}^I$ and $f_{awbs}^I := f_{wbs}^I$. In fact, the subsystems NWBS and AWBS need for BP, SP, and GP power lines, which functionality is part of the assumption of the WBS. The last step addresses the verification of the proof obligation for f_{ewbs}^I which is unsat, expressing the fact that it has no dependencies to the other fault ports. According to this result, Fig. 1 shows that EWBS is not dependent to any assumptions of the WBS i.e., it does not need any power sources.

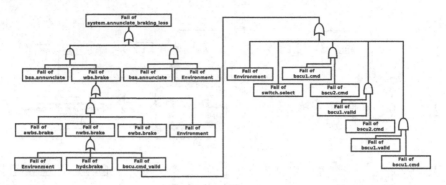

Fig. 4. Fault tree of an unannunciated loss of all wheel braking: automatically generated

6   Contract-Based Fault Tree Analysis

6.1   Contract-Based Fault Tree Generation

Given the extension of the system contract refinement, the FT is automatically generated. The top level event is the failure f_S^O of a non-leaf component S. It is labeled with "Fail of C_S", where C_S is the contract of S. The intermediate events are similarly labeled with the failure of the guarantees of the components that are used in the contract refinement and are not further refined. The failure of the system environment is labeled with "Fail of Environment". The leaves of the tree are basic events, representing the failure of the system's assumption and the failures of the guarantees of contracts that are not further refined. If the architecture is extended further in a step-wise way by decomposing some leaves components, these basic events can become intermediate and be refined further by exploiting the extended contract refinement.

The FT is generated starting from the top level event f_S^O and linking it to the intermediate events present in $\gamma^X(f_S^O)$. Formally, if f is a basic event, then the FT is atomic: $FT(f) := f$; if f is an intermediate event, then $FT(f_S^O) := f_S^O \mapsto \gamma^X(f_S^O)$. Thus, the FT is defined recursively until reaching the basic events. To simplify the tree, we do not label the failure of the assumption of intermediate components. Therefore, if U is not the system component and f_U^I is present in the tree, we replace it with $\gamma^X(f_U^I)$. Note that the same failure may appear in different branches of the FT – this is standard in FTA – hence, in the above top-down procedure we only need to expand one occurrence of the same failure. We also assume that in the relationship among the failures there is no circular dependency. Usually, such dependencies may be broken by introducing time delays [26]. We leave modeling of faults with temporal dynamics and dealing with circular dependencies to future work.

Example 6 (Automatic generation of WBS FT). By applying contract refinement to the WBS example, we obtain the FT in Fig. 4. As it can be seen from Table 1, there is nearly a one-to-one mapping with the FT presented in Fig. 2 – the only differences are that: (i) in the contract-based FT the failure of the environment is considered also for the sub-components that depends to it, and this provides a more detailed system failure explanation; (ii) the monitoring function is more detailed in our model.

Table 1. Failure of contracts description

Failure of Contract	Description
system.annunciate_braking_loss	Unannunciated loss of All Wheel Braking.
bsa.annunciate	Loss of Annunciation Capability.
wbs.brake	Loss of All Wheel Braking.
nwbs.brake	Normal Brake System does not operate.
awbs.brake	Alternate Brake System does not operate.
ewbs.brake	Emergency Brake System does not operate.
hydr.brake	Loss of Normal Brake System Hydraulic Components.
bscu.cmd_valid	Loss of BSCU Ability to Command Braking.
switch.select	Switch Failure Contributes to Loss of Braking Commands.
bscu1.cmd	Loss of BSCU sub system 1.
bscu1.valid	Loss of monitoring for BSCU sub system 1.
bscu2.cmd	Loss of BSCU sub system 2.
bscu2.valid	Loss of monitoring for BSCU sub system 2.

6.2   CBSA Cut-Sets Semantics

We notice that, in the generated FT, the cut sets local to a single component decomposition are minimal by construction. Here, we consider the cut sets of the whole FT that are obtained by replacing intermediate events with their definition in the FT. We call them flattened cut sets, since they can be represented as a two-level FT. They are defined in terms of the failures of the basic components and of the system environment.

Let *leaves* be the basic components of the architecture and let *root* the (root) system component. We denote with $\mathcal{F}$ the set of basic failure ports, i.e., $\mathcal{F} = \{f_l^O\}_{l \in leaves} \cup \{f_{root}^I\}$, and we identify a fault configuration with an assignment to these parameters. A cut set is therefore a fault configuration of a trace violating the top-level guarantee.

Given a failure port f_S (either input or output) of a component S in the architecture, let us define $\gamma^{X*}(f_S)$ as the iterative application of γ^X to f_S until reaching a fixpoint, i.e., a Boolean combination of failures in $\mathcal{F}$ only. $\gamma^{X*}(f_S)$ defines the set of flattened cut sets obtained with CBSA. We prove that every cut set (in the standard sense) is also a flattened cut set for CBSA.

Theorem 2. *Let* $L^X = \mathcal{L}(\gamma^*(\bigwedge_{l \in leaves}(\mathcal{G}_l^X) \wedge \mathcal{A}_{root}^X))$.
If $FC \in CS(L^X, \neg(\mathcal{G}_S), \mathcal{F})$, *then* $FC^\top \models \gamma^{X*}(f_S^O)$.

Here, L^X represents the extension of the system architecture in a MBSA-like fashion, where the guarantees of leaf components and the root assumption are extended locally without explicit constraints among component failures (hence, γ^* is used instead of γ^{X*}). The converse is not true in general. In fact, for the contract refinement to be correct, it is sufficient that the contract of the composite component is weaker than the composition of those of the subcomponents. However, this may create cut sets that are present considering the weaker contract, while are they ruled out by the composition.

6.3   Relationship between Contracts and Generated Fault Trees

We remark that the FT generated with the proposed approach is clearly sensitive to the contracts and can be used to improve the CBD. For example, in the contract specification of the WBS proposed in [19], each redundant sub-BSCU guarantees that the input pedal application is followed by the braking command or the Validity Monitor set to invalid within a given time bound. Following this approach, the proposed procedure generates a FT in which each sub-BSCU is a single point of failure. In fact, a failure of its contract means that it can keep the Validity Monitor set to true without ever braking. This contrasts with [4]. The FT shown in Fig. 4 is actually obtained with an improved specification, where we separated the functional part of the contract from the monitoring of safety, providing a contract that says that every pedal application is followed by the braking command and another contract demanding that the Validity Monitor is set to invalid if the pedal is applied but the brake is never commanded.

7 Implementation and Experiments

We implemented our methodology on top of OCRA [15], a tool for architectural design based on CBD. The OCRA language allows the user to specify contracts (written in various temporal logics of different expressiveness, including LTL and HRELTL [16]), and associate them to architectural components. The correctness of refinements is reduced to a set of proof obligations (as per Section 4.3) – temporal satisfiability checks that are carried out by nuXmv [22], the underlying verification platform, which provides reasoning capabilities via BDD-, SAT-, and SMT-based techniques.

We extended OCRA in the following directions. First, we implemented primitives to automatically extend the architectural description by means of symbolic fault injection, extending the ports and the contracts. Second, we implemented the procedure for the synthesis of the interconnections between failure ports among different levels, as per Section 5. Finally, we implemented the procedure to extract FTs from the extended models, as per Section 6. The algorithms are based on pure BDD [18], in addition to a combination of Bounded Model Checking (BMC) [8] and BDD. In particular, the BMC+BDD approach first computes MCSs up to a specific k-depth using BMC, and then a BDD based routine is run to generate the remaining results.

We first evaluated the CBSA approach by modeling (several variants of) the WBS case-study in OCRA[2]. The analysis demonstrated very useful to provide feedback on the structure of the contracts. In fact, as described in Section 6.3, we could improve over the first version of the WBS model described in [19,17]. We then compared our approach with the "flat" MBSA approach implemented in xSAP- a re-implementation of FSAP[12]. xSAP supports FTA for behavioral models (finite state machines written in the SMV language). We refer to the xSAP approach as *monolithic*, since it generates FTs that are "flat"(i.e., presented as DNF of the MCSs). In OCRA, FTs can be generated from behavioral models, by associating each leaf component with an SMV implementation, where the activation of failure modes causes the violation of contracts. For the evaluation, we associated concrete implementations to the leaf WBS components. We first evaluated the tightness of the contract extension. As described in Section 6, CBSA can provide a "pessimistic" interpretation of the system failure, due to the hierarchical partitioning imposed by contract decomposition. Indeed, our results confirm that this is the case for the WBS: if the concrete implementations happen to operate correctly

---

[2] The models and the binaries necessary to reproduce the experiments described in this paper can be download at https://es.fbk.eu/people/mattarei/dist/ATVA14/

even if the power is not provided, then the monolithic approach provides a tighter set of MCSs. However, if the concrete implementations are such that a loss of power implies a loss of functional behavior, then both techniques result in the same sets of MCSs. We also compared the scalability of the monolithic and the CBSA approach for FTA. We considered a parameterized version of the WBS, by varying the total number of faults (M), and the upper bound for the cycles needed to wait until performing an emer-

Table 2. Scalability comparison

M	9	10	11	12	13	...	29
MCS	6	11	22	42	50	...	3316
CBSA.BD	701	701	701	702	702	702	703
Mono.BD	619	1106	3180	T.O.	T.O.	T.O.	T.O.
CBSA.BB	1.8	1.8	1.8	1.8	1.8	1.8	1.8
Mono.BB	3.1	3.4	4.1	4.6	4.9	...	582

gency reaction (N). The experiments were run on an Intel Xeon E3-1270 at 3.40GHz. We first varied the delay N (with $M = 9$). With $N = 10$, CBSA takes 11m40s (BDD), and 2s (BMC+BDD, with k=20), whereas the monolithic approach takes 14m and 7s, respectively. For $N = 15$, CBSA times do not vary, while the monolithic approach requires more than 50m (BDD), and 15s (BMC+BDD). The stability in performance shown by the CBSA approach is motivated by the fact that the time needed to compute the FT is mainly spent during the contracts evaluation, whereas analyzing the leaves takes always less than 1s. We then fixed $N = 5$ and varied M from 9 to 29. The results are reported in Table 2, where "BD" and "BB" stand for BDD and BMC+BDD (with k=20). CBSA is subject only to a marginal degradation in performance, since the variation is local to the computation of the FTs for the leaves. In contrast, the monolithic method passes from 10m19s to timing out after one hour for $M = 12$ (BDD), and from 3s to 582s (BMC+BDD). This degradation is directly correlated to the increased number of MCSs, that are enumerated by the monolithic approach. As a final remark, notice that the CBSA approach is fully incremental: the only variation required when exploring different implementations is in constructing the FTs resulting from the analysis of each finite state machine with respect to its contracts. This contrasts with the considerable efforts required in the monolithic approach, that needs to be repeated for each different implementation.

8   Conclusions

In this paper we proposed a new, formal methodology for safety assessment based on CBD and automated fault injection. This approach is able to generate automatically hierarchical FTs mimicking system decomposition, and overcomes two key shortcomings of traditional MBSA [13], namely the lack of structure of the generated FTs, and the poor scalability. Moreover, it provides full support to the informal, manual state of the practice, and it can provide important feedback in the early stages of system design.

As future work, we will investigate methods to pinpoint situations where the hierarchical decomposition leads to over-constraining, and to generate suitable diagnostic information. Second, we will generalize fault injection with the introduction of more fine-grained failure dynamics based on temporal patterns and the use of specific fault models (similar to the contract extension with "exceptional" behavior [14]). We will investigate aspects related to fault propagation [1] and extend the framework to consider richer contract specification languages to enable quantitative evaluation of FTs.

References

1. Abdelwahed, S., Karsai, G., Mahadevan, N., Ofsthun, S.C.: Practical Implementation of Diagnosis Systems Using Timed Failure Propagation Graph Models. IEEE T. Instrumentation and Measurement 58(2), 240–247 (2009)
2. Abrial, J.R.: The B-book: Assigning Programs to Meanings. Cambridge Univ. Press (1996)
3. ARP4754A Guidelines for Development of Civil Aircraft and Systems. SAE (December 2010)
4. ARP4761 Guidelines and Methods for Conducting the Safety Assessment Process on Civil Airborne Systems and Equipment. SAE (December 1996)
5. Banach, R., Bozzano, M.: The Mechanical Generation of Fault Trees for Reactive Systems via Retrenchment II: Clocked and Feedback Circuits. FAC 25(4), 609–657 (2013)
6. Bate, I., Hawkins, R., McDermid, J.A.: A Contract-based Approach to Designing Safe Systems. In: SCS 2000, pp. 25–36 (2003)
7. Benveniste, A., Caillaud, B., Ferrari, A., Mangeruca, L., Passerone, R., Sofronis, C.: Multiple Viewpoint Contract-Based Specification and Design. In: de Boer, F.S., Bonsangue, M.M., Graf, S., de Roever, W.-P. (eds.) FMCO 2007. LNCS, vol. 5382, pp. 200–225. Springer, Heidelberg (2008)
8. Biere, A., Cimatti, A., Clarke, E.M., Zhu, Y.: Symbolic model checking without BDDs. In: Cleaveland, W.R. (ed.) TACAS 1999. LNCS, vol. 1579, pp. 193–207. Springer, Heidelberg (1999)
9. Bozzano, M., Cimatti, A., Katoen, J.P., Nguyen, V.Y., Noll, T., Roveri, M.: Safety, dependability and performance analysis of extended AADL models. The Computer Journal 54(5), 754–775 (2011)
10. Bozzano, M., Cimatti, A., Lisagor, O., Mattarei, C., Mover, S., Roveri, M., Tonetta, S.: Symbolic Model Checking and Safety Assessment of Altarica models. ECEASST 46 (2011)
11. Bozzano, M., Cimatti, A., Tapparo, F.: Symbolic fault tree analysis for reactive systems. In: Namjoshi, K.S., Yoneda, T., Higashino, T., Okamura, Y. (eds.) ATVA 2007. LNCS, vol. 4762, pp. 162–176. Springer, Heidelberg (2007)
12. Bozzano, M., Villafiorita, A.: The FSAP/NuSMV-SA Safety Analysis Platform. STTT 9(1), 5–24 (2007)
13. Bozzano, M., Villafiorita, A.: Design and Safety Assessment of Critical Systems. CRC Press (Taylor and Francis), an Auerbach Book (2010)
14. Broy, M.: Towards a Theory of Architectural Contracts: - Schemes and Patterns of Assumption/Promise Based System Specification. In: Software and Systems Safety - Specification and Verification, pp. 33–87. IOS Press (2011)
15. Cimatti, A., Dorigatti, M., Tonetta, S.: OCRA: A Tool for Checking the Refinement of Temporal Contracts. In: ASE, pp. 702–705. IEEE (2013)
16. Cimatti, A., Roveri, M., Tonetta, S.: Requirements validation for hybrid systems. In: Bouajjani, A., Maler, O. (eds.) CAV 2009. LNCS, vol. 5643, pp. 188–203. Springer, Heidelberg (2009)
17. Cimatti, A., Tonetta, S.: A property-based proof system for contract-based design. In: SEAA, pp. 21–28 (2012)

18. Clarke, E.M., Emerson, E.A., Sistla, A.P.: Automatic verification of finite-state concurrent systems using temporal logic specifications. ACM TOPLAS 8(2), 244–263 (1986)
19. Damm, W., Hungar, H., Josko, B., Peikenkamp, T., Stierand, I.: Using contract-based component specifications for virtual integration testing and architecture design. In: DATE, pp. 1023–1028 (2011)
20. McKelvin Jr., M.L., Eirea, G., Pinello, C., Kanajan, S., Sangiovanni-Vincentelli, A.: A formal approach to fault tree synthesis for the analysis of distributed fault tolerant systems. In: EMSOFT, pp. 237–246. ACM (2005)
21. The MISSA Project, http://www.missa-fp7.eu
22. nuXmv: a new eXtended model verifier, https://nuxmv.fbk.eu
23. Pinello, C., Carloni, L.P., Sangiovanni-Vincentelli, A.: Fault-tolerant deployment of embedded software for cost-sensitive real-time feedback-control applications. In: DATE, p. 21164. IEEE Computer Society (2004)
24. Pnueli, A.: The temporal logic of programs. In: Foundations of Computer Science (FOCS 1977), pp. 46–57. IEEE Computer Society Press (1977)
25. Siddiqi, S.A., Huang, J.: Hierarchical Diagnosis of Multiple Faults. In: IJCAI, pp. 581–586 (2007)
26. Vesely, W., Stamatelatos, M., Dugan, J., Fragola, J., Minarick III, J., Railsback, J.: Fault Tree Handbook with Aerospace Applications. Technical report, NASA (2002)

Verification of Markov Decision Processes Using Learning Algorithms[*]

Tomáš Brázdil[1], Krishnendu Chatterjee[2], Martin Chmelík[2], Vojtěch Forejt[3],
Jan Křetínský[2], Marta Kwiatkowska[3], David Parker[4], and Mateusz Ujma[3]

[1] Masaryk University, Brno, Czech Republic
[2] IST, Austria
[3] University of Oxford, UK
[4] University of Birmingham, UK

Abstract. We present a general framework for applying machine-learning algorithms to the verification of Markov decision processes (MDPs). The primary goal of these techniques is to improve performance by avoiding an exhaustive exploration of the state space. Our framework focuses on probabilistic reachability, which is a core property for verification, and is illustrated through two distinct instantiations. The first assumes that full knowledge of the MDP is available, and performs a heuristic-driven partial exploration of the model, yielding precise lower and upper bounds on the required probability. The second tackles the case where we may only sample the MDP, and yields probabilistic guarantees, again in terms of both the lower and upper bounds, which provides efficient stopping criteria for the approximation. The latter is the first extension of statistical model checking for unbounded properties in MDPs. In contrast with other related techniques, our approach is not restricted to time-bounded (finite-horizon) or discounted properties, nor does it assume any particular properties of the MDP. We also show how our methods extend to LTL objectives. We present experimental results showing the performance of our framework on several examples.

1 Introduction

Markov decision processes (MDPs) are a widely used model for the formal verification of systems that exhibit stochastic behaviour. This may arise due to the possibility of failures (e.g. of physical system components), unpredictable events (e.g. messages sent across a lossy medium), or uncertainty about the environment (e.g. unreliable sensors in a robot). It may also stem from the explicit use of randomisation, such as probabilistic routing in gossip protocols or random back-off in wireless communication protocols.

Verification of MDPs against temporal logics such as PCTL and LTL typically reduces to the computation of optimal (minimum or maximum) reachability probabilities, either on the MDP itself or its product with some deterministic ω-automaton. Optimal

---

[*] This research was funded in part by the European Research Council (ERC) under grant agreement 267989 (QUAREM), 246967 (VERIWARE) and 279307 (Graph Games), by the EU FP7 project HIERATIC, by the Austrian Science Fund (FWF) projects S11402-N23 (RiSE), S11407-N23 (RiSE) and P23499-N23, by the Czech Science Foundation grant No P202/12/P612, by EPSRC project EP/K038575/1 and by the Microsoft faculty fellows award.

F. Cassez and J.-F. Raskin (Eds.): ATVA 2014, LNCS 8837, pp. 98–114, 2014.

reachability probabilities (and a corresponding optimal strategy for the MDP) can be computed in polynomial time through a reduction to linear programming, although in practice verification tools often use dynamic programming techniques, such as value iteration which approximates the values up to some pre-specified convergence criterion.

The efficiency or feasibility of verification is often limited by excessive time or space requirements, caused by the need to store a full model in memory. Common approaches to tackling this include: symbolic model checking, which uses efficient data structures to construct and manipulate a compact representation of the model; abstraction refinement, which constructs a sequence of increasingly precise approximations, bypassing construction of the full model using decision procedures such as SAT or SMT; and statistical model checking [37,19], which uses Monte Carlo simulation to generate approximate results of verification that hold with high probability.

In this paper, we explore the opportunities offered by learning-based methods, as used in fields such as planning or reinforcement learning [36]. In particular, we focus on algorithms that explore an MDP by generating trajectories through it and, whilst doing so, produce increasingly precise approximations for some property of interest (in this case, reachability probabilities). The approximate values, along with other information, are used as heuristics to guide the model exploration so as to minimise the solution time and the portion of the model that needs to be considered.

We present a general framework for applying such algorithms to the verification of MDPs. Then, we consider two distinct instantiations that operate under different assumptions concerning the availability of knowledge about the MDP, and produce different classes of results. We distinguish between *complete information*, where full knowledge of the MDP is available (but not necessarily generated and stored), and *limited information*, where (in simple terms) we can only sample trajectories of the MDP.

The first algorithm assumes complete information and is based on *real-time dynamic programming* (RTDP) [3]. In its basic form, this only generates approximations in the form of lower bounds (on maximum reachability probabilities). While this may suffice in some scenarios (e.g. planning), in the context of verification we typically require more precise guarantees. So we consider bounded RTDP (BRTDP) [30], which supplements this with an additional upper bound. The second algorithm assumes limited information and is based on *delayed Q-learning* (DQL) [35]. Again, we produce both lower and upper bounds but, in contrast to BRTDP, where these are guaranteed to be correct, DQL offers probably approximately correct (PAC) results, i.e., there is a nonzero probability that the bounds are incorrect.

Typically, MDP solution methods based on learning or heuristics make assumptions about the structure of the model. For example, the presence of end components [15] (subsets of states where it is possible to remain indefinitely with probability 1) can result in convergence to incorrect values. Our techniques are applicable to arbitrary MDPs. We first handle the case of MDPs that contain no end components (except for trivial designated goal or sink states). Then, we adapt this to the general case by means of *on-the-fly* detection of end components, which is one of the main technical contributions of the paper. We also show how our techniques extend to LTL objectives and thus also to minimum reachability probabilities.

Our DQL-based method, which yields PAC results, can be seen as an instance of statistical model checking [37,19], a technique that has received considerable attention. Until recently, most work in this area focused on purely probabilistic models, without nondeterminism, but several approaches have now been presented for statistical model checking of nondeterministic models [13,14,27,4,28,18,29]. However, these methods all consider either time-bounded properties or use discounting to ensure convergence (see below for a summary). The techniques in this paper are the first for statistical model checking of unbounded properties on MDPs.

We have implemented our framework within the PRISM tool [25]. This paper concludes with experimental results for an implementation of our BRTDP-based approach that demonstrate considerable speed-ups over the fastest methods in PRISM.

Detailed proofs omitted due to lack of space are available in [7].

1.1 Related Work

In fields such as planning and artificial intelligence, many learning-based and heuristic-driven solution methods for MDPs have been developed. In the *complete information* setting, examples include RTDP [3] and BRTDP [30], as discussed above, which generate lower and lower/upper bounds on values, respectively. Most algorithms make certain assumptions in order to ensure convergence, for example through the use of a discount factor or by restricting to so-called Stochastic Shortest Path (SSP) problems, whereas we target arbitrary MDPs without discounting. More recently, an approach called FRET [24] was proposed for a generalisation of SSP, but this gives only a one-sided (lower) bound. We are not aware of any attempts to apply or adapt such methods in the context of probabilistic verification. A related paper is [1], which applies heuristic search methods to MDPs, but for generating probabilistic counterexamples.

As mentioned above, in the *limited information* setting, our algorithm based on delayed Q-learning (DQL) yields PAC results, similar to those obtained from *statistical model checking* [37,19,34]. This is an active area of research with a variety of tools [21,8,6,5]. In contrast with our work, most techniques focus on time-bounded properties, e.g., using bounded LTL, rather than *unbounded* properties. Several approaches have been proposed to transform checking of unbounded properties into testing of bounded properties, for example, [38,17,33,32]. However, these focus on purely probabilistic models, without nondeterminism, and do not apply to MDPs. In [4], unbounded properties are analysed for MDPs with spurious nondeterminism, where the way it is resolved does not affect the desired property.

More generally, the development of statistical model checking techniques for probabilistic models with *nondeterminism*, such as MDPs, is an important topic, treated in several recent papers. One approach is to give the nondeterminism a probabilistic semantics, e.g., using a uniform distribution instead, as for timed automata in [13,14,27]. Others [28,18], like this paper, aim to quantify over all strategies and produce an ε-optimal strategy. The work in [28] and [18] deals with the problem in the setting of discounted (and for the purposes of approximation thus bounded) or bounded properties, respectively. In the latter work, candidates for optimal schedulers are generated and gradually improved, but "at any given point we cannot quantify how close to optimal the candidate scheduler is" and "the algorithm does not estimate the maximum probability of the property" (cited from [29]). Further, [29] considers compact representation of schedulers, but again focuses only on (time) bounded properties.

Since statistical model checking is simulation-based, one of the most important difficulties is the analysis of *rare events*. This issue is, of course, also relevant for our approach; see the section on experimental results. Rare events have been addressed using methods such as importance sampling [17,20] and importance splitting [22].

End components in MDPs can be collapsed either for algorithmic correctness [15] or efficiency [11] (where only lower bounds on maximum reachability probabilities are considered). Asymptotically efficient ways to detect them are given in [10,9].

2 Basics about MDPs and Learning Algorithms

We begin with basic background material on MDPs and some fundamental definitions for our learning framework. We use $\mathbb{N}$, $\mathbb{Q}$, and $\mathbb{R}$ to denote the sets of all non-negative integers, rational numbers and real numbers respectively. $Dist(X)$ is the set of all rational probability distributions over a finite or countable set X, i.e., the functions $f : X \to [0,1] \cap \mathbb{Q}$ such that $\sum_{x \in X} f(x) = 1$, and $supp(f)$ denotes the *support* of f.

2.1 Markov Decision Processes

We work with *Markov decision processes* (MDPs), a widely used model to capture both nondeterminism (e.g., for control or concurrency) and probability.

Definition 1. *An* MDP *is a tuple* $\mathsf{M} = \langle S, \bar{s}, A, E, \Delta \rangle$, *where S is a finite set of* states, $\bar{s} \in S$ *is an* initial state, *A is a finite set of* actions, $E : S \to 2^A$ *assigns non-empty sets of* enabled *actions to all states, and* $\Delta : S \times A \to Dist(S)$ *is a (partial)* probabilistic transition function *defined for all s and a where $a \in E(s)$.*

Remark 1. For simplicity of presentation we assume w.l.o.g. that, for every action $a \in A$, there is at most one state s such that $a \in E(s)$, i.e., $E(s) \cap E(s') = \emptyset$ for $s \neq s'$. If there *are* states s, s' such that $a \in E(s) \cap E(s')$, we can always rename the actions as $(s, a) \in E(s)$, and $(s', a) \in E(s')$, so that the MDP satisfies our assumption.

An *infinite path* of an MDP M is an infinite sequence $\omega = s_0 a_0 s_1 a_1 \ldots$ such that $a_i \in E(s_i)$ and $\Delta(s_i, a_i)(s_{i+1}) > 0$ for every $i \in \mathbb{N}$. A *finite path* is a finite prefix of an infinite path ending in a state. We use $last(\omega)$ to denote the last state of a finite path ω. We denote by $IPath$ (resp. $FPath$) the set of all infinite (resp. finite) paths, and by $IPath_s$ (resp. $FPath_s$) the set of infinite (resp. finite) paths starting in a state s.

A state s is *terminal* if all actions $a \in E(s)$ satisfy $\Delta(s, a)(s) = 1$. An *end component* (EC) of M is a pair (S', A') where $S' \subseteq S$ and $A' \subseteq \bigcup_{s \in S'} E(s)$ such that: (1) if $\Delta(s, a)(s') > 0$ for some $s \in S'$ and $a \in A'$, then $s' \in S'$; and (2) for all $s, s' \in S'$ there is a path $\omega = s_0 a_0 \ldots s_n$ such that $s_0 = s$, $s_n = s'$ and for all $0 \leq i < n$ we have $a_i \in A'$. A *maximal end component* (MEC) is an EC that is maximal with respect to the point-wise subset ordering.

Strategies. A *strategy* of MDP M is a function $\sigma : FPath \to Dist(A)$ satisfying $supp(\sigma(\omega)) \subseteq E(last(\omega))$ for every $\omega \in FPath$. Intuitively, the strategy resolves the choices of actions in each finite path by choosing (possibly at random) an action enabled in the last state of the path. We write Σ_M for the set of all strategies in M. In standard fashion [23], a strategy σ induces, for any initial state s, a probability measure $Pr^\sigma_{M,s}$ over $IPath_s$. A strategy σ is *memoryless* if $\sigma(\omega)$ depends only on $last(\omega)$.

Objectives and values. Given a set $F \subseteq S$ of target states, *bounded reachability* for step k, denoted by $\Diamond^{\le k}F$, refers to the set of all infinite paths that reach a state in F within k steps, and *unbounded reachability*, denoted by $\Diamond F$, refers to the set of all infinite paths that reach a state in F. Note that $\Diamond F = \bigcup_{k \ge 0} \Diamond^{\le k}F$. We consider the *reachability probability* $Pr^\sigma_{M,s}(\Diamond F)$, and strategies that maximise this probability. We denote by $V(s)$ the *value* in s, defined by $\sup_{\sigma \in \Sigma_M} Pr^\sigma_{M,s}(\Diamond F)$. Given $\varepsilon \ge 0$, we say that a strategy σ is ε-optimal in s if $Pr^\sigma_{M,s}(\Diamond F) + \varepsilon \ge V(s)$, and we call a 0-optimal strategy *optimal*. It is known [31] that, for every MDP and set F, there is a memoryless optimal strategy for $\Diamond F$. We are interested in strategies that approximate the value function, i.e., ε-optimal strategies for some $\varepsilon > 0$.

2.2 Learning Algorithms for MDPs

In this paper, we study a class of learning-based algorithms that stochastically approximate the value function of an MDP. Let us fix, for this section, an MDP M $= \langle S, \bar{s}, A, E, \Delta \rangle$ and target states $F \subseteq S$. We denote by $V : S \times A \to [0, 1]$ the *value function* for state-action pairs of M, defined for all (s, a) where $s \in S$ and $a \in E(s)$:

$$V(s, a) := \sum_{s' \in S} \Delta(s, a)(s') \cdot V(s').$$

Intuitively, $V(s, a)$ is the value in s assuming that the first action performed is a. A *learning algorithm* $\mathcal{A}$ simulates executions of M, and iteratively updates upper and lower approximations $U : S \times A \to [0, 1]$ and $L : S \times A \to [0, 1]$, respectively, of the value function $V : S \times A \to [0, 1]$.

The functions U and L are initialised to appropriate values so that $L(s, a) \le V(s, a) \le U(s, a)$ for all $s \in S$ and $a \in A$. During the computation of $\mathcal{A}$, simulated executions start in the initial state $\bar{s}$ and move from state to state according to choices made by the algorithm. The values of $U(s, a)$ and $L(s, a)$ are updated for the states s visited by the simulated execution. Since $\max_{a \in E(s)} U(s, a)$ and $\max_{a \in E(s)} L(s, a)$ represent upper and lower bound on $V(s)$, a learning algorithm $\mathcal{A}$ terminates when $\max_{a \in E(\bar{s})} U(\bar{s}, a) - \max_{a \in E(\bar{s})} L(\bar{s}, a) < \varepsilon$ where the *precision* $\varepsilon > 0$ is given to the algorithm as an argument. Note that, because U and L are possibly updated based on the simulations, the computation of the learning algorithm may be randomised and even give incorrect results with some probability.

Definition 2. *Denote by* $\mathcal{A}(\varepsilon)$ *the instance of learning algorithm* $\mathcal{A}$ *with precision* ε. *We say that* $\mathcal{A}$ converges *surely (resp. almost surely) if, for every* $\varepsilon > 0$*, the computation of* $\mathcal{A}(\varepsilon)$ *surely (resp. almost surely) terminates, and* $L(\bar{s}, a) \le V(\bar{s}, a) \le U(\bar{s}, a)$ *holds upon termination.*

In some cases, almost-sure convergence cannot be guaranteed, so we demand that the computation terminates correctly with sufficiently high probability. In such cases, we assume the algorithm is also given a *confidence* $\delta > 0$ as an argument.

Definition 3. *Denote by $\mathcal{A}(\varepsilon, \delta)$ the instance of learning algorithm $\mathcal{A}$ with precision ε and confidence δ. We say that $\mathcal{A}$ is* probably approximately correct (PAC) *if, for every $\varepsilon > 0$ and every $\delta > 0$, with probability at least $1 - \delta$, the computation of $\mathcal{A}(\varepsilon, \delta)$ terminates with $L(\bar{s}, a) \leq V(\bar{s}, a) \leq U(\bar{s}, a)$.*

The function U defines a memoryless strategy σ_U which in every state s chooses all actions a maximising the value $U(s, a)$ over $E(s)$ uniformly at random. The strategy σ_U is used in some of the algorithms and also contributes to the output.

Remark 2. If the value function is defined as the infimum over strategies (as in [30]), then the strategy chooses actions to minimise the lower value. Since we consider the dual case of supremum over strategies, the choice of σ_U is to maximise the upper value.

We also need to specify what knowledge about the MDP M is available to the learning algorithm. We distinguish the following two distinct cases.

Definition 4. *A learning algorithm has* limited information *about M if it knows only the initial state $\bar{s}$, a number $K \geq |S|$, a number $E_m \geq \max_{s \in S} |E(s)|$, a number $0 < q \leq p_{\min}$, where $p_{\min} = \min\{\Delta(s, a)(s') \mid s \in S, a \in E(s), s' \in supp(\Delta(s, a))\}$, and the function E (more precisely, given a state s, the learning procedure can ask an oracle for $E(s)$). We assume that the algorithm may simulate an execution of M starting with $\bar{s}$ and choosing enabled actions in individual steps.*

Definition 5. *A learning algorithm has* complete information *about M if it knows the complete MDP M.*

Note that the MDPs we consider are "fully observable", so even in the limited information case strategies can make decisions based on the precise state of the system.

3   MDPs without End Components

We first present algorithms for MDPs *without* ECs, which considerably simplifies the adaptation of BRTDP and DQL to unbounded reachability objectives. Later, in Section 4, we extend our methods to deal with arbitrary MDPs (*with* ECs). Let us fix an MDP M $= \langle S, \bar{s}, A, E, \Delta \rangle$ and a target set F. Formally, we assume the following.

Assumption-EC. MDP M has no ECs, except two trivial ones containing distinguished terminal states 1 and 0, respectively, with $F = \{1\}$, $V(1) = 1$ and $V(0) = 0$.

3.1   Our Framework

We start by formalising a general framework for learning algorithms, as outlined in the previous section. We then instantiate this and obtain two learning algorithms: BRTDP and DQL. Our framework is presented as Algorithm 1, and works as follows. Recall that functions U and L store the current upper and lower bounds on the value function V. Each iteration of the outer loop is divided into two phases: EXPLORE and UPDATE. In the EXPLORE phase (lines 5 - 10), the algorithm samples a finite path ω in M from $\bar{s}$ to a state in $\{1, 0\}$ by always randomly choosing one of the enabled actions that maximises

---

Algorithm 1. Learning algorithm (for MDPs with no ECs)

1: **Inputs:** An EC-free MDP M
2: $U(\cdot,\cdot) \leftarrow 1, L(\cdot,\cdot) \leftarrow 0$
3: $L(1,\cdot) \leftarrow 1, U(0,\cdot) \leftarrow 0$ ▷ INITIALISE
4: **repeat**
5:     $\omega \leftarrow \bar{s}$ /* EXPLORE phase */
6:     **repeat**
7:         $a \leftarrow$ sampled uniformly from $\arg\max_{a \in E(last(\omega))} U(last(\omega),a)$
8:         $s \leftarrow$ sampled according to $\Delta(last(\omega),a)$ ▷ GETSUCC(ω,a)
9:         $\omega \leftarrow \omega\, a\, s$
10:     **until** $s \in \{1,0\}$ ▷ TERMINATEPATH(ω)
11:     **repeat** /* UPDATE phase */
12:         $s' \leftarrow pop(\omega)$
13:         $a \leftarrow pop(\omega)$
14:         $s \leftarrow last(\omega)$
15:         UPDATE($(s,a),s'$)
16:     **until** $\omega = \bar{s}$
17: **until** $\max_{a \in E(\bar{s})} U(\bar{s},a) - \max_{a \in E(\bar{s})} L(\bar{s},a) < \varepsilon$ ▷ TERMINATE

---

the U value, and sampling the successor state using the probabilistic transition function. In the UPDATE phase (lines 11 - 16), the algorithm updates U and L on the state-action pairs along the path in a backward manner. Here, the function *pop* pops and returns the last letter of the given sequence.

3.2 Instantiations: BRTDP and DQL

Our two algorithm instantiations, BRTDP and DQL, differ in the definition of UPDATE.

Unbounded Reachability with BRTDP. We obtain BRTDP by instantiating UPDATE with Algorithm 2, which requires complete information about the MDP. Intuitively, UPDATE computes new values of $U(s,a)$ and $L(s,a)$ by taking the weighted average of the corresponding U and L values, respectively, over all successors of s via action a. Formally, denote $U(s) = \max_{a \in E(s)} U(s,a)$ and $L(s) = \max_{a \in E(s)} L(s,a)$.

Algorithm 2. BRTDP instantiation of Algorithm 1

1: **procedure** UPDATE($(s,a),\cdot$)
2:     $U(s,a) := \sum_{s' \in S} \Delta(s,a)(s')U(s')$
3:     $L(s,a) := \sum_{s' \in S} \Delta(s,a)(s')L(s')$

The following theorem says that BRTDP satisfies the conditions of Definition 2 and never returns incorrect results.

Theorem 1. *The algorithm BRTDP converges almost surely under Assumption-EC.*

Remark 3. Note that, in the EXPLORE phase, an action maximising the value of U is chosen and the successor is sampled according to the probabilistic transition function of M. However, we can consider various modifications. Actions and successors may be chosen in different ways (e.g., for GETSUCC), for instance, uniformly at random, in a round-robin fashion, or assigning various probabilities (bounded from below by some fixed $p > 0$) to all possibilities in any biased way. In order to guarantee almost-sure convergence, some conditions have to be satisfied. Intuitively we require, that the state-action pairs used by ε-optimal strategies have to be chosen enough times. If this condition is satisfied then the almost-sure convergence is preserved and the practical running times may significantly improve. For details, see Section 5.

Remark 4. The previous BRTDP algorithm is only applicable if the transition probabilities are known. However, if complete information is not known, but $\Delta(s, a)$ can be repeatedly sampled for any s and a, then a variant of BRTDP can be shown to be probably approximately correct.

Unbounded Reachability with DQL. Often, complete information about the MDP is unavailable, repeated sampling is not possible, and we have to deal with only limited information about M (see Definition 4). For this scenario, we use DQL, which can be obtained by instantiating UPDATE with Algorithm 3.

Algorithm 3. DQL (delay m, estimator precision $\bar{\varepsilon}$) instantiation of Algorithm 1

1: **procedure** UPDATE$((s, a), s')$
2:     **if** $c(s, a) = m$ **and** LEARN(s, a) **then**
3:         **if** $accum_m^U(s, a)/m < U(s, a) - 2\bar{\varepsilon}$ **then**
4:             $U(s, a) \leftarrow accum_m^U(s, a)/m + \bar{\varepsilon}$
5:             $accum_m^U(s, a) = 0$
6:         **if** $accum_m^L(s, a)/m > L(s, a) + 2\bar{\varepsilon}$ **then**
7:             $L(s, a) \leftarrow accum_m^L(s, a)/m - \bar{\varepsilon}$
8:             $accum_m^L(s, a) = 0$
9:         $c(s, a) = 0$
10:    **else**
11:        $accum_m^U(s, a) \leftarrow accum_m^U(s, a) + U(s')$
12:        $accum_m^L(s, a) \leftarrow accum_m^L(s, a) + L(s')$
13:        $c(s, a) \leftarrow c(s, a) + 1$

Macro LEARN(s, a) is true in the kth call of UPDATE$((s, a), \cdot)$ if, since the $(k - 2m)$th call of UPDATE$((s, a), \cdot)$, line 4 was not executed in any call of UPDATE$(\cdot, \cdot)$.

The main idea behind DQL is as follows. As the probabilistic transition function is not known, we cannot update $U(s, a)$ and $L(s, a)$ with the actual values $\sum_{s' \in S} \Delta(s, a)(s')U(s')$ and $\sum_{s' \in S} \Delta(s, a)(s')L(s')$, respectively. However, we can instead use simulations executed in the EXPLORE phase of Algorithm 1 to estimate these values. Namely, we use $accum_m^U(s, a)/m$ to estimate $\sum_{s' \in S} \Delta(s, a)(s')U(s')$ where $accum_m^U(s, a)$ is the sum of the U values of the last m immediate successors of (s, a) seen during the EXPLORE phase. Note that the delay m must be chosen large enough for the estimates to be sufficiently close, i.e., $\bar{\varepsilon}$-close, to the real values.

So, in addition to $U(s, a)$ and $L(s, a)$, the algorithm uses new variables $accum_m^U(s, a)$ and $accum_m^L(s, a)$ to accumulate $U(s, a)$ and $L(s, a)$ values, respectively, and a counter $c(s, a)$ recording the number of invocations of a in s since the last update (all these variables are initialised to 0 at the beginning of computation). Assume that a has been invoked in s during the EXPLORE phase of Algorithm 1,

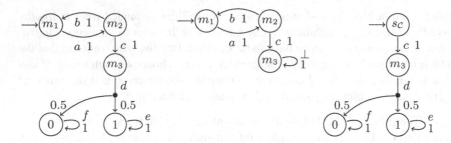

Fig. 1. MDP M with an EC (left), MDP $M^{\{m_1,m_2\}}$ constructed from M in on-the-fly BRTDP (centre), and MDP M′ obtained from M by collapsing $\mathcal{C} = (\{m_1, m_2\}, \{a, b\})$ (right)

which means that UPDATE$((s, a), s')$ is eventually called in the UPDATE phase of Algorithm 1 with the corresponding successor s' of (s, a). If $c(s, a) = m$ at that time, a has been invoked in s precisely m times since the last update concerning (s, a) and the procedure UPDATE$((s, a), s')$ updates $U(s, a)$ with $accum_m^U(s, a)/m$ plus an appropriate constant $\bar\varepsilon$ (unless LEARN is false). Here, the purpose of adding $\bar\varepsilon$ is to make $U(s, a)$ stay above the real value $V(s, a)$ with high probability. If $c(s, a) < m$, then UPDATE$((s, a), s')$ simply accumulates $U(s')$ into $accum_m^U(s, a)$ and increases the counter $c(s, a)$. The $L(s, a)$ values are estimated by $accum_m^L(s, a)/m$ in a similar way, just subtracting $\bar\varepsilon$ from $accum_m^L(s, a)$. The procedure requires m and $\bar\varepsilon$ as inputs, and they are chosen depending on ε and δ; more precisely, we choose $\bar\varepsilon = \frac{\varepsilon \cdot (p_{\min}/E_m)^{|S|}}{12|S|}$ and $m = \frac{\ln(6|S||A|(1+\frac{|S||A|}{\bar\varepsilon})/\delta)}{2\bar\varepsilon^2}$ and establish that DQL is probably approximately correct. The parameters m and $\bar\varepsilon$ can be conservatively approximated using only the limited information about the MDP (i.e. using K, E_m and q). Even though the algorithm has limited information about M, we still establish the following theorem.

Theorem 2. *DQL is probably approximately correct under Assumption-EC.*

Bounded Reachability. Algorithm 1 can be trivially adapted to handle bounded reachability properties by preprocessing the input MDP in standard fashion. Namely, every state is equipped with a bounded counter with values ranging from 0 to k where k is the step bound, the current value denoting the number of steps taken so far. All target states remain targets for all counter values, and every non-target state with counter value k becomes rejecting. Then, to determine the k-step reachability in the original MDP, we compute the (unbounded) reachability in the new MDP. Although this means that the number of states is multiplied by $k + 1$, in practice the size of the explored part of the model can be small.

4   Unrestricted MDPs

We first illustrate with an example that the algorithms BRTDP and DQL as presented in Section 3 may not converge when there are ECs in the MDP.

Example 1. Consider the MDP M in Fig. 1 (left) with EC $(\{m_1, m_2\}, \{a, b\})$. The values in states m_1, m_2 are $V(m_1) = V(m_2) = 0.5$ but the upper bounds are

$U(m_1) = U(m_2) = 1$ for every iteration. This is because $U(m_1, a) = U(m_2, b) = 1$ and both algorithms greedily choose the action with the highest upper bound. Thus, in every iteration t of the algorithm, the error for the initial state m_1 is $U(m_1) - V(m_1) = \frac{1}{2}$ and the algorithm does not converge. In general, any state in an EC has upper bound 1 since, by definition, there are actions that guarantee the next state is in the EC, i.e., is a state with upper bound 1. This argument holds even for standard value iteration with values initialised to 1.

One way of dealing with general MDPs is to preprocess them to identify all MECs [10,9] and "collapse" them into single states (see e.g. [15,11]). These algorithms require that the graph model is known and explore the whole state space, but this may not be possible either due to limited information (see Definition 4) or because the model is too large. Hence, we propose a modification to the algorithms from the previous sections that allows us to deal with ECs "on-the-fly". We first describe the collapsing of a set of states and then present a crucial lemma that allows us to identify ECs to collapse.

Collapsing States. In the following, we say that an MDP $M' = \langle S', \bar{s}', A', E', \Delta' \rangle$ is obtained from $M = \langle S, \bar{s}, A, E, \Delta \rangle$ by *collapsing* a tuple (R, B), where $R \subseteq S$ and $B \subseteq A$ with $B \subseteq \bigcup_{s \in R} E(s)$ if:

- $S' = (S \setminus R) \cup \{s_{(R,B)}\}$,
- $\bar{s}'$ is either $s_{(R,B)}$ or $\bar{s}$, depending on whether $\bar{s} \in R$ or not,
- $A' = A \setminus B$,
- $E'(s) = E(s)$, for $s \in S \setminus R$; $E'(s_{(R,B)}) = \bigcup_{s \in R} E(s) \setminus B$,
- Δ' is defined for all $s \in S'$ and $a \in E'(s)$ by:
  - $\Delta'(s, a)(s') = \Delta(s, a)(s')$ for $s, s' \neq s_{(R,B)}$,
  - $\Delta'(s, a)(s_{(R,B)}) = \sum_{s' \in R} \Delta(s, a)(s')$ for $s \neq s_{(R,B)}$,
  - $\Delta'(s_{(R,B)}, a)(s') = \Delta(s, a)(s')$ for $s' \neq s_{(R,B)}$ and s the unique state with $a \in E(s)$ (see Remark 1),
  - $\Delta'(s_{(R,B)}, a)(s_{(R,B)}) = \sum_{s' \in R} \Delta(s, a)(s')$ where s is the unique state with $a \in E(s)$.

We denote the above transformation, which creates M' from M, as the COLLAPSE function, i.e., COLLAPSE(R, B). As a special case, given a state s and a terminal state $s' \in \{0, 1\}$, we use MAKETERMINAL(s, s') as shorthand for COLLAPSE$(\{s, s'\}, E(s))$, where the new state is renamed to s'. Intuitively, after MAKETERMINAL(s, s'), every transition previously leading to state s will now lead to the terminal state s'.

For practical purposes, it is important to note that the collapsing does not need to be implemented explicitly, but can be done by keeping a separate data structure which stores information about the collapsed states.

Identifying ECs from Simulations. Our modifications will identify ECs "on-the-fly" through simulations that get stuck in them. The next lemma establishes the identification principle. To this end, for a path ω, let us denote by $Appear(\omega, i)$ the tuple (S_i, A_i) of M such that $s \in S_i$ and $a \in A_i(s)$ if and only if (s, a) occurs in ω more than i times.

Lemma 1. *Let* $c = \exp\left(-\left(p_{\min}/E_m\right)^\kappa / \kappa\right)$, *where* $\kappa = KE_m + 1$, *and let* $i \geq \kappa$. *Assume that the* EXPLORE *phase in Algorithm 1 terminates with probability less than 1. Then, provided the* EXPLORE *phase does not terminate within* $3i^3$ *iterations, the conditional probability that* $Appear(\omega, i)$ *is an EC is at least* $1 - 2c^i i^3 \cdot (p_{\min}/E_m)^{-\kappa}$.

The above lemma allows us to modify the EXPLORE phase of Algorithm 1 in such a way that simulations will be used to identify ECs. The ECs discovered will subsequently be collapsed. We first present the overall skeleton (Algorithm 4) for treating ECs "on-the-fly", which consists of two parts: (i) identification of ECs; and (ii) processing them. The instantiations for BRTDP and DQL will differ in the identification phase. Hence, before proceeding to the individual identification algorithms, we first establish the correctness of the processing phase.

Algorithm 4. Extension for general MDPs

1: **function** ON-THE-FLY-EC
2:     $\mathcal{M} \leftarrow$ IDENTIFYECS   ▷ IDENTIFICATION OF ECS
3:     **for all** $(R, B) \in \mathcal{M}$ **do**   ▷ PROCESS ECS
4:         COLLAPSE(R, B)
5:         **for all** $s \in R$ and $a \in E(s) \setminus B$ **do**
6:             $U(s_{(R,B)}, a) \leftarrow U(s, a)$
7:             $L(s_{(R,B)}, a) \leftarrow L(s, a)$
8:         **if** $R \cap F \neq \emptyset$ **then**
9:             MAKETERMINAL$(s_{(R,B)}, 1)$
10:        **else if** no actions enabled in $s_{(R,B)}$ **then**
11:            MAKETERMINAL$(s_{(R,B)}, 0)$

Lemma 2. *Assume (R, B) is an EC in MDP M, V_M the value before the PROCESS ECs procedure in Algorithm 4, and $V_{M'}$ the value after the procedure, then:*
- *for $i \in \{0, 1\}$ if MAKETERMINAL$(s_{(R,B)}, i)$ is called, then $\forall s \in R : V_M(s) = i$,*
- *$\forall s \in S \setminus R : V_M(s) = V_{M'}(s)$,*
- *$\forall s \in R : V_M(s) = V_{M'}(s_{(R,B)})$.*

Interpretation of Collapsing. Intuitively, once an EC (R, B) is collapsed, the algorithm in the EXPLORE phase can choose a state $s \in R$ and action $a \in E(s) \setminus B$ to leave the EC. This is simulated in the EXPLORE phase by considering all actions of the EC uniformly at random until s is reached, and then action a is chosen. Since (R, B) is an EC, playing all actions of B uniformly at random ensures s is almost surely reached. Note that the steps made inside a collapsed EC do not count towards the length of the explored path.

Now, we present the on-the-fly versions of BRTDP and DQL. For each case, we describe: (i) modification of Algorithm 1; (ii) identification of ECs; and (iii) correctness.

4.1 Complete Information (BRTDP)

Modification of Algorithm 1. To obtain BRTDP working with unrestricted MDPs, we modify Algorithm 1 as follows: for iteration i of the EXPLORE phase, we insert a check after line 9 such that, if the length of the path ω explored (i.e., the number of states) is k_i (see below), then we invoke the ON-THE-FLY-EC function for BRTDP. The ON-THE-FLY-EC function possibly modifies the MDP by processing (collapsing) some ECs as described in Algorithm 4. After the ON-THE-FLY-EC function terminates, we interrupt the current EXPLORE phase, and start the EXPLORE phase for the $i+1$-th iteration (i.e., generating a new path again, starting from $\bar{s}$ in the modified MDP). To complete the description we describe the choice of k_i and identification of ECs.

Choice of k_i. Because computing ECs can be expensive, we do not call ON-THE-FLY-EC every time a new state is explored, but only after every k_i steps of the repeat-until loop at lines 6–10 in iteration i. The specific value of k_i can be decided experimentally and change as the computation progresses. A theoretical bound for k_i to ensure that there is an EC with high probability can be obtained from Lemma 1.

Identification of ECs. Given the current explored path ω, let (T, G) be $Appear(\omega, 0)$, that is, the set of states and actions explored in ω. To obtain the ECs from the set T of explored states, we use Algorithm 5. This computes an auxiliary MDP $\mathsf{M}^T = \langle T', \bar{s}, A', E', \Delta' \rangle$ defined as follows:

- $T' = T \cup \{t \mid \exists s \in T, a \in E(s) \text{ such that } \Delta(s, a)(t) > 0\}$,
- $A' = \bigcup_{s \in T} E(s) \cup \{\bot\}$,
- $E'(s) = E(s)$ if $s \in T$ and $E'(s) = \{\bot\}$ otherwise,
- $\Delta'(s, a) = \Delta(s, a)$ if $s \in T$, and $\Delta'(s, \bot)(s) = 1$ otherwise.

It then computes all MECs of M^T that are contained in T and identifies them as ECs. The following lemma states that each of these is indeed an EC in the original MDP.

Algorithm 5. Identification of ECs for BRTDP

1: **function** IDENTIFYECS(M, T)
2:     compute M^T
3:     $\mathcal{M}' \leftarrow$ MECs of M^T
4:     $\mathcal{M} \leftarrow \{(R, B) \in \mathcal{M}' \mid R \subseteq T\}$

Lemma 3. *Let* M, M^T *be the MDPs from the construction above and* T *be the set of explored states. Then every MEC* (R, B) *in* M^T *such that* $R \subseteq T$ *is an EC in* M.

Finally, we establish that the modified algorithm, which we refer to as *on-the-fly BRTDP*, almost surely converges; the proof is an extension of Theorem 1.

Theorem 3. *On-the-fly BRTDP converges almost surely for all MDPs.*

Example 2. Let us describe the execution of the on-the-fly BRTDP on the MDP M from Fig. 1 (left). Choose $k_i \geq 6$ for all i. The loop at lines 6 to 10 of Algorithm 1 generates a path ω that contains some (possibly zero) number of loops $m_1 a m_2 b$ followed by $m_1 a m_2 c m_3 d t$ where $t \in \{0, 1\}$. In the subsequent UPDATE phase, we set $U(m_3, d) = L(m_3, d) = 0.5$ and then $U(m_2, c) = L(m_2, c) = 0.5$; none of the other values change. In the second iteration of the loop at lines 6 to 10, the path $\omega' = m_1 a m_2 b m_1 a m_2 b \ldots$ is being generated, and the newly inserted check for ON-THE-FLY-EC will be triggered once ω achieves the length k_i.

The algorithm now aims to identify ECs in the MDP based on the part of the MDP explored so far. To do so, the MDP M^T for the set $T = \{m_1, m_2\}$ is constructed and we depict it in Fig. 1 (centre). We then run MEC detection on M^T, finding that $(\{m_1, m_2\}, \{a, b\})$ is an EC, and so it gets collapsed according to the COLLAPSE procedure. This gives the MDP M' from Fig. 1 (right).

The execution then continues with M'. A new path is generated at lines 6 to 10 of Algorithm 1; suppose it is $\omega'' = s_C c m_3 d0$. In the UPDATE phase we then update the value $U(s_C, d) = L(s_C, d) = 0.5$, which makes the condition at the last line of Algorithm 1 satisfied, and the algorithm finishes, having computed the correct value.

4.2 Limited Information (DQL)

Modification of Algorithm 1 and Identification of ECs. The modification of Algorithm 1 is done exactly as for the modification of BRDTP (i.e., we insert a check after line 9 of EXPLORE, which invokes the ON-THE-FLY-EC function if the length of path ω exceeds k_i). In iteration i, we set k_i as $3\ell_i^3$, for some ℓ_i (to be described later). The identification of the EC is as follows: we consider $Appear(\omega, \ell_i)$, the set of states and actions that have appeared more than ℓ_i times in the explored path ω, which is of length $3\ell_i^3$, and identify the set as an EC; i.e., $\mathcal{M}$ in line 2 of Algorithm 4 is defined as the set containing the single tuple $Appear(\omega, \ell_i)$. We refer to the algorithm as *on-the-fly DQL*.

Choice of ℓ_i and Correctness. The choice of ℓ_i is as follows. Note that, in iteration i, the error probability, obtained from Lemma 1, is at most $2c^{\ell_i}\ell_i^3 \cdot (p_{\min}/E_m)^{-\kappa}$ and we choose ℓ_i such that $2c^{\ell_i}\ell_i^3 \cdot (p_{\min}/E_m)^{-\kappa} \leq \frac{\delta/2}{2^i}$, where δ is the confidence. Note that, since $c < 1$, we have that c^{ℓ_i} decreases exponentially, and hence for every i such ℓ_i exists. It follows that the total error of the algorithm due to the on-the-fly EC collapsing is at most $\delta/2$. It follows from the proof of Theorem 2 that for on-the-fly DQL the error is at most δ if we use the same $\bar{\varepsilon}$ as for DQL, but now with DQL confidence $\delta/4$, i.e., with $m = \frac{\ln(24|S||A|(1+\frac{|S||A|}{\varepsilon})/\delta)}{2\bar{\varepsilon}^2}$. As before, these numbers can be conservatively approximated using the limited information.

Theorem 4. *On-the-fly DQL is probably approximately correct for all MDPs.*

Example 3. Let us now briefly explain the execution of on-the-fly DQL on the MDP M from Fig. 1 (left). At first, paths of the same form as ω in Example 2 will be generated and there will be no change to U and L, because in any call to UPDATE (see Algorithm 3) for states $s \in \{m_1, m_2\}$ with $c(s, a) = m$ the values accumulated in $accum_m^U(s, a)/m$ and $accum_m^L(s, a)/m$ are the same as the values already held, namely 1 and 0, respectively.

At some point, we call UPDATE for the tuple (m_3, d) with $c(m_3, d) = m$, which will result in the change of $U(m_3, d)$ and $L(m_3, d)$. Note, that at this point, the numbers $accum_m^U(s, d)/m$ and $accum_m^L(s, d)/m$ are both equal to the proportion of generated paths that visited the state 1. This number will, with high probability, be very close to 0.5, say 0.499. We thus set $U(m_3, d) = 0.499 + \varepsilon$ and $L(m_3, d) = 0.499 - \varepsilon$.

We then keep generating paths of the same form and at some point also update $U(m_2, c)$ and $L(m_2, c)$ to precisely $0.499 + \varepsilon$ and $0.499 - \varepsilon$, respectively. The subsequently generated path will be looping on m_1 and m_2, and once it is of length ℓ_i, we identify $(\{m_1, m_2\}, \{a, b\})$ as an EC due to the definition of $Appear(\omega, \ell_i)$. We then get the MDP from Fig. 1 (right), which we use to generate new paths, until the upper and lower bounds on value in the new initial state are within the required bound.

4.3 Extension to LTL

So far we have focused on reachability, but our techniques also extend to linear temporal logic (LTL) objectives. By translating an LTL formula to an equivalent deterministic ω-automaton, verifying MDPs with LTL objectives reduces to analysis of MDPs with ω-regular conditions such as Rabin acceptance conditions. A Rabin acceptance condition consists of a set $\{(M_1, N_1) \ldots (M_d, N_d)\}$ of d pairs (M_i, N_i), where each $M_i \subseteq S$ and $N_i \subseteq S$. The acceptance condition requires that, for some $1 \leq i \leq d$, states in M_i are visited infinitely often and states in N_i are visited finitely often.

Value computation for MDPs with Rabin objectives reduces to optimal reachability of *winning* ECs, where an EC (R, B) is winning if $R \cap M_i \neq \emptyset$ and $R \cap N_i = \emptyset$ for some $1 \leq i \leq d$ [12]. Thus, extending our results from reachability to Rabin objectives requires processing of ECs for Rabin objectives (line 3-11 of Algorithm 4), which is done as follows. Once an EC (R, B) is identified, we first obtain the EC in the original MDP (i.e., obtain the set of states and actions corresponding to the EC in the original MDP) as $(\overline{R}, \overline{B})$ and then determine if there is a sub-EC of $(\overline{R}, \overline{B})$ that is winning using standard algorithms for MDPs with Rabin objectives [2]; and if so then we merge the whole EC as in line 9 of Algorithm 4; if not, and, moreover, there is no action out of the EC, we merge as in line 11 of Algorithm 4. This modified EC processing yields on-the-fly BRTDP and DQL algorithms for MDPs with Rabin objectives.

5 Experimental Results

Implementation. We have developed an implementation of our learning-based framework within the PRISM model checker [25], building upon its simulation engine for generating trajectories and explicit probabilistic model checking engine for storing visited states and U and L values. We focus on the complete-information case (i.e., BRTDP), for which we can perform a more meaningful comparison with PRISM. We implement Algorithms 1 and 2, and the on-the-fly EC detection algorithm of Sec. 4, with the optimisation of taking T as the set of all states explored so far.

We consider three distinct variants of the learning algorithm by modifying the GET-SUCC function in Algorithm 1, which is the heuristic responsible for picking a successor state s' after choosing some action a in each state s of a trajectory. The first variant takes the unmodified GETSUCC, selecting s' at random according to the distribution $\Delta(s, a)$. This behaviour follows the one of the original RTDP algorithm [3]. The second uses the heuristic proposed for BRTDP in [30], selecting the successor $s' \in supp(\Delta(s, a))$ that maximises the difference $U(s') - L(s')$ between bounds for those states (M-D). For the third, we propose an alternative approach that systematically chooses all successors s' in a round-robin (R-R) fashion, and guarantees termination with certainty.

Results. We evaluated our implementation on four existing benchmark models, using a machine with a 2.8GHz Xeon processor and 32GB of RAM, running Fedora 14. We use three models from the PRISM benchmark suite [26]: *zeroconf*, *wlan*, and *firewire_impl_dl*; and a fourth one from [16]: *mer*. The first three use unbounded probabilistic reachability properties; the fourth a time-bounded probabilistic reachability.

Table 1. Verification times using BRTDP (three different heuristics) and PRISM

Name [param.s]	Param. values	Num. states	Time (s)				Visited states		
			PRISM	RTDP	M-D	R-R	RTDP	M-D	R-R
zeroconf [N, K]	20, 10	3,001,911	129.9	7.40	1.47	1.83	760	2007	2570
	20, 14	4,427,159	218.2	12.4	2.18	2.26	977	3728	3028
	20, 18	5,477,150	303.8	71.5	3.89	3.73	1411	5487	3704
wlan [BOFF]	4	345,000	7.35	0.53	0.48	0.54	2018	1377	1443
	5	1,295,218	22.3	0.55	0.45	0.54	2053	1349	1542
	6	5,007,548	82.9	0.50	0.43	0.49	1995	1313	1398
firewire_impl_dl [delay, deadline]	36, 200	6,719,773	63.8	2.85	2.62	2.26	26,508	28,474	22,038
	36, 240	13,366,666	145.4	8.37	7.69	6.72	25,214	26,680	20,219
	36, 280	19,213,802	245.4	9.29	7.90	7.39	32,214	28,463	25,565
mer [N, q]	3000, 0.0001	17,722,564	158.5	67.0	2.42	4.44	1950	3116	3729
	3000, 0.9999	17,722,564	157.7	10.9	2.82	6.80	2902	4643	4608
	4500, 0.0001	26,583,064	250.7	67.3	2.41	4.42	1950	3118	3729
	4500, 0.9999	26,583,064	246.6	10.9	2.84	6.79	2900	4644	4608

The latter is used to show differences between heuristics in the case of MDPs containing rare events, e.g., MDPs where failures occur with very low probability. All models, properties and logs are available online at [39].

We run BRTDP and compare its performance to PRISM. We terminate it when the bounds L and U differ by at most ε for the initial state of the MDP. We use $\varepsilon = 10^{-6}$ in all cases except *zeroconf*, where $\varepsilon = 10^{-8}$ is used since the actual values are very small. For PRISM, we use its fastest engine, which is the "sparse" engine, running value iteration. This is terminated when the values for all states in successive iterations differ by at most ε. Strictly speaking, this is not guaranteed to produce an ε-optimal strategy (e.g. in the case of very slow numerical convergence), but on all these examples it does.

The experimental results are summarised in Table 1. For each model, we give the number of states in the full model, the time for PRISM (model construction, precomputation of zero/one states and value iteration) and time and number of visited states for BRTDP with each of the three heuristics described earlier. Some heuristics perform random exploration and therefore all results have been averaged over 20 runs.

We see that our method outperforms PRISM on all four benchmarks. The improvements in execution time on these benchmarks are possible because the algorithm is able to construct an ε-optimal policy whilst exploring only a portion of the state space. The number of states visited by the algorithm is at least two orders of magnitude smaller than the total size of the model (column 'Num. states'). These numbers do not vary greatly between heuristics.

The RTDP heuristic is generally the slowest of the three, and tends to be sensitive to the probabilities in the model. In the *mer* example, changing the parameter q can mean that some states, which are crucial for the convergence of the algorithm, are no longer visited due to low probabilities on incoming transitions. This results in a considerable slow-down, and is a potential problem for MDPs containing rare events. The M-D and R-R heuristics perform very similarly, despite being quite different (one is randomised, the other deterministic). Both perform consistently well on these examples.

6 Conclusions

We have presented a framework for verifying MDPs using learning algorithms. Building upon methods from the literature, we provide novel techniques to analyse unbounded probabilistic reachability properties of arbitrary MDPs, yielding either exact bounds, in the case of complete information, or PAC bounds, in the case of limited information. Given our general framework, one possible direction would be to explore other learning algorithms in the context of verification. Another direction of future work is to explore whether learning algorithms can be combined with symbolic methods for probabilistic verification.

Acknowledgement. We thank Arnd Hartmanns and anonymous reviewers for careful reading and valuable feedback.

References

1. Aljazzar, H., Leue, S.: Generation of counterexamples for model checking of Markov decision processes. In: QEST, pp. 197–206 (2009)
2. Baier, C., Katoen, J.P.: Principles of model checking. MIT Press (2008)
3. Barto, A.G., Bradtke, S.J., Singh, S.P.: Learning to act using real-time dynamic programming. Artificial Intelligence 72(1-2), 81–138 (1995)
4. Bogdoll, J., Ferrer Fioriti, L.M., Hartmanns, A., Hermanns, H.: Partial order methods for statistical model checking and simulation. In: Bruni, R., Dingel, J. (eds.) FMOODS/FORTE 2011. LNCS, vol. 6722, pp. 59–74. Springer, Heidelberg (2011)
5. Bogdoll, J., Hartmanns, A., Hermanns, H.: Simulation and statistical model checking for modestly nondeterministic models. In: Schmitt, J.B. (ed.) MMB & DFT 2012. LNCS, vol. 7201, pp. 249–252. Springer, Heidelberg (2012)
6. Boyer, B., Corre, K., Legay, A., Sedwards, S.: PLASMA-lab: A flexible, distributable statistical model checking library. In: Joshi, K., Siegle, M., Stoelinga, M., D'Argenio, P.R. (eds.) QEST 2013. LNCS, vol. 8054, pp. 160–164. Springer, Heidelberg (2013)
7. Brázdil, T., Chatterjee, K., Chmelìk, M., Forejt, V., Křetínský, J., Kwiatkowska, M.Z., Parker, D., Ujma, M.: Verification of Markov decision processes using learning algorithms. CoRR abs/1402.2967 (2014)
8. Bulychev, P.E., David, A., Larsen, K.G., Mikucionis, M., Poulsen, D.B., Legay, A., Wang, Z.: UPPAAL-SMC: Statistical model checking for priced timed automata. In: QAPL (2012)
9. Chatterjee, K., Henzinger, M.: An $O(n^2)$ algorithm for alternating Büchi games. In: SODA, pp. 1386–1399 (2012)
10. Chatterjee, K., Henzinger, M.: Faster and dynamic algorithms for maximal end-component decomposition and related graph problems in probabilistic verification. In: SODA (2011)
11. Ciesinski, F., Baier, C., Grosser, M., Klein, J.: Reduction techniques for model checking Markov decision processes. In: QEST, pp. 45–54 (2008)
12. Courcoubetis, C., Yannakakis, M.: Markov decision processes and regular events (extended abstract). In: Paterson, M. (ed.) ICALP 1990. LNCS, vol. 443, pp. 336–349. Springer, Heidelberg (1990)
13. David, A., Larsen, K.G., Legay, A., Mikučionis, M., Poulsen, D.B., van Vliet, J., Wang, Z.: Statistical model checking for networks of priced timed automata. In: Fahrenberg, U., Tripakis, S. (eds.) FORMATS 2011. LNCS, vol. 6919, pp. 80–96. Springer, Heidelberg (2011)
14. David, A., Larsen, K.G., Legay, A., Mikučionis, M., Wang, Z.: Time for statistical model checking of real-time systems. In: Gopalakrishnan, G., Qadeer, S. (eds.) CAV 2011. LNCS, vol. 6806, pp. 349–355. Springer, Heidelberg (2011)
15. De Alfaro, L.: Formal verification of probabilistic systems. Ph.D. thesis (1997)

16. Feng, L., Kwiatkowska, M., Parker, D.: Automated learning of probabilistic assumptions for compositional reasoning. In: Giannakopoulou, D., Orejas, F. (eds.) FASE 2011. LNCS, vol. 6603, pp. 2–17. Springer, Heidelberg (2011)

17. He, R., Jennings, P., Basu, S., Ghosh, A.P., Wu, H.: A bounded statistical approach for model checking of unbounded until properties. In: ASE, pp. 225–234 (2010)

18. Henriques, D., Martins, J., Zuliani, P., Platzer, A., Clarke, E.M.: Statistical model checking for Markov decision processes. In: QEST, pp. 84–93 (2012)

19. Hérault, T., Lassaigne, R., Magniette, F., Peyronnet, S.: Approximate probabilistic model checking. In: Steffen, B., Levi, G. (eds.) VMCAI 2004. LNCS, vol. 2937, pp. 73–84. Springer, Heidelberg (2004)

20. Jegourel, C., Legay, A., Sedwards, S.: Cross-entropy optimisation of importance sampling parameters for statistical model checking. In: Madhusudan, P., Seshia, S.A. (eds.) CAV 2012. LNCS, vol. 7358, pp. 327–342. Springer, Heidelberg (2012)

21. Jegourel, C., Legay, A., Sedwards, S.: A platform for high performance statistical model checking – PLASMA. In: Flanagan, C., König, B. (eds.) TACAS 2012. LNCS, vol. 7214, pp. 498–503. Springer, Heidelberg (2012)

22. Jegourel, C., Legay, A., Sedwards, S.: Importance splitting for statistical model checking rare properties. In: Sharygina, N., Veith, H. (eds.) CAV 2013. LNCS, vol. 8044, pp. 576–591. Springer, Heidelberg (2013)

23. Kemeny, J., Snell, J., Knapp, A.: Denumerable Markov Chains. Springer (1976)

24. Kolobov, A., Mausam, Weld, D.S., Geffner, H.: Heuristic search for generalized stochastic shortest path MDPS. In: ICAPS (2011)

25. Kwiatkowska, M., Norman, G., Parker, D.: PRISM 4.0: Verification of probabilistic real-time systems. In: Gopalakrishnan, G., Qadeer, S. (eds.) CAV 2011. LNCS, vol. 6806, pp. 585–591. Springer, Heidelberg (2011)

26. Kwiatkowska, M., Norman, G., Parker, D.: The PRISM benchmark suite. In: QEST, pp. 203–204 (2012)

27. Larsen, K.G.: Priced timed automata and statistical model checking. In: Johnsen, E.B., Petre, L. (eds.) IFM 2013. LNCS, vol. 7940, pp. 154–161. Springer, Heidelberg (2013)

28. Lassaigne, R., Peyronnet, S.: Approximate planning and verification for large Markov decision processes. In: SAC, pp. 1314–1319 (2012)

29. Legay, A., Sedwards, S.: Lightweight Monte Carlo algorithm for Markov decision processes. CoRR abs/1310.3609 (2013)

30. McMahan, H.B., Likhachev, M., Gordon, G.J.: Bounded real-time dynamic programming: RTDP with monotone upper bounds and performance guarantees. In: ICML (2005)

31. Puterman, M.: Markov Decision Processes. Wiley (1994)

32. El Rabih, D., Pekergin, N.: Statistical model checking using perfect simulation. In: Liu, Z., Ravn, A.P. (eds.) ATVA 2009. LNCS, vol. 5799, pp. 120–134. Springer, Heidelberg (2009)

33. Sen, K., Viswanathan, M., Agha, G.: On statistical model checking of stochastic systems. In: Etessami, K., Rajamani, S.K. (eds.) CAV 2005. LNCS, vol. 3576, pp. 266–280. Springer, Heidelberg (2005)

34. Sen, K., Viswanathan, M., Agha, G.: Statistical model checking of black-box probabilistic systems. In: Alur, R., Peled, D.A. (eds.) CAV 2004. LNCS, vol. 3114, pp. 202–215. Springer, Heidelberg (2004)

35. Strehl, A.L., Li, L., Wiewiora, E., Langford, J., Littman, M.L.: PAC model-free reinforcement learning. In: ICML, pp. 881–888 (2006)

36. Sutton, R., Barto, A.: Reinforcement Learning: An Introduction. MIT Press (1998)

37. Younes, H., Simmons, R.: Probabilistic verification of discrete event systems using acceptance sampling. In: Brinksma, E., Larsen, K.G. (eds.) CAV 2002. LNCS, vol. 2404, pp. 223–235. Springer, Heidelberg (2002)

38. Younes, H.L.S., Clarke, E.M., Zuliani, P.: Statistical verification of probabilistic properties with unbounded until. In: Davies, J. (ed.) SBMF 2010. LNCS, vol. 6527, pp. 144–160. Springer, Heidelberg (2011)

39. http://www.prismmodelchecker.org/files/atva14learn/

Test Coverage Estimation Using Threshold Accepting

Thao Dang and Noa Shalev

VERIMAG/CNRS,
Centre Equation
2 Avenue de Vignate, 38610 Gières, France
{Thao.Dang,Noa.Shalev}@imag.fr

Abstract. This paper is concerned with model-based testing of hybrid systems. In our previous work [6], we proposed a test generation algorithm, called gRRT, guided by a coverage measure defined using the star discrepancy notion. An important ingredient in this algorithm is a procedure for dynamically estimating the coverage, which is done based on a box partition of the continuous state space. The goal of this estimation is to identify the areas in the state space which have not been sufficiently visited. A drawback of this guiding method is that its complexity depends on the number of boxes in the partition, which needs to be fine enough to guarantee a good coverage estimate. Thus in high dimensions the method can become very costly. To enhance the scalability of the algorithm gRRT we propose in this paper a new guiding method, motivated by the observation that trying to optimize the coverage in each exploration step is, on one hand, computationally costly, and on the other hand, not always a good choice since this may make the system try to expand in the directions which are not reachable (due to the controllability of the system). Instead of considering all the boxes in the partition, we propose to use a randomized search to quickly find a region that yields a high local discrepancy value. This randomized search is based on threshold accepting, a well-known integer optimization heuristic. We also present some experimental results obtained on a challenging circuit benchmark and a number of randomly generated examples, which shows that the new guiding method allows achieving better time and coverage efficiency.

1 Introduction

Model-Based Development is a pervasive approach for developing and testing embedded systems. Techniques for analyzing dynamical systems are essential for proving correctness of safety-critical applications of embedded systems. Existing testing and validation techniques for such systems are costly if high confidence in the results is expected and they can still fail to discover all the behaviors that can have a detrimental effect on safety and performance of the system. This paper addresses the problem of efficiently testing the behaviors of hybrid

F. Cassez and J.-F. Raskin (Eds.): ATVA 2014, LNCS 8837, pp. 115–128, 2014.

dynamical systems (that is, systems combining continuous and discrete dynamics). Hybrid systems have been widely accepted as a mathematical model for many applications in embedded systems. The particular focus of this paper is on enhancing the coverage-guided test generation technique proposed in [6]. This technique combines an adaptation of the successful robotic motion planning technique RRT (Rapidly-exploring Random Tree) [15,16] with a guiding tool based on the star discrepancy coverage. The resulting algorithm is called gRRT (for "guided RRT"). It has been successfully applied to a number of analog circuits and control applications. Although the algorithm can handle large systems with complex dynamics (described for example using nonlinear differential algebraic equations), its coverage analysis becomes computationally costly in high dimensions. Indeed, an important ingredient of this coverage-guided algorithm is a procedure for estimating the star discrepancy of a point set, which is done based on a box partition of the continuous state space. The goal of this estimation is mainly to identify the areas in the state space which are not sufficiently visited. This information is then used to guide the exploration by steering the system towards these areas. A drawback of this guiding method is that its complexity depends on the number of boxes in the partition, which needs to be fine enough to guarantee a good coverage estimate. Thus in high dimensions the method can become very costly.

To enhance the scalability of the test generation algorithm gRRT we propose in this paper a new guiding method, motivated by the observation that trying to optimize the coverage in each exploration step is, on one hand, computationally costly, and on the other hand, not always a good choice since this may make the system try to expand in the directions which are not reachable (due to the controllability of the system). The essence of our new guiding method is as follows. Instead of considering all the boxes in the partition, we use a randomized search to quickly find a region that yields a high local discrepancy value (which corresponds to a low local coverage). This randomized search is based on threshold accepting, a well-known integer optimization heuristic [7]. Although this guiding method is less accurate in terms of coverage estimation, it can identify critical areas and additionally consumes less computational time and thus allows the algorithm to visit more states.

The rest of the paper is structured as follows. In the first section, we recall our testing problem and the test generation algorithm gRRT. We then explain our new guiding method. Finally we present some experimental results obtained for a ring oscillator circuit, a challenging analog circuit benchmark, and for a number of randomly generated examples.

Before continuing, we briefly discuss related works. Hybrid systems testing has recently attracted the intention of many researchers, which is attested by numerous publications (see for example [10,11,18,14,19] and references therein). The RRT algorithm has been used to solve a variety of related reachability problems, such as hybrid systems planning, control, verification and testing (see for example [10,11,9,4,18]). Randomized testing using the cross-entropy method is proposed in [20]. Our idea of using threshold accepting to estimate the star discrepancy is similar in spirit to a randomized approach proposed in [1]. This approach, based on a variant of Simulated Annealing, is used to minimize the distance of the system trajectories to some set violating a property of interest. While our guiding procedure simultaneously exploits the spatial structure of many different trajectories in a step-by-step manner over time, this approach considers trajectory by trajectory. Note that threshold accepting is similar to Hill Climbing, which has been used in test data generation for software testing [17]. In our work, due to the approximate nature of the coverage estimation and additionally to the fact that the evolution of the coverage is constrained by the system dynamics, we do not seek a globally optimal solution in each intermediate step but use a local search method to quickly produce a locally optimal solution.

2   Test Generation Problem

For clarity of presentation, we explain the new guiding method only for continuous systems since their extension to hybrid systems is straightforward, which will be discussed later. We consider a continuous system described by the following differential equation:

$$\dot{x}(t) = f(x(t), u(t))$$

where

- $x \in \mathcal{X} \subseteq \mathbb{R}^n$ is the continuous state evolving inside some bounded state space $\mathcal{X}$,
- $u(\cdot) \in \mathcal{U}$ is the input of the form $u : \mathbb{R}^+ \to U \subset \mathbb{R}^{n_u}$. The set $\mathcal{U}$ is the set of admissible inputs. Since we are interested in implementing the tester as a program, $\mathcal{U}$ contains piecewise constant functions. The input is assumed to be controllable by the tester.

The non-determinism in the input is useful for describing disturbances from the environment and imprecision in modelling and implementation. We use the usual assumption that the function f is Lipschitz continuous.

A *test case* in our framework is represented by a tree where each node is associated with a state, and each edge of the tree is associated with the a control input value. To execute such a test case, the tester applies a control input sequence to the system, measures the corresponding sequence of states, and decides whether the system under test conforms to the specification.

The main steps of the coverage-guided test generation algorithm gRRT [6] are summarized in Algorithm 1.

Algorithm 1. Abstract Algorithm of gRRT

Step 1: a goal state x_{goal} is sampled from the state space;
Step 2: a neighbor state x_{init} of the goal state x_{goal} is determined;
Step 3: from x_{init} an appropriate control input u is applied for a time step h to steer the system towards the goal state x_{goal}.

The sampling process in Step 1 is guided so that the goal state lies in a region where the local coverage of the visited states is still low (the notions of coverage will be recalled in the subsequent paragraph). The above abstract procedure can be applied to hybrid systems. Indeed, to sample a goal hybrid state, one can first sample a location (or a discrete mode) based on the current continuous coverage at each location. A location with low continuous coverage has a higher probability of being sampled. Once a goal location is chosen, it remains to sample a goal continuous state in the state space of that location, which is the problem we want to solve more efficiently in this work. Therefore, as mentioned earlier, for clarity of presentation, in the rest of the paper we consider only continuous systems and the solution proposed here can be readily used in the gRRT algorithm for hybrid systems, as described in [6].

To discuss the goal state sampling process, we first recall the coverage notion. We assume that the state space is a box

$$\mathcal{B} = [l_1, L_1] \times \ldots \times [l_n, L_n] \subset \mathbb{R}^n.$$

Let P be a set of k points inside $\mathcal{B}$, which represent a set of visited states. Let $\mathcal{J}$ be the set of all sub-boxes J of the form $J = \prod_{i=1}^{n} [l_i, y_i]$ with $y_i \in [l_i, L_i]$. The local discrepancy of the point set P with respect to the sub-box J is defined as follows:

$$D(P, J) = \left| \frac{A(P, J)}{k} - \frac{vol(J)}{vol(\mathcal{B})} \right|$$

where $A(P, J)$ is the number of points of P that are inside J, and $vol(J)$ is the volume of the box J. The star discrepancy of P with respect to the box $\mathcal{B}$ is defined as:

$$D^*(P, \mathcal{B}) = sup_{J \in \mathcal{J}} D(P, J). \tag{1}$$

The star discrepancy of P with respect to a box $\mathcal{B}$ satisfies $0 < D^*(P, \mathcal{B}) \leq 1$. Intuitively, the star discrepancy is a measure for the irregularity of a set of points. A large value $D^*(P, \mathcal{B})$ means that the points in P are not much equidistributed over $\mathcal{B}$, and the coverage of P is defined as: $Cov(P) = 1 - D^*(P, \mathcal{B})$.

Discrepancy Estimation. The star discrepancy is an important notion in equidistribution theory as well as in quasi-Monte Carlo techniques (see for example [3]). Computing the star discrepancy is not an easy problem (see for example [8]). Many theoretical results for one dimensional point sets cannot be generalized to higher dimensions, and among the fastest algorithms, the one proposed in [8] has time complexity $\mathcal{O}(k^{1+n/2})$ where k is the number of points and n is the dimension. It is known that the problem of computing the star discrepancy of arbitrary point sets is NP-hard [12].

The current version of gRRT does not try to exactly compute the star discrepancy but estimate a lower bound and an upper bound. These bounds and the information obtained from their estimation indicate the areas in the state space that need to be explored more and the algorithm thus favors the goal state sampling in these areas. This estimation is done using a method, published in [21], which considers a finite box partition of the box $\mathcal{B}$ (instead of an infinite number of all sub-boxes as in the definition of the star discrepancy (1)). This partition allows determining an upper bound and a lower bound of the local discrepancy value for each box as well as of the star discrepancy. Then, a probability distribution is defined for the boxes based on their local discrepancy values. Since our new guiding method uses the same construction of box partition and the upper bound, we recall some important definitions.

A box partition of $\mathcal{B}$ is a set of boxes $\Pi = \{b^1, \ldots, b^{n_b}\}$ such that $\bigcup_{i=1}^{n_b} b^i = \mathcal{B}$ and the interiors of the boxes b^i do not intersect. Given a box $b = [\alpha_1, \beta_1] \times \ldots \times [\alpha_n, \beta_n] \in \Pi$, we define

$$b^+ = [l_1, \beta_1] \times \ldots \times [l_n, \beta_n],$$
$$b^- = [l_1, \alpha_1] \times \ldots \times [l_n, \alpha_n].$$

Figure 1 provides an illustration of these definitions.

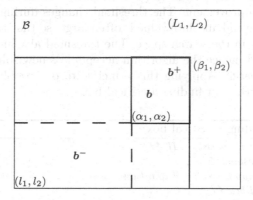

Fig. 1. Illustration of the boxes b^- and b^+

In [21] it is proven that for any finite box partition Π of $\mathcal{B}$, an upper bound $B(P, \Pi)$ of the star discrepancy $D^*(P, \mathcal{B})$ of the point set P with respect to $\mathcal{B}$ can be determined as follows:

$$B(P, \Pi) = \max_{b \in \Pi} \kappa(b, P) \tag{2}$$

where

$$\kappa(b, P) = \max\{\frac{A(P, b^+)}{k} - \frac{vol(b^-)}{vol(\mathcal{B})}, \frac{vol(b^+)}{vol(\mathcal{B})} - \frac{A(P, b^-)}{k}\}. \tag{3}$$

3   Search for a Critical Box

To improve time efficiency of the goal state sampling process, we propose a randomized search method, called threshold accepting [7]. The goal of this search method is to find a box in the partition that corresponds to a good approximate solution of (2). We call it a *critical box*, that is a box with high local discrepancy. This box is then used as the sampling space for the next goal state (since it is of interest to reduce the local discrepancy of this critical box). It is important to emphasize that for a system with "limited controllability", that is from a given state not all directions are reachable, a best solution of (2) may repeatedly lead to the same blocking situation where the algorithm keeps adding the states close to the previously visited ones. Hence, picking only critical boxes (representing a sub-optimal solution) allows a more flexible expansion of the tree in the reachable space.

Essentially, the threshold accepting algorithm [7] starts with a randomly chosen feasible solution and then picks randomly a neighbor solution as a new candidate solution. If the difference between this neighbor solution and the current one is larger than some non-positive threshold, the algorithm moves to this neighbor solution; otherwise, it stays with the current solution and selects again a new neighbour. The algorithm stops after a fixed number of iterations, or if there is no more improvement. The threshold changes during the execution of the algorithm. Its initial absolute value is often large, so that the algorithm may explore more freely in the search space. The threshold absolute values are then gradually decreased; hence the algorithm accepts less new solutions and finally works as a local search. Applying this principle to our problem (2), we derive the following algorithm for finding a critical box.

Algorithm 2. Finding a critical box

/* Input: point set P, partition Π */
   initial threshold Δ_κ^0 */
   maximal number i_{max} of iterations */
/* Output: critical box */

$j = 0$
$b = urandom(\Pi)$ /* uniformly sampling an initial box */
$i_f = 0$
repeat
   $b' = candidateSampling(\mathcal{N}(b, d))$ /* sampling a new candidate box
                                              from the neighborhood of the current box */
   if $(\kappa(b', P) - \kappa(b, P) > \Delta_\kappa^j)$ **then**
      $b = b'$
      $i_f = 0$
   else
      $i_f + +$
   end if
   $\Delta_\kappa^{j+1} = update(\Delta_\kappa^j)$ /* updating the threshold Δ_κ */
   $j + +$
until $j = j_{max}$
RETURN b

First the algorithm chooses uniformly at random a box b from the partition Π and its local bound $\kappa(b, P)$ is computed as in (3). Then a number i_{max} of iterations are executed. In each iteration, a neighborhood of b is determined and within this neighborhood a box b' is chosen at random and then its local bound is computed. If its difference from the bound of the current box b is greater than the current threshold Δ_κ^j, the box b is replaced by b'. In the following, we explain the important ingredients of the algorithm, namely defining the neighborhood $\mathcal{N}(b, d)$, sampling a new candidate box from the neighborhood, and updating the threshold.

3.1 Defining a Neighborhood

The coordinates of the boxes in the partition Π form a grid

$$\mathcal{G}(\Pi) = \mathcal{G}_1 \times \ldots \times \mathcal{G}_n$$

such that for each dimension $i \in \{1, \ldots, n\}$ $\mathcal{G}_i$ is the sequence of all the left and right bounds of the boxes in Π, sorted in an increasing order. Let $\mathcal{G}_i(j)$ denote the jth element of $\mathcal{G}_i$, and for a real number $\alpha \in \mathcal{G}_i$, $\iota_i(\alpha)$ is the order of α in the sequence $\mathcal{G}_i$.

Let $b = [\lambda_1, \rho_1] \times \ldots \times [\lambda_n, \rho_n]$ be a box in Π and $d \in \mathbb{Z}$ be a vector of n positive integers, we define a box that envelops b by a grid-distance d as

$$E(b, d) = [\mathcal{G}_1(\iota_1(\lambda_1) - d), \mathcal{G}_1(\iota_1(\rho_1) + d)] \times \ldots$$
$$\times [\mathcal{G}_n(\iota_n(\lambda_n) - d), \mathcal{G}_n(\iota_n(\rho_n) + d)]$$

Then the neighborhood of b is the set of all the boxes in Π that have non-empty intersection with $E(b, d)$, that is

$$\mathcal{N}(b, d) = \{b' \cap E(b, d) \neq \emptyset \mid b' \in \Pi\}.$$

A new candidate box b' is then chosen from the set $\mathcal{N}(b, d)$. In the following we explain the procedure of sampling such a candidate box.

3.2 Selecting a New Candidate Box

We remark that for a box $b \in \Pi$ to be a solution to the optimization problem (2), the coordinates of its upper bound must be sufficiently large so that the volume of b^+ is at least v, where v is a constant in $(0, \prod_{i=1}^{n}(L_i - l_i))$. Therefore, the coordinates of the upper vertex of b^+ should be at least $v^{1/n}$. Hence, in high dimensions it is more appropriate to favor the selection of candidate boxes with larger upper vertex coordinates. To this end, we follow a two step procedure:

1. We first sample a point in the enveloping box according to a probability distribution that reflects the effect of dimension n. This point indicates the candidate box in the neighborhood to select in the next step. More concretely, let the enveloping box be denoted as

$$E(b, d) = [l_1^E, L_1^E] \times \ldots \times [l_n^E, L_n^E].$$

Let y be a point sampled uniformly in the unit box $[0,1]^n$, this point y is then mapped to a point x in the enveloping box $E(\boldsymbol{b}, d)$ by the following function:

$$\forall i \in \{1, \dots, n\} : x_i = (\, ((L_i^E)^n - (l_i^E)^n)y_i + (l_i^E)^n \,)^{1/n}$$

2. Then the box in $\mathcal{N}(\boldsymbol{b}, d)$ that contains x is chosen as the next candidate box. In case the box containing x is $\boldsymbol{b}$ itself, we discard this sample and start the sampling again.

3.3   Threshold Update

Threshold accepting has already been used for approximating the star discrepancy of a point set in [22,13]. These approximation techniques were developed to study point sets (often called good lattice point sets) generated specifically for approximating integrands using Monte Carlo and quasi-Monte Carlo methods. They use monotonically increasing (non-positive) threshold sequences that are generated from empirical distributions and each threshold value is used for J iterations in order to stabilize the search at this threshold value. These threshold sequences are experimentally proven to be efficient for such particular point sets.

Nevertheless, in our problem, we do not have prior knowledge of the point sets generated by the system under test and, in addition, the box structure of the partition might not capture well the global contour of such point sets. Therefore, we can relax the condition for updating the candidate box. If the current box $\boldsymbol{b}$ does not get updated after a number of trials, the threshold sequence is slightly decreased, which helps the algorithm to avoid being stuck in a situation where most neighboring boxes of the current box have smaller values of κ. The amount of decrease can grow with the number of update failures (indicated by the counter i_f in the algorithm). On the other hand, whenever the box is updated, the counter i_f is set to 0 and the threshold is increased. This can be captured by the following *update* function:

$$update(\Delta_\kappa^j) = ((\frac{i_f}{m})^p - 1)\Delta(1 - \frac{j}{j_{max}})^q)$$

where m, p, q, Δ are parameters to fine-tune the growth rate of the threshold. The above update function does not depend on Δ_κ^j but it is also possible to define an update function that depends on the previous threshold values.

Whenever i_f is reset to 0, the threshold takes the most negative value, thus giving the algorithm the possibility to move around rapidly. The threshold then rises from this negative value until the current box is updated again. Although using monotonic threshold sequence allows enjoying the convergence properties of threshold accepting [7], we do not want to run too many iterations; it is thus more important to move more freely in the search space.

4   Goal State Sampling and Neighbor State Computation

Algorithm 2 finds a critical box with high local discrepancy. We can now exploit this information to reduce its local discrepancy, by sampling a goal state x_{goal} uniformly within this box, in Step 1 of Algorithm 1. Now we proceed with Step 2 of Algorithm 1, that is finding a neighbor state of x_{goal}.

Note that $A(P, b)$ is the number of points of P which are inside b. We associate with each box $b \subseteq \Pi$ a number $A^*(b)$ such that

$$\frac{vol(b)}{vol(\mathcal{B})} = \frac{A^*(b)}{k}.$$

We denote

$$\Delta_A(b) = A(P, b) - A^*(b). \tag{4}$$

The sign of $\Delta_A(b)$ reflects a 'lack' or an 'excess' of points in the box b, and its absolute value indicates how significant the lack or the excess is. We can rewrite the definition of the upper bound given by (2) as follows:

$$B(P, \Pi) = \frac{1}{k} \max_{b \in \Pi} \Delta_A^m(b) \tag{5}$$

where $\Delta_A^m(b) = \max\{\Delta_A^+(b), \Delta_A^-(b)\}$ and

$$\Delta_A^+(b) = A(P, b^+) - A^*(b^-),$$
$$\Delta_A^-(b) = A^*(b^+) - A(P, b^-).$$

We observe that adding a point in b increases $\Delta_A^+(b)$ but does not affect $\Delta_A^-(b)$. There are two cases:

- If $\Delta_A^-(b) > \Delta_A^+(b)$, $\Delta_A^m(b) = \Delta_A^-(b)$ and it is preferable that the next point is added to b^-, that is we favor the selection of a neighbor state which is near the set b^-.
- If $\Delta_A^+(b) > \Delta_A^-(b)$, $\Delta_A^m(b) = \Delta_A^+(b)$ and it is preferable that the next point is added to the area outside b^+, that is we favor the selection of a neighbor state which is near the set $\mathcal{B} \setminus b^+$.

Before proceeding with experimental results we briefly discuss the computational complexity of the new method. In this method, the box partition Π is used to store the visited points, as in the previous star discrepancy estimation method. However, when a new point is added, while the previous method needs to update the local star discrepancy bounds for all the sub-boxes that are affected by the addition of the new point (see for example the equation (3)), the randomized search method only needs to determine the local discrepancy values for the boxes that are selected during the search. This explains an improvement in time efficiency of the new method.

5   Experimental Results

In this section, we describe two experiments. In the first experiment we applied the new guiding method to a circuit which has been used as a benchmark for evaluating circuit validation methods. The goal of the second experiment is to evaluate the performance of the method on high dimensional systems.

The circuit benchmark in the first experiment is a variant of standard ring oscillators. A standard ring oscillator oscillates only if it has an odd number of stages. To obtain an oscillator with an even number of stages, a modification is introduced in the form of additional inverter pairs which form bridges within the original oscillator (see Figure 2). This circuit can oscillate only under the following condition: the ratio of the sizes of the transistors comprising the main feedback chain to the sizes of the transistors comprising the bridge must be within certain limit. For the circuit provided by Rambus, simulation results show that when this ratio is roughly in the interval $[0.4, 2.2]$ periodic oscillations occur, and when this ratio approaches the extreme values of the interval, the circuit exhibits dampened oscillations; and when the ratio is outside the interval, the circuit stabilizes and does not oscillate. A research challenge is to see whether the current state of the art of verification techniques could show that with wrong transistor sizes, the circuit does not oscillate properly. The circuit is specified as a SPICE netlist.

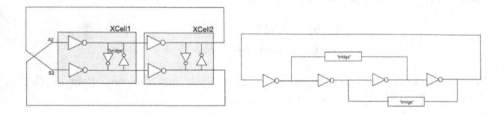

Fig. 2. Rambus ring oscillator (in two different views)

We have implemented the new guiding algorithm and integrated it in the tool HTG for test generation[1]. We now briefly describe the main features of the tool. The tool can accept as input a hybrid automaton. In view of validation of analog and mixed-signal circuits, the tool is connected to a parser that can handle SPICE netlists, an industrial standard circuit specification formalism. The tool can generate test cases using the gRRT algorithm combined with random walk sampling [5]. It can also be used for test execution in practical settings with partial observability as well as sensor and actuator imprecisions.

First we apply our new guiding method to the same circuit but with two ratio values: 2.1 and 2.2. In this example, the input of the system is the disturbance on the source voltage and we also generate test cases for two disturbance ranges

---

[1] https://sites.google.com/site/htgtestgenerationtool/home

$[-0.01, 0.01]$ and $[-0.2, 0.2]$. In this experiment we set the grid-distance of the enveloping box d to be $1/4$ of the total number $|P|$ of points in P if $|P| \geq 100$, and to be $1/8$ of that total number if it is larger than 100. The parameters of the threshold update function are $m = 100$, $p = 2$, $j_{max} = 1000$, $q = 0.5$ and the initial threshold $\Delta_\kappa^0 = -0.1$. These values are commonly used in threshold updating.

All the figures that follow depict the evolution of the voltage output of the first transistor. Figure 3 shows that with ratio 2.1 the circuit oscillates even under the large range of disturbances. When the ratio is 2.2, the oscillations are much more sensitive to the disturbances, as shown in Figure 4.

We also compared the new guiding method and the previous method, which shows that for the same number of visited points, the new guiding method is more time efficient and in addition achieves better coverage. Indeed, the new guiding method detects a larger variation of the values of the low level voltage (see Figure 5). Indeed, with the old guiding method, the computation time is $125.69s$, the minimal low value is -2.975, and the maximal low value is -2.3976. With the new method, the computation time is $116.39s$, the minimal low value is -2.9882 and the maximal low value is -2.379.

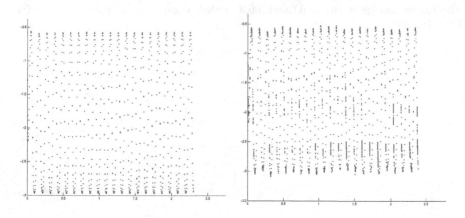

Fig. 3. Result of the new guiding method for the circuit with ratio 2.1, disturbances on the source voltage ± 0.01 (left) and ± 0.2 (right), computation times $81.29s$ (left) and $84.84s$ (right)

We proceed with the second experiment, the goal of which is to compare the new guiding method with threshold accepting (denoted by TA for short) and the guiding method based on the star discrepancy estimation (denoted by SDE) [6]. To this end, we created a continuous system the dynamics of which is described by a system of linear differential equations with uncertain input. The matrices are of Jordan form where each block has a randomly generated value between $[-1, 1]$. It is important to note that the algorithm does not exploit the linearity of the dynamics. We can observe from the results that to achieve a similar level of coverage, the method TA is more time efficient, as shown in Table 6. In this

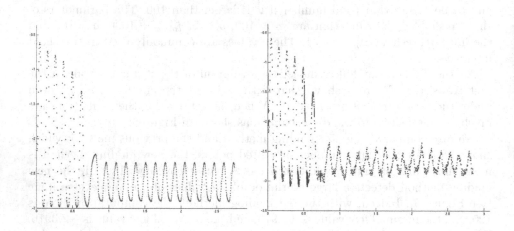

Fig. 4. Result of the new guiding method for the circuit with ratio 2.2, disturbances on the source voltage ±0.01 (left) and ±0.2 (right), computation times 83.51s (left) and 90s (right)

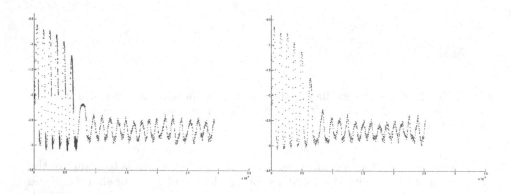

Fig. 5. Results of the old (left) and new (right) guiding methods for the circuit with ratio 2.2, disturbance on the source voltage ±0.2

experiment, we let the number of iterations be 10000. Again the parameters for threshold accepting are the same as in the first experiment: the grid-distance $d = \frac{1}{4}|P|$ if $|P| \geq 100$, and $d = \frac{1}{8}|P|$ if $|P| < 100$; $m = 100$, $p = 2$, $j_{max} = 1000$, $q = 0.5$ and the initial threshold $\Delta_\kappa^0 = -0.1$. The second and fourth columns of Table 6 contain the numbers of states satisfying the condition defining the state space. Indeed, when the reachable space is much smaller than the whole state space, a guiding method with low coverage tends to explore the states near the boundary of the reachable space and results in the new states which are too close to the previously visited states and are then not included.

dim	nb states TA	time(s) TA	nb states SDE	time(s) SDE
50	8127	4.51	6999	10.77
100	8424	13.57	5417	45.45
200	7968	32.98	6617	48.92

Fig. 6. Experimental results for a continuous system in various dimensions. The second and third columns contain the computation times and the numbers of generated states for the method TA, and the last two columns contain the results for the method SDE.

6 Conclusion

In this paper we presented a new method for guiding the process of test generation using the star discrepancy coverage. The method is based on the threshold accepting heuristic. The experimental results are promising and we intend to pursue this work further in two directions. One concerns a study of the convergence of the global test generation algorithm with respect to the probability of visiting any reachable state. In addition, we want to find the procedures for defining the threshold sequence and neighborhood structure that reflects the controllability of the system dynamics.

References

1. Abbas, H., Fainekos, G.: Convergence Proofs for Simulated Annealing Falsification of Safety Properties. In: Proc. of 50th Annual Allerton Conference on Communication, Control, and Computing, Monticello, IL (October 2012)
2. Alur, R., Courcoubetis, C., Halbwachs, N., Henzinger, T.A., Ho, P.-H., Nicollin, X., Olivero, A., Sifakis, J., Yovine, S.: The algorithmic analysis of hybrid systems. Theoretical Computer Science 138(1), 3–34 (1995)
3. Beck, J., Chen, W.W.L.: Irregularities of distribution. In: Acta Arithmetica, UK, Cambridge University Press (1997)
4. Branicky, M., Curtiss, M., Levine, J., Morgan, S.: Sampling-based reachability algorithms for control and verification of complex systems. In: Thirteenth Yale Workshop on Adaptive and Learning Systems (2005)

5. Dang, T., Shalev, N.: State estimation and property-guided exploration for hybrid systems testing. In: Nielsen, B., Weise, C. (eds.) ICTSS 2012. LNCS, vol. 7641, pp. 152–167. Springer, Heidelberg (2012)
6. Dang, T., Nahhal, T.: Coverage-guided test generation for continuous and hybrid systems. Formal Methods in System Design 34(2), 183–213 (2009)
7. Dueck, G., Scheuer, T.: Threshold accepting: A general purpose optimization algorithm appearing superior to simulated annealing. Journal of Computational Physics 90(1), 161–175 (1990)
8. Dobkin, D., Eppstein, D.: Computing the discrepancy. In: SCG 1993: Proceedings of the Ninth Annual Symposium on Computational Geometry, pp. 47–52. ACM Press, New York (1993)
9. Kim, J., Esposito, J., Kumar, V.: Sampling-based algorithm for testing and validating robot controllers. Int. J. Rob. Res. 25(12), 1257–1272 (2006)
10. Esposito, J., Kim, J.W., Kumar, V.: Adaptive RRTs for validating hybrid robotic control systems. In: Proceedings Workshop on Algorithmic Foundations of Robotics, Zeist, The Netherlands (July 2004)
11. Bhatia, A., Frazzoli, E.: Incremental search methods for reachability analysis of continuous and hybrid systems. In: Alur, R., Pappas, G.J. (eds.) HSCC 2004. LNCS, vol. 2993, pp. 142–156. Springer, Heidelberg (2004)
12. Gnewuch, M., Srivastav, A., Winzen, C.: Finding optimal volume subintervals with k points and calculating the star discrepancy are NP-hard problems. J. Complexity 25(2), 115–127 (2009)
13. Gnewuch, M., Wahlström, M., Winzen, C.: SIAM Journal of Numerical Analysis 50, 781–807 (2012)
14. Julius, A., Fainekos, G.E., Anand, M., Lee, I., Pappas, G.J.: Robust test generation and coverage for hybrid systems. In: Bemporad, A., Bicchi, A., Buttazzo, G. (eds.) HSCC 2007. LNCS, vol. 4416, pp. 329–342. Springer, Heidelberg (2007)
15. Kuffner, J., LaValle, S.: RRT-connect: An efficient approach to single-query path planning. In: Proc. IEEE Int'l Conf. on Robotics and Automation (ICRA 2000), San Francisco, CA (April 2000)
16. LaValle, S., Kuffner, J.: Rapidly-exploring random trees: Progress and prospects. In: Workshop on the Algorithmic Foundations of Robotics (2000)
17. Mcinn, P.: Search-based Software Test Data Generation: A Survey: Research Articles. Softw. Test. Verif. Reliab. 14(2), 105–156
18. Plaku, E., Kavraki, L.E., Vardi, M.Y.: Hybrid systems: From verification to falsification. In: Damm, W., Hermanns, H. (eds.) CAV 2007. LNCS, vol. 4590, pp. 463–476. Springer, Heidelberg (2007)
19. Plaku, E., Kavraki, L.E., Vardi, M.Y.: Hybrid Systems: From Verification to Falsification by Combining Motion Planning and Discrete Search. Formal Methods in System Design 34(2), 157–182 (2009)
20. Sankaranarayanan, S., Fainekos, G.: Falsification of Temporal Properties of Hybrid Systems Using the Cross-Entropy Method. In: Proceedings of the ACM International Conference on Hybrid Systems: Computation and Control, Beijing, China (April 2012)
21. Thiémard, E.: An algorithm to compute bounds for the star discrepancy. J. Complexity 17(4), 850–880 (2001)
22. Winker, P., Fang, K.: Application of Threshold-Accepting to the Evaluation of the Discrepancy of a Set of Points. SIAM Journal on Numerical Analysis 34, 2028–2042 (1997)

On Time with Minimal Expected Cost!

Alexandre David[1], Peter G. Jensen[1], Kim Guldstrand Larsen[1], Axel Legay[2],
Didier Lime[3], Mathias Grund Sørensen[1], and Jakob H. Taankvist[1]

[1] Aalborg University, Denmark
[2] INRIA Rennes, France
[3] École Centrale de Nantes, IRCCyN, Nantes, France
{adavid,kgl}@cs.aau.dk, {pgje09,mgso09,jtaank09}@student.aau.dk,
axel.legay@inria.fr, didier.lime@irccyn.ec-nantes.fr

Abstract. (Priced) timed games are two-player quantitative games involving an environment assumed to be completely antogonistic. Classical analysis consists in the synthesis of strategies ensuring safety, time-bounded or cost-bounded reachability objectives. Assuming a randomized environment, the (priced) timed game essentially defines an infinite-state Markov (reward) decision proces. In this setting the objective is classically to find a strategy that will minimize the expected reachability cost, but with no guarantees on worst-case behaviour. In this paper, we provide efficient methods for computing reachability strategies that will both ensure worst case time-bounds *as well as* provide (near-) minimal expected cost. Our method extends the synthesis algorithms of the synthesis tool UPPAAL-TIGA with suitable adapted reinforcement learning techniques, that exhibits several orders of magnitude improvements w.r.t. previously known automated methods.

1 Motivation

Sparse time and resources are common problems to projects in almost any domain, ranging from manufacturing to office work-flow and program parallelization. In a real world setting, the duration of a process is dependent on the tasks it is composed of. The durations and arrival pattern of tasks are not static, but uncertain by nature. Furthermore, tasks are often solved by different agents running in parallel, creating races for shared resources. A scheduler is needed to handle these conflict situations.

The above type of scheduling problem may conveniently be represented as a timed game (TG) [27], being a two-player quantitative game involving an adversary (modeling the environment – here the tasks) which is assumed to be completely antagonistic. Classical analysis consists in the synthesis of strategies ensuring safety or time-bounded reachability objectives. In all cases, decidability for TGs are obtained from the existence of equivalent finite-state games constructed using the classical notion of regions for timed automata [3]. Moreover, efficient symbolic on-the-fly algorithms using have been developed and implemented as found in UPPAAL-TIGA [4]. The assignment of resources to tasks incurs a cost – e.g. energy-consumption. This naturally leads to the extended

F. Cassez and J.-F. Raskin (Eds.): ATVA 2014, LNCS 8837, pp. 129–145, 2014.

setting of *priced* timed games [10,11] (PTG), for which – unfortunately – the corresponding synthesis problem of cost-bounded reachability strategies is undecidable in general [13], with the one-clock case being a notable exception [11].

Now, assuming a randomized environment – e.g. where the duration of tasks are stochastic – the (priced) timed game essentially defines an infinite-state Markov (reward) decision process, here named (priced) timed Markov decision processes (PTMDP). In this setting the objective is to find a strategy that will minimize the expected reachability cost, but with no guarantees on worst-case behavior.

In this paper, we provide efficient methods for synthesizing reachability strategies for PTMDPs that subject to guaranteeing a given worst case time-bound, will provide (near-) minimal expected reachability cost.

Assume a (deterministic) strategy has been synthesized guaranteeing a given time-bound, we may – as a first attempt – apply statistical model checking as found in UPPAAL SMC [16], to estimate the expected reachability cost in the (priced) timed game under the given strategy. Statistical model checking [26] is a highly scalable technique which achieves its estimates by random sampling of runs, the number of which depending on the desired precision and confidence. However, there may be several strategies guaranteeing the given time-bound and we want the one with minimal expected reachability cost. For this much more ambitious goal, we apply suitable adapted reinforcement learning techniques: starting from a uniformized version of the *most permissive* strategy guaranteeing the given time bound, the learning technique iteratively improves the strategy – by observing the effect of control-choices in sampled runs – until a strategy with satisfactory expected reachability-cost is found. Crucial to the efficiency of our simulation-based synthesis method is the effective and space-efficient representation and manipulation of strategies. Besides the symbolic (zone-based) representation used for TGs, we consider a number of techniques well-known from Machine Intelligence (covariance matrices, logistic regression) as well as a new splitting data-structure of ours. The resulting method is implemented in a new version of UPPAAL-TIGA that supports the statistical model-checking techniques of UPPAAL. The experimental evaluation has been performed on a large collection of job-shop-like problems (so-called Duration Probabilistic Automata) demonstrating several order or magnitude improvements with respect to previous exact synthesis methods [22].

Example. Consider the PTMDP of Fig. 1 modeling a process consisting of a sequence of two uncontrollable steps (indicated by dashed edges), r, d, with a possible control action (indicated by full edges), a, b, w being taken after the first step. The first step r is taken between 0 and 100 time-units according to a uniform distribution[1] as can be seen by the invariant x<=100 and the absent guard, and with cost-rate c'==0. In the next step, the controller may suggest to play any of the time-action pairs (d, a), (d, b) with $d \leq 100$ or $(100, w)$. These

---

[1] Following the stochastic semantics for timed automata components applied in UPPAAL SMC.

will be in competition with the uniformly distributed choices of the environment $(e, \mathbf{d})$ with $e \in [90, 100]$. It is clear that in terms of worst-case time, the best choice for the controller is $(100, \mathbf{w})$ with 200 as worst-case overall time. In contrast, the worst choice for the controller is $(100, \mathbf{b})$ with 340 as worst-case time.

For expected cost, the optimal and worst choices are $(0, \mathbf{b})$ respectively $(90, \mathbf{a})$ with $2 * 80 = 160$ respectively $4 * 90 + 3 * 90 = 630$ as expected remaining reachability cost due to the uniform distributions resolving the delays. Thus, in case there is no upper time bound to be guaranteed (or it is above 240) the cost-optimal strategy will be to choose $\mathbf{b}$ immediately, yielding an expected cost of 160.

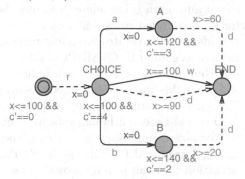

Fig. 1. A Priced Timed MDP

Now assume that the END location must be reached within an upper time-bound of 210. The on-the-fly method of UPPAAL-TIGA (exploiting early termination) may (in fact will) produce the strategy which deterministically chooses $(100, \mathbf{w})$. This clearly meets the given upper time-bound, and yields an expected reachability cost of $4 * 95 = 380$. The most permissive strategy guaranteeing the time-bound 210 (also obtainable by UPPAAL-TIGA) will have the choice depend on the time-point t when CHOICE is reached: if $t > 90$ only $(100, \mathbf{w})$ is a legal choice; if $70 < t \leq 90$ also $(d, \mathbf{a})$ with $d \leq 90 - t$ are legal choices, and finally if $t \leq 70$ also $(e, \mathbf{b})$ with $e \leq 70 - t$ are legal. The strategy with minimal expected reachability cost while guaranteeing the time-bound 210, will (obviously) deterministically make the "cheapest" legal choice for a given value of t, i.e. $(100, \mathbf{w})$ for $t > 90$, $(0, \mathbf{a})$ when $70 < t \leq 90$, and $(0, \mathbf{b})$ when $t \leq 70$. This yields 204 as minimum expected value

Related Work. A number of models combining continuous time and Markov decision processes have previously been proposed. We mention some of these below, and point out that they are all special cases of our proposed PTMDP formalism.

Probabilistic timed automata (PrTA) [21,24] extends the fully non-deterministic formalism of timed automata with probabilistic resolution of discrete choices, thus providing an infinite-state MDP with choices of dealys to be resolved by the strategy. Decidability for PrTA w.r.t. optimal (minimum and maximum) reachability probabilities as well as general model checking with respect to PCTL are obtained using region-constructions. Tool support for analysis of PrTAs are provided in PRISM [23]. More recently, cost-bounded reachability for priced extensions of PrTAs has been considered, showing undecidability for more than 3 clocks [6] and with the semi-decision algorithmic based tool FORTUNA [7].

Continuous-time Markov decision processes (CTMDPs) are also special cases of PTMDPs, where the delay choice of the environment is always made according to exponential distributions, and with choices of the strategy being instantaneous. In the setting of CTMDPs a number of bounded reachability synthesis problems has been recently addressed. In [19] multi-dimensional maximal cost-bounded reachability probability over CTMDPs are considered, offering a numerical approximation algorithm. In [8] a marriage of CTMDPs with timed automata is considered showing the existence of finite optimal schedulers for time-bounded reachability objectives. In [12], stochastic real-time games are considered where states are partitioned into environment nodes - where the behaviour is similar to CTMDPs - and control nodes - where one player chooses a distribution over actions, which induces a probability distribution for the next state. For this game model, objectives are given by deterministic timed automata (DTA), with results focusing on qualitative properties.

Our real-time synthesis problem – aiming at optimal expected cost subject to worst-case time bounds – extends the notion of *beyond* worst-case synthesis in [14] introduced for finite state MDPs, with consideration of minimizing expectation of mean-payoff (shown to be in NP∩coNP) as well reachability cost (shown to be NP-hard). The DPA formalisms considered in [22] is a proper subclass of PTMDP of this paper. In [22] exact methods for synthesizing strategies with minimal expected completion time are given and implemented. However, no worst-case guarantees are considered. As we shall demonstrate our reinforcement learning method produces identical solutions and with an order of magnitude time-improvement. [25] uses a version of Kearns algorithm to find a memoryless scheduler for expecting reward, however with no implementation provided, and no real-time consideration. Our use of statistical model checking for learning optimal strategies of PTMDPs extends that of [20] from finite-state MDPs to the setting of timed game automata based, infinite state MDPs requiring the use of symbolic strategies. Finally, statistical model checking has been used for confluent MDPs in [9].

2   Priced Timed Markov Decision Processes

Priced Timed Games [27] are two-player games played on (priced) timed automata [3,5]. Here we recall the basic results. Let $X = \{x, y, ...\}$ be a finite set of clock. We define $\mathcal{B}(X)$ as the set of clock constraints over X generated by grammar: $g, g_1, g_2 ::= x \bowtie n \mid x - y \bowtie n \mid g_1 \wedge g_2$, where $x, y \in X$ are clocks, $n \in \mathbb{N}$ and $\bowtie \in \{\leq, <, =, >, \geq\}$.

Definition 1. *A* Priced Timed Automaton *(PTA)* $\mathcal{A} = (L, \ell_0, X, \Sigma, E, P, Inv)$ *is a tuple where L is a finite set of locations, $\ell_0 \in L$ is the initial location, X is a finite set of non-negative real-valued clocks, Σ is a finite set of actions, $E \subseteq L \times \mathcal{B}(X) \times \Sigma \times 2^X \times L$ is a finite set of edges, $P : L \to \mathbb{N}$ assigns a price-rate to each location, and $Inv : L \to \mathcal{B}(X)$ sets an invariant for each location.*

The semantics of a PTA $\mathcal{A}$ is a *priced transition system* $S_{\mathcal{A}} = (Q, q_0, \Sigma, \to)$, where the set of states Q consists of pairs (ℓ, v) with $\ell \in L$ and $v \in \mathbb{R}_{\geq 0}^X$ such that $v \models Inv(\ell)\}$, and $q_0 = (\ell_0, 0)$ is the initial state. Σ is a finite set of actions, and $\to \subseteq Q \times (\Sigma \cup \mathbb{R}_{\geq 0}) \times \mathbb{R}_{\geq 0} \times Q$ is the priced transition relation defined separately for action $a \in \Sigma$ and delay $d \in \mathbb{R}_{\geq 0}$ as:

- $(\ell, v) \xrightarrow{a}_0 (\ell', v')$ if there is an edge $(\ell \xrightarrow{g,\alpha,r} \ell') \in E$ such that $v \models g$, $v' = v[r \mapsto 0]$ and $v' \models Inv(\ell')$,
- $(\ell, v) \xrightarrow{d}_p (\ell, v + d)$, where $p = P(\ell) \cdot d$, $v \models Inv(\ell)$ and $v + d \models Inv(\ell)$.

Thus, the price of an action-transition is 0, whereas the price of a delay transition is proportional to the delay according to the price-rate of the given location. We shall omit price-subscripts when the actual price do not matter. We shall assume that $S_{\mathcal{A}}$ is *deterministic* in the sense that any state $q \in Q$ has at most one successor q^α for any action or delay $\alpha \in (\Sigma \cup \mathbb{R}_{\geq 0})$. A *run* of a PTA $\mathcal{A}$ is an alternating sequence of priced action and delay transitions of its priced transition system $S_{\mathcal{A}}$: $\pi = q_0 \xrightarrow{d_0}_{p_0} q'_0 \xrightarrow{a_0}_0 q_1 \xrightarrow{d_1}_{p_1} q'_1 \xrightarrow{a_1}_0 \cdots \xrightarrow{d_{n-1}}_{p_{n-1}} q'_{n-1} \xrightarrow{a_{n-1}}_0$ $q_n \cdots$, where $a_i \in \Sigma$, $d_i, p_i \in \mathbb{R}_{\geq 0}$, and q_i is a state (ℓ_{q_i}, v_{q_i}). We denote the set of runs of $\mathcal{A}$ as $Exec_{\mathcal{A}}$, and $Exec_{\mathcal{A}}^f$ ($Exec_{\mathcal{A}}^m$) for the set of its finite (maximal) runs. For a run π we denote by $\pi[i]$ the state q_i, and by $\pi|_i$ ($\pi|^i$) the prefix (suffix) of π ending (starting) at q_i. For a finite run π, $C(\pi)$ denotes its total accumulated cost $\sum_{i=0}^{n-1} p_i$. Similarly $T(\pi)$ denotes the total accumulated time $\sum_{i=0}^{n-1} d_i$. An infinite run π is said to be cost-divergent provided $\lim_{n \to \infty} \sum_{i=0}^{n-1} p_i = +\infty$. We say that $\mathcal{A}$ is (cost-) non-Zeno provided every infinite run is time-(cost-)divergent.

Definition 2. *A Priced Timed Game $\mathcal{G}$ (PTG) is a PTA whose actions Σ are partitioned into controllable (Σ_c) and uncontrollable (Σ_u) actions.*

We note, that for PTAs and PTGs with $P(\ell) = 1$ in all locations ℓ, we obtain standard timed automata (TA) and timed games (TG). Given a (P)TG $\mathcal{G}$, a set of goal-locations $G \subseteq L$ and a cost- (time-) bound $B \in \mathbb{R}_{\geq 0}$, the (G, B) *cost- (time-) bounded reachability control problem* for $\mathcal{G}$ consists in finding a *strategy* σ that will enforce G to be reached within accumulated cost (time) B. Informally, a strategy σ decides to continue a run π either by a proposed controllable action $a \in \Sigma_c$ or by a delay - indicated by the symbol λ. The formal definition of this control problem is based on definitions of *strategy* and *outcome*.

Definition 3. *A strategy σ over a PTG $\mathcal{G}$ is a partial function from $Exec_{\mathcal{G}}^f$ to $\mathcal{P}(\Sigma_c \cup \{\lambda\}) \setminus \{\emptyset\}$ such that for any finite run π ending in state $q = last(\pi)$, if $a \in \sigma(\pi) \cap \Sigma_c$, then there must exist a transition $q \xrightarrow{a} q'$ in $S_{\mathcal{G}}$.*

Given a PTG $\mathcal{G}$ and a strategy σ over $\mathcal{G}$, the outcome $Out(\sigma)$ is the subset of $Exec_{\mathcal{G}}$ defined inductively by $q_0 \in Out(\sigma)$, and:

- If $\pi \in Out(\sigma)$ then $\pi' = \pi \xrightarrow{e} q' \in Out(\sigma)$ if $\pi' = Excel_{\mathcal{G}}$ and either one of the following three conditions hold:
  1. $e \in \Sigma_u$, or
  2. $e \in \Sigma_c$ and $e \in \sigma(\pi)$, or
  3. $e \in \mathbb{R}_{\geq 0}$ and for all $e' < e$, $last(\pi) \xrightarrow{e'} q'$ for some q' s.t. $\sigma(\pi \xrightarrow{e'} q') \ni \lambda$.

Let (G, B) be a cost- (time-) bounded reachability objective for $\mathcal{G}$. We say that a maximal, finite run π is *winning* w.r.t. (G, B), if $last(\pi) \in G \times \mathbb{R}_{\geq 0}^X$ and

$C(\pi) \leq B$. A strategy σ over $\mathcal{G}$ is a *winning strategy* if all runs in $Out(\sigma)$ are winning (w.r.t. (G, B)).

A *memoryless strategy* σ only depends on the last state of a run, e.g. whenever $last(\pi) = last(\pi')$, then $\sigma(\pi) = \sigma(\pi')$. For unbounded reachability and safety objectives for TGs, memoryless strategies suffices [27], For TGs with an additional clock `time`, which is never reset (here named *clocked* TGs), memoryless strategies even suffices for time-bounded reachability objectives.

The notion of strategy in Def. 3 is non-deterministic, thus inducing a natural order of *permissiveness*: $\sigma \preceq \sigma'$ iff $\sigma(\pi) \subseteq \sigma'(\pi)$ for any finite run π. *Deterministic* strategies – returning singleton-sets for each run – are least permissive. For safety objectives – being maximal fixed-points – strategies are closed under point-wise union, yielding (unique) *most permissive strategies*. For TGs being non-Zeno, time-bounded reachability objectives *are* safety properties.

Theorem 1. *Let $\mathcal{G}$ be a non-Zeno, clocked TG. If a time-bounded reachability objective (G, T) has a winning strategy, then it has (a) deterministic, memoryless winning strategies, and (b) a (unique) most permissive, memoryless winning strategy $\sigma_{\mathcal{G}}^p(G, T)$.*

The tool UPPAAL-TIGA [4] provides on-the-fly, symbolic (zone-based) algorithms for computing both types of memoryless safety strategies for TGs. For PTGs, the synthesis problem for cost-bounded reachability problems is in general undecidable [13].

Priced Timed Markov Decision Processes. The definition of outcome of a strategy in the previous Section assumes that an environment behaves completely antagonistically. We will now assume a randomized environment, where the choices of delay and uncontrollable actions are stochastic according to a (delay,action)-density function for a given state.

Definition 4. *A Priced Timed Markov Decision Process (PTMDP) is a pair $\mathcal{M} = \langle \mathcal{G}, \mu^u \rangle$, where $\mathcal{G} = (L, \ell_0, X, \Sigma_c, \Sigma_u, E, P, Inv)$ is a PTG, and μ^u is a family of density-functions, $\{\mu_q^u : \exists \ell \exists v.q = (\ell, v)\}$, with $\mu_q^u(d, u) \in \mathbb{R}_{\geq 0}$ assigning the density of the environment aiming at taking the uncontrollable action $u \in \Sigma_u$ after a delay of d from state q.*

In the above definition, it is tacitly assumed that $\mu_q^u(d, u) > 0$ only if $q \xrightarrow{d,u}$ in $\mathcal{G}$. Also, we shall *wlog* for time-bounded reachability objectives assume that $\sum_u (\int_{t \geq 0} \mu_q^u(t, u) dt) = 1^2$. In case the environment wants to perform an action deterministically after an exact delay d, μ_q^u will involve the use of Dirac delta function (see [15]).

The presence of the stochastic component μ^u makes a PTMDP a de facto infinite state Markov decision process. Here we seek strategies that will minimize the expected accumulated cost of reaching a given goal set G.

---

[2] For a time-bounded reachability objective (G, T), we may without affecting controllability assume that each location has each action (controllable or uncontrollable) action enabled after T.

Definition 5. *A stochastic strategy μ^c for a PTMDP $\mathcal{M} = \langle \mathcal{G}, \mu^u \rangle$ is a family of density-functions, $\{\mu^c_q : \exists \ell \exists v . q = (\ell, v)\}$, with $\mu^c_q(d, c) \in \mathbb{R}_{\geq 0}$ assigning the density of the controller aiming at taking the controllable action $c \in \Sigma_c$ after a delay of d from state q.*

Again it is tacitly assumed that $\mu^c_q(d, c) > 0$ only if $q \xrightarrow{d,c}$ in $\mathcal{G}$. Now, a PTMDP $\mathcal{M} = \langle \mathcal{G}, \mu^u \rangle$ and a stochastic strategy μ^c defines a race between the environment and the control strategy, where the outcome is settled by the two competing density-functions. More precisely, the combination of $\mathcal{M}$ and μ^c defines a probability measure $\mathbb{P}_{\mathcal{M}, \mu^c}$ on (certain) sets of runs.

For $\ell_i \in L$ and $I_i = [l_i, u_i]$ with $l_i, u_i \in \mathbb{Q}$, $i = 0..n$, we denote the *cylinder set* by $\mathcal{C}(q, I_0 \ell_0 I_1 \cdots I_{n-1} \ell_n)$ consisting of all maximal runs having a prefix of the form: $q \xrightarrow{d_0} \xrightarrow{a_0} (\ell_1, v_1) \xrightarrow{d_1} \xrightarrow{a_1} \cdots \xrightarrow{d_{n-1}} \xrightarrow{a_{n-1}} (\ell_n, v_n)$ where $d_i \in I_i$ for all $i < n$. Providing the basis for a σ-algebra, we now inductively define the probability measure for such sets of runs[3]:

$$
\mathbb{P}_{\langle \mathcal{G}, \mu^u \rangle, \mu^c}\big(\mathcal{C}(q, I_0 \ell_0 I_1 \cdots I_{n-1} \ell_n) \big) =
$$
$$
\sum_{\substack{p \in \{u,c\} \\ \ell_q \xrightarrow{a} \ell_1}} \sum_{a \in \Sigma_p} \int_{t \in I_0} \mu^p_q(t, a) \cdot \Big(\int_{\tau > t} \mu^{\bar{p}}_q(\tau) d\tau \Big) \cdot \mathbb{P}_{\langle \mathcal{G}, \mu^u \rangle, \mu^c}\big(\mathcal{C}((q^t)^a, \mathcal{C}(I_1 \cdots I_{n-1} \ell_n) \big) \, dt
$$

The above definition requires a few words of explanation: the outermost sums divide into cases according to who wins the race of the first action (c or u), and which action a the winner will perform. Next, we integrate over all the legal delays the winner may choose according to the given interval I_0 using the relevant density-function. Independently, the non-winning player ($\bar{p}$) must choose a larger delay; hence the product of the probability that this will happen. Finally, the probability of runs according to the remaining cylinder $I_1 \ell_1, \cdots, I_{n-1} \ell_n$ from the new state $(q^t)^a$ is taken into account.

Now let $\pi \in Exec^m$ and let G be as set of goal locations. Then $C_G(\pi) = min\{C(\pi|_i) : \pi[i] \in G\}$ denotes the accumulated cost before π reaches G[4]. Now C_G is a random variable, which for a given stochastic strategy, μ^c, will have expected value $\mathbb{E}^{\mathcal{M}}_{\mu^c}(C_G)$ given by the Lesbegue integral $\int_{\pi \in Exec^m} C_G(\pi) \mathbb{P}_{\mathcal{M}, \mu^c}(d\pi)$. Now, we want a (near-optimal) stochastic strategy μ^o that minimizes this expected value, subject to guaranteeing T as a worst-case reachability time-bound – or alternatively – subject to μ^o being a stochastic refinement ($\prec$[5]) of the most permissive time-bounded reachability strategy $\sigma^p(G, T)$ for $\mathcal{M}$. That is $\mathbb{E}^{\mathcal{M}}_T(C_G) = \inf \big\{ \mathbb{E}^{\mathcal{M}}_{\mu^c}(C_G) \mid \mu^c \prec \sigma^p(G, T) \big\}$. We note that letting μ^c range over deterministic strategies σ^d suffices in attaining $\mathbb{E}^{\mathcal{M}}_T(C_G)$.

---

[3] With the base case, e.g. $n = 0$, being 1.

[4] Note that $C_G(\pi)$ will be infinite in case π does not reach G. However, this case will never happen in our usages.

[5] $\mu^c \prec \sigma$ iff $\mu^c_q(d, a) > 0$ only if $\lambda \in \sigma(q^e)$ for all $e < d$ and $a \in \sigma(q^d)$.

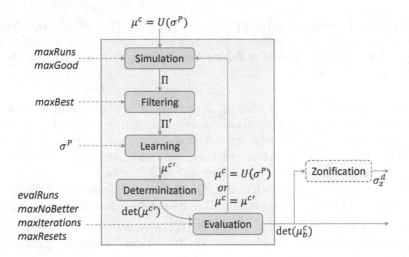

Fig. 2. Optimal scheduler approximation using reinforcement learning

3   Optimal Scheduler Approximation

Given a PTMDP $\mathcal{M}$ and a time-bounded reachability goal (G, T), we present a method for approximating $\mathbb{E}_T^{\mathcal{M}}(C_G)$ by computing a (deterministic) scheduler obtained using reinforced learning. In general, the technique of statistical model-checking (SMC) is used to generate runs according to a given stochastic semantics and then to analyze their outcomes w.r.t some property or expectation. In our context, given a PTMDP $\mathcal{M}$ and stochastic control strategy μ^c, we use SMC to generate runs that are used both to estimate $\mathbb{E}_{\mu^c}^{\mathcal{M}}(C_G)$ and to iteratively improve μ^c towards μ^o. We combine the techniques of UPPAAL-TIGA to guarantee a given time-bound and UPPAAL SMC for expected-cost optimality. The core concept is similar to [20] but differs on the goal of the scheduler. We also differ on the termination criteria since our algorithm can reset itself to get out of local minima. We start with an overview of the procedure:

Figure 2 shows the general flow of the algorithm. The idea is to reinforce a current stochastic strategy representing distributions over controllable actions noted μ^c. This strategy is initialized to a uniform strategy noted $U(\sigma^P)$ based on a most permissive (zone-based) strategy σ^P obtained from UPPAAL-TIGA. This strategy allows all possible moves that still guarantee the controller to meet its goal within the given time-bound. The algorithm reinforces μ^c with $\mu^{c\prime}$ unless $\mu^{c\prime}$ is not improving too many times in a row, in which case it is reset to the initial uniform strategy. When it is improving and it is better than the currently *best* known strategy μ_b^c, then it replaces it. A strategy is better if it exhibits a lower expected cost.

The different steps are detailed as follows. First, the *simulation* step uses UPPAAL SMC to generate at most *maxGood* good runs that are used for learning. To do so, at most *maxRuns* runs in total are generated. The result is a set of runs

Π. It may happen that Π is empty, in which case μ^c is reset and the simulation is restarted. This is not depicted on the figure. Second, the set of runs Π is then *filtered* where at most *maxBest best* runs among those are kept. We retain the subset $\Pi' \subseteq \Pi$ of runs that have minimum cost. In practice this is done with a heap structure to keep a set of *maxBest* runs with their associated costs used for ordering the runs.

Then, central to the algorithm, comes the *learning* phase where the actual algorithm depends on the data structure used to represent μ^c. This phase computes a new $\mu^{c'}$ and we detail in the following section different ways to represent μ^c. Also, the strategy σ^P from UPPAAL-TIGA is used here to ensure that any learned strategy still guarantees the required bound.

The resulting strategy is then *determinized* before being *evaluated*. This step uses UPPAAL SMC again to evaluate the expected time (or cost) for the reinforced strategy $det(\mu^{c'})$ on a number of *evalRuns* runs. The resulting $\mu^{c'}$ may have a lower cost than μ^c, in which case we update μ^c (and possibly the best known strategy μ_b^c if it is better than this one too). However, if $\mu^{c'}$ is not better than μ^c *maxNoBetter* times then we reset it to $\mu^c = U(\sigma^P)$. This makes sure that the reinforcement learning does not get stuck into local minima. Finally, the algorithm loops at most *maxIteration* times if μ^c has been reset no more than *maxResets* times.

When the algorithm stops, the best known deterministic strategy $det(\mu_b^c)$ is outputted. It is then possible to "zonify" the strategy, meaning to approximate it with the zone-based representation σ_z^d used in UPPAAL-TIGA, thus allowing for model checking of additional properties.

4   Strategies: Data Structures, Algorithms and Learning

Non-determistic Strategies. Crucial to our reinforcement learning algorithm Fig. 2 is the efficient representation and manipulation of control strategies. In UPPAAL-TIGA, non-deterministic strategies are represented using zones, e.g. sets Z of valuations described by a guard in $\mathcal{B}(X)$. In a representation R, each location ℓ has an associated finite set $R_\ell = \{(Z_1, a_1), \ldots, (Z_k, a_k)\}$ of zone-action pairs, where $a_i \in \Sigma_c \cup \{\lambda\}$. Now R represents the strategy σ_R where $\sigma_R((\ell, v)) \ni a$ iff $(Z, a) \in R_\ell$ for some Z with $v \in Z$. In UPPAAL-TIGA R is efficiently implemented as a hash-table with the location ℓ as key, and using difference bounded matrices (DBMs) [17] for representing zones.

For a non-deterministic strategy σ and (l, v) a state, we write $(l, v) \xrightarrow{d}_\sigma$ to denote that σ allows a delay of d, i.e. for all $d' < d, \lambda \in \sigma(l, v + d')$. Similarly, we write $(l, v) \xrightarrow{c}_\sigma$ to denote that the controllable action c is allowed, i.e. $c \in \sigma(l, v)$. Uniformization and zonification are operations between non-deterministic and stochastic strategies. *Uniformization* is an operation that refines a non-deterministic strategy σ into a stochastic strategy μ^σ, subject to the condition that $\mu_{(l,v)}^\sigma(d, c) > 0$ if and only if $(l, v) \xrightarrow{d}_\sigma \xrightarrow{c}_\sigma$. Several implementations of uniformization may easily be obtained from the representation of a non-deterministic strategy. Dually, *zonification* is an operation that abstracts a stochastic strategy μ into a non-determistic strategy σ_R, with a zone-based representation R, and subject to the condition that whenever $\mu_{(l,v)}(d,c) > 0$ then $(l,v) \xrightarrow{d}_{\sigma_R} \xrightarrow{c}_{\sigma_R}$.

Stochastic and Non-Lazy Strategies. For stochastic strategies, we shall in the following restrict our attention to so-called *non-lazy* strategies[6], μ^c, where the controller either urgently decides on an action, i.e. $\mu_q^c(d,a) = 0$ if $d > 0$, or prefer to wait until the environment makes a move, i.e. $\mu_{(\ell,v)}^c(d,a) = 0$ whenever $v(\texttt{time}) + d \leq T$ with T being the time-bound of the reachability property in question. We shall use $\texttt{w}$ to denote such an indefinite delay choice. Thus, for non-lazy stochastic strategies, the functionality may be recast as discrete probability distributions, i.e. $\mu_q^c : (\Sigma_c \cup \{\texttt{w}\}) \rightarrow [0,1]$. In particular, we note that any non-lazy, stochastic strategy can trivially be transformed to a deterministic strategy by always selecting the action with the highest probability.

In the following we introduce three different data structuring and learning algorithms for stochastic strategies. Given that memoryless strategies suffices, we will learn a set of sub-strategies $\mu_\ell^c = \{\mu_q^c : \exists v.q = (\ell,v)\}$, where $\ell \in L$. The sub-strategies are then learned solely from a set of *(action,valuation)* pairs. Given a set of runs Π the relevant information for the sub-strategy μ_ℓ^c is given as In_ℓ:

$$In_\ell = \{(s_n,v) \in (\Sigma_c \cup \mathbb{R}) \times \mathbb{R}_{\geq 0}^X \mid (q_0 \xrightarrow{s_0} p_0 \cdots \xrightarrow{s_{n-1}} p_{n-1} (\ell,v) \xrightarrow{s_n} p_n \cdots) \in \Pi\}$$

Thus, in the following we only describe methods for learning sub-strategies.

Sample Mean and Covariance. For each controllable action c and location ℓ, we approximate the set of points representing clock valuations from which that action was successfully taken in ℓ by its sample mean and covariance matrix. Suppose we have N points corresponding to clock valuations $v_1, \ldots, v_N$. The sample mean vector $\overline{v}$ is the arithmetic mean, component-wise, for all the points: $\overline{v} = \frac{1}{N} \sum_{k=1}^{N} v_k$. The sample covariance matrix is defined as the square matrix $Q = [q_{ij}] = \frac{1}{N-1} \sum_{k=1}^{N} (v_k - \overline{v})(v_k - \overline{v})^T$.

Intuitively, if the sample covariance q_{ij} between two clocks x_i and x_j is positive, then bigger (resp. smaller) values of x_i correspond to bigger (resp. smaller) values of x_j. If it is negative, then the bigger (resp. smaller) values of x_i correspond to the smaller (resp. bigger) values of x_j. If it is zero then there is no such relation between the values of those two variables.

Note that the covariance matrix has size n^2 where n is the number of clocks but it is symmetric. Furthermore, for the matrix to be significant we need at least $n(n+1)/2$ sample points that correspond to the number of (potentially) different elements in the matrix, otherwise we default to using only the mean vector.

---

[6] In [22] it is shown that non-lazy strategies suffices for optimal scheduling of so-called DPAs.

Distribution. The purpose of this representation is to derive a distance from an arbitrary point to this "set" that is used to compute a weight for each controllable action. For a given valuation, such a distance $d(v)$ is evaluated as follows: $d(v)^2 = (u-\overline{v})^T Q^{-1}(u-\overline{v})$. If there are too few sample points then we default to using the Euclidian distance to the mean $\overline{v}$. The weight is then given by $w(v) = N \cdot e^{-d(v)}$. The weights for the different actions define a probability distribution.

Algorithm and Complexity. When generating runs using SMC, controllable actions are chosen according to the represented distribution that is initialized to be uniform. The time complexity is $O(n^2)$, n being the number of clocks. For the learning phase, the covariance matrix is computed using the filtered "best" samples. Then we need to invert it (once) before the next learning phase. The time complexity is $O(n^3)$. This is done for every action.

Logistic Regression. We consider a sub strategy μ_ℓ^c where the only options are either to take a transition (a) or wait until the environment takes a transition (w) (the case with more options is addressed later). The goal is to learn the weights $\beta_0, \beta_1, \ldots, \beta_{|X|} \in \mathbb{R}$ to use in the logistic function: Equation 4.

$$f(v) = \frac{1}{1 + e^{-(\beta_0 + \beta_1 \cdot v(x_1) + \cdots + \beta_{|X|} \cdot v(x_{|X|}))}},$$

where $x_1, \ldots, x_{|X|} \in X$. This function, combined with the learned weights $\beta_0, \beta_1, \ldots, \beta_{|X|}$, defines a stochastic sub-strategy s.t. $\mu_{(\ell,v)}^c(a) = f(v)$ and $\mu_{(\ell,v)}^c(w) = 1 - f(v)$. Using Figure 3 we here give an intuition on how, given an input set In_ℓ, we learn the weights $\beta_0, \ldots, \beta_{|X|}$ (for details, see [18]). We assume that there exists only two options (a and w) in the location ℓ, and (for simplicity and *wlog*) a single clock in the system. For each input $(s_n, v) \in In_\ell$:

- If $s_n = a$, construct a point at $(v(x), 1)$ where $x \in X$ is the clock. These are the triangles in Figure 3.
- Otherwise, construct a point at $(v(x), 0)$ where $x \in X$ is the clock. These are the circles in Figure 3.

We use L1-regularized logistic regression provided by LIBLINEAR [18] for fitting the function to the constructed points. The output of this process is the weights $\beta_0, \beta_1, \ldots, \beta_{|X|}$ and the result is shown in Figure 3. In the case of more than two options (e.g. if we also had an action b) we use the one-versus-all method. This method learns a function for each action[7].

Complexity. The complexity of fitting the points using this method is $O(|In_\ell| + i)$ [29], where i is the number of iterations before the fitting algorithm converges thus for multiple actions, the complexity for learning is $O(c \cdot (|In_\ell| + i))$ where c is the number of options. We need to store $c \cdot |X|$ weights per location, this is the space complexity.

---

[7] If e.g. we have three actions, a, b and w, we will learn three functions, one which is a versus b and w, one which is b versus a and w, and one which is w versus a and b.

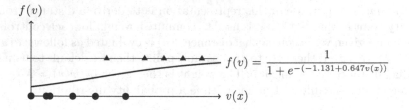

$f(v)$

$$f(v) = \frac{1}{1 + e^{-(-1.131 + 0.647v(x))}}$$

$v(x)$

Fig. 3. Example of logistic regression with one clock x and two options a and w. For valuation v, $f(v)$ gives the probability of selecting action a (triangle) and $1 - f(v)$ gives the probability of selecting action w (circle). The probabilities are equal at $v(x) = 1.747$ because $f(0.5) = 1.747$.

Splitting. Here we represent a sub-strategy as a binary tree, where an internal node is a four-tuple $(x, s, low, high)$, where low and $high$ are either internal nodes or leaf nodes, $x \in X$ is the clock we split on and $s \in \mathbb{R}_{>0}$ is the discriminating value for the clock. A leaf node is a function W mapping actions, a, from $\Sigma_c \cup \{w\}$ to weights, $W(a) \in \mathbb{R}_{>0}$. Figure 4 shows an example of a tree with a splitting for the clock x at value 2. For a given clock valuation v, the tree is traversed to the leaf node W to which it "belongs", with W represented by the pairs $(a, W(a))$ with $W(a) > 0$. This defines a stochastic sub-strategy μ_ℓ^c s.t. $\mu_{\ell,v}^c(a) = W(a)/\sum_{b \in \Sigma_c \cup \{w\}} W(b)$ for all $a \in \Sigma_c \cup \{w\}$. Initially, the tree consists of only a single leaf node assigning weight 1 to all actions. In each iteration of the learning algorithm presented in Section 3, a percentage of the leaf nodes are split on one clock according to the following algorithm:

1. *Select nodes to split.* Given a set In_ℓ, count how many of these did not perform the action with the highest weight in the corresponding leaf node. The leaf nodes over all locations with the highest counts are chosen for splitting, the remaining have their weights updated using reinforced learning.
2. *Select clock to split on.* For each node to split:
   (a) Let In_l^n be the runs from In_l which satisfy the constraints of the tree, to this leaf node.
   (b) For every clock $x \in X$:
      i. Find the minimum and maximum $v(x)$ where $(s_n, v) \in In_l^n$ and call the average of these two s.
      ii. In the set $\{(s_n, v) \in In_\ell^n \mid v(x) \leq s\}$ count for each $a \in \Sigma_c \cup \{w\}$ how many runs choose a. Insert these points in a vector. Make a corresponding vector for the set $\{(s_n, v) \in In_\ell^n \mid v(x) > s\}$.
      iii. Compute Euclidean distance of the vectors.
3. *Update tree.* For clock x and split s with largest Euclidian distance, split the leaf node by replacing the node itself with internal node $(x, s, low, high)$ where low and $high$ are new leaf nodes. Compute weights using reinforced learning for the new leaf nodes.

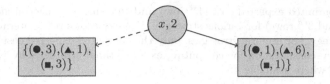

Fig. 4. A binary tree with a splitting on clock x and value 2

Complexity. The complexity of step 1 is $O(nl \cdot |\Pi|)$ where nl is the current number of leafs in the tree, and Π is the number of good runs in the batch. The complexity of step 2 is $O(nl \cdot |X| \cdot |\Pi|)$ and the complexity of step 3 is $O(|\Pi|)$. This means the complete complexity of the whole learning is $O(nl \cdot |X| \cdot |\Pi|)$. In step 1 we select a percentage of the clocks to split on, thus the space complexity of this method is exponential in the worst case, however we bound this by not allowing splitting a leaf on a clock with a range shorter than a predefined (small) constant.

5 Experiments

We now present experiments for evaluating the algorithms proposed in Section 4. Table 1 shows a selection of results. The results are elaborated in the following sections. The full set of results will be available in a full version of this paper to be found on arXiv.org of Cornell University. In each of the experiments, we use 2000 runs pr. iteration. We have evaluated the learned strategies using UPPAAL SMC, also with 2000 runs.

Small Examples. The first row in Table 1 shows the statistics for the motivational example in Figure 1, for obtaining the optimal strategy w.r.t. expected cost under the constraint that END is guaranteed to be reached within 210 time units. Recall from Section 1 that the optimal expected cost for this case is 204. An optimal strategy according to SMC is found using all the methods, achieving an expected cost very close to the optimal expected cost.

The second row shows the statistics for a Go-To-Work example from [14]. We first use UPPAAL-TIGA to ensure that you are guaranteed to get to work in 60 time units and then minimize the expected *time* for going to work under this constraint. The three different methods find strategies with the same expected time, the splitting is the fastest and uses slightly less memory than the others.

Duration Probabilistic Automata. In Section 1, we initially mentioned a type of scheduling problems where tasks have uncertainty in execution time and depends no an amount of resources. This class of job-shop-like scheduling problems can be represented as Duration Probabilistic Automata (DPAs) [22]. A DPA is a multiset of resources and a set of Simple Duration Probabilistic Automata (SDPAs). An SDPA is a series of tasks which cannot be executed in parallel, be preempted and must be executed according to some order. Each task requires a multiset of resources and has a uniformly distributed duration with a

Table 1. Computed expected cost (1st row) and time/memory consumption for synthesis (2nd and 3rd rows) for various strategies. 4th row shows resets/iterations to find optimal strategy. For uniform strategies, only the computed expected cost is reported. Time/memory consumption for computing exact optimal strategies by Kempf et al. [22] reported where available.

Model	Uniform	Co-variance	Splitting	Regression	Exact [22]
Motivational	404.299	205.169	206.328	203.721	
example		33.78s	30.55s	42.61s	
		8.17MB	15.79MB	8.46MB	
		2/82	4/109	1/52	
	38.64	32.69	32.81	32.81	
GoWork		9.8s	24.41s	14.18s	
		7.96MB	8.38MB	8.08MB	
		5/72	0/10	4/71	
	18.08	17.53	17.34	17.38	
p0s3p1s4_4		28.84s	27.06s	51.92s	1062.77s
		8.75MB	17.25MB	8.88MB	145.47MB
		3/54	3/40	2/58	
	18.56	17.75	16.90	16.83	
p0s3p1s4_16		36.67s	46.13s	69.51s	176.15s
		8.63MB	14.38MB	9.07MB	35.60MB
		6/119	0/22	0/27	
	19.90	19.27	19.21	19.27	
p0s4p1s4_5		45.91s	47.1s	60.11s	8547.52s
		9.03MB	26.11MB	9.23MB	486.92MB
		1/31	3/86	5/115	
	3946.76	2213.35	2303.47	2218.34	
ran-4-3		196.19s	242.7s	330.64s	
		19.65MB	124.06MB	20.28MB	
		2/59	1/37	3/141	
	8068.02	4111.77	4221.75	3641.61	
ran-4-4		323.35s	281.58s	459.08s	
		34.46MB	167.66MB	28.88MB	
		5/190	6/159	5/194	
	3965.73	2765.19	2780.45	2765.77	
tiga-ran-4-3		230.06s	351.45s	337.39s	
		17.44MB	127.10MB	25.23MB	
		4/88	5/165	6/164	
	8058.78	6343.45	6307.29	6358.3	
tiga-ran-4-4		262.09s	323.7s	270.93s	
		26.37MB	170.63MB	20.76MB	
		2/32	5/121	2/30	

given time-interval. The DPA scheduling problem is now: given a configuration of an DPA, which SDPA should be allocated which resources at what time in order to minimize expected completion time? For this scheduling problem, Kempf et al. [22] provide a method for exact optimal scheduler synthesis under uncertainty. We will use their results as a benchmark. Poulsen et al. [28] provides a method for translating DPA into TAs with a uniform scheduler, it is trivial to adapt this for translating DPAs into PTMPDs.

Qualitative Comparison. Rows 3-5 show the statistics of obtaining the optimal strategy for three small models (2 processes, 2 tasks) from Kemp et al. [22][8] using our approach. If we examine the synthesized strategies, we see that these are in fact the same strategies as those found using the exact computation (with decision boundaries located within 0.5 time units of the optimal boundaries). We also observe that even though an optimal strategy is found, this does not affect the expected time significantly. Furthermore, the exact computation of [22] for these models took between 176 − 8547 seconds, whereas our method synthesize optimal strategies in less than 70 seconds in each case, thus an order of magnitude faster and less memory-consuming.

Scalability Comparison. For testing the method on larger models, we randomly generate a number of larger DPAs (3-5 processes, 3-5 tasks). On two of these DPAs we first ran UPPAAL-TIGA to find the best possible worst case time guarantee (rows 8, 9 in Table 1). Then on all four (rows 6 − 9 in Table 1) we ran the three different methods to synthesize a strategy with near-minimal expected completion-cost subject to the possible time-bound guarantee.

Generally we observe, that it is specific to the example which method performs the best. We observe that all three methods are able to learn a strategy which is significantly better than the uniformly random strategy. We see that in the examples, where we constrain the allowed strategies using UPPAAL-TIGA only little overhead is incurred, but the strategy we learn does not improve as much as otherwise. This is natural as UPPAAL-TIGA constrain the choices we are allowed to learn.

6   Conclusion and Future Works

In this paper, we have presented a new technique that combines classical controller synthesis with reinforcement learning to compute strategies that provide near optimal expected cost *and* time-bound guarantees. Our experiments show very good results on the class of DPA models. The framework presented is general and not limited to neither DPAs or PTMDPs. In particular, if a time-bound is not required then we can omit the UPPAAL-TIGA step and apply our technique to hybrid MDPs by utilizing UPPAAL SMC's support for stochastic hybrid systems [15]. Future works include developing suitable data structures for more general classes of strategies than non-lazy ones. Though our method is guaranteed to converge to the optimal strategy (under the assumption of non-lazyness), it would be usefull if an estimation of how close a given proposed solution is to the optimal one. However, given the difficulty in obtaining such error-bounds in much simpler cases such as job-shop and task-graph scheduling [2,1], we believe that this will be very difficult.

---

[8] Models and results available
    at http://www-verimag.imag.fr/PROJECTS/TEMPO/DATA/201304_dpa/

References

1. Abdeddaïm, Y., Kerbaa, A., Maler, O.: Task graph scheduling using timed automata. In: IPDPS, p. 237. IEEE Computer Society (2003)
2. Abdeddaïm, Y., Maler, O.: Job-shop scheduling using timed automata. In: Berry, G., Comon, H., Finkel, A. (eds.) CAV 2001. LNCS, vol. 2102, pp. 478–492. Springer, Heidelberg (2001)
3. Alur, R., Dill, D.L.: A theory of timed automata. Theor. Comput. Sci. 126(2), 183–235 (1994)
4. Behrmann, G., Cougnard, A., David, A., Fleury, E., Larsen, K.G., Lime, D.: UPPAAL-Tiga: Time for playing games! In: Damm, W., Hermanns, H. (eds.) CAV 2007. LNCS, vol. 4590, pp. 121–125. Springer, Heidelberg (2007)
5. Behrmann, G., Fehnker, A., Hune, T., Larsen, K.G., Pettersson, P., Romijn, J., Vaandrager, F.W.: Minimum-cost reachability for priced timed automata. In: Di Benedetto, M.D., Sangiovanni-Vincentelli, A.L. (eds.) HSCC 2001. LNCS, vol. 2034, pp. 147–161. Springer, Heidelberg (2001)
6. Berendsen, J., Chen, T., Jansen, D.N.: Undecidability of cost-bounded reachability in priced probabilistic timed automata. In: Chen, J., Cooper, S.B. (eds.) TAMC 2009. LNCS, vol. 5532, pp. 128–137. Springer, Heidelberg (2009)
7. Berendsen, J., Jansen, D.N., Vaandrager, F.W.: Fortuna: Model checking priced probabilistic timed automata. In: QEST, pp. 273–281. IEEE Computer Society (2010)
8. Bertrand, N., Schewe, S.: Playing optimally on timed automata with random delays. In: Jurdziński, M., Ničković, D. (eds.) FORMATS 2012. LNCS, vol. 7595, pp. 43–58. Springer, Heidelberg (2012)
9. Bogdoll, J., Hartmanns, A., Hermanns, H.: Simulation and statistical model checking for modestly nondeterministic models. In: Schmitt, J.B. (ed.) MMB & DFT 2012. LNCS, vol. 7201, pp. 249–252. Springer, Heidelberg (2012)
10. Bouyer, P., Cassez, F., Fleury, E., Larsen, K.G.: Synthesis of optimal strategies using hytech. Electr. Notes Theor. Comput. Sci. 119(1), 11–31 (2005)
11. Bouyer, P., Larsen, K.G., Markey, N., Rasmussen, J.I.: Almost optimal strategies in one clock priced timed games. In: Arun-Kumar, S., Garg, N. (eds.) FSTTCS 2006. LNCS, vol. 4337, pp. 345–356. Springer, Heidelberg (2006)
12. Brázdil, T., Krcál, J., Kretínský, J., Kucera, A., Rehák, V.: Measuring performance of continuous-time stochastic processes using timed automata. In: Caccamo, M., Frazzoli, E., Grosu, R. (eds.) HSCC, pp. 33–42. ACM (2011)
13. Brihaye, T., Bruyère, V., Raskin, J.F.: On optimal timed strategies. In: Pettersson, P., Yi, W. (eds.) FORMATS 2005. LNCS, vol. 3829, pp. 49–64. Springer, Heidelberg (2005)
14. Bruyère, V., Filiot, E., Randour, M., Raskin, J.F.: Meet your expectations with guarantees: Beyond worst-case synthesis in quantitative games. In: Mayr, E.W., Portier, N. (eds.) STACS. LIPIcs, vol. 25, pp. 199–213. Schloss Dagstuhl - Leibniz-Zentrum fuer Informatik (2014)
15. David, A., Du, D., Larsen, K.G., Legay, A., Mikucionis, M., Poulsen, D.B., Sedwards, S.: Statistical model checking for stochastic hybrid systems. In: Bartocci, E., Bortolussi, L. (eds.) HSB. EPTCS, vol. 92, pp. 122–136 (2012)
16. David, A., Larsen, K.G., Legay, A., Mikučionis, M., Wang, Z.: Time for statistical model checking of real-time systems. In: Gopalakrishnan, G., Qadeer, S. (eds.) CAV 2011. LNCS, vol. 6806, pp. 349–355. Springer, Heidelberg (2011)

17. Dill, D.L.: Timing assumptions and verification of finite-state concurrent systems. In: Sifakis, J. (ed.) CAV 1989. LNCS, vol. 407, pp. 197–212. Springer, Heidelberg (1990)

18. Fan, R.E., Chang, K.W., Hsieh, C.J., Wang, X.R., Lin, C.J.: LIBLINEAR: A library for large linear classification. Journal of Machine Learning Research 9, 1871–1874 (2008)

19. Fu, H.: Maximal cost-bounded reachability probability on continuous-time markov decision processes. In: Muscholl, A. (ed.) FOSSACS 2014. LNCS, vol. 8412, pp. 73–87. Springer, Heidelberg (2014)

20. Henriques, D., Martins, J., Zuliani, P., Platzer, A., Clarke, E.: Statistical model checking for markov decision processes. In: 2012 Ninth International Conference on Quantitative Evaluation of Systems (QEST), pp. 84–93 (2012)

21. Jensen, H.E., Gregersen, H.: Model checking probabilistic real time systems. Nordic Workshop on Programming Theory 7, 247–261 (1996)

22. Kempf, J.F., Bozga, M., Maler, O.: As soon as probable: Optimal scheduling under stochastic uncertainty. In: Piterman, N., Smolka, S.A. (eds.) TACAS 2013. LNCS, vol. 7795, pp. 385–400. Springer, Heidelberg (2013)

23. Kwiatkowska, M.Z., Norman, G., Parker, D.: Probabilistic symbolic model checking with prism: A hybrid approach. In: Katoen, J.-P., Stevens, P. (eds.) TACAS 2002. LNCS, vol. 2280, pp. 52–66. Springer, Heidelberg (2002)

24. Kwiatkowska, M.Z., Norman, G., Segala, R., Sproston, J.: Verifying quantitative properties of continuous probabilistic timed automata. In: Palamidessi, C. (ed.) CONCUR 2000. LNCS, vol. 1877, pp. 123–137. Springer, Heidelberg (2000)

25. Lassaigne, R., Peyronnet, S.: Approximate planning and verification for large markov decision processes. In: Ossowski, S., Lecca, P. (eds.) SAC, pp. 1314–1319. ACM (2012)

26. Legay, A., Delahaye, B., Bensalem, S.: Statistical model checking: An overview. In: Barringer, H., et al. (eds.) RV 2010. LNCS, vol. 6418, pp. 122–135. Springer, Heidelberg (2010)

27. Maler, O., Pnueli, A., Sifakis, J.: On the synthesis of discrete controllers for timed systems (an extended abstract). In: Mayr, E.W., Puech, C. (eds.) STACS 1995. LNCS, vol. 900, pp. 229–242. Springer, Heidelberg (1995)

28. Poulsen, D.B., van Vliet, J.: Duration probabilistic automata, http://www.cs.aau.dk/~adavid/smc/DurationProbabilisticAutomata.pdf

29. Yuan, G.X., Ho, C.H., Lin, C.J.: An improved glmnet for l1-regularized logistic regression. In: Proceedings of the 17th ACM SIGKDD International Conference on Knowledge Discovery and Data Mining, KDD 2011, pp. 33–41. ACM, New York (2011), http://doi.acm.org/10.1145/2020408.2020421

Fast Debugging of PRISM Models*

Christian Dehnert[1], Nils Jansen[1], Ralf Wimmer[2],
Erika Ábrahám[1], and Joost-Pieter Katoen[1]

[1] RWTH Aachen University, Germany
{dehnert,nils.jansen,abraham,katoen}@cs.rwth-aachen.de
[2] Albert-Ludwigs-Universität Freiburg, Germany
wimmer@informatik.uni-freiburg.de

Abstract. In addition to rigorously checking whether a system conforms to a specification, model checking can provide valuable feedback in the form of succinct and understandable counterexamples. In the context of probabilistic systems, path- and subsystem-based counterexamples at the state-space level can be of limited use in debugging. As many probabilistic systems are described in a guarded command language like the one used by the popular model checker PRISM, a technique identifying a subset of critical commands has recently been proposed. Based on repeatedly solving MAXSAT instances, our novel approach to computing a minimal critical command set achieves a speed-up of up to five orders of magnitude over the previously existing technique.

1 Introduction

Algorithmic counterexample generation is a key component of modern model checkers. Counterexamples are pivotal for debugging—experience has shown that counterexamples are the single most effective feature to convince system engineers about the value of formal verification [11]. They are an essential ingredient in counterexample-guided abstraction refinement [10] (CEGAR) and can be effectively used in model-based testing. Prominent model checkers such as SPIN and NUSMV include powerful facilities to generate counterexamples in various formats. Such counterexamples are typically provided at the modeling level, like a diagram indicating how the change of model variables yields a property violation, or a message sequence chart illustrating the failing scenario. Substantial efforts have been made to generate succinct counterexamples, often at the price of an increased time complexity [14,17,26]. Despite the growing popularity of probabilistic model checkers, such facilities are absent in tools such as PRISM [22] and MRMC[21]. This paper presents an efficient scalable technique for computing minimal counterexamples for the PRISM modeling language.

* This work is partly supported by the Excellence Initiative of the German federal and state governments, the EU-FP7 projects CARP and SENSATION, the EU FP7-IRSES project MEALS, and by the German Research Council (DFG) as part of the Transregional Collaborative Research Center AVACS (SFB/TR 14).

F. Cassez and J.-F. Raskin (Eds.): ATVA 2014, LNCS 8837, pp. 146–162, 2014.

Counterexample generation for probabilistic models is not easy. Showing that the reachability probability of a bad state b does not stay below a given threshold λ requires a set of finite paths leading to b, whose probability mass exceeds λ. Computing minimal sets is a k-shortest path problem [16] and can be done using heuristics [1] or bounded model checking [29] and may be enhanced by post-processing steps, such as building a fault-tree to better explain the causality in the model [23]. A viable alternative is to determine minimal critical subsystems [30,31], i.e., model fragments for which the likelihood of reaching b already exceeds λ. The drawback of most approaches in the literature is that they work at the state space level. As the size of sets of finite paths can be doubly exponential in the number of states [16], and minimal critical subsystems can have thousands of states [30], state-based diagnostic feedback is often incomprehensible and not effectively usable in CEGAR approaches for probabilistic systems [18,9]. Although symbolic approaches diminish this problem to some extent, the resulting counterexamples are still too large to handle [19].

We therefore take a radically different approach, and generate *counterexamples as* PRISM *probabilistic programs*. Our approach basically deletes commands of a PRISM probabilistic program yielding a *smallest* PRISM probabilistic program violating the reachability property at hand. PRISM uses a stochastic version of Alur and Henzinger's reactive modules [2] as modeling language. A module description consists of a set of guarded commands providing discrete probabilistic choices. The semantics of a module is a probabilistic automaton [27], a compositional variant of Markov decision processes. A PRISM probabilistic program consists of several modules that communicate by shared variables or using synchronization on common actions. (Remark that our approach is also applicable to other modeling formalisms for probabilistic automata such as PIOA [8], process algebra [20] and the graphical component-wise representation of systems as possible in UPPAAL [7].)

The problem considered is: determine a minimal set of guarded commands of a given PRISM probabilistic program (constituting a PRISM sub-program) that refutes the reachability property at hand. This problem is NP-hard [32]. We present an *incremental* approach for computing minimal critical command sets. The basic idea of our approach is to deduce necessary conditions for an optimal solution by a static analysis of the probabilistic program. We then use a MAXSAT solver to compute a smallest set of commands that is in accordance with these constraints. The resulting PRISM probabilistic program is model checked against the property at hand. If the reachability property is violated, the program constitutes the desired minimal critical command set. Otherwise, it is excluded from the search space and further conditions on the optimal solution are deduced. This paper presents the technical details of the approach and establishes its correctness. We report on a prototype implementation and show the practical applicability of our incremental MAXSAT approach on a number of PRISM benchmark case studies. The experimental results show that our approach scales to models with millions of states and achieves a speed-up of up to five orders of magnitude in comparison to a mixed-integer linear programming approach [32].

Whereas this paper focuses on reachability probabilities, our approach can be easily extended to properties φ that are monotonic in the sense that if $\mathcal{A}$ is a sub-PA of $\mathcal{A}'$ and $\mathcal{A} \not\models \varphi$, then also $\mathcal{A}' \not\models \varphi$.

2   Preliminaries

2.1   Probabilistic Automata

Let S be a countable set. A *probability distribution* over S is a function $\mu \colon S \to [0,1]$ such that $\sum_{s \in S} \mu(s) = 1$. We denote by $Dist(S)$ the set of all probability distributions over S. A distribution μ is called *Dirac* if there exists an element $s \in S$ with $\mu(s) = 1$ and $\mu(s') = 0$ for all $s' \in S$ with $s \neq s'$.

Definition 1 (Probabilistic Automaton [27]). *A probabilistic automaton (PA) is a tuple $\mathcal{A} = (S, s_{\mathrm{init}}, Act, \mathbf{P})$ where S is a finite set of states, $s_{\mathrm{init}} \in S$ is the initial state, Act is a finite set of actions, and $\mathbf{P} : S \to 2^{Act \times Dist(S)}$ is a probabilistic transition relation such that $\mathbf{P}(s)$ is finite for all $s \in S$.*

Intuitively, the evolution of a probabilistic automaton is as follows. Starting in the initial state s_{init}, a transition $(\alpha, \mu) \in \mathbf{P}(s_{\mathrm{init}})$ is chosen nondeterministically. Then, the successor state $s' \in S$ is determined probabilistically according to the probability distribution μ. Repeating this process in s' yields the next state and so on. To prevent deadlocks, we require $\mathbf{P}(s) \neq \emptyset$ for all $s \in S$.

Let $\mathrm{succ}_{\mathcal{A}}(s, \alpha, \mu) = \{s' \in S \mid \mu(s') > 0\}$ for $(\alpha, \mu) \in \mathbf{P}(s)$, $\mathrm{succ}_{\mathcal{A}}(s) = \bigcup_{(\alpha, \mu) \in \mathbf{P}(s)} \mathrm{succ}_{\mathcal{A}}(s, \alpha, \mu)$, and $\mathrm{pred}_{\mathcal{A}}(s) = \{s' \in S \mid \exists (\alpha, \mu) \in \mathbf{P}(s') : \mu(s) > 0\}$. We will omit the subscript $\mathcal{A}$ if the PA is clear from the context.

An (infinite) path π in a PA $\mathcal{A}$ is an infinite sequence $s_0(\alpha_0, \mu_0) s_1(\alpha_1, \mu_1) \ldots$ such that $(\alpha_i, \mu_i) \in \mathbf{P}(s_i)$ and $s_{i+1} \in \mathrm{succ}(s_i, \alpha_i, \mu_i)$ for all $i \geq 0$. A finite path ρ in $\mathcal{A}$ is a finite prefix $s_0(\alpha_0, \mu_0) s_1(\alpha_1, \mu_1) \ldots s_n$ of an infinite path π in $\mathcal{A}$ and its last state is denoted $last(\rho) = s_n$. Let $\pi[i]$ denote the ith state in path π. The sets of all infinite and finite paths in $\mathcal{A}$ starting in $s \in S$ are denoted by $\mathrm{Path}_{\mathcal{A}}(s)$ and $\mathrm{Path}_{\mathcal{A}}^{\mathrm{fin}}(s)$, respectively.

Example 1. Figure 2 on page 152 shows an example PA with five states. For instance, the state s_1 has a nondeterministic choice between the two transitions (reset, $\mu_{s_{\mathrm{init}}}$) and (proc, μ_{proc}) where $\mu_{s_{\mathrm{init}}}$ is the Dirac distribution at s_{init} and μ_{proc} is given by $\mu_{\mathrm{proc}}(s_3) = 0.99$ and $\mu_{\mathrm{proc}}(s_4) = 0.01$.

To define a suitable probability measure on PAs, the nondeterminism has to be resolved by *schedulers*.

Definition 2 (Scheduler). *A scheduler for a PA $\mathcal{A} = (S, s_{\mathrm{init}}, Act, \mathbf{P})$ is a function $\sigma \colon \mathrm{Path}_{\mathcal{A}}^{\mathrm{fin}}(s_{\mathrm{init}}) \to Dist(Act \times Dist(S))$ mapping each finite path $\rho \in \mathrm{Path}_{\mathcal{A}}^{\mathrm{fin}}(s_{\mathrm{init}})$ in $\mathcal{A}$ to a probability distribution over transitions such that $\sigma(\rho)(\alpha, \mu) > 0$ implies $(\alpha, \mu) \in \mathbf{P}(last(\rho))$.*

Intuitively, a scheduler resolves the nondeterminism in a PA by assigning probabilities to the nondeterministic choices available in the last state of a given finite path. It therefore reduces the nondeterministic model to a fully probabilistic one. Given a PA $\mathcal{A}$ and a scheduler σ for $\mathcal{A}$, a standard probability measure on paths, which we denote by $\Pr^{\sigma}_{s_{\text{init}},\mathcal{A}}$ (or, briefly, $\Pr^{\sigma}_{\mathcal{A}}$), can be defined [4].

In the context of this paper we are interested in *probabilistic reachability properties*: is the probability to reach a set $T \subseteq S$ of target states from s_{init} at most $\lambda \in [0,1]$? This property is denoted by $\mathcal{P}_{\leq \lambda}(\Diamond T)$. Note that checking arbitrary ω-regular properties can be reduced to checking reachability properties, see [4] for details. $\mathcal{A}$ satisfies a probabilistic reachability property $\mathcal{P}_{\leq \lambda}(\Diamond T)$, denoted $\mathcal{A} \models \mathcal{P}_{\leq \lambda}(\Diamond T)$, if $\Pr^{\sigma}_{\mathcal{A}}(\Diamond T) := \Pr^{\sigma}_{\mathcal{A}}(\{\pi \in \text{Path}_{\mathcal{A}}(s_{\text{init}}) \mid \exists i : \pi[i] \in T\}) \leq \lambda$ for all schedulers σ. Algorithmically, the maximal reachability probability $\Pr^{\max}_{\mathcal{A}}(\Diamond T) := \sup_{\sigma} \Pr^{\sigma}_{\mathcal{A}}(\Diamond T)$ is computed using standard techniques, such as value or policy iteration [5,25], and compared against the bound λ.

2.2 PRISM's Probabilistic Guarded Command Language

For a set *Var* of Boolean variables, let $\mathcal{N}_{Var}$ denote the set of all variable *valuations*, i.e., the set of functions $\nu : Var \to \{0,1\}$.

Definition 3 (Probabilistic Program, Module, Command). *A probabilistic program is a tuple* $\mathfrak{P} = (Var, \nu_{\text{init}}, \mathbf{M})$ *where Var is a finite set of Boolean variables[1], $\nu_{\text{init}} \in \mathcal{N}_{Var}$ is the initial variable valuation, and $\mathbf{M} = \{M_1, \ldots, M_k\}$ is a finite set of modules.*

A module is a tuple $M_i = (Var_i, Act_i, C_i)$ where for $1 \leq i, j \leq k$ $Var_i \subseteq Var$ is a finite set of Boolean variables such that $Var_i \cap Var_j = \emptyset$ for $i \neq j$, Act_i is a finite set of synchronizing actions, and C_i is a finite set of commands. Additionally, to be consistent with the program, we require $Var = \bigcup_{j=1}^{k} Var_j$.

Let $\tau \notin \bigcup_{i=1}^{k} Act_i$ denote the internal non-synchronizing action. A command $c \in C_i$ is of the form $c = [\alpha]\ g\ \to\ p_1 : f_1 + \ldots + p_n : f_n$, where $\alpha \in Act_i \,\dot{\cup}\, \{\tau\}$ is the action of c that is referred to as act(c), g is a Boolean predicate over Var (called the guard of c), denoted by grd(c), $p_j \in [0,1]$ is a rational number such that $\sum_{i=1}^{n} p_i = 1$, and $f_j : \mathcal{N}_{Var} \to \mathcal{N}_{Var_i}$ is an update function that assigns to each variable of the module a new value based on the values of all variables in the program for all $1 \leq j \leq n$.

Note that each variable $v \in Var_i$ may be written only by the module M_i, but the update may depend on variables of other modules. The restriction $(Var_i, Act_i, C_i \cap C)$ of module M_i to a set C of commands is denoted $M_i|_C$ and $\mathfrak{P}|_C = (Var, \nu_{\text{init}}, \{M_1|_C, \ldots, M_k|_C\})$ is the restriction of the whole program to this set of commands.

A model with $k > 1$ modules is equivalent to a model with a single module resulting from the *parallel composition* $M_1 \parallel \cdots \parallel M_k$ of all modules. Intuitively, the parallel composition of two modules corresponds to a new module that enables all non-synchronizing behavior of the two modules as well as the composition of all command-pairs that need to synchronize because of a common action

---

[1] Note that for PRISM, the variables do not have to be Boolean. However, as finite variable domains are required, every program can be transformed into one only having Boolean variables.

---

module coin
  f: **bool init** 0; c: **bool init** 0;
  [flip] $\neg f \rightarrow 0.5 : (f' = 1)\&(c' = 1) + 0.5 : (f' = 1)\&(c' = 0);$ (c_1)
  [reset] $f \wedge \neg c \rightarrow 1 : (f' = 0);$ (c_2)
  [proc] $f \rightarrow 0.99 : (f' = 1) + 0.01 : (c' = 1);$ (c_3)
endmodule
module processor
  p: **bool init** 0;
  [proc] $\neg p \rightarrow 1 : (p' = 1);$ (c_4)
  [loop] $p \rightarrow 1 : (p' = 1);$ (c_5)
  [reset] $true \rightarrow 1 : (p' = 0);$ (c_6)
endmodule

Fig. 1. A probabilistic program $\mathfrak{P}_{Ex}$ in PRISM's input language

name. Formally, the binary composition $M_i \parallel M_j = (Var_i \cup Var_j, Act_i \cup Act_j, C)$ of two modules M_i and M_j with $i \neq j$ has the set of commands

$$C = \{c \mid c \in C_i \cup C_j \wedge \text{act}(c) \in (\{\tau\} \cup Act_i \ominus Act_j)\}$$
$$\cup \{c \otimes c' \mid c \in C_1 \wedge c' \in C_2 \wedge \text{act}(c) = \text{act}(c') \in Act_i \cap Act_j\}$$

where $A \ominus B$ is the symmetric difference of the sets A and B. The composition $c \otimes c'$ of two commands $c = [\alpha] \, g \rightarrow p_1 : f_1 + \ldots + p_n : f_n$ and $c' = [\alpha] \, g' \rightarrow p'_1 : f'_1 + \ldots + p'_m : f'_m$ with the same action α is defined as

$$c \otimes c' = [\alpha] \, g \wedge g' \quad \rightarrow \quad \sum_{i=1}^{n} \sum_{j=1}^{m} p_i \cdot p'_j : f_i \oplus f'_j.$$

Here, the composition $f_r \oplus f_s : \mathcal{N}_{Var} \rightarrow \mathcal{N}_{Var_i \cup Var_j}$ of two update functions $f_r : \mathcal{N}_{Var} \rightarrow \mathcal{N}_{Var_i}$ and $f_s : \mathcal{N}_{Var} \rightarrow \mathcal{N}_{Var_j}$ is defined by

$$(f_r \oplus f_s)(\nu)(v) = \begin{cases} f_r(\nu)(v), & \text{if } v \in Var_i, \\ f_s(\nu)(v), & \text{otherwise.} \end{cases}$$

Example 2. Figure 1 shows a probabilistic program $\mathfrak{P}_{Ex}$ with two modules coin and processor. It models a system that first does a coin flip and then processes some data. While doing so, it may erroneously modify the coin. Depending on the outcome of the coin flip, the system may reset to the initial configuration. The program uses three variables $Var_{Ex} = \{f, c, p\}$ that indicate whether a coin has been flipped (f), the coin shows tails ($c = 0$) or heads ($c = 1$) and whether some data was processed (p). Initially the module coin can do a coin flip (command c_1). Then, both modules can process some data by synchronizing on the proc action (c_3 and c_4). However, the processing step can by mistake set the coin to show heads with probability 0.01 (c_3). Additionally, if the coin showed tails, the coin flip can be undone by a reset (c_2 and c_6). Finally, if data has been processed the system may loop forever (c_5).

The semantics of a probabilistic program $\mathfrak{P} = (Var, \nu_{\text{init}}, \{M\})$ with only one module $M = (Var, Act, C)$ is defined in terms of a PA $\mathcal{A} = [\![\mathfrak{P}]\!] = (S, s_{\text{init}}, Act, \mathbf{P})$. $S = \mathcal{N}_{Var}$ is the set of all valuations of the program variables[2]. Hence, each state $s \in S$ can be seen as a bit vector $(x_1, \ldots, x_m)$ with x_i being the value of the variable $v_i \in Var = \{v_1, \ldots, v_m\}$. The initial state s_{init} of the PA corresponds to the initial valuation ν_{init} of variables in the program. A guard g defines a subset $S_g \subseteq S$ of states in which the guard evaluates to true. Now, a command $c = [\alpha]\ g \to p_1 : f_1 + \ldots + p_n : f_n$ induces a probability distribution $\mu_{s,c} \in Dist(S)$ for all states $s \in S_g$ by setting

$$\mu_{s,c}(s') = \sum_{\{i\,|\,1\leq i\leq n \wedge f_i(s)=s'\}} p_i$$

for each $s' \in S$. The transition relation $\mathbf{P}$ is then defined for all $s \in S$ by

$$\mathbf{P}(s) = \{(\alpha, \mu_{s,c}) \,|\, \exists c \in C : \text{act}(c) = \alpha \wedge s \in S_{\text{grd}(c)}\}\ .$$

We say that the transition $(\alpha, \mu_{s,c})$ is *generated* by the command c. In case c resulted from the parallel composition of a set of commands C from a probabilistic program with more than one module, we say that the commands in C (jointly) generate the transition. From now on we assume a labeling function $L : S \times Act \times Dist(S) \to 2^{Lab}$ that labels each transition $(\alpha, \mu) \in \mathbf{P}(s)$ with a set of labels $L(s, \alpha, \mu) \subseteq Lab = \{\ell_c \,|\, \exists i \in \{1, \ldots, k\} : c \in C_i\}$ to indicate which commands generated the transition. Note that in case of synchronization the labeling of a transition is a set with more than one element. In order to distinguish the transitions generated by different commands later on, we create different copies of the transition and label them appropriately, if a particular transition is generated by different commands or command sets. We will abbreviate the set of states $\{s \in S \,|\, \exists(\alpha, \mu) \in \mathbf{P}(s) : c \in L(s, \alpha, \mu)\}$ that have an outgoing transition generated by $c \in C$ by $\text{src}(c)$. Analogously, we let $\text{dst}(c)$ be the set of states that have an incoming transition (α, μ) from some state s' with $c \in L(s', \alpha, \mu)$. If a state s has no command enabled, i.e. $s \notin S_{\text{grd}(c)}$ for any $c \in C$, the state is equipped with a self-loop transition (α_s, μ_s) where $\alpha_s \notin Act$ is a new action and μ_s is the Dirac distribution on s. For all transitions added this way, we let $L(s, \alpha_s, \mu_s) = \emptyset$ to reflect that they were not generated by any command, but were added to avoid deadlock states.

Example 3. $\mathcal{A} = [\![\mathfrak{P}_{\text{Ex}}]\!]$ is depicted in Figure 2 where all unreachable states are omitted. The states of the automaton are given by the valuations of the variables in the form $\langle f, c, p \rangle$ and the arrows between the states define the transition relation $\mathbf{P}$, where the highlighting of arrows only becomes relevant in a following example and can be ignored for now. Assume that the probabilistic reachability property $\varphi = \mathcal{P}_{\leq 0.5}(\Diamond\{s_4\})$ is given. Clearly, $\mathcal{A} \not\models \varphi$, because, for example,

---

[2] Actually, PRISM programs also allow to specify discrete-time and continuous-time Markov chains (DTMCs and CTMCs, respectively) and probabilistic timed-automata (PTA). While this paper focuses on PAs, our technique can be readily applied to DTMCs and PTA and also on CTMCs if the guards of commands are non-overlapping.

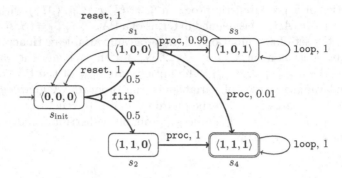

Fig. 2. The reachable fragment of the probabilistic automaton $[\![\mathfrak{P}_{\mathrm{Ex}}]\!]$

$\mathrm{Pr}_{\mathcal{A}}^{\sigma}(\lozenge\{s_4\}) = 0.505$ for the scheduler σ that chooses the `proc` action in both s_1 and s_2 and loops in s_3 and s_4.

Critical command sets. Consider a probabilistic program $\mathfrak{P} = (\mathit{Var}, \nu_{\mathrm{init}}, \{M = (\mathit{Var}, \mathit{Act}, C)\})$, its associated PA $\mathcal{A} = [\![\mathfrak{P}]\!] = (S, s_{\mathrm{init}}, \mathit{Act}, \mathbf{P})$, and the reachability property $\varphi = \mathcal{P}_{\leq\lambda}(\lozenge T)$ for a set of target states $T \subseteq S$. We assume φ to be violated by $[\![\mathfrak{P}]\!]$, i.e., $\mathcal{A} \not\models \varphi$. We aim at identifying a set $C' \subseteq C$ of commands such that the program restricted to these commands still violates the property φ, i.e., $[\![\mathfrak{P}|_{C'}]\!] \not\models \varphi$. We call these subsets of commands *critical command sets*, as they induce a critical fragment of the probabilistic automaton that already proves the violation of the property.

Example 4. Reconsider the probabilistic automaton $[\![\mathfrak{P}_{\mathrm{Ex}}]\!]$ and the probabilistic reachability property $\varphi = \mathcal{P}_{\leq 0.5}(\lozenge\{s_4\})$ given in Example 3. While the program $\mathfrak{P}_{\mathrm{Ex}}$ has 5 commands, the commands $C_{\mathrm{Ex}}^* = \{c_1, c_3, c_4\}$ are already critical, because $[\![\mathfrak{P}_{\mathrm{Ex}}|_{C_{\mathrm{Ex}}^*}]\!] \not\models \varphi$. The transitions of the restricted model are drawn as bold arrows in Figure 2.

2.3 MAXSAT

Given two finite sets Φ, Ψ of propositional formulae over variables Var such that Ψ is satisfiable, the goal is to determine an assignment $\nu \in \mathcal{N}_{\mathit{Var}}$ which satisfies all formulae in Ψ and a maximal number of formulae in Φ, i.e., $\mathrm{MAXSAT}(\Phi, \Psi) = \nu$ such that $\nu \models \Theta \cup \Psi$ where $\Theta \in \mathrm{argmax}_{\Phi' \subseteq \Phi}\{|\Phi'| \mid \Phi' \cup \Psi \text{ is satisfiable}\}$. Note that by negating each formula in Φ, i.e., letting $\overline{\Phi} = \{\neg\varphi \mid \varphi \in \Phi\}$, $\mathrm{MAXSAT}(\overline{\Phi}, \Psi)$ yields an assignment that satisfies a minimal number of formulae of Φ while still satisfying all constraints in Ψ. Consequently, we let $\mathrm{MINSAT}(\Phi, \Psi) := \mathrm{MAXSAT}(\overline{\Phi}, \Psi)$. There are different techniques to solve the MAXSAT problem for a given instance, but we focus on a counter-based technique that is particularly suited if an instance needs to be solved repeatedly after adding additional constraints. For further details, we refer to [13].

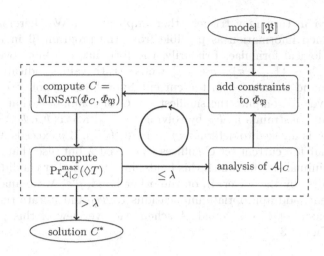

Fig. 3. A schematic overview of our MAXSAT-based approach

3 Computing Minimal Critical Command Sets

In this section we present our novel approach to compute a critical command set as introduced in Section 2.2. For the remainder of this section, let $\mathfrak{P} = (Var, \nu_{\text{init}}, \mathbf{M})$ with $\mathbf{M} = \{M_1, \ldots, M_k\}$ be a probabilistic program with modules $M_i = (Var_i, Act_i, C_i)$ for $1 \leq i \leq k$. Let $\mathcal{A} = [\![\mathfrak{P}]\!] = (S, s_{\text{init}}, Act, \mathbf{P})$ and $\mathcal{A}|_C = [\![\mathfrak{P}|_C]\!]$ for a given set C of commands. We assume that the labeling L of transitions with command labels according to Section 2.2 is given. Furthermore, let $T \subseteq S$ be a set of target states and $\lambda \in [0, 1]$ such that $\mathcal{A} \not\models \mathcal{P}_{\leq\lambda}(\lozenge T)$ in order to guarantee the existence of a critical command set. The task is to compute a *minimal* critical command set, i. e., a smallest set C^* of commands such that $\mathcal{A}|_{C^*} \not\models \mathcal{P}_{\leq\lambda}(\lozenge T)$ or, equivalently, $\text{Pr}^{\max}_{\mathcal{A}|_{C^*}}(\lozenge T) > \lambda$. The fact that this problem is NP-hard in the size of the probabilistic program can be shown by a reduction from exact 3-cover (X3C) very similar to the one in [32]. Note that a solution C^* of this problem is not unique as there may be more than one set of commands of size $|C^*|$ that suffices to violate the reachability property.

3.1 Algorithm

Basic idea. Clearly, for realistic problems, an enumeration of all possible command sets is infeasible. Hence, it is crucial to obtain additional information from the model to rapidly guide the search. For example, if an optimal solution C^* contains a synchronizing command c of module M_i, it must also contain at least one command of each module M_j that needs to synchronize with c, i. e., $\text{act}(c) \in Act_j$. Likewise, if a command c does not lead to a target state in T directly, adding c to the set C^* implies that it must also contain at least one command (or command combination) that may directly follow

c in $\mathcal{A}$, which in turn may trigger other implications. We therefore strive to encode as much information as possible from the program $\mathfrak{P}$ in the form of a set $\Phi_{\mathfrak{P}}$ of logical formulae. Primarily, the formulae are built over variables $\Phi_C := \{x_c \mid \exists i \in \{1, \ldots, k\} : c \in C_i\}$ whose truth values indicate whether a certain command is included in the current hypothesis or not. We then use a MAXSAT solver to compute the smallest set C of commands that is in accordance with all constraints in $\Phi_{\mathfrak{P}}$ by solving $C = \text{MINSAT}(\Phi_C, \Phi_{\mathfrak{P}})$.[3] Finally, a model checker is invoked to determine $p = \text{Pr}_{\mathcal{A}|C}^{\max}(\Diamond T)$. If p exceeds λ, we do not only know that the current set C suffices to exceed λ but also that C is among the sets of minimal size for which this holds, because smaller candidate sets are enumerated first by the solver. If, on the other hand, $p \leq \lambda$, we analyze why C was insufficient, add appropriate implications to $\Phi_{\mathfrak{P}}$ and iterate the algorithm until a sufficient set C was found. A schematic overview of this procedure is depicted in Figure 3.

3.2   Building the Initial Constraint System $\Phi_{\mathfrak{P}}$

As previously mentioned, the first step of our algorithm consists of statically deriving information about the model $\mathcal{A} = [\![\mathfrak{P}]\!]$ to guide the search for a minimal critical command set C^*. Note that it suffices to consider the reachable state space of $\mathcal{A}$ for all the constraints we derive.

Guaranteed commands. For typical models, some commands need to be taken along all paths from the initial state to a target state. It is thus beneficial to determine this set in a preprocessing step to the actual search and thereby possibly prune large parts of the search space. We therefore compute the set of *guaranteed commands* using a standard fixed point analysis [24] on $\mathcal{A}$.

Example 5. All paths that lead to the target state in $[\![\mathfrak{P}_{\text{Ex}}]\!]$ must go along transitions generated by the commands c_1, c_3 and c_4, so it is a priori known that a solution must contain all of them.

Synchronization implications. By the semantics of the program $\mathfrak{P}$, it is required that a synchronizing command c in module M_i can only generate a transition together with synchronizing commands c_j of all modules M_j, $i \neq j$, with $\text{act}(c) \in Act_j$. Consequently, we can conclude that any optimal solution C^* with $c \in C^*$ must also contain at least one command c_j of each synchronizing module such that the commands c and c_j are simultaneously enabled. Formally, we assert

$$x_c \to \bigvee_{\substack{s \in \text{src}(c) \\ \ell_c \in L(s,\alpha,\mu)}} \bigvee_{(\alpha,\mu) \in \mathbf{P}(s)} \bigwedge_{\substack{\ell_{c'} \in L(s,\alpha,\mu) \\ c \neq c'}} x_{c'} \qquad \text{for all } M_i \in \mathbf{M} \text{ and } c \in C_i. \qquad (1)$$

---

[3] Formally, this is not entirely correct, since MINSAT returns a satisfying assignment. More formally, we let $C = \{c \mid \nu(x_c) = 1\}$ where $\nu = \text{MINSAT}(\Phi_C, \Phi_{\mathfrak{P}})$.

Example 6. In $\mathfrak{P}_{\text{Ex}}$, the command c_3 in the first module and c_4 in the second module need to synchronize in order to generate a transition. The synchronization implications $x_{c_3} \to x_{c_4}$ and $x_{c_4} \to x_{c_3}$ ensure that candidate sets must either contain both or none of the two commands.

Successor and predecessor implications. Observe that a candidate set C is surely sub-optimal if $c \in C$ only participates in generating transitions in $\mathcal{A}|_C$ that lead to non-target states without outgoing transitions. In this case, no path from the initial state to a target state can visit a transition that was generated by c and, hence, c can be dropped from C without affecting the reachability probability. Thus, we can assert that each $c \in C$ either possibly leads to a target state directly or leads to some state that has a non-empty transition set. Hence, we add for all $M_i \in \mathbf{M}$ and $c \in C_i$ with $\text{dst}(c) \cap T = \emptyset$ the constraint

$$x_c \to \bigvee_{s' \in \text{dst}(c)} \bigvee_{(\alpha,\mu) \in \mathbf{P}(s')} \bigwedge_{\substack{\ell_{c'} \in L(s',\alpha,\mu) \\ c \neq c'}} x_{c'} \tag{2}$$

to $\Phi_{\mathfrak{P}}$. Analogously, for each command c' that is not enabled in the initial state, i.e., $s_{\text{init}} \notin \text{src}(c')$, we select a combination of commands that leads to some state $s \in \text{src}(c')$ by enforcing

$$x_{c'} \to \bigvee_{s \in \text{src}(c')} \bigvee_{s' \in \text{pred}(s)} \bigvee_{\substack{(\alpha,\mu) \in \mathbf{P}(s') \\ s \in \text{succ}(s',\alpha,\mu)}} \bigwedge_{\substack{\ell_c \in L(s',\alpha,\mu) \\ c \neq c'}} x_c \tag{3}$$

As slight variations of these implications, we can encode that at least one of the transitions of the initial state and at least one transition that has a target state as a direct successor are generated by (a subset of) C.

Example 7. In our running example $\mathfrak{P}_{\text{Ex}}$, the command c_1 must be used in order to reach states that have c_3 enabled. Consequently, we can add the predecessor implication $x_{c_3} \to x_{c_1}$. Likewise, all transitions generated by c_2 must be preceded by either a transition generated by c_1 or by the synchronization of c_3 and c_4, so $x_{c_2} \to x_{c_1} \vee (x_{c_3} \wedge x_{c_4})$ can be added to $\Phi_{\mathfrak{P}_{\text{Ex}}}$. Finally, since the initial state must have an outgoing transition, we can assert x_{c_1}. Note that these are only a few of the constraints that can be constructed for $\mathfrak{P}_{\text{Ex}}$.

Extended backward implications. Reconsider the probabilistic program $\mathfrak{P}_{\text{Ex}}$. Our previously presented backward implications assert that if a candidate set C contains command c_2, it also contains either c_1 or both c_3 and c_4, because both command combinations may directly precede c_2. However, it is obvious that c_1 must always be executed before c_2, because otherwise the guard of c_2 never becomes true. Put differently, only command c_1 "enables" c_2 and should therefore be implied by the choice of c_2.

More formally, we say that a set of commands C' *enables* a non-synchronizing command c if there is at least one state s such that (i) $s \notin \text{src}(c)$, (ii) there is an

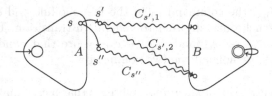

Fig. 4. A restricted model with only unreachable target states

$(\alpha, \mu) \in \mathbf{P}(s)$ with $L(s, \alpha, \mu) = C'$ and a successor state $s' \in \mathrm{succ}(s, \alpha, \mu)$ such that $s' \in \mathrm{src}(c)$, (iii) c is not enabled in the initial state, i.e., $s_{\mathrm{init}} \notin \mathrm{src}(c)$. Let $\mathrm{enab}(c)$ denote the set of all command sets that enable c. We can then assert

$$x_c \rightarrow \bigvee_{C' \in \mathrm{enab}(c)} \bigwedge_{c' \in C'} x_{c'} \tag{4}$$

for all commands c with $s_{\mathrm{init}} \notin \mathrm{src}(c)$ without ruling out optimal solutions. A similar, yet more involved implication can also be asserted for synchronizing commands, but is omitted for the sake of simplicity.

Enforce reachability of a target state. Using a similar construction as the one in [32], reachability of a target state can be encoded in the constraints if a MaxSmt solver is used.

3.3 Analysis of Insufficient Command Sets

After the initial constraint set was constructed, a MinSat problem is solved to obtain a smallest command set C that adheres to these constraints. The restricted model $\mathcal{A}|_C$ is then dispatched to a model checker to verify or refute $\mathcal{P}_{\leq\lambda}(\Diamond T)$. If the reachability probability in $\mathcal{A}|_C$ exceeds λ, a solution for the minimal critical command set problem has been found, because the set C is, by construction, the smallest candidate set. However, in the more likely event of not exceeding λ, we aim to derive additional constraints from the constrained model that guide the solver towards a solution with a higher reachability probability. While it is easily possible to rule out just the current (insufficient) candidate set C by adding a formula to $\Phi_{\mathfrak{B}}$, we strive to rule out more insufficient candidate sets to guide the search. We illustrate this procedure for the case where the reachability probability is zero, i.e., the target states are unreachable altogether (which can, of course, only happen if the constraints to enforce reachability of a target state are not used). A similar reasoning can be applied in case the probability is non-zero. Assume that the current candidate C induces a restricted model $\mathcal{A}|_C$ in which the target states are unreachable. Figure 4 sketches the shape of $\mathcal{A}|_C$ in this scenario where A is the set of states reachable from the initial state and B is formed by all states that can reach a target state. In order to increase the probability of reaching T, any future candidate set $C' \supsetneq C$ must generate a path from A to B in $\mathcal{A}|_{C'}$ in order to reach a target state. More concretely, we do not need to consider all states in A but rather those states that are on the border $border_C(A, B)$ of A, meaning that they possess a transition in the unrestricted model $\mathcal{A}$ that is (i) not present in $\mathcal{A}|_C$, (ii) leaves the set A and (iii) is the first transition of a finite path that ends in B. The states in question can be obtained using efficient graph searches that are essentially breadth-first searches. Having identified these states, we perform a usually cheap analysis that for a given state s determines the set of commands $C_{s \rightsquigarrow B}$ that need to be taken along all paths from s to some state $s' \in B$. We could then assert

$$\bigwedge_{c \in C} x_c \to \bigvee_{s \in border_C(A,B)} \bigwedge_{c \in C_{s \rightsquigarrow B}} x_c \tag{5}$$

to express that any future candidate $C' \supsetneq C$ must contain all commands necessary for reaching B from some state $s \in border_C(A, B)$. However, as the sets $C_{s \rightsquigarrow B}$ are possibly empty, the above constraint does not necessarily eliminate any candidate (not even C). Hence, to guarantee elimination of C as a candidate, we take an intermediate step from a border state s to some state $s' \notin A$ to ensure some transition leaving A is generated. Formally, this leads to the constraint

$$\bigwedge_{c \in C} x_c \to \bigvee_{\substack{s \in border_C(A,B)}} \bigvee_{\substack{(\alpha,\mu) \in P(s)}} \bigvee_{\substack{s' \in succ(s,\alpha,\mu) \\ s' \notin A}} \Big(\underbrace{\bigwedge_{\ell_c \in L(s,\alpha,\mu)} x_c}_{s \to s'} \wedge \underbrace{\bigwedge_{c' \in C_{s' \rightsquigarrow B}} x_{c'}}_{s' \rightsquigarrow B} \Big).$$

Example 8. Assume that the solver found the candidate set $C = \{c_1\}$ while searching for a critical command set in $\mathfrak{P}_{\mathrm{Ex}}$ for φ. This would not be possible if all previously mentioned constraints are added, but is assumed for the sake of simplicity. Then, $\mathcal{A}|_C$ comprises the three reachable states $A = \{s_{\mathrm{init}}, s_1, s_2\}$, the latter two of which are on the $border_C(A, \{s_4\})$. Since all transitions leaving the two states s_1 and s_2 towards s_4 are jointly generated by the commands c_3 and c_4, we add the constraint $x_{c_1} \to x_{c_3} \wedge x_{c_4}$ to rule out C.

3.4   Correctness and Completeness

The *correctness* of our approach basically depends on the fact, that all possible sets of commands are incrementally enumerated until one set fits the requirement given by the violated property. If no additional constraints are used, the MAXSAT method starts with the minimal possible subset of commands and increases this size until the model checker reports the violation of the property for the then optimal set of commands C^*. *Completeness* of the algorithm holds, as all candidates are enumerated at most once and there are finitely many candidate command sets.

What remains to be argued is that all constraints in the set $\Phi_{\mathfrak{P}}$ are correct in the sense that each optimal solution C^* of the critical command set problem necessarily satisfies all of these constraints. Put differently, every constraint $\varphi \in \Phi_{\mathfrak{P}}$ only restricts the solution space such that no optimal solution, i. e., no *minimal* *critical command set*, is ruled out. Due to the page limit, we abstain from giving a formal proof, but refer to Sections 3.2 and 3.3 where the correctness of all constraints is explained.

4   Evaluation

Implementation. We implemented our technique in roughly 1000 lines of C++ code. The prototype was developed in the context of a model checker under development. We employ the counter-based MAXSAT procedure described in Section 2.3 using Z3 4.3 [12] as the underlying SAT/SMT solver. To provide a fair comparison, we additionally implemented the MILP-based approach [32] using the commercial solver Gurobi 5.6 [15]. We also added the detection of guaranteed commands (see Section 3.2) as an optimization to the MILP approach and added the resulting information to the problem encoding. As proposed in [32], we added the so-called *scheduler cuts*, an additional set of constraints to rule out suboptimal solutions, to the MILP encoding, because they strongly tend to improve the performance of the solver. According to [32], all other cuts may have a mixed influence on the performance of the solver and were thus omitted.

Case studies. For the evaluation of the prototype we used four benchmarks that were all previously considered in [32]. They can be found on PRISM's website.

▶ Consensus Protocol. The probabilistic program coin(N, K) models the shared coin protocol of a randomized consensus algorithm [3]. It is used to determine a preference between two choices, each of which appears with a certain probability. The shared coin protocol is parametrized in the number N of involved processes and a constant $K > 1$. Internally, the protocol is based on flipping a coin to come to a decision. We consider the property $\mathcal{P}_{<\lambda}(\Diamond(\text{finished} \wedge \text{all\_coins\_equal\_1}))$ that is satisfied if the probability to finish the protocol with all coins showing the value 1 is below λ.

▶ Wireless LAN. The case study wlan(B, D) concerns the two-way handshake mechanism of the IEEE 802.11 Wireless LAN protocol. Two stations try to send data, but run into a collision. Therefore they enter the randomized exponential backoff scheme. Parameter B denotes the maximally allowed value of the backoff counter. We check the property $\mathcal{P}_{<\lambda}(\Diamond(\text{num\_collisions} = D))$, putting an upper bound on the probability that the maximal number of collisions D occurs.

▶ CSMA. The csma(N, B) model concerns the IEEE 802.3 CSMA/CD network protocol with N the number of processes wanting to access a common channel and B is the maximal value of the backoff counter. We check that the probability of all stations successfully sending their messages before a collision with maximal backoff occurs is less than λ, i.e., $\mathcal{P}_{<\lambda}(\neg\text{collision } U \text{ delivered})$.

▶ Firewire. Finally, fw(N) models the Tree Identify Protocol of the IEEE 1394 High Performance Serial Bus (called "FireWire") [28]. It is a leader election protocol that is executed each time a node enters or leaves the network. The parameter N denotes the delay of the wire. We check $\mathcal{P}_{<\lambda}(\Diamond\text{leader\_elected})$, i.e., that the probability of finally electing a leader is below λ.

Table 1. The results of the experiments

model	states	trans.	λ/p^*	comm.	$|C^*|$	MILP[32] Time	MILP[32] Mem.	MaxSat Time	MaxSat Mem.	enum.
coin(2, 2)	272	492	0.4 / 0.56	10 (4)	9	TO	> 0.04	**0.08**	**0.02**	54%
coin(4, 4)	43136	144352	0.4 / 0.54	20 (8)	17	TO	> 2.60	**1876**	**0.07**	50%
coin(4, 6)	63616	213472	0.4 / 0.53	20 (8)	17	TO	> 6.70	**6231**	**0.09**	50%
coin(6, 2)	1258240	6236736	0.4 / 0.59	30 (12)	–	TO	> 8.36	TO	> 1.54	–
csma(2, 4)	7958	10594	0.5 / 0.999	38 (21)	36	31.4	0.07	**2.26**	**0.04**	0.09%
csma(4, 2)	761962	1327068	0.4 / 0.78	68 (22)	53	TO	> 9.60	**18272**	**0.92**	3.9E-9%
fw(1)	1743	2199	0.5 / 1	64 (6)	24	207.25	0.16	**16.14**	**0.05**	1.4E-10%
fw(10)	17190	29366	0.5 / 1	64 (6)	24	9196	0.84	**90.47**	**0.07**	1.4E-10%
fw(36)	212268	481792	0.5 / 1	64 (6)	24	TO	> 3.20	**1542**	**0.34**	1.4E-10%
wlan(0, 2)	6063	10619	0.1 / 0.184	42 (22)	33	TO	> 1.99	**1.6**	**0.03**	0.02%
wlan(2, 4)	59416	119957	4E-4 / 7.9E-4	48 (26)	39	TO	> 4.03	**50.27**	**0.07**	0.01%
wlan(6, 6)	5007670	11475920	1E-7 / 2.2E-7	52 (30)	43	ERR	–	**5035**	**3.86**	0.01%

Experimental results. All experiments were conducted on an Intel Core i7 920 quadcore processor clocked at 2.66 GHz with 12 GB RAM running Mac OS 10.9. We set a timeout of 12 hours for each individual (single-threaded) experiment. Table 1 summarizes the results of our experiments. Next to some model statistics about the particular model, the considered probability bound λ and the maximal reachability probability p^* of the unrestricted model are shown. Furthermore, we give the number of relevant commands of the probabilistic program and how many of them are guaranteed commands (see Section 3.2). Here, relevant means that they appear on at least one path from the initial to a target state. The size of an optimal solution C^* as well as the runtimes and memory consumption (in seconds and gigabytes, respectively) of both the MILP- and the MaxSat-based approach are listed in the following five columns, where TO indicates a timeout. For the MILP approach [32], we performed experiments with and without using the scheduler cuts and report on the best of these results. Encoding reachability of a target state (see Section 3.2) tended to be rather expensive for Z3: in almost all cases it slowed down the overall computation and thus we list the times obtained without adding these constraints. For all considered models the MaxSat approach significantly outperforms the MILP-based technique. While for the fw and csma models the speed-up is about one to two orders of magnitude, for the coin and wlan case studies it goes as high as five orders of magnitude. Enabling the multi-threading capabilities of Gurobi (8 threads on our machine) did not change the order of improvement we obtained. Furthermore it can be seen that the MaxSat approach consistently uses one order of magnitude less memory. For the largest wlan example, Gurobi reported a wrong result ($|C^*| = 38$). Performing model checking on the restricted model revealed that the computed command set does not suffice to violate the property. After careful inspection of our implementation and considering that all other results coincide, we believe this is due to numerical instabilities in the solving technique that could not be eliminated by setting its tolerances to the lowest possible value. Finally, to indicate to what extent the constraints in our new approach guide the search as opposed to an unguided enumeration of candidate sets, Table 1 also shows the fraction $\frac{\ell}{\sum_{i=0}^{k}\binom{n}{i}}$ (column enum.) where ℓ is the number of candidate sets enumerated, k is the number of commands in C^* minus the guaranteed commands, and n is the number of all relevant but not guaranteed commands. It represents the ratio of candidate sets that were tested to all candidate sets with at most $|C^*|$ commands that contain all guaranteed commands. Hence, it indicates which fragment of the search space could be pruned. For all case studies except the `coin` models, the constraints avoided huge parts of the search space. Interestingly, despite exploring more than half of the search space, the MAXSAT approach is still much faster on the `coin` examples, which is due to the efficient underlying testing procedure for candidate sets.

Further, it is noteworthy that, depending on the model, the analysis of insufficient command sets (see Section 3.3) consumes the largest fraction of the runtime: for the `csma` and `fw` examples more than 80 % of the runtime is spent on it, whereas for the other examples it only contributes a very small fraction to the overall runtime, which is then clearly dominated by model checking.

Since it is a known characteristic of MILP solvers that good solutions are found quickly, but the solver is unable to prove their optimality in reasonable time, we also examined the solution progress of `Gurobi` on the models for which it times out. For the smaller to medium-sized models, for example `wlan(0,2)` and `fw(10)`, the MILP solver finds a solution of optimal size in 4 and 388 seconds, respectively, but then fails at proving optimality. However, for the largest models of each case study that could be solved within time by the MAXSAT approach, `Gurobi` is unable to find any solution until the time limit is reached.

5   Conclusion

We have presented a novel technique for computing counterexamples at the modeling level of probabilistic programs, which we believe to complement existing counterexample techniques in the probabilistic setting. In contrast to the previous approach tackling the minimal command set problem, our new technique substantially improves computation time and memory consumption and scales to systems with millions of states. Furthermore, it can be readily applied to the wider range of monotonic properties by introducing problem-specific constraints. However, the performance of the technique can still be improved. It is easily parallelizable and could therefore benefit from accelerators like GPUs. More sophisticated analysis techniques of candidate sets that failed to exceed the probability threshold could be both more efficient to compute and more beneficial with respect to the number of suboptimal sets that could be pruned. Moreover, the computed counterexamples can be further reduced in size by applying branch minimization [32]. Future work also includes possible applications in techniques that are guided by counterexamples, such as CEGAR [18,9] or assume-guarantee reasoning [6].

References

1. Aljazzar, H., Leue, S.: Directed explicit state-space search in the generation of counterexamples for stochastic model checking. IEEE Trans. on Software Engineering 36(1), 37–60 (2010)
2. Alur, R., Henzinger, T.A.: Reactive modules. Formal Methods in System Design 15(1), 7–48 (1999)
3. Aspnes, J., Herlihy, M.: Fast randomized consensus using shared memory. Journal of Algorithms 11(3), 441–461 (1990)
4. Baier, C., Katoen, J.-P.: Principles of Model Checking. MIT Press (2008)
5. Bellman, R.: Dynamic Programming, 1st edn. Princeton University Press, Princeton (1957)
6. Gheorghiu Bobaru, M., Păsăreanu, C.S., Giannakopoulou, D.: Automated assume-guarantee reasoning by abstraction refinement. In: Gupta, A., Malik, S. (eds.) CAV 2008. LNCS, vol. 5123, pp. 135–148. Springer, Heidelberg (2008)
7. Bulychev, P., David, A., Guldstrand Larsen, K., Legay, A., Mikučionis, M., Bøgsted Poulsen, D.: Checking and distributing statistical model checking. In: Goodloe, A.E., Person, S. (eds.) NFM 2012. LNCS, vol. 7226, pp. 449–463. Springer, Heidelberg (2012)
8. Canetti, R., Cheung, L., Kaynar, D.K., Liskov, M., Lynch, N.A., Pereira, O., Segala, R.: Analyzing security protocols using time-bounded task-PIOAs. Discrete Event Dynamic Systems 18(1), 111–159 (2008)
9. Chatterjee, K., Chmelík, M., Daca, P.: CEGAR for qualitative analysis of probabilistic systems. In: Biere, A., Bloem, R. (eds.) CAV 2014. LNCS, vol. 8559, pp. 473–490. Springer, Heidelberg (2014)
10. Clarke, E.M., Grumberg, O., Jha, S., Lu, Y., Veith, H.: Counterexample-guided abstraction refinement. In: Emerson, E.A., Sistla, A.P. (eds.) CAV 2000. LNCS, vol. 1855, pp. 154–169. Springer, Heidelberg (2000)
11. Clarke, E.M., Veith, H.: Counterexamples revisited: Principles, algorithms, applications. In: Dershowitz, N. (ed.) Verification: Theory and Practice. LNCS, vol. 2772, pp. 208–224. Springer, Heidelberg (2004)
12. de Moura, L.M., Bjørner, N.: Z3: An efficient SMT solver. In: Ramakrishnan, C.R., Rehof, J. (eds.) TACAS 2008. LNCS, vol. 4963, pp. 337–340. Springer, Heidelberg (2008)
13. Fu, Z., Malik, S.: On solving the partial MAX-SAT problem. In: Biere, A., Gomes, C.P. (eds.) SAT 2006. LNCS, vol. 4121, pp. 252–265. Springer, Heidelberg (2006)
14. Gastin, P., Moro, P.: Minimal counterexample generation for SPIN. In: Bošnački, D., Edelkamp, S. (eds.) SPIN 2007. LNCS, vol. 4595, pp. 24–38. Springer, Heidelberg (2007)
15. Gurobi optimization, inc.: Gurobi optimizer reference manual version 5.6 (2014), http://www.gurobi.com/resources/documentation
16. Han, T., Katoen, J.-P., Damman, B.: Counterexample generation in probabilistic model checking. IEEE Trans. on Software Engineering 35(2), 241–257 (2009)
17. Hansen, H., Geldenhuys, J.: Cheap and small counterexamples. In: Proc. of SEFM, pp. 53–62. IEEE Computer Society (2008)
18. Hermanns, H., Wachter, B., Zhang, L.: Probabilistic CEGAR. In: Gupta, A., Malik, S. (eds.) CAV 2008. LNCS, vol. 5123, pp. 162–175. Springer, Heidelberg (2008)
19. Jansen, N., Wimmer, R., Ábrahám, E., Zajzon, B., Katoen, J.-P., Becker, B.: Symbolic counterexample generation for large discrete-time Markov chains. Science of Computer Programming 91(A), 90–114 (2014)

20. Katoen, J.-P., van de Pol, J., Stoelinga, M., Timmer, M.: A linear process-algebraic format with data for probabilistic automata. Theoretical Computer Science 413(1), 36–57 (2012)
21. Katoen, J.-P., Zapreev, I.S., Hahn, E.M., Hermanns, H., Jansen, D.N.: The ins and outs of the probabilistic model checker MRMC. Performance Evaluation 68(2), 90–104 (2011)
22. Kwiatkowska, M., Norman, G., Parker, D.: PRISM 4.0: Verification of probabilistic real-time systems. In: Gopalakrishnan, G., Qadeer, S. (eds.) CAV 2011. LNCS, vol. 6806, pp. 585–591. Springer, Heidelberg (2011)
23. Leitner-Fischer, F., Leue, S.: Probabilistic fault tree synthesis using causality computation. IJCCBS 4(2), 119–143 (2013)
24. Nielson, F., Nielson, H.R., Hankin, C.: Principles of program analysis (2. corr. print). Springer (2005)
25. Puterman, M.L.: Markov Decision Processes: Discrete Stochastic Dynamic Programming, 1st edn. John Wiley & Sons, Inc., New York (1994)
26. Schuppan, V., Biere, A.: Shortest counterexamples for symbolic model checking of LTL with past. In: Halbwachs, N., Zuck, L.D. (eds.) TACAS 2005. LNCS, vol. 3440, pp. 493–509. Springer, Heidelberg (2005)
27. Segala, R., Lynch, N.A.: Probabilistic simulations for probabilistic processes. Nordic Journal of Computing 2(2), 250–273 (1995)
28. Stoelinga, M.: Fun with firewire: A comparative study of formal verification methods applied to the IEEE 1394 root contention protocol. Formal Aspects of Computing 14(3), 328–337 (2003)
29. Wimmer, R., Braitling, B., Becker, B.: Counterexample generation for discrete-time Markov chains using bounded model checking. In: Jones, N.D., Müller-Olm, M. (eds.) VMCAI 2009. LNCS, vol. 5403, pp. 366–380. Springer, Heidelberg (2009)
30. Wimmer, R., Jansen, N., Ábrahám, E., Becker, B., Katoen, J.-P.: Minimal critical subsystems for discrete-time Markov models. In: Flanagan, C., König, B. (eds.) TACAS 2012. LNCS, vol. 7214, pp. 299–314. Springer, Heidelberg (2012)
31. Wimmer, R., Jansen, N., Ábrahám, E., Katoen, J.-P., Becker, B.: Minimal counterexamples for linear-time probabilistic verification. Theoretical Computer Science (2014), doi:10.1016/j.tcs.2014.06.020 (accepted for publication)
32. Wimmer, R., Jansen, N., Vorpahl, A., Ábrahám, E., Katoen, J.-P., Becker, B.: High-level counterexamples for probabilistic automata. In: Joshi, K., Siegle, M., Stoelinga, M., D'Argenio, P.R. (eds.) QEST 2013. LNCS, vol. 8054, pp. 18–33. Springer, Heidelberg (2013)

ACME: Automata with Counters, Monoids and Equivalence*

Nathanaël Fijalkow[1,2] and Denis Kuperberg[2]

[1] LIAFA, Paris 7
[2] University of Warsaw

Abstract. We present ACME, a tool implementing algebraic techniques to solve decision problems from automata theory. The core generic algorithm takes as input an automaton and computes its stabilization monoid, which is a generalization of its transition monoid.

Using the stabilization monoid, one can solve many problems: determine whether a B-automaton (which is a special kind of automata with counters) is limited, whether two B-automata are equivalent, and whether a probabilistic leaktight automaton has value 1.

The dedicated webpage where the tool ACME can be downloaded is

http://www.liafa.univ-paris-diderot.fr/~nath/acme.htm.

1 Stabilization Monoids for B- and Probabilistic Automata

The notion of stabilization monoids appears in two distinct contexts. It has first been developed in the theory of regular cost functions, introduced by Colcombet [Col09, Col13]. The underlying ideas have then been transferred to the setting of probabilistic automata [FGO12].

1.1 Stabilization Monoids in the Theory of Regular Cost Functions

At the heart of the theory of regular cost functions lies the equivalence between different formalisms: a logical formalism, cost MSO, two automata model, B- and S-automata, and an algebraic counterpart, stabilization monoids.

Here we briefly describe the model of B-automata, and their transformations to stabilization monoid. This automaton model generalizes the non-deterministic automata by adding a finite set of counters. Instead of accepting or rejecting a word as a non-deterministic automaton does, a B-automaton associates an integer value to each input word. Formally, a B-automaton is a tuple $\mathcal{A} = \langle A, Q, \Gamma, I, F, \Delta \rangle$, where A is a finite alphabet, Q is a finite set of states, Γ is a finite set of counters, $I \subseteq Q$ is the set of initial

---

* The research leading to these results has received funding from the French ANR project 2010 BLAN 0202 02 FREC, the European Union's Seventh Framework Programme (FP7/2007-2013) under grant agreement 259454 (GALE) and 239850 (SOSNA).

F. Cassez and J.-F. Raskin (Eds.): ATVA 2014, LNCS 8837, pp. 163–167, 2014.
© Springer International Publishing Switzerland 2014

states, $F \subseteq Q$ is the set of final states, and $\Delta \subseteq Q \times A \times \{\mathbf{ic}, \varepsilon, \mathbf{r}\}^\Gamma \times Q$ is the set of transitions.

A transition (p, a, τ, q) allows the automaton to go from state p to state q while reading letter a and performing action $\tau(\gamma)$ on counter γ. Action $\mathbf{ic}$ increments the current counter value by 1, ε leaves the counter unchanged, and $\mathbf{r}$ resets the counter to 0.

The value of a run is the maximal value assumed by any of the counters during the run. The semantics of a B-automaton $\mathcal{A}$ is defined on a word w by $\llbracket \mathcal{A} \rrbracket (w) = \inf\{\mathrm{val}(\rho) \mid \rho$ is a run of $\mathcal{A}$ on $w\}$. In other words, the automaton uses the non determinism to minimize the value among all runs. In particular, if $\mathcal{A}$ has no run on w, then $\llbracket \mathcal{A} \rrbracket (w) = \infty$.

The main decision problem in the theory of regular cost functions is the limitedness problem. We say that a B-automaton $\mathcal{A}$ is *limited* if there exists N such that for all words w, if $\llbracket \mathcal{A} \rrbracket (w) < \infty$, then $\llbracket \mathcal{A} \rrbracket (w) < N$.

One way to solve the limitedness problem is by computing the stabilization monoid. It is a monoid of matrices over the semiring of counter actions $\{\mathbf{ic}, \varepsilon, \mathbf{r}, \omega\}^\Gamma$. There are two operations on matrices: a binary composition called product, giving the monoid structure, and a unary operation called stabilization. The stabilization monoid of a B-automaton is the set of matrices containing the matrices corresponding to each letter, and closed under the two operations, product and stabilization. As shown in [Col09, Col13], the stabilization monoid of a B-automaton $\mathcal{A}$ contains an unlimited witness if and only if it is not limited, implying a conceptually simple solution to the limitedness problem: compute the stabilization monoid and check for the existence of unlimited witnesses.

1.2 Stabilization Monoids for Probabilistic Automata

The notion of stabilization monoids also appeared for probabilistic automata, for the Markov Monoid Algorithm. This algorithm was introduced in [FGO12] to partially solves the value 1 problem: given a probabilistic automaton $\mathcal{A}$, does there exist $(u_n)_{n \in \mathbb{N}}$ a sequence of words such that $\lim_n \mathbb{P}_\mathcal{A}(u_n) = 1$?

Although the value 1 problem is undecidable, it has been shown that the Markov Monoid Algorithm correctly determines whether a probabilistic automaton has value 1 under the *leaktight* restriction. It has been recently shown that all classes of probabilistic automata for which the value 1 problem has been shown decidable are included in the class of leaktight automata [FGKO14], hence the Markov Monoid Algorithm is the *most correct* algorithm known to (partially) solve the value 1 problem.

As for the case of B-automata, the stabilization monoid of a probabilistic automaton is the set of matrices containing the matrices corresponding to each letter, and closed under the two operations, product and stabilization.

Note that the main point is that both the products and the stabilizations depend on which type of automata is considered, B-automata or probabilistic automata.

2   Computing the Stabilization Monoid of an Automaton

We report here on some implementation issues regarding the following algorithmic task:

We are given as input:

- A finite set of matrices S,
- A binary associative operation on matrices, the product, denoted $\cdot$,
- A unary operation on matrices, the stabilization, denoted $\sharp$.

The aim is to compute the closure of S under product and stabilization, called the stabilization monoid generated by S.

Our choice of OCaml allowed for a generic implementation of the algorithm.

Note that if we ignore the stabilization operation, this reduces to computing the monoid generated by a finite set of matrices, *i.e.* the transition monoid of a non-deterministic automaton. It is well-known that this monoid can be exponential in the size of the automaton, so the crucial aspect here is space optimization.

In our application, the initial set of matrices is given by matrices M_a for $a \in A$, where A is the finite alphabet of the automaton. Hence we naturally associate to every element of the stabilization monoid a $\sharp$-expression: $(M_a \cdot M_b^{\sharp} \cdot M_a)^{\sharp}$ is associated to $(ab^{\sharp}a)^{\sharp}$. Many $\sharp$-expressions actually correspond to the same matrix: for instance, it may be that $(M_a \cdot M_a \cdot M_b)^{\sharp} = M_a^{\sharp}$; in such case, we would like to associate this matrix to the $\sharp$-expression $a^{\sharp}$, which is "simpler" than $(aab)^{\sharp}$.

There are two data structures: a table and a queue. The table is of fixed size (a large prime number), and is used to keep track of all the matrices found so far, through their hash value. The queue stores the elements to be treated. The pseudo-code of the algorithm is presented in Algorithm 1.

3   Minimizing the Stabilization Monoid

To test whether two B-automata are equivalent, we follow [CKL10]: for both automata we construct its stabilization monoid, then we minimize them and check whether the minimal stabilization monoids are isomorphic.

We do not explain in details how to check whether two stabilization monoids are isomorphic. This is in general a very hard problem, theoretically not well understood; for instance there is no polynomial-time algorithm to check whether two groups are isomorphic. Our setting here makes the task much easier, as we look for an isomorphism extending two given morphisms (associating to each letter an element), leading to a simple linear-time algorithm.

Data: $S = \{M_a \mid a \in A\}$
Result: The stabilization monoid generated by S
Initialization: an empty table T and an empty queue Q;
for $a \in A$ **do**
> push (a, M_a) onto Q for every $a \in A$;
> add M_a to T;

end
while Q *is not empty* **do**
> let (s, M) the first element in Q;
> search M in T (through its hash value);
> **if** M *is not in* T *(new)* **then**
> > add M to T;
> > **for** $N \in T$ **do**
> > > push $M \cdot N$ onto Q;
> > > push $N \cdot M$ onto Q;
> >
> > **end**
> > push $M^\sharp$ onto Q;
>
> **end**

end

Algorithm 1. Computing the stabilization monoid

Let M be a stabilization monoid, whose elements are denoted $m_1, \cdots, m_n$, and an ideal $I \subseteq M$. The algorithm constructs an increasing sequence of partitions, starting from the partition that separates I from $M \setminus I$.

Consider a partition P of the elements. For an element $m \in M$, we denote by $[m]_P$ its equivalence class with respect to P. The type of m with respect to P is the following vector of equivalence classes:

$$([m]_P, \, [m^{\omega\sharp}]_P, [m \cdot m_1]_P, \cdots, [m \cdot m_n]_P, [m_1 \cdot m]_P, \cdots, [m_n \cdot m]_P) \, .$$

Note that the second component uses the $\omega\sharp$ operator, defined using the $\sharp$ operator. Relying on the $\sharp$ operator would not be correct, as it is partial (only defined for idempotent elements).

Using the types, we construct a larger partition P', such that two elements are equivalent for P' if they have the same type with respect to P.

There are three data structures: two *union-find* tables to handle partitions of the elements and a table of types. We present in Algorithm 2 a pseudo-code of the minimization algorithm.

> **Data**: A stabilization monoid $(M, \cdot, \sharp)$, an ideal $I \subseteq M$
> **Result**: The minimal stabilization monoid with respect to (M, I)
> Initialization: a partition P separating I and $M \setminus I$ and an empty table T of types;
> **while** *unstable* **do**
> > Compute the types (with respect to P) in T;
> > Create a new partition P' such that two elements are equivalent for P' if they have the same types;
> > $P \longleftarrow P'$;
>
> **end**

Algorithm 2. Minimizing the stabilization monoid

References

[CKL10]   Colcombet, T., Kuperberg, D., Lombardy, S.: Regular temporal cost functions. In: Abramsky, S., Gavoille, C., Kirchner, C., Meyer auf der Heide, F., Spirakis, P.G. (eds.) ICALP 2010, Part II. LNCS, vol. 6199, pp. 563–574. Springer, Heidelberg (2010)

[Col09]   Colcombet, T.: The theory of stabilisation monoids and regular cost functions. In: Albers, S., Marchetti-Spaccamela, A., Matias, Y., Nikoletseas, S., Thomas, W. (eds.) ICALP 2009, Part II. LNCS, vol. 5556, pp. 139–150. Springer, Heidelberg (2009)

[Col13]   Colcombet, T.: Regular cost-functions, part I: Logic and algebra over words. Logical Methods in Computer Science 9(3) (2013)

[FGKO14]   Fijalkow, N., Gimbert, H., Kelmendi, E., Oualhadj, Y.: Deciding the value 1 problem for probabilistic leaktight automata (2014)

[FGO12]   Fijalkow, N., Gimbert, H., Oualhadj, Y.: Deciding the value 1 problem for probabilistic leaktight automata. In: LICS, pp. 295–304 (2012)

Modelling and Analysis of Markov Reward Automata

Dennis Guck[1], Mark Timmer[1], Hassan Hatefi[2],
Enno Ruijters[1], and Mariëlle Stoelinga[1]

[1] Formal Methods and Tools, University of Twente, The Netherlands
[2] Dependable Systems and Software, Saarland University, Germany

Abstract. Costs and rewards are important ingredients for many types of systems, modelling critical aspects like energy consumption, task completion, repair costs, and memory usage. This paper introduces Markov reward automata, an extension of Markov automata that allows the modelling of systems incorporating *rewards* (or *costs*) in addition to nondeterminism, discrete probabilistic choice and continuous stochastic timing. Rewards come in two flavours: action rewards, acquired instantaneously when taking a transition; and state rewards, acquired while residing in a state. We present algorithms to optimise three reward functions: the expected cumulative reward until a goal is reached, the expected cumulative reward until a certain time bound, and the long-run average reward. We have implemented these algorithms in the SCOOP/IMCA tool chain and show their feasibility via several case studies.

1 Introduction

The design of computer systems involves many trade offs: Is it cost-effective to use multiple processors to increase availability and performance? Should we carry out preventive maintenance to save future repair costs? Can we reduce the clock speed to save energy, while still meeting the required performance bounds? How can we best schedule a task set so that the operational costs are minimised? Such optimisation questions typically involve the following ingredients: (1) rewards or costs, to measure the quality of the solution; (2) (stochastic) timing to model speed or delay; (3) discrete probability to model random phenomena like failures; and (4) nondeterminism to model the choices in the optimisation process.

This paper introduces Markov reward automata (MRAs), a novel model that combines the ingredients mentioned above. It is obtained by adding rewards to the formalism of Markov automata (MAs) [15]. We support two types of rewards: *Action rewards* are obtained directly when taking a transition, and *state rewards* model the reward per time unit while residing in a state. Such reward extensions have shown valuable in the past for less expressive models, for instance leading to the tool MRMC [24] for model checking reward-based properties over CTMCs [21] and DTMCs [1] with rewards. With our MRA model we provide a natural combination of the EMPA [3] and PEPA [9] reward formalisms.

F. Cassez and J.-F. Raskin (Eds.): ATVA 2014, LNCS 8837, pp. 168–184, 2014.
© Springer International Publishing Switzerland 2014

By generalising MAs, MRAs provide a well-defined semantics for generalised stochastic Petri nets (GSPNs) [13], dynamic fault trees [4] and the domain-specific language AADL [5]. Recent work also demonstrated that MAs (and hence MRAs as well) are suitable for modelling and analysing distributed algorithms such as a leader election protocol, performance models such as a polling system and hardware models such as a processor grid [31].

Model checking algorithms for MAs against Continuous Stochastic Logic (CSL) properties were discussed in [20]. Notions of strong, weak and branching bisimulation were defined to equate behaviourally equivalent MAs [15,28,12,31], and the process-algebraic language MAPA was introduced for easily specifying large MAs in a concise manner [32]. Several types of reduction techniques [34,33] have been defined for the MAPA language and implemented in the tool SCOOP, optimising specifications to decrease the state space of the corresponding MAs while staying bisimilar [30,18]. This way, MAs can be generated efficiently in a direct way (as opposed to first generating a large model and then reducing), thus partly circumventing the omnipresent state space explosion. Additionally, the game-based abstraction refinement technique developed in [6] provides a sound approximation of time-bounded reachability over a substantially reduced abstract model. The tool IMCA [17,18] was developed to analyse the concrete MAs that are generated by SCOOP. It includes algorithms for computing time-bounded reachability probabilities, expected times and long-run averages for sets of goal states within an MA.

While the framework in place already works well for computing probabilities and expected durations, it did not yet support rewards or costs. Therefore, we extend the MAPA language from MAs to the realm of MRAs and extend most of SCOOP's reduction techniques to efficiently generate them. Further, we present algorithms for three optimisation problems over MRAs. That is, we resolve the nondeterministic choices in the MRA such that one of three optimisation criteria is minimised (or maximised): (1) the expected cumulative reward to reach a set of goal states, (2) the expected cumulative reward until a given time bound, and (3) the long-run average reward.

The current paper is a first step towards a fully quantitative system design formalism. As such, we focus on positive rewards. Negative rewards, more complex optimisation criteria, as well as the handling of several rewards as multi-optimisation problem are important topics for future research. For a more detailed version of this paper with extended proofs we refer to [19].

2   Markov Reward Automata

MAs were introduced as the union of Interactive Markov Chains (IMCs) [23] and Probabilistic Automata (PAs) [27]. Hence, they feature nondeterminism, as well as Markovian rates and discrete probabilistic choice. We extend this model with reward functions for both the states and the transitions.

Definition 1 (Background). *A probability distribution over a countable set S is a function $\mu\colon S \to [0,1]$ such that $\sum_{s\in S}\mu(s) = 1$. For $S' \subseteq S$, let*

$\mu(S') = \sum_{s \in S'} \mu(s)$. We write $\mathbb{1}_s$ for the Dirac distribution for s determined by $\mathbb{1}_s(s) = 1$. We use $\mathsf{Distr}(S)$ to denote the set of all probability distributions over S.

Given an equivalence relation $R \subseteq S \times S$, we write $[s]_R$ for the equivalence class of s induced by R, i.e., $[s]_R = \{s' \in S \mid (s, s') \in R\}$. Given two probability distributions $\mu, \mu' \in \mathsf{Distr}(S)$ and an equivalence relation R, we write $\mu \equiv_R \mu'$ to denote that $\mu([s]_R) = \mu'([s]_R)$ for every $s \in S$.

2.1   Markov Reward Automata

Before defining MRAs, we recall the definition of MAs. It assumes a countable universe of actions Act, with $\tau \in Act$ the invisible internal action.

Definition 2 (Markov Automata). A Markov automaton (MA) is a tuple $\mathcal{M} = \langle S, s^0, A, \hookrightarrow, \rightsquigarrow \rangle$, where

- S is a countable set of states, of which $s^0 \in S$ is the initial state;
- $A \subseteq Act$ is a countable set of actions, including τ;
- $\hookrightarrow \subseteq S \times A \times \mathsf{Distr}(S)$ is the probabilistic transition relation;
- $\rightsquigarrow \subseteq S \times \mathbb{R}_{>0} \times S$ is the Markovian transition relation;

If $(s, \alpha, \mu) \in \hookrightarrow$, we write $s \xrightarrow{\alpha} \mu$ and say that action α can be executed from state s, after which the probability to go to each $s' \in S$ is $\mu(s')$. If $(s, \lambda, s') \in \rightsquigarrow$, we write $s \xrightarrow{\lambda} s'$ and say that s moves to s' with rate λ.

A state $s \in S$ that has at least one transition $s \xrightarrow{a} \mu$ is called *probabilistic*. A state that has at least one transition $s \xrightarrow{\lambda} s'$ is called *Markovian*. Note that a state could be both probabilistic and Markovian.

The *rate* between two states $s, s' \in S$ is $\mathbf{R}(s, s') = \sum_{(s, \lambda, s') \in \rightsquigarrow} \lambda$, and the *outgoing rate of* s is $E(s) = \sum_{s' \in S} \mathbf{R}(s, s')$. We require $E(s) < \infty$ for every state $s \in S$. If $E(s) > 0$, the *branching probability distribution* after this delay is denoted by $\mathbb{P}_s$ and defined by $\mathbb{P}_s(s') = \frac{\mathbf{R}(s, s')}{E(s)}$ for every $s' \in S$. By definition of the exponential distribution, the probability of leaving a state s within t time units is given by $1 - e^{-E(s) \cdot t}$ (given $E(s) > 0$), after which the next state is chosen according to $\mathbb{P}_s$. Further, we denote by $A(s)$ the set of all enabled actions in state s.

MAs adhere to the *maximal progress assumption*, prescribing τ-transitions to never be delayed. Hence, a state that has at least one outgoing τ-transition can never take a Markovian transition. This fact is captured below in the definition of extended transitions, which is used to provide a uniform manner for dealing with both probabilistic and Markovian transitions.

Definition 3 (Extended action set). Let $\mathcal{M} = \langle S, s^0, A, \hookrightarrow, \rightsquigarrow \rangle$ be an MA, then the extended action set of $\mathcal{M}$ is given by $A^\chi = A \cup \{\chi(r) \mid r \in \mathbb{R}_{>0}\}$. The actions $\chi(r)$ represent exit rates and are used to distinguish probabilistic and Markovian transitions. For $\alpha = \chi(\lambda)$, we define $E(\alpha) = \lambda$. If $\alpha \in A$, we set $E(\alpha) = 0$. Given a state $s \in S$ and an action $\alpha \in A^\chi$, we write $s \xrightarrow{\alpha} \mu$ if either

- $\alpha \in A$ and $s \xhookrightarrow{\alpha} \mu$, or
- $\alpha = \chi(E(s))$, $E(s) > 0$, $\mu = \mathbb{P}_s$ and there is no μ' such that $s \xhookrightarrow{\tau} \mu'$.

A transition $s \xrightarrow{\alpha} \mu$ is called an extended transition. We use $s \xrightarrow{\alpha} t$ to denote $s \xrightarrow{\alpha} \mathbb{1}_t$, and write $s \to t$ if there is at least one action α such that $s \xrightarrow{\alpha} t$. We write $s \xrightarrow{\alpha,\mu} s'$ if there is an extended transition $s \xrightarrow{\alpha} \mu$ such that $\mu(s') > 0$.

Note that each state has an extended transition per probabilistic transition, while it has only one for all its Markovian transitions together (if there are any).

We now formally introduce the MRA. For simplicity of the reward functions, we chose to define MRAs in terms of extended actions. Hence, instead of two separate probabilistic and Markovian transition relations, there is only one transition relation. This also simplifies the notion of bisimulation introduced later.

Definition 4 (Markov Reward Automata). A Markov Reward Automaton (MRA) is a tuple $\mathcal{M} = \langle S, s^0, A, T, \rho \rangle$, where

- S is a countable set of states, of which $s^0 \in S$ is the initial state;
- $A \subseteq Act$ is a countable set of actions;
- $T \subseteq S \times A^\chi \times \mathbb{R}_{\geq 0} \times \mathsf{Distr}(S)$ is the transition relation including action rewards;
- $\rho \colon S \to \mathbb{R}_{\geq 0}$ is the state-reward function.

We require for each $s \in S$ that there is at most one transition labeled with $\chi(\cdot)$. Further, we require that T is countable and write $s \xrightarrow{\alpha}_r \mu$ if $(s, \alpha, r, \mu) \in T$.

The function ρ associates a real number to each state. This number may be zero, indicating the absence of a reward. The state-based rewards are gained *while being in a state*, and are proportional to the duration of this stay. The action-based rewards are gained instantaneously *when taking a transition* and are included directly in the transition relation.

2.2 Paths, Policies and Rewards

As for traditional labelled transition systems (LTSs), the behaviour of MAs and MRAs can also be expressed by means of paths. A *path* in $\mathcal{M}$ is a finite sequence $\pi^{\text{fin}} = s_0 \xrightarrow{a_1,\mu_1,t_1}_{r_1} s_1 \xrightarrow{a_2,\mu_2,t_2}_{r_2} \cdots \xrightarrow{a_n,\mu_n,t_n}_{r_n} s_n$ from some state s_0 to a state s_n $(n \geq 0)$, or an infinite sequence $\pi^{\text{inf}} = s_0 \xrightarrow{a_1,\mu_1,t_1}_{r_1} s_1 \xrightarrow{a_2,\mu_2,t_2}_{r_2} s_2 \xrightarrow{a_3,\mu_3,t_3} \cdots$, with $s_i \in S$ for all $0 \leq i \leq n$ and all $0 \leq i$, respectively. The step $s_i \xrightarrow{a_i,\mu_i,t_i}_{r_i} s_{i+1}$ denotes that after residing t_i time units in s_i, the MRA has moved via action a_i and probability distribution μ_i to s_{i+1} obtaining r_i action reward. We use $prefix(\pi, t)$ to denote the prefix of path π up to and including time t, formally $prefix(\pi, t) = s_0 \xrightarrow{a_1,\mu_1,t_1}_{r_1} \cdots \xrightarrow{a_i,\mu_i,t_i}_{r_i} s_i$ such that $t_1 + \cdots + t_i \leq t$ and $t_1 + \cdots + t_i + t_{i+1} > t$. We use $step(\pi, i)$ to denote the transition $s_{i-1} \xrightarrow{a_i}_{r_i} \mu_i$. When π is finite we define $|\pi| = n$, $last(\pi) = s_n$, and for every path $\pi[i] = s_i$. Further, we denote by π^j the path π up to and including state s_j. Let *paths** and *paths* denote the set of finite and infinite paths, respectively. We define the *total reward* of a finite path π by

$$reward(\pi) = \sum_{i=1}^{|\pi|} \rho(\pi[i-1]) \cdot t_i + r_i \tag{1}$$

Rewards can be used to model many quantitative systems aspects, like energy consumption, memory usage, deployment or maintenance costs, etc. The total reward of a path (e.g, total amount of energy consumed) is obtained by adding all rewards along that path, that is, all state rewards multiplied by the sojourn times of the corresponding states plus all action rewards on the path.

Policies. Policies resolve the nondeterministic choices in an MRA, i.e., make a choice over the outgoing probabilistic transitions in a state. Given a policy, the behaviour of an MRA is fully probabilistic. Formally, a *policy*, ranged over by D, is a measurable function such that $D\colon paths^* \to \mathsf{Distr}(T)$ and $D(\pi)$ chooses only from transitions that emanate from $last(\pi)$. The information on which basis a policy resolves the choices yields different classes. Let GM denote the class of general measurable policies. A stationary deterministic policy is a mapping $D\colon S \to T$ such that $D(s)$ chooses only from transitions that emanate from s; such policies always take the same transition in a state s. A time-dependent policy may decide on the basis of the states visited so far and their timings. For more details about different classes of policies and their relations we refer to [26]. Given a policy D and an initial state s, a measurable set of paths is equipped with the probability measure $\mathrm{Pr}_{s,D}$.

2.3 Strong Bisimulation

We define a notion of strong bisimulation for MRAs. As for LTSs, PAs, IMCs and MAs, it equates systems the are equivalent in the sense that every step of one system can be mimicked by the other, and vice versa.

Definition 5 (Strong bisimulation). *Given an MRA $\mathcal{M} = \langle S, s^0, A, T, \rho \rangle$, an equivalence relation $R \subseteq S \times S$ is a strong bisimulation for $\mathcal{M}$ if for every $(s, s') \in R$ and all $\alpha \in A^\chi, \mu \in \mathsf{Distr}(S), r \in \mathbb{R}_{\geq 0}$, it holds that $\rho(s) = \rho(s')$ and*

$$s \xrightarrow{\alpha}_r \mu \implies \exists \mu' \in \mathsf{Distr}(S) \,.\, s' \xrightarrow{\alpha}_r \mu' \wedge \mu \equiv_R \mu'$$

Two states $s, s' \in S$ are strongly bisimilar (denoted by $s \approx s'$) if there exists a strong bisimulation R for $\mathcal{M}$ such that $(s, s') \in R$. Two MAs $\mathcal{M}, \mathcal{M}'$ are strongly bisimilar (denoted by $\mathcal{M} \approx \mathcal{M}'$) if their initial states are strongly bisimilar in their disjoint union.

Clearly, when setting all state-based and action-based rewards to 0, MRAs coincide with MAs. Additionally, our definition of strong bisimulation then reduces to the definition of strong bisimulation for MAs. Since it was already shown in [14] that strong bisimulation for MAs coincides with the corresponding notions for all subclasses of MAs, this also holds for our definition. Hence, it safely generalises the existing notions of strong bisimulation.

3 Quantitative Analysis

This section shows how to perform quantitative analyses on MRAs. We will focus on three common reward measures: (1) The expected cumulative reward until reaching a set of goal states, (2) the expected cumulative reward until a given time-bound, and (3) the long-run average reward. Typical examples where these algorithms can be used are respectively: to minimise the average energy consumption needed to download and install a medium-size software update; to minimise the average maintenance cost of a railroad line over the first year of deployment; and to maximise the yearly revenues of a data center over a long time horizon. In the following we lift the algorithms from [18] to the realm of rewards. We focus on maximising the properties. The minimisation problem can be solved similarly — namely, by replacing max by min and sup by inf below.

3.1 Notation and Preprocessing

Throughout this section, we consider a fixed MRA $\mathcal{M}$ with state space S and a set of goal states $G \subseteq S$. To facilitate the algorithms, we first perform three preprocessing steps. (1) We consider only closed MRAs, which are not subject to further interaction. Therefore, we hide all actions (renaming them to τ), focussing on their induced rewards. (2) Due to the maximal progress assumption, a Markovian transition will never be executed from a state with outgoing τ-transitions. Hence, we remove such Markovian transitions. Thus, each state either has one outgoing Markovian transition or only probabilistic outgoing transitions. We call these states Markovian and probabilistic respectively, and use MS and PS to denote the sets of Markovian and probabilistic states. (3) To distinguish the different τ-transitions emerging from a state $s \in PS$, we assume w.l.o.g. that these are numbered from 1 to n_s, where n_s is the number of outgoing transitions. We write $\mu_s^{\tau_i}$ for the distribution induced by taking τ_i in state s and we write $r_s^{\tau_i}$ for the reward. For Markovian transitions we write $\mathbb{P}_s$ and r_s, respectively.

3.2 Goal-Bounded Expected Cumulative Reward

We are interested in the minimal and maximal expected cumulative reward until reaching a set of goal states $G \subseteq S$. That is, we accumulate the state and transition rewards until a state in G is reached; if no state in G is reached, we keep on accumulating rewards.

The random variable $V_G \colon paths \to \mathbb{R}_{\geq 0}^{\infty}$ yields the accumulated reward before first visiting some state in G. For an infinite path π, we define

$$V_G(\pi) = \begin{cases} reward(\pi^j) & \text{if } \pi[j] \in G \wedge \forall i < j.\ \pi[i] \notin G \\ reward(\pi) & \text{if } \forall i.\ \pi[i] \notin G \end{cases}$$

The maximal expected reward to reach G from $s \in S$ is then defined as

$$\mathsf{eR}^{\max}(s, G) = \sup_{D \in GM} \mathbb{E}_{s,D}(V_G) = \sup_{D \in GM} \int_{paths} V_G(\pi) \Pr_{s,D}(d\pi) \qquad (2)$$

where D is an arbitrary policy on $\mathcal{M}$.

To compute $\mathsf{eR}^{\max}$ we turn it into a classical Bellman equation: For all goal states, no more reward is accumulated, so their expected reward is zero. For Markovian states $s \notin G$, the state reward of s is weighted with the expected sojourn time in s plus the expected reward accumulated via its successor states plus the transition reward to them. For a probabilistic state $s \notin G$, we select the action that maximises the expected cumulative reward. Note that, since the accumulated reward is only relevant until reaching a state in G, we may turn all states in G into absorbing Markovian states.

Theorem 1 (Bellman equation). *The function* $\mathsf{eR}^{\max} \colon S \to \mathbb{R}^{\infty}_{\geq 0}$ *is the unique fixed point of the Bellman equation*

$$v(s) = \begin{cases} \frac{\rho(s)}{E(s)} + \sum_{s' \in S} \mathbb{P}_s(s') \cdot (v(s') + r_s) & \text{if } s \in MS \setminus G \\ \max_{\alpha \in A(s)} \sum_{s' \in S} \mu_s^{\alpha}(s') \cdot (v(s') + r_s^{\alpha}) & \text{if } s \in PS \setminus G \\ 0 & \text{if } s \in G. \end{cases}$$

A direct consequence of Theorem 1 is that the supremum in (2) is attained by a stationary deterministic policy. Moreover, this result enables us to use standard solution techniques such as value iteration and linear programming to compute $\mathsf{eR}^{\max}(s, G)$. Note that by assigning $\rho(s) = 1$ to all $s \in MS$ and setting all other rewards to 0, we compute the expected time to reach a set of goal states.

3.3 Time-Bounded Expected Cumulative Reward

A time-bounded reward is the reward gained until a time bound t is reached and is denoted by the random variable $reward(\cdot, t)$. For an infinite path π, we first find the prefix of π up to t and then compute the reward using (1), i. e.

$$reward(\pi, t) = reward(prefix(\pi, t)) \qquad (3)$$

The maximum time-bounded reward then is the maximum expected reward gained within some interval $I = [0, b]$, starting from some initial state s:

$$\mathcal{R}^{\max}(s, b) = \sup_{D \in GM} \int_{paths} reward(\pi, b) \Pr_{s,D}(d\pi) \qquad (4)$$

Similar to time-bounded reachability there is a fixed point characterisation (FPC) for computing the optimal reward within some interval of time. Here we focus on the maximum case; the minimum can be extracted similarly.

Lemma 2 (Fixed Point Characterisation). *Given a Markov reward automaton $\mathcal{M}$ and a time bound $b \geq 0$. The maximum expected cumulative reward from state $s \in S$ until time bound b is the least fixed point of higher order operator $\Omega \colon (S \times \mathbb{R}_{\geq 0} \mapsto \mathbb{R}_{\geq 0}) \mapsto (S \times \mathbb{R}_{\geq 0} \mapsto \mathbb{R}_{\geq 0})$, such that*

$$\Omega(F)(s,b) = \begin{cases} \left(r_s + \frac{\rho(s)}{E(s)}\right)\left(1 - e^{-E(s)b}\right) \\ \quad + \int_0^b E(s)e^{-E(s)t}\sum_{s'\in S}\mathbb{P}_s(s')F(s',b-t)\,dt & s \in MS \wedge b \neq 0 \\ \max_{\alpha \in A(s)}\left(r_s^\alpha + \sum_{s'\in S}\mu_s^\alpha(s')F(s',b)\right) & s \in PS \\ 0 & otherwise. \end{cases}$$

This FPC is a generalisation of that for time-bounded reachability [18, Lemma 1], taking both action and state rewards into account. The proof goes along the same lines as that of [25, Theorem 6.1].

Discretisation. Similar to time-bounded reachability, the FPC is not algorithmically tractable and needs to be discretised: we have to divide the time horizon $[0, b]$ into a (generally large) number of equidistant time steps, each of length $0 < \delta \leq b$, such that $b = k\delta$ for some $k \in \mathbb{N}$. First, we express $\mathcal{R}^{\max}(s, b)$ in terms of its behaviour in the first discretisation step $[0, \delta)$. To do so, we partition the paths from s into the set $\mathcal{P}_1$ of paths that make their first Markovian jump in $[0, \delta)$ and the set $\mathcal{P}_2$ of paths that do not. We write $\mathcal{R}^{\max}(s, b)$ as the sum of

1. The expected reward obtained in $[0, \delta)$ by paths from $\mathcal{P}_1$
2. The expected reward obtained in $[\delta, b]$ by paths from $\mathcal{P}_1$
3. The expected reward obtained in $[0, \delta)$ by paths from $\mathcal{P}_2$
4. The expected reward obtained in $[\delta, b]$ by paths from $\mathcal{P}_2$

It turns out to be convenient to combine the first three items, denoted by $A(s, b)$, since the resulting term resembles the expression in Lemma 2:

$$A(s,b) = \rho(s)\delta e^{-E(s)\delta} + \int_0^\delta E(s)e^{-E(s)t}\left(\rho(s)t + r_s + \sum_{s'\in S}\mathbb{P}_s(s')\mathcal{R}^{\max}(s',b-t)\right)dt$$

$$= \left(r_s + \frac{\rho(s)}{E(s)}\right)\left(1 - e^{-E(s)\delta}\right) + \int_0^\delta E(s)e^{-E(s)t}\sum_{s'\in S}\mathbb{P}_s(s')\mathcal{R}^{\max}(s',b-t)\,dt \quad (5)$$

where the first equality follows directly from the definition of $A(s, b)$ and the second equality is along the same lines as the proof of Lemma 2. It can easily be seen that $\mathcal{R}^{\max}(s, b) = A(s, b) + e^{-E(s)\delta}\mathcal{R}^{\max}(s, b - \delta)$.

Exact computation of $A(s, b)$ is in general still intractable due to the term $\mathcal{R}^{\max}(s', b - t)$. However, if the discretisation constant δ is very small, then, with high probability, at most one Markovian jump happens in each discretisation step. Hence, the reward gained by paths having multiple Markovian jumps within at least one such interval is negligible and can be omitted from the computation, while introducing only a small error. Technically, that means that we don't have to remember the remaining time within a discretisation step after a Markovian jump has happened. We can therefore discretise $A(s, b)$ into $\tilde{A}_\delta(s, k)$

and $\mathcal{R}^{\max}(s, b)$ into $\tilde{\mathcal{R}}_\delta^{\max}(s, k)$, just counting the number of discretisation steps k that are left instead of the actual time bound b:

$$\tilde{\mathcal{R}}_\delta^{\max}(s, k) = \tilde{A}_\delta(s, k) + e^{-E(s)\delta} \tilde{\mathcal{R}}_\delta^{\max}(s, k-1), \quad s \in MS \qquad (6)$$

where $\tilde{A}_\delta(s, k)$ is defined by

$$\tilde{A}_\delta(s, k) = \left(r_s + \frac{\rho(s)}{E(s)}\right)\left(1 - e^{-E(s)\delta}\right) + \int_0^\delta E(s)e^{-E(s)t} \sum_{s' \in S} \mathbb{P}_s(s')\tilde{\mathcal{R}}_\delta^{\max}(s', k-1) \, dt$$

$$= \left(r_s + \frac{\rho(s)}{E(s)} + \sum_{s' \in S} \mathbb{P}_s(s')\tilde{\mathcal{R}}_\delta^{\max}(s', k-1)\right)\left(1 - e^{-E(s)\delta}\right) \qquad (7)$$

Note that we used $\tilde{\mathcal{R}}_\delta^{\max}(s, k-1)$ instead of both $\mathcal{R}^{\max}(s, b-\delta)$ and $\mathcal{R}^{\max}(s, b-t)$.

Eq. (6) and (7) help us to establish a tractable discretised version of the FPC described in Lemma 2 and to formally define the discretised maximum time-bounded reward afterwards:

Definition 6 (Discretised Maximum Time-Bounded Reward). *Let $\mathcal{M}$ be an MRA, $b \geq 0$ a time bound and $\delta > 0$ a discretisation step such that $b = k\delta$ for some $k \in \mathbb{N}$. The discretised maximum time bounded cumulative reward, $\tilde{\mathcal{R}}_\delta^{\max}$, is defined as the least fixed point of higher order operator $\Omega_\delta \colon (S \times \mathbb{N} \mapsto \mathbb{R}_{\geq 0}) \mapsto (S \times \mathbb{N} \mapsto \mathbb{R}_{\geq 0})$, such that*

$$\Omega_\delta(F)(s, k) = \begin{cases} \left(r_s + \frac{\rho(s)}{E(s)} + \sum_{s' \in S} \mathbb{P}_s(s')F(s', k-1)\right)\left(1 - e^{-E(s)\delta}\right) \\ \quad + e^{-E(s)\delta}F(s, k-1) & s \in MS \wedge k \neq 0 \\ \max_{\alpha \in A(s)} \left(r_s^\alpha + \sum_{s' \in S} \mu_s^\alpha(s')F(s', k)\right) & s \in PS \\ 0 & otherwise. \end{cases}$$

The reason behind the tractability of $\tilde{\mathcal{R}}_\delta^{\max}$ is hidden in Eq. (7). It brings two simplifications to the computation. First, it implies that $\tilde{\mathcal{R}}_\delta^{\max}$ is the conditional expected reward given that each step carries at most one Markovian transition. Second, it neglects to compute the reward after the first Markovian jump and simply assume that it is zero. We have shown the formal specification of the simplifications in [19, Lemma C1]. With the help of these simplifications, reward computation becomes tractable but indeed inexact.

The accuracy of $\tilde{\mathcal{R}}_\delta^{\max}$ depends on some parameters including the step size δ. The smaller δ is, the better the quality of discretisation is. It is possible to quantify the quality of the discretisation. To this end we need first to define some parameters of MRA. For a given MRA $\mathcal{M}$, assume that λ is the maximum exit rate of any Markovian state, i.e. $\lambda = \max_{s \in MS} E(s)$, and $\rho_{\max}$ is maximum state reward of any Markovian state, i.e. $\rho_{\max} = \max_{s \in MS} \rho(s)$. Moreover we define $r_{\max}$ as the maximum action reward that can be gained between two consecutive Markovian jumps. The value can be computed via Theorem 1, where we set Markovian states as the goal states. Given that $\mathsf{eR}^{\max}(s, MS)$ has already been computed, we define $r(s) = r_s + \sum_{s' \in S} \mathsf{eR}^{\max}(s', MS)$ for $s \in MS$, and $r(s) = \mathsf{eR}^{\max}(s, MS)$ otherwise. Finally we have $r_{\max} = \max_{s \in S} r(s)$. Note that in practice we use a value iteration algorithm to compute $r_{\max}$. With all of the parameters known, the following theorem quantifies the quality of the abstraction.

Theorem 3. *Let $\mathcal{M}$ be an MRA, $b \geq 0$ be a time bound, $\delta > 0$ be a discretisation step such that $b = k\delta$ for some $k \in \mathbb{N}$. Then for all $s \in S$:*

$$\tilde{\mathcal{R}}_\delta^{\max}(s, k) \leq \mathcal{R}^{\max}(s, b) \leq \tilde{\mathcal{R}}_\delta^{\max}(s, k) + \frac{b\lambda}{2}(\rho_{\max} + r_{\max}\lambda)(1 + \frac{b\lambda}{2})\delta$$

3.4 Long-Run Average Reward

Next, we are interested in the average cumulative reward induced by a set of goal states $G \subseteq S$ in the long-run. Hence, all state and action rewards for states $s \in S \setminus G$ are set to 0. We define the random variable $\mathcal{L}_\mathcal{M} : paths \to \mathbb{R}_{\geq 0}$ as the long-run reward over paths in MRA $\mathcal{M}$. For an infinite path π let

$$\mathcal{L}_\mathcal{M}(\pi) = \lim_{t \to \infty} \frac{1}{t} \cdot reward(\pi, t).$$

Then, the maximal long-run average reward on $\mathcal{M}$ starting in state $s \in S$ is:

$$\mathsf{LRR}_\mathcal{M}^{\max}(s) = \sup_{D \in GM} \mathbb{E}_{s,D}(\mathcal{L}_\mathcal{M}) = \sup_{D \in GM} \int_{paths} \mathcal{L}_\mathcal{M}(\pi) \Pr_{s,D}(d\pi). \qquad (8)$$

The computation of the expected long-run reward can be split into three steps:

1. Determine all maximal end components of MRA $\mathcal{M}$;
2. Determine $\mathsf{LRR}_{\mathcal{M}_i}^{\max}$ for each maximal end component $\mathcal{M}_i$;
3. Reduce the computation of $\mathsf{LRR}_\mathcal{M}^{\max}(s)$ to an SSP problem.

A sub-MRA $\mathcal{M}$ is a pair (S', K) where $S' \in S$ and K is a function that assigns to each state $s \in S'$ a non-empty set of actions, such that for all $\alpha \in K(s)$, $s \xrightarrow{\alpha} \mu$ with $\mu(s') > 0$ implies $s' \in S'$. An *end component* is a sub-MRA whose underlying graph is strongly connected; it is maximal (a *MEC*) w.r.t. K if it is not contained in any other end component (S'', K). In this section we focus on the second step. The first step can be performed by a graph-based algorithm [8,10] and the third step is as in [18].

A MEC can be seen as a unichain MRA: an MRA that yields a strongly connected graph structure under any stationary deterministic policy.

Theorem 4. *For a unichain MRA $\mathcal{M}$, for each $s \in S$ the value of $\mathsf{LRR}_\mathcal{M}^{\max}(s)$ equals*

$$\mathsf{LRR}_\mathcal{M}^{\max} = \sup_D \sum_{s \in S} \left(\rho(s) \cdot \mathsf{LRA}^D(s) + r_s^{D(s)} \cdot \nu^D(s) \right)$$

where ν is the frequency of passing through a state, defined by

$$\nu^D(s) = \begin{cases} \mathsf{LRA}^D(s) \cdot E(s) & \text{if } s \in MS \\ \sum_{s' \in S} \nu^D(s') \cdot \mu_{s'}^{D(s')}(s) & \text{if } s \in PS \end{cases}$$

and $\mathsf{LRA}^D(s)$ is the long-run average time spent in state s under stationary deterministic policy D.

Thus, the frequency of passing through a Markovian state equals the long-run average time spent in s times the exit rate, and for a probabilistic state it is the accumulation of the frequencies of the incoming transitions. Hence, the long-run reward gathered by a state s is defined by the state reward weighted with the average time spent in s and the action reward weighted by the frequency of passing through the state. Since in a unichain MRA $\mathcal{M}$, for any two states s, s', $\mathsf{LRR}_{\mathcal{M}}^{\max}(s)$ and $\mathsf{LRR}_{\mathcal{M}}^{\max}(s')$ coincides, we omit the starting state and just write $\mathsf{LRR}_{\mathcal{M}}^{\max}$. Note that probabilistic states are left immediately, so $\mathsf{LRA}^{D}(s) = 0$ if $s \in PS$. Further, by assigning $\rho(s) = 1$ to all $s \in MS \cap G$ and setting all other rewards to 0, we compute the long-run average time spent in a set of goal states.

Theorem 5. *The long-run average reward of a unichain MRA coincides with the limit of the time-bounded expected cumulative reward, such that* $\mathsf{LRR}^{D}(s) = \lim\limits_{t \to \infty} \frac{1}{t}\mathcal{R}^{D}(s,t)$.

For the equation from Theorem 4 it would be too expensive to compute for all possible policies and for each state the long-run average time as well as the frequency of passing through a state and weigh those with the associated rewards. Instead, we compute $\mathsf{LRR}_{\mathcal{M}}^{\max}$ by solving a system of linear inequations following the concepts of [10]. Given a unichain MRA $\mathcal{M}$, let k denote the optimal average reward accumulated in the long-run and executing the optimal policy. Then, for all $s \in S$ there is a function $h(s)$ that describes a differential cost per visit to state s, such that a system of inequations can be constructed as follows:

Minimise k subject to:

$$
\begin{cases}
h(s_i) = \frac{\overline{\rho}(s_i)}{E(s_i)} - \frac{k}{E(s_i)} + \sum\limits_{s_j \in S} \mathbb{P}_{s_i}(s_j) \cdot h(s_j) & \text{if } s_i \in MS \\
h(s_i) \geq r_{s_i}^{\alpha} + \sum\limits_{s_j \in S} \mu_{s_i}^{\alpha}(s_j) \cdot h(s_j) & \text{if } s_i \in PS \wedge \forall \alpha \in A(s_i)
\end{cases}
\tag{9}
$$

where the state and action reward of Markovian states are combined as $\overline{\rho}(s_i) = \rho(s_i) + (r_{s_i} \cdot E(s_i))$. Standard linear programming algorithms, e.g., the simplex method [35], can be applied to solve the above system of linear equations.

To obtain the long-run average reward in an arbitrary MRA, we have to weigh the obtained long-run rewards in each maximal end component with the probability to reach those from s. This is equivalent to the third step in the long-run average computation of [18]. Further, for the discrete time setting [7] considers multiple long-run average objectives.

4   MAPA with Rewards

The Markov Automata Process Algebra (MAPA) language allows MAs to be generated in an efficient and effective manner [31]. It is based on μCRL [16], allowing the standard process-algebraic constructs such as nondeterministic choice and action prefix to be used in a data-rich context: processes are equipped with a set of variables over user-definable data types, and actions can be parameterised based on the values of these variables. Additionally, conditions can be used to restrict behaviour, and nondeterministic choices over data types are possible. MAPA adds two operators to μCRL: a probabilistic choice over data types and a Markovian delay (both possibly depending on data parameters).

We extended MAPA by accompanying it with rewards. Due to the action-based approach of process algebra, there is a clear separation between the action-based and state-based rewards. *Action-based rewards* are just added as decorations to the actions in the process-algebraic specification: we use $a[r]\sum_{x:D} f : p$ to denote an action a having reward r, continuing as process p (where the variable x gets a value from its domain D based on a probabilistic expression f). We refer to [31] for a detailed exposition of the syntax and semantics of MAPA; this is trivially generalised to incorporate the action-based rewards.

State-based rewards are dealt with separately. They can be assigned to *conditions*; each state that fulfills a reward's condition is then assigned that reward. If a state satisfies multiple conditions, the rewards are accumulated.

4.1 MaMa Extensions

Since realistic systems often consist of a very large number of states, we do not want to construct their MRA models manually. Rather, we prefer to specify them as the parallel composition of multiple components. This approach was applied earlier to generate MAs, using a tool called SCOOP [30,18,31]. It generates MAs from MAPA specifications, applying several reduction techniques in the process. The underlying philosophy is to already reduce on the specification, not having to first generate a large model before being able to minimise. The parallel composition of MRAs is described in the technical report [19] and is equivalent to [11] for the probabilistic transitions.

We extended SCOOP to parse action-based and state-based rewards. Action-based rewards are stored as part of the transitions, while state-based rewards are represented internally by self-loops. Additionally, we generalised most of its reduction techniques to take into account the new rewards. The following reduction techniques are now also applicable to MRAs:

Dead variable reduction. This technique resets variables if their value is not needed anymore until they are overwritten. Instead of only checking whether a variable is used in conditions or actions, we generalised this technique to also check if it is used in reward expressions.

Maximal progress reduction. This technique removes Markovian transitions from states also having τ-transitions. It can be applied unchanged to MRAs.

Basic reduction techniques. The basic reduction techniques omit variables that are never changed, omit nondeterministic choices that only have one option and simplify expressions where possible. These three techniques were easily generalised by taking the reward expressions into account as well.

Confluence reduction was not yet generalised, as it is based on a much more complicated notion of bisimulation (that is not yet available for MRAs).

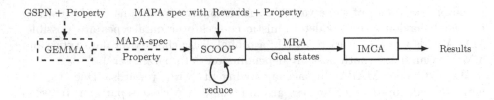

Fig. 1. Analysing Markov Reward Automata using the MaMa tool chain

SCOOP takes both the action-based and state-based rewards into account when generating an input file for the IMCA toolset. This toolset implements several algorithms for computing reward-based properties, as detailed before. The connection of the tool-chain is depicted in Figure 1.

5   Case Studies

To assess the performance of the algorithms and implementation, we provide two case studies: A server polling system based on [29], and a fault-tolerant workstation cluster based on [22]. Rewards were added to both examples. The experiments were conducted on a 2.2 GHz Intel® Core™ i7-2670QM processor with 8 GB RAM, running Linux.

Polling system. Figure 2 shows the MAPA specification of the polling system. It consists of two stations, each providing a job queue, and one server. When the server polls a job from a station, there is a 10% chance that it will erroneously remain in the queue. An impulse reward of 0.1 is given each time a server takes a job, and a reward of 0.01 per time unit is given for each job in the queue. The rewards are meant to be interpreted as costs in this example, for having a job processed and for taking up server memory, respectively.

Tables 1 and 3 show the results obtained by the MaMa tool-chain when analysing for different queue sizes Q and different numbers of job types N. The

---

constant $queueSize = Q, nrOfJobTypes = N$
type $Stations = \{1, 2\}, \; Jobs = \{1, \ldots, nrOfJobTypes\}$

$Station(i : Stations, q : Queue, size : \{0..queueSize\})$
  $= size < queueSize \Rightarrow (2i + 1) \cdot \sum_{j:Jobs} arrive(j) \cdot Station(i, enqueue(q, j), size + 1)$
  $+ \; size > 0 \qquad\qquad \Rightarrow deliver(i, head(q)) \sum_{k \in \{1,9\}} \frac{k}{10} : k = 1 \Rightarrow Station(i, q, size)$
  $\qquad\qquad\qquad\qquad\qquad\qquad\qquad + k = 9 \Rightarrow Station(i, tail(q), size - 1)$

$Server = \sum_{n:Stations} \sum_{j:Jobs} poll(n, j)[\underline{0.1}] \cdot (2 * j) \cdot finish(j) \cdot Server$

$\gamma(poll, deliver) = copy \qquad\qquad$ // actions *poll* and *deliver* synchronise and yield action *copy*

$System = \tau_{\{copy, arrive, finish\}} (\partial_{\{poll, deliver\}} (Station(1, empty, 0) \parallel Station(2, empty, 0) \parallel Server))$

state reward true $\rightarrow size_1 * 0.01 + size_2 * 0.01$

Fig. 2. MAPA specification of a nondeterministic polling system

Table 1. Time-bounded rewards for the polling system (T in seconds)

Q N	T_{lim}	Time-bounded reward			
		min	T(min)	max	T(max)
2 3	1	0.626	0.46	0.814	0.46
2 3	2	0.914	1.64	1.389	1.66
2 3	10	1.005	161.73	2.189	166.59
3 3	1	0.681	4.90	0.893	4.75
3 3	2	1.121	16.69	1.754	17.11
3 3	10	1.314	1653	4.425	1687

Table 2. Time-bounded rewards for the workstation cluster (T in seconds)

N Q	T_{lim}	Time-bounded reward			
		min	T(min)	max	T(max)
4 3	10	0.0126	5.47	0.0126	5.53
4 3	20	0.0267	38.58	0.0267	38.98
4 3	50	0.0701	579.66	0.0701	576.13
4 3	100	0.143	4607	0.143	4540
4 5	10	0.0114	4.17	0.0114	4.23
4 5	20	0.0232	28.54	0.0232	28.75
4 5	50	0.0584	444.39	0.0584	442.63
4 5	100	0.1154	3520.18	0.1154	3521.70

goal states for the expected reward are those when both queues are full. The error-bound for the time-bounded reward analysis was set to 0.1.

The tables show that the minimal reward does not depend on the number of job types, while the maximal reward does. The long-run reward computation is, for this example, considerably slower than the expected reward, and both increase more than linear with the number of states. The time-bounded reward is more affected by the time bound than the number of states, and the computation time does not significantly differ between the maximal and minimal queries.

Workstation Cluster. The second case study is based on a fault-tolerant workstation cluster, described as a GSPN in [25]. Using the GEMMA [2] tool, the GSPN was converted into a MAPA specification.

The workstation cluster consists of two groups of N workstations, each group connected by one switch. The two groups are connected to each other by a backbone. Workstations, switches and the backbone experience exponentially distributed failures, and can be repaired one at a time. If multiple components are eligible for repair at the same time, the choice is nondeterministic. The overall cluster is considered operational if at least Q workstations are operational and connected to each other. Rewards have been added to the system to simulate the costs of repairs and downtime. Repairing a workstation has cost 0.3, a switch costs 0.1, and the backbone costs 1 to repair. If fewer than Q workstations are operational and connected, a cost of 1 per unit time is incurred.

Tables 2 and 4 show the analysis results for this example. The goal states for the expected reward are the states where not enough operational workstations are connected. The error bound for the time-bounded reward analysis was 0.1. For this example, the long-run rewards are quicker to compute than the expected rewards. The long-run rewards do not vary much with the scheduler, since multiple simultaneous failures are rare in this system. This also explains the large expected rewards when Q is low: many repairs will occur before the cluster fails. The time-bounded rewards also show almost no dependence on the scheduler.

Table 3. Long-run and expected rewards for the polling system (T in seconds)

Q	N	$\|S\|$	$\|G\|$	Long-run reward				Expected reward			
				min	T(min)	max	T(max)	min	T(min)	max	T(max)
2	3	1159	405	0.731	0.61	1.048	0.43	0.735	0.28	2.110	0.43
2	4	3488	1536	0.731	3.76	1.119	2.21	0.735	0.93	3.227	2.01
3	3	11122	3645	0.750	95.60	1.107	19.14	1.034	3.14	4.752	8.14
3	4	57632	24576	0.750	5154.6	1.198	705.8	1.034	31.80	8.878	95.87
4	2	5706	1024	0.769	38.03	0.968	5.73	1.330	3.12	4.199	3.12
4	3	102247	32805		Timeout(2h)			1.330	63.24	9.654	192.18

Table 4. Long-run and expected rewards for the workstation cluster (T in seconds)

N	Q	$\|S\|$	$\|G\|$	Long-run reward				Expected reward			
				min	T(min)	max	T(max)	min	T(min)	max	T(max)
4	3	1439	1008	0.00145	0.49	0.00145	0.60	2717	158.5	2718	138.2
4	5	1439	621	0.00501	0.45	0.00505	0.61	1.714	0.56	1.714	0.59
4	8	1439	1438	0.00701	0.48	0.00705	0.64	0	0.50	0	0.50
8	6	4876	3584	0.00145	2.18	0.00145	3.71	2896	783.7	2896	786.6
8	8	4876	4415	0.00146	1.93	0.00147	3.34	285.5	57.13	285.5	54.33
8	10	4883	4783	0.00501	1.92	0.00505	3.36	1.714	2.31	1.714	2.33
8	16	4895	4894	0.00701	2.09	0.00705	3.89	0	2.43	0	2.19

6   Conclusions and Future Work

We introduced the Markov Reward Automaton (MRA), an extension of the Markov Automaton (MA) featuring both state-based and action-based rewards (or, equivalently, costs). We defined strong bisimulation for MRAs, and validated it by stating that our notion coincides with the traditional notions of strong bisimulation for MAs. We generalised the MAPA language to efficiently model MRAs by process-algebraic specifications, and extended the SCOOP tool to automatically generate MRAs from these specifications. Furthermore, we presented three algorithms, for computing the expected reward until reaching a set of goal states, for computing the expected reward until reaching a time-bound, and for computing the long-run average reward while visiting a set of states. Our modelling framework and algorithms allow for a wide variety of systems—featuring nondeterminism, discrete probabilistic choice, continuous stochastic timing and action-based and state-based rewards—to be efficiently modelled, generated and analysed.

Future work will focus on developing weak notions of bisimulation for MRAs, possibly allowing the generalisation of confluence reduction. For quantitative analysis, future work will focus on considering negative rewards, optimisations with respect to time and reward-bounded reachability properties, as well as the handling of several rewards as multi-optimisation problems.

Acknowledgement. This work has been supported by the NWO project SYRUP (612.063.817), by the STW-ProRail partnership program ExploRail under the project ArRangeer (12238), by the DFG/NWO bilateral project ROCKS

(DN 63-257), by the German Research Council (DFG) as part of the Transregional Collaborative Research Center "Automatic Verification and Analysis of Complex Systems" (SFB/TR 14 AVACS), and by the European Union Seventh Framework Programmes under grant agreement no. 295261 (MEALS), 318490 (SENSATION) and 318003 (TREsPASS). We would like to thank Joost-Pieter Katoen for the fruitful discussions.

References

1. Andova, S., Hermanns, H., Katoen, J.-P.: Discrete-time rewards model-checked. In: Larsen, K.G., Niebert, P. (eds.) FORMATS 2003. LNCS, vol. 2791, pp. 88–104. Springer, Heidelberg (2004)
2. Bamberg, R.: Non-deterministic generalised stochastic Petri nets modelling and analysis. Master's thesis, University of Twente (2012)
3. Bernardo, M.: An algebra-based method to associate rewards with EMPA terms. In: Degano, P., Gorrieri, R., Marchetti-Spaccamela, A. (eds.) ICALP 1997. LNCS, vol. 1256, pp. 358–368. Springer, Heidelberg (1997)
4. Boudali, H., Crouzen, P., Stoelinga, M.I.A.: A rigorous, compositional, and extensible framework for dynamic fault tree analysis. IEEE Transactions on Dependable and Secure Computing 7(2), 128–143 (2010)
5. Bozzano, M., Cimatti, A., Katoen, J.-P., Nguyen, V.Y., Noll, T., Roveri, M.: Safety, dependability and performance analysis of extended AADL models. The Computer Journal 54(5), 754–775 (2011)
6. Braitling, B., Fioriti, L.M.F., Hatefi, H., Wimmer, R., Becker, B., Hermanns, H.: MeGARA: Menu-based game abstraction and abstraction refinement of Markov automata. In: QAPL. EPTCS, vol. 154, pp. 48–63 (2014)
7. Brazdil, T., Brozek, V., Chatterjee, K., Forejt, V., Kucera, A.: Two views on multiple mean-payoff objectives in Markov decision processes. In: LICS, pp. 33–42. IEEE (2011)
8. Chatterjee, K., Henzinger, M.: Faster and dynamic algorithms for maximal end-component decomposition and related graph problems in probabilistic verification. In: SODA, pp. 1318–1336. SIAM (2011)
9. Clark, G.: Formalising the specification of rewards with PEPA. In: PAPM, pp. 139–160 (1996)
10. de Alfaro, L.: Formal Verification of Probabilistic Systems. PhD thesis, Stanford University (1997)
11. Deng, Y., Hennessy, M.: Compositional reasoning for weighted Markov decision processes. Science of Computer Programming 78(12), 2537–2579 (2013), Special Section on International Software Product Line Conference 2010 and Fundamentals of Software Engineering (selected papers of FSEN 2011)
12. Deng, Y., Hennessy, M.: On the semantics of Markov automata. Information and Computation 222, 139–168 (2013)
13. Eisentraut, C., Hermanns, H., Katoen, J.-P., Zhang, L.: A semantics for every GSPN. In: Colom, J.-M., Desel, J. (eds.) PETRI NETS 2013. LNCS, vol. 7927, pp. 90–109. Springer, Heidelberg (2013)
14. Eisentraut, C., Hermanns, H., Zhang, L.: Concurrency and composition in a stochastic world. In: Gastin, P., Laroussinie, F. (eds.) CONCUR 2010. LNCS, vol. 6269, pp. 21–39. Springer, Heidelberg (2010)
15. Eisentraut, C., Hermanns, H., Zhang, L.: On probabilistic automata in continuous time. In: LICS, pp. 342–351. IEEE (2010)

16. Groote, J.F., Ponse, A.: The syntax and semantics of μCRL. In: ACP, Workshops in Computing, pp. 26–62. Springer (1995)
17. Guck, D., Han, T., Katoen, J.-P., Neuhäußer, M.R.: Quantitative timed analysis of interactive Markov chains. In: Goodloe, A.E., Person, S. (eds.) NFM 2012. LNCS, vol. 7226, pp. 8–23. Springer, Heidelberg (2012)
18. Guck, D., Hatefi, H., Hermanns, H., Katoen, J.-P., Timmer, M.: Modelling, reduction and analysis of Markov automata. In: Joshi, K., Siegle, M., Stoelinga, M., D'Argenio, P.R. (eds.) QEST 2013. LNCS, vol. 8054, pp. 55–71. Springer, Heidelberg (2013)
19. Guck, D., Timmer, M., Hatefi, H., Ruijters, E.J.J., Stoelinga, M.I.A.: Modelling and analysis of Markov reward automata (extended version). Technical Report TR-CTIT-14-06, CTIT, University of Twente, Enschede (2014)
20. Hatefi, H., Hermanns, H.: Model checking algorithms for Markov automata. Electronic Communications of the EASST 53 (2012)
21. Haverkort, B.R., Cloth, L., Hermanns, H., Katoen, J.-P., Baier, C.: Model checking performability properties. In: DSN, pp. 103–112. IEEE (2002)
22. Haverkort, B.R., Hermanns, H., Katoen, J.-P.: On the use of model checking techniques for dependability evaluation. In: SRDS, pp. 228–237. IEEE (2000)
23. Hermanns, H. (ed.): Interactive Markov Chains. LNCS, vol. 2428. Springer, Heidelberg (2002)
24. Katoen, J.-P., Zapreev, I.S., Hahn, E.M., Hermanns, H., Jansen, D.N.: The ins and outs of the probabilistic model checker MRMC. Performance Evaluation 68(2), 90–104 (2011)
25. Neuhäußer, M.R.: Model Checking Nondeterministic and Randomly Timed Systems. PhD thesis, University of Twente (2010)
26. Neuhäußer, M.R., Stoelinga, M.I.A., Katoen, J.-P.: Delayed nondeterminism in continuous-time Markov decision processes. In: de Alfaro, L. (ed.) FOSSACS 2009. LNCS, vol. 5504, pp. 364–379. Springer, Heidelberg (2009)
27. Segala, R.: Modeling and Verification of Randomized Distributed Real-Time Systems. PhD thesis, Massachusetts Institute of Technology (1995)
28. Song, L., Zhang, L., Godskesen, J.C.: Late weak bisimulation for Markov automata. Technical report, ArXiv e-prints (2012)
29. Srinivasan, M.M.: Nondeterministic polling systems. Management Science 37(6), 667–681 (1991)
30. Timmer, M.: SCOOP: A tool for symbolic optimisations of probabilistic processes. In: QEST, pp. 149–150. IEEE (2011)
31. Timmer, M.: Efficient Modelling, Generation and Analysis of Markov Automata. PhD thesis, University of Twente (2013)
32. Timmer, M., Katoen, J.-P., van de Pol, J.C., Stoelinga, M.I.A.: Efficient modelling and generation of Markov automata. In: Koutny, M., Ulidowski, I. (eds.) CONCUR 2012. LNCS, vol. 7454, pp. 364–379. Springer, Heidelberg (2012)
33. Timmer, M., van de Pol, J., Stoelinga, M.I.A.: Confluence reduction for Markov automata. In: Braberman, V., Fribourg, L. (eds.) FORMATS 2013. LNCS, vol. 8053, pp. 243–257. Springer, Heidelberg (2013)
34. van de Pol, J., Timmer, M.: State space reduction of linear processes using control flow reconstruction. In: Liu, Z., Ravn, A.P. (eds.) ATVA 2009. LNCS, vol. 5799, pp. 54–68. Springer, Heidelberg (2009)
35. Wunderling, R.: Paralleler und objektorientierter Simplex-Algorithmus. PhD thesis, Technische Universität Berlin (1996)

Extensional Crisis and Proving Identity*

Ashutosh Gupta[1], Laura Kovács[2], Bernhard Kragl[1,3], and Andrei Voronkov[4]

[1] IST Austria, Klosterneuburg, Austria
[2] Chalmers University of Technology, Gothenburg, Sweden
[3] Vienna University of Technology, Vienna, Austria
[4] The University of Manchester, Manchester, UK

Abstract. Extensionality axioms are common when reasoning about data collections, such as arrays and functions in program analysis, or sets in mathematics. An extensionality axiom asserts that two collections are equal if they consist of the same elements at the same indices. Using extensionality is often required to show that two collections are equal. A typical example is the set theory theorem $(\forall x)(\forall y)x \cup y = y \cup x$. Interestingly, while humans have no problem with proving such set identities using extensionality, they are very hard for superposition theorem provers because of the calculi they use. In this paper we show how addition of a new inference rule, called extensionality resolution, allows first-order theorem provers to easily solve problems no modern first-order theorem prover can solve. We illustrate this by running the VAMPIRE theorem prover with extensionality resolution on a number of set theory and array problems. Extensionality resolution helps VAMPIRE to solve problems from the TPTP library of first-order problems that were never solved before by any prover.

1 Introduction

Software verification involves reasoning about data collections, such as arrays, sets, and functions. Many modern programming languages support native collection types or have standard libraries for collection types. Many interesting properties of collections are expressed using both quantifiers and theory specific predicates and functions. Unless these properties fall into a decidable theory supported by existing satisfiability modulo theories (SMT) solvers or theorem provers, verifying them requires a combination of reasoning with quantifiers and collection-specific reasoning.

For proving properties of collections one often needs to use *extensionality axioms* asserting that two collections are equal if and only if they consist of the same elements at the same indices. A typical example is the set theory theorem $(\forall x)(\forall y)x \cup y = y \cup x$, asserting that set union is commutative and therefore the union of two sets x and y is the same as the union of y and x. To prove this theorem, in addition to using the definition of the union operation (see Section 2), one needs to use the property that sets containing the same elements are equal. This property is asserted by the extensionality axiom of set theory.

* This research was supported in part by the European Research Council (ERC) under grant agreement 267989 (QUAREM), the Swedish VR grant D0497701, the Austrian National Research Network RiSE (FWF grants S11402-N23 and S11410-N23), and the WWTF PROSEED grant ICT C-050.

F. Cassez and J.-F. Raskin (Eds.): ATVA 2014, LNCS 8837, pp. 185–200, 2014.

Interestingly, while humans have no problem with proving such set identities using extensionality, they are very hard for superposition-based theorem provers because of the calculi they use. The technical details of why it is so are presented in the next section. To overcome this limitation, we need specialized methods of reasoning with extensionality, preferably those not requiring radical changes in the underlying inference mechanism and implementation of superposition.

In this paper we present a new inference rule, called *extensionality resolution*, which allows first-order theorem provers to easily solve problems no modern first-order theorem prover can solve (Section 3). Our approach requires no substantial changes in the implementation of superposition, and introduces no additional constraints on the orderings used by the theorem prover. Building extensionality resolution in a theorem prover needs efficient recognition and treatment of extensionality axioms. We analyze various forms of extensionality axioms and describe various choices made, and corresponding options, for extensionality resolution (Section 4).

We implemented our approach in the first-order theorem prover VAMPIRE [15] and evaluated our method on a number of challenging examples from set theory and reasoning about arrays (Section 5). Our experiments show significant improvements on problems containing extensionality axioms: for example, many problems proved by the new implementation in essentially no time could not be proved by any of the existing first-order provers, including VAMPIRE without extensionality resolution. In particular, we found 12 problems from the TPTP library of first-order problems [21] that were never proved before by any existing prover in any previous edition of the CASC world championship for automated theorem proving [22].

2 Motivating Examples

In this section we explain why theories with extensionality axioms require special treatment in superposition theorem provers.

We assume some basic understanding of first-order theorem proving and the superposition calculus, see, e.g. [3,16] or [15]. Throughout this paper we denote the equality predicate by $=$ and the empty clause by $\Box$. We write $s \neq t$ to mean $\neg(s = t)$, and similarly for every binary predicate written in infix notation. Superposition calculi deal with selection functions: in every non-empty clause at least one literal is selected. Unlike [3], we impose no restrictions on literal selection.

Set Theory. We start with an axiomatization of set theory and will refer to this axiomatization in the rest of the paper. The set theory will use the membership predicate $\in$ and the subset predicate $\subseteq$, the constant $\varnothing$ denoting the empty set, and operations $\cup$ (union), $\cap$ (intersection), $-$ (difference), $\triangle$ (symmetric difference), and complement, denoted by over-lining the expression it is applied to (that is, the complement of a set x is denoted by $\overline{x}$). An axiomatization of set theory with these predicates and operations is shown in Figure 2. We denote set variables by x, y, z and set elements by e.

Example 1. The commutativity of union is a valid property of sets and a logical consequence of the set theory axiomatization:

$$(\forall x)(\forall y)\ x \cup y = y \cup x. \tag{1}$$

$$(\forall x)(\forall y)((\forall e)(e \in x \leftrightarrow e \in y) \to x = y) \qquad \text{(extensionality)}$$
$$(\forall x)(\forall y)(x \subseteq y \leftrightarrow (\forall e)(e \in x \to e \in y)) \qquad \text{(definition of subset)}$$
$$(\forall e)(e \notin \varnothing) \qquad \text{(definition of the empty set)}$$
$$(\forall x)(\forall y)(\forall e)(e \in x \cup y \leftrightarrow e \in x \vee e \in y) \qquad \text{(definition of union)}$$
$$(\forall x)(\forall y)(\forall e)(e \in x \cap y \leftrightarrow e \in x \wedge e \in y) \qquad \text{(definition of intersection)}$$
$$(\forall x)(\forall y)(\forall e)(e \in x - y \leftrightarrow e \in x \wedge e \notin y) \qquad \text{(definition of set difference)}$$
$$(\forall x)(\forall y)(\forall e)(e \in x \triangle y \leftrightarrow (e \in x \leftrightarrow e \notin y)) \qquad \text{(definition of symmetric difference)}$$
$$(\forall x)(\forall e)(e \in \overline{x} \leftrightarrow e \notin x) \qquad \text{(definition of complement)}$$

Fig. 1. Set Theory Axiomatization

This identity is problem 2 in our problem suite of Section 5. Proving such properties poses no problem to humans. We present an example of a human proof.

(1) Take two arbitrary sets a and b. We have to prove $a \cup b = b \cup a$.
(2) By extensionality, to prove (1) we should take an arbitrary element e and prove that $e \in a \cup b$ if and only if $e \in b \cup a$.
(3) We will prove that $e \in a \cup b$ implies $e \in b \cup a$, the reverse direction is obvious.
(4) To this end, assume $e \in a \cup b$. Then, by the definition of union, $e \in a$ or $e \in b$. Again, by the definition of union, both $e \in a$ implies $e \in b \cup a$ and $e \in b$ implies $e \in b \cup a$. In both cases we have $e \in b \cup a$, so we are done.

The given proof is almost trivial. Apart from the application of extensionality (step 2) and skolemization (introduction of constant a, b, e), it uses the definition of union and propositional inferences.

What is interesting is that this problem is hard for first-order theorem provers. If we use our full axiomatization of set theory, none of the top three first-order provers according to the CASC-24 theorem proving competition of last year [22], that is VAMPIRE [15], E [20] and IPROVER [14], can solve it. If we only use the relevant axioms, that is extensionality and the definition of union, these three provers can prove the problem, however not immediately, with runtimes ranging from 0.24 to 27.18 seconds.

If we take slightly more complex set identities, the best first-order theorem provers cannot solve them within reasonable time. We next give such an example.

Example 2. Consider the following conditional identity:

$$(\forall x)(\forall y)(\forall z)(x \cap y \subseteq z \wedge z \subseteq x \cup y \to (x \cup y) \cap (\overline{x} \cup z) = y \cup z) \qquad (2)$$

The above formula cannot be proved by any existing theorem prover within a 1 hour time limit. This formula is problem 25 in our problem suite of Section 5.

It is not hard to analyze the reason for the failure of superposition provers for examples requiring extensionality, such as Example 2: it is the treatment of the extensionality axioms. Suppose that we use a superposition theorem prover and use the standard skolemization and CNF transformation algorithms. Then one of the clauses derived from the extensionality axiom of Figure 2 is:

$$f(x, y) \notin x \vee f(x, y) \notin y \vee x = y. \qquad (3)$$

Here f is a skolem function. This clause is also required for a computer proof, since without it the resulting set of clauses is satisfiable.

Independently of the ordering used by a theorem prover, $x = y$ will be the smallest literal in clause (3). Since it is also positive, no superposition prover will select this literal. Thus, the way the clause will be used by superposition provers is to derive a new set identity from already proved membership literals $s \in t$ by instantiating $x = y$. Note that it will be used in the same way independently of whether the goal is $a \cup b = b \cup a$ or any other set identity. This essentially means that the only way to prove $a \cup b = b \cup a$ is to saturate the rest of the clauses until $x \cup y = y \cup x$ is derived, and likewise for all other set identities! This explains why theorem provers are very inefficient when an application of extensionality is required to prove a set identity.

Arrays. We now give an example of extensionality reasoning over arrays. The standard axiomatization of the theory of arrays also contains an extensionality axiom of the form

$$(\forall x)(\forall y)((\forall i)\ select(x, i) = select(y, i)) \rightarrow x = y), \tag{4}$$

where x, y denote array variables, i is an array index and $select$ the standard select/read function over arrays. Note that this axiom is different from that of sets because arrays are essentially maps and two maps are equal if they contain the same elements at the same indices.

Example 3. Consider the following formula expressing the valid property that the result of updating an array at two different indices does not depend on the order of updates:

$$i_1 \neq i_2 \rightarrow store(store(a, i_1, v_1), i_2, v_2) = store(store(a, i_2, v_2), i_1, v_1). \tag{5}$$

Here, $store$ is the standard store/write function over arrays.

Again, this problem (and similar problems for a larger number of updates) is very hard for theorem provers, see Section 5. The explanation of why it is hard is the same as for sets: the extensionality axiom is used in "the wrong direction" because the literal $x = y$ in axiom (4) is never selected.

Solutions? Though extensionality is important for reasoning about collections, and collection types are first-class in nearly all modern programming languages, reasoning with extensionality is hard for theorem provers because of the (otherwise very efficient) superposition calculus implementation.

The above discussion may suggest that one simple solution would be to select $x = y$ in clauses derived from an extensionality axiom. Note that selecting *only* $x = y$ will result in a loss of completeness, so we can assume that it is selected *in addition* to the literals a theorem prover normally selects. It is not hard to see that this solution effectively makes provers fail on most problems. The reason is that superposition from a variable, resulting from selecting $x = y$, can be done in *every non-variable term*. For example, consider the clause

$$e \in x - y \lor e \in x \lor e \notin y, \tag{6}$$

obtained by converting the set difference axiom of Figure 2 into CNF and suppose that the first literal is selected in it. A superposition step from the extensionality clause (3) into this clause gives

$$f(x - y, z) \notin x - y \lor f(x - y, z) \notin z \lor e \in z \lor e \in x \lor e \notin y. \qquad (7)$$

Note the size of the new clause and also that it contains new occurrences of $x - y$, to which we can apply extensionality again.

From the above example it is easy to see that selecting $x = y$ in the extensionality clause (3) will result in a rapid blow-up of the search space by large clauses. The solution we propose and defend in this paper is to add a special generating inference rule for treating extensionality, called *extensionality resolution*, which requires relatively simple changes in the architecture of a superposition theorem prover.

3   Reasoning in First-Order Theories with Extensionality Axioms

In this section we explain our solution to problems arising in reasoning with extensionality axioms. For doing so, we introduce the new inference rule *extensionality resolution* and show how to integrate it into a superposition theorem prover.

Suppose that we have a partial function *ext_rec*, called *extensionality recognizer*, such that for every clause C, *ext_rec*(C) either is undefined, or returns the single positive equality among variables $x = y$ from C. We will also sometimes use *ext_rec* as a boolean function, meaning that it is true iff it is defined. We call an *extensionality clause* any clause C for which *ext_rec*(C) holds. Note that every clause derived from an extensionality axiom contains a single positive equality among variables, but in general not every clause containing such an equality corresponds to an extensionality axiom, see Section 4.

The *extensionality resolution* rule is the following inference rule:

$$\frac{x = y \lor C \quad s \neq t \lor D}{C\theta \lor D} , \qquad (8)$$

where

1. *ext_rec*$(x = y \lor C) = (x = y)$, hence, $x = y \lor C$ is an extensionality clause;
2. $s \neq t$ is selected in $s \neq t \lor D$;
3. θ is the substitution $\{x \mapsto s, y \mapsto t\}$.

Note that, since equality is symmetric, there are two inferences between the premises of (8); one is given above and the other one is with the substitution $\{x \mapsto t, y \mapsto s\}$.

Example 4. Consider two clauses: clause (3) and the unit clause $a \cup b \neq b \cup a$. Suppose that the former clause is recognized as an extensionality clause. Then the following inference is an instance of extensionality resolution:

$$\frac{f(x, y) \notin x \lor f(x, y) \notin y \lor x = y \quad a \cup b \neq b \cup a}{f(a \cup b, b \cup a) \notin a \cup b \lor f(a \cup b, b \cup a) \notin b \cup a} .$$

input: *init*: set of clauses;
var *active*, *passive*, *unprocessed* : = ∅: set of clauses;
var *given*, *new*: clause;
unprocessed : = *init*;
loop
  while *unprocessed* ≠ ∅
    new : =*pop*(*unprocessed*);
    if *new* = □ **then return** *unsatisfiable*;
    if *retained*(*new*) **then**   *(* retention test *)*
      simplify *new* by clauses in *active* ∪ *passive* ;   *(* forward simplification *)*
      if *new* = □ **then return** *unsatisfiable*;
      if *retained*(*new*) **then**   *(* another retention test *)*
        delete and simplify clauses in *active* and   *(* backward simplification *)*
                       passive using *new*;
        move the simplified clauses to *unprocessed*;
        add *new* to *passive*;
  if *passive* = ∅ **then return** *satisfiable* or *unknown*;
  given : = *select*(*passive*);   *(* clause selection *)*
  move *given* from *passive* to *active*;
  unprocessed : =*forward_infer*(*given*, *active*);   *(* forward generating inferences *)*
  add *backward_infer*(*given*, *active*) to *unprocessed*;   *(* backward generating inferences *)*

Fig. 2. Otter Saturation Algorithm

Given a clause with a selected literal $s \neq t$, which can be considered as a request to prove $s = t$, extensionality resolution replaces it by an instance of the premises of extensionality. This example shows that an application of extensionality resolution achieves the same effect as the use of extensionality in the "human" proof of Example 1.

Let us now explain how extensionality resolution can be integrated in a saturation algorithm of a superposition theorem prover. The key questions to consider is when the rule is applied and whether this rule requires term indexing or other algorithms to be performed. The implementation is similar for all saturation algorithms; for ease of presentation we will describe it only for the Otter saturation algorithm [15]. For an overview of saturation algorithms we refer to [18,15].

A simplified description of the Otter saturation algorithm is shown in Figure 2. It uses three kinds of inferences: *generating*, which add new clauses to the search space; *simplifying*, which replace existing clauses by new ones, and *deletion*, which delete clauses from the search space. The algorithms maintains three sets of clauses:

1. *active*: the set of clauses to which generating inferences have already been applied;
2. *passive*: clauses that are retained by the prover (that is, not deleted);
3. *unprocessed*: clauses that are in a queue for a retention test.

At each step, the algorithm either processes a clause *new*, picked from *unprocessed*, or performs generating inferences with the so-called *given clause given*, which is the clause most recently added to *active*.

All operations performed by the saturation algorithm that may take considerable time to execute are normally implemented using *term indexing*, that is, by building a special

input: *init*: set of clauses;
var *active, passive, unprocessed* : = ∅: set of clauses;
var *given, new*: clause;
√ **var** *neg_equal, ext* : = ∅: set of clauses;
unprocessed : = *init*;
loop
  while *unprocessed* ≠ ∅
   new : =*pop*(*unprocessed*);
   if *new* = □ **then** **return** *unsatisfiable*;
   if *retained*(*new*) **then**   *(* retention test *)*
    simplify *new* by clauses in *active* ∪ *passive* ;   *(* forward simplification *)*
    if *new* = □ **then** **return** *unsatisfiable*;
    if *retained*(*new*) **then**   *(* another retention test *)*
     delete and simplify clauses in *active* and   *(* backward simplification *)*
                       passive using *new*;
     move the simplified clauses to *unprocessed*;
     add *new* to *passive*;
   if *passive* = ∅ **then** **return** *satisfiable* or *unknown*;
   given : = *select*(*passive*);   *(* clause selection *)*
   move *given* from *passive* to *active*;
   unprocessed : =*forward_infer*(*given, active*);   *(* forward generating inferences *)*
√ **if** *given* has a negative selected equality **then**
√   add *given* to *neg_equal*;
√   add to *unprocessed* all conclusions of extensionality resolution inferences
√   between clauses in *ext* and *given*;
   add *backward_infer*(*given, active*) to *unprocessed*; *(* backward generating inferences *)*
√ **if** *ext_rec*(*given*) **then**
√   add *given* to *ext*;
√   add to *unprocessed* all conclusions of extensionality resolution inferences
√   between *given* and clauses in *neg_equal*;

Fig. 3. Otter Saturation Algorithm with Extensionality Resolution parts marked by √

purpose index data structure that makes the operation faster. For example, all theorem provers with built-in equality reasoning have an index for forward demodulation.

Extensionality resolution is a generating inference rule, so the relevant lines of the saturation algorithm are the ones at the bottom, referring to generating inferences. The same saturation algorithm with extensionality resolution related parts marked by √ is shown in Figure 3.

As one can see from the algorithm in Figure 3, extensionality resolution is easy to integrate into superposition theorem provers. The reason is that it requires no sophisticated indexing to find candidates for inferences: extensionality resolution applies to *every* extensionality clause and *every* clause with a negative selected equality literal.

Therefore, we only have to maintain two collections: *neg_equal* of active clauses having a negative selected equality literal and *ext* of extensionality clauses as recognized by the function *ext_rec*. Another addition to the saturation algorithm, not shown in Figure 3, is that deleted or simplified clauses belonging to any of these collections should be deleted from the collections too. An easy way to implement this is to ignore such deletions when they occur and instead check the storage class of a clause (that is active, passive, unprocessed or deleted) when we iterate through the collection during generating inferences. If during such an iteration we discover a clause that is no more active, we remove it from the collection and perform no generating inferences with it.

4   Recognizing Extensionality Axioms

One of the key questions for building extensionality reasoning into a theorem prover is the recognition of extensionality clauses, i.e. the concrete choice of ext_rec. Every clause containing a single positive equality between two different variables $x = y$ is a potential extensionality clause.

To understand this, we analyzed problems in the TPTP library of about 14,000 first-order problems [21] . It turned out that the TPTP library contains about 6,000 different axioms (mainly formulas, not clauses) that can result in a clause containing a positive equality among variables. By different here we mean up to variable renaming. One can consider other equivalence relations among axioms, such as using commutativity and associativity of $\wedge$ or $\vee$, or closure under renaming of predicate and function symbols, for which the number of different axioms will be smaller. Anyhow, having 6,000 different axioms in about 14,000 problems shows that such axioms are very common.

The most commonly used examples of extensionality axioms are the already discussed set and array extensionality axioms. In addition to them, set theory axiomatizations often contain the subset-based extensionality axiom $x \subseteq y \wedge y \subseteq x \rightarrow x = y$.

Contrary to these intended extensionality axioms, there is one kind of axioms which is dangerous to consider as extensionality: constructor axioms, describing that some function symbol is a constructor. Constructor axioms are central in theories of algebraic data types. For example, consider an axiom describing a property of pairs $pair(x_1, x_2) = pair(y_1, y_2) \rightarrow x_1 = y_1$, or a similar axiom for the successor function $succ(x) = succ(y) \rightarrow x = y$. If we regard the latter as an extensionality axiom, extensionality resolution allows one to derive from any inequality $s \neq t$ the inequality $succ(s) \neq succ(t)$, which, in turn, allows one to derive $succ(succ(s)) \neq succ(succ(t))$ and so on. This will clutter the search space with bigger and bigger clauses. Hence, clauses derived from constructor axioms must not be recognized as extensionality clauses. We achieve this by excluding clauses having a negative equality of the same sort as $x = y$. However, in unsorted problems, i.e. every term has the same sort, we would for example also lose the array extensionality axiom.

The clause $i = j \vee select(store(x, i, e), j) = select(x, j)$ from the axiomatization of arrays is also certainly not intended to be an extensionality axiom. From this example we derive the option to exclude clauses having a positive equality other than the one among variables.

Another common formula is the definition of a non-strict order: $x \leq y \leftrightarrow x < y \vee x = y$. We did not yet investigate how considering this axiom as an extensionality axiom affects the search space, and consider such an investigation an interesting task for future work.

In addition to the above mentioned potential extensionality axioms, there is a large variety of such axioms in the TPTP library, including very long ones. One example, coming from the Mizar library, is

$$(\forall x_0)(\forall x_1)(\forall x_2)(\forall x_3)(\forall x_4)$$
$$((v1\_funct\_1(x_1) \wedge v1\_funct\_2(x_1, k2\_zfmisc\_1(x_0, x_0), x_0) \wedge$$
$$v1\_funct\_1(x_2) \wedge v1\_funct\_2(x_2, k2\_zfmisc\_1(x_0, x_0), x_0) \wedge$$
$$m1\_subset\_1(x_3, x_0) \wedge m1\_relset\_1(x_1, k2\_zfmisc\_1(x_0, x_0), x_0) \wedge$$
$$m1\_subset\_1(x_4, x_0) \wedge m1\_relset\_1(x_2, k2\_zfmisc\_1(x_0, x_0), x_0)) \rightarrow$$
$$(\forall x_4)(\forall x_6)(\forall x_7)(\forall x_8)(\forall x_9)($$
$$g3\_vectsp\_1(x_0, x_1, x_2, x_3, x_4) = g3\_vectsp\_1(x_5, x_6, x_7, x_8, x_9) \rightarrow$$
$$(x_0 = x_5 \wedge x_1 = x_6 \wedge x_2 = x_7 \wedge x_3 = x_8 \wedge x_4 = x_9))).$$

Another example comes from problems generated automatically by parsing natural language sentences:

$$x_4 = x_6 \vee ssSkC0 \vee \neg in(x_6, x_7) \vee \neg front(x_7) \vee \neg furniture(x_7) \vee \neg seat(x_7) \vee$$
$$\neg fellow(x_6) \vee \neg man(x_6) \vee \neg young(x_6) \vee \neg seat(x_5) \vee \neg furniture(x_5) \vee \neg front(x_5) \vee$$
$$\neg in(x_4, x_5) \vee \neg young(x_4) \vee \neg man(x_4) \vee \neg fellow(x_4) \vee \neg in(x_2, x_3) \vee \neg city(x_3) \vee$$
$$\neg hollywood(x_3) \vee \neg event(x_2) \vee \neg barrel(x_2, x_1) \vee \neg down(x_2, x_0) \vee \neg old(x_1) \vee$$
$$\neg dirty(x_1) \vee \neg white(x_1) \vee \neg car(x_1) \vee \neg chevy(x_1) \vee \neg street(x_0) \vee \neg way(x_0) \vee$$
$$\neg lonely(x_0).$$

These examples give rise to an option for limiting the number of literals in an extensionality clause.

Based on our analysis in this section, there are a number of options for recognizing extensionality clauses. In Section 5 we show two combinations of these options are useful for solving distinct problems.

5 Experimental Results

We implemented extensionality resolution in VAMPIRE. Our implementation required about 1,000 lines of C++ code on top of the existing VAMPIRE code. The extended VAMPIRE is available as binary at [1] and will be merged in the next official release of VAMPIRE. In the sequel, we refer to our extended VAMPIRE implementation as VAMPIRE[EX].

In this section we report on our experimental results obtained by evaluating extensionality resolution on three collections of benchmarks: (i) handcrafted hard set theory problems, (ii) array problems from the SMT-LIB library [6], and (iii) first-order problems of the TPTP library [21]. Our results are summarized in Tables 1–3, and detailed below.

On the set theory problems our implementation significantly outperforms all theorem provers that were competing in the last year's theorem proving system competition CASC-24 [22]. VAMPIRE[EX] efficiently solves all the set theory problems, while every other prover including the original VAMPIRE solves less than half of the problems (Table 1). We also tried the SMT solver Z3, which failed to prove any of our set theory problems.

When evaluating VAMPIRE[EX] on array problems taken from the SMT-LIB library, VAMPIRE[EX] solved more problems than all existing first-order theorem provers (Table 2). The SMT solver Z3 outperformed VAMPIRE[EX] if we encode these array problems as problems from the theory of arrays with extensionality, in which case Z3 can use its decision procedure for this theory.

1. $x \cap y = y \cap x$
2. $x \cup y = y \cup x$
3. $x \cap y = ((x \cup y) - (x - y)) - (y - x)$
4. $\overline{(\overline{x})} = x$
5. $x = x \cap (x \cup y)$
6. $x = x \cup (x \cap y)$
7. $(x \cap y) - z = (x - z) \cap (y - z)$
8. $\overline{x \cup y} = \overline{x} \cap \overline{y}$
9. $\overline{x \cap y} = \overline{x} \cup \overline{y}$
10. $x \cup (y \cap z) = (x \cup y) \cap (x \cup z)$
11. $x \cap (y \cup z) = (x \cap y) \cup (x \cap z)$
12. $x \subseteq y \rightarrow x \cup y = y$
13. $x \subseteq y \rightarrow x \cap y = x$
14. $x \subseteq y \rightarrow x - y = \emptyset$
15. $x \subseteq y \rightarrow y - x = y - (x \cap y)$
16. $x \cup y \subseteq z \rightarrow z - (x \triangle y) = (x \cap y) \cup (z - (x \cup y))$
17. $x \triangle y = \emptyset \rightarrow x = y$
18. $z - (x \triangle y) = (x \cap (y \cap z)) \cup (z - (x \cup y))$
19. $(x - y) \cap (x \triangle y) = x \cap \overline{y}$

20. $x \triangle y = (x - y) \cup (y - x)$
21. $(x \triangle y) \triangle z = x \triangle (y \triangle z)$
22. $(x \triangle y) \triangle z = ((x - (y \cup z)) \cup (y - (x \cup z))) \cup ((z - (x \cup y)) \cup (x \cap (y \cap z)))$
23. $((x \cup y) \cap (\overline{x} \cup z)) = (y - x) \cup (x \cap z)$
24. $(\exists x)(((x \cup y) \cap (\overline{x} \cup z)) = y \cup z)$
25. $(x \cap y) \subseteq z \subseteq (x \cup y) \rightarrow ((x \cup y) \cap (\overline{x} \cup z)) = y \cup z$
26. $x \subseteq y \rightarrow (z - x) - y = z - y$
27. $x \subseteq y \rightarrow (z - y) - x = z - y$
28. $x \subseteq y \rightarrow z - (y \cup x) = z - y$
29. $x \subseteq y \rightarrow z - (y \cap x) = z - x$
30. $x \subseteq y \rightarrow (z - y) \cap x = \emptyset$
31. $x \subseteq y \rightarrow (z - x) \cap y = z \cap (y - x)$
32. $x \subseteq y \subseteq z \rightarrow (z - x) \cap y = y - x$
33. $x - y = x \cap \overline{y}$
34. $x \cap \emptyset = \emptyset$
35. $x \cup \emptyset = x$
36. $x \subseteq y \rightarrow (\exists z)(y - z = x)$

Fig. 4. Collection of 36 handcrafted set theory problems. All variables without explicit quantification are universally quantified.

On the TPTP library, VAMPIRE[EX] solved 84 problems not solved by the CASC version of VAMPIRE (Table 3). Even more, 12 of these problems have rating 1, which means that no existing prover, either first-order or SMT, can solve them.

The rest of this section describes in detail our experiments. All results were obtained on a GridEngine managed cluster system at IST Austria. Each run of a prover on a problem was assigned a dedicated 2.3 GHz core and 10 GB RAM with the time limit of 60 seconds.

Set Theory Experiments. We handcrafted 36 set identity problems given in Figure 4, which also include the problems presented in Section 2. For proving the problems, we created TPTP files containing the set theory axioms from Figure 2 as TPTP axioms and the problem to be proved as a TPTP conjecture.

Table 1 shows the runtimes and the number of problems solved by VAMPIRE[EX] compared to all but two provers participating in the first-order theorems (FOF) and typed first-order theorems (TFA) divisions of the CASC-24 competition.[1] The only provers which we did not compare with VAMPIRE[EX] were PROVER9 and SPASS+T, for the following reasons: PROVER9 depends on the directory structure of the CASC system and the TPTP library, thus it did not run on our test system; SPASS+T only accepts problems containing arithmetic. Since not all provers participating in CASC-24 support typed formulas, we have also generated untyped versions of the problems. As a

---

[1] We used the exact programs and command calls as in the competition, up to adaptions of the absolute file paths to our test system.

Table 1. Runtimes in seconds of provers on the set theory problems from Figure 4. Empty entries mean timeout after 60 seconds. The first row indicates whether the prover was run on typed (TFF) or untyped (FOF) problems. The last row counts the number of solved problems.

#	VAMPIRE^{EX} (TFF)	VAMPIRE^{EX} (FOF)	IPROVER (FOF)	PRINCESS (TFF)	PRINCESS (FOF)	VAMPIRE (TFF)	VAMPIRE (FOF)	CVC4 (FOF)	E (FOF)	MUSCADET (FOF)	ZIPPER-POSITION (FOF)	BEAGLE (TFF)	BEAGLE (FOF)	E-KR-HYPER (FOF)
1	0.02	0.08	13.70	7.78	7.61					0.10				
2	0.01	0.02		7.92	8.22				41.54					
3	0.06	0.29												
4	0.02	0.07	1.47	9.36	9.45	0.21	0.24	30.24	1.38	0.65				
5	0.02	0.25	0.89	17.19	14.64	1.92		56.05	33.98	0.10				
6	0.02	0.25	0.29	15.41	10.97			54.40						
7	0.03	0.03												
8	0.02	0.08												
9	0.02	0.09												
10	0.04	0.09												
11	0.04	0.27												
12	0.02	0.25	0.58	15.36	14.66	0.39	0.40	50.52						
13	0.02	0.02	1.10	15.23	15.13	0.14	0.17	30.34	0.35	0.09				
14	0.02	0.07	2.44	7.80	8.09	0.02	0.03		0.07	0.09	10.59	6.85	7.88	
15	0.02	0.03	13.80	8.55	8.04	0.12	0.15	32.15	1.55					
16	3.41	4.14												
17	0.01	0.09				0.02	0.02	30.94	24.31		0.44			
18	0.94	1.08												
19	0.03	0.04												
20	0.02	0.25												
21	0.03	0.25												
22	1.73	1.76												
23	0.24	0.50												
24	0.15	0.42				0.43	0.26							
25	0.05	0.05												
26	0.05	0.10												
27	0.03	0.08	11.80	25.80	20.97				52.47					
28	0.06	0.31	11.80	33.73	37.05	0.80	0.72	34.32						
29	0.03	0.04	38.63			0.22	0.26	31.33	1.64					
30	0.02	0.08	3.32	12.36	11.53	0.06	0.07		27.54	0.11	23.30			
31	0.03	0.27												
32	0.04	0.09												
33	0.02	0.01	23.28	20.92	21.00									
34	0.02	0.01	0.50	6.71	6.71	0.02	0.02	30.29	0.03	0.08	0.59	2.22	2.21	
35	0.02	0.02	8.23	6.87	7.24	0.23	0.25	30.34	30.23					
36	0.02	0.03	1.50			20.86	21.01	44.77						
	36	36	16	15	15	14	13	13	11	7	4	2	2	0

result, theorem provers supporting typed formulas were then evaluated on both typed and untyped problems.

Our results show that only VAMPIRE^{EX} could solve all problems, and 17 problems could not be solved by any other prover. Moreover, VAMPIRE^{EX} is very fast: out of the 36 typed problems, only 5 took more than 0.1 seconds and only 2 took more than 1 second.

In our experiments with typed formulas, type information reduces the number of well-formed formulas and therefore the search space. Hence VAMPIRE^{EX} is generally faster on typed problems, in our experiments by 4.18 seconds in total. The total

Table 2. Evaluation of extensionality resolution on array problems. Runtimes are in seconds.

Prover	solved	runtime
VAMPIRE^{EX}	154	1193.85
VAMPIRE	107	1020.76
E	81	600.01
BEAGLE	16	185.44
ZIPPERPOSITION	15	49.27
PRINCESS	10	35.02
IPROVER	9	47.13
CVC4	8	0.36
E-KRHYPER	8	1.26
MUSCADET	4	0.41
Z3	277	64.25

runtime of VAMPIRE^{EX} on all typed problems was 7.33 seconds. Among the problems also solved by VAMPIRE, VAMPIRE^{EX} is always faster.

Finally, Table 1 does not compare VAMPIRE^{EX} with SMT solvers for the reason that these set theory problems use both quantifiers and theories. We however note that the use of quantifiers in the set theory axiomatization caused SMT solvers, in particular Z3, to fail on all these examples. Z3 provides a special encoding [11] for sets that allows some of the problems to be encoded as quantifier free and we believe that a comparison with this encoding is unfair.

Array Experiments. For evaluating VAMPIRE^{EX} on array problems, we used all the 278 unsatisfiable problems from the QF_AX category of quantifier-free formulas over the theory of arrays with extensionality of SMT-LIB. We translated these problems into the TPTP syntax. Table 2 reports on the results of VAMPIRE^{EX} on these problems and compares them to the results obtained by the other first-order provers and the SMT solver Z3, which solves all of them but one using a decision procedure for the theory. However, we feel that arrays with extensionality are not very interesting for applications, since we failed to find natural examples of problems that require such extensionality, apart from those that state that the results of updating arrays at distinct indexes does not depend on the order of updates (for example, all problems in the QF_AX category of SMT-LIB are such problems).

For array experiments we were interested whether VAMPIRE^{EX} can outperform first-order provers without extensionality resolution. Table 2 shows that the number of array problems it solves is significantly larger than that of all other first-order provers, thus confirming the power of our approach to extensionality reasoning.

The TPTP Library Experiments. VAMPIRE uses a collection of strategies to prove hard problems and our new inference rule adds new possible options in the repertoire of VAMPIRE. Based on the discussion of Section 4, we introduced two new options for the VAMPIRE strategies to control the recognition of extensionality clauses in VAMPIRE^{EX}, namely known and all. The option known only recognizes clauses

Table 3. Experiments with various options for recognizing extensionality clauses in VAMPIRE[EX]

Strategies	solved	uniquely solved	
original	4015	156	
original+known	3870	8	} 84
original+all	3747	50	

obtained from the set and array extensionality axioms, as well as the subset-based set extensionality axiom. The option all applies the criteria given in Section 4.

We ran experiments on all 7224 TPTP problems that may contain an equality between variables. Our results are summarized in Table 3, where the first row reports on using VAMPIRE[EX] with the original collection of strategies of VAMPIRE. The second row uses VAMPIRE[EX] in the combination of the option known and the original strategies of VAMPIRE, whereas the third row uses the option all with the original strategies of VAMPIRE.

The original strategies solved 4015 problems, and 156 were uniquely solved by these collection of strategies. The original+known and original+all solved 3870 and 3747 problems, respectively. They uniquely solved 8 and 50 problems respectively. Using however original+known and original+all in combination, VAMPIRE[EX] solved 84 problems which were not solved by the original collection of strategies original. We have listed these 84 problems in Table 4. Out of these 84 solved problems, 12 problems are rated with difficulty 1 in the CASC system competition. That is, these 12 problems were never solved in any previous CASC competition by any existing prover, including all existing first-order provers and the SMT solvers Z3 and CVC4 [5]. VAMPIRE[EX] hence outperforms all modern solvers when it comes to reasoning with both theories and quantifiers.

Note that for first-order theorem provers the average number of problems solved by a strategy does not mean much in general. The reason is that these provers show the best performance when they treat problems by a cocktail of strategies. Normally, if a problem is solvable by a prover, there is a strategy that solves it in nearly no time, so running many short-lived strategies gives better results than running a small number of strategies for longer times. When we introduce a new option to a theorem prover, the main question is, if this option can complement the cocktail of strategies so that more problems are solved by these strategies all together. This means that an option that solves many unique problems is, in general, much more valuable than an option solving many problems on the average.

Our results indicate that the use extensionality resolution in first-order theorem proving can solve a significant number of problems not solvable without it. Therefore it is a powerful addition to the toolbox of first-order theorem proving methods. Further extensive experiments with combining extensionality resolution with various other options are required for better understanding of how it can be integrated in first-order provers.

Table 4. Fields and ratings of TPTP problems only solved by VAMPIRE with extensionality resolution

Field	Subfield	Problem	Rating
Computer Science	Commonsense Reasoning	CRS075+6	0.97
Computer Science	Commonsense Reasoning	CRS076+2	0.97
Computer Science	Commonsense Reasoning	CRS076+6	1.00
Computer Science	Commonsense Reasoning	CRS076+7	1.00
Computer Science	Commonsense Reasoning	CRS078+2	1.00
Computer Science	Commonsense Reasoning	CRS079+6	0.97
Computer Science	Commonsense Reasoning	CRS080+1	0.97
Computer Science	Commonsense Reasoning	CRS080+2	1.00
Computer Science	Commonsense Reasoning	CRS081+4	0.93
Computer Science	Commonsense Reasoning	CRS083+4	0.90
Computer Science	Commonsense Reasoning	CRS083+6	0.97
Computer Science	Commonsense Reasoning	CRS084+2	0.93
Computer Science	Commonsense Reasoning	CRS084+4	0.93
Computer Science	Commonsense Reasoning	CRS084+5	0.93
Computer Science	Commonsense Reasoning	CRS088+1	0.97
Computer Science	Commonsense Reasoning	CRS088+2	1.00
Computer Science	Commonsense Reasoning	CRS088+4	0.93
Computer Science	Commonsense Reasoning	CRS088+6	1.00
Computer Science	Commonsense Reasoning	CRS089+6	1.00
Computer Science	Commonsense Reasoning	CRS092+6	1.00
Computer Science	Commonsense Reasoning	CRS093+4	0.93
Computer Science	Commonsense Reasoning	CRS093+6	1.00
Computer Science	Commonsense Reasoning	CRS093+7	1.00
Computer Science	Commonsense Reasoning	CRS094+6	0.97
Computer Science	Commonsense Reasoning	CRS109+6	0.93
Computer Science	Commonsense Reasoning	CRS118+6	0.97
Computer Science	Commonsense Reasoning	CSR057+5	0.97
Computer Science	Software Creation	SWC021-1	0.64
Computer Science	Software Creation	SWC160-1	0.93
Computer Science	Software Verification	SWV474+1	0.83
Computer Science	Software Verification	SWV845-1	0.86
Computer Science	Software Verification Continued	SWW284+1	0.87
Logic	Combinatory Logic	COL081-1	0.64
Mathematics	Algebra/Lattices	LAT298+1	0.90
Mathematics	Algebra/Lattices	LAT324+1	0.80
Mathematics	Category Theory	CAT009-1	0.00
Mathematics	Category Theory	CAT010-1	0.00
Mathematics	Graph Theory	GRA007+1	0.60
Mathematics	Graph Theory	GRA007+2	0.63
Mathematics	Number Theory	NUM459+1	0.70
Mathematics	Number Theory	NUM493+1	0.87
Mathematics	Number Theory	NUM493+3	0.97
Mathematics	Number Theory	NUM495+1	0.60
Mathematics	Number Theory	NUM508+3	0.63
Mathematics	Number Theory	NUM515+1	1.00
Mathematics	Number Theory	NUM515+3	1.00
Mathematics	Number Theory	NUM517+3	0.70
Mathematics	Number Theory	NUM535+1	0.63
Mathematics	Number Theory	NUM542+1	0.83
Mathematics	Number Theory	NUM544+1	0.90
Mathematics	Set Theory	SET018+1	0.90
Mathematics	Set Theory	SET041-3	0.36
Mathematics	Set Theory	SET066-6	1.00
Mathematics	Set Theory	SET066-7	1.00
Mathematics	Set Theory	SET069-6	0.93
Mathematics	Set Theory	SET069-7	0.93
Mathematics	Set Theory	SET070-6	0.93
Mathematics	Set Theory	SET070-7	0.93
Mathematics	Set Theory	SET097-7	0.64
Mathematics	Set Theory	SET099+1	0.87
Mathematics	Set Theory	SET128-6	0.71
Mathematics	Set Theory	SET157-6	0.71
Mathematics	Set Theory	SET262-6	0.86
Mathematics	Set Theory	SET497-6	0.71
Mathematics	Set Theory	SET510-6	0.43
Mathematics	Set Theory	SET606+3	0.53
Mathematics	Set Theory	SET613+3	0.83
Mathematics	Set Theory	SET634+3	0.67
Mathematics	Set Theory	SET671+3	0.90
Mathematics	Set Theory	SET673+3	0.90
Mathematics	Set Theory	SET674+3	0.90
Mathematics	Set Theory	SET831-1	0.86
Mathematics	Set Theory	SET837-1	0.93
Mathematics	Set Theory Continued	SEU007+1	1.00
Mathematics	Set Theory Continued	SEU049+1	0.87
Mathematics	Set Theory Continued	SEU058+1	0.93
Mathematics	Set Theory Continued	SEU059+1	0.97
Mathematics	Set Theory Continued	SEU073+1	1.00
Mathematics	Set Theory Continued	SEU194+1	0.70
Mathematics	Set Theory Continued	SEU205+1	0.97
Mathematics	Set Theory Continued	SEU265+2	0.97
Mathematics	Set Theory Continued	SEU283+1	0.73
Mathematics	Set Theory Continued	SEU384+1	0.90
Social Sciences	Social Choice Theory	SCT162+1	0.87

6   Related Work

Reasoning with both theories and quantifiers is considered as a major challenge in the theorem proving and SMT communities. SMT solvers can process very large formulas in ground decidable theories [10,5]. Quantifier reasoning in SMT solvers is implemented using trigger-based E-matching, which is not as powerful as the use of unification in superposition calculi. Combining quantifiers with theories based on SMT solving is described in [17,19].

Unlike SMT reasoning, first-order theorem provers are very efficient in handling quantifiers but weak in theory reasoning. Paper [4] introduces the hierarchical superposition calculus by combining the superposition calculus with black-box style theory reasoning. This approach has been further extended in [7] for first-order reasoning modulo background theories under the assumption that theory terms are ground. A similar approach is also addressed in the instantiation-based theorem proving method of [12,14], where quantifier-free instances of the first-order problem are generated. These ground instances are passed to the reasoning engine of the background theory for proving unsatisfiability of the original quantified problem. In case of satisfiability, the original problem is refined based on the generated ground model and new instances are next generated. All mentioned approaches separate the theory-specific and quantifier reasoning. This is not the case with our work, where theory reasoning using extensionality is a natural extension of the superposition calculus.

Our work is dedicated to first-order reasoning about collections, such as sets and arrays. It is partially motivated by program analysis, since collection types are first-class types in many programming languages and nearly every programming languages has collection libraries. While there has been a considerable amount of work on deciding universal theories of collection types, including using superposition provers [2] and decidability or undecidability of their extensions [9,13], our work is different since we consider collections in first-order logic with quantifiers. As many others, we are trying to bridge the gap between quantifier and theory reasoning, but in a way that is friendly to existing architectures of first-order theorem provers. Unlike [2], we impose no additional constraints on the used simplification ordering and can deal with arbitrary axioms on top of array axioms.

In a way, our approach is similar to the one of [8], where it is proposed to extend the resolution calculus by theory-specific rules, which do not change the underlying inference mechanisms. Indeed, our implementation of extensionality resolution requires relatively simple changes in saturation algorithms.

7   Conclusion

We examined why reasoning with extensionality axioms is hard for superposition-based theorem provers and proposed a new inference rule, called *extensionality resolution*, to improve their performance on problems containing such axioms. Our experimental results show that first-order provers with extensionality resolution can easily solve problems in reasoning with sets and arrays that were unsolvable by all existing theorem provers and, also much harder versions of these problems. Our results contribute to one of the main problems in modern theorem proving: efficiently solving problems using both quantifiers and theories.

References

1. Experimental results of this paper, http://vprover.org/extres
2. Armando, A., Bonacina, M.P., Ranise, S., Schulz, S.: New Results on Rewrite-Based Satisfiability Procedures. ACM Trans. Comput. Log. 10(1) (2009)
3. Bachmair, L., Ganzinger, H.: Resolution Theorem Proving. In: Handbook of Automated Reasoning, pp. 19–99. Elsevier and MIT Press (2001)
4. Bachmair, L., Ganzinger, H., Waldmann, U.: Refutational Theorem Proving for Hierarchic First-Order Theories. Appl. Algebra Eng. Commun. Comput. 5, 193–212 (1994)
5. Barrett, C., Conway, C.L., Deters, M., Hadarean, L., Jovanović, D., King, T., Reynolds, A., Tinelli, C.: CVC4. In: Gopalakrishnan, G., Qadeer, S. (eds.) CAV 2011. LNCS, vol. 6806, pp. 171–177. Springer, Heidelberg (2011)
6. Barrett, C., Stump, A., Tinelli, C.: The Satisfiability Modulo Theories Library (SMT-LIB) (2010), www.SMT-LIB.org
7. Baumgartner, P., Waldmann, U.: Hierarchic Superposition with Weak Abstraction. In: Bonacina, M.P. (ed.) CADE 2013. LNCS, vol. 7898, pp. 39–57. Springer, Heidelberg (2013)
8. Bledsoe, W.W., Boyer, R.S.: Computer Proofs of Limit Theorems. In: Proc. of IJCAI, pp. 586–600 (1971)
9. Bradley, A.R., Manna, Z., Sipma, H.B.: What's Decidable About Arrays? In: Emerson, E.A., Namjoshi, K.S. (eds.) VMCAI 2006. LNCS, vol. 3855, pp. 427–442. Springer, Heidelberg (2006)
10. de Moura, L., Bjørner, N.: Z3: An Efficient SMT Solver. In: Ramakrishnan, C.R., Rehof, J. (eds.) TACAS 2008. LNCS, vol. 4963, pp. 337–340. Springer, Heidelberg (2008)
11. de Moura, L., Bjørner, N.: Generalized, efficient array decision procedures. In: FMCAD, pp. 45–52. IEEE (2009)
12. Ganzinger, H., Korovin, K.: Theory Instantiation. In: Hermann, M., Voronkov, A. (eds.) LPAR 2006. LNCS (LNAI), vol. 4246, pp. 497–511. Springer, Heidelberg (2006)
13. Habermehl, P., Iosif, R., Vojnar, T.: What Else Is Decidable about Integer Arrays? In: Amadio, R.M. (ed.) FOSSACS 2008. LNCS, vol. 4962, pp. 474–489. Springer, Heidelberg (2008)
14. Korovin, K.: iProver – An Instantiation-Based Theorem Prover for First-Order Logic (System Description). In: Armando, A., Baumgartner, P., Dowek, G. (eds.) IJCAR 2008. LNCS (LNAI), vol. 5195, pp. 292–298. Springer, Heidelberg (2008)
15. Kovács, L., Voronkov, A.: First-Order Theorem Proving and VAMPIRE. In: Sharygina, N., Veith, H. (eds.) CAV 2013. LNCS, vol. 8044, pp. 1–35. Springer, Heidelberg (2013)
16. Nieuwenhuis, R., Rubio, A.: Paramodulation-Based Theorem Proving. In: Robinson, A., Voronkov, A. (eds.) Handbook of Automated Reasoning, vol. I, ch. 7, pp. 371–443. Elsevier Science (2001)
17. Prevosto, V., Waldmann, U.: SPASS+T. In: Proc. of ESCoR, pp. 18–33 (2006)
18. Riazanov, A., Voronkov, A.: Limited Resource Strategy in Resolution Theorem Proving. J. of Symbolic Computation 36(1-2), 101–115 (2003)
19. Rümmer, P.: E-Matching with Free Variables. In: Bjørner, N., Voronkov, A. (eds.) LPAR-18 2012. LNCS, vol. 7180, pp. 359–374. Springer, Heidelberg (2012)
20. Schulz, S.: System Description: E 1.8. In: McMillan, K., Middeldorp, A., Voronkov, A. (eds.) LPAR-19 2013. LNCS, vol. 8312, pp. 735–743. Springer, Heidelberg (2013)
21. Sutcliffe, G.: The TPTP Problem Library and Associated Infrastructure. J. Autom. Reasoning 43(4), 337–362 (2009)
22. Sutcliffe, G., Suttner, C.: The State of CASC. AI Communications 19(1), 35–48 (2006)

Deciding Entailments in Inductive Separation Logic with Tree Automata

Radu Iosif[1], Adam Rogalewicz[2], and Tomáš Vojnar[2]

[1] University Grenoble Alpes, CNRS, VERIMAG, Grenoble, France
[2] FIT, Brno University of Technology, IT4Innovations Centre of Excellence, Czech Republic

Abstract. Separation Logic (SL) with inductive definitions is a natural formalism for specifying complex recursive data structures, used in compositional verification of programs manipulating such structures. The key ingredient of any automated verification procedure based on SL is the decidability of the entailment problem. In this work, we reduce the entailment problem for a non-trivial subset of SL describing trees (and beyond) to the language inclusion of tree automata (TA). Our reduction provides tight complexity bounds for the problem and shows that entailment in our fragment is EXPTIME-complete. For practical purposes, we leverage from recent advances in automata theory, such as inclusion checking for non-deterministic TA avoiding explicit determinization. We implemented our method and present promising preliminary experimental results.

1 Introduction

Separation Logic (SL) [22] is a logical framework for describing recursive mutable data structures. The attractiveness of SL as a specification formalism comes from the possibility of writing higher-order *inductive definitions* that are natural for describing the most common recursive data structures, such as singly- or doubly-linked lists (SLLs/DLLs), trees, hash maps (lists of lists), and more complex variations thereof, such as nested and overlaid structures (e.g. lists with head and tail pointers, skip-lists, trees with linked leaves, etc.). In addition to being an appealing specification tool, SL is particularly suited for compositional reasoning about programs. Indeed, the principle of *local reasoning* allows one to verify different elements (functions, threads) of a program, operating on disjoint parts of the memory, and to combine the results a-posteriori, into succinct verification conditions.

However, the expressive power of SL comes at the price of undecidability [6]. To avoid this problem, most SL dialects used by various tools (e.g. SPACE INVADER [2], PREDATOR [9], or INFER [7]) use hard-coded predicates, describing SLLs and DLLs, for which entailments are, in general, tractable [8]. For graph structures of bounded tree width, a general decidability result was presented in [14]. Entailment in this fragment is EXPTIME-hard, as proven in [1].

In this paper, we present a novel decision procedure for a restriction of the decidable SL fragment from [14], describing recursive structures in which *all edges are local with respect to a spanning tree*. Examples of such structures include SLLs, DLLs, trees and trees with parent pointers, etc. For structures outside of this class (e.g. skip-lists or trees with linked leaves), our procedure is sound (namely, if the answer of the procedure is

F. Cassez and J.-F. Raskin (Eds.): ATVA 2014, LNCS 8837, pp. 201–218, 2014.

positive, then the entailment holds), but not complete (the answer might be negative and the entailment could still hold). In terms of program verification, such a lack of completeness in the entailment prover can lead to non-termination or false positives, but will not cause unsoundness (i.e. classify a buggy program as correct).

The method described in the paper belongs to the class of *automata-theoretic* decision techniques: We translate an entailment problem $\varphi \models \psi$ into a language inclusion problem $\mathcal{L}(A_\varphi) \subseteq \mathcal{L}(A_\psi)$ for tree automata (TA) A_φ and A_ψ that (roughly speaking) encode the sets of models of φ and ψ, respectively. Yet, a naïve translation of the inductive definitions of SL into TA encounters a *polymorphic representation* problem: the same set of structures can be defined in several different ways, and TA simply mirroring the definition will not report the entailment. For example, DLLs with selectors next and prev for the next and previous nodes, respectively, can be described by a forward unfolding of the inductive definition: $\mathrm{DLL}(head, prev, tail, next) \equiv \exists x.\ head \mapsto (x, prev) * \mathrm{DLL}(x, head, tail, next) \mid \mathbf{emp} \wedge head = tail \wedge prev = next$, as well as by a backward unfolding of the definition: $\mathrm{DLL}_{rev}(head, prev, tail, next) \equiv \exists x.\ tail \mapsto (next, x) * \mathrm{DLL}_{rev}(head, prev, x, tail) \mid \mathbf{emp} \wedge head = tail \wedge prev = next$. Also, one can define a DLL starting with a node in the middle and unfolding backward to the left of this node and forward to the right: $\mathrm{DLL}_{mid}(head, prev, tail, next) \equiv \exists x, y, z.\ \mathrm{DLL}(y, x, tail, next) * \mathrm{DLL}_{rev}(head, prev, z, x)$. The circular entailment: $\mathrm{DLL}(\mathsf{a}, \mathsf{b}, \mathsf{c}, \mathsf{d}) \models \mathrm{DLL}_{rev}(\mathsf{a}, \mathsf{b}, \mathsf{c}, \mathsf{d}) \models \mathrm{DLL}_{mid}(\mathsf{a}, \mathsf{b}, \mathsf{c}, \mathsf{d}) \models \mathrm{DLL}(\mathsf{a}, \mathsf{b}, \mathsf{c}, \mathsf{d})$ holds, but a naïve structural translation to TA might not detect this fact. To bridge this gap, we define a closure operation on TA, called *canonical rotation*, which adds all possible representations of a given inductive definition, encoded as a tree automaton.

The translation from SL to TA provides also tight complexity bounds, showing that entailment in the local fragment of SL with inductive definitions is EXPTIME-complete. Moreover, we implemented our method using the VATA [17] tree automata library, which leverages from recent advances in non-deterministic language inclusion for TA [4], and obtained quite encouraging experimental results.

Related Work. Given the large body of literature on logics for describing mutable data structures, we need to restrict this section to the related work that focuses on SL [22]. The first (proof-theoretic) decidability result for SL on a restricted fragment defining only SLLs was reported in [3], which describe a co-NP algorithm. The full basic SL without recursive definitions, but with the magic wand operator was found to be undecidable when interpreted *in any memory model* [6]. A PTIME entailment procedure for SL with list predicates is given in [8]. Their method was extended to reason about nested and overlaid lists in [11]. More recently, entailments in an important SL fragment with hardcoded SLL/DLL predicates were reduced to Satisfiability Modulo Theories (SMT) problems, leveraging from recent advances in SMT technology [20,18]. The work reported in [10] deals with entailments between inductive SL formulae describing nested list structures. It uses a combination of graphs and TA to encode models of SL, but it does not deal with the problem of polymorphic representation. Recently, a decision procedure for entailments in a fragment of multi-sorted first-order logic with reachability, hard-coded trees and frame specifications, called GRIT (Graph Reachability and Inverted Trees) has been reported in [21]. Due to the restriction of the transitive closure to one function symbol (parent pointer), the expressive power of their logic, without data constraints, is strictly lower than ours (regular properties of trees cannot be encoded in GRIT). However, GRIT can be extended with data, which has not been, so far, considered for SL.

Closer to our work on SL with user-provided *inductive definitions* is the fragment used in the tool SLEEK, which implements a semi-algorithmic entailment check, based on unfoldings and unifications [19]. Along this line of work, the theorem prover CY-CLIST builds entailment proofs using a sequent calculus. Neither SLEEK nor CYCLIST are complete for a given fragment of SL, and, moreover, these tools do not address the polymorphic representation problem.

Our previous work [14] gave a general decidability result for SL with inductive definitions interpreted over graph-like structures, under several necessary restrictions, based on a reduction from SL to Monadic Second Order Logic (MSOL) on graphs of bounded tree width. Decidability of MSOL on such graphs relies on a combinatorial reduction to MSOL on trees (see [12] for a proof of Courcelle's theorem). Altogether, using the method from [14] causes a blowup of several exponentials in the size of the input problem and is unlikely to produce an effective decision procedure.

The work [1] provides a rather complete picture of complexity for the entailment in various SL fragments with inductive definitions, including EXPTIME-hardness of the decidable fragment of [14], but provides no upper bound. The EXPTIME-completeness result in this paper provides an upper bound for a fragment of *local definitions*, and strengthens the EXPTIME-hard lower bound as well, i.e. it is showed that even the entailment between local definitions is EXPTIME-hard.

2   Definitions

The set of natural numbers is denoted by $\mathbb{N}$. If $\mathbf{x} = \langle x_1,\ldots,x_n \rangle$ and $\mathbf{y} = \langle y_1,\ldots,y_m \rangle$ are tuples, $\mathbf{x} \cdot \mathbf{y} = \langle x_1,\ldots,x_n,y_1,\ldots,y_m \rangle$ denotes their concatenation, $|\mathbf{x}| = n$ denotes the length of $\mathbf{x}$, and $(\mathbf{x})_i = x_i$ denotes the i-th element of $\mathbf{x}$. For a partial function $f : A \rightharpoonup B$, and $\bot \notin B$, we denote by $f(x) = \bot$ the fact that f is undefined at some point $x \in A$. The domain of f is denoted $dom(f) = \{x \in A \mid f(x) \neq \bot\}$, and the image of f is denoted as $img(f) = \{y \in B \mid \exists x \in A \cdot f(x) = y\}$. By $f : A \rightharpoonup_{fin} B$, we denote any partial function whose domain is finite. Given two partial functions f,g defined on disjoint domains, i.e. $dom(f) \cap dom(g) = \emptyset$, we denote by $f \oplus g$ their union.

States. We consider $Var = \{x,y,z,\ldots\}$ to be a countably infinite set of *variables* and **nil** $\in Var$ be a designated variable. Let Loc be a countably infinite set of locations and $null \in Loc$ be a designated location.

Definition 1. *A* state *is a pair* $\langle s,h \rangle$ *where* $s : Var \rightharpoonup Loc$ *is a partial function mapping pointer variables into locations such that* $s(\mathbf{nil}) = null$, *and* $h : Loc \rightharpoonup_{fin} \mathbb{N} \rightharpoonup_{fin} Loc$ *is a finite partial function such that (i)* $null \notin dom(h)$ *and (ii) for all* $\ell \in dom(h)$ *there exists* $k \in \mathbb{N}$ *such that* $(h(\ell))(k) \neq \bot$.

Given a state $S = \langle s,h \rangle$, s is called the *store* and h the *heap*. For any $l,l' \in Loc$, we write $\ell \xrightarrow{k}_S \ell'$ instead of $(h(\ell))(k) = \ell'$ for any $k \in \mathbb{N}$ called a *selector*. We call the triple $\ell \xrightarrow{k}_S \ell'$ an *edge* of S. When the S subscript is obvious from the context, we sometimes omit it. Let $Img(h) = \bigcup_{\ell \in Loc} img(h(\ell))$ be the set of locations which are destinations of some edge in h. A location $\ell \in Loc$ is said to be *allocated* in $\langle s, h \rangle$ if $\ell \in dom(h)$ (i.e. it is the source of an edge). The location is called *dangling* in $\langle s, h \rangle$ if $\ell \in [img(s) \cup Img(h)] \setminus dom(h)$, i.e. it is referenced by a store variable or reachable from an allocated location in the heap, but it is not allocated in the heap itself. The set $loc(S) = img(s) \cup dom(h) \cup Img(h)$ is the set of all locations either allocated or referenced in the state S.

For any two states $S_1 = \langle s_1, h_1 \rangle$ and $S_2 = \langle s_2, h_2 \rangle$ such that (i) s_1 and s_2 agree on the evaluation of common variables ($\forall x \in dom(s_1) \cap dom(s_2) . s_1(x) = s_2(x)$) and (ii) h_1 and h_2 have disjoint domains ($dom(h_1) \cap dom(h_2) = \emptyset$), we denote by $S_1 \uplus S_2 = \langle s_1 \cup s_2, h_1 \oplus h_2 \rangle$ the *disjoint union* of S_1 and S_2. The disjoint union is undefined if one of the above conditions does not hold.

Trees and Tree Automata. Let Σ be a countable alphabet and $\mathbb{N}^*$ be the set of sequences of natural numbers. Let $\varepsilon \in \mathbb{N}^*$ denote the empty sequence and $p.q$ denote the concatenation of two sequences $p, q \in \mathbb{N}^*$. We say that p is a *prefix* of q if $q = p.q'$ for some $q' \in \mathbb{N}^*$. A set $X \subseteq \mathbb{N}^*$ is *prefix-closed* iff $p \in X \Rightarrow q \in X$ for each prefix q of p.

A *tree* t over Σ is a finite partial function $t : \mathbb{N}^* \rightharpoonup_{fin} \Sigma$ such that $dom(t)$ is a finite prefix-closed subset of $\mathbb{N}^*$ and, for each $p \in dom(t)$ and $i \in \mathbb{N}$, we have $t(p.i) \neq \bot$ only if $t(p.j) \neq \bot$, for all $0 \leq j < i$. The sequences $p \in dom(t)$ are called *positions* in the following. Given two positions $p, q \in dom(t)$, we say that q is the i-th successor (child) of p if $q = p.i$, for some $i \in \mathbb{N}$. We denote by $\mathcal{D}(t) = \{-1, 0, \ldots, N\}$ the *direction alphabet* of t, where $N = \max\{i \in \mathbb{N} \mid \exists p \in \mathbb{N}^* . p.i \in dom(t)\}$, and we let $\mathcal{D}_+(t) = \mathcal{D}(t) \setminus \{-1\}$. By convention, we have $(p.i).(-1) = p$, for all $p \in \mathbb{N}^*$ and $i \in \mathcal{D}_+(t)$. Given a tree t and a position $p \in dom(t)$, we define the *arity* of the position p as $\#_t(p) = \max\{d \in \mathcal{D}_+(t) \mid p.d \in dom(t)\} + 1$.

A (finite, non-deterministic, bottom-up) *tree automaton* (abbreviated as TA in the following) is a quadruple $A = \langle Q, \Sigma, \Delta, F \rangle$, where Σ is a finite alphabet, Q is a finite set of *states*, $F \subseteq Q$ is a set of *final states*, Σ is an alphabet, and Δ is a set of *transition rules* of the form $\sigma(q_1, \ldots, q_n) \rightarrow q$, for $\sigma \in \Sigma$, and $q, q_1, \ldots, q_n \in Q$. Given a tree automaton $A = \langle Q, \Sigma, \Delta, F \rangle$, for each rule $\rho = (\sigma(q_1, \ldots, q_n) \rightarrow q)$, we define its size as $|\rho| = n + 1$. The size of the tree automaton is $|A| = \sum_{\rho \in \Delta} |\rho|$. A *run* of A over a tree $t : \mathbb{N}^* \rightharpoonup_{fin} \Sigma$ is a function $\pi : dom(t) \rightarrow Q$ such that, for each node $p \in dom(t)$, where $q = \pi(p)$, if $q_i = \pi(p.i)$ for $1 \leq i \leq n$, then Δ has a rule $(t(p))(q_1, \ldots, q_n) \rightarrow q$. We write $t \xRightarrow{\pi} q$ to denote that π is a run of A over t such that $\pi(\varepsilon) = q$. We use $t \Rightarrow q$ to denote that $t \xRightarrow{\pi} q$ for some run π. The *language* of A is defined as $\mathcal{L}(A) = \{t \mid \exists q \in F, t \Rightarrow q\}$.

2.1 Separation Logic

The syntax of *basic formulae* of Separation Logic (SL) is given below:

$$\alpha \in Var \setminus \{\mathbf{nil}\};\ x \in Var;$$
$$\Pi ::= \alpha = x \mid \Pi_1 \wedge \Pi_2$$
$$\Sigma ::= \mathbf{emp} \mid \alpha \mapsto (x_1, \ldots, x_n) \mid \Sigma_1 * \Sigma_2 , \text{ for some } n > 0$$
$$\varphi ::= \Sigma \wedge \Pi \mid \exists x . \varphi$$

A formula of the form $\bigwedge_{i=1}^{n} \alpha_i = x_i$ defined by the Π nonterminal in the syntax above is said to be *pure*. The atomic proposition **emp**, or any formula of the form $\bigstar_{i=1}^{k} \alpha_i \mapsto$

$(x_{i,1}, \ldots, x_{i,n_i})$, for some $k > 0$, is said to be *spatial*. A variable x is said to be *free* in φ if it does not occur under the scope of any existential quantifier. We denote by $FV(\varphi)$ the set of free variables. A variable $\alpha \in FV(\Sigma) \setminus \{\mathbf{nil}\}$ is said to be *allocated* (respectively, *referenced*) in a spatial formula Σ if it occurs on the left-hand (respectively, right-hand) side of a proposition $\alpha \mapsto (x_1, \ldots, x_n)$ of Σ.

In the following, we shall use two equality relations. The *syntactic equality*, denoted $\sigma \equiv \varsigma$, means that σ and ς are the same syntactic object (formula, variable, tuple of variables, etc.). On the other hand, by writing $x =_\Pi y$, for two variables $x, y \in Var$ and a pure formula Π, we mean that the equality of the values of x and y is implied by Π.

A system of *inductive definitions* (inductive system) $\mathcal{P}$ is a set of rules of the form

$$\left\{ P_i(x_{i,1}, \ldots, x_{i,n_i}) \equiv |_{j=1}^{m_i} R_{i,j}(x_{i,1}, \ldots, x_{i,n_i}) \right\}_{i=1}^k \qquad (1)$$

where $\{P_1, \ldots, P_k\}$ is a set of *predicates*, $x_{i,1}, \ldots, x_{i,n_i}$ are called *formal parameters*, and the formulae $R_{i,j}$ are called the *rules* of P_i. Each rule is of the form $R_{i,j}(\mathbf{x}) \equiv \exists \mathbf{z} . \Sigma * P_{i_1}(\mathbf{y}_1) * \ldots * P_{i_m}(\mathbf{y}_m) \wedge \Pi$, where $\mathbf{x} \cap \mathbf{z} = \emptyset$, and the following holds:

1. $\Sigma \not\equiv \mathbf{emp}$ is a non-empty spatial formula[1], called the *head* of $R_{i,j}$.
2. $P_{i_1}(\mathbf{y}_1), \ldots, P_{i_m}(\mathbf{y}_m)$ is a tuple of *predicate occurrences*, called the *tail* of $R_{i,j}$, where $|\mathbf{y}_j| = n_{i_j}$, for all $1 \leq j \leq m$.
3. Π is a pure formula, restricted such that, for all formal parameters $\beta \in \mathbf{x}$, we allow only equalities of the form $\alpha =_\Pi \beta$, where α is allocated in Σ.[2]
4. for all $1 \leq r, s \leq m$, if $x_{i,k} \in \mathbf{y}_r$, $x_{i,l} \in \mathbf{y}_s$, and $x_{i,k} =_\Pi x_{i,l}$, for some $1 \leq k, l \leq n_i$, then $r = s$; a formal parameter of a rule cannot be passed to two or more subsequent occurrences of predicates in that rule.[3]

The size of a rule R is denoted by $|R|$ and defined inductively as follows: $|\alpha = x| = 1$, $|\mathbf{emp}| = 1$, $|\alpha \mapsto (x_1, \ldots, x_n)| = n + 1$, $|\varphi \bullet \psi| = |\varphi| + |\psi|$, $|\exists x . \varphi| = |\varphi| + 1$, and $|P(x_1, \ldots, x_n)| = n$. Here, $\alpha \in Var \setminus \{\mathbf{nil}\}$, $x, x_1, \ldots, x_n \in Var$, and $\bullet \in \{*, \wedge\}$. The size of an inductive system (1) is defined as $|\mathcal{P}| = \sum_{i=1}^k \sum_{j=1}^{m_i} |R_{i,j}|$. A *rooted system* $\langle \mathcal{P}, P_i \rangle$ is an inductive system $\mathcal{P}$ with a designated predicate $P_i \in \mathcal{P}$.

Example 1. To illustrate the use of inductive definitions (with the above restrictions), we first show how to define a predicate $\mathrm{DLL}(hd, p, tl, n)$ describing doubly-linked lists of length at least one. As depicted on the top of Fig. 1, the formal parameter hd points to the first allocated node of such a list, p to the node pointed to by the *prev* selector of hd, tl

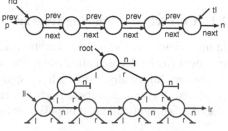

Fig. 1. Top: A DLL. Bottom: A TLL

to the last node of the list (possibly equal to hd), and n to the node pointed to by the *next* selector from tl. This predicate can be defined as follows: $\mathrm{DLL}(hd, p, tl, n) \equiv hd \mapsto (n, p) \wedge hd = tl \mid \exists x. hd \mapsto (x, p) * \mathrm{DLL}(x, hd, tl, n)$.

---

[1] In practice, we allow frontier or root rules to have **empty** heads.

[2] This restriction can be lifted at the expense of an exponential blowup in the size of the TA.

[3] The restriction can be lifted by testing double allocation as in [14] (with an exponential cost).

Another example is the predicate $\text{TLL}(r, ll, lr)$ describing binary trees with linked leaves whose root is pointed to by the formal parameter r, the left-most leaf is pointed to by ll, and the right-most leaf points to lr as shown in the bottom of Fig. 1: $\text{TLL}(r, ll, lr) \equiv r \mapsto (\textbf{nil}, \textbf{nil}, lr) \land r = ll \mid \exists x, y, z. \ r \mapsto (x, y, \textbf{nil}) * \text{TLL}(x, ll, z) * \text{TLL}(y, z, lr)$. ∎

The semantics of SL is given by the *model relation* $\models$, defined inductively, on the structure of formulae, as follows:

$$
\begin{aligned}
S &\models \textbf{emp} &&\Longleftrightarrow dom(h) = \emptyset \\
S &\models \alpha \mapsto (x_1, \ldots, x_n) &&\Longleftrightarrow s = \{(\alpha, \ell_0), (x_1, \ell_1), \ldots, (x_n, \ell_n)\} \text{ and} \\
&&& \quad h = \{\langle \ell_0, \lambda i . \text{ if } 1 \le i \le n \text{ then } \ell_i \text{ else } \bot \rangle\} \\
&&& \quad \text{for some } \ell_0, \ell_1, \ldots, \ell_n \in Loc \\
S &\models \varphi_1 * \varphi_2 &&\Longleftrightarrow S_1 \models \varphi_1 \text{ and } S_2 \models \varphi_2 \text{ for some } S_1, S_2 : S_1 \uplus S_2 = S \\
S &\models \exists x . \varphi &&\Longleftrightarrow \langle s[x \leftarrow \ell], h \rangle \models \varphi \text{ for some } \ell \in Loc \\
S &\models P_i(x_{i,1}, \ldots, x_{i,n_i}) &&\Longleftrightarrow S \models R_{i,j}(x_{i,1}, \ldots, x_{i,n_i}), \text{ for some } 1 \le j \le m_i, \text{ in (1)}
\end{aligned}
$$

The semantics of $=$ and $\land$ are classical for first order logic. Note that we adopt here the *strict semantics*, in which a points-to relation $\alpha \mapsto (x_1, \ldots, x_n)$ holds in a state consisting of a single cell pointed to by α that has exactly n outgoing edges $s(\alpha) \xrightarrow{k}_s s(x_k)$, $1 \le k \le n$, leading either towards the single allocated location $s(x_k)$ (if $s(x_k) = s(\alpha)$) or towards dangling locations (if $s(x_k) \neq s(\alpha)$). The empty heap is specified by $\textbf{emp}$.

A state S is a model of a predicate P_i iff it is a model of one of its rules $R_{i,j}$. For a state S that is a model of $R_{i,j}$, the inductive definition of the semantics implies existence of a finite *unfolding tree*: this is a tree labeled with rules of the system in such a way that, whenever a node is labeled by a rule with a tail $P_{i_1}(\mathbf{y}_1), \ldots, P_{i_m}(\mathbf{y}_m)$, it has exactly m children such that the j-th child, for $1 \le j \le m$, is labeled with a rule of P_{i_j} (see the middle part of Fig. 2—a formal definition is given in [16].

Given an inductive system $\mathcal{P}$, predicates $P_i(x_1, \ldots, x_n)$ and $P_j(y_1, \ldots, y_n)$ of $\mathcal{P}$ with the same number of formal parameters n, and a tuple of variables $\mathbf{x}$ where $|\mathbf{x}| = n$, the *entailment problem* is defined as follows: $P_i(\mathbf{x}) \models_{\mathcal{P}} P_j(\mathbf{x}) : \forall S . S \models P_i(\mathbf{x}) \Rightarrow S \models P_j(\mathbf{x})$.

2.2 Connectivity, Spanning Trees and Local States

In this section, we define two conditions ensuring that entailments in the restricted SL fragment can be decided effectively. The notion of a *spanning tree* is central for these definitions. Informally, a state S has a spanning tree t if all allocated locations of S can be placed in t such that there is always an edge in S in between every two locations placed in a parent-child pair of positions (see Fig. 2 for two spanning trees).

Definition 2. *Given a state* $S = \langle s, h \rangle$, *a spanning tree of* S *is a bijective tree* $t : \mathbb{N}^* \to dom(h)$ *such that* $\forall p \in dom(t) \forall d \in \mathcal{D}_+(t) . \ p.d \in dom(t) \Rightarrow \exists k \in \mathbb{N} . \ t(p) \xrightarrow{k}_s t(p.d)$.

Given an inductive system $\mathcal{P}$, let $S = \langle s, h \rangle$ be a state and $P_i \in \mathcal{P}$ be an inductive definition such that $S \models P_i$. Our first restriction, called *connectivity* (Def. 3), ensures that the unfolding tree of the definition of P_i is also a spanning tree of S (cf. Fig. 2, middle). In other words, each location $\ell \in dom(h)$ is created by an atomic proposition of the form $\alpha \mapsto (x_1, \ldots, x_n)$ from the unfolding tree of the definition P_i, and, moreover, by Def. 2, there exists an edge $\ell \xrightarrow{k}_S \ell'$ for any parent-child pair of positions in this tree (cf. the next edges in Fig. 2).

For a basic quantifier-free SL formula $\varphi \equiv \Sigma \wedge \Pi$ and two variables $x, y \in FV(\varphi)$, we say that y is φ-*reachable* from x iff there is a sequence $x =_\Pi \alpha_0, \ldots, \alpha_m =_\Pi y$, for some $m \geq 0$, such that, for each $0 \leq i < m$, $\alpha_i \mapsto (\beta_{i,1}, \ldots, \beta_{i,p_i})$ is an atomic proposition in Σ, and $\beta_{i,s} =_\Pi \alpha_{i+1}$, for some $1 \leq s \leq p_i$. A variable $x \in FV(\Sigma)$ is called a *root* of Σ if every variable $y \in FV(\Sigma)$ is φ-reachable from x.

Definition 3. *Given a system* $\mathcal{P} = \{P_i \equiv |_{j=1}^{m_i} R_{i,j}\}_{i=1}^n$ *of inductive definitions, a rule* $R_{i,j}(x_{i,1}, \ldots, x_{i,k}) \equiv \exists \mathbf{z} \ . \ \Sigma * P_{i_1}(\mathbf{y}_1) * \ldots * P_{i_m}(\mathbf{y}_m) \wedge \Pi$ *of a predicate* $P_i(x_{i,1}, \ldots, x_{i,k})$ *is connected iff there exists a formal parameter* $x_{i,\ell}$ *of* P_i, $1 \leq \ell \leq k$, *such that (i)* $x_{i,\ell}$ *is a root of* Σ *and (ii) for each* $j = 1, \ldots, m$, *there exists* $0 \leq s < |\mathbf{y}_j|$ *such that* $(\mathbf{y}_j)_s$ *is* $(\Sigma \wedge \Pi)$-*reachable from* $x_{i,\ell}$ *and* $x_{i_j,s}$ *is a root of the head of each rule of* P_{i_j}. *The system* $\mathcal{P}$ *is said to be* connected *if all its rules are connected.*

For instance, the DLL and TLL systems from Ex. 1 are both connected. Our second restriction, called *locality*, ensures that every edge $\ell \xrightarrow{k}_S \ell'$, between allocated locations $\ell, \ell' \in dom(h)$, involves locations that are mapped to a parent-child pair of positions in some spanning tree of S.

Definition 4. *Let* $S = \langle s, h \rangle$ *be a state and* $t : \mathbb{N}^* \to dom(h)$ *be a spanning tree of* S. *An edge* $\ell \xrightarrow{k}_S \ell'$ *with* $\ell, \ell' \in dom(h)$ *is said to be* local w.r.t. *a spanning tree* t *iff there exist* $p \in dom(t)$ *and* $d \in \mathcal{D}(t) \cup \{\varepsilon\}$ *such that* $t(p) = \ell$ *and* $t(p.d) = \ell'$. *The tree* t *is a* local spanning tree *of* S *iff* t *is a spanning tree of* S *and* S *has only local edges w.r.t.* t. *The state* S *is* local *iff it has a local spanning tree.*

For instance, the DLL system of Ex. 1 is local, while the TLL system is not (e.g. the n edges between leaves cannot be mapped to parent-child pairs in the spanning tree that is obtained by taking the l and r edges of the TLL). In this paper, we address the locality problem by giving a sufficient condition (a syntactic check of the inductive system, prior to the generation of TA) able to decide the locality on all of the practical examples considered (Sec. 3.2). The decidability of locality of general inductive systems is an interesting open problem, considered for future research.

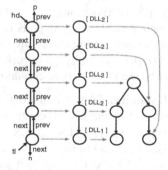

Fig. 2. Two spanning trees of a DLL. The middle one is an unfolding tree when labeled by $DLL_1 \equiv hd \mapsto (n, p) \wedge hd = tl$ and $DLL_2 \equiv \exists x. \ hd \mapsto (x, p) * DLL(x, hd, tl, n)$.

Definition 5. *A system* $\mathcal{P} = \{P_i(x_{i,1}, \ldots, x_{i,n_i})\}_{i=1}^k$ *is said to be* local *if and only if each formal parameter* $x_{i,j}$ *of a predicate* P_i *is either (i) allocated in each rule of* P_i *and* $(\mathbf{y})_j$ *is referenced at each occurrence* $P_i(\mathbf{y})$, *or (ii) referenced in each rule of* P_i *and* $(\mathbf{y})_j$ *is allocated at each occurrence* $P_i(\mathbf{y})$.

This gives a sufficient (but not necessary) condition ensuring that any state S, such that $S \models P_i$, has a local spanning tree, if $\mathcal{P}$ is a connected local system. The condition is effective and easily implemented (see Sec. 3.2) by the translation from SL to TA.

3   From Separation Logic to Tree Automata

The first step of our entailment decision procedure is building a TA for a given inductive system. Roughly speaking, the TA we build recognizes unfolding trees of the inductive system. The alphabet of such a TA consists of small basic SL formulae describing the neighborhood of each allocated variable, together with a specification of the connections between each such formula and its parent and children in the unfolding tree. Each alphabet symbol in the TA is called a *tile*. Due to technical details related to the encoding of states as trees of SL formulae, the most space in this section is dedicated to the definition of tiles. Once the tile alphabet is defined, the states of the TA correspond naturally to the predicates of the inductive system, and the transition rules correspond to the rules of the system.

3.1   Tiles, Canonical Tiles, and Quasi-canonical Tiles

A *tile* is a tuple $T = \langle \varphi, \mathbf{x}_{-1}, \mathbf{x}_0, \ldots, \mathbf{x}_{d-1} \rangle$, for some $d \geq 0$, where φ is a basic SL formula, and each $\mathbf{x}_i$ is a tuple of pairwise distinct variables, called a *port*. We further assume that all ports contain only free variables from φ and that they are pairwise disjoint. The variables from $\mathbf{x}_{-1}$ are said to be *incoming*, the ones from $\mathbf{x}_0, \ldots, \mathbf{x}_{d-1}$ are said to be *outgoing*, and the ones from $\mathbf{par}(T) = FV(\varphi) \setminus (\mathbf{x}_{-1} \cup \ldots \cup \mathbf{x}_{d-1})$ are called *parameters*. The *arity* of a tile $T = \langle \varphi, \mathbf{x}_{-1}, \ldots, \mathbf{x}_{d-1} \rangle$ is the number of outgoing ports, denoted by $\#(T) = d$. We denote $\mathbf{form}(T) \equiv \varphi$ and $\mathbf{port}_i(T) \equiv \mathbf{x}_i$, for all $-1 \leq i < d$.

Given tiles $T_1 = \langle \varphi, \mathbf{x}_{-1}, \ldots, \mathbf{x}_{d-1} \rangle$ and $T_2 = \langle \phi, \mathbf{y}_{-1}, \ldots, \mathbf{y}_{e-1} \rangle$ such that $FV(\varphi) \cap FV(\phi) = \emptyset$, we define the *i-composition*, for some $0 \leq i < d$, such that $|\mathbf{x}_i| = |\mathbf{y}_{-1}|$: $T_1 \circledast_i T_2 = \langle \psi, \mathbf{x}_{-1}, \ldots \mathbf{x}_{i-1}, \mathbf{y}_0, \ldots, \mathbf{y}_{e-1}, \mathbf{x}_{i+1}, \ldots, \mathbf{x}_{d-1} \rangle$ where $\psi \equiv \exists \mathbf{x}_i \exists \mathbf{y}_{-1} . \varphi * \phi \wedge \mathbf{x}_i = \mathbf{y}_{-1}$.[4] For a position $q \in \mathbb{N}^*$ and a tile T, we denote by $T^{\langle q \rangle}$ the tile obtained by renaming each variable x in the ports of T by $x^{\langle q \rangle}$. A tree t labeled with tiles corresponds to a tile defined inductively, for any $p \in dom(t)$, as: $\mathcal{T}(t,p) = t(p)^{\langle p \rangle} \circledast_0 \mathcal{T}(t,p.0) \circledast_1 \mathcal{T}(t,p.1) \ldots \circledast_{\#(p)-1} \mathcal{T}(t,p.(\#_t(p)-1))$. The SL formula $\Phi(t) \equiv \mathbf{form}(\mathcal{T}(t,\varepsilon))$ is said to be the *characteristic formula* of t.

Canonical Tiles. We first define a class of tiles that encode local states (Def. 4) with respect to the underlying tile-labeled spanning trees. We denote by $T = \langle (\exists z) \ z \mapsto (y_0, \ldots, y_{m-1}) \wedge \Pi, \mathbf{x}_{-1}, \ldots, \mathbf{x}_{d-1} \rangle$ a tile whose spatial formula is either (i) $\exists z . z \mapsto (y_0, \ldots, y_{m-1})$ or (ii) $z \mapsto (y_0, \ldots, y_{m-1})$ with $z \in \mathbf{par}(T)$. A tile $T = \langle (\exists z) \ z \mapsto (y_0, \ldots, y_{m-1}) \wedge \Pi, \mathbf{x}_{-1}, \ldots, \mathbf{x}_{d-1} \rangle$ is said to be *canonical* if each port $\mathbf{x}_i$ can be factorized as $\mathbf{x}_i^{fw} \cdot \mathbf{x}_i^{bw}$ (distinguishing *forward* links going from the root to the leaves and *backward* links going in the opposite direction, respectively) such that:

1. $\mathbf{x}_{-1}^{bw} \equiv \langle y_{h_0}, \ldots, y_{h_k} \rangle$, for some ordered sequence $0 \leq h_0 < \ldots < h_k < m$, i.e. the backward incoming tuple consists only of variables referenced by the unique allocated variable z, ordered by the corresponding selectors.

2. For all $0 \leq i < d$, $\mathbf{x}_i^{fw} \equiv \langle y_{j_0}, \ldots, y_{j_{k_i}} \rangle$, for some ordered sequence $0 \leq j_0 < \ldots < j_{k_i} < m$. As above, each forward outgoing tuple consists of variables referenced by the unique allocated variable z, ordered by the corresponding selectors.

---

[4] For two tuples $\mathbf{x} = \langle x_1, \ldots, x_k \rangle$ and $\mathbf{y} = \langle y_1, \ldots, y_k \rangle$, we write $\mathbf{x} = \mathbf{y}$ for $\bigwedge_{i=1}^k x_i = y_i$.

3. For all $0 \leq i, j < d$, if $(\mathbf{x}_i^{fw})_0 \equiv y_p$ and $(\mathbf{x}_j^{fw})_0 \equiv y_q$, for some $0 \leq p < q < m$ (i.e. $y_p \not\equiv y_q$), then $i < j$. This means that the forward outgoing tuples are ordered by the selectors referencing their first element.

4. $(\mathbf{x}_{-1}^{fw} \cup \mathbf{x}_0^{bw} \cup \ldots \cup \mathbf{x}_{d-1}^{bw}) \cap \{y_0, \ldots, y_{m-1}\} = \emptyset$ and $\Pi \equiv \mathbf{x}_{-1}^{fw} = z \wedge \bigwedge_{i=0}^{d-1} \mathbf{x}_i^{bw} = z$.[5]

We denote by $\mathbf{port}_i^{fw}(T)$ and $\mathbf{port}_i^{bw}(T)$ the tuples $\mathbf{x}_i^{fw}$ and $\mathbf{x}_i^{bw}$, respectively, for all $-1 \leq i < d$. The set of canonical tiles is denoted as $\mathcal{T}^c$.

Definition 6. *A tree* $t : \mathbb{N}^* \rightharpoonup_{fin} \mathcal{T}^c$ *is called* canonical *iff* $\#(t(p)) = \#_t(p)$ *for any* $p \in dom(t)$ *and, moreover, for each* $0 \leq i < \#_t(p)$, $|\mathbf{port}_i^{fw}(t(p))| = |\mathbf{port}_{-1}^{fw}(t(p.i))|$ *and* $|\mathbf{port}_i^{bw}(t(p))| = |\mathbf{port}_{-1}^{bw}(t(p.i))|$.

An important property of canonical trees is that each state that is a model of the characteristic formula $\Phi(t)$ of a canonical tree t (i.e. $S \models \Phi(t)$) can be uniquely described by a *local spanning tree* $u : dom(t) \to Loc$, which has the same structure as t, i.e. $dom(u) = dom(t)$. Intuitively, this is because each variable y_i, referenced in an atomic proposition $z \mapsto (y_0, \ldots, y_{m-1})$ in a canonical tile, is allocated only if it belongs to the backward part of the incoming port $\mathbf{x}_{-1}^{bw}$ or the forward part of some outgoing port $\mathbf{x}_i^{fw}$. In the first case, y_i is equal to the variable allocated by the parent tile, and in the second case, it is equal to the variable allocated by the i-th child. An immediate consequence is that any two models of $\Phi(t)$ differ only by a renaming of the allocated locations, i.e. they are identical up to isomorphism.

Example 2 (cont. of Ex. 1). To illustrate the notion of canonical trees, Fig. 3 shows two canonical trees for a given DLL. The tiles are depicted as big rectangles containing the appropriate basic formula as well as the input and output ports. In all ports, the first variable is in the forward and the second in the backward part.

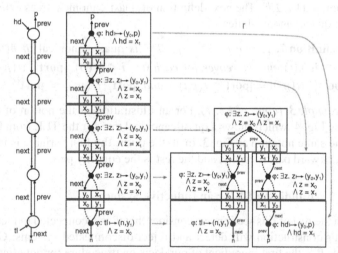

Fig. 3. The DLL from Fig. 1 with two of its canonical trees (related by a canonical rotation r)

Quasi-canonical tiles. We next define a class of tiles that encode non-local states in order to extend our decision procedure to handle entailments between non-local inductive systems. In addition to local edges between neighboring tiles, quasi-canonical tiles

---

[5] For a tuple $\mathbf{x} = \langle x_1, \ldots, x_k \rangle$, we write $\mathbf{x} = z$ for $\bigwedge_{i=1}^{k} x_i = z$.

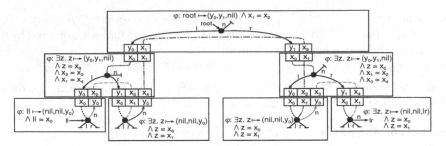

Fig. 4. A quasi-canonically tiled tree for the tree with linked leaves from Fig. 1

allow to define sequences of equalities between remote tiles. This extension is used to specify non-local edges within the state. A tile $T = \langle \varphi \wedge \Pi, \mathbf{x}_{-1}, \ldots, \mathbf{x}_{d-1} \rangle$ is said to be *quasi-canonical* if and only if each port $\mathbf{x}_i$ can be factorized as $\mathbf{x}_i^{fw} \cdot \mathbf{x}_i^{bw} \cdot \mathbf{x}_i^{eq}$, $\langle \varphi, \mathbf{x}_{-1}^{fw} \cdot \mathbf{x}_{-1}^{bw}, \ldots, \mathbf{x}_{d-1}^{fw} \cdot \mathbf{x}_{d-1}^{bw} \rangle$ is a canonical tile, Π is pure formula, and:

1. for each $0 \leq i < |\mathbf{x}_{-1}^{eq}|$, either $(\mathbf{x}_{-1}^{eq})_i \in FV(\varphi)$ or $(\mathbf{x}_{-1}^{eq})_i =_\Pi (\mathbf{x}_k^{eq})_j$ for some unique indices $0 \leq k < d$ and $0 \leq j < |\mathbf{x}_k^{fw}|$.
2. for each $0 \leq k < d$ and each $0 \leq j < |\mathbf{x}_k^{eq}|$, either $(\mathbf{x}_k^{eq})_j \in FV(\varphi)$ or exactly one of the following holds: (i) $(\mathbf{x}_k^{eq})_j =_\Pi (\mathbf{x}_{-1}^{eq})_i$ for some unique index $0 \leq i < |\mathbf{x}_{-1}^{eq}|$ or (ii) $(\mathbf{x}_k^{eq})_j =_\Pi (\mathbf{x}_r^{eq})_s$ for some unique indices $0 \leq r < d$ and $0 \leq s < |\mathbf{x}_r^{eq}|$.
3. For any $x, y \in \bigcup_{i=-1}^{d-1} \mathbf{x}_i^{eq}$, we have $x =_\Pi y$ only in one of the cases above.

We denote $\mathbf{port}_i^{eq}(T) \equiv \mathbf{x}_i^{eq}$, for all $-1 \leq i < d$. The set of quasi-canonical tiles is denoted by $\mathcal{T}^{qc}$. The next definition of quasi-canonical trees extends Def. 6 to the case of quasi-canonical tiles.

Definition 7. *A tree* $t : \mathbb{N}^* \rightharpoonup_{fin} \mathcal{T}^{qc}$ *is* quasi-canonical *iff* $\#(t(p)) = \#_t(p)$ *for any* $p \in dom(t)$ *and, moreover, for each* $0 \leq i < \#_t(p)$, $|\mathbf{port}_i^{fw}(t(p))| = |\mathbf{port}_{-1}^{fw}(t(p.i))|$, $|\mathbf{port}_i^{bw}(t(p))| = |\mathbf{port}_{-1}^{bw}(t(p.i))|$, *and* $|\mathbf{port}_i^{eq}(t(p))| = |\mathbf{port}_{-1}^{eq}(t(p.i))|$.

Example 3 (cont. of Ex. 1). For an illustration of the notion of quasi-canonical trees, see Fig. 4, which shows a quasi-canonical tree for the TLL from Fig. 1. The figure uses the same notation as Fig. 3. In all the ports, the first variable is in the forward part, the backward part is empty, and the rest is the equality part. ∎

3.2 Building a TA for an Inductive System

In the rest of this section, we consider that $\mathcal{P}$ is a connected inductive system (Def. 3)— our construction will detect and reject disconnected systems. Given a rooted system $\langle \mathcal{P}, P_r \rangle$, the first ingredient of our decision procedure for entailments is a procedure for building a TA that recognizes all unfolding trees of the inductive definition of P_r in the system $\mathcal{P}$. The first steps of the procedure implement a *specialization* of the rooted system with respect to a tuple $\overline{\alpha} = \langle \alpha_1, \ldots, \alpha_{n_r} \rangle$ of actual parameters for P_r, not used in $\mathcal{P}$. For space reasons, the specialization steps are described only informally here (for a detailed description of these steps, see [16]).

The first step is an elimination of existentially quantified variables that occur within equalities with formal parameters or allocated variables from all rules of $\mathcal{P}$. Second, each rule of $\mathcal{P}$ whose head consists of more than one atomic proposition $\alpha \mapsto (x_1, \ldots, x_n)$ is split into several new rules, containing exactly one such atomic proposition. At this point, any disconnected inductive system (Def. 3) passed to the procedure is detected and rejected. The final specialization step consists in propagating the actual parameters $\overline{\alpha}$ through the rules. A formal parameter $x_{i,k}$ of a rule $R_{i,j}(x_{i,1}, \ldots, x_{i,n_i}) \equiv \exists \mathbf{z} . \Sigma * P_{i_1}(\mathbf{y}_1) * \ldots * P_{i_m}(\mathbf{y}_m) \wedge \Pi$ is *directly propagated* to some (unique) parameter of a predicate occurrence P_{i_j}, for some $1 \leq j \leq m$, if and only if $x_{i,k} \notin FV(\Sigma)$ and $x_{i,k} \equiv (\mathbf{y}_{i_j})_\ell$, for some $0 \leq \ell < |\mathbf{y}_{i_j}|$, i.e. $x_{i,k}$ is neither allocated nor pointed to by the head of the rule before being passed on to P_{i_j}. We denote direct propagation of parameters by the relation $x_{i,k} \rightsquigarrow x_{i_j,\ell}$ where $x_{i_j,\ell}$ is the formal parameter of P_{i_j} which is mapped to the occurrence of $(\mathbf{y}_{i_j})_\ell$. We say that $x_{i,k}$ is *propagated* to $x_{r,s}$ if $x_{i,k} \rightsquigarrow^* x_{r,s}$ where $\rightsquigarrow^*$ denotes the reflexive and transitive closure of the $\rightsquigarrow$ relation. Finally, we replace each variable y of $\mathcal{P}$ by the actual parameter α_j provided that $x_{r,j} \rightsquigarrow^* y$. It is not hard to show that the specialization procedure runs in time $O(|\mathcal{P}|)$, hence the size of the output system is increased by a linear factor only.

Example 4 (cont. of Ex. 1). As an example of specialization, let us consider the predicate DLL from Ex. 1, with parameters DLL$(\mathsf{a}, \mathsf{b}, \mathsf{c}, \mathsf{d})$. After the parameter elimination and renaming the newly created predicates, we have a call Q_1 (without parameters) of the following inductive system:

$$Q_1() \equiv \mathsf{a} \mapsto (\mathsf{d}, \mathsf{b}) \wedge \mathsf{a} = \mathsf{c} \mid \exists x. \mathsf{a} \mapsto (x, \mathsf{b}) * Q_2(x, \mathsf{a})$$
$$Q_2(hd, p) \equiv hd \mapsto (\mathsf{d}, p) \wedge hd = \mathsf{c} \mid \exists x. hd \mapsto (x, p) * Q_2(x, hd) \qquad \blacksquare$$

We are now ready to describe the construction of a TA for a specialized rooted system $\langle \mathcal{P}, P_r \rangle$. First, for each predicate $P_j(x_{j,1}, \ldots, x_{j,n_j}) \in \mathcal{P}$, we compute several sets of parameters, called *signatures*: $\mathtt{sig}_j^{fw} = \{x_{j,k} \mid x_{j,k}$ is allocated in each rule of P_j, and $(\mathbf{y})_k$ is referenced in each occurrence $P_j(\mathbf{y})$ of $P_j\}$, $\mathtt{sig}_j^{bw} = \{x_{j,k} \mid x_{j,k}$ is referenced in each rule of P_j, and $(\mathbf{y})_k$ is allocated at each occurrence $P_j(\mathbf{y})$ of $P_j\}$, and, finally, $\mathtt{sig}_j^{eq} = \{x_{j,1}, \ldots, x_{j,n_j}\} \setminus (\mathtt{sig}_j^{fw} \cup \mathtt{sig}_j^{bw})$. The signatures of an inductive system can be used to implement the *locality test* (Def. 5): the system $\mathcal{P} = \{P_1, \ldots, P_k\}$ is local if and only if $\mathtt{sig}_i^{eq} = \emptyset$ for each $1 \leq i \leq k$.

Example 5 (cont. of Ex. 4). The signatures for the system in Ex. 4 are: $\mathtt{sig}_1^{fw} = \mathtt{sig}_1^{bw} = \mathtt{sig}_1^{eq} = \emptyset$ and $\mathtt{sig}_2^{fw} = \{hd\}, \mathtt{sig}_2^{bw} = \{p\}, \mathtt{sig}_2^{eq} = \emptyset$. The fact that, for each $i = 1, 2$, we have $\mathtt{sig}_i^{eq} = \emptyset$ implies that the DLL system is local. $\qquad \blacksquare$

The procedure for building a TA from a rooted system $\langle \mathcal{P}, P_r \rangle$ with actual parameters $\overline{\alpha}$ is denoted as SL2TA$(\mathcal{P}, P_r, \overline{\alpha})$ in the following. For each rule $R_{j,\ell}$ in the system, the SL2TA procedure creates a quasi-canonical tile whose incoming and outgoing ports $\mathbf{x}_i$ are factorized as $\mathbf{x}_i^{fw} \cdot \mathbf{x}_i^{bw} \cdot \mathbf{x}_i^{eq}$ according to the precomputed signatures $\mathtt{sig}_j^{fw}, \mathtt{sig}_j^{bw}$, and $\mathtt{sig}_j^{eq}$, respectively. The backward part of the input port $\mathbf{x}_{-1}^{bw}$ and the forward parts of the output ports $\{\mathbf{x}_i^{fw}\}_{i \geq 0}$ are sorted according to the order of incoming selector edges from the single points-to formula which constitutes the head of the rule. The output ports $\{\mathbf{x}_i\}_{i \geq 0}$ are sorted within the tile according to the order of the selector edges pointing to $(\mathbf{x}_i^{fw})_0$ for each $i \geq 0$. Finally, each predicate name P_i is associated with a state q_i, and for each inductive rule, the procedure creates a transition rule in the TA. The final state of the TA then corresponds to the root of the system (see Algorithm in [16]). The invariant used to prove the correctness of this construction is that whenever the TA reaches a state q_i it reads an unfolding tree whose root is labeled with a rule $R_{i,j}$ of the definition of a predicate P_i. The following lemma summarizes the TA construction:

Lemma 1. *Given a rooted system $\langle \mathcal{P}, P_r(x_{r,1}, \ldots, x_{r,n_r}) \rangle$ where $\mathcal{P} = \{P_i\}_{i=1}^k$ is a connected inductive system, $1 \leq r \leq k$, and $\overline{\alpha} = \langle \alpha_1, \ldots, \alpha_{n_i} \rangle$ is a tuple of variables not in $\mathcal{P}$, let $A = \text{SL2TA}(\mathcal{P}, P_r, \overline{\alpha})$. Then, for every state S, we have $S \models P_r(\overline{\alpha})$ iff there exists $t \in \mathcal{L}(A)$ such that $S \models \Phi(t)$. Moreover, $|A| = O(|\mathcal{P}|)$.*

Example 6 (cont. of Ex. 5). For the specialized inductive system $\mathcal{P} =$

$$\Delta = \left\{ \begin{array}{ll} \langle \mathbf{a} \mapsto (\mathbf{d},\mathbf{b}) \wedge \mathbf{a} = \mathbf{c}, \emptyset \rangle () \to q_1 & \langle \mathbf{a} \mapsto (x,\mathbf{b}), \emptyset, (x,\mathbf{a}) \rangle (q_2) \to q_1 \\ \langle \exists hd'.hd' \mapsto (\mathbf{d},p) \wedge hd = \mathbf{c} \wedge hd' = hd, (hd,p) \rangle () & \to q_2 \\ \langle \exists hd'.hd' \mapsto (x,p) \wedge hd' = hd, (hd,p), (x,hd) \rangle (q_2) & \to q_2 \end{array} \right\}$$

$\{Q_1, Q_2\}$ from Ex. 4, we obtain the TA $A = \text{SL2TA}(\mathcal{P}, Q_1, \langle \mathbf{a}, \mathbf{b}, \mathbf{c}, \mathbf{d} \rangle) = \langle \Sigma, \{q_1, q_2\}, \Delta, \{q_1\} \rangle$ where Δ is shown above. ∎

4   Rotation of Tree Automata

In this section we deal with polymorphic representations of states, i.e. situations when a state can be represented by different spanning trees, with different tilings. In this section we show that, for states with local spanning trees only (Def. 4), these trees are related by a *rotation* relation.

4.1   Rotation as a Transformation of TA

We start by defining rotation as a relation on trees. Intuitively, two trees t_1 and t_2 are related by a rotation whenever we can obtain t_2 from t_1 by picking a position $p \in dom(t_1)$ and making it the root of t_2, while maintaining in t_2 all edges from t_1 (Fig. 5).

Definition 8. *Given two trees $t_1, t_2 : \mathbb{N}^* \rightharpoonup_{fin} \Sigma$ and a bijective mapping $r : dom(t_1) \to dom(t_2)$, we say that t_2 is an r-rotation of t_1, denoted by $t_1 \sim_r t_2$ if and only if: $\forall p \in dom(t_1) \forall d \in \mathcal{D}_+(t_1) : p.d \in dom(t_1) \Rightarrow \exists e \in \mathcal{D}(t_2) . r(p.d) = r(p).e$. We write $t_1 \sim t_2$ if there exists a bijective mapping $r : dom(t_1) \to dom(t_2)$ such that $t_1 \sim_r t_2$.*

An example of a rotation r of a tree t_1 to a tree t_2 such that $r(\varepsilon) = 2$, $r(0) = \varepsilon$, $r(1) = 20$, $r(00) = 0$, and $r(01) = 1$ is shown in Fig. 5. Note that, e.g., for $p = \varepsilon \in dom(t_1)$ and $d = 0 \in \mathcal{D}_+(t_1)$, where $p.d = \varepsilon.0 \in dom(t_1)$, we get $e = -1 \in \mathcal{D}(t_2)$, and $r(\varepsilon.0) = 2.(-1) = \varepsilon$.

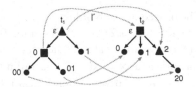

Fig. 5. An example of a rotation

In the rest of this section, we define rotation on canonical and quasi-canonical trees. These definitions are refinements of Def. 8. Namely, the change in the structure of the tree is mirrored by a change in the tile alphabet labeling the tree in order to preserve the state which is represented by the (quasi-)canonical tree.

A *substitution* is an injective partial function $\sigma : Var \rightharpoonup_{fin} Var$. Given a basic formula φ and a substitution σ, we denote by $\varphi[\sigma]$ the result of simultaneously replacing each variable x (not necessarily free) that occurs in φ by $\sigma(x)$. For instance, if $\sigma(x) = y$, $\sigma(y) = z$, and $\sigma(z) = t$, then $(\exists x, y . x \mapsto (y,z) \wedge z = x)[\sigma] \equiv \exists y, z . y \mapsto (z,t) \wedge t = y$.

Definition 9. *Given two canonical trees $t, u : \mathbb{N}^* \rightharpoonup_{fin} \mathcal{T}^c$ and a bijective mapping $r : dom(t) \rightarrow dom(u)$, we say that u is a canonical rotation of t, denoted $t \sim^c_r u$, if and only if $t \sim_r u$ and there exists a substitution $\sigma_p : Var \rightharpoonup_{fin} Var$ for each $p \in dom(t)$ such that $\mathbf{form}(t(p))[\sigma_p] \equiv \mathbf{form}(u(r(p)))$ and, for all $0 \leq i < \#_t(p)$, there exists $j \in \mathcal{D}(u)$ such that $r(p.i) = r(p).j$ and:*

$$\mathbf{port}^{fw}_i(t(p))[\sigma_p] \equiv \textit{if } j \geq 0 \textit{ then } \mathbf{port}^{fw}_j(u(r(p))) \textit{ else } \mathbf{port}^{bw}_{-1}(u(r(p)))$$
$$\mathbf{port}^{bw}_i(t(p))[\sigma_p] \equiv \textit{if } j \geq 0 \textit{ then } \mathbf{port}^{bw}_j(u(r(p))) \textit{ else } \mathbf{port}^{fw}_{-1}(u(r(p)))$$

We write $t \sim^c u$ if there exists a mapping r such that $t \sim^c_r u$.

Example 7 (cont. of Ex. 2). The notion of canonical rotation is illustrated by the canonical rotation r relating the two canonical trees of a DLL shown in Fig. 3. In its case, the variable substitutions are simply the identity in each node. Note, in particular, that when the tile 0 of the left tree (i.e., the second one from the top) gets rotated to the tile 1 of the right tree (i.e., the right successor of the root), the input and output ports get swapped and so do their forward and backward parts.   ∎

The following lemma is the key for proving completeness of our entailment checking for local inductive systems: if a (local) state is a model of the characteristic formulae of two different canonical trees, then these trees must be related by canonical rotation.

Lemma 2. *Let $t : \mathbb{N}^* \rightharpoonup_{fin} \mathcal{T}^c$ be a canonical tree and $S = \langle s, h \rangle$ be a state such that $S \models \Phi(t)$. Then, for any canonical tree $u : \mathbb{N}^* \rightharpoonup_{fin} \mathcal{T}^c$, we have $S \models \Phi(u)$ iff $t \sim^c u$.*

In the following, we extend the notion of rotation to quasi-canonical trees:

Definition 10. *Given two quasi-canonical trees $t, u : \mathbb{N}^* \rightharpoonup_{fin} \mathcal{T}^{qc}$ and a bijective mapping $r : dom(t) \rightarrow dom(u)$, we say that u is a quasi-canonical rotation of t, denoted $t \sim^{qc}_r u$, if and only if $t \sim^c_r u$ and $|\mathbf{port}^{eq}_i(t(p))| = |\mathbf{port}^{eq}_j(u(r(p)))|$ for all $p \in dom(t)$ and all $0 \leq i < \#_t(p), -1 \leq j < \#_t(p)$ such that $r(p.i) = r(p).j$. We write $t \sim^{qc} u$ if there exists a mapping r such that $t \sim^{qc}_r u$.*

The increase in expressivity (i.e. the possibility of defining non-local edges) comes at the cost of a loss of completeness. The following lemma generalizes the necessity direction ($\Leftarrow$) of Lemma 2 for quasi-canonical tiles. Notice that the sufficiency ($\Rightarrow$) direction does not hold in general.

Lemma 3. *Let $t, u : \mathbb{N}^* \rightharpoonup_{fin} \mathcal{T}^{qc}$ be quasi-canonical trees such that $t \sim^{qc} u$. For all states S, if $S \models \Phi(t)$, then $S \models \Phi(u)$.*

Algorithm 1. Rotation Closure of Quasi-canonical TA

input a quasi-canonical TA $A = \langle Q, \Sigma, \Delta, F \rangle$
output a TA A^r where:
$\mathcal{L}(A^r) = \{u : \mathbb{N}^* \rightharpoonup_{fin} \mathcal{T}^{qc} \mid \exists t \in \mathcal{L}(A) \ . \ u \sim^{qc} t\}$
function ROTATETA(A)
$\quad A^r \leftarrow A$
$\quad$ **assume** $A^r \equiv \langle Q_r, \Sigma, \Delta_r, F_r \rangle$
$\quad$ **for all** $\rho \in \Delta$ **do**
$\quad\quad$ **assume** $\rho \equiv T(q_0, \dots, q_k) \to q$
$\quad\quad$ **assume** $T \equiv \langle \varphi, \mathbf{x}_{-1}, \mathbf{x}_0, \dots, \mathbf{x}_k \rangle$
$\quad\quad$ **if** $\mathbf{x}_{-1} \neq \emptyset$ **or** $q \notin F$ **then**
$\quad\quad\quad$ **assume** $\mathbf{x}_{-1} \equiv \mathbf{x}_{-1}^{fw} \cdot \mathbf{x}_{-1}^{bw} \cdot \mathbf{x}_{-1}^{eq}$
$\quad\quad\quad$ **if** $\mathbf{x}_{-1}^{bw} \neq \emptyset$ **then**
$\quad\quad\quad\quad Q^{rev} \leftarrow \{q^{rev} \mid q \in Q\}$
$\quad\quad\quad\quad (Q_\rho, \Delta_\rho) \leftarrow (Q \cup Q^{rev} \cup \{q_\rho^f\}, \Delta)$
$\quad\quad\quad\quad p \leftarrow$ POSITIONOF$(\mathbf{x}_{-1}^{bw}, \varphi)$
$\quad\quad\quad\quad \mathbf{x}_{swap} \leftarrow \mathbf{x}_{-1}^{bw} \cdot \mathbf{x}_{-1}^{fw} \cdot \mathbf{x}_{-1}^{eq}$
$\quad\quad\quad\quad T_{new} \leftarrow \langle \varphi, \langle \rangle, \mathbf{x}_0, \dots, \mathbf{x}_p, \mathbf{x}_{swap}, \dots, \mathbf{x}_k \rangle$
$\quad\quad\quad\quad \Delta_\rho \leftarrow \Delta_\rho \cup \{T_{new}(q_0 \dots q_p, q^{rev} \dots q_k) \to q_\rho^f\}$
$\quad\quad\quad\quad (\Delta_\rho, \_) \leftarrow$ ROTTR$(q, \Delta, \Delta_\rho, \emptyset, F)$
$\quad\quad\quad\quad A_\rho \leftarrow \langle Q_\rho, \Sigma, \Delta_\rho, \{q_\rho^f\} \rangle$
$\quad\quad\quad\quad A^r \leftarrow A^r \cup A_\delta$
$\quad$ **return** A^r

function ROTTR$(q, \Delta, \Delta_{new}, \mathsf{V}, F)$
$\quad \mathsf{V} \leftarrow \mathsf{V} \cup \{q\}$
$\quad$ **for all** $(U(s_0, \dots, s_\ell) \to s) \in \Delta$ **do**
$\quad\quad$ **for all** $0 \leq j \leq \ell$ such that $s_j = q$ **do**
$\quad\quad\quad$ **assume** $U = \langle \varphi, \mathbf{x}_{-1}, \mathbf{x}_0, \dots, \mathbf{x}_j, \dots, \mathbf{x}_\ell \rangle$
$\quad\quad\quad$ **assume** $\mathbf{x}_j \equiv \mathbf{x}_j^{fw} \cdot \mathbf{x}_j^{bw} \cdot \mathbf{x}_j^{eq}$
$\quad\quad\quad$ **if** $\mathbf{x}_{-1} = \emptyset$ **and** $s \in F$ **then**
$\quad\quad\quad\quad \mathbf{x}_{swap} \leftarrow \mathbf{x}_j^{bw} \cdot \mathbf{x}_j^{fw} \cdot \mathbf{x}_j^{eq}$
$\quad\quad\quad\quad U' \leftarrow \langle \varphi, \mathbf{x}_{swap}, \mathbf{x}_0, \dots, \mathbf{x}_{j-1}, \mathbf{x}_{j+1}, \dots, \mathbf{x}_\ell \rangle$
$\quad\quad\quad\quad \Delta_{new} \leftarrow \Delta_{new} \cup \{U'(s_0 \dots s_{j-1} \dots s_\ell) \to q^{rev}\}$
$\quad\quad\quad$ **else**
$\quad\quad\quad\quad \mathbf{x}_{-1} \equiv \mathbf{x}_{-1}^{fw} \cdot \mathbf{x}_{-1}^{bw} \cdot \mathbf{x}_{-1}^{eq}$
$\quad\quad\quad\quad$ **if** $\mathbf{x}_{-1}^{bw} \neq \emptyset$ **then**
$\quad\quad\quad\quad\quad$ ports $\leftarrow \langle \mathbf{x}_0, \dots, \mathbf{x}_{j-1}, \mathbf{x}_{j+1}, \dots, \mathbf{x}_\ell \rangle$
$\quad\quad\quad\quad\quad$ states $\leftarrow (s_0, \dots, s_{j-1}, s_{j+1}, \dots, s_\ell)$
$\quad\quad\quad\quad\quad \mathbf{x}_{swap} \leftarrow \mathbf{x}_{-1}^{bw} \cdot \mathbf{x}_{-1}^{fw} \cdot \mathbf{x}_{-1}^{eq}$
$\quad\quad\quad\quad\quad p \leftarrow$ INSERTOUTPORT$(\mathbf{x}_{swap}, $ports$, \varphi)$
$\quad\quad\quad\quad\quad$ INSERTLHSSTATE$(s^{rev}, $states$, p)$
$\quad\quad\quad\quad\quad U_{new} \leftarrow \langle \varphi, \mathbf{x}_j^{bw} \cdot \mathbf{x}_j^{fw} \cdot \mathbf{x}_j^{eq}, $ports$\rangle$
$\quad\quad\quad\quad\quad \Delta_{new} \leftarrow \Delta_{new} \cup \{U_{new}($states$) \to q^{rev}\}$
$\quad\quad\quad\quad\quad$ **if** $s \notin \mathsf{V}$ **then**
$\quad\quad\quad\quad\quad\quad (\Delta_{new}, \mathsf{V}) \leftarrow$ ROTTR$(s, \Delta, \Delta_{new}, \mathsf{V}, F)$
$\quad$ **return** $(\Delta_{new}, \mathsf{V})$

4.2 Implementing Rotation as a Transformation of TA

This section describes the algorithm that produces the closure of a quasi-canonical tree automaton (i.e. a tree automaton recognizing quasi-canonical trees only) under rotation. The result is a TA that recognizes all trees $u : \mathbb{N}^* \rightharpoonup_{fin} \mathcal{T}^{qc}$ such that $t \sim^{qc} u$ for some tree t recognized by the input TA $A = \langle Q, \Sigma, \Delta, F \rangle$. Algorithm 1 (the ROTATETA procedure) describes the rotation closure whose result is a language-theoretic union of A and the TA A_ρ, one for each rule ρ of A. The idea behind the construction of $A_\rho = \langle Q_\rho, \Sigma, \Delta_\rho, \{q_\rho^f\} \rangle$ can be understood by considering a tree $t \in \mathcal{L}(A)$, a run $\pi :$ $dom(t) \to Q$, and a position $p \in dom(t)$, which is labeled with the right hand side of the rule $\rho = T(q_1, \dots, q_k) \to q$ of A. Then $\mathcal{L}(A_\rho)$ will contain the rotated tree u, i.e. $t \sim_r^{qc} u$, where the significant position p is mapped into the root of u by the rotation function r, i.e. $r(p) = \varepsilon$. To this end, we introduce a new rule $T_{new}(q_0, \dots, q^{rev}, \dots, q_k) \to q_\rho^f$ where the tile T_{new} mirrors the change in the structure of T at position p, and $q^{rev} \in Q_\rho$ is a fresh state corresponding to q. The construction of A_ρ continues recursively (procedure ROTTR), by considering every rule of A that has q on the left hand side: $U(q_1', \dots, q, \dots, q_\ell') \to s$. This rule is changed by swapping the roles of q and s and producing a rule $U_{new}(q_1', \dots, s^{rev}, \dots q_\ell') \to q^{rev}$ where U_{new} mirrors the change in the structure of U. Intuitively, the states $\{q^{rev} \mid q \in Q\}$ mark the unique path from the root of u to $r(\varepsilon) \in dom(u)$. The recursion stops when either (i) s is a final state of A, (ii) The tile U does not specify a forward edge in the direction marked by q, or (iii) all states of A have been visited.

Lemma 4. *Let* $A = \langle Q, \mathcal{T}^{qc}, \Delta, F \rangle$ *be a TA, and* $A^r =$ ROTATETA(A) *be the TA defining the rotation closure of* A. *Then* $\mathcal{L}(A^r) = \{u \mid u : \mathbb{N}^* \rightharpoonup_{fin} \mathcal{T}^{qc}, \exists t \in \mathcal{L}(A) \ . \ u \sim^{qc} t\}$. *Moreover,* $|A^r| = O(|A|^2)$.

The main result of this paper is given by the following theorem. The entailment problem for inductive systems is reduced, in polynomial time, to a language inclusion problem for tree automata. The inclusion test is always sound (if the answer is yes, the entailment holds), and complete, if the right-hand side is a local system (Def. 4).

Theorem 1. *Let* $\mathcal{P} = \left\{ P_i \equiv |_{j=1}^{m_i} R_{i,j} \right\}_{i=1}^{k}$ *be a connected inductive system. Then, for any two predicates* $P_i(x_{i,1},\ldots,x_{i,n_i})$ *and* $P_j(x_{j,1},\ldots,x_{j,n_j})$ *of* $\mathcal{P}$ *such that* $n_i = n_j$, *and for any tuple of variables* $\overline{\alpha} = \langle \alpha_1,\ldots,\alpha_{n_i} \rangle$ *not used in* $\mathcal{P}$, *the following holds for* $A_1 = \text{SL2TA}(\mathcal{P}, P_i, \overline{\alpha})$ *and* $A_2 = \text{SL2TA}(\mathcal{P}, P_j, \overline{\alpha})$:
- **(Soundness)** $P_i(\overline{\alpha}) \models_{\mathcal{P}} P_j(\overline{\alpha})$ *if* $\mathcal{L}(A_1) \subseteq \mathcal{L}(A_2^r)$ *and*
- **(Completness)** $P_i(\overline{\alpha}) \models_{\mathcal{P}} P_j(\overline{\alpha})$ *only if* $\mathcal{L}(A_1) \subseteq \mathcal{L}(A_2^r)$ *provided* $\langle \mathcal{P}, P_j \rangle$ *is local.*

Example 8 (cont. of Ex. 6). When applied on the tree automaton A, the operation of rotation closure produces the

$$
\Delta = \left\{
\begin{array}{lr}
\langle a \mapsto (b,d) \wedge a = c, \emptyset \rangle () \to q_1 & \langle a \mapsto (x,b), \emptyset, (x,a) \rangle (q_2) \to q_1 \\
\langle \exists hd'.hd' \mapsto (d,p) \wedge hd = c \wedge hd' = hd, (hd,p) \rangle () & \to q_2 \\
\langle \exists hd'.hd' \mapsto (x,p) \wedge hd' = hd, (hd,p), (x,hd) \rangle (q_2) & \to q_2 \\
\langle \exists hd'.hd' \mapsto (d,p) \wedge hd = c \wedge hd' = hd, \emptyset, (p,hd) \rangle (q_2^{rev}) & \to q_{fin} \\
\langle a \mapsto (x,b), (a,x) \rangle () & \to q_2^{rev} \\
\langle \exists hd'.hd' \mapsto (x,p) \wedge hd' = hd, (hd,x), (p,hd) \rangle (q_2^{rev}) & \to q_2^{rev} \\
\langle \exists hd'.hd' \mapsto (x,p) \wedge hd' = hd, \emptyset, (x,hd), (p,hd) \rangle (q_2, q_2^{rev}) & \to q_{fin}
\end{array}
\right\}
$$

tree automaton $A^r = \langle \Sigma, \{q_1, q_2, q_2^{rev}, q_{fin}\}, \Delta, \{q_1, q_{fin}\} \rangle$ *where* Δ *is shown above.* ∎

5 Complexity

In this section, we provide tight complexity bounds for the entailment problem in the fragment of SL with inductive definitions under consideration, i.e., with the *connectivity* and *locality* restrictions. The first result shows the need for *connectivity* within the system: allowing disconnected rules leads to undecidability of the entailment problem. As a remark, the general undecidability of entailments for SL with inductive definitions has already been proven in [1]. Our proof stresses the fact that undecidability occurs due the lack of connectivity within some rules.

Theorem 2. *Entailment is undecidable for inductive systems with disconnected rules.*

The second result of this section provides tight complexity bounds for the entailment problem for local connected systems. We must point out that EXPTIME-hardness of entailments in the fragment of [14] was already proved in [1]. The result below is stronger since the fragment under consideration is a restriction of the fragment from [14] obtained by applying the locality condition.

Theorem 3. *Entailment is EXPTIME-complete for local connected inductive systems.*

6 Experiments

We implemented a prototype tool called SLIDE (Separation Logic with Inductive DEfinitions) [15] that takes as input two rooted systems $\langle \mathcal{P}_{lhs}, P_{lhs} \rangle$ and $\langle \mathcal{P}_{rhs}, P_{rhs} \rangle$ and tests the validity of the entailment $P_{lhs} \models_{\mathcal{P}_{lhs} \cup \mathcal{P}_{rhs}} P_{rhs}$. Table 1 lists the entailment queries on which we tried out our tool; all examples are public and available on the web [15]. The upper part of the table contains local systems, whereas the bottom part contains

Table 1. Experimental results. The upper table contains local systems, while the lower table non-local ones. Sizes of initial TA (col. 3,4) and rotated TA (col. 5) are in numbers of states/transitions.

Entailment $LHS \models RHS$	Answer	$\|A_{lhs}\|$	$\|A_{rhs}\|$	$\|A^r_{rhs}\|$
$DLL(a,nil,c,nil) \models DLL_{rev}(a,nil,c,nil)$	True	2/4	2/4	5/8
$DLL_{rev}(a,nil,c,nil) \models DLL_{mid}(a,nil,c,nil)$	True	2/4	4/8	12/18
$DLL_{mid}(a,nil,c,nil) \models DLL(a,nil,c,nil)$	True	4/8	2/4	5/8
$\exists x,n,b.\ x \mapsto (n,b) * DLL_{rev}(a,nil,b,x) * DLL(n,x,c,nil) \models DLL(a,nil,c,nil)$	True	3/5	2/4	5/8
$DLL(a,nil,c,nil) \models \exists x,n,b.\ x \mapsto (n,b) * DLL_{rev}(a,nil,b,x) * DLL(n,x,c,nil)$	False	2/4	3/5	9/13
$\exists y,a.\ x \mapsto (y,nil) * y \mapsto (a,x) * DLL(a,y,c,nil) \models DLL(x,nil,c,nil)$	True	3/4	2/4	5/8
$DLL(x,nil,c,nil) \models \exists y,a.\ x \mapsto (nil,y) * y \mapsto (a,x) * DLL(a,y,c,nil)$	False	2/4	3/4	8/10
$\exists x,b.DLL(x,b,c,nil) * DLL_{rev}(a,nil,b,x) \models DLL(a,nil,c,nil)$	True	3/6	2/4	5/8
$DLL(a,nil,c,nil) \models DLL_{0+}(a,nil,c,nil)$	True	2/4	2/4	5/8
$TREE_{pp}(a,nil) \models TREE^{rev}_{pp}(a,nil)$	True	2/4	3/8	6/11
$TREE^{rev}_{pp}(a,nil) \models TREE_{pp}(a,nil)$	True	3/8	2/4	5/10
$TLL_{pp}(a,nil,c,nil) \models TLL^{rev}_{pp}(a,nil,c,nil)$	True	4/8	4/8	13/22
$TLL^{rev}_{pp}(a,nil,c,nil) \models TLL_{pp}(a,nil,c,nil)$	True	4/8	4/8	13/22
$\exists l,r,z.\ a \mapsto (l,r,nil,nil) * TLL(l,c,z) * TLL(r,z,nil) \models TLL(a,c,nil)$	True	4/7	4/8	13/22
$TLL(a,c,nil) \models \exists l,r,z.\ a \mapsto (l,r,nil,nil) * TLL(l,c,z) * TLL(r,z,nil)$	False	4/8	4/7	13/21

non-local systems. Apart from the DLL and TLL predicates from Sect. 2.1, the considered entailment queries contain the following predicates: DLL_{rev} (resp. DLL_{mid}) that encodes a DLL from the end (resp. middle), DLL_{0+} that encodes a possibly empty DLL, $TREE_{pp}$ encoding trees with parent pointers, $TREE^{rev}_{pp}$ that encodes trees with parent pointers defined starting with an arbitrary leaf, TLL_{pp} encoding TLLs with parent pointers, and TLL^{rev}_{pp} which encodes TLLs with parent pointers starting from their leftmost leaf. Columns $|A_{lhs}|$, $|A_{rhs}|$, and $|A^r_{rhs}|$ of Table 1 provide information about the number of states/transitions of the respective TA. The tool answered all queries correctly (despite the incompleteness for non-local systems), and the running times were all under 1 sec. on a standard PC (Intel Core2 CPU, 3GHz, 4GB RAM).

We also compared the SLIDE tool to the CYCLIST [5] theorem prover on the examples from the CYCLIST distribution [13]. Both tools run in less than 1 sec. on the examples from their common fragment of SL. CYCLIST does not handle examples where rotation is needed, while SLIDE fails on examples that generate an unbounded number of dangling pointers and are outside of the decidable fragment of [14].

7 Conclusion

We presented a novel decision procedure for the entailment problem in a non-trivial subset of SL with inductive predicates, which deals with the problem that the same recursive structure may be represented differently, when viewed from different entry points. To this end, we use a special operation, which closes a given TA representation w.r.t. the rotations of its spanning trees. Our procedure is sound and complete for inductive systems with local edges. We have implemented a prototype tool which we tested through a number of non-trivial experiments, with encouraging results.

Acknowledgment. This work was supported by the Czech Science Foundation under the project 14-11384S, the EU/Czech IT4Innovations Centre of Excellence project CZ.1.05/1.1.00/02.0070, and the internal BUT projects FIT-S-12-1 and FIT-S-14-2486.

References

1. Antonopoulos, T., Gorogiannis, N., Haase, C., Kanovich, M., Ouaknine, J.: Foundations for decision problems in separation logic with general inductive predicates. In: Muscholl, A. (ed.) FOSSACS 2014. LNCS, vol. 8412, pp. 411–425. Springer, Heidelberg (2014)
2. Berdine, J., Calcagno, C., Cook, B., Distefano, D., O'Hearn, P.W., Wies, T., Yang, H.: Shape analysis for composite data structures. In: Damm, W., Hermanns, H. (eds.) CAV 2007. LNCS, vol. 4590, pp. 178–192. Springer, Heidelberg (2007)
3. Berdine, J., Calcagno, C., O'Hearn, P.W.: A decidable fragment of separation logic. In: Lodaya, K., Mahajan, M. (eds.) FSTTCS 2004. LNCS, vol. 3328, pp. 97–109. Springer, Heidelberg (2004)
4. Bouajjani, A., Habermehl, P., Holík, L., Touili, T., Vojnar, T.: Antichain-based universality and inclusion testing over nondeterministic finite tree automata. In: Ibarra, O.H., Ravikumar, B. (eds.) CIAA 2008. LNCS, vol. 5148, pp. 57–67. Springer, Heidelberg (2008)
5. Brotherston, J., Gorogiannis, N., Petersen, R.L.: A generic cyclic theorem prover. In: Jhala, R., Igarashi, A. (eds.) APLAS 2012. LNCS, vol. 7705, pp. 350–367. Springer, Heidelberg (2012)
6. Brotherston, J., Kanovich, M.: Undecidability of propositional separation logic and its neighbours. In: Proceedings of the 2010 25th Annual IEEE Symposium on Logic in Computer Science, LICS 2010, pp. 130–139 (2010)
7. Calcagno, C., Distefano, D.: Infer: An automatic program verifier for memory safety of C programs. In: Bobaru, M., Havelund, K., Holzmann, G.J., Joshi, R. (eds.) NFM 2011. LNCS, vol. 6617, pp. 459–465. Springer, Heidelberg (2011)
8. Cook, B., Haase, C., Ouaknine, J., Parkinson, M., Worrell, J.: Tractable reasoning in a fragment of separation logic. In: Katoen, J.-P., König, B. (eds.) CONCUR 2011. LNCS, vol. 6901, pp. 235–249. Springer, Heidelberg (2011)
9. Dudka, K., Peringer, P., Vojnar, T.: Predator: A practical tool for checking manipulation of dynamic data structures using separation logic. In: Gopalakrishnan, G., Qadeer, S. (eds.) CAV 2011. LNCS, vol. 6806, pp. 372–378. Springer, Heidelberg (2011)
10. Enea, C., Lengál, O., Sighireanu, M., Vojnar, T.: Compositional Entailment Checking for a Fragment of Separation Logic. Technical Report FIT-TR-2014-01, FIT, Brno University of Technology (2014)
11. Enea, C., Saveluc, V., Sighireanu, M.: Compositional invariant checking for overlaid and nested linked lists. In: Felleisen, M., Gardner, P. (eds.) ESOP 2013. LNCS, vol. 7792, pp. 129–148. Springer, Heidelberg (2013)
12. Flum, J., Grohe, M.: Parameterized Complexity Theory. Springer-Verlag New York, Inc. (2006)
13. Gorogiannis, N.: Cyclist: a cyclic theorem prover framework, https://github.com/ngorogiannis/cyclist/
14. Iosif, R., Rogalewicz, A., Simacek, J.: The tree width of separation logic with recursive definitions. In: Bonacina, M.P. (ed.) CADE 2013. LNCS, vol. 7898, pp. 21–38. Springer, Heidelberg (2013)
15. Iosif, R., Rogalewicz, A., Vojnar, T.: Slide: Separation logic with inductive definitions, http://www.fit.vutbr.cz/research/groups/verifit/tools/slide/
16. Iosif, R., Rogalewicz, A., Vojnar, T.: Deciding entailments in inductive separation logic with tree automata. CoRR, abs/1402.2127 (2014)
17. Lengal, O., Simacek, J., Vojnar, T.: Vata: a tree automata library, http://www.fit.vutbr.cz/research/groups/verifit/tools/libvata/

18. Navarro Pérez, J.A., Rybalchenko, A.: Separation logic modulo theories. In: Shan, C.-C. (ed.) APLAS 2013. LNCS, vol. 8301, pp. 90–106. Springer, Heidelberg (2013)
19. Nguyen, H.H., Chin, W.-N.: Enhancing program verification with lemmas. In: Gupta, A., Malik, S. (eds.) CAV 2008. LNCS, vol. 5123, pp. 355–369. Springer, Heidelberg (2008)
20. Piskac, R., Wies, T., Zufferey, D.: Automating separation logic using SMT. In: Sharygina, N., Veith, H. (eds.) CAV 2013. LNCS, vol. 8044, pp. 773–789. Springer, Heidelberg (2013)
21. Piskac, R., Wies, T., Zufferey, D.: Automating separation logic with trees and data. In: Biere, A., Bloem, R. (eds.) CAV 2014. LNCS, vol. 8559, pp. 711–728. Springer, Heidelberg (2014)
22. Reynolds, J.: Separation Logic: A Logic for Shared Mutable Data Structures. In: Proc. of LICS 2002. IEEE CS Press (2002)

Liveness Analysis for Parameterised Boolean Equation Systems

Jeroen J.A. Keiren[1], Wieger Wesselink[2], and Tim A.C. Willemse[2]

[1] VU University Amsterdam, The Netherlands
`j.j.a.keiren@vu.nl`
[2] Eindhoven University of Technology, The Netherlands
`{j.w.wesselink,t.a.c.willemse}@tue.nl`

Abstract. We present a sound static analysis technique for fighting the combinatorial explosion of parameterised Boolean equation systems (PBESs). These essentially are systems of mutually recursive fixed point equations ranging over first-order logic formulae. Our method detects parameters that are not live by analysing a control flow graph of a PBES, and it subsequently eliminates such parameters. We show that a naive approach to constructing a control flow graph, needed for the analysis, may suffer from an exponential blow-up, and we define an approximate analysis that avoids this problem. The effectiveness of our techniques is evaluated using a number of case studies.

1 Introduction

Parameterised Boolean equation systems (PBESs) [7] are systems of fixpoint equations that range over first-order formulae; they are essentially an equational variation of *Least Fixpoint Logic (LFP)*. Fixpoint logics such as PBESs have applications in database theory and computer aided verification. For instance, the CADP [6] and mCRL2 [4] toolsets use PBESs for model checking and equivalence checking and in [2] PBESs are used to solve Datalog queries.

In practice, the predominant problem for PBESs is evaluating (henceforth referred to as *solving*) them so as to answer the decision problem encoded in them. There are a variety of techniques for solving PBESs, see [7], but the most straightforward method is by instantiation to a *Boolean equation system (BES)* [10], and then solving this BES. This process is similar to the explicit generation of a behavioural state space from its symbolic description, and it suffers from a combinatorial explosion that is akin to the state space explosion problem. Combatting this combinatorial explosion is therefore instrumental in speeding up the process of solving the problems encoded by PBESs.

While several static analysis techniques have been described using fixpoint logics, see *e.g.* [3], with the exception of the static analysis techniques for PBESs, described in [12], no such techniques seem to have been employed to simplify expressions in fixpoint logics.

Our main contribution in this paper is a static analysis method for PBESs that significantly improves over the aforementioned techniques for simplifying PBESs. In our method, we construct a *control flow graph* (CFG) for a given PBES and subsequently

F. Cassez and J.-F. Raskin (Eds.): ATVA 2014, LNCS 8837, pp. 219–234, 2014.

apply state space reduction techniques [5,16], combined with liveness analysis techniques from compiler technology [1]. These typically scrutinise syntactic descriptions of behaviour to detect and eliminate variables that at some point become irrelevant (dead, not live) to the behaviour, thereby decreasing the complexity.

The notion of control flow of a PBES is not self-evident: formulae in fixpoint logics (such as PBESs) do not have a notion of a program counter. Our notion of control flow is based on the concept of *control flow parameters* (CFPs), which induce a CFG. Similar notions exist in the context of state space exploration, see *e.g.* [14], but so far, no such concept exists for fixpoint logics.

The size of the CFGs is potentially exponential in the number of CFPs. We therefore also describe a modification of our analysis—in which reductive power is traded against a lower complexity—that does not suffer from this problem. Our static analysis technique allows for solving PBESs using instantiation that hitherto could not be solved this way, either because the underlying BESs would be infinite or they would be extremely large. We show that our methods are sound; *i.e.*, simplifying PBESs using our analyses leads to PBESs with the same solution.

Our static analysis techniques have been implemented in the mCRL2 toolset [4] and applied to a set of model checking and equivalence checking problems. Our experiments show that the implementations outperform existing static analysis techniques for PBESs [12] in terms of reductive power, and that reductions of almost 100% of the size of the underlying BESs can be achieved. Our experiments confirm that the optimised version sometimes achieves slightly less reduction than our non-optimised version, but is faster. Furthermore, in cases where no additional reduction is achieved compared to existing techniques, the overhead is mostly negligible.

Structure of the Paper. In Section 2 we give a cursory overview of basic PBES theory and in Section 3, we present an example to illustrate the difficulty of using instantiation to solve a PBES and to sketch our solution. In Section 4 we describe our construction of control flow graphs for PBESs and in Section 5 we describe our live parameter analysis. We present an optimisation of the analysis in Section 6. The approach is evaluated in Section 7, and Section 8 concludes. We refer to [9] for proofs and additional results.

2   Preliminaries

Throughout this paper, we work in a setting of *abstract data types* with non-empty data sorts $D_1, D_2, \ldots$, and operations on these sorts, and a set $\mathcal{D}$ of sorted data variables. We write vectors in boldface, *e.g.* d is used to denote a vector of data variables. We write d_i to denote the i-th element of a vector d.

A semantic set $\mathbb{D}$ is associated to every sort D, such that each term of sort D, and all operations on D are mapped to the elements and operations of $\mathbb{D}$ they represent. *Ground terms* are terms that do not contain data variables. For terms that contain data variables, we use an environment δ that maps each variable from $\mathcal{D}$ to a value of the associated type. We assume an interpretation function $\llbracket \_ \rrbracket$ that maps every term t of sort D to the data element $\llbracket t \rrbracket \delta$ it represents, where the extensions of δ to open terms and vectors are standard. Environment updates are denoted $\delta[v/d]$, where $\delta[v/d](d') = v$ if $d' = d$, and $\delta(d')$ otherwise.

We specifically assume the existence of a sort B with elements *true* and *false* representing the Booleans $\mathbb{B}$ and a sort $N = \{0, 1, 2, \ldots\}$ representing the natural numbers $\mathbb{N}$. For these sorts, we assume that the usual operators are available and, for readability, these are written the same as their semantic counterparts.

Parameterised Boolean equation systems [11] are sequences of fixed-point equations ranging over *predicate formulae*. The latter are first-order formulae extended with predicate variables, in which the non-logical symbols are taken from the data language.

Definition 1. Predicate formulae *are defined through the following grammar:*

$$\varphi, \psi ::= b \mid X(e) \mid \varphi \wedge \psi \mid \varphi \vee \psi \mid \forall d\colon D.\varphi \mid \exists d\colon D.\varphi$$

in which b is a data term of sort B, $X(e)$ is a predicate variable instance (PVI) in which X is a predicate variable of sort $D \to B$, taken from some sufficiently large set $\mathcal{P}$ of predicate variables, and e is a vector of data terms of sort D. The interpretation of a predicate formula φ in the context of a predicate environment $\eta\colon \mathcal{P} \to \mathbb{D} \to \mathbb{B}$ and a data environment δ is denoted as $[\![\varphi]\!]\eta\delta$, where:

$$[\![b]\!]\eta\delta = \begin{cases} true & if\ \delta(b) \\ false & otherwise \end{cases} \qquad [\![X(e)]\!]\eta\delta = \begin{cases} true & if\ \eta(X)(\delta(e)) \\ false & otherwise \end{cases}$$

$$[\![\phi \wedge \psi]\!]\eta\delta = [\![\phi]\!]\eta\delta\ and\ [\![\psi]\!]\eta\delta\ hold \qquad [\![\phi \vee \psi]\!]\eta\delta = [\![\phi]\!]\eta\delta\ or\ [\![\psi]\!]\eta\delta\ hold$$

$$[\![\forall d\colon D.\ \phi]\!]\eta\delta = for\ all\ v \in \mathbb{D},\ [\![\phi]\!]\eta\delta[v/d]\ holds$$

$$[\![\exists d\colon D.\ \phi]\!]\eta\delta = for\ some\ v \in \mathbb{D},\ [\![\phi]\!]\eta\delta[v/d]\ holds$$

We assume the usual precedence rules for the logical operators. *Logical equivalence* between two predicate formulae φ, ψ, denoted $\varphi \equiv \psi$, is defined as $[\![\varphi]\!]\eta\delta = [\![\psi]\!]\eta\delta$ for all η, δ. Freely occurring data variables in φ are denoted by $FV(\varphi)$. We refer to $X(e)$ occurring in a predicate formula as a *predicate variable instance* (PVI).

Definition 2. *PBESs are defined by the following grammar:*

$$\mathcal{E} ::= \emptyset \mid (\nu X(d\colon D) = \varphi)\mathcal{E} \mid (\mu X(d\colon D) = \varphi)\mathcal{E}$$

in which $\emptyset$ denotes the empty equation system; μ and ν are the least and greatest fixed point signs, respectively; X is a sorted predicate variable of sort $D \to B$, d is a vector of formal parameters, and φ is a predicate formula. We henceforth omit a trailing $\emptyset$.

By convention φ_X denotes the right-hand side of the defining equation for X in a PBES $\mathcal{E}$; $\mathrm{par}(X)$ denotes the set of *formal parameters* of X; and we assume that $FV(\varphi_X) \subseteq \mathrm{par}(X)$, and that $\mathrm{par}(X)$ is disjoint from the set of quantified variables. By superscripting a formal parameter with the predicate variable to which it belongs, we distinguish between formal parameters for different predicate variables, *i.e.*, we write d^X when $d \in \mathrm{par}(X)$. We write σ to stand for either μ or ν.

The set of *bound predicate variables* of some PBES $\mathcal{E}$, denoted $\mathrm{bnd}(\mathcal{E})$, is the set of predicate variables occurring at the left-hand sides of the equations in $\mathcal{E}$. Throughout this paper, we deal with PBESs that are both *well-formed*, i.e. for every $X \in \mathrm{bnd}(\mathcal{E})$ there is exactly one equation in $\mathcal{E}$, and *closed*, i.e. for every $X \in \mathrm{bnd}(\mathcal{E})$, only predicate variables taken from $\mathrm{bnd}(\mathcal{E})$ occur in φ_X.

To each PBES $\mathcal{E}$ we associate a *top assertion*, denoted $\mathbf{init}\ X(\boldsymbol{v})$, where we require $X \in \mathsf{bnd}(\mathcal{E})$. For a parameter $\boldsymbol{d}_m \in \mathsf{par}(X)$ for the top assertion $\mathbf{init}\ X(\boldsymbol{v})$ we define the value $\mathsf{init}(\boldsymbol{d}_m)$ as $\boldsymbol{v}_m$.

We next define a PBES's semantics. Let $\mathbb{B}^{\mathbb{D}}$ denote the set of functions $f\colon \mathbb{D} \to \mathbb{B}$, and define the ordering $\sqsubseteq$ as $f \sqsubseteq g$ iff for all $\boldsymbol{v} \in \mathbb{D}$, $f(\boldsymbol{v})$ implies $g(\boldsymbol{v})$. For a given pair of environments δ, η, a predicate formula φ gives rise to a predicate transformer T on the complete lattice $(\mathbb{B}^{\mathbb{D}}, \sqsubseteq)$ as follows: $T(f) = \lambda \boldsymbol{v} \in \mathbb{D}.\llbracket \varphi \rrbracket \eta[f/X]\delta[\boldsymbol{v}/\boldsymbol{d}]$.

Since the predicate transformers defined this way are monotone, their extremal fixed points exist. We denote the least fixed point of a given predicate transformer T by μT, and the greatest fixed point of T is denoted νT.

Definition 3. *The solution of an equation system in the context of a predicate environment η and data environment δ is defined inductively as follows:*

$$\llbracket \emptyset \rrbracket \eta \delta = \eta$$
$$\llbracket (\mu X(\boldsymbol{d}\colon \boldsymbol{D}) = \varphi_X)\mathcal{E} \rrbracket \eta \delta = \llbracket \mathcal{E} \rrbracket \eta[\mu T/X]\delta$$
$$\llbracket (\nu X(\boldsymbol{d}\colon \boldsymbol{D}) = \varphi_X)\mathcal{E} \rrbracket \eta \delta = \llbracket \mathcal{E} \rrbracket \eta[\nu T/X]\delta$$

with $T(f) = \lambda \boldsymbol{v} \in \mathbb{D}.\llbracket \varphi_X \rrbracket (\llbracket \mathcal{E} \rrbracket \eta[f/X]\delta)\delta[\boldsymbol{v}/\boldsymbol{d}]$

The solution prioritises the fixed point signs of left-most equations over the fixed point signs of equations that follow, while respecting the equations. Bound predicate variables of closed PBESs have a solution that is independent of the predicate and data environments in which it is evaluated. We therefore omit these environments and write $\llbracket \mathcal{E} \rrbracket(X)$ instead of $\llbracket \mathcal{E} \rrbracket \eta \delta(X)$.

3   A Motivating Example

In practice, solving PBESs proceeds via *instantiating* [13] into *Boolean equation systems (BESs)*, for which solving is decidable. The latter is the fragment of PBESs with equations that range over propositions only, *i.e.*, formulae without data and quantification. Instantiating a PBES to a BES is akin to state space exploration and suffers from a similar combinatorial explosion. Reducing the time spent on it is thus instrumental in speeding up, or even enabling the solving process. We illustrate this using the following (academic) example, which we also use as our running example:

$$\nu X(i,j,k,l\colon N) = (i \neq 1 \lor j \neq 1 \lor X(2,j,k,l+1)) \land \forall m\colon N.Z(i,2,m+k,k)$$
$$\mu Y(i,j,k,l\colon N) = k = 1 \lor (i = 2 \land X(1,j,k,l))$$
$$\nu Z(i,j,k,l\colon N) = (k < 10 \lor j = 2) \land (j \neq 2 \lor Y(1,1,l,1)) \land Y(2,2,1,l)$$

The presence of PVIs $X(2,j,k,l+1)$ and $Z(i,2,m+k,k)$ in X's equation means the solution to $X(1,1,1,1)$ depends on the solutions to $X(2,1,1,2)$ and $Z(1,2,v+1,1)$, for all values v, see Fig. 1. Instantiation finds these dependencies by simplifying the right-hand side of X when its parameters have been assigned value 1:

$$(1 \neq 1 \lor 1 \neq 1 \lor X(2,1,1,1+1)) \land \forall m\colon N.Z(1,2,m+1,1)$$

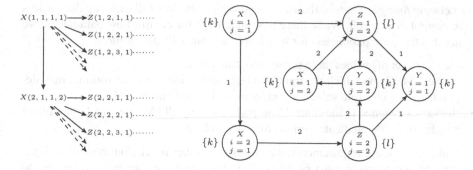

Fig. 1. Dependency graph   **Fig. 2.** Control flow graph for the running example

Since for an infinite number of different arguments the solution to Z must be computed, instantiation does not terminate. The problem is with the third parameter (k) of Z. We cannot simply assume that values assigned to the third parameter of Z do not matter; in fact, only when $j = 2$, Z's right-hand side predicate formula does not depend on k's value. This is where our developed method will come into play: it automatically determines that it is sound to replace PVI $Z(i, 2, m + k, k)$ by, e.g., $Z(i, 2, 1, k)$ and to remove the universal quantifier, enabling us to solve $X(1, 1, 1, 1)$ using instantiation.

Our technique uses a *Control Flow Graph* (CFG) underlying the PBES for analysing which parameters of a PBES are *live*. The CFG is a finite abstraction of the dependency graph that would result from instantiating a PBES. For instance, when ignoring the third and fourth parameters in our example PBES, we find that the solution to $X(1, 1, *, *)$ depends on the first PVI, leading to $X(2, 1, *, *)$ and the second PVI in X's equation, leading to $Z(1, 2, *, *)$. In the same way we can determine the dependencies for $Z(1, 2, *, *)$, resulting in the finite structure depicted in Fig. 2. The subsequent liveness analysis annotates each vertex with a label indicating which parameters cannot (cheaply) be excluded from having an impact on the solution to the equation system; these are assumed to be live. Using these labels, we modify the PBES automatically.

Constructing a good CFG is a major difficulty, which we address in Section 4. The liveness analysis and the subsequent modification of the analysed PBES is described in Section 5. Since the CFG constructed in Section 4 can still suffer from a combinatorial explosion, we present an optimisation of our analysis in Section 6.

4 Constructing Control Flow Graphs for PBESs

The vertices in the control flow graph we constructed in the previous section represent the values assigned to a subset of the equations' formal parameters whereas an edge between two vertices captures the dependencies among (partially instantiated) equations. The better the control flow graph approximates the dependency graph resulting from an instantiation, the more precise the resulting liveness analysis.

Since computing a precise control flow graph is expensive, the problem is to compute the graph effectively and to balance precision and cost. To this end, we first identify a set of *control flow parameters*; the values to these parameters will make up the vertices in the control flow graph. While there is some choice for control flow parameters, we require that these are parameters for which we can *statically* determine:

1. the (finite set of) values these parameters can assume,
2. the set of PVIs on which the truth of a right-hand side predicate formula may depend, given a concrete value for each control flow parameter, and
3. the values assigned to the control flow parameters by all PVIs on which the truth of a right-hand side predicate formula may depend.

In addition to these requirements, we impose one other restriction: control flow parameters of one equation must be *mutually independent*; *i.e.*, we have to be able to determine their values independently of each other. Apart from being a natural requirement for a control flow parameter, it enables us to devise optimisations of our liveness analysis.

We now formalise these ideas. First, we characterise three partial functions that together allow to relate values of formal parameters to the dependency of a formula on a given PVI. Our formalisation of these partial functions is based on the following observation: if in a formula φ, we can replace a particular PVI $X(e)$ with the subformula $\psi \wedge X(e)$ without this affecting the truth value of φ, we know that φ's truth value only depends on $X(e)$'s whenever ψ holds. We will choose ψ such that it allows us to pinpoint exactly what value a formal parameter of an equation has (or will be assigned through a PVI). Using these functions, we then identify our control flow parameters by eliminating variables that do not meet all of the aforementioned requirements.

In order to reason about individual PVIs occurring in predicate formulae we introduce the notation necessary to do so. Let $\mathsf{npred}(\varphi)$ denote the number of PVIs occurring in a predicate formula φ. The function $\mathsf{PVI}(\varphi, i)$ is the formula representing the ith PVI in φ, of which $\mathsf{pv}(\varphi, i)$ is the name and $\mathsf{arg}(\varphi, i)$ represents the term that appears as the argument of the instance. In general $\mathsf{arg}(\varphi, i)$ is a vector, of which we denote the jth argument by $\mathsf{arg}_j(\varphi, i)$. Given predicate formula ψ we write $\varphi[i \mapsto \psi]$ to indicate that the PVI at position i is replaced syntactically by ψ in φ.

Definition 4. *Let* $s\colon \mathcal{P} \times \mathbb{N} \times \mathbb{N} \to D$, $t\colon \mathcal{P} \times \mathbb{N} \times \mathbb{N} \to D$, *and* $c\colon \mathcal{P} \times \mathbb{N} \times \mathbb{N} \to \mathbb{N}$ *be partial functions, where* D *is the union of all ground terms. The triple* (s, t, c) *is a* unicity constraint *for PBES* $\mathcal{E}$ *if for all* $X \in \mathsf{bnd}(\mathcal{E})$, $i, j, k \in \mathbb{N}$ *and ground terms* e:

- *(source) if* $s(X, i, j) = e$ *then* $\varphi_X \equiv \varphi_X[i \mapsto (d_j = e \wedge \mathsf{PVI}(\varphi_X, i))]$,
- *(target) if* $t(X, i, j) = e$ *then* $\varphi_X \equiv \varphi_X[i \mapsto (\mathsf{arg}_j(\varphi_X, i) = e \wedge \mathsf{PVI}(\varphi_X, i))]$,
- *(copy) if* $c(X, i, j) = k$ *then* $\varphi_X \equiv \varphi_X[i \mapsto (\mathsf{arg}_k(\varphi_X, i) = d_j \wedge \mathsf{PVI}(\varphi_X, i))]$.

Observe that indeed, function s states that, when defined, formal parameter d_j must have value $s(X, i, j)$ for φ_X's truth value to depend on that of $\mathsf{PVI}(\varphi_X, i)$. In the same vein $t(X, i, j)$, if defined, gives the fixed value of the jth formal parameter of $\mathsf{pv}(\varphi_X, i)$. Whenever $c(X, i, j) = k$ the value of variable d_j is transparently copied to position k in the ith predicate variable instance of φ_X. Since s, t and c are partial functions, we do not require them to be defined; we use $\perp$ to indicate this.

Example 1. A unicity constraint (s, t, c) for our running example could be one that assigns $s(X, 1, 2) = 1$, since parameter j^X must be 1 to make X's right-hand side formula depend on PVI $X(2, j, k, l + 1)$. We can set $t(X, 1, 2) = 1$, as one can deduce that parameter j^X is set to 1 by the PVI $X(2, j, k, l + 1)$; furthermore, we can set $c(Z, 1, 4) = 3$, as parameter k^Y is set to l^Z's value by PVI $Y(1, 1, l, 1)$.

From hereon, we assume that $\mathcal{E}$ is an arbitrary PBES with (source, target, copy) a unicity constraint we can deduce for it. Notice that for each formal parameter for which either source or target is defined for some PVI, we have a finite set of values that this parameter can assume. However, at this point we do not yet know whether this set of values is exhaustive: it may be that some PVIs may cause the parameter to take on arbitrary values. Below, we will narrow down for which parameters we *can* ensure that the set of values is exhaustive. First, we eliminate formal parameters that do not meet conditions 1–3 for PVIs that induce self-dependencies for an equation.

Definition 5. *A parameter $d_n \in$ par(X) is a* local control flow parameter *(LCFP) if for all i such that* pv$(\varphi_X, i) = X$, *either* source(X, i, n) *and* target(X, i, n) *are defined, or* copy$(X, i, n) = n$.

Example 2. Formal parameter l^X in our running example does not meet the conditions of Def. 5 and is therefore not an LCFP. All other parameters in all other equations are still LCFPs since X is the only equation with a self-dependency.

From the formal parameters that are LCFPs, we next eliminate those parameters that do not meet conditions 1–3 for PVIs that induce dependencies among *different* equations.

Definition 6. *A parameter $d_n \in$ par(X) is a* global control flow parameter *(GCFP) if it is an LCFP, and for all $Y \in$ bnd$(\mathcal{E}) \setminus \{X\}$ and all i such that* pv$(\varphi_Y, i) = X$, *either* target(Y, i, n) *is defined, or* copy$(Y, i, m) = n$ *for some GCFP $d_m \in$ par(Y).*

The above definition is recursive in nature: if a parameter does not meet the GCFP conditions then this may result in another parameter also not meeting the GCFP conditions. Any set of parameters that meets the GCFP conditions is a good set, but larger sets possibly lead to better information about the control flow in a PBES.

Example 3. Formal parameter k^Z in our running example is not a GCFP since in PVI $Z(i, 2, m + k, k)$ from X's equation, the value assigned to k^Z cannot be determined.

The parameters that meet the GCFP conditions satisfy the conditions 1–3 that we imposed on control flow parameters: they assume a finite set of values, we can deduce which PVIs may affect the truth of a right-hand side predicate formula, and we can deduce how these parameters evolve as a result of all PVIs in a PBES. However, we may still have parameters of a given equation that are mutually dependent. Note that this dependency can only arise as a result of copying parameters: in all other cases, the functions source and target provide the information to deduce concrete values.

Example 4. GCFP k^Y affects GCFP k^X's value through PVI $X(1, j, k, l)$; likewise, k^X affects l^Z's value through PVI $Z(i, 2, m + k, k)$. Through the PVI $Y(2, 2, 1, l)$ in Z's equation, GCFP l^Z affects GCFPs l^Y value. Thus, k^Y affects l^Y's value transitively.

We identify parameters that, through copying, may become mutually dependent. To this end, we use a relation $\sim$, to indicate that GCFPs are *related*. Let d_n^X and d_m^Y be GCFPs; these are *related*, denoted $d_n^X \sim d_m^Y$, if $n =$ copy(Y, i, m) for some i. Next, we characterise when a set of GCFPs does not introduce mutual dependencies.

Definition 7. *Let C be a set of GCFPs, and let $\sim^*$ denote the reflexive, symmetric and transitive closure of $\sim$ on C. Assume $\approx \subseteq C \times C$ is an equivalence relation that subsumes $\sim^*$; i.e., that satisfies $\sim^* \subseteq \approx$. Then the pair $\langle C, \approx \rangle$ defines a* control structure *if for all $X \in \mathsf{bnd}(\mathcal{E})$ and all $d, d' \in C \cap \mathsf{par}(X)$, if $d \approx d'$, then $d = d'$.*

We say that a unicity constraint is a *witness* to a control structure $\langle C, \approx \rangle$ if the latter can be deduced from the unicity constraint through Definitions 5–7. The equivalence $\approx$ in a control structure also serves to identify GCFPs that take on the same role in *different* equations: we say that two parameters $c, c' \in C$ are *identical* if $c \approx c'$. As a last step, we formally define our notion of a control flow parameter.

Definition 8. *A formal parameter c is a* control flow parameter *(CFP) if there is a control structure $\langle C, \approx \rangle$ such that $c \in C$.*

Example 5. There is a unicity constraint that identifies that parameter i^X is copied to i^Z in our running example. Then necessarily $i^Z \sim i^X$ and thus $i^X \approx i^Z$ for a control structure $\langle C, \approx \rangle$ with $i^X, i^Z \in C$. However, i^X and i^Y do not have to be related, but we have the option to define $\approx$ so that they are. The structure $\langle \{i^X, j^X, i^Y, j^Y, i^Z, j^Z\}, \approx \rangle$ for which $\approx$ relates all (and only) identically named parameters is a control structure.

Using a control structure $\langle C, \approx \rangle$, we can ensure that all equations have the same set of CFPs. This can be done by assigning unique names to identical CFPs and by adding CFPs that do not appear in an equation as formal parameters for this equation. Without loss of generality we therefore continue to work under the following assumption.

Assumption 1. *The set of CFPs is the same for every equation in a PBES $\mathcal{E}$; i.e., for all $X, Y \in \mathsf{bnd}(\mathcal{E})$, $d^X \in \mathsf{par}(X)$ is a CFP iff $d^Y \in \mathsf{par}(Y)$ is a CFP, and $d^X \approx d^Y$.*

From hereon, we call any formal parameter that is not a control flow parameter a *data parameter*. We make this distinction explicit by partitioning $\mathcal{D}$ into CFPs $\mathcal{C}$ and data parameters $\mathcal{D}^{DP}$. As a consequence of Assumption 1, we may assume that every PBES we consider has equations with the same sequence of CFPs; *i.e.*, all equations are of the form $\sigma X(c\colon C, d^X\colon D^X) = \varphi_X(c, d^X)$, where c is the (vector of) CFPs, and d^X is the (vector of) data parameters of the equation for X.

Using the CFPs, we next construct a control flow graph. Vertices in this graph represent valuations for the vector of CFPs and the edges capture dependencies on PVIs. The set of potential valuations for the CFPs is bounded by $\mathsf{values}(c_k)$, defined as:

$$\{\mathsf{init}(c_k)\} \cup \bigcup_{i \in \mathbb{N}, X \in \mathsf{bnd}(\mathcal{E})} \{v \in D \mid \mathsf{source}(X, i, k) = v \vee \mathsf{target}(X, i, k) = v\}.$$

We generalise values to the vector c in the obvious way.

Definition 9. *The* control flow graph *(CFG) of $\mathcal{E}$ is a directed graph $(V, \rightarrow)$ with:*

- $V \subseteq \mathsf{bnd}(\mathcal{E}) \times \mathsf{values}(c)$.
- $\rightarrow \subseteq V \times \mathbb{N} \times V$ *is the least relation for which, whenever $(X, v) \xrightarrow{i} (\mathsf{pv}(\varphi_X, i), w)$ then for every k either:*

- $\mathsf{source}(X, i, k) = v_k$ and $\mathsf{target}(X, i, k) = w_k$, or
- $\mathsf{source}(X, i, k) = \bot$, $\mathsf{copy}(X, i, k) = k$ and $v_k = w_k$, or
- $\mathsf{source}(X, i, k) = \bot$, and $\mathsf{target}(X, i, k) = w_k$.

We refer to the vertices in the CFG as *locations*. Note that a CFG is finite since the set values(c) is finite. Furthermore, CFGs are complete in the sense that all PVIs on which the truth of some φ_X may depend when $c = v$ are neighbours of location (X, v).

Example 6. Using the CFPs identified earlier and an appropriate unicity constraint, we can obtain the CFG depicted in Fig. 2 for our running example.

Implementation. CFGs are defined in terms of CFPs, which in turn are obtained from a unicity constraint. Our definition of a unicity constraint is not constructive. However, a unicity constraint can be derived from *guards* for a PVI. Computing the exact guard, *i.e.* the strongest formula ψ satisfying $\varphi \equiv \varphi[i \mapsto (\psi \wedge \mathsf{PVI}(\varphi, i))]$, is computationally hard. We can efficiently approximate it such that $\varphi \equiv \varphi[i \mapsto (\mathsf{guard}^i(\varphi) \wedge \mathsf{PVI}(\varphi, i))]$; *i.e.*, $\mathsf{PVI}(\varphi, i)$ is relevant to φ's truth value only if $\mathsf{guard}^i(\varphi)$ is satisfiable, as follows:

Definition 10. *Let φ be a predicate formula. We define the guard of the i-th PVI in φ, denoted $\mathsf{guard}^i(\varphi)$, inductively as follows:*

$$\mathsf{guard}^i(b) = \mathit{false} \qquad\qquad \mathsf{guard}^i(Y) = \mathit{true}$$

$$\mathsf{guard}^i(\forall d: D.\varphi) = \mathsf{guard}^i(\varphi) \qquad \mathsf{guard}^i(\exists d: D.\varphi) = \mathsf{guard}^i(\varphi)$$

$$\mathsf{guard}^i(\varphi \wedge \psi) = \begin{cases} s(\varphi) \wedge \mathsf{guard}^{i-\mathsf{npred}(\varphi)}(\psi) & \mathit{if}\ i > \mathsf{npred}(\varphi) \\ s(\psi) \wedge \mathsf{guard}^i(\varphi) & \mathit{if}\ i \leq \mathsf{npred}(\varphi) \end{cases}$$

$$\mathsf{guard}^i(\varphi \vee \psi) = \begin{cases} s(\neg\varphi) \wedge \mathsf{guard}^{i-\mathsf{npred}(\varphi)}(\psi) & \mathit{if}\ i > \mathsf{npred}(\varphi) \\ s(\neg\psi) \wedge \mathsf{guard}^i(\varphi) & \mathit{if}\ i \leq \mathsf{npred}(\varphi) \end{cases}$$

where $s(\varphi) = \varphi$ if $\mathsf{npred}(\varphi) = 0$, and true otherwise.

Example 7. In the running example $\mathsf{guard}^1(\varphi_X) = \mathit{true} \wedge \neg(i \neq 1) \wedge \neg(j \neq 1) \wedge \mathit{true}$.

A good heuristic for defining the unicity constraints is looking for positive occurrences of constraints of the form $d = e$ in the guards and using this information to see if the arguments of PVIs reduce to constants.

5 Data Flow Analysis

Our liveness analysis is built on top of CFGs constructed using Def. 9. The analysis proceeds as follows: for each location in the CFG, we first identify the data parameters that may directly affect the truth value of the corresponding predicate formula. Then we inductively identify data parameters that can affect such parameters through PVIs as live as well. Upon termination, each location is labelled by the *live* parameters at that location. The set $\mathsf{sig}(\varphi)$ of parameters that affect the truth value of a predicate formula φ, *i.e.*, those parameters that occur in Boolean data terms, are approximated as follows:

$$\begin{array}{ll} \mathsf{sig}(b) = FV(b) & \mathsf{sig}(Y(e)) = \emptyset \\ \mathsf{sig}(\varphi \wedge \psi) = \mathsf{sig}(\varphi) \cup \mathsf{sig}(\psi) & \mathsf{sig}(\varphi \vee \psi) = \mathsf{sig}(\varphi) \cup \mathsf{sig}(\psi) \\ \mathsf{sig}(\exists d\colon D.\varphi) = \mathsf{sig}(\varphi) \setminus \{d\} & \mathsf{sig}(\forall d\colon D.\varphi) = \mathsf{sig}(\varphi) \setminus \{d\} \end{array}$$

Observe that $\mathsf{sig}(\varphi)$ is not invariant under logical equivalence. We use this fact to our advantage: we assume the existence of a function simplify for which we require $\mathsf{simplify}(\varphi) \equiv \varphi$, and $\mathsf{sig}(\mathsf{simplify}(\varphi)) \subseteq \mathsf{sig}(\varphi)$. An appropriately chosen function simplify may help to narrow down the parameters that affect the truth value of predicate formulae in our base case; in the worst case the function leaves φ unchanged. Labelling the CFG with live variables is achieved as follows:

Definition 11. *Let $\mathcal{E}$ be a PBES and let $(V, \to)$ be its CFG. The labelling $L\colon V \to \mathbb{P}(\mathcal{D}^{DP})$ is defined as $L(X, v) = \bigcup_{n \in \mathbb{N}} L^n(X, v)$, with L^n inductively defined as:*

$$L^0(X, v) = \mathsf{sig}(\mathsf{simplify}(\varphi_X[c := v]))$$
$$L^{n+1}(X, v) = L^n(X, v) \cup \{d \in \mathsf{par}(X) \cap \mathcal{D}^{DP} \mid \exists i \in \mathbb{N}, (Y, w) \in V :$$
$$(X, v) \overset{i}{\to} (Y, w) \wedge \exists d_\ell \in L^n(Y, w) : d \in FV(\mathsf{arg}_\ell(\varphi_X, i))\}$$

The set $L(X, v)$ approximates the set of parameters potentially live at location (X, v); all other data parameters are guaranteed to be "dead", *i.e.*, irrelevant.

Example 8. The labelling computed for our running example is depicted in Fig. 2. One can cheaply establish that $k^Z \notin L^0(Z, 1, 2)$ since assigning value 2 to j^Z in Z's right-hand side effectively allows to reduce subformula $(k < 10 \vee j = 2)$ to *true*. We have $l \in L^1(Z, 1, 2)$ since we have $k^Y \in L^0(Y, 1, 1)$.

A parameter d that is not live at a location can be assigned a fixed default value. To this end the corresponding data argument of the PVIs that lead to that location are replaced by a default value $\mathsf{init}(d)$. This is achieved by function Reset, defined below:

Definition 12. *Let $\mathcal{E}$ be a PBES, let $(V, \to)$ be its CFG, with labelling L. The PBES $\mathsf{Reset}_L(\mathcal{E})$ is obtained from $\mathcal{E}$ by replacing every PVI $X(e, e')$ in every φ_X of $\mathcal{E}$ by the formula $\bigwedge_{v \in \mathsf{values}(c)} (v \neq e \vee X(e, \mathsf{Reset}_L^{(X,v)}(e')))$. The function $\mathsf{Reset}_L^{(X,v)}(e')$ is defined positionally as follows:*

$$\text{if } d_i \in L(X, v) \text{ we set } \mathsf{Reset}_L^{(X,v)}(e')_i = e'_i, \text{ else } \mathsf{Reset}_L^{(X,v)}(e')_i = \mathsf{init}(d_i).$$

Resetting dead parameters preserves the solution of the PBES, as we claim below.

Theorem 1. *Let $\mathcal{E}$ be a PBES, and L a labelling. For all predicate variables X, and ground terms v and w: $[\![\mathcal{E}]\!](X([\![v]\!], [\![w]\!])) = [\![\mathsf{Reset}_L(\mathcal{E})]\!](X([\![v]\!], [\![w]\!]))$.*

Proof sketch. We define a relation R^L such that $(X, [\![v]\!], [\![w]\!]) R^L (Y, [\![v']\!], [\![w']\!])$ if and only if $X = Y$, $[\![v]\!] = [\![v']\!]$, and $\forall d_k \in L(X, v) : [\![w_k]\!] = [\![w'_k]\!]$. This relation is a *consistent correlation* [15]; the result then follows. See [9] for a detailed proof.   □

As a consequence of the above theorem, instantiation of a PBES may become feasible where this was not the case for the original PBES. This is nicely illustrated by our running example, which now indeed can be instantiated to a BES.

Example 9. Observe that parameter k^Z is not labelled in any of the Z locations. This means that X's right-hand side essentially changes to:

$$(i \neq 1 \vee j \neq 1 \vee X(2, j, k, l + 1)) \wedge$$
$$\forall m \colon N.(i \neq 1 \vee Z(i, 2, 1, k)) \wedge \forall m \colon N.(i \neq 2 \vee Z(i, 2, 1, k))$$

Since variable m no longer occurs in the above formula, the quantifier can be eliminated. Applying the reset function on the entire PBES leads to a PBES that we *can* instantiate to a BES (in contrast to the original PBES), allowing us to compute that the solution to $X(1, 1, 1, 1)$ is *true*. This BES has only 7 equations.

6   Optimisation

Constructing a CFG can suffer from a combinatorial explosion; *e.g.*, the size of the CFG underlying the following PBES is exponential in the number of detected CFPs.

$$\nu X(i_1, \ldots, i_n \colon B) \;=\; (i_1 \wedge X(false, \ldots, i_n)) \vee (\neg i_1 \wedge X(true, \ldots, i_n)) \vee$$
$$\cdots \vee (i_n \wedge X(i_1, \ldots, false)) \vee (\neg i_n \wedge X(i_1, \ldots, true))$$

In this section we develop an alternative to the analysis of the previous section which mitigates the combinatorial explosion but still yields sound results. The correctness of our alternative is based on the following proposition, which states that resetting using any labelling that approximates that of Def. 11 is sound.

Proposition 1. *Let, for given PBES $\mathcal{E}$, $(V, \rightarrow)$ be a CFG with labelling L, and let L' be a labelling such that $L(X, \boldsymbol{v}) \subseteq L'(X, \boldsymbol{v})$ for all $(X, \boldsymbol{v})$. Then for all $X, \boldsymbol{v}$ and $\boldsymbol{w}$:*
$$[\![\mathcal{E}]\!](X([\![\boldsymbol{v}]\!], [\![\boldsymbol{w}]\!])) = [\![\mathsf{Reset}_{L'}(\mathcal{E})]\!](X([\![\boldsymbol{v}]\!], [\![\boldsymbol{w}]\!]))$$

The idea is to analyse a CFG consisting of disjoint subgraphs for each individual CFP, where each subgraph captures which PVIs are under the control of a CFP: only if the CFP can confirm whether a predicate formula potentially depends on a PVI, there will be an edge in the graph. As before, let $\mathcal{E}$ be an arbitrary but fixed PBES, (source, target, copy) a unicity constraint derived from $\mathcal{E}$, and $\boldsymbol{c}$ a vector of CFPs.

Definition 13. *The* local *control flow graph (LCFG) is a graph $(V^l, \hookrightarrow)$ with:*
- $V^l = \{(X, n, v) \mid X \in \mathsf{bnd}(\mathcal{E}) \wedge n \leq |\boldsymbol{c}| \wedge v \in \mathsf{values}(\boldsymbol{c}_n)\}$, *and*
- $\hookrightarrow \,\subseteq V^l \times \mathbb{N} \times V^l$ *is the least relation satisfying $(X, n, v) \overset{i}{\hookrightarrow} (\mathsf{pv}(\varphi_X, i), n, w)$ if:*
  - source$(X, i, n) = v$ *and* target$(X, i, n) = w$, *or*
  - source$(X, i, n) = \bot$, $\mathsf{pv}(\varphi_X, i) \neq X$ *and* target$(X, i, n) = w$, *or*
  - source$(X, i, n) = \bot$, $\mathsf{pv}(\varphi_X, i) \neq X$ *and* copy$(X, i, n) = n$ *and* $v = w$.

We write $(X, n, v) \overset{i}{\hookrightarrow}$ if there exists some (Y, m, w) such that $(X, n, v) \overset{i}{\hookrightarrow} (Y, m, w)$. Note that the size of an LCFG is $\mathcal{O}(|\mathsf{bnd}(\mathcal{E})| \times |\boldsymbol{c}| \times \max\{|\mathsf{values}(\boldsymbol{c}_k)| \mid 0 \leq k \leq |\boldsymbol{c}|\})$.

Example 10. For our running example, we obtain the following LCFG.

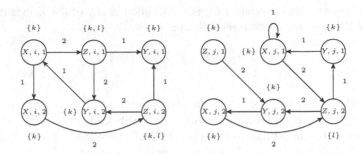

We next describe how to label the LCFG in such a way that the labelling meets the condition of Proposition 1, ensuring soundness of our liveness analysis. The idea of using LCFGs is that in practice, the use and alteration of a data parameter is entirely determined by a single CFP, and that only on "synchronisation points" of two CFPs (when the values of the two CFPs are such that they both confirm that a formula may depend on the same PVI) there is exchange of information in the data parameters.

We first formalise when a data parameter is involved in a recursion (*i.e.*, when the parameter may affect whether a formula depends on a PVI, or when a PVI may modify the data parameter through a self-dependency or uses it to change another parameter). Let $X \in \mathsf{bnd}(\mathcal{E})$ be an arbitrary bound predicate variable in the PBES $\mathcal{E}$.

Definition 14. *Denote* $\mathsf{PVI}(\varphi_X, i)$ *by* $Y(e)$. *Parameter* $d_j \in \mathsf{par}(X)$ *is:*
- *used for* $Y(e)$ *if* $d_j \in FV(\mathsf{guard}^i(\varphi_X))$;
- *used in* $Y(e)$ *if for some* k, *we have* $d_j \in FV(e_k)$, *($k \neq j$ if $X = Y$)* ;
- *changed by* $Y(e)$ *if both* $X = Y$ *and* $d_j \neq e_j$.

Example 11. In the running example, k is used for $\mathsf{PVI}(\varphi_Y, 1)$. Parameter l is used in $\mathsf{PVI}(\varphi_Z, 1)$ and it is changed by $\mathsf{PVI}(\varphi_X, 1)$.

The PVIs using or modifying some data parameter constitute the parameter's dataflow. A data parameter *belongs to* a CFP if its complete dataflow is controlled by that CFP.

Definition 15. *CFP* c_j *rules* $\mathsf{PVI}(\varphi_X, i)$ *if* $(X, j, v) \stackrel{i}{\hookrightarrow}$ *for some* v. *Let* $d \in \mathsf{par}(X) \cap \mathcal{D}^{DP}$ *be a data parameter;* d *belongs to* c_j *if and only if:*
- *whenever* d *is used for or in* $\mathsf{PVI}(\varphi_X, i)$, *$c_j$ rules* $\mathsf{PVI}(\varphi_X, i)$, *and*
- *whenever* d *is changed by* $\mathsf{PVI}(\varphi_X, i)$, *$c_j$ rules* $\mathsf{PVI}(\varphi_X, i)$.

The set of data parameters that belong to c_j *is denoted by* $\mathsf{belongs}(c_j)$.

Example 12. In all equations in our running example, k and l both belong to both i and j. Consider, *e.g.*, $\mathsf{PVI}(\varphi_X, 2)$, for which k is used; this PVI is ruled by i, which is witnessed by the edge $(X, i, 2) \stackrel{2}{\hookrightarrow} (Z, i, 2)$.

By adding dummy CFPs that can only take on one value, we can ensure that every data parameter belongs to at least one CFP. For simplicity and without loss of generality, we can therefore continue to work under the following assumption.

Assumption 2. *Each data parameter in an equation belongs to at least one CFP.*

We next describe how to conduct the liveness analysis using the LCFG. Every live data parameter is only labelled in those subgraphs corresponding to the CFPs to which it belongs. The labelling itself is constructed in much the same way as was done in the previous section. Our base case labels a vertex (X, n, v) with those parameters that belong to the CFP and that are significant in φ_X when c_n has value v. The backwards reachability now distinguishes two cases, based on whether the influence on live variables is internal to the CFP or via an external CFP.

Definition 16. Let $(V^l, \hookrightarrow)$ be a LCFG for PBES $\mathcal{E}$. The labelling $L_l \colon V^l \to \mathbb{P}(\mathcal{D}^{DP})$ is defined as $L_l(X, n, v) = \bigcup_{k \in \mathbb{N}} L_l^k(X, n, v)$, with L_l^k inductively defined as:

$$
\begin{aligned}
L_l^0(X, n, v) &= \{d \in \mathsf{belongs}(c_n) \mid d \in \mathsf{sig}(\mathsf{simplify}(\varphi_X[c_n := v]))\} \\
L_l^{k+1}(X, n, v) &= L_l^k(X, n, v) \\
&\quad \cup \{d \in \mathsf{belongs}(c_n) \mid \exists i, w \text{ such that } \exists d_\ell^Y \in L_l^k(Y, n, w) : \\
&\qquad (X, n, v) \overset{i}{\hookrightarrow} (Y, n, w) \wedge d \in FV(\mathsf{arg}_\ell(\varphi_X, i))\} \\
&\quad \cup \{d \in \mathsf{belongs}(c_n) \mid \exists i, m, v', w \text{ such that } (X, n, v) \overset{i}{\hookrightarrow} \\
&\qquad \wedge \exists d_\ell^Y \in L_l^k(Y, m, w') : d_\ell^Y \notin \mathsf{belongs}(c_n) \\
&\qquad \wedge (X, m, v') \overset{i}{\hookrightarrow} (Y, m, w') \wedge d \in FV(\mathsf{arg}_\ell(\varphi_X, i))\}
\end{aligned}
$$

Example 13. In the LCFG for the running example, initially k occurs in the labelling of all Y and Z nodes, except for $(Z, j, 2)$, since when $j = 2$, $k < 10 \vee j = 2$ is satisfied regardless of the value of k. The final labelling is shown in the graph in Example 10.

On top of this labelling we define the induced labelling $L_l(X, v)$, defined as $d \in L_l(X, v)$ iff for all k for which $d \in \mathsf{belongs}(c_k)$ we have $d \in L_l(X, k, v_k)$. This labelling over-approximates the labelling of Def. 11; *i.e.*, we have $L(X, v) \subseteq L_l(X, v)$ for all (X, v). The induced labelling L_l can remain implicit; in an implementation, the labelling constructed by Def. 16 can be used directly, sidestepping a combinatorial explosion. Combined with Prop. 1, this leads to the following theorem.

Theorem 2. We have $[\![\mathcal{E}]\!](X([\![v]\!], [\![w]\!])) = [\![\mathsf{Reset}_{L_l}(\mathcal{E})]\!](X([\![v]\!], [\![w]\!]))$ for all predicate variables X and ground terms v and w.

Example 14. Using the labelling from Example 13, we obtain $L_l(Z, v, 2) = \{l\}$ for $v \in \{1, 2\}$, and $L_l(X, v) = \{k\}$ for all other X, v. Observe that, for the reachable part shown in Figure 2, this coincides with the labelling obtained using the global algorithm. For the example, this analysis thus yields the same reduction as the analysis in Section 5.

7   Case Studies

We implemented our techniques in the tool `pbesstategraph` of the mCRL2 toolset [4]. Here, we report on the tool's effectiveness in simplifying the PBESs originating from model checking problems and behavioural equivalence checking problems: we compare sizes of the BESs underlying the original PBESs to those for the PBESs obtained after running the tool `pbesparelm` (implementing the techniques from [12]) and those for the PBESs obtained after running our tool. Furthermore, we compare the total times needed for reducing the PBES, instantiating it into a BES, and solving this BES.

Table 1. Sizes of the BESs underlying (1) the original PBESs, and the reduced PBESs using (2) `pbesparelm`, (3) `pbesstategraph` (global) and (4) `pbesstategraph` (local). For the original PBES, we report the number of generated BES equations, and the time required for generating and solving the resulting BES. For the other PBESs, we state the total reduction in percentages (*i.e.*, $100*(|original| - |reduced|)/|original|$), and the reduction of the times (in percentages, computed in the same way), where for times we additionally include the `pbesstategraph/parelm` running times. Verdict $\sqrt{}$ indicates the problem has solution *true*; $\times$ indicates it is *false*.

		Sizes				Times				Verdict
	$\|D\|$	Original	parelm	st.graph (global)	st.graph (local)	Original	parelm	st.graph (global)	st.graph (local)	
Model Checking Problems										
No deadlock										
Onebit	2	81,921	86%	89%	89%	15.7	90%	85%	90%	$\sqrt{}$
	4	742,401	98%	99%	99%	188.5	99%	99%	99%	$\sqrt{}$
Hesselink	2	540,737	100%	100%	100%	64.9	99%	95%	99%	$\sqrt{}$
	3	13,834,801	100%	100%	100%	2776.3	100%	100%	100%	$\sqrt{}$
No spontaneous generation of messages										
Onebit	2	185,089	83%	88%	88%	36.4	87%	85%	88%	$\sqrt{}$
	4	5,588,481	98%	99%	99%	1178.4	99%	99%	99%	$\sqrt{}$
Messages that are read are inevitably sent										
Onebit	2	153,985	63%	73%	73%	30.8	70%	62%	73%	$\times$
	4	1,549,057	88%	92%	92%	369.6	89%	90%	92%	$\times$
Messages can overtake one another										
Onebit	2	164,353	63%	73%	70%	36.4	70%	67%	79%	$\times$
	4	1,735,681	88%	92%	90%	332.0	88%	88%	90%	$\times$
Values written to the register can be read										
Hesselink	2	1,093,761	1%	92%	92%	132.8	-3%	90%	91%	$\sqrt{}$
	3	27,876,961	1%	98%	98%	5362.9	25%	98%	99%	$\sqrt{}$
Equivalence Checking Problems										
Branching bisimulation equivalence										
ABP-CABP	2	31,265	0%	3%	0%	3.9	-4%	-1880%	-167%	$\sqrt{}$
	4	73,665	0%	5%	0%	8.7	-7%	-1410%	-72%	$\sqrt{}$
Buf-Onebit	2	844,033	16%	23%	23%	112.1	30%	28%	31%	$\sqrt{}$
	4	8,754,689	32%	44%	44%	1344.6	35%	44%	37%	$\sqrt{}$
Hesselink I-S	2	21,062,529	0%	93%	93%	4133.6	0%	74%	91%	$\times$
Weak bisimulation equivalence										
ABP-CABP	2	50,713	2%	6%	2%	5.3	2%	-1338%	-136%	$\sqrt{}$
	4	117,337	3%	10%	3%	13.0	4%	-862%	-75%	$\sqrt{}$
Buf-Onebit	2	966,897	27%	33%	33%	111.6	20%	29%	28%	$\sqrt{}$
	4	9,868,225	41%	51%	51%	1531.1	34%	49%	52%	$\sqrt{}$
Hesselink I-S	2	29,868,273	4%	93%	93%	5171.7	7%	79%	94%	$\times$

Our cases are taken from the literature. We here present a selection of the results. For the model checking problems, we considered the *Onebit* protocol, which is a complex sliding window protocol, and Hesselink's handshake register [8]. Both protocols are parametric in the set of values that can be read and written. A selection of properties of varying complexity and varying nesting degree, expressed in the data-enhanced modal μ-calculus are checked.[1] For the behavioural equivalence checking problems, we

---

[1] The formulae are contained in [9]; here we use textual characterisations instead.

considered a number of communication protocols such as the *Alternating Bit Protocol* (ABP), the *Concurrent Alternating Bit Protocol* (CABP), a two-place buffer (Buf) and the aforementioned Onebit protocol. Moreover, we compare an implementation of Hesselink's register to a specification of the protocol that is correct with respect to trace equivalence (but for which currently no PBES encoding exists) but not with respect to the two types of behavioural equivalence checking problems we consider here: branching bisimilarity and weak bisimilarity.

The experiments were performed on a 64-bit Linux machine with kernel version 2.6.27, consisting of 14 Intel® Xeon© E5520 Processors running at 2.27GHz, and 1TB of shared main memory. In this system 7 servers are aggregated to appear as a single machine using vSMP software (each node has 2 CPUs and 144GB of main memory). In our experiments we run up to 24 tools simultaneously, but within each tool no multi-core features are used. We used revision 12637 of the mCRL2 toolset.[2]

The results are reported in Table 1; higher percentages mean better reductions/smaller runtimes. The experiments confirm our technique can achieve as much as an additional reduction of about 97% over pbesparelm, see the model checking and equivalence problems for Hesselink's register. Compared to the sizes of the BESs underlying the original PBESs, the reductions can be immense. Furthermore, reducing the PBES using the local stategraph algorithm, instantiating, and subsequently solving it is typically faster than using the global stategraph algorithm, even when the reduction achieved by the first is less. For the equivalence checking cases, when no reduction is achieved the local version of stategraph sometimes results in substantially larger running times than parelm, which in turn already adds an overhead compared to the original; however, for the cases in which this happens the original running time is around or below 10 seconds, so the observed increase may be due to inaccuracies in measuring.

8 Conclusions and Future Work

We described a static analysis technique for PBESs that uses a notion of control flow to determine when data parameters become irrelevant. Using this information, the PBES can be simplified, leading to smaller underlying BESs. Our static analysis technique enables the solving of PBESs using instantiation that so far could not be solved this way as shown by our running example. Compared to existing techniques, our new static analysis technique can lead to additional reductions of up-to 97% in practical cases, as illustrated by our experiments. Furthermore, if a reduction can be achieved the technique can significantly speed up instantiation and solving, and in case no reduction is possible, it typically does not negatively impact the total running time.

Several techniques described in this paper can be used to enhance existing reduction techniques for PBESs. For instance, our notion of a *guard* of a predicate variable instance in a PBES can be put to use to cheaply improve on the heuristics for constant elimination [12]. Moreover, we believe that our (re)construction of control flow graphs from PBESs can be used to automatically generate invariants for PBESs. The theory on invariants for PBESs is well-established, but still lacks proper tool support.

---

[2] The complete scripts for our test setup are available at
https://github.com/jkeiren/pbesstategraph-experiments

Acknowledgments. The authors would like to thank Wan Fokkink and Sjoerd Cranen for remarks on earlier drafts of this paper that greatly helped improving the presentation of the material.

References

1. Aho, A.V., Sethi, R., Ullman, J.D.: Compilers: Principles, Techniques, and Tools. Addison-Wesley (1986)
2. Alpuente, M., Feliú, M.A., Joubert, C., Villanueva, A.: Datalog-based program analysis with BES and RWL. In: de Moor, O., Gottlob, G., Furche, T., Sellers, A. (eds.) Datalog 2010. LNCS, vol. 6702, pp. 1–20. Springer, Heidelberg (2011)
3. Cousot, P., Cousot, R.: Abstract interpretation: A unified lattice model for static analysis of programs by construction or approximation of fixpoints. In: POPL 1977, pp. 238–252. ACM, New York (1977)
4. Cranen, S., Groote, J.F., Keiren, J.J.A., Stappers, F.P.M., de Vink, E.P., Wesselink, W., Willemse, T.A.C.: An overview of the mCRL2 toolset and its recent advances. In: Piterman, N., Smolka, S.A. (eds.) TACAS 2013. LNCS, vol. 7795, pp. 199–213. Springer, Heidelberg (2013)
5. Fernandez, J.-C., Bozga, M., Ghirvu, L.: State space reduction based on live variables analysis. Science of Computer Programming 47(2-3), 203–220 (2003)
6. Garavel, H., Lang, F., Mateescu, R., Serwe, W.: CADP 2010: A toolbox for the construction and analysis of distributed processes. In: Abdulla, P.A., Leino, K.R.M. (eds.) TACAS 2011. LNCS, vol. 6605, pp. 372–387. Springer, Heidelberg (2011)
7. Groote, J.F., Willemse, T.A.C.: Parameterised boolean equation systems. Theoretical Computer Science 343(3), 332–369 (2005)
8. Hesselink, W.H.: Invariants for the construction of a handshake register. Information Processing Letters 68, 173–177 (1998)
9. Keiren, J.J.A., Wesselink, J.W., Willemse, T.A.C.: Improved static analysis of parameterised boolean equation systems using control flow reconstruction. arXiv:1304.6482 [cs.LO] (2013)
10. Mader, A.: Verification of Modal Properties Using Boolean Equation Systems. PhD thesis, Technische Universität München (1997)
11. Mateescu, R.: Vérification des propriétés temporelles des programmes parallèles. PhD thesis, Institut National Polytechnique de Grenoble (1998)
12. Orzan, S., Wesselink, W., Willemse, T.A.C.: Static Analysis Techniques for Parameterised Boolean Equation Systems. In: Kowalewski, S., Philippou, A. (eds.) TACAS 2009. LNCS, vol. 5505, pp. 230–245. Springer, Heidelberg (2009)
13. Ploeger, B., Wesselink, W., Willemse, T.A.C.: Verification of reactive systems via instantiation of parameterised Boolean equation systems. Information and Computation 209(4), 637–663 (2011)
14. van de Pol, J., Timmer, M.: State Space Reduction of Linear Processes Using Control Flow Reconstruction. In: Liu, Z., Ravn, A.P. (eds.) ATVA 2009. LNCS, vol. 5799, pp. 54–68. Springer, Heidelberg (2009)
15. Willemse, T.A.C.: Consistent Correlations for Parameterised Boolean Equation Systems with Applications in Correctness Proofs for Manipulations. In: Gastin, P., Laroussinie, F. (eds.) CONCUR 2010. LNCS, vol. 6269, pp. 584–598. Springer, Heidelberg (2010)
16. Yorav, K., Grumberg, O.: Static Analysis for State-Space Reductions Preserving Temporal Logics. Formal Methods in System Design 25(1), 67–96 (2004)

Rabinizer 3: Safraless Translation of LTL to Small Deterministic Automata[*]

Zuzana Komárková[1] and Jan Křetínský[2]

[1] Faculty of Informatics, Masaryk University, Brno, Czech Republic
[2] IST, Austria

Abstract. We present a tool for translating LTL formulae into deterministic ω-automata. It is the first tool that covers the whole LTL that does not use Safra's determinization or any of its variants. This leads to smaller automata. There are several outputs of the tool: firstly, deterministic Rabin automata, which are the standard input for probabilistic model checking, e.g. for the probabilistic model-checker PRISM; secondly, deterministic *generalized* Rabin automata, which can also be used for probabilistic model checking and are sometimes by orders of magnitude smaller. We also link our tool to PRISM and show that this leads to a significant speed-up of probabilistic LTL model checking, especially with the generalized Rabin automata.

1 Introduction

The automata-theoretic approach to model checking is a very successful concept, which found its way to real industrial practice. The key idea is that a property to be checked on a given system is transformed into an automaton and the product of the automaton and the original system is then examined. Since real systems are often huge it is important that the automata used are very small, so that the product is not too large to be processed or even fit in the memory. Therefore, a lot of effort has been invested in transforming popular specification languages, such as *linear temporal logic* (LTL) [Pnu77], to small automata [Cou99, DGV99, EH00, SB00, GO01, GL02, Fri03, BKŘS12, DL13].

The property automata are usually non-deterministic Büchi automata (NBA) as they can express all LTL properties and are quite succinct. However, for purposes of quantitative probabilistic LTL model checking or of LTL synthesis, *deterministic* automata are needed [BK08]. To this end, we can transform NBA to deterministic Rabin automata (DRA) using Safra's determinization procedure or its variants [Saf88, Pit06, Sch09] implemented in [Kle, KNP11, TTH13]. The disadvantage of this approach is that the blow-up is often exponential even for

[*] This research was funded in part by the European Research Council (ERC) under grant agreement 267989 (QUAREM), the Austrian Science Fund (FWF) project S11402-N23 (RiSE), and the Czech Science Foundation, grant No. P202/12/G061. Jan Křetínský is on leave from Faculty of Informatics, Masaryk University, Brno, Czech Republic.

F. Cassez and J.-F. Raskin (Eds.): ATVA 2014, LNCS 8837, pp. 235–241, 2014.

simple formulae despite various heuristics [KB07]. Therefore, practically more efficient procedures have been designed for *fragments* of LTL [KE12, KLG13, BBKS13]. A comparison of currently available translators into deterministic automata [Kle, GKE12, KLG13, BBKS13] can be found in [BKS13].

While our technique for the (**F**, **G**)-fragment [KE12, GKE12] was extended to some larger fragments [KLG13], an occurrence of the **U** operator in the scope of the **G** operator posed a fundamental problem for the approach. Recently [EK14], we have shown how to modify the techniques of [KE12] to the whole LTL, using a more complex procedure. In this paper, we present its implementation together with several optimizations: `Rabinizer 3`, the first tool to translate LTL formulae directly to deterministic automata not employing any automata determinization procedure. Thus after partial solutions of `Rabinizer` [GKE12] based on [KE12], and `Rabinizer 2` [KLG13], we finally reach our ultimate goal set up from the very start.

Firstly, we optimize the construction of the state space given in [EK14]. We also implement the construction of the acceptance condition of the automata. As the condition is defined by an exponentially large description, several optimizations were needed to compute it efficiently and to obtain an equivalent small condition. Our optimizations lead to automata and acceptance conditions no larger than those generated by tools for fragments of LTL.

Furthermore, we provide an interface between our tool and `PRISM` [KNP11], the leading probabilistic model checker, resulting in a faster tool for probabilistic LTL model checking. While `PRISM` uses DRA produced by a re-implementation of `ltl2dstar` [Kle], our tool produces not only DRA, but also *generalized DRA* (DGRA). They are often much smaller and can also be used for probabilistic model checking for virtually no extra cost [CGK13]. Moreover, since the algorithm for probabilistic LTL model checking through DGRA has the same structure as for DRA, it was possible to implement it reusing the `PRISM` code.

`Rabinizer 3` as well as the extended `PRISM` are available at [R3].

2   Tool and Experimental Results

Principles and Optimizations. The key idea of the approach of [EK14] is to have (i) one "master" automaton monitoring the formula that at each step needs to be satisfied, and (ii) one "slave" automaton for each subformula of the form $\mathbf{G}\psi$ monitoring whether ψ holds true at *all but finitely many* positions in the word.[1] They all run synchronously in parallel; the slaves are organized recursively, providing information to the slaves of larger formulae and finally also to the master.

Example 1. Consider $\varphi = (a \land \mathbf{F}\mathbf{G}b) \lor (\mathbf{F}a \land \mathbf{F}\mathbf{G}c)$. Upon reading $\{a, b\}$, the master moves to $\mathbf{F}\mathbf{G}b \lor \mathbf{F}\mathbf{G}c$ and the slave for $\mathbf{F}\mathbf{G}b$ records it has seen a b. If we

---

[1] This approach bears some similarity with temporal testers [KPoR98, PZ08], which non-deterministically guess satisfaction at each point and later check the guesses. In contrast, Mojmir automata [EK14] used here are deterministic and thus can provide the information to the master only through acceptance.

read $\emptyset$ instead, the master would move to $\mathbf{F}a \wedge \mathbf{FG}c$. Apparently, in this state, it makes no sense any more to monitor whether $\mathbf{FG}b$ holds or not. Moreover, we can postpone checking $\mathbf{FG}c$ until we see an a.

Both observations of the previous example lead to optimizations saving unnecessary states. The former was considered already in [KLG13]. The latter is similar to [BBDL+13], where a similar effect is achieved by graph analysis of the automata. In contrast, here we can detect the same situation much more easily using the logical structure of the state space. Thus for instance, for the formula $\mathbf{F}a \wedge \mathbf{GF}(b \wedge \mathbf{XXX}b)$ the size drops from 16 states in [EK14] to 9 here. Further, an optimization of the initial states of slaves leads to a similar saving, e.g., for $\mathbf{GF}((a \wedge \mathbf{XXX}a) \vee (\neg a \wedge \mathbf{XXX}\neg a))$ from 15 to 8 states.

A major advantage of our approach is that it can generate deterministic *generalized* Rabin automata [KE12, CGK13].

Definition 1 (DGRA). *A deterministic generalized Rabin automaton (DGRA) is a deterministic ω-automaton with an acceptance condition of the form*

$$\bigvee_{i=1}^{k} (Fin_i, \bigwedge_{j=1}^{k_i} Inf_i^j)$$

A run visiting exactly set S of states infinitely often is accepting, if for some i, $S \cap Fin_i = \emptyset$ and $S \cap Inf_i^j \neq \emptyset$ for all $j = 1, \ldots, k_i$.

Hence, DRA are DGRA with all k_i equal to 1. Similarly, we can define *transition-based* DGRA (DTGRA), where the acceptance sets Fin_i, Inf_i^j are sets of transitions. We use both variants and the transition-based acceptance often saves even more, see Table 1 for examples of fairness constraints. The lower part of the table illustrates the effect of the optimizations: the size of DTGRA due to unoptimized [EK14] for ψ_1 and ψ_2 is 11 and 32, respectively, compared to 3 and 16 using the new optimizations. For more experiments, see the web-page of the tool [R3].

The generalized Rabin acceptance condition arises naturally from the product of Rabin conditions for each slave and one global co-Büchi condition. Unfortunately, due to the global consition it is a disjunction over all *subsets* of G-subformulae and various subsets of slaves' states. Therefore, it is large. However, after simplifying the pairs, removing pairs simulated by other pairs and several other steps, we often decrease the number of pairs down to the actual Rabin index [KPB95], i.e. the minimal possible number for the given language, as illustrated in Table 1.

Outputs. Given a formula, Rabinizer 3 can output the corresponding DTGRA, DGRA and DRA. Several output formats are available, such as the ltl2dstar format, the dot format for visualization, or the PRISM format. Optional labels on states display the internal logical structure of the automaton. Transitions can be displayed either explicitly or more compactly using BDDs, e.g. $a + b$ stands for three transitions, namely under $\{a\}$, $\{b\}$, and $\{a, b\}$.

Table 1. Experimental comparisons on fairness constraints (upper part) and two formulae of [EK14] (lower part). We display number of states and acceptance pairs for ltl2dstar and Rabinizer 3 producing different types of automata, all with the same number of pairs. Here $\psi_1 = \mathbf{FG}(((a \wedge \mathbf{XX}b) \wedge \mathbf{GF}b)\mathbf{U}\mathbf{G}(\mathbf{XX}!c \vee \mathbf{XX}(a \wedge b)))$ and $\psi_2 = \mathbf{G}(!q \vee (((!s \vee r) \vee \mathbf{X}(\mathbf{G}(!t \vee r)\vee!r\mathbf{U}(r \wedge (!t \vee r))))\mathbf{U}(r \vee p) \vee \mathbf{G}((!s \vee \mathbf{XG}!t))))$, the latter being φ_{40} "1 cause-2 effect precedence chain" of Spec Patterns [SP].

Formula	ltl2dstar		Rabinizer 3			
	DRA states	pairs	DRA st.	DGRA st.	DTGRA st.	pairs
$\mathbf{FG}a \vee \mathbf{GF}b$	4	2	4	4	1	2
$(\mathbf{FG}a \vee \mathbf{GF}b) \wedge (\mathbf{FG}c \vee \mathbf{GF}d)$	11324	8	21	16	1	4
$\bigwedge_{i=1}^{3}(\mathbf{GF}a_i \rightarrow \mathbf{GF}b_i)$	1 304 706	10	511	64	1	8
$\bigwedge_{i=1}^{3}(\mathbf{GF}a_i \rightarrow \mathbf{GF}a_{i+1})$	153 558	8	58	17	1	8
ψ_1	40	4	4	4	3	1
ψ_2	314	7	21	21	16	4

Probabilistic Model Checking. We follow up on our experimental implementation of [CGK13] for DGRA and DRA. We provide Java classes allowing for linking any tool with an appropriate output text format to be used in PRISM.

Since we also produce transition-based DGRA, our experimental results reveal an interesting observation. Although state-based DGRA are larger than their transition-based counterpart DTGRA, the respective product is not much larger (often not at all), see Table 2. For instance, consider the case when the only extra information that DGRA carries in states, compared to DTGRA, is the labeling of the last transition taken. Then this information is absorbed in the product, as the system's states carry their labeling anyway. Therefore, in this relatively frequent case for simpler formulae (like the one in Table 2), there is no difference in sizes of products with DGRA and DTGRA.

Table 2. Model checking Pnueli-Zuck mutex protocol with 5 processes (altogether 308 800 states) from the benchmark set [KNP11] for the property that either all processes 1-4 enter the critical section infinitely often, or process 5 asks to enter it only finitely often

	ltl2dstar DRA	R.3 DRA	R.3 DGRA	R.3 DTGRA
Automaton size (and nr. of pairs)	196 (5)	11 (2)	33 (2)	1 (2)
Product size	13 826 588	1 100 608	308 800	308 800

Further, notice that the DGRA in Table 2 is larger than the DRA obtained by degeneralization of DTGRA and subsequent transformation to a state-based automaton. However, the product with the DGRA is of the size of the original system, while for DRA it is larger! This demonstrates the superiority of generalized Rabin automata over standard Rabin automata with respect to the product size and thus also computation time, which is superlinear in the size. For details, further experiments, and the implementation, see [R3].

3   Conclusion

We present the first tool translating the whole LTL directly to deterministic ω-automata, while not employing any automata determinization procedure. This often results in much smaller DRA. Moreover, the power of DGRA is now available for the whole LTL as well. Together with our modification of PRISM, this allows for further speed up of probabilistic model checking as demonstrated by experimental results.

Acknowledgement. We would like to thank Javier Esparza, Vojtěch Forejt, Mojmír Křetínský, Marta Kwiatkowska, and Dave Parker for discussions and feedback and Andreas Gaiser and Ruslán Ledesma Garza for pieces of code we could reuse.

References

[BBDL+13] Babiak, T., Badie, T., Duret-Lutz, A., Křetínský, M., Strejček, J.: Compositional approach to suspension and other improvements to LTL translation. In: Bartocci, E., Ramakrishnan, C.R. (eds.) SPIN 2013. LNCS, vol. 7976, pp. 81–98. Springer, Heidelberg (2013)

[BBKS13] Babiak, T., Blahoudek, F., Křetínský, M., Strejček, J.: Effective translation of LTL to deterministic Rabin automata: Beyond the (F, G)-fragment. In: Van Hung, D., Ogawa, M. (eds.) ATVA 2013. LNCS, vol. 8172, pp. 24–39. Springer, Heidelberg (2013)

[BK08] Baier, C., Katoen, J.-P.: Principles of model checking. MIT Press (2008)

[BKŘS12] Babiak, T., Křetínský, M., Řehák, V., Strejček, J.: LTL to Büchi automata translation: Fast and more deterministic. In: Flanagan, C., König, B. (eds.) TACAS 2012. LNCS, vol. 7214, pp. 95–109. Springer, Heidelberg (2012)

[BKS13] Blahoudek, F., Křetínský, M., Strejček, J.: Comparison of LTL to deterministic Rabin automata translators. In: McMillan, K., Middeldorp, A., Voronkov, A. (eds.) LPAR-19 2013. LNCS, vol. 8312, pp. 164–172. Springer, Heidelberg (2013)

[CGK13] Chatterjee, K., Gaiser, A., Křetínský, J.: Automata with generalized Rabin pairs for probabilistic model checking and LTL synthesis. In: Sharygina, N., Veith, H. (eds.) CAV 2013. LNCS, vol. 8044, pp. 559–575. Springer, Heidelberg (2013)

[Cou99] Couvreur, J.-M.: On-the-fly verification of linear temporal logic. In: Wing, J.M., Woodcock, J. (eds.) FM 1999. LNCS, vol. 1708, pp. 253–271. Springer, Heidelberg (1999)

[DGV99] Daniele, M., Giunchiglia, F., Vardi, M.Y.: Improved automata generation for linear temporal logic. In: Halbwachs, N., Peled, D.A. (eds.) CAV 1999. LNCS, vol. 1633, pp. 249–260. Springer, Heidelberg (1999)

[DL13] Duret-Lutz, A.: Manipulating LTL formulas using spot 1.0. In: Van Hung, D., Ogawa, M. (eds.) ATVA 2013. LNCS, vol. 8172, pp. 442–445. Springer, Heidelberg (2013)

[EH00]   Etessami, K., Holzmann, G.J.: Optimizing Büchi automata. In: Palamidessi, C. (ed.) CONCUR 2000. LNCS, vol. 1877, pp. 153–167. Springer, Heidelberg (2000)

[EK14]   Esparza, J., Křetínský, J.: From LTL to Deterministic Automata: A Safraless Compositional Approach. In: Biere, A., Bloem, R. (eds.) CAV 2014. LNCS, vol. 8559, pp. 192–208. Springer, Heidelberg (2014)

[Fri03]   Fritz, C.: Constructing Büchi automata from linear temporal logic using simulation relations for alternating Büchi automata. In: Ibarra, O.H., Dang, Z. (eds.) CIAA 2003. LNCS, vol. 2759, pp. 35–48. Springer, Heidelberg (2003)

[GKE12]   Gaiser, A., Křetínský, J., Esparza, J.: Rabinizer: Small deterministic automata for LTL(F,G). In: Chakraborty, S., Mukund, M. (eds.) ATVA 2012. LNCS, vol. 7561, pp. 72–76. Springer, Heidelberg (2012)

[GL02]   Giannakopoulou, D., Lerda, F.: From states to transitions: Improving translation of LTL formulae to Büchi automata. In: Peled, D.A., Vardi, M.Y. (eds.) FORTE 2002. LNCS, vol. 2529, pp. 308–326. Springer, Heidelberg (2002)

[GO01]   Gastin, P., Oddoux, D.: Fast LTL to Büchi automata translation. In: Berry, G., Comon, H., Finkel, A. (eds.) CAV 2001. LNCS, vol. 2102, pp. 53–65. Springer, Heidelberg (2001), at http://www.lsv.ens-cachan.fr/~gastin/ltl2ba/

[KB07]   Klein, J., Baier, C.: On-the-fly stuttering in the construction of deterministic ω-automata. In: Holub, J., Žďárek, J. (eds.) CIAA 2007. LNCS, vol. 4783, pp. 51–61. Springer, Heidelberg (2007)

[KE12]   Křetínský, J., Esparza, J.: Deterministic automata for the (F,G)-fragment of LTL. In: Madhusudan, P., Seshia, S.A. (eds.) CAV 2012. LNCS, vol. 7358, pp. 7–22. Springer, Heidelberg (2012)

[Kle]   Klein, J.: ltl2dstar - LTL to deterministic Streett and Rabin automata, http://www.ltl2dstar.de/

[KLG13]   Křetínský, J., Garza, R.L.: Rabinizer 2: Small deterministic automata for LTL\GU. In: Van Hung, D., Ogawa, M. (eds.) ATVA 2013. LNCS, vol. 8172, pp. 446–450. Springer, Heidelberg (2013)

[KNP11]   Kwiatkowska, M., Norman, G., Parker, D.: PRISM 4.0: Verification of probabilistic real-time systems. In: Gopalakrishnan, G., Qadeer, S. (eds.) CAV 2011. LNCS, vol. 6806, pp. 585–591. Springer, Heidelberg (2011)

[KPB95]   Krishnan, S.C., Puri, A., Brayton, R.K.: Structural complexity of ω-automata. In: Mayr, E.W., Puech, C. (eds.) STACS 1995. LNCS, vol. 900, pp. 143–156. Springer, Heidelberg (1995)

[KPoR98]   Kesten, Y., Pnueli, A., Raviv, L.-O.: Algorithmic verification of linear temporal logic specifications. In: Larsen, K.G., Skyum, S., Winskel, G. (eds.) ICALP 1998. LNCS, vol. 1443, pp. 1–16. Springer, Heidelberg (1998)

[Pit06]   Piterman, N.: From nondeterministic Büchi and Streett automata to deterministic parity automata. In: LICS, pp. 255–264 (2006)

[Pnu77]   Pnueli, A.: The temporal logic of programs. In: FOCS, pp. 46–57 (1977)

[PZ08]   Pnueli, A., Zaks, A.: On the merits of temporal testers. In: Grumberg, O., Veith, H. (eds.) 25MC Festschrift. LNCS, vol. 5000, pp. 172–195. Springer, Heidelberg (2008)

[R3]   Rabinizer 3, https://www7.in.tum.de/~kretinsk/rabinizer3.html
[Saf88]   Safra, S.: On the complexity of ω-automata. In: FOCS, pp. 319–327 (1988)
[SB00]   Somenzi, F., Bloem, R.: Efficient Büchi automata from LTL formulae.
            In: Emerson, E.A., Sistla, A.P. (eds.) CAV 2000. LNCS, vol. 1855, pp.
            248–263. Springer, Heidelberg (2000)
[Sch09]   Schewe, S.: Tighter bounds for the determinisation of Büchi automata.
            In: de Alfaro, L. (ed.) FOSSACS 2009. LNCS, vol. 5504, pp. 167–181.
            Springer, Heidelberg (2009)
[SP]   Spec Patterns: Property pattern mappings for LTL,
            http://patterns.projects.cis.ksu.edu/documentation/
            patterns/ltl.shtml
[TTH13]   Tsai, M.-H., Tsay, Y.-K., Hwang, Y.-S.: GOAL for games, omega-
            automata, and logics. In: Sharygina, N., Veith, H. (eds.) CAV 2013. LNCS,
            vol. 8044, pp. 883–889. Springer, Heidelberg (2013)

PeCAn: Compositional Verification of Petri Nets Made Easy*

Dinh-Thuan Le[1], Huu-Vu Nguyen[1], Van-Tinh Nguyen[1], Phuong-Nam Mai[1],
Bao-Trung Pham-Duy[1], Thanh-Tho Quan[1], Étienne André[2],
Laure Petrucci[2], and Yang Liu[3]

[1] HoChiMinh City University of Technology, Vietnam
[2] Université Paris 13, Sorbonne Paris Cité, LIPN, CNRS,
Villetaneuse, France
[3] Nanyang Technological University, Singapore

Abstract. This paper introduces PeCAn, a tool supporting compositional verification of Petri nets. Beyond classical features (such as on-the-fly analysis and synchronisation between multiple Petri nets), PeCAn generates Symbolic Observation Graphs (SOG), and uses their composition to support modular abstractions of multiple Petri nets for more efficient verification. Furthermore, PeCAn implements an incremental strategy based on counter-examples for model-checking, thus improving significantly the cost of execution time and memory space. PeCAn also provides users with the visualisation of the input Petri nets and their corresponding SOGs. We experimented PeCAn with benchmark datasets from the Petri Nets' model checking contests, showing promising results.

Keywords: Compositional verification, Petri nets, SOG.

1 Introduction

A Petri net (PN) [7] is a graphical mathematical language which efficiently supports the modelling and verification of distributed systems. Basically, a Petri net is a directed bipartite graph, featuring transitions and places. As Petri nets are widely used in research and industry communities, there are several tools developed to help users specify and verify Petri nets, in particularly LoLa [10], Snoopy [5], TAPAAL [3], CosyVerif [1], CPN Tools [12] or JPetriNet[1]. Although most of the tools work with basic place/transitions PNs, some of them cater for some advanced forms of PNs such as timed, coloured, or stochastic PNs.

In this paper, we present PeCAn (<u>Pe</u>tri net <u>C</u>ompositional <u>An</u>alyser), a tool supporting verification of Petri nets in a compositional manner. PeCAn can take as input Petri Net models described in PNML, one of the most popular languages

---

* This work is partially supported by the STIC-Asie project CATS ("Compositional Analysis of Timed Systems").
[1] http://jpetrinet.sourceforge.net

F. Cassez and J.-F. Raskin (Eds.): ATVA 2014, LNCS 8837, pp. 242–247, 2014.

to describe Petri Nets nowadays. The properties to be checked are expressed as LTL formulae. PeCAn offers the following features:

- PeCAn allows users to compose a complex PN from multiple concurrent PNs and then verify the composed PN against a given property.
- PeCAn is able to generate Symbolic Observation Graphs (SOG) [4] from the actual PNs. Therefore, PeCAn supports verification of modular PNs by composing SOGs of separate components.
- PeCAn implements the incremental strategy based on counter-examples when verifying the generated SOG [2]. Thus, the cost of execution time and memory space is significantly reduced.

2   Modular Verification

In this section, we take the example presented in [8] to demonstrate how to use PeCAn to verify Petri nets. Even though PeCAn can verify a single Petri net as other existing tools do, in this paper we only focus on compositional verification of PeCAn, i.e. verifying a Petri net composed by multiple synchronised modules.

We assume that the original Petri net is already decomposed by users into modules. PeCAn allows users to verify an arbitrary composition of predefined modules. In order to do so, they must define synchronised transitions by the same name between modules. Figure 1b gives an example of a system decomposed into three modules through synchronised transitions. This system can be described easily in a modular style by PeCAn. In this example, modules A and B have two transitions with the same name (F1, F3) meaning that these two transitions must be synchronised. Similarly, a synchronised transition, F2, is shared by modules B and C, also declared by the same name in PeCAn.

When the module composition and the LTL property are defined, users can choose to perform the verification using one of the following methods:

Basic LTL Verification. The modules are synchronised together based on the user specification. Then the synchronised modules are converted into an LTS model and verified on-the-fly by the PAT model checking library [11].

SOG-based Verification. In this method, we do not directly verify the synchronised modules. Instead, we produce a corresponding SOG and use it for the verification. If a counter-example is found, it is verified again on the original Petri net to check whether it is an actual counter-example.

Incremental SOG-based Verification. It is similar to the SOG-based Verification method. However, we do not generate the SOG for the whole synchronisation of modules. Instead, we incrementally synchronise two modules first and verify the corresponding SOG. If no counter-example is found, we incrementally synchronise one more module and repeat the SOG-based verification step, until a counter-example is found or all modules are synchronised and verified (see [2]).

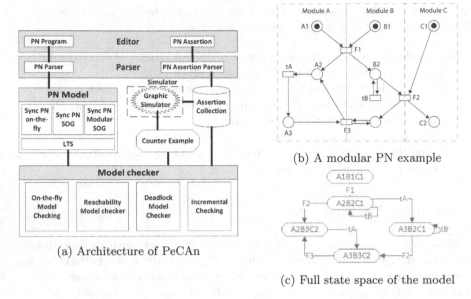

(a) Architecture of PeCAn

(b) A modular PN example

(c) Full state space of the model

Fig. 1. Architecture of PeCAn and example with state space

3   Architecture

The architecture of PeCAn, given in Figure 1a, is described as follows:

Editor Layer. Allows users to describe PNs by a (i) PNML specification or (ii) graph-based visualisation. Users can design an arbitrary number of modules as well as any composition between them.

Parser Layer. Parses the architectures of the PNs from the Editor Layer and converts the Petri net models as well as properties to check into an internal representation for the Semantic Layer.

Semantic Layer. Responsible for generating the corresponding LTS of the input Petri nets, in order to be model checked by the next layer. The three approaches of Basic LTL Verification, SOG-based Verification and Incremental SOG-based Verification are then implemented as three sub-modules: *Sync PN on-the-fly*, *Sync PN SOG* and *Sync PN Modular SOG*.

Model Checker Layer. We make use of the PAT model checking library [11] for this layer. This library takes an LTS as input, and verifies the properties.

4   Functionality Comparison and Experiments

We finally present some comparative discussion and experiments of our tool with other similar approaches. Since PeCAn takes PNML as input, we collected

Table 1. Available tools that support PNML models

No	Tool	PNML format supported	GUI editor	Deadlock checking	User-defined LTL checking	Simulation
1	PeCAn	✓	✓	✓	✓	✓
2	PNEditor[2]	✓	✓	×	×	
3	Snoopy[3]	×[4]	✓	×	×	✓
4	PNML Framework[5]	✓	✓		?[6]	
5	ProM framework[7]	✓	✓	×	?[8]	×
6	P3[9]	✓		×		
7	ePNK[10]	✓	✓	?[11]		
8	Tina[12]	✓	×	×	✓	✓

other PN verification tools also supporting PNML. We selected the tools listed at http://www.informatik.uni-hamburg.de/TGI/PetriNets/tools/ and supporting PNML. As shown in Table 1, very few tools can support PNML specification and perform full LTL verification.

We then experimented PeCAn with benchmark datasets downloaded from the Model Checking contest [6][13]. Results, as display in Table 2 showed that PeCAn can endure some remarkably large model sizes. When a counter-example is found, PeCAn can terminate quickly with significantly less resources usage.

Lastly, we also compared the performance of PeCAn in terms of the (symbolic) states and transitions generated by the SOG-based approach. The results are presented in Figures 2a and 2b respectively. Results show that the SOG-based approach of PeCAn usually reduces the number of states, and always significantly reduces the number of transitions when compared to the standard approach. In fact, the number of generated transitions is always significantly reduced, leading to a substantial gain of time when applying a model checking algorithm. The tool and all experiments can be downloaded from [9].

---

[2] http://www.pneditor.org/download/pneditor-0.64.jar
[3] http://www-dssz.informatik.tu-cottbus.de/track/download.php?id=136
[4] Claimed as coming soon
[5] http://pnml.lip6.fr
[6] Depends on analysis tool using PNML Framework
[7] http://www.promtools.org/prom6/
[8] Claimed to be done via plugins, but we could not find where.
[9] http://www.sfu.ca/~dgasevic/projects/P3net/Download.htm
[10] http://www.imm.dtu.dk/~ekki/projects/ePNK/
[11] It could not load Eclipse after installation
[12] http://projects.laas.fr/tina//download.php
[13] http://mcc.lip6.fr/

Table 2. Experiments with deadlock models: PeCAn does not need to explore the whole state space

No	Model	Parameter	State space	Number of Reached Markings	Number of Transition Firings	Time (s)	Memory (KB)
1	CSRepetitions	2	7.424	32	31	0.015	8,962
2	CSRepetitions	3	1.341×10^8	117	116	0.078	10,465
3	CSRepetitions	4	unknown	291	290	0.202	16,033
4	CSRepetitions	5	unknown	1,274	1,283	0.642	43,289
5	CSRepetitions	7	unknown	2,148	2,147	2.367	135,809
6	CSRepetitions	8	unknown	7,242	7,241	20.836	1,056,194
7	Eratosthenes	10	32	12	19	0.191	8,635
8	Eratosthenes	20	2,048	28	60	0.015	8,929
9	Eratosthenes	50	1.718×10^{10}	287	821	0.071	11,451
10	Eratosthenes	100	1.899×10^{22}	1,236	4,099	0.539	23,446
11	Eratosthenes	200	1.142×10^{46}	3,614	13,007	4.794	91,365
12	Eratosthenes	500	4.13×10^{121}	24,236	88,363	76.082	899,525
13	HouseContruction	2	1,501	74	73	0.119	9,100
14	HouseContruction	5	unknown	209	208	0.031	10,095
15	HouseContruction	10	$1,664 \times 10^9$	434	433	0.018	10,354
16	HouseContruction	20	1.367×10^{13}	884	883	0.052	13,481
17	HouseContruction	50	unknown	2,234	2,233	0.121	17,747
18	HouseContruction	100	unknown	4,484	4,483	0.294	20,059
19	HouseContruction	200	unknown	8,984	8,983	0.471	32,975
20	HouseContruction	500	unknown	22,484	22,483	1.48	63,711
21	PermAdmissibility	1	52,537	41	40	0.183	10,437
22	PermAdmissibility	2	unknown	253	252	0.098	13,243
23	PermAdmissibility	5	unknown	1,025	1,024	0.363	25,011
24	PermAdmissibility	10	unknown	2,372	2,371	0.869	45,072
25	PermAdmissibility	20	unknown	5,027	5,026	2.021	87,138
26	PermAdmissibility	50	unknown	12,912	12,911	4.901	201,224
27	Philosopher	5	243	68	84	0.007	9,274
28	Philosopher	10	59,049	7,242	10,576	1.057	42,935
29	Philosopher	20	3.487×10^9	Time out after 7200s			

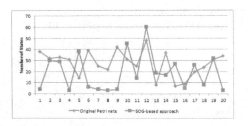

(a) Number of states

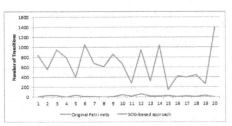

(b) Number of transitions

Fig. 2. Experimental results on a set of Petri nets

Acknowledgments. All our thanks to the PAT team [11] for their help in interfacing our tool with the PAT library.

References

1. André, É., Hillah, L.-M., Hulin-Hubard, F., Kordon, F., Lembachar, Y., Linard, A., Petrucci, L.: CosyVerif: An open source extensible verification environment. In: ICECCS, pp. 33–36. IEEE Computer Society (2013)
2. André, É., Klai, K., Ochi, H., Petrucci, L.: A counterexample-based incremental and modular verification approach. In: Calinescu, R., Garlan, D. (eds.) Monterey Workshop 2012. LNCS, vol. 7539, pp. 283–302. Springer, Heidelberg (2012)
3. Byg, J., Jørgensen, K.Y., Srba, J.: TAPAAL: Editor, simulator and verifier of timed-arc Petri nets. In: Liu, Z., Ravn, A.P. (eds.) ATVA 2009. LNCS, vol. 5799, pp. 84–89. Springer, Heidelberg (2009)
4. Haddad, S., Ilié, J.-M., Klai, K.: Design and evaluation of a symbolic and abstraction-based model checker. In: Wang, F. (ed.) ATVA 2004. LNCS, vol. 3299, pp. 196–210. Springer, Heidelberg (2004)
5. Heiner, M., Richter, R., Schwarick, M.: Snoopy: A tool to design and animate/simulate graph-based formalisms. In: SimuTools, vol. 15 (2008)
6. Kordon, F., Linard, A., Beccuti, M., Buchs, D., Fronc, L., Hillah, L.-M., Hulin-Hubard, F., Legond-Aubry, F., Lohmann, N., Marechal, A., Paviot-Adet, E., Pommereau, F., Rodríguez, C., Rohr, C., Thierry-Mieg, Y., Wimmel, H., Wolf, K.: Model checking contest @ Petri nets, report on the 2013 edition. CoRR, abs/1309.2485 (2013)
7. Kozura, V.E., Nepomniaschy, V.A., Novikov, R.M.: Verification of distributed systems modelled by high-level Petri nets. In: PARELEC, pp. 61–66 (2002)
8. Lakos, C., Petrucci, L.: Modular state spaces for prioritised Petri nets. In: Calinescu, R., Jackson, E. (eds.) Monterey Workshop 2010. LNCS, vol. 6662, pp. 136–156. Springer, Heidelberg (2011)
9. Le, D.-T.: PeCAn Web page (2014),
   http://cse.hcmut.edu.vn/~save/project/pn-ver/start
10. Schmidt, K.: Distributed verification with LoLA. Fund. Inf. 54(2-3), 253–262 (2003)
11. Sun, J., Liu, Y., Dong, J.S., Pang, J.: PAT: Towards flexible verification under fairness. In: Bouajjani, A., Maler, O. (eds.) CAV 2009. LNCS, vol. 5643, pp. 709–714. Springer, Heidelberg (2009)
12. Westergaard, M.: CPN Tools 4: Multi-formalism and extensibility. In: Colom, J.-M., Desel, J. (eds.) PETRI NETS 2013. LNCS, vol. 7927, pp. 400–409. Springer, Heidelberg (2013)

The Context-Freeness Problem Is coNP-Complete for Flat Counter Systems*

Jérôme Leroux[1], Vincent Penelle[2], and Grégoire Sutre[1]

[1] Univ. Bordeaux & CNRS, LaBRI, UMR 5800, Talence, France
[2] Univ. Paris Est & CNRS, LIGM, UMR 8049, Marne-la-Vallée, France

Abstract. Bounded languages have recently proved to be an important class of languages for the analysis of Turing-powerful models. For instance, bounded context-free languages are used to under-approximate the behaviors of recursive programs. Ginsburg and Spanier have shown in 1966 that a bounded language $L \subseteq a_1^* \cdots a_d^*$ is context-free if, and only if, its Parikh image is a stratifiable semilinear set. However, the question whether a semilinear set is stratifiable, hereafter called the stratifiability problem, was left open, and remains so. In this paper, we give a partial answer to this problem. We focus on semilinear sets that are given as finite systems of linear inequalities, and we show that stratifiability is coNP-complete in this case. Then, we apply our techniques to the context-freeness problem for flat counter systems, that asks whether the trace language of a counter system intersected with a bounded regular language is context-free. As main result of the paper, we show that this problem is coNP-complete.

1 Introduction

The class of bounded languages was introduced in 1964 by Ginsburg and Spanier to study context-free languages [11]. Nowadays, this class plays an important role in the analysis of Turing-powerful models. Recall that a language is *bounded* if it is contained in $\sigma_1^* \cdots \sigma_d^*$ for some words $\sigma_1, \ldots, \sigma_d$. The restriction of a model to behaviors contained in a bounded language produces a so-called *flat* model that is often amenable to automatic verification. Indeed, the reachability sets of such restrictions are usually computable through *acceleration techniques* [3,4,8,1,10,2,5]. Following the same approach, bounded languages have recently been used for the analysis of recursive concurrent systems, and more generally as a way to unify various recent and promising "bounded verification" techniques [9].

In these applications, the class of semilinear bounded languages is central. Recall that a *semilinear set* is a finite union of sets of the form $\boldsymbol{b} + \mathbb{N}\boldsymbol{p}_1 + \cdots + \mathbb{N}\boldsymbol{p}_k$ where $\boldsymbol{b}, \boldsymbol{p}_1, \ldots, \boldsymbol{p}_k$ are vectors in $\mathbb{N}^d$. Semilinear sets coincide with the sets definable in Presburger arithmetic [13]. A *semilinear bounded language* is a language of the form $\{\sigma_1^{n_1} \cdots \sigma_d^{n_d} \mid (n_1, \ldots, n_d) \in \boldsymbol{S}\}$ where $\sigma_1, \ldots, \sigma_d$ are words and $\boldsymbol{S}$ is a semilinear set. The class of semilinear bounded languages admits several

---

* This work was supported by the ANR project REACHARD (ANR-11-BS02-001).

F. Cassez and J.-F. Raskin (Eds.): ATVA 2014, LNCS 8837, pp. 248–263, 2014.
© Springer International Publishing Switzerland 2014

characterizations through language acceptors [6,16,9]. From a language-theoretic viewpoint, semilinear bounded languages are incomparable with context-free languages. Indeed, the language $\{a^n b^n c^n \mid n \in \mathbb{N}\}$ is well-known to be non-context-free, and, conversely, the language $\{a, b\}^*$ is not a bounded language. However, bounded context-free languages are semilinear bounded languages, by Parikh's theorem and closure under inverse morphism of context-free languages.

Ginsburg and Spanier have established in [13,14] a characterization of bounded context-free languages in terms of semilinear sets satisfying a "stratification" requirement. We call such semilinear sets *stratifiable*. The existence of a decision procedure for determining whether a given semilinear set is stratifiable was left open in [13,14], and has remained open since then. Rephrased in terms of languages, this decision problem is equivalent to the question whether a given semilinear bounded language is context-free. The latter problem is known to be decidable for some subclasses of semilinear bounded languages, with a notable example being the trace languages of flat Petri nets. In fact, the context-freeness problem is decidable for trace languages of arbitrary Petri nets [22,18], and was recently shown to be ExpSpace-complete for them [19].

Contributions. In this paper, we provide a partial answer to the question whether a given semilinear set is stratifiable, hereafter called the stratifiability problem. We focus on semilinear sets that are integral polyhedra, in other words, that are given as finite systems of linear inequalities. Our contributions are twofold.

As main technical result of the paper, we show that the stratifiability problem for integral polyhedra is coNP-complete. The proof is decomposed in two steps. First, we reduce the stratifiability of an integral polyhedron $\{x \in \mathbb{N}^d \mid Ax \geq b\}$ to a stratification-like property, called *nestedness*, that only involves the matrix A. We then provide a criterion for nestedness, and show how to express this criterion by a polynomial-size quantifier-free formula in the first-order theory of the rational numbers with addition and order. This way, we obtain that the stratifiability problem for integral polyhedra is solvable in coNP. The proof of coNP-hardness is by reduction from the emptiness problem for integral polyhedra.

Building on this result, we then investigate the context-freeness problem for flat counter systems, that asks whether the trace language of a counter system intersected with a bounded regular language is context-free. In our setting, *counter systems* are a generalization of Petri nets where transitions are guarded by integral polyhedra. Such guards can express zero tests, so counter systems are Turing-powerful since they subsume Minsky machines. By exploiting the restriction to bounded languages required by flatness, we show that the context-freeness problem for flat counter systems is coNP-complete, and remains so for flat Petri nets.

Related Work. The class of semilinear bounded languages was recently characterized through various language acceptors, namely, Parikh automata [6], reversal-bounded counter machines [16], and multi-head pushdown automata [9]. The class of semilinear sets was shown in [20] to coincide with the finite intersections of stratifiable semilinear sets. It follows that the class of bounded context-free languages is a generating class for the semilinear bounded languages. In [17], the stratifiability problem is shown to be equivalent to the existence of a 0-synchronized n-tape pushdown automaton equivalent to a given n-tape finite-state automaton whose language is contained in $a_1^* \times \cdots \times a_n^*$. In a recent paper [18], we proved that the trace language of a Petri net is context-free if, and only if, it has a context-free intersection with every bounded regular language. Building on this characterization, we then established in [19] that the context-freeness problem for Petri nets is EXPSPACE-complete, but the complexity was left open for the subcase of flat Petri nets. Here, we show that the context-freeness problem for flat Petri nets is coNP-complete. Related to our work is the question whether a given model is a posteriori flat, in other words, whether the set of all its behaviors is a bounded language. This question is shown in [7] to be decidable for the class of complete and deterministic well-structured transition systems.

Outline. The paper is organized as follows. Preliminary notations are given in Section 2. We recall the definition of stratifiable semilinear sets in Section 3. The stratifiability problem for integral polyhedra is shown to be decidable in Section 4, and it is proved to be coNP-complete in Section 5. We then address the context-freeness problem for flat counter systems, and show in Section 6 that it is coNP-complete. Section 7 concludes the paper with directions for future work.

2   Preliminaries

We let $\mathbb{N}$, $\mathbb{Z}$ and $\mathbb{Q}$ denote the usual sets of *nonnegative integers, integers* and *rational numbers*, respectively. We write $\mathbb{N}_1$ for the set of *positive integers* and $\mathbb{Q}_{\geq 0}$ for the set of *nonnegative rational numbers*. Vectors (of rational numbers), sets of vectors and matrices are typeset in bold face. The ith *component* of a vector v is written $v(i)$. The *support* of a vector v, written $\mathsf{supp}(v)$, is the set of indices i such that $v(i) \neq 0$. We let e_i denote the ith *unit vector*, defined by $e_i(i) = 1$ and $e_i(j) = 0$ for all indices $j \neq i$.

A *partial-order* on a set S is a binary relation $\preceq$ on S that is reflexive, antisymmetric and transitive. As usual, we write $s \prec t$ when $s \preceq t$ and $t \not\preceq s$. A *well-partial-order* on S is a partial-order $\preceq$ on S such that every infinite sequence $s_0, s_1, s_2, \ldots$ in S contains an increasing pair $s_i \preceq s_j$ with $i < j$.

3   Stratifiable Semilinear Sets

Building on earlier work with Spanier [13], Ginsburg provides, in his book [14], a characterization of bounded context-free languages in terms of semilinear sets satisfying a "stratification" requirement. We call such semilinear sets *stratifiable*. The existence of a decision procedure for determining whether a given semilinear set is stratifiable was left open in [13,14], and has remained open since then. We provide a partial answer to this problem in Sections 4 and 5. Before that, we recall in this section the definition of stratifiable semilinear sets, and how they can be used to characterize bounded context-free languages.

Given a finite set $P = \{p_1, \ldots, p_k\}$ of vectors in $\mathbb{N}^d$, we let $P^\star$ denote the set of finite sums of vectors in P, i.e., $P^\star = \mathbb{N}p_1 + \cdots + \mathbb{N}p_k$. A *linear set* is a set of the form $b + P^\star$ where b is a vector in $\mathbb{N}^d$ and P is a finite subset of $\mathbb{N}^d$. The vector b is called the *basis*, and the vectors in P are called *periods*. A *semilinear set* is a finite union of linear sets. Recall that semilinear sets coincide with the sets definable in $\mathsf{FO}\,(\mathbb{N}, 0, 1, +, \leq)$, also known as Presburger arithmetic [13].

Definition 3.1 ([13,14]). *A finite subset P of $\mathbb{N}^d$ is stratified if every vector in P has at most two non-zero components, and it holds that*

$$p(r) \neq 0 \land p(t) \neq 0 \land q(s) \neq 0 \land q(u) \neq 0 \;\; \Rightarrow \;\; \neg(r < s < t < u)$$

for every vectors $p, q \in P$ and indices $r, s, t, u \in \{1, \ldots, d\}$.

Example 3.2. The following examples are from [14]. The set $\{(2, 1, 0), (0, 3, 3)\}$ is stratified, but the set $\{(1, 1, 1), (1, 0, 2)\}$ is not stratified, since $(1, 1, 1)$ has three non-zero components. The set $\{(3, 0, 0, 2), (0, 1, 5, 0), (4, 7, 0, 0)\}$ is stratified, but the set $\{(2, 0, 3, 0), (0, 3, 0, 2)\}$ is not stratified. □

We call a semilinear set stratifiable when it is a finite union of linear sets, each with a stratified set of periods. Formally, a semilinear set S is *stratifiable* if there exits a finite family $\{(b_i, P_i)\}_{i \in I}$ of vectors b_i in $\mathbb{N}^d$ and finite stratified subsets P_i of $\mathbb{N}^d$ such that $S = \bigcup_{i \in I}(b_i + P_i^\star)$. The following lemma shows that stratifiable semilinear sets enjoy nice closure properties.

Lemma 3.3. *The class of stratifiable semilinear sets is closed under union, under projection, under inverse projection, and under intersection with Cartesian products of intervals.*

Proof. These closure properties are easily derived from the definition of stratifiable semilinear sets. □

The *stratifiability problem* asks whether a given semilinear set S is stratifiable. The decidability of the stratifiability problem was raised in [13,14], and has been open for nearly fifty years. Stratifiability is linked to the following characterization of bounded context-free languages.

We consider words over a finite alphabet Σ. Recall that a language $L \subseteq \Sigma^*$ is *bounded* if $L \subseteq \sigma_1^* \cdots \sigma_d^*$ for some words $\sigma_1, \ldots, \sigma_d$ in Σ^*. In his book [14], Ginsburg characterizes which bounded languages are context-free, in terms of semilinear sets. The reader is referred to [14] for further details.

Theorem 3.4 ([14, p. 162]). *Consider a language $L \subseteq \sigma_1^* \cdots \sigma_d^*$, where each $\sigma_i \in \Sigma^*$. Then L is context-free if, and only if, the set of all vectors $(n_1, \ldots, n_d)$ in $\mathbb{N}^d$ such that $\sigma_1^{n_1} \cdots \sigma_d^{n_d} \in L$ is a stratifiable semilinear set.*

Example 3.5. Take $\Sigma = \{a, b, c\}$. The language $\{a^n b^m c^n \mid n, m \in \mathbb{N}\}$ is context-free since the set $\{(n_1, n_2, n_3) \in \mathbb{N}^3 \mid n_1 = n_3\}$ is the linear set $P^\star$ where $P = \{(1, 0, 1), (0, 1, 0)\}$ is stratified. The language $\{a^n b^n c^n \mid n \in \mathbb{N}\}$ is known to be non-context-free. This means the semilinear set $\mathbb{N}(1, 1, 1)$ is not stratifiable. $\qquad \square$

4   Decidability of Stratifiability for Integral Polyhedra

In this section, we show that stratifiability is decidable for a subclass of semilinear sets, namely the sets of integral solutions of finite systems of linear inequalities. Formally, an *integral polyhedron* is a set of the form $\{x \in \mathbb{N}^d \mid Ax \geq b\}$ where $A \in \mathbb{Z}^{n \times d}$ is a matrix and $b \in \mathbb{Z}^d$ is a vector. Every linear system $Ax \geq b$ can be encoded into Presburger arithmetic, so integral polyhedra are semilinear sets. The *stratifiability problem for integral polyhedra* asks, given a matrix $A \in \mathbb{Z}^{n \times d}$ and a vector $b \in \mathbb{Z}^d$, both encoded in binary, whether the integral polyhedron $\{x \in \mathbb{N}^d \mid Ax \geq b\}$ is stratifiable. The remainder of this section reduces this problem to a decision problem that only involves the matrix $A \in \mathbb{Z}^{n \times d}$.

First, we show that stratifiability for integral polyhedra can be reduced to the particular case of homogeneous linear inequalities. Formally, an *integral cone* is a set of the form $\{x \in \mathbb{N}^d \mid Ax \geq 0\}$ where $A \in \mathbb{Z}^{n \times d}$ is a matrix. The following lemma shows that every integral cone is a linear set, and provides a way to decompose integral polyhedra into integral cones.

Lemma 4.1 ([21, p. 237]). *For every matrix $A \in \mathbb{Z}^{n \times d}$ and every vector $b \in \mathbb{Z}^d$, there exists two finite subsets B and P of $\mathbb{N}^d$ such that:*

$$\{x \in \mathbb{N}^d \mid Ax \geq b\} = B + P^\star \qquad and \qquad P^\star = \{x \in \mathbb{N}^d \mid Ax \geq 0\}$$

We have considered so far integral solutions of finite systems of linear inequalities. To simplify our analysis, we now move from integers to rational numbers. A *cone* is a set of the form $\{x \in \mathbb{Q}_{\geq 0}^d \mid Ax \geq 0\}$ where $A \in \mathbb{Z}^{n \times d}$ is a matrix. Given a finite set $P = \{p_1, \ldots, p_k\}$ of vectors in $\mathbb{N}^d$, we let $P^\triangleleft$ denote the set of linear combinations of vectors in P with nonnegative rational coefficients, i.e., $P^\triangleleft = \mathbb{Q}_{\geq 0} p_1 + \cdots + \mathbb{Q}_{\geq 0} p_k$. Put differently, $P^\triangleleft$ is defined as $P^\star$ except that $\mathbb{Q}_{\geq 0} p_i$ replaces $\mathbb{N} p_i$. Observe that $P^\triangleleft = \mathbb{Q}_{\geq 0} P^\star$ for every finite subset P of $\mathbb{N}^d$. Let us recall the following well-known property.

Property 4.2 (Farkas-Minkowski-Weyl Theorem). A subset X of $\mathbb{Q}_{\geq 0}^d$ is a cone if, and only if, $X = P^\triangleleft$ for some finite subset P of $\mathbb{N}^d$.

In order to extract the asymptotic directions of an integral polyhedron, we associate to every finite subset $P \subseteq \mathbb{N}^d$ a partial-order $\sqsubseteq_P$ on $\mathbb{N}^d$ defined by $x \sqsubseteq_P y$ if $y \in x + P^\star$. Observe that when $P = \{e_1, \ldots, e_d\}$, the partial-order $\sqsubseteq_P$ coincides with the classical partial order $\leq$ on $\mathbb{N}^d$, which is known to be a well-partial-order on $\mathbb{N}^d = \mathbb{N}^d \cap P^\triangleleft$, by Dickson's lemma. This observation can be generalized to any finite subset P of $\mathbb{N}^d$, as follows. We refer the reader to the proof of Lemma 1.2 from [15] for details.

Lemma 4.3 ([15]). *The partial-order $\sqsubseteq_P$ on $\mathbb{N}^d$ is a well-partial-order on $\mathbb{N}^d \cap P^\lhd$, for every finite subset P of $\mathbb{N}^d$.*

To show that the stratifiability problem for integral polyhedra is decidable, we decompose cones into "maximal stratifiable parts". The formal definition of these parts requires some additional notations. A binary relation R on $\{1, \ldots, d\}$ is called *nested* if it satisfies the two following conditions:

$$(s, t) \in R \;\Rightarrow\; s \leq t \tag{1}$$

$$(r, t) \in R \wedge (s, u) \in R \;\Rightarrow\; \neg(r < s < t < u) \tag{2}$$

An example of a nested relation is depicted in Figure 1a. Given a cone $X \subseteq \mathbb{Q}_{\geq 0}^d$ and a nested binary relation R on $\{1, \ldots, d\}$, we introduce the set X_R defined as follows:

$$X_R = \sum_{r \in R} X_r$$

where, for each pair $r = (s, t)$ of indices satisfying $1 \leq s \leq t \leq d$, the set X_r is given by:

$$X_r = \left\{ x \in X \;\middle|\; \bigwedge_{j \notin \{s,t\}} x(j) = 0 \right\}$$

Intuitively, the "maximal stratifiable parts" mentioned previously are the sets X_R. The "stratification" property of X_R is expressed by the following lemma.

Lemma 4.4. *For every cone $X \subseteq \mathbb{Q}_{\geq 0}^d$ and every nested binary relation R on $\{1, \ldots, d\}$, it holds that $X_R = P_R^\lhd$ for some finite stratified subset P_R of $\mathbb{N}^d$.*

Proof. Consider a cone $X = \{x \in \mathbb{Q}_{\geq 0}^d \mid Ax \geq 0\}$ and a nested binary relation R on $\{1, \ldots, d\}$. First, notice that X_r is a cone for every $r = (s, t)$ in R. Indeed, every constraint $x(j) = 0$ may be expressed as the conjunction of $x(j) \geq 0$ and $-x(j) \geq 0$. By adding these inequalities to the matrix A for every $j \notin \{s, t\}$, we obtain a matrix witnessing that X_r is a cone. It follows from Property 4.2 that $X_r = P_r^\lhd$ for some finite subset $P_r \subseteq \mathbb{N}^d$. Therefore, $X_R = P_R^\lhd$ where P_R is the finite subset of $\mathbb{N}^d$ defined by $P_R = \bigcup_{r \in R} P_r$. Since R is nested, we derive that P_R is stratified, which concludes the proof of the lemma. $\qquad \square$

We are now ready to provide a decidable characterization of stratifiable integral polyhedra. Given a cone $X \subseteq \mathbb{Q}_{\geq 0}^d$, we say that X is *nested* if $X = \bigcup_R X_R$. It is understood that the union ranges over nested binary relations on $\{1, \ldots, d\}$. Observe that each X_R is contained in X, since cones are closed under addition. So nestedness only requires that X is contained in $\bigcup_R X_R$. The *cone nestedness problem* asks, given a matrix $A \in \mathbb{Z}^{n \times d}$ encoded in binary, whether the cone $\{x \in \mathbb{Q}_{\geq 0}^d \mid Ax \geq 0\}$ is nested.

Theorem 4.5. *An integral polyhedron $\{x \in \mathbb{N}^d \mid Ax \geq b\}$ is stratifiable if, and only if, it is empty or the cone $\{x \in \mathbb{Q}_{\geq 0}^d \mid Ax \geq 0\}$ is nested.*

Proof. For brevity, we let S denote the integral polyhedron $\{x \in \mathbb{N}^d \mid Ax \geq b\}$, and X denote its associated cone $\{x \in \mathbb{Q}_{\geq 0}^d \mid Ax \geq 0\}$.

We first prove the "if" direction of the theorem. If S is empty then it is trivially stratifiable. Let us assume that X is nested. According to Lemma 4.1, the integral polyhedron S can be decomposed into a sum $S = B + H$ where $B \subseteq \mathbb{N}^d$ is a finite set and H is the integral cone $\{x \in \mathbb{N}^d \mid Ax \geq 0\}$. Observe that $X = \bigcup_R X_R$ since X is nested, and that $H \subseteq X$ by definition. We derive that H can be decomposed into $H = \bigcup_R H_R$ where $H_R = H \cap X_R$. By Lemma 4.4, there exists a finite stratified set $P_R \subseteq \mathbb{N}^d$ such that $X_R = P_R^\triangleleft$. Lemma 4.3 entails that $\sqsubseteq_{P_R}$ is a well-partial-order on $\mathbb{N}^d \cap X_R$. It follows that the set of minimal elements of H_R for this well-partial-order is a finite set. Moreover, writing B_R this finite set, we obtain that $H_R \subseteq B_R + P_R^\star$. We have proved the inclusion $H \subseteq \bigcup_R (B_R + P_R^\star)$. Since the converse inclusion is immediate, the set H is stratifiable. From $S = B + H$, we deduce that S is stratifiable.

We now prove the "only if" direction of the theorem. Let us assume that S is non-empty and stratifiable. Since S is stratifiable, it can be decomposed into $\bigcup_{i \in I} (b_i + P_i^\star)$ where I is finite, $b_i \in \mathbb{N}^d$ and $P_i \subseteq \mathbb{N}^d$ is a finite stratified set.

Let us first show that $P_i^\star \subseteq \bigcup_R X_R$. Define R_i to be the set of pairs (s, t), with $1 \leq s \leq t \leq d$, such that $p(s) \neq 0 \wedge p(t) \neq 0$ for some vector $p \in P_i$. It is readily seen that R_i is a nested binary relation on $\{1, \ldots, d\}$, since P_i is stratified. Let $p \in P_i$. For each $n \in \mathbb{N}$, it holds that $b_i + np \in S$. Thus, $Ab_i + nAp \geq b$ for every $n \in \mathbb{N}$. We deduce that $Ap \geq 0$, hence, $p \in X$. By definition of R_i, we get that $p \in X_{R_i}$. Since X_{R_i} is closed under addition, we obtain that $P_i^\star \subseteq X_{R_i}$.

To prove that $X \subseteq \bigcup_R X_R$, it is enough to show that $\mathbb{N}^d \cap X \subseteq \bigcup_R X_R$, since cones are closed under multiplication with nonnegative rational numbers. Let $x \in \mathbb{N}^d \cap X$. Since S is non-empty, there exists $s \in S$. For every $n \in \mathbb{N}$, we have $A(s + nx) \geq b$, hence, $s + nx \in S$. By the pigeon-hole principle, there exists $i \in I$ and an infinite set $N \subseteq \mathbb{N}$ such that $s + nx \in b_i + P_i^\star$ for every $n \in N$. Lemma 4.3 entails that $\sqsubseteq_{P_i}$ is a well-partial-order on $\mathbb{N}^d \cap P_i^\triangleleft$. Since $x_n = s - b_i + nx$ is in $P_i^\star \subseteq \mathbb{N}^d \cap P_i^\triangleleft$ for every $n \in \mathbb{N}$, we deduce that there exists $n, m \in N$ such that $n < m$ and $x_n \sqsubseteq_{P_i} x_m$. It follows that $(m - n)x = x_m - x_n \in P_i^\star$. Since $P_i^\star \subseteq \bigcup_R X_R$, we obtain that $x \in \bigcup_R X_R$. We have shown that $\mathbb{N}^d \cap X \subseteq \bigcup_R X_R$, and we conclude that X is nested. $\square$

Given a cone $X = \{x \in \mathbb{Q}_{\geq 0}^d \mid Ax \geq 0\}$, we may compute from the matrix A a formula in the theory $\mathrm{FO}\,(\bar{\mathbb{Q}}, 0, 1, +, \leq)$ expressing the equality $X = \bigcup_R X_R$. Since this theory is decidable by Fourier-Motzkin quantifier elimination, we obtain that the cone nestedness problem is decidable. It follows from Theorem 4.5 that the stratifiability problem for integral polyhedra is decidable. We show, in the next section, that this problem is coNP-complete.

5   A Criterion for Cone Nestedness Decidable in coNP

We provide, in this section, a criterion for checking whether a given cone is nested. This criterion leads to a coNP decision procedure for the cone nestedness

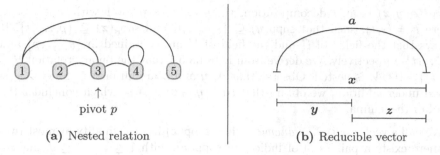

(a) Nested relation

(b) Reducible vector

Fig. 1. Decomposition of nested relations and of reducible vectors

problem, and similarly for the stratifiability problem for integral polyhedra. We also show that the latter upper bound is tight.

To every cone $X \subseteq \mathbb{Q}_{\geq 0}^d$, we associate the set $\widehat{X} = \bigcup_R X_R$. Recall that X is non-nested precisely when $X \not\subseteq \widehat{X}$. We show that non-nestedness of a cone X can always be witnessed by a vector in $X \setminus \widehat{X}$ of a special form. We will need the following easy facts. An illustration of the first lemma is given in Figure 1a.

Lemma 5.1. *Assume that $d \geq 3$. A binary relation R on $\{1, \ldots, d\}$ is nested if, and only if, there exist a pivot p with $1 < p < d$ and two nested binary relations U and V on $\{1, \ldots, p\}$ and $\{p, \ldots, d\}$, respectively, such that $R \subseteq \{(1, d)\} \cup U \cup V$.*

Lemma 5.2. *For every $x \in \widehat{X}$, there exists a nested binary relation R on[1] $\mathsf{supp}(x)$ such that $x \in X_R$.*

Proof (sketch). If $x \in \widehat{X}$ then $x = \sum_{r \in R} x_r$ for some nested binary relation R on $\{1, \ldots, d\}$ and some vectors $x_r \in X_r$. We can assume, w.l.o.g., that $x_r(s) \neq 0$ and $x_r(t) \neq 0$ for each pair $r = (s, t)$. Indeed, if $x_r = 0$ then r can be removed from R, and, otherwise, if $x_r(s) = 0$ or $x_r(t) = 0$ then r can be replaced by (t, t) or (s, s), respectively. It follows that R is a nested binary relation on $\mathsf{supp}(x)$. □

Consider a cone $X \subseteq \mathbb{Q}_{\geq 0}^d$. Given a pair $r = (s, t)$ of indices with $1 \leq s \leq t \leq d$, we call *r-decomposition*[2] any triple (a, y, z) of vectors in $X_r \times X \times X$ such that $\mathsf{supp}(y) \subseteq \{s, \ldots, p\}$ and $\mathsf{supp}(z) \subseteq \{p, \ldots, t\}$ for some pivot p satisfying $s < p < t$. Since cones are closed under addition, the vector $a + y + z$ is in X for every decomposition (a, y, z). The following lemma shows that membership in $\widehat{X}$ is also preserved by decomposition.

Lemma 5.3. *For every r-decomposition (a, y, z), it holds that $(a + y + z) \in \widehat{X}$ if $y \in \widehat{X}$ and $z \in \widehat{X}$.*

Proof. Assume that $y \in \widehat{X}$ and $z \in \widehat{X}$. By Lemma 5.2, there exists two nested binary relations U on $\mathsf{supp}(y)$ and V on $\mathsf{supp}(z)$ such that $y \in X_U$ and $z \in X_V$.

---

[1] Recall that $\mathsf{supp}(v)$ denotes the support of v, i.e, the set of indices i with $v(i) \neq 0$.
[2] This notion is defined relative to a cone X, which is left implicit to reduce clutter.

Since (a, y, z) is an r-decomposition, there exists a pivot p with $s < p < t$, where $r = (s, t)$, such that $\mathsf{supp}(y) \subseteq \{s, \ldots, p\}$ and $\mathsf{supp}(z) \subseteq \{p, \ldots, t\}$. It follows that the field[3] of U and the field of V are contained in $\{s, \ldots, p\}$ and $\{p, \ldots, t\}$, respectively. We derive from Lemma 5.1 that the binary relation $R = \{(s, t)\} \cup U \cup V$ is nested. Observe that a, y and z are all in X_R. Since X_R is closed under addition, we obtain that $(a + y + z) \in X_R$, which concludes the proof of the lemma. □

We call a vector $x \in X$ *reducible*[4] when $\mathsf{supp}(x)$ has cardinality at most two, or there exists a pair (s, t) of indices in $\mathsf{supp}(x)$, with $1 \leq s \leq t \leq d$, and an (s, t)-decomposition (a, y, z) such that $x = a + y + z$. The latter condition is depicted in Figure 1b. Note that this condition entails that $\mathsf{supp}(x) \subseteq \{s, \ldots, t\}$. A vector $x \in X$ is called *irreducible*[4] when it is not reducible. The following theorem characterizes which cones are nested, in terms of irreducible vectors. Before that, we illustrate these notions on a few examples.

Example 5.4. Let X and Y be the cones given by $X = \{x \in \mathbb{Q}_{\geq 0}^3 \mid x(1) = x(3)\}$ and $Y = \{x \in \mathbb{Q}_{\geq 0}^3 \mid x(1) = x(2) = x(3)\}$. The vector $(1, 0, 1)$ is reducible for both cones, since it contains only two non-zero components. The vector $(1, 1, 1)$ is reducible for X. This is witnessed by the $(1, 3)$-decomposition (a, y, y) where $a = (1, 0, 1)$ and $y = (0, 0.5, 0)$. The same vector $(1, 1, 1)$ is irreducible for Y. □

Theorem 5.5. *A cone is nested if, and only if, it contains no irreducible vector.*

Proof. Consider a cone $X \subseteq \mathbb{Q}_{\geq 0}^d$. We first prove the "only if" direction of the theorem. Assume that X is nested, and let $x \in X$. If $\mathsf{supp}(x)$ has cardinality at most two, then x is trivially reducible. Suppose, on the contrary, that x contains at least three non-zero components. Since $X \subseteq \widehat{X}$, we obtain from Lemma 5.2 that there exists a nested binary relation R on $\mathsf{supp}(x)$ such that $x \in X_R$. Moreover, R is not empty since $x \neq 0$. Let F denote the field[5] of R, and define $s = \min F$ and $t = \max F$. Observe that both s and t are in $\mathsf{supp}(x)$. Notice also that $t \geq s + 2$ since x contains at least three non-zero components. We derive from Lemma 5.1 that there exist a pivot p with $s < p < t$, a nested binary relation U on $\{s, \ldots, p\}$ and a nested binary relation V on $\{p, \ldots, t\}$, such that $R \subseteq \{(s, t)\} \cup U \cup V$. We derive that $x \in (X_{(s,t)} + X_U + X_V)$, which entails that x is reducible.

Let us now prove the "if" direction of the theorem. Assume that X is not nested. This means that $X \not\subseteq \widehat{X}$. Among the vectors x in $X \setminus \widehat{X}$, pick one such that $\mathsf{supp}(x)$ is minimal for inclusion. Let us show that x is irreducible. By contradiction, suppose that x is reducible. Observe that $\mathsf{supp}(x)$ has cardinality at least three since $x \in (X \setminus \widehat{X})$. Therefore, there exists a pair (s, t) of indices in $\mathsf{supp}(x)$, with $1 \leq s \leq t \leq d$, and an (s, t)-decomposition (a, y, z) such that $x = a + y + z$. It is readily seen that $\mathsf{supp}(y)$ and $\mathsf{supp}(z)$ are both strictly contained in $\mathsf{supp}(x)$. By minimality of x, we get that y and z are in $\widehat{X}$. We derive from Lemma 5.3 that $x \in \widehat{X}$, which contradicts the assumption that x is in $X \setminus \widehat{X}$. □

---

[3] The *field* of a binary relation is the union of its domain and range.

The previous theorem allows us to reduce the cone nestedness problem to the question whether a given cone contains only reducible vectors. In the remainder of this section, we explain how to solve the latter problem in coNP. Consider a matrix $A \in \mathbb{Z}^{n \times d}$ encoded in binary, and let $X = \{x \in \mathbb{Q}_{\geq 0}^d \mid Ax \geq 0\}$. We build, in time polynomial in the size of A, a quantifier-free formula[4] $\rho(x)$ in FO $(\mathbb{Q}, 0, 1, +, \leq)$ that is valid if, and only if, X contains only reducible vectors. This will entail a coNP upper bound for the cone nestedness problem, since satisfiability of quantifier-free formulas in FO $(\mathbb{Q}, 0, 1, +, \leq)$ is solvable in NP (see, e.g., [21, p. 120]). First, we build a formula $\varphi(x)$, containing quantifiers, whose models are precisely the vectors in X that are reducible. Let B be the the matrix in $\mathbb{Z}^{(n+d) \times d}$ obtained from A by appending the identity matrix to the bottom of A. Note that $X = \{x \in \mathbb{Q}^d \mid Bx \geq 0\}$. The formula $\varphi(x)$ is:

$$Bx \geq 0 \land \bigvee_{1 \leq s \leq t \leq d} \left[\left(\bigwedge_{i \notin \{s,t\}} x(i) = 0 \right) \lor (x(s) > 0 \land x(t) > 0 \land \psi_{B,s,t}(x)) \right]$$

where, for each pair (s,t) of indices with $1 \leq s \leq t \leq d$, the formula $\psi_{B,s,t}(x)$, given below, expresses that there exists an (s,t)-decomposition (a, y, z) such that $x = a + y + z$. The formula $\psi_{B,s,t}(x)$ is:

$$\left(\bigwedge_{i<s \lor i>t} x(i) = 0 \right) \land \bigvee_{p=s+1}^{t-1} \exists \mu \, \exists \nu \, \exists \pi \left[\begin{array}{ll} B(\mu e_s + \nu e_t) & \geq 0 \\ B\left(\sum_{s \leq i < p} x(i)e_i - \mu e_s + \pi e_p \right) & \geq 0 \\ B\left(\sum_{p \leq i \leq t} x(i)e_i - \pi e_p - \nu e_t \right) & \geq 0 \end{array} \right\}$$

Here, it is understood that the sub-formula in brackets stands for the conjunction of the three systems of linear inequalities. It is routinely checked that, for every vector $x \in \mathbb{Q}^d$, the formula $\varphi(x)$ holds if, and only if, x is a reducible vector of X. Notice that each disjunct $\exists \mu \exists \nu \exists \pi [\cdots]$ contains a constant number of quantifiers, namely three. So, with Fourier-Motzkin quantifier elimination, we can transform, in polynomial time, each formula $\psi_{B,s,t}(x)$ into an equivalent quantifier-free formula $\psi'_{B,s,t}(x)$. Let $\varphi'(x)$ denote the formula obtained from the definition of $\varphi(x)$ by replacing each $\psi_{B,s,t}(x)$ by $\psi'_{B,s,t}(x)$. The desired formula $\rho(x)$ is $(Bx \geq 0) \Rightarrow \varphi'(x)$. We have shown the following theorem.

Theorem 5.6. *The cone nestedness problem is solvable in coNP.*

We now have all the necessary ingredients to prove the following corollary, which is the main technical result of the paper.

Corollary 5.7. *The stratifiability problem for integral polyhedra is coNP-complete.*

---

[4] In this paper, we assume that all integer constants in formulas are encoded in binary.

Proof. We start by recalling that the emptiness problem for integral polyhedra is coNP-complete (see, e.g., [21, p. 245]). This problem asks, given a matrix $A \in \mathbb{Z}^{n \times d}$ and a vector $b \in \mathbb{Z}^d$, both encoded in binary, whether the integral polyhedron $\{x \in \mathbb{N}^d \mid Ax \geq b\}$ is empty.

Let us now prove the corollary. The upper bound follows from Theorem 4.5, Theorem 5.6, and closure under union of coNP. The lower bound is obtained by reduction from the emptiness problem for integral polyhedra. First of all, we observe that by increasing d by 3 and by slightly modifying the pair (A, b), the emptiness problem for integral polyhedra can be reduced, in linear time, to the particular case of integral polyhedra X satisfying the following condition:

$$X = \emptyset \quad \text{or} \quad \{(x(1), x(2), x(3)) \mid x \in X\} = \mathbb{N}(1, 1, 1) \tag{3}$$

Recall that the linear set $\mathbb{N}(1, 1, 1)$ is not stratifiable (see Example 3.5). It follows from Lemma 3.3 that every integral polyhedron satisfying (3) is empty if, and only if, it is stratifiable. We have thus reduced, in linear time, the emptiness problem for integral polyhedra to the stratifiability problem for them.   □

6   Application to Flat Counter Systems

In this section, we investigate the context-freeness problem for flat counter systems. This problem asks whether the trace language of a given counter system intersected with a given bounded regular language is context-free. In our setting, counter systems are a generalization of Petri nets where transitions are guarded by integral polyhedra. Such guards can express zero tests, so counter systems subsume Minsky machines and, therefore, are Turing-powerful. We show that the context-freeness problem for flat counter systems is coNP-complete, and remains so for flat Petri nets.

We exploit the restriction to bounded languages required by flatness to reduce the context-freeness problem for flat counter systems to the stratifiability problem for integral polyhedra. This reduction is performed in two steps. It is well-known that bounded regular languages are finite unions of languages of the form $w_1 \sigma_1^+ \cdots w_d \sigma_d^+$ [12]. As a first step, we consider a subproblem of the context-freeness problem for flat counter systems, where the given bounded regular language is of the form $w_1 \sigma_1^+ \cdots w_d \sigma_d^+$. We provide a reduction of this subproblem to the stratifiability problem for integral polyhedra. The context-freeness problem for flat counter systems is then reduced to this subproblem by providing polynomial bounds on the size of the languages $w_1 \sigma_1^+ \cdots w_d \sigma_d^+$.

A counter system is a formal model manipulating a finite set of counters ranging over the natural numbers. Given a number of counters $c \in \mathbb{N}$, a *configuration* is a vector $x \in \mathbb{N}^c$, and a *transition* is a triple $\theta = (A, b, v)$ where $A \in \mathbb{Z}^{m \times c}$ is a matrix, and $b \in \mathbb{Z}^m$ and $v \in \mathbb{Z}^c$ are two vectors. Informally, a transition (A, b, v) represents the guarded translation "$Ax \geq b$; $x := x + v$; $x \geq 0$".

Formally, a *counter system* is a triple $S = \langle c, \Theta, x_{\text{init}} \rangle$ where $c \in \mathbb{N}$ is a number of counters, $\Theta \subseteq \mathbb{Z}^{m \times c} \times \mathbb{Z}^m \times \mathbb{Z}^c$ is a finite set of transitions, and $x_{\text{init}} \in \mathbb{N}^c$ is an *initial* configuration. The operational semantics of $\mathcal{S}$ is given by the labeled transition relation $\rightarrow \subseteq \mathbb{N}^c \times \Theta \times \mathbb{N}^c$, defined by $x \xrightarrow{(A, b, v)} y$ if $Ax \geq b$ and $y = x + v$. A *run* is a finite, alternating sequence $(x_0, \theta_1, x_1, \ldots, \theta_k, x_k)$ of configurations and transitions, satisfying $x_{i-1} \xrightarrow{\theta_i} x_i$ for all i. The word $\theta_1 \cdots \theta_k$ is called the *label* of the run. We introduce, for every word $\sigma \in \Theta^*$, the binary relation $\xrightarrow{\sigma}$ between configurations, defined by $x \xrightarrow{\sigma} y$ if there exists a run from x to y labeled by σ. A *trace* from a configuration x is the label of some run that starts with x. We let $\mathcal{T}(\mathcal{S}, x)$ denote the set of all traces from x. The set $\mathcal{T}(\mathcal{S}, x_{\text{init}})$ of all traces from the initial configuration, shortly written $\mathcal{T}(\mathcal{S})$, is called the *trace language* of $\mathcal{S}$. The *context-freeness problem for counter systems* asks whether the trace language of a given counter system is context-free. This problem is easily shown to be undecidable, by reduction from the reachability problem for (deterministic) Minsky machines.

For the subclass of Petri nets, the context-freeness problem was shown to be decidable by Schwer in [22]. In our settings, a Petri net is a counter system $\langle c, \Theta, x_{\text{init}} \rangle$ where Θ is a set of transitions of the form (A, b, v) such that A is the identity matrix. Informally, Petri net transitions are guarded translations "$x \geq b$; $x := x + v$; $x \geq 0$". In a recent paper [18], we revisited the context-freeness problem for Petri nets, and gave a simpler proof of decidability based on bounded regular languages. We showed that the trace language of a Petri net is context-free if, and only if, it has a context-free intersection with every bounded regular language. Based on this characterization, the context-freeness problem for Petri nets was then shown to be EXPSPACE-complete [19]. However, the complexity of the context-freeness problem for flat Petri nets was left open.

This motivates our study of the *context-freeness problem for flat counter systems*. Formally, we define this problem as follows:

Input: a counter system $\mathcal{S} = \langle c, \Theta, x_{\text{init}} \rangle$, and a finite-state automaton[5] $\mathcal{A}$ recognizing a bounded regular language $L(\mathcal{A}) \subseteq \Theta^*$,
Output: whether the language $\mathcal{T}(\mathcal{S}) \cap L(\mathcal{A})$ is context-free.

The size of the input is the obvious one, where integers are encoded in binary. In the sequel, this problem is reduced to a subproblem, called the *context-freeness problem for flat-linear counter systems*, which is defined as follows:

Input: a counter system $\mathcal{S} = \langle c, \Theta, x_{\text{init}} \rangle$, and a finite sequence $w_1, \sigma_1, \ldots, w_d, \sigma_d$ of words in Θ^*,
Output: whether the language $\mathcal{T}(\mathcal{S}) \cap w_1 \sigma_1^+ \cdots w_d \sigma_d^+$ is context-free.

The size of the input is, again, the obvious one, with integers encoded in binary. The decidability of this last problem requires the following variant of Ginsburg's characterization of bounded context-free languages (cf. Theorem 3.4).

---

[5] Recall that a *finite-state automaton* is a quintuple $\mathcal{A} = \langle Q, I, F, \Sigma, \rightarrow \rangle$ where Q is a finite set of *states*, $I \subseteq Q$ and $F \subseteq Q$ are finite sets of *initial* and *final* states, Σ is a finite alphabet, and $\rightarrow \subseteq Q \times \Sigma \times Q$ is a finite set of *transitions*. We let $L(\mathcal{A})$ denote the language recognized by $\mathcal{A}$.

Lemma 6.1. *Consider a language $L \subseteq w_1\sigma_1^+ \cdots w_d\sigma_d^+$, where each $w_i \in \Sigma^*$ and each $\sigma_i \in \Sigma^*$. Then L is context-free if, and only if, the set of all vectors $(n_1, \ldots, n_d)$ in $\mathbb{N}_1^d$ such that $w_1\sigma_1^{n_1} \cdots w_d\sigma_d^{n_d} \in L$ is a stratifiable semilinear set.*

The context-freeness problem for flat-linear counter systems is shown to be decidable in coNP by a polynomial-time reduction to the stratifiability problem for integral polyhedra, which is solvable in coNP by Corollary 5.7. Let us consider an input of this problem, namely a counter system $\mathcal{S} = \langle c, \Theta, \boldsymbol{x}_{\text{init}} \rangle$ and a finite sequence $w_1, \sigma_1, \ldots, w_d, \sigma_d$ of words in Θ^*. By Lemma 6.1, the language $L = \mathcal{T}(\mathcal{S}) \cap w_1\sigma_1^+ \cdots w_d\sigma_d^+$ is context-free if, and only if, the following set is stratifiable:

$$N = \{(n_1, \ldots, n_d) \in \mathbb{N}_1^d \mid w_1\sigma_1^{n_d} \cdots w_d\sigma_d^{n_d} \in \mathcal{T}(\mathcal{S})\}$$

This set is shown to be an integral polyhedron in Corollary 6.3. This result follows from the following "acceleration" lemma.

Lemma 6.2. *There exists a polynomial-time algorithm that, given a counter system $\mathcal{S} = \langle c, \Theta, \boldsymbol{x}_{init} \rangle$ and a word $\sigma \in \Theta^*$, computes a matrix $\boldsymbol{A} \in \mathbb{Z}^{n \times c}$ and three vectors $\boldsymbol{a}, \boldsymbol{b} \in \mathbb{Z}^n$ and $\boldsymbol{v} \in \mathbb{Z}^c$ such that:*

$$\boldsymbol{x} \xrightarrow{\sigma^n} \boldsymbol{y} \quad \Longleftrightarrow \quad \boldsymbol{A}\boldsymbol{x} + n\boldsymbol{a} \geq \boldsymbol{b} \wedge \boldsymbol{y} = \boldsymbol{x} + n\boldsymbol{v}$$

for every $\boldsymbol{x}, \boldsymbol{y} \in \mathbb{N}^c$ and $n \in \mathbb{N}_1$.

Proof (sketch). By encoding the effect of a word $\sigma \in \Theta^*$ into a single transition, we deduce the lemma thanks to [2]. The crucial observation is the convexity of the guard of this transition. $\square$

Corollary 6.3. *There exists a polynomial-time algorithm that, given a counter system $\mathcal{S} = \langle c, \Theta, \boldsymbol{x}_{init} \rangle$ and a sequence $w_1, \sigma_1, \ldots, w_d, \sigma_d$ of words in Θ^*, computes a matrix $\boldsymbol{A} \in \mathbb{Z}^{n \times d}$ and a vector $\boldsymbol{b} \in \mathbb{Z}^n$ such that:*

$$w_1\sigma_1^{n_1} \cdots w_d\sigma_d^{n_d} \in \mathcal{T}(\mathcal{S}) \quad \Longleftrightarrow \quad \boldsymbol{A}(n_1, \ldots, n_d) \geq \boldsymbol{b}$$

for every $n_1, \ldots, n_d \in \mathbb{N}_1$.

Proof. We derive in polynomial time from Lemma 6.2, a tuple $(\boldsymbol{A}_i, \boldsymbol{a}_i, \boldsymbol{b}_i, \boldsymbol{v}_i)$ such that for every $n \in \mathbb{N}_1$ and any $\boldsymbol{x}, \boldsymbol{y} \in \mathbb{N}^c$ we have $\boldsymbol{x} \xrightarrow{\sigma_i^n} \boldsymbol{y}$ if, and only if, $\boldsymbol{A}_i\boldsymbol{x} + n\boldsymbol{a}_i \geq \boldsymbol{b}_i$ and $\boldsymbol{y} = \boldsymbol{x} + n_i\boldsymbol{v}_i$. In polynomial time, we compute transitions $\theta_i = (\boldsymbol{B}_i, \boldsymbol{c}_i, \boldsymbol{u}_i)$ such that the binary relation $\xrightarrow{w_i}$ is equal to $\xrightarrow{\theta_i}$. The word $w_1\sigma_1^{n_1} \cdots w_d\sigma_d^{n_d}$ is a trace from $\boldsymbol{x}_{\text{init}}$ with $n_1, \ldots, n_d \in \mathbb{N}_1$ if, and only if, the following linear system is satisfiable where $\boldsymbol{y}_i = \boldsymbol{x}_{\text{init}} + \sum_{1 \leq j < i}(\boldsymbol{u}_j + n_j\boldsymbol{v}_j)$ and $\boldsymbol{x}_i = \boldsymbol{y}_i + \boldsymbol{u}_i$:

$$\bigwedge_{i=1}^{d} \boldsymbol{B}_i\boldsymbol{y}_i \geq \boldsymbol{c}_i \wedge \boldsymbol{A}_i\boldsymbol{x}_i + n_i\boldsymbol{a}_i \geq \boldsymbol{b}_i$$

Now, just observe that such a linear system can be written as a linear system of the form $\boldsymbol{A}(n_1, \ldots, n_d) \geq \boldsymbol{b}$. $\square$

We deduce the following theorem.

Theorem 6.4. *The context-freeness problem for flat-linear counter systems is coNP-complete.*

Proof. Since the language L is context-free if, and only if, the integral polyhedron N is stratifiable, it follows from Corollary 5.7 that the context-freeness problem for flat-linear counter systems is in coNP. The problem is shown to be coNP-hard by a direct reduction from the stratifiability problem for integral polyhedra, which is coNP-hard by Corollary 5.7. □

The context-freeness problem for flat counter systems can be reduced to the flat-linear case thanks to the following lemma, which provides polynomial bounds on the decomposition of bounded regular languages into languages of the form $w_1\sigma_1^+ \cdots w_d\sigma_d^+$.

Lemma 6.5. *Let $\mathcal{A}$ be a finite-state automaton. If $L(\mathcal{A})$ is bounded then it is the union of the languages $w_1\sigma_1^+ \cdots w_d\sigma_d^+$ such that $\mathcal{A}$ contains an accepting run $q_0 \xrightarrow{w_1} q_1 \xrightarrow{\sigma_1} q_1 \cdots q_{d-1} \xrightarrow{w_d} q_d \xrightarrow{\sigma_d} q_d$ with $d + |w_1\sigma_1 \cdots w_d\sigma_d| \leq 6|Q|^3$.*

Proof (sketch). The proof is obtained by first proving that $|w_1\sigma_1|, \ldots, |w_d\sigma_d|$ are bounded by $|Q|$. The lemma follows from the bound $d \leq |Q|^2 + 1$ with a pigeon-hole argument. □

Now, consider an instance $(\mathcal{S}, \mathcal{A})$ of the context-freeness problem for flat counter systems. Recall that $L(\mathcal{A})$ is bounded. We derive from the previous Lemma that $\mathcal{T}(\mathcal{S}) \cap L(\mathcal{A})$ is not context-free if, and only if, there exists an accepting run $q_0 \xrightarrow{w_1} q_1 \xrightarrow{\sigma_1} q_1 \cdots q_{d-1} \xrightarrow{w_d} q_d \xrightarrow{\sigma_d} q_d$ in $\mathcal{A}$ of polynomial length such that $\mathcal{T}(\mathcal{S}) \cap w_1\sigma_1^+ \cdots w_d\sigma_d^+$ is not context-free. Since non-context-freeness of $\mathcal{T}(\mathcal{S}) \cap w_1\sigma_1^+ \cdots w_d\sigma_d^+$ can be checked in NP, we obtain that the context-freeness problem for flat counter systems is in coNP. A matching lower bound is obtained by reduction from 3-SAT.

Lemma 6.6. *The context-freeness problem for flat Petri nets[6] is coNP-hard.*

Proof (sketch). Given a 3-SAT formula φ, an instance $(\mathcal{S}, \mathcal{A})$ of the context-freeness problem for flat Petri nets is computed in polynomial time in such a way that the language $\mathcal{T}(\mathcal{S}) \cap L(\mathcal{A})$ is non-empty, and in this case not context-free, if, and only if, the formula φ is satisfiable. Since 3-SAT is NP-hard, the context-freeness problem for flat Petri nets is coNP-hard. □

We have shown the following theorem, which is the second main result of the paper.

Theorem 6.7. *The context-freeness problem for flat counter systems is coNP-complete, and remains so for flat Petri nets.*

---

[6] The *context-freeness problem for flat Petri nets* is defined exactly as the context-freeness problem for flat counter systems except that the input counter system is required to be a Petri net.

Remark 6.8. Our setting requires a single initial configuration. Let us consider a variant without any specific initial configuration. An *uninitialized counter system* is a pair $\mathcal{S} = \langle c, \Theta \rangle$ where $c \in \mathbb{N}$ is a number of counters and Θ is a finite set of transitions. Its *trace language* is defined by $\mathcal{T}(\mathcal{S}) = \bigcup_{\boldsymbol{x}_{init} \in \mathbb{N}^c} \mathcal{T}(\mathcal{S}, \boldsymbol{x}_{init})$. The *context-freeness problem for uninitialized flat counter systems* is defined exactly as the context-freeness problem for flat counter systems except that it takes an uninitialized counter system as input. This problem can be shown to be decidable by adapting techniques developed in this paper. In fact, just observe that the set $\boldsymbol{N} = \{(n_1, \ldots, n_d) \in \mathbb{N}_1^d \mid w_1 \sigma_1^{n_1} \cdots w_d \sigma_d^{n_d} \in \mathcal{T}(\mathcal{S})\}$ can be denoted by a Presburger formula $\varphi(n_1, \ldots, n_d) = \exists \boldsymbol{x}_{init}\ \boldsymbol{A}(\boldsymbol{x}_{init}, n_1, \ldots, n_d) \geq \boldsymbol{b}$ for a matrix $\boldsymbol{A}$ and a vector $\boldsymbol{b}$ that are both computable in polynomial time. Decidability of the context-freeness problem for uninitialized flat counter systems follows by quantifier elimination on φ. However, the complexity is open.   □

7   Conclusions and Future Work

The decidability of the stratifiability problem for semilinear sets was raised in [13,14] almost fifty years ago, and is still open. Rephrased in terms of languages, this decision problem is equivalent to the question whether a given semilinear bounded language is context-free. In this paper, we have shown that the stratifiability problem for the subclass of integral polyhedra is coNP-complete. Building on this result, we have then established that the context-freeness problem for flat counter systems is coNP-complete, and remains coNP-hard for the subcase of flat Petri nets.

To solve the stratifiability problem for integral polyhedra, we have reduced it to the particular case of integral cones. While the latter is in coNP, its exact complexity is open.

References

1. Annichini, A., Bouajjani, A., Sighireanu, M.: TReX: A tool for reachability analysis of complex systems. In: Berry, G., Comon, H., Finkel, A. (eds.) CAV 2001. LNCS, vol. 2102, pp. 368–372. Springer, Heidelberg (2001)
2. Bardin, S., Finkel, A., Leroux, J., Petrucci, L.: Fast: acceleration from theory to practice. Int. J. Software Tools Technology Transfer (STTT) 10(5), 401–424 (2008)
3. Boigelot, B., Wolper, P.: Symbolic verification with periodic sets. In: Dill, D.L. (ed.) CAV 1994. LNCS, vol. 818, pp. 55–67. Springer, Heidelberg (1994)
4. Bouajjani, A., Habermehl, P.: Symbolic reachability analysis of FIFO-channel systems with nonregular sets of configurations. Theor. Comput. Sci. 221(1-2), 211–250 (1999)
5. Bozga, M., Iosif, R., Konečný, F.: Fast acceleration of ultimately periodic relations. In: Touili, T., Cook, B., Jackson, P. (eds.) CAV 2010. LNCS, vol. 6174, pp. 227–242. Springer, Heidelberg (2010)
6. Cadilhac, M., Finkel, A., McKenzie, P.: Bounded parikh automata. Int. J. Found. Comput. Sci. 23(8), 1691–1710 (2012)

7. Chambart, P., Finkel, A., Schmitz, S.: Forward analysis and model checking for trace bounded WSTS. In: Kristensen, L.M., Petrucci, L. (eds.) PETRI NETS 2011. LNCS, vol. 6709, pp. 49–68. Springer, Heidelberg (2011)
8. Comon, H., Jurski, Y.: Multiple counters automata, safety analysis and Presburger arithmetic. In: Vardi, M.Y. (ed.) CAV 1998. LNCS, vol. 1427, pp. 268–279. Springer, Heidelberg (1998)
9. Esparza, J., Ganty, P., Majumdar, R.: A perfect model for bounded verification. In: Proc. LICS 2012, pp. 285–294. IEEE Computer Society (2012)
10. Finkel, A., Iyer, S.P., Sutre, G.: Well-abstracted transition systems: Application to FIFO automata. Information and Computation 181(1), 1–31 (2003)
11. Ginsburg, S., Spanier, E.H.: Bounded ALGOL-like languages. Trans. Amer. Math. Soc. 113, 333–368 (1964)
12. Ginsburg, S., Spanier, E.H.: Bounded regular sets. Proc. Amer. Math. Soc. 17(5), 1043–1049 (1966)
13. Ginsburg, S., Spanier, E.H.: Semigroups, Presburger formulas and languages. Pacific J. Math. 16(2), 285–296 (1966)
14. Ginsburg, S.: The Mathematical Theory of Context-Free Languages. McGraw-Hill (1966)
15. Hopcroft, J., Pansiot, J.J.: On the reachability problem for 5-dimensional vector addition systems. Theor. Comput. Sci. 8(2), 135–159 (1979)
16. Ibarra, O.H., Seki, S.: Characterizations of bounded semilinear languages by one-way and two-way deterministic machines. Int. J. Found. Comput. Sci. 23(6), 1291–1306 (2012)
17. Ibarra, O.H., Seki, S.: On the open problem of Ginsburg concerning semilinear sets and related problems. Theor. Comput. Sci. 501, 11–19 (2013)
18. Leroux, J., Penelle, V., Sutre, G.: On the context-freeness problem for vector addition systems. In: Proc. LICS 2013, pp. 43–52. IEEE Computer Society (2013)
19. Leroux, J., Praveen, M., Sutre, G.: A relational trace logic for vector addition systems with application to context-freeness. In: D'Argenio, P.R., Melgratti, H. (eds.) CONCUR 2013. LNCS, vol. 8052, pp. 137–151. Springer, Heidelberg (2013)
20. Liu, L., Weiner, P.: A characterization of semilinear sets. J. Comput. Syst. Sci. 4(4), 299–307 (1970)
21. Schrijver, A.: Theory of Linear and Integer Programming. John Wiley and Sons, New York (1987)
22. Schwer, S.R.: The context-freeness of the languages associated with vector addition systems is decidable. Theor. Comput. Sci. 98(2), 199–247 (1992)

Efficiently and Completely Verifying Synchronized Consistency Models[*]

Yi Lv[1], Luming Sun[1], Xiaochun Ye[2], Dongrui Fan[2], and Peng Wu[1]

[1] State Key Laboratory of Computer Science,
Institute of Software, Chinese Academy of Sciences, China
[2] State Key Laboratory of Computer Architecture,
Institute of Computing Technology, Chinese Academy of Sciences, China

Abstract. The physical time order information can help verifying the memory model of a multiprocessor system rather efficiently. But we find that this time order based approach is limited to the sequential consistency model. For most relaxed memory models, an incompatible time order may possibly result in a false negative verdict. In this paper, we extend the original time order based approach to synchronized consistency models, and propose an active frontier approach to rule out such false verdicts based on a reasonably relaxed time order. Our approach can be applied to most known memory models, especially to those with non-atomic write operations, while nevertheless retaining the efficiency of the original time order based approach. We implement our approach in a Memory Order Dynamic Verifier (MODV). A case study with an industrial Godson-T many-core processor demonstrates the effectiveness and efficiency of our approach. Several bugs of the design of this processor are also found by MODV.

1 Introduction

With the increasingly aggressive development of hardware optimization technologies, most multi-core processors support relaxed memory models for the sake of high performance. Synchronized consistency models, such as release consistency [1] and scope consistency [2], were usually deployed in software Distributed Shared Memory (DSM) systems. Recently, these models have been implemented at the hardware level by many-core systems [3] and network-on-chip based multi-core systems [4,5]. These systems allow out-of-order executions of the memory access operations within lock protected code sections. Such relaxation would trigger more nondeterministic executions dramatically, hence making it more difficult to verify these relaxed memory models. The verification problem of synchronized consistency models has been rarely studied so far due to its high complexity.

---

[*] This work is partially supported by the National Natural Science Foundation of China under Grants No.61272135, No.61100015, No.61204047, No.61100069, and No.61161130530.

F. Cassez and J.-F. Raskin (Eds.): ATVA 2014, LNCS 8837, pp. 264–280, 2014.

A common way to verify the memory model of a multiprocessor system is by running concurrent test programs on the system and then checking whether their executions comply with the memory model under concern. Test programs can be pre-specified or generated randomly. A directed constraint graph can be constructed on the memory access operations in an execution. The edges of the graph represent the order between these operations as permitted by the memory model under concern. In this way, a cycle in the graph would mean a violation of the memory model under concern.

The problem of verifying an execution against a memory model is NP-complete in general [6]. It has been shown that for a constant number of processors, it can take just linear time (in the number of operations) to solve this problem with the aid of the pending period information of operations [7,8]. The pending period of an operation is the interval between the time when the operation is *issued* and the time when the operation is *committed*. Intuitively, two operations in an execution can be ordered in the physical time if one of them is committed before the other one is issued.

However, we find that this time order based approach does not even apply to the total store order (TSO) memory model [9] because it implicitly assumes that the time order along an execution is compatible with the memory model under concern. This underlying assumption does not apply to the TSO/x86 memory model. Fig. 1 shows a typical execution on an x86 microprocessor [10]. In this execution, the write operation w_{11} (respectively, w_{21}) writes the value 1 to the memory address A (respec-

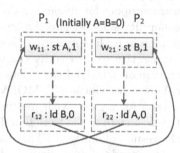

Fig. 1. A False Cycle

tively, B) on processor P_1 (respectively, P_2). But the read operation r_{12} (respectively, r_{22}) still reads the initial value 0 at the memory address B (respectively, A). In Fig. 1, the solid edges represent the TSO edges, while the dashed boxes indicates the pending periods of the operations. These dashed boxes are not overlapped, hence inducing the time order edges (represented by the dashed edges in Fig. 1). The original time order based approach in [7,8] would treat the cycle of edges in Fig. 1 as a violation of the TSO/x86 memory model. This would also happen to synchronized consistency models, which neither guarantee write operations to be atomic. Therefore, the original time order based approach is limited to the sequential consistency (SC) memory model.

In this paper, we extend the original time order based approach to synchronized consistency models. Given an execution, the synchronization operations accessing the same locks are mutually exclusive to each other under synchronized consistency models. Therefore, these operations need to be executed in a sequentially consistent way. This also applies to the write operations accessing the same addresses. Our approach aims to find total orders between these synchronization operations and between these write operations, in order to justify the execution against the synchronized consistency model under concern. To avoid the above false negative results by the original time order based approach, we relax the notion of time order so that the write operations in an execution can be ordered approximately in the time when these operations are globally visible to all processors. In this way, the relaxed time order along the execution is compatible with the relaxed memory models that do not guarantee write operations to be atomic.

We then propose an active frontier approach to deal with synchronized consistency models based on the notion of relaxed time order. Those operations that should be executed sequentially are identified in separate and composed into active frontiers based on their relaxed pending period information. Our approach is proved to be sound and complete, in the sense that it can indeed find the necessary total orders as a witness if the given execution complies with the synchronized consistency model under concern, and vice versa. As far as we know, our approach provides the first efficient solution for the verification problem of synchronized consistency models.

A precise implementation of our approach would require extra dedicated hardware support for retrieving the time information of executions. For the sake of generality and cost-effectiveness, we implement an over-approximation of our approach in a Memory Order Dynamic Verifier (MODV). As the main case study, we use this tool to verify the memory model of Godson-T, a many-core architecture of industrial size. Memory accesses inside any region were assumed to be coherent for Godson-T. MODV finds that such coherence is actually not guaranteed for regions with multiple locks. This ambiguity has been confirmed by the designers of Godson-T and corrected in its programming manual based on the results of our work. This case study shows that MODV can handle hundreds of thousands of operations on 16 cores in minutes.

2   Related Work

We refer to [11] and [12] for a survey on memory consistency models. Synchronized consistency models such as release consistency [1], entry consistency [13], scope consistency [2] and location consistency [14] have also been uniformly defined in [12] in an axiomatic style.

An empirical approach was presented in [15] to generate litmus tests automatically for multi-core processors. Formal verification techniques have been applied to verify concurrent programs for memory models. To name a few, [16] used the explicit model checker Murφ for operational memory models; while [17] used a SAT solver for axiomatic memory models. [18] presented a verification approach for store buffer safety by non-intrusively monitoring the sequential consistent executions of concurrent programs. However, these techniques still suffer from the scalability issue.

Dynamic analysis has gained more attention for the verification problem of memory consistency models. It can be broadly classified into two categories: hardware-assisted and software-based methods. In hardware-assisted methods, the runtime information such as read mapping and write order can be directly collected through auxiliary hardware. Consequently, efficient verification algorithms can be developed with the time complexity of $O(n)$, where n is the number of the operations in the given execution [19,20,21]. However, this advantage is often offset by extra design effort and silicon area consumption, as well as performance loss, on the hardware level.

On the contrary, software-based methods avoid such nontrivial hardware support by deriving the runtime information from the given execution. The first software-based method was the frontier graph method presented in [6] for the SC memory model. Its time complexity is $O(n^p)$, where p is the number of processors. A sound but incomplete algorithm for the TSO memory model was first proposed in [22] with the time complexity of $O(n^5)$. This algorithm was extended in [23] based on the concept of vector clocks, with the time complexity reduced to $O(pn^3)$. The vector clocks in [23] is computed out by splitting the given execution into virtual SC processors. Another more efficient implementation of [22] was presented in [24] with the time complexity of $O(n^4)$. Furthermore, a backtracking algorithm was proposed in [25] to make the software-based methods complete. The time complexity of this backtracking algorithm is $O(n^p/p^p \times pn^3)$.

The most closely related work to ours are [7,8], where the additional pending period information was exploited for the sake of efficiency. But their approaches are sound only for the SC memory model and may report false negative results for the memory models that do not guarantee write operations to be atomic.

3   Synchronized Consistency Models

In this section, we introduce the memory orders of synchronized consistency models [12]. Herein, we consider four types of operations: read, write, acquire and release. Suppose a multiprocessor system consists of $p \geq 1$ processors with a shared memory. Let A, B denote a memory address, and l denote a lock.

A read operation r in the form of "$ld\ A, i$" reads the value i from the memory address A, while a write operation w in the form of "$st\ B, i$" writes the value i to the memory address B.[1] Let $add(r)$ and $val(r)$ be the memory address that r accesses and the value that r reads, respectively. Similarly, let $addr(w)$ and $val(w)$ be the memory address that w accesses and the value that w writes, respectively. Read and write operations are referred to as memory operations in this paper.

An acquire operation s^a in the form of "$acq\ l$" acquires the lock l, while a release operation s^r in the form of "$rel\ l$" releases it. Let $lock(s^a)$ and $lock(s^r)$ be the locks that s^a and s^r access, respectively. Acquire and release operations are referred to as synchronization operations, denoted s, in this paper. These operations can be used together to implement other atomic synchronization operations, such as barrier operations.

Let u, v denote an operation in general, and $\mathbb{O}$ be the set of all operations. An execution of the system is a tuple $\sigma = (\sigma_1, \ldots, \sigma_p)$, where $\sigma_i = u_{i,1} \ldots u_{i,n_i}$ is a finite sequence of operations on the i-th processor with $1 \leq i \leq p, n_i \geq 1$.

---

[1] Without loss of generality, we assume that all written values are different.

On each σ_i, acquire and release operations should appear in pairs for the same locks. A fragment of σ_i from an acquire operation s^a to its accompanying release operation s^r constitutes a *synchronization session*, denoted $S = (s^a, s^r)$. Similarly, let $lock(S)$ be the lock that protects the synchronization session S, i.e., $lock(S) = lock(s^a) = lock(s^r)$.

An execution of the system is obtained typically by running a concurrent test program on the system. In an execution σ, two operations u and v of the same processor constitute a *program order* pair, denoted $u \xrightarrow{P} v$, if u is executed before v as dictated by the program. We use the notion of *constraint function* [24] to specify the program order that must be abided under a memory model. A constraint function $cf : \mathbb{O} \times \mathbb{O} \rightarrow Boolean$ of a memory model is defined such that $cf(u, v) = true$ if u must be executed before v under the memory model. In weak consistency, two write operations w_1 and w_2 with $addr(w_1) = addr(w_2)$ must be executed in their program order. In release consistency, an acquire operation s^a must be executed before any read operation r such that $s^a \xrightarrow{P} r$; while in scope consistency, this only happens when s^a and r belong to the same synchronization session.

With the above notations, we now define the axioms of memory orders of synchronized consistency models. A synchronized consistency model with its constraint function cf requires the following partial orders to be satisfied by any execution σ of the system:

Writes-to Order. A write operation w and a read operation r of two different processors constitute a *writes-to order* pair, denoted $w \xrightarrow{Wt} r$, if r reads the value that w writes, i.e., $val(r) = val(w)$.

Local Order. Two operations u and v of the same processor constitute a *local order* pair, denoted $u \xrightarrow{L} v$, if $u \xrightarrow{P} v$ and one of the following two conditions holds:
  - $cf(u, v) = true$ if either u or v is a memory operation;
  - u and v are both synchronization operations with $lock(u) = lock(v)$.

Synchronization Order. Given two synchronization sessions $S = (s^a, s^r)$ and $S' = (s'^a, s'^r)$ with $lock(S) = lock(S')$, S and S' must be mutually exclusive to each other. This can be formally defined as $(s^r \xrightarrow{Syn} s'^a) \oplus (s'^r \xrightarrow{Syn} s^a)$, where $\oplus$ is the exclusive disjunction operator. Consequently, the synchronized sessions protected by the same lock should be able to be serialized in a total synchronization order.

Coherence Order. Given two write operations w_1 and w_2 with $addr(w_1) = addr(w_2)$, w_1 and w_2 should be able to be serialized. This can be formally defined as $(w_1 \xrightarrow{Co} w_2) \oplus (w_2 \xrightarrow{Co} w_1)$. Then, a read operation r and a write operation w with $addr(r) = addr(w)$ constitute an *inferred* coherence order pair, denoted $r \xrightarrow{Co} w$, if there is a write operation w' such that $w' \xrightarrow{Co} w$ and $val(w') = val(r)$.

This axiom of coherence order was referred to as *write atomicity* in [11], *coherence* in [12,26,27] and *store atomicity* in [7]. Similarly, a total coherence order should exist between the write operations that access the same memory address. In this paper, we include this axiom for the generality of our approach. It is not supported by all synchronized consistency models. Whenever this axiom is included, a local order pair $w \xrightarrow{L} w'$ should hold for any write operations w and w' such that $w \xrightarrow{P} w'$ and $addr(w) = addr(w')$.

Global Order. The transitive closure of the above orders is referred to as global order in this paper. Two operations u and v constitute a *global order* pair, denoted $u \xrightarrow{G} v$, if $(u \xrightarrow{Wt} v)$, or $(u \xrightarrow{L} v)$, or $(u \xrightarrow{Syn} v)$, or $(u \xrightarrow{Co} v)$, or there exists an operation u' along the execution such that $u \xrightarrow{G} u'$ and $u' \xrightarrow{G} v$.

Herein, the axiomatic definitions of *Local Order* and *Synchronization Order* are similar to those in [12]. Alternatively, synchronized consistency models can be defined by a "view" method, where each processor has its own view of memory orders of operations [12]. This method has been applied to characterize POWER processors [27]. The memory orders defined in this section can be easily transformed as a linear view order for each processor over all of its operations, together with all the write and synchronization operations of the other processors. In this case, all the processors would share the same view of inter-processor writes-to, synchronization and coherence orders.

4 Baseline Algorithm

Given an execution of a multiprocessor system and a synchronized consistency model with its constraint function, we aim to develop an algorithm that can decide whether the execution complies with the synchronized consistency model. In this section we propose a baseline algorithm for this purpose with an extended notion of frontier.

As in [22,23,24,25], we model the given execution as a constraint graph (V, E), where V is a finite set of nodes representing the operations in the given execution, and $E \subseteq V \times V$ is a finite set of edges representing the ordered pairs of these operations. For brevity, we refer to the operations and the corresponding nodes by the same notation. Then, for two operations u and v, $(u, v) \in E$ if $u \xrightarrow{G} v$.

For the orders defined in Section 3, the corresponding edges can be categorized into two classes: static and dynamic edges. The writes-to and local order edges are static in the sense that these edges are fixed in the constraint graph and can be determined directly by the given execution. On the contrary, the synchronization and coherence order edges have to be constructed tentatively in order to establish the necessary total synchronization and coherence orders.

We extend the notion of frontier [6] to present the search routine for the dynamic edges that can fit in certain total synchronization and coherence orders. For an execution $\sigma = (\sigma_1, \ldots, \sigma_p)$, let $addr(\sigma)$ and $lock(\sigma)$ be the set of the addresses and locks accessed in σ, respectively. Let $\sigma_i|_A$ be the projection of σ_i on the write operations accessing the address $A \in addr(\sigma)$, and $\sigma_i|_l$ be the projection of σ_i on the synchronization operations accessing the lock $l \in lock(\sigma)$.

Without loss of generality, let A_j and l_k range over the addresses in $addr(\sigma)$ and the locks in $lock(\sigma)$, respectively, with $1 \leq j \leq |addr(\sigma)|$ and $1 \leq k \leq |lock(\sigma)|$. Then, a *frontier* is a tuple $f = (w_{11}, \ldots, w_{p|addr(\sigma)|}, s_{11}, \ldots, s_{p|lock(\sigma)|})$, where w_{ij} is a write operation on the i-th processor with $addr(w_{ij}) = A_j$ and s_{ik} is a synchronization operation on the i-th processor with $lock(s_{ik}) = l_k$ for $1 \leq i \leq p, 1 \leq j \leq |addr(\sigma)|, 1 \leq k \leq |lock(\sigma)|$.

Intuitively, in a frontier f, there is one and only one write operation on each processor that accesses each memory address, as well as one and only one synchronization operation on each processor that accesses each lock. A next frontier $f' = f\{u'/u\}$ results from f by replacing u in f with u' such that u and u' belong to the same i-th processor (for some $1 \leq i \leq p$) and u' is the follow-up operation of u on $\sigma_i|_{addr(u)}$ (if u is a write operation) or $\sigma_i|_{lock(u)}$ (if u is a synchronization operation). Then, u' is referred to as the *active* operation of f'. Especially, we attach the beginning operation $\perp$ before the first operation of each $\sigma_i|_{A_j}$ and $\sigma_i|_{l_k}$, and the ending operation $\top$ after the last operation of each $\sigma_i|_{A_j}$ and $\sigma_i|_{l_k}$. The beginning frontier (denoted $f_\perp$) and the ending frontier (denoted $f_\top$) are the ones consisting of $p(|addr(\sigma)| + |lock(\sigma)|)$ beginning and ending operations, respectively.

The baseline algorithm is shown in Algorithm 1. In this algorithm, the static edges are added first and then checked for a possible cycle (Lines 1-2). It can be seen that the constraint graph is acyclic at Line 4. Then, dynamic edges are searched for through a recursive function ExploreFrontier (Line 5).

Algorithm 1. Baseline Algorithm

Input: an execution and the constraint function of a memory model
Output: true if no cycle has been detected, and false otherwise

1 Add writes-to and local order edges;
2 **if** *the above static edges result in a cycle* **then**
3 | **return** false;
4 $f_0 \leftarrow$ the beginning frontier;
5 $sat \leftarrow$ ExploreFrontier(f_0);
6 **return** sat;

The function ExploreFrontier, shown in Function 2, explores all the possible frontiers in a depth-first manner. At Line 8, a synchronization order edge is added tentatively between the two latest visited synchronization sessions accessing $lock(u')$; while at Line 12, a coherence order edge is added tentatively between the two latest visited write operations accessing $addr(u')$, together with the coherence order edges inferred from it. Then, the newly added dynamic edges are checked for a possible cycle in the current constraint graph (Line 13). Such a cycle would invalidate the newly added dynamic edges. Hence, if a cycle is detected, the newly added dynamic edges are then removed (Line 14). If all the next frontiers of f have been explored without achieving an acyclic constraint graph, then the function ExploreFrontier returns back to its caller with the negative result at Line 19. If this means to return to Algorithm 1, then there is no way to establish a total synchronization order and a total coherence order over the given execution.

Function 2. ExploreFrontier(f)

Input: a frontier f
Output: true if no cycle has been detected, and false otherwise
1 **if** f *is the ending frontier* **then**
2 | **return** true;
3 $res \leftarrow$ false;
4 **for** *each next frontier f' of f* **do**
5 | $u' \leftarrow$ the active operation of f';
6 | **switch** (u') **do**
7 | **case** u' *is an acquire operation*
8 | Add the edge $s^r \xrightarrow{Syn} u'$, where s^r is the last active release operation with $lock(s^r) = lock(u')$;
9 | **case** u' *is a write operation*
10 | $w \leftarrow$ the last active write operation with $addr(w) = addr(u')$;
11 | **for** *each r such that $val(r) = val(w)$* **do**
12 | Add the edges $w \xrightarrow{Co} u'$ and $r \xrightarrow{Co} u'$;
13 | **if** FindPath(u', u') **then**
14 | Remove the newly added edge(s);
15 | **else**
16 | $res \leftarrow$ ExploreFrontier(f');
17 | **if** res **then**
18 | break;
19 **return** res;

If the ending frontier is eventually reached, then the function `ExploreFrontier` returns directly the positive result (Line 2), which will be carried over to Algorithm 1 through Line 18. In this case, the necessary total synchronization and coherence orders have just been established for the given execution.

As shown in Function 3, we implement the cycle checking function `FindPath`(u, v) in a straightforward way for the baseline algorithm. It is meant to find a path from u to v in the current constraint graph. A cycle passing through an operation u' can then be detected by calling this function with (u', u').

Function 3. FindPath(u, v)

Input: operations u and v
Output: true if there is a path from u to v, and false otherwise
1 **for** *each v' such that $u \xrightarrow{G} v'$* **do**
2 | **if** $v' = v$ *or* FindPath(v', v) **then**
3 | **return** true;
4 **return** false;

It can be seen that the baseline algorithm is sound and complete for synchronized consistency models, in the sense that it returns false if and only if the given execution does not satisfy the memory model under concern. This can be proved in the similar way as in [25]. But the baseline algorithm would scale poorly because of the combinatorial explosion of the number of frontiers to be explored. Suppose the given execution σ contains n operations on p processors. Then, the baseline algorithm needs to explore at most $O(n^{p(|addr(\sigma)|+|lock(\sigma)|)})$ frontiers. Each time a frontier is confronted, it takes at most $O(n)$ time to check if the newly added dynamic edge(s) would cause a cycle. Moreover, it takes at most $O(n^2)$ time to check whether static edges may result in a cycle. Hence, the worst time complexity is $O(n^2 + n^{p(|addr(\sigma)|+|lock(\sigma)|)+1})$ in total.

5   Exploiting Time Order Information

Apparently the baseline algorithm can not deal with large executions efficiently. In this section we first recall and relax the definition of time order for synchronized consistency models. Then, we present an improvement of the baseline algorithm by taking into account the relaxed time order of the given execution.

In a multiprocessor system with a unique global physical clock, an operation can neither affect others before being issued (namely, entering the instruction window of a processor); nor can be affected after having been committed (namely, having retired from the instruction window of the processor). For an operation u, let $t_e(u)$ and $t_c(u)$ denote the *enter time* when u is issued and the *commit time* when u is committed, respectively. Obviously, $t_e(u) < t_c(u)$ for any operation u. The *pending period* of the operation u is the time interval $[t_e(u), t_c(u)]$. Then, two operations with disjoint pending periods can be ordered in physical time. This can be formalized as the *time order* T such that $u \xrightarrow{T} v$ if $t_c(u) \le t_e(v)$, otherwise $u \xrightarrow{T} v$.

The notion of time order defines a natural order between the operations along the given execution. The time order edges can be determined implicitly by checking the enter and commit time of the related operations.

However, as shown in Fig. 1, the time order is not naturally compatible with the global order in general. According to the definitions in Section 3, the two solid edges in Fig. 1 are actually coherence order edges, which are inferred from the fact that r_{22} and r_{12} read the initial value 0 of A and B, respectively. Then, w_{11} (respectively, w_{21}) is committed when it writes to the internal write buffer of the processor P_1 (respectively, P_2). At this moment, w_{11} (respectively, w_{21}) has not been performed globally. Hence, the values written by w_{11} and w_{21} are not yet visible to all the processors.

Let $t_p(u)$ denote the *performed time* when the operation u is performed globally and is visible to all processors. A read operation is performed globally when it fetches a value from the specified memory address, while a write operation is performed globally when it stores the specified value to the main memory (or the L2 cache for a multi-core processor). A synchronization operation is performed globally when it gets the access to the specified lock. Hence, it can be seen that all but non-atomic write operations would take effect before being committed. Obviously, $t_e(u) < t_p(u)$ for any operation u.

If the time order can be rectified by replacing the commit time of an operation with its performed time, the cycle in Fig. 1 can then be eliminated, as shown in Fig. 2 (where the dashed boxes surrounding the write operations are enlarged to indicate their expanded pending periods).

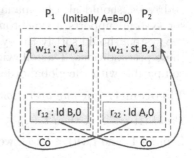

Fig. 2. False Cycle is Eliminated

However, the performed time of a write operation can not be observed directly from the given execution. We choose to approximate it based on the pending period information of the related read operations and its follow-up operations.

Definition 1 (Relaxed Time Order). *The* relaxed commit time *of an operation u, denoted $t_{rc}(u)$, is defined as follows:*

- *if u is a read or synchronization operation, $t_{rc}(u) = t_c(u)$;*
- *if u is a write operation, $t_{rc}(u) = \min_{v \in N(u)} t_{rc}(v)$ if $N(u) \neq \emptyset$, where $N(u) = \{v \mid u \xrightarrow{Wt} v, \text{ or } u \xrightarrow{L} v\}$; otherwise, $t_{rc}(u) = t_\infty$, where t_∞ is a sufficiently large time constant such that any operation in the given execution will be performed by then.*

Accordingly, the relaxed pending period *of the operation u is the time interval $[t_e(u), t_{rc}(u)]$. Any operations u and v constitute a relaxed time order* pair, *denoted $u \xrightarrow{RT} v$, if $t_{rc}(u) \leq t_e(v)$; otherwise, $u \xrightarrow{RT} v$.*

The following lemma shows that the relaxed pending period of an operation u covers its performed time, i.e., $t_e(u) < t_p(u) \leq t_{rc}(u)$. The details of its proof can be found in the technical report [28].

Lemma 1. $t_p(u) \leq t_{rc}(u)$ *for any operation u.*

Moreover, it is generally accepted that a multiprocessor system should be designed to be able to guarantee certain physical time constraints under its memory model [7,8]. Definition 2 summarizes the time constraints for the implementation mechanisms of multiprocessor systems.

Definition 2 (Preconditions of Time Order). *For any operations u and v:*

1. *If $u \xrightarrow{P} v$, then u is issued no later than v, i.e., $t_e(u) \leq t_e(v)$.*
2. *If $u \xrightarrow{G} v$, then u is performed no later than v, i.e., $t_p(u) \leq t_p(v)$.*

These preconditions are defined following the same principles as in the original time order based approach [7,8]. For a read operations r and a write operation w, if $w \xrightarrow{Wt} r$, then r can only fetch the value $val(w)$ after w stores it into the main memory. Hence, $t_p(w) \leq t_p(r)$. Similarly, synchronization operations accessing the same locks, as well as write operations accessing the same memory addresses, should also be managed in a serializable manner. If a multiprocessor system supports a synchronized consistency model, then any execution of the system should satisfy the synchronized consistency model without violating these preconditions. The following theorem shows that the relaxed time order is compatible with the global order under the preconditions in Definition 2.

Theorem 1. *For any operations u and v, $u \xrightarrow{G} v$ implies $v \xrightarrow{RT} u$.*

Proof. If $u \xrightarrow{G} v$, then $t_p(u) \le t_p(v)$ by Definition 2. Since $t_p(v) \le t_{rc}(v)$ (by Lemma 1) and $t_e(u) < t_p(u)$, we have $t_e(u) < t_{rc}(v)$, i.e., $v \xrightarrow{RT} u$. □

We now present the final algorithm that can take advantages of the relaxed time order. In addition to the given execution and the constraint function of the memory model under concern, the time information of the execution is required as part of the input to the final algorithm. This time information will be preprocessed by the final algorithm to compute the relaxed pending periods of the operations. Then, the final algorithm proceeds as the baseline algorithm, except replacing the function ExploreFrontier of the baseline algorithm with the function ExploreActiveFrontier, shown in Function 4.

Function 4. ExploreActiveFrontier(f)

Input: a frontier f
Output: true if no cycle has been detected, and false otherwise

1 **if** *f is the ending frontier* **then**
2 | **return** true;
3 $res \leftarrow$ false;
4 **for** *each next active frontier f' of f* **do**
5 | $u' \leftarrow$ the active operation of f';
6 | **switch** (u') **do**
7 | | **case** *u' is an acquire operation*
8 | | | Add the edge $s^r \xrightarrow{Syn} u'$, where s^r is the last active release operation with $lock(s^r) = lock(u')$;
9 | | **case** *u' is a write operation*
10 | | | $w \leftarrow$ the last active write operation with $addr(w) = addr(u')$;
11 | | | **for** *each r such that $val(r) = val(w)$* **do**
12 | | | | **if** $u' \xrightarrow{RT} r$ **then**
13 | | | | | **return** res;
14 | | | **for** *each r such that $val(r) = val(w)$ and $u' \xrightarrow{RT} r$* **do**
15 | | | | Add the edges $w \xrightarrow{Co} u'$ and $r \xrightarrow{Co} u'$;
16 | | **if** FindTimedPath(u', u') **then**
17 | | | Remove the newly added edges;
18 | | **else**
19 | | | $res \leftarrow$ ExploreActiveFrontier(f');
20 | | | **if** res **then**
21 | | | | break;
22 **return** res;

At Line 4 of Function 4, only active frontiers need to be explored. Given an execution σ, the *active period of a write operation* w on the i-th processor is the time interval $[t_e(w), t_{rc}(w')]$, where w' is the follow-up write operation of w in $\sigma_i|_{addr(w)}$; while the *active period of a synchronization operation* s on the i-th processor is the time interval $[t_e(s), t_{rc}(s')]$, where s' is the follow-up synchronization operation of s in $\sigma_i|_{lock(s)}$. Then, a frontier f is *active* if each operation in f is in the active period of each other operation in f. The notion of active frontier is inspired by the notion of feasible frontier in [8]. But [8] concerns only the SC memory model and assumes the pending periods of two consecutive operations on the same processor are always overlapped.

In this way, the frontiers that are not active under the physical time can be ignored without missing any chance to establish the correctness of the given execution. At Line 13 of Function 4, a cycle is detected with $r \xrightarrow{Co} u'$ and $u' \xrightarrow{RT} r$. This is contrary to Theorem 1, which directly means a violation of the given memory model under the preconditions in Definition 2. At Line 16 of Function 4, a new cycle checking function FindTimedPath is called to check for a possible cycle in the current constraint graph under the relaxed time order.

The function FindTimedPath (u, v), shown in Function 5, only needs to examine the operations within the relaxed pending period of the operation v. For any operation v' such that $u \xrightarrow{G} v'$, if it is committed before the relaxed pending period of the operation v, then there exists a relaxed time order edge from v' to v, i.e., $v' \xrightarrow{RT} v$. Thus, a timed path $u \xrightarrow{G} v' \xrightarrow{RT} v$ is resulting from the current constraint graph (at Line 3 of Function 5). If $u = v$, this path constitutes a cycle that invalidates the newly added dynamic edges. In this way, the subsequent global order edges from v' need not to be further checked. For an operation v' issued after the relaxed pending period of the operation v, the global order edge $u \xrightarrow{G} v'$ would be considered as a time order edge for later cycle checking.

Function 5. FindTimedPath(u, v)

Input: operations u and v
Output: true if there is a path backing to u from v, and false otherwise
1 **for** *each v' such that $u \xrightarrow{G} v'$ and $v \xrightarrow{RT} v'$* **do**
2 | **if** $v' = v$ *or* $v' \xrightarrow{RT} v$ *or* FindTimedPath(v', v) **then**
3 | | **return** true;
4 **return** false;

Since the relaxed time order is compatible with the global order, it can be seen that the final algorithm is sound and complete, as stated in the following theorem. The details of its proof can be found in the technical report [28].

Theorem 2 (Soundness and Completeness of the Final Algorithm). *The final algorithm presented in this section returns false if and only if the given execution does not satisfy the given synchronized consistency model under the preconditions in Definition 2.*

Time Complexity. Suppose in the relaxed pending period of an operation, there are C operations running on each processor. C is usually a hardware-dependant constant [7]. Then, at most $O(nC^{p(|addr(\sigma)|+|lock(\sigma)|)-1})$ active frontiers need to be explored. Similarly, when an active frontier is confronted, it would only take $O(pC)$ time to check for a possible cycle within the relaxed pending period of the latest active operation. So the upper bound of the time complexity of active frontier traversal is $O(npC^{p(|addr(\sigma)|+|lock(\sigma)|)})$. Furthermore, it would take at most $O(n^2)$ time to relax the pending periods of write operations. Recall that it would also take at most $O(n^2)$ time to check whether static edges may cause a cycle. Hence, the worst time complexity of this final algorithm is $O(2n^2 + npC^{p(|addr(\sigma)|+|lock(\sigma)|)})$ in total. Obviously, the final algorithm would scale much better with large executions than the baseline algorithm.

6   Experimental Results

It can be seen that a precise implementation of the final algorithm would closely depend on the time information of executions. However, it requires extra hardware support with specific internal registers to retrieve the enter time and commit time of each operation. Similar to [8], we uses the general performance counter sampling mechanism to over-approximate the pending period information of operations. Hence, the soundness of the final algorithm is preserved under this approximation. We have developed a Memory Order Dynamic Verifier (MODV) to implement our algorithms.[2] Through combining different constraint functions and axiomatic rules of memory orders, MODV can support various memory models, including SC, TSO/x86 and typical synchronized consistency models.

Performance counters have been supported by most industrial processors. In a multiprocessor system, the values of performance counters can be scanned out from its internal registers through certain debug interface. The pending period information of each operation can be computed out through scanning performance counters periodically, though the actual time order information may be lost partially during the consecutive scans. The tighter the performance counter scan period is, the more precise the pending period information obtained can be. But, a tight scan period would exert too much pressure on the system performance. The performance counter scan period is set to be 600 cycles per scan in the following experiments.

As the main case study, we use MODV to verify the memory model of the Godson-T many-core architecture [3]. Godson-T is a many-core processor with 64 homogeneous processing cores, each of which has a 16KB private instruction cache and a 32KB local memory. Moreover, a dedicated synchronization manager provides architectural support for mutual exclusion and barrier synchronization. The memory model of Godson-T is a variant of scope consistency. Godson-T uses a region-based cache coherence (RCC) protocol to support large-scale parallelism. A region is exactly a synchronization session defined in this paper.

---

[2] MODV is available at http://lcs.ios.ac.cn/~lvyi/MODV/index.html

MODV has found several bugs in the design of Godson-T. One of them is related to Godson-T's memory model. Memory accesses inside any region were assumed to be coherent for Godson-T. But actually this is not guaranteed for regions with multiple locks. MODV finds this bug through an execution shown in Fig. 3 (with simplification for clarity). In this execution, $w_{13} \xrightarrow{Wt} r_{22}$ because r_{22} reads the value of w_{13}; Similarly, $w_{12} \xrightarrow{Wt} r_{33}$. Then, since $w_{12} \xrightarrow{L} w_{13}$, an inferred coherence order edge exists between r_{33} and w_{13}, i.e., $r_{33} \xrightarrow{Co} w_{13}$. Moreover, $r_{22} \xrightarrow{RT} r_{33}$ because $t_{rc}(r_{22}) < t_e(r_{33})$. Hence, the cycle $w_{13} \xrightarrow{Wt} r_{22} \xrightarrow{RT} r_{33} \xrightarrow{Co} w_{13}$ is detected.

The reason of this cycle is as follows. When a processor writes a value into a memory address in a region, it first stores the value into its internal cache, and then writes through into the memory (L2 cache) immediately. If a processor reads a memory address for the first time in a region, it first invalidates its cache, and then reads the value from the memory directly. For the subsequent read operations to the same memory address in the same region, it will read the value from its cache. Therefore, r_{32} and

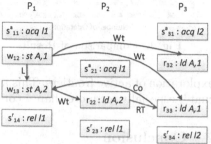

Fig. 3. A Bug of Godson-T

r_{33} reads the value 1 from the memory and from P_3's cache, respectively. In the meanwhile, the values of the same memory address at the memory and at P_2's cache are both 2. Hence, the memory system of Godson-T is not cache coherent for regions with multiple locks.

We then illustrate the performance of our algorithms with large scale test programs. All the experiments have been carried out on a Linux server with four 8-core 2.4GHz Intel Xeon processors and 48GB memory. To validate synchronization and coherence orders together, we randomly generate concurrent test programs with 60% load instructions and 30% store instructions for 2 different addresses, and 10% synchronization instructions for one lock. Branch instructions are not used in these programs.

Fig. 4 shows the average performance of the baseline and final algorithms for up to 100K operations on 2 cores. It can be seen that the final algorithm performs much better than the baseline algorithm when the number of operations increases. As a matter of fact, for no less than 4K operations on no less than 4 cores, the baseline algorithm often cannot return within 8 hours. Fig. 5 shows the average performance of the final algorithm on 2, 4, 8 and 16 cores. It can be seen that with the aid of the relaxed time order, the final algorithm also scales well with the increasing numbers of cores.

The fluctuations in Fig. 5 are because the information derived from consecutive scans is an over-approximation of the pending periods of the operations. The lost time order information would result in extra backtracking during the

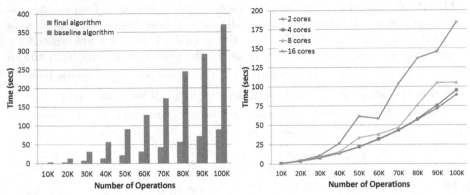

Fig. 4. Comparison of Results   **Fig. 5.** Performance Test

exploration of active frontiers. This makes the time consumption of MODV fluctuate, especially for more than 4 cores.

7   Conclusion

We present in this paper a relaxed time order based active frontier approach for verifying synchronized consistency models. The original notion of frontier is expanded with the memory addresses and the locks accessed along an execution. Then, we integrate this extended frontier approach with the pending period information of operations. The notion of active frontier is introduced to reduce the number of frontiers to be explored and the number of operations to be examined for cycle checking. In literature, the notion of time order has not yet been widely appreciated due to its incompatibility issue. Our approach addresses this issue by relaxing the time order of the given execution in a conservative way. On one hand, our approach is sound in the sense that it would not produce false negative results for memory models with non-atomic write operations. On the other hand, our approach is also complete in the sense that it can guarantee to detect a cycle if the given execution does not comply with the memory model under concern.

Without loss of generality and cost-effectiveness, we have implemented an over-approximation of our approach in a verification tool MODV. The tool preserves the soundness of our approach, and can be easily customized to support various memory models with user-defined constraint functions and user-selected memory orders. We have used MODV to verify the memory model of the Godson-T many-core processor, and found that Godson-T does not support the coherence order for regions with multiple locks. This bug has been confirmed by the designers of Godson-T. Its programming manual has been revised based on the results of our work. This case study shows that our approach is very efficient in practice for detecting subtle bugs in multiprocessor systems.

Our approach exploits the advantages of time order for verifying a wider range of memory models. As the future work, we will investigate the memory models of the POWER and ARM architectures, where write operations are also not guaranteed to be atomic.

References

1. Gharachorloo, K., Lenoski, D., Laudon, J., Gibbons, P., Gupta, A., Hennessy, J.: Memory consistency and event ordering in scalable shared-memory multiprocessors. In: Baer, J., Snyder, L., Goodman, J.R. (eds.) ISCA 1990, pp. 15–26. ACM (1990)
2. Iftode, L., Singh, J.P., Li, K.: Scope consistency: A bridge between release consistency and entry consistency. Theory of Computing Systems 31(4), 451–473 (1998)
3. Fan, D., Zhang, H., Wang, D., Ye, X., Song, F., Li, G., Sun, N.: Godson-T: An efficient many-core processor exploring thread-level parallelism. IEEE Micro 32(2), 38–47 (2012)
4. Naeem, A., Jantsch, A., Lu, Z.: Scalability analysis of memory consistency models in NoC-based distributed shared memory SoCs. IEEE Transactions on Computer-Aided Design of Integrated Circuits and Systems 32(5), 760–773 (2013)
5. Hansson, A., Goossens, K., Bekooij, M., Huisken, J.: CoMPSoC: A template for composable and predictable multi-processor system on chips. ACM Trans. Des. Autom. Electron. Syst. 14(1), 2:1–2:24 (2009)
6. Gibbons, P.B., Korach, E.: On testing cache-coherent shared memories. In: SPAA 1994, pp. 177–188. ACM (1994)
7. Chen, Y., Lv, Y., Hu, W., Chen, T., Shen, H., Wang, P., Pan, H.: Fast complete memory consistency verification. In: HPCA 2009, pp. 381–392. IEEE Computer Society (2009)
8. Hu, W., Chen, Y., Chen, T., Qian, C., Li, L.: Linear time memory consistency verification. IEEE Transactions on Computers 61(4), 502–516 (2012)
9. Sindhu, P., Frailong, J.M., Cekleov, M.: Formal specification of memory models. In: Dubois, M., Thakkar, S. (eds.) Scalable Shared Memory Multiprocessors, US, pp. 25–41. Springer, Heidelberg (1992)
10. Sorin, D.J., Hill, M.D., Wood, D.A.: A primer on memory consistency and cache coherence. Synthesis Lectures on Computer Architecture 6(3), 1–212 (2011)
11. Adve, S.V., Gharachorloo, K.: Shared memory consistency models: A tutorial. IEEE Computer 29, 66–76 (1996)
12. Robert, C.S., Gary, J.N.: A unified theory of shared memory consistency. J. ACM 51(5), 800–849 (2004)
13. Bershad, B., Zekauskas, M., Sawdon, W.: The Midway distributed shared memory system. In: COMPCON 1993. Digest of Papers, pp. 528–537 (1993)
14. Gao, G., Sarkar, V.: Location consistency: a new memory model and cache consistency protocol. IEEE Transactions on Computers 49(8), 798–813 (2000)
15. Alglave, J., Maranget, L., Sarkar, S., Sewell, P.: Litmus: Running tests against hardware. In: Abdulla, P.A., Leino, K.R.M. (eds.) TACAS 2011. LNCS, vol. 6605, pp. 41–44. Springer, Heidelberg (2011)
16. Park, S., Dill, D.L.: An executable specification, analyzer and verifier for RMO (relaxed memory order). In: SPAA 1995, pp. 34–41. ACM (1995)
17. Yang, Y., Gopalakrishnan, G., Lindstrom, G., Slind, K.: Nemos: a framework for axiomatic and executable specifications of memory consistency models. In: IPDPS 2004, pp. 31–40. IEEE Computer Society (2004)

18. Burckhardt, S., Musuvathi, M.: Effective program verification for relaxed memory models. In: Gupta, A., Malik, S. (eds.) CAV 2008. LNCS, vol. 5123, pp. 107–120. Springer, Heidelberg (2008)

19. Meixner, A., Sorin, D.: Dynamic verification of memory consistency in cache-coherent multithreaded computer architectures. IEEE Transactions on Dependable and Secure Computing 6(1), 18–31 (2009)

20. Lu, S., Tucek, J., Qin, F., Zhou, Y.: AVIO: Detecting atomicity violations via access-interleaving invariants. IEEE Micro 27(1), 26–35 (2007)

21. DeOrio, A., Wagner, I., Bertacco, V.: Dacota: Post-silicon validation of the memory subsystem in multi-core designs. In: HPCA 2009, pp. 405–416. IEEE Computer Society (2009)

22. Hangal, S., Vahia, D., Manovit, C., Lu, J.Y.J.: TSOtool: A program for verifying memory systems using the memory consistency model. In: ISCA 2004, pp. 114–123. IEEE Computer Society (2004)

23. Manovit, C., Hangal, S.: Efficient algorithms for verifying memory consistency. In: SPAA 2005, pp. 245–252. ACM (2005)

24. Roy, A., Zeisset, S., Fleckenstein, C., Huang, J.: Fast and generalized polynomial time memory consistency verification. In: Ball, T., Jones, R.B. (eds.) CAV 2006. LNCS, vol. 4144, pp. 503–516. Springer, Heidelberg (2006)

25. Manovit, C., Hangal, S.: Completely verifying memory consistency of test program executions. In: HPCA 2006, pp. 166–175. IEEE Computer Society (2006)

26. Alglave, J., Fox, A., Ishtiaq, S., Myreen, M.O., Sarkar, S., Sewell, P., Nardelli, F.Z.: The semantics of POWER and ARM multiprocessor machine code. In: Proceedings of the 4th Workshop on Declarative Aspects of Multicore Programming, DAMP 2009, pp. 13–24. ACM (2009)

27. Mador-Haim, S., et al.: An axiomatic memory model for POWER multiprocessors. In: Madhusudan, P., Seshia, S.A. (eds.) CAV 2012. LNCS, vol. 7358, pp. 495–512. Springer, Heidelberg (2012)

28. Lv, Y., Sun, L., Ye, X., Fan, D., Wu, P.: Efficiently and completely verifying synchronized consistency models. Technical Report ISCAS-SKLCS-14-07, State Key Laboratory of Computer Science, Institute of Software, Chinese Academy of Sciences (2014), http://lcs.ios.ac.cn/~lvyi/MODV/files/ISCAS-SKLCS-14-07.pdf

Symmetry Reduction in Infinite Games
with Finite Branching*

Nicolas Markey[1] and Steen Vester[2]

[1] LSV, CNRS & ENS Cachan, France
markey@lsv.ens-cachan.fr
[2] Technical University of Denmark, Kgs. Lyngby, Denmark
stve@dtu.dk

Abstract. Symmetry reductions have been applied extensively for the verification of finite-state concurrent systems and hardware designs using model-checking of temporal logics such as LTL, CTL and CTL*, as well as real-time and probabilistic-system model-checking. In this paper we extend the technique to handle infinite-state games on graphs with finite branching where the objectives of the players can be very general. As particular applications, it is shown that the technique can be applied to reduce the state space in parity games as well as when doing model-checking of the temporal logic ATL*.

1 Introduction

Symmetry reduction techniques have been introduced in model-checking around twenty years ago for combatting the state-space explosion in systems that posses some amount of symmetry [6,9,11,5]. The idea is to merge states of a system that behave in the same way with respect to a given property φ. This provides a smaller model of the system which exhibits the same behaviors as the original model with respect to φ; therefore model-checking can be performed on the smaller model, yielding a more efficient verification procedure since the original model need not be constructed. While the technique does not guarantee a great efficiency improvement in general, it has been applied to a large number of practical cases with great success [11,5,6,10,13,15]. These applications include extensions from traditional model-checking of finite-state transition systems to real-time systems [10] and probabilistic systems [13]. It seems that many naturally occuring instances of model-checking of concurrent and hardware systems contain symmetry and therefore the technique is very applicable.

In this paper, we extend symmetry reduction for transition systems to symmetry reduction of games. Games can be used to naturally model concurrent and reactive systems and have applications in the synthesis of programs. We expect that on practical instances, symmetry reduction in games should be as applicable as it has been in model-checking of temporal logics. Our contribution is to extend the symmetry reduction technique introduced in [9,6] to games. A central

---

* Partly supported by ERC Starting Grant EQualIS and EU FP7 project Cassting.

F. Cassez and J.-F. Raskin (Eds.): ATVA 2014, LNCS 8837, pp. 281–296, 2014.

result in these papers is a correspondence lemma that describes a correspondence between paths in an original model M and in a reduced model M^G. This correspondence is used to conclude that CTL* model-checking can be performed in the reduced model instead of the original model. In our setting, the correspondence lemma describes a correspondence between *strategies* in an original game $\mathcal{M}$ and in a reduced game $\mathcal{M}^G$. This lemma can then be used to establish a correspondence between winning strategies in the original game and in the reduced game for many different types of objectives. In particular, it follows from this that ATL* model-checking can be performed in the reduced game, and that parity games can be reduced while preserving existence of winning strategies. However, the technique is applicable for a much more general set of objectives. The proof that the reduction works for games is technically more involved than for finite-state transition systems, due to the possible irregular behaviours of an opponent player. This phenomenon leads us to apply König's Lemma [12] in order to prove the correspondence between the original game and the reduced game. In addition, our approach does not restrict to finite-state games but also works for games played on infinite graphs, provided that they have finite branching. This includes weighted games (e.g. with energy or mean-payoff objectives), pushdown games, games played on VASS, etc.

2   Preliminaries

In this paper, we consider turn-based games played by two players I and II on a graph with finite branching.

Definition 1. *A 2-player turn-based game structure is a tuple* $\mathcal{M} = (S, R, S_I, S_{II})$ *where*

- S *is a set of states;*
- $R \subseteq S \times S$ *is a total transition relation such that for each state* $s \in S$ *there is only a finite number of states* $t \in S$ *such that* $(s, t) \in R$;
- S_I *and* S_{II} *is a partition of* S, *i.e.* $S_I \cup S_{II} = S$ *and* $S_I \cap S_{II} = \emptyset$.

Whenever we write *game structure* (or simply *game*) in the following, we mean 2-player turn-based game structure with finite branching, unless otherwise stated. We say that a state s is owned by player $P \in \{I, II\}$ if $s \in S_P$. A game is played by placing a token on an initial state s_0. Then it proceeds for an infinite number of rounds where in each round, the player owning the current state (the state on which the token is currently placed) must choose to move the token to a state t such that $(s, t) \in R$.

We denote by S^*, S^+ and S^ω the set of finite sequences of states, the set of non-empty finite sequences of states and the set of infinite sequences of states respectively. For a sequence $\rho = s_0 s_1 \ldots$ of states we define $\rho_i = s_i$, $\rho_{\leq i} = s_0 \ldots s_i$ and $\rho_{\geq i} = s_i s_{i+1} \ldots$. When ρ is finite, i.e. $\rho = s_0 \ldots s_\ell$ we write $\text{last}(\rho) = s_\ell$ and $|\rho| = \ell$. A play is a sequence $s_0 s_1 \ldots \in S^\omega$ such that $(s_i, s_{i+1}) \in R$ for all $i \geq 0$. The set of all plays is denoted $\text{Play}_{\mathcal{M}}$. For $s_0 \in S$, the set of plays with initial state s_0 is denoted $\text{Play}_{\mathcal{M}}(s_0)$. A history is a prefix of a play. The set of all histories (resp. histories with initial state s_0) is denoted $\text{Hist}_{\mathcal{M}}$ (resp. $\text{Hist}_{\mathcal{M}}(s_0)$). A strategy for player $P \in \{\text{I}, \text{II}\}$ is a partial mapping $\sigma_P \colon \text{Hist}_{\mathcal{M}} \to S$ defined for all histories $h \in \text{Hist}_{\mathcal{M}}$ such that $\text{last}(h) \in S_P$, with the requirement that $(\text{last}(h), \sigma_P(h)) \in R$. We say that a play (resp. history) $\rho = s_0 s_1 \ldots$ (resp. $\rho = s_0 \ldots s_\ell$) is compatible with a strategy σ_P for player $P \in \{\text{I}, \text{II}\}$ if $\sigma_P(\rho_{\leq i}) = \rho_{i+1}$ for all $i \geq 0$ (resp. $0 \leq i < \ell$) such that $\rho_i \in S_P$. We write $\text{Play}(s_0, \sigma_P)$ (resp. $\text{Hist}(s_0, \sigma_P)$) for the set of plays (resp. histories) starting in s_0 that are compatible with σ_P. An objective is a set $\Omega \subseteq \text{Play}_{\mathcal{M}}$ of plays. A play ρ satisfies an objective Ω iff $\rho \in \Omega$. We say that σ_P is a winning strategy for player $P \in \{\text{I}, \text{II}\}$ from state s_0 with objective Ω if $\text{Play}(s_0, \sigma_P) \subseteq \Omega$. If such a strategy exists, we say that s_0 is a winning state for player P with objective Ω. The set of winning states for player P with objective Ω in game $\mathcal{M}$ is denoted $W_{\mathcal{M}}^P(\Omega)$.

3   Symmetry Reduction

In the following we fix a game $\mathcal{M} = (S, R, S_{\text{I}}, S_{\text{II}})$.

Definition 2. *A permutation π of S is a symmetry for $\mathcal{M}$ if for all $s, s' \in S$*

1. *$(s, s') \in R \Leftrightarrow (\pi(s), \pi(s')) \in R$*
2. *$s \in S_{\text{I}} \Leftrightarrow \pi(s) \in S_{\text{I}}$*

Let $\text{Sym}_{\mathcal{M}}$ be the set of all symmetries in $\mathcal{M}$. We call a set G of symmetries a *symmetry group* if $(G, \circ)$ is a group, where $\circ$ is the composition operator defined by $(f \circ g)(x) = f(g(x))$. We consider G to be a fixed symmetry group in the rest of this section.

Definition 3. *The orbit $\theta(s)$ of a state s induced by G is given by*

$$\theta(s) = \{s' \in S \mid \exists \pi \in G. \ \pi(s) = s'\}.$$

Notice that when $s' \in \theta(s)$, then also $s \in \theta(s')$. The orbits induce an equivalence relation $\sim_G$ defined by $s \sim_G s'$ if, and only if, $s \in \theta(s')$. The reason for $\sim_G$ being an equivalence relation is that G is a group. The orbit $\theta(s)$ can be thought of as a set of states that have the same behavior as s with respect to the symmetry defined by G. For a sequence $\rho = s_0 s_1 \ldots$ of states we define $\theta(\rho) = \theta(s_0)\theta(s_1) \ldots$ From each orbit $\theta(s)$, we choose a unique state $\text{rep}(\theta(s)) \in \theta(s)$ as a representative of the orbit. For a strategy σ of player $P \in \{\text{I}, \text{II}\}$, an initial state s_0 and a sequence $t_0 \ldots t_\ell$ of orbits, we choose a unique representative history $\text{rep}_{s_0, \sigma}(t_0 \ldots t_\ell) = s_0 \ldots s_\ell$ that is compatible with σ and such that $s_i \in t_i$ for all $0 \leq i \leq \ell$, provided that such a history exists; notice that the sequence $t_0 \ldots t_\ell$ is arbitrary, so that it could be the case that no such representative exists. In the later case, we let $\text{rep}_{s_0, \sigma}(t_0 \ldots t_\ell) = \perp$.

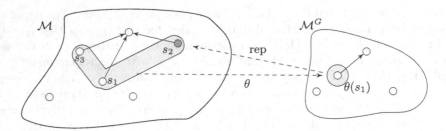

Fig. 1. Schematic representation of symmetry reduction, with three states s_1, s_2 and s_3 being in the same orbit in $\mathcal{M}$, and identified as the same state $\theta(s_1)$ in $\mathcal{M}^G$, with s_2 as its representative

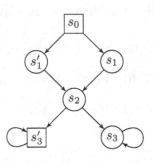

Notice that representative histories can not always "respect" prefixes (in the sense that the k-th prefix of the representative of a history is the representative of k-th prefix of that history): consider the game opposite, and the strategy σ that in s_2 goes to s_3 if s_1 was visited and to s_3' otherwise. There is a symmetry exchanging states s_1 and s_1' (and leaving the other states unchanged). Now, consider the sequence $h = \theta(s_0)\theta(s_1)\theta(s_2)$, and fix some representative for it (either $s_0 s_1 s_2$ or $s_0 s_1' s_2$). Then the extensions of h with $\theta(s_3)$ and $\theta(s_3')$ both have σ-compatible representatives, but one of them will not respect prefixes.

We are now ready to define the notion of a quotient game.

Definition 4. *Given a game* $\mathcal{M} = (S, R, S_{\mathrm{I}}, S_{\mathrm{II}})$ *and a symmetry group* G, *we define the quotient game* $\mathcal{M}^G = (S^G, R^G, S_{\mathrm{I}}^G, S_{\mathrm{II}}^G)$ *by*

- $S^G = \{\theta(s) \mid s \in S\}$
- $R^G = \{(\theta(s), \theta(s')) \mid (s, s') \in R\}$
- $S_P^G = \{\theta(s) \mid s \in S_P\}$ *for* $P \in \{\mathrm{I}, \mathrm{II}\}$

Notice that $\mathcal{M}^G$ is indeed a game structure: symmetries respect the partition of S into S_{I} and S_{II}, and therefore S_{I}^G and S_{II}^G also constitute a partition of S^G. Also, R^G is total and has finite branching.

Example 1. Consider the game $\mathcal{M} = (S, R, S_{\mathrm{I}}, S_{\mathrm{II}})$ to the left in Fig. 2 and define

$$G = \left\{ \pi \in \mathrm{Sym}_{\mathcal{M}} \middle| \begin{array}{l} \pi(s_0, s_1, s_2, s_3, s_4, s_5) = (s_0, s_1, s_2, s_3, s_4, s_5) \\ \pi(s_0, s_1, s_2, s_3, s_4, s_5) = (s_0, s_4, s_2, s_3, s_1, s_5) \\ \pi(s_0, s_1, s_2, s_3, s_4, s_5) = (s_0, s_1, s_3, s_2, s_4, s_5) \\ \pi(s_0, s_1, s_2, s_3, s_4, s_5) = (s_0, s_4, s_3, s_2, s_1, s_5) \end{array} \right\}$$

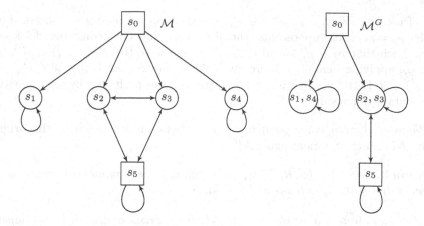

Fig. 2. A game $\mathcal{M}$ to the left that has symmetric properties and the quotient game $\mathcal{M}^G$ induced by G on the right

It is easy to see that G is a symmetry group. G now induces the orbits $\{s_0\}, \{s_5\}, \{s_2, s_3\}, \{s_1, s_4\}$. This gives rise to the quotient game $\mathcal{M}^G$ to the right in Fig. 2. Note how the construction gives us a smaller game that still has many of the structural properties of the original game.

We begin with two simple lemmas, which are not particular to our game setting and actually correspond to Lemma 3.1 of [9]. We reprove them here for the sake of completeness.

The first lemma shows a correspondence between transitions in the reduced game and transitions in the original game:

Lemma 1. *Let $(t, t') \in R^G$ be a transition in $\mathcal{M}^G$, and $s \in t$. Then there is a state s' of $\mathcal{M}$ such that $s' \in t'$ and $(s, s') \in R$.*

Proof. By definition of R^G, from the transition (t, t') in R^G, we get the existence of a transition (u, u') in R, with $u \in t$ and $u' \in t'$. Now, since s and u are in t, there is a symmetry π such that $s = \pi(u)$. By definition of a symmetry, we then have $(\pi(u), \pi(u')) \in R$ and $\pi(u') \in t'$ (because $u' \in t'$), so that letting $s' = \pi(u')$ proves the lemma.

We can extend the above correspondence to plays:

Lemma 2. *Let $\mathcal{M} = (S, R, S_{\mathrm{I}}, S_{\mathrm{II}})$ be a game and G be a symmetry group. Then*

1. *For each play $\rho \in \mathrm{Play}_{\mathcal{M}}$, there exists a play $\rho' \in \mathrm{Play}_{\mathcal{M}^G}$ such that $\rho_i \in \rho'_i$ for all $i \geq 0$;*
2. *For each play $\rho' \in \mathrm{Play}_{\mathcal{M}^G}$, and for each $s \in \rho'_0$, there exists a play $\rho \in \mathrm{Play}_{\mathcal{M}}(s)$ such that $\rho_i \in \rho'_i$ for all $i \geq 0$.*

Proof. (1) Suppose $\rho \in \mathrm{Play}_{\mathcal{M}}$. Then for every $i \geq 0$ we have $(\rho_i, \rho_{i+1}) \in R$. This implies that $(\theta(\rho_i), \theta(\rho_{i+1})) \in R^G$. Thus, $\theta(\rho) \in \mathrm{Play}_{\mathcal{M}^G}$. Since $\rho_i \in \theta(\rho_i)$ the result follows.

(2) Pick $\rho' \in \text{Play}_{\mathcal{M}^G}$, and $s \in \rho'_0$. We construct a play ρ as follows. First, we let $\rho_0 = s$. Next, suppose that the history $\rho_{\leq i}$ has been constructed for some $i \geq 0$ such that $\rho_j \in \rho'_j$ for all $0 \leq j \leq i$. We have that $(\rho'_i, \rho'_{i+1}) \in R^G$, and $\rho_i \in \rho'_i$; applying Lemma 1, there must exist a state s' such that $s' \in \rho'_{i+1}$ and $(\rho_i, s') \in R$. Letting $\rho_{i+1} = s'$, we have extended our prefix $\rho_{\leq i}$ by one transition. This entails our result.   □

We now show a correspondence lemma between strategies in the original game $\mathcal{M}$ and the quotient game $\mathcal{M}^G$.

Lemma 3. *Let $\mathcal{M} = (S, R, S_{\text{I}}, S_{\text{II}})$ be a game, G be a symmetry group, $s_0 \in S$ be an initial state, $t_0 = \theta(s_0)$ and $P \in \{\text{I}, \text{II}\}$. Then*

1. *For any strategy σ of player P in $\mathcal{M}$, there exists a strategy σ' of player P in $\mathcal{M}^G$ such that, for all $t_0 t_1 \ldots \in \text{Play}_{\mathcal{M}^G}(t_0, \sigma')$, there exists $s_0 s_1 \ldots \in \text{Play}_{\mathcal{M}}(s_0, \sigma)$ where $s_i \in t_i$ for all $i \geq 0$;*
2. *For any strategy σ' of player P in $\mathcal{M}^G$, there exists a strategy σ of player P in $\mathcal{M}$ such that, for all $s_0 s_1 \ldots \in \text{Play}_{\mathcal{M}}(s_0, \sigma)$, there exists a play $t_0 t_1 \ldots \in \text{Play}_{\mathcal{M}^G}(t_0, \sigma')$ where $s_i \in t_i$ for all $i \geq 0$.*

Proof. (1) Let σ be a strategy for player $P \in \{\text{I}, \text{II}\}$ in the original game $\mathcal{M}$. From this we construct a strategy σ' for player P in the quotient game $\mathcal{M}^G$ by

$$\sigma'(h) = \theta(\sigma(\text{rep}_{s_0, \sigma}(h)))$$

for all $h \in \text{Hist}_{\mathcal{M}^G}$ such that $\text{rep}_{s_0, \sigma}(h) \neq \bot$ and arbitrarily when $\text{rep}_{s_0, \sigma}(h) = \bot$. This strategy is well-defined, i.e., it is coherent with the transition relation. Indeed, when $\text{rep}_{s_0, \sigma}(h) \neq \bot$, we have

$$(\text{last}(\text{rep}_{s_0, \sigma}(h)), \sigma(\text{rep}_{s_0, \sigma}(h))) \in R$$
$$\Rightarrow (\theta(\text{last}(\text{rep}_{s_0, \sigma}(h))), \theta(\sigma(\text{rep}_{s_0, \sigma}(h)))) \in R^G$$
$$\Rightarrow (\text{last}(h), \sigma'(h)) \in R^G.$$

This means that there is a legal transition to the successor state prescribed by the strategy σ'.

Now, let $\rho = t_0 t_1 \ldots \in \text{Play}_{\mathcal{M}^G}(t_0, \sigma')$ be an arbitrary play compatible with σ' in $\mathcal{M}^G$ from t_0. We construct a directed tree T where the root is labelled by $u_0 = s_0$ and where the labelling of the infinite paths in T are exactly the plays compatible with σ in $\mathcal{M}$ from s_0. From this tree we obtain a new tree T_ρ by cutting away from T part of the branches labelled $u_0 u_1 \ldots$ on which there exists $i \geq 0$ such that $u_i \notin t_i$. If j is the smallest number such that $u_j \notin t_j$ then the nodes labelled $u_j u_{j+1} \ldots$ are removed. The situation is illustrated in Fig. 3. We assume for a contradiction that T_ρ has finite height ℓ. This means that there must be a branch in the tree labelled by the history $\text{rep}_{s_0, \sigma}(t_0, \ldots, t_\ell) = u_0 \ldots u_\ell$, because if we had $\text{rep}_{s_0, \sigma}(t_0, \ldots, t_\ell) = \bot$ then T_ρ would have had height smaller than ℓ. There are now two cases to consider:

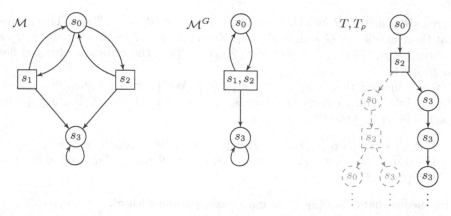

Fig. 3. From left to right is drawn the original game $\mathcal{M}$, the quotient arena $\mathcal{M}^G$ and the trees T, T_ρ where $G = \{(s_0, s_1, s_2, s_3), (s_0, s_2, s_1, s_3)\}$, $\sigma(h) = s_2$ for all histories h ending in s_0, and $\rho = \theta(s_0)\theta(s_1)\theta(s_3)^\omega$. T and T_ρ are drawn together: T is the whole tree, while T_ρ only consists of the solid black nodes.

- Suppose $u_\ell \in S_P$. Then due to the definition of σ' we get

$$\sigma(u_0 \ldots u_\ell) = \sigma(\mathrm{rep}_{s_0,\sigma}(t_0 \ldots t_\ell)) \in \sigma'(t_0 \ldots t_\ell) = t_{\ell+1}.$$

Since $u_0 \ldots u_\ell \sigma(s_0 \ldots s_\ell)$ is compatible with σ and $u_i \in t_i$ for $0 \le i \le \ell$ then $u_0 \ldots u_\ell \sigma(s_0 \ldots s_\ell)$ is the labelling of a path in T_ρ, which gives a contradiction since it has length $\ell + 1$.
- Suppose $u_\ell \notin S_P$. Applying Lemma 1 for $(t_\ell, t_{\ell+1}) \in R_G$ and u_l, we get a state $v \in t_{\ell+1}$ such that $(u_\ell, v) \in R$. Since u_ℓ is not in S_P, we get that $u_0 \ldots u_\ell v$ is compatible with σ, so that it is the labelling of a path in T_ρ of length $\ell + 1$. This gives a contradiction as well.

This means that the height of T_ρ is unbounded. Still, it could be the case that all branches are finite, in case the tree has infinite branching. Assuming T_ρ is finitely branching, it must have an infinite path according to König's Lemma. Let the labelling of such a path be $s_0 s_1 \ldots$ Since $s_0 s_1 \ldots$ is the labelling of an infinite path in T_ρ, it is a play compatible with σ, since all infinite paths in T_ρ are infinite paths in T. Moreover, since it is an infinite path in T_ρ, it satisfies $s_i \in t_i$ for all $i \ge 0$, because otherwise it would not be present in T_ρ. This proves the first part since $t_0 t_1 \ldots$ was an arbitrary play compatible with σ'.

(2) Let σ' be a strategy for player P in $\mathcal{M}^G$. Define σ from this in such a way that

$$\sigma(s_0 \ldots s_\ell) \in \sigma'(\theta(s_0) \ldots \theta(s_\ell))$$

for all histories $s_0 \ldots s_\ell$ in $\mathcal{M}$ with $s_\ell \in S_I$. Note that when $s_0 \ldots s_\ell$ is a history in $\mathcal{M}$ then $\theta(s_0) \ldots \theta(s_\ell)$ is a history in $\mathcal{M}^G$. Further, we need to check that there exists a state $s \in \sigma'(\theta(s_0) \ldots \theta(s_\ell))$ such that $(s_\ell, s) \in R$ in order for the definition to make sense. This can be seen as follows. Since $(\theta(s_\ell), \sigma'(\theta(s_0) \ldots \theta(s_\ell))) \in R^G$

there exists $(u, v) \in R$ such that $u \in \theta(s_\ell)$ and $v \in \sigma'(\theta(s_0) \ldots \theta(s_\ell))$. This means that there exists $\pi \in G$ with $\pi(u) = s_\ell$. Now, $(u, v) \in R \Rightarrow (\pi(u), \pi(v)) \in R \Rightarrow (s_\ell, \pi(v)) \in R$. Since $\pi(v) \in \theta(v) = \sigma'(\theta(s_0) \ldots \theta(s_\ell))$ the state $s = \pi(v)$ satisfies the property.

Now, suppose that $s_0 s_1 \ldots \in \text{Play}_{\mathcal{M}}(\sigma)$. We prove that $\theta(s_0)\theta(s_1) \ldots \in \text{Play}_{\mathcal{M}^G}(\sigma')$, which entails (2) since $s_i \in \theta(s_i)$ for all $i \geq 0$. For any prefix $\theta(s_0) \ldots \theta(s_\ell)$ we have that

- If $\theta(s_\ell) \notin S_P^G$ then $(s_\ell, s_{\ell+1}) \in R$ implies that $(\theta(s_\ell), \theta(s_{\ell+1})) \in R^G$.
- If $\theta(s_\ell) \in S_P^G$ then $s_{\ell+1} = \sigma(s_0 \ldots s_\ell) \in \sigma'(\theta(s_0) \ldots \theta(s_\ell)) \Rightarrow \theta(s_{\ell+1}) = \sigma'(\theta(s_0) \ldots \theta(s_\ell))$

This means that $\theta(s_0)\theta(s_1) \ldots$ is indeed compatible with σ'. $\qquad \square$

This lemma leads to desirable properties of the quotient game when certain types of objectives are considered.

Definition 5. *A symmetry group G preserves the objective Ω if for any two plays $s_0 s_1 \ldots$ and $s_0' s_1' \ldots$ in $\text{Play}_{\mathcal{M}}$, if $s_0 s_1 \ldots \in \Omega$ and $s_i \sim_G s_i'$ for all $i \geq 0$, then also $s_0' s_1' \ldots \in \Omega$.*

If Ω is an objective and G is a symmetry group that preserves it, then we denote by Ω^G the objective in the quotient game $\mathcal{M}^G$ defined as $\Omega^G = \{\theta(s_0)\theta(s_1) \ldots \mid s_0 s_1 \ldots \in \Omega\}$. Lemma 3 gives us the following.

Theorem 1. *Let $\mathcal{M}$ be a game, G be a symmetry group that preserves the objective Ω, $P \in \{\text{I}, \text{II}\}$ and $s_0 \in S$. Then*

$$s_0 \in W_{\mathcal{M}}^P(\Omega) \text{ if, and only if, } \theta(s_0) \in W_{\mathcal{M}^G}^P(\Omega^G).$$

Proof. $(\Rightarrow)$ Suppose player P has a winning strategy σ in $\mathcal{M}$ with objective Ω from state s_0. Then $\text{Play}_{\mathcal{M}}(s_0, \sigma) \subseteq \Omega$. According to Lemma 3 there is a strategy σ' for player P in $\mathcal{M}^G$ such that for a given play $t_0 t_1 \ldots \in \text{Play}_{\mathcal{M}^G}(\theta(s_0), \sigma')$ there exists a play $s_0 s_1 \ldots \in \text{Play}_{\mathcal{M}}(s_0, \sigma)$ with $s_i \in t_i$ for all $i \geq 0$. Since G preserves Ω and $\text{Play}_{\mathcal{M}}(s, \sigma) \subseteq \Omega$ this means that $t_0 t_1 \ldots \in \Omega^G$. Since $t_0 t_1 \ldots$ is an arbitrary play compatible with σ' from $\theta(s_0)$ we have $\text{Play}_{\mathcal{M}^G}(\theta(s_0), \sigma') \subseteq \Omega^G$ and thus $\theta(s_0) \in W_{\mathcal{M}^G}^P(\theta(s_0), \sigma')$.

$(\Leftarrow)$ Suppose player P has a winning strategy σ' in $\mathcal{M}^G$ with objective Ω^G from state $\theta(s_0)$. Then $\text{Play}_{\mathcal{M}^G}(\theta(s_0), \sigma') \subseteq \Omega^G$. According to Lemma 3 there is a strategy σ for player P in $\mathcal{M}$ such that for a given play $s_0 s_1 \ldots \in \text{Play}_{\mathcal{M}}(s_0, \sigma)$ there exists a play $t_0 t_1 \ldots \in \text{Play}_{\mathcal{M}^G}(\theta(s_0), \sigma')$ with $s_i \in t_i$ for all $i \geq 0$. Since G preserves Ω and $\text{Play}_{\mathcal{M}^G}(\theta(s_0), \sigma') \subseteq \Omega^G$ this means that $s_0 s_1 \ldots \in \Omega$. Since $s_0 s_1 \ldots$ is an arbitrary play compatible with σ from s_0 we have $\text{Play}_{\mathcal{M}}(s_0, \sigma) \subseteq \Omega$ and thus $s_0 \in W_{\mathcal{M}}^P(s_0, \sigma)$. $\qquad \square$

Corollary 1. *Let $\mathcal{M}$ be a game, G be a symmetry group that preserves the objective Ω, $P \in \{\text{I}, \text{II}\}$ and $s, s' \in S$ be such that $s \sim_G s'$. Then*

$$s \in W_{\mathcal{M}}^P(\Omega) \text{ if, and only if, } s' \in W_{\mathcal{M}}^P(\Omega).$$

We have now shown the main result of this paper, namely that a winning strategy exists in the original game if, and only if, it exists in the quotient game. This also implies that there is a winning strategy from a state s in the original game if, and only if, there is a winning strategy from another state s' that belongs to the same orbit. For transition systems the correspondence between existence of paths in the original system and the quotient system as shown in Lemma 2 was enough to show that model-checking of a CTL* formula in the original system can be reduced to model-checking the same formula in the quotient system if the symmetry group preserves the labelling [9,6]. However, due to the possible behaviors of an opponent player we have had to generalize this result in Lemma 3 which directly leads to Theorem 1. It will be used in Section 4 to show that we can extend the symmetry reduction approach to ATL*, even for infinite-state games. Since we apply König's Lemma in the proof, we have assumed that the games are finitely branching. We leave it as an open problem whether the technique can be generalized to infinitely branching games as well.

4   Applications

In this section we illustrate some examples of applications of Theorem 1. We look at symmetry reductions for parity games and games with properties defined in temporal logics. We also consider an example of an infinite game with a corresponding quotient game that is finite. This makes it possible for us to decide existence of winning strategies in the original game by using standard techniques on the quotient game. Notice that this could be applied to infinite-state games such as games on counter- or pushdown systems, etc. (provided that we have a suitable symmetry group at hand).

4.1   Parity Games

Let $\mathcal{M} = (S, R, S_\mathrm{I}, S_\mathrm{II})$ be a game and let $c\colon S \to \{0, \ldots, k\}$ be a coloring function that assigns a color to each state of the game. From this, the corresponding parity objective is given by $\Omega_c = \{s_0 s_1 \ldots \in \mathrm{Play}_{\mathcal{M}} \mid \min \mathrm{Inf}\{c(s_i) \mid i \in \mathbb{N}\}$ is odd$\}$, where Inf takes as input an infinite sequence and returns the set of items that appear infinitely many times in this sequence. A parity game is a game with a parity objective [8]. We say that a symmetry group G preserves c if for all $s, s' \in S$ we have $s \sim_G s' \Rightarrow c(s) = c(s')$. When G preserves c, we define a coloring function c^G on the set of orbits by $c^G(t) = c(\mathrm{rep}(t))$ for all orbits t. Using Theorem 1 we now get the following result for parity games when we have a symmetry group preserving the coloring function.

Proposition 1. *Let $\mathcal{M} = (S, R, S_\mathrm{I}, S_\mathrm{II})$ be a game, $c\colon S \to \{0, \ldots, k\}$ be a coloring function, G be a symmetry group that preserves c, $s \in S$, and $P \in \{\mathrm{I}, \mathrm{II}\}$. Then*

1. G preserves the objective Ω_c,
2. $\Omega_c^G = \{\theta(s_0)\theta(s_1) \ldots \in \mathrm{Play}_{\mathcal{M}^G} \mid \min \mathrm{Inf}\{c^G(\theta(s_i)) \mid i \in \mathbb{N}\}$ is odd$\}$,

3. $s \in W^P_{\mathcal{M}}(\Omega_c)$ *if, and only if,* $\theta(s) \in W^P_{\mathcal{M}^G}(\Omega^G_c)$.

Proof. (1) Suppose $s_0 s_1 \ldots \in \Omega$ and $s'_0 s'_1 \ldots \in \text{Play}_{\mathcal{M}}$ satisfy $s_i \sim_G s'_i$ for all $i \geq 0$. Then $\min \text{Inf}\{c(s'_i) \mid i \in \mathbb{N}\} = \min \text{Inf}\{c(s_i) \mid i \in \mathbb{N}\}$ is odd since G preserves c. Thus, $s'_0 s'_1 \ldots \in \Omega_c$ and G preserves Ω_c.
(2) This can be seen as follows

$$
\begin{aligned}
\Omega^G_c &= \{\theta(s_0)\theta(s_1)\ldots \in \text{Play}_{\mathcal{M}^G} \mid s_0 s_1 \ldots \in \Omega_c\} \\
&= \{\theta(s_0)\theta(s_1)\ldots \in \text{Play}_{\mathcal{M}^G} \mid \min \text{Inf}\{c(s_i) \mid i \in \mathbb{N}\} \text{ is odd}\} \\
&= \{\theta(s_0)\theta(s_1)\ldots \in \text{Play}_{\mathcal{M}^G} \mid \min \text{Inf}\{c(\text{rep}(\theta(s_i))) \mid i \in \mathbb{N}\} \text{ is odd}\} \\
&= \{\theta(s_0)\theta(s_1)\ldots \in \text{Play}_{\mathcal{M}^G} \mid \min \text{Inf}\{c^G(\theta(s_i)) \mid i \in \mathbb{N}\} \text{ is odd}\}
\end{aligned}
$$

(3) From (1), we have that G preserves Ω_c and thus, we get the result by applying Theorem 1.   □

This means that if we have a symmetry group that preserves the coloring function we can decide existence of winning strategies in a parity game by deciding existence of winning strategies in the quotient game. Furthermore, the quotient game is also a parity game and it has the same number of colors as the original game.

Example 2. Consider again the game $\mathcal{M}$ from Example 1. Let a coloring function c be defined by $c(s_0) = c(s_1) = c(s_5) = 0$ and $c(s_2) = c(s_3) = c(s_4) = 1$. Then the symmetry group G defined in the example does not preserve c since $s_1 \sim_G s_4$ but $c(s_1) \neq c(s_4)$. However, we can define a (smaller) symmetry group G' that preserves c by

$$
G' = \left\{ \pi \in \text{Sym}_{\mathcal{M}} \left| \begin{array}{l} \pi(s_0, s_1, s_2, s_3, s_4, s_5) = (s_0, s_1, s_2, s_3, s_4, s_5) \\ \pi(s_0, s_1, s_2, s_3, s_4, s_5) = (s_0, s_1, s_3, s_2, s_4, s_5) \end{array} \right. \right\}
$$

This does not give as great a reduction as G, but on the other hand it preserves the existence of winning strategies for parity conditions defined by c.

4.2   Alternating-Time Temporal Logic

We will show that the symmetry reduction technique can be applied for model-checking of the alternating-time temporal logic ATL* [1,2] as well. In this section let Agt = $\{\text{I, II}\}$ be a fixed set of players and let AP be a finite set of proposition symbols. Then ATL* state formulas are defined by the grammar

$$
\varphi ::= p \mid \neg\varphi_1 \mid \varphi_1 \vee \varphi_2 \mid \langle\!\langle A \rangle\!\rangle \psi_1
$$

where $p \in$ AP is a proposition symbol, $A \subseteq$ Agt is a set of players, φ_1, φ_2 are ATL* state formulas and ψ_1 is an ATL* path formula. ATL* path formulae are defined by the grammar

$$
\psi ::= \varphi_1 \mid \neg\psi_1 \mid \psi_1 \vee \psi_2 \mid \mathbf{X}\psi_1 \mid \psi_1 \mathbf{U}\psi_2
$$

where φ_1 is an ATL* state formula and ψ_1 and ψ_2 are ATL* path formulas. State formulas are interpreted over states of a game whereas path formulas are interpreted over plays of a game. For all games $\mathcal{M} = (S, R, S_I, S_{II})$, labelling functions $L\colon S \to 2^{AP}$, all states $s \in S$, all plays $\rho \in \mathrm{Play}_{\mathcal{M}}$, all propositions $p \in AP$, all state formulas φ_1, φ_2 and all path formulas ψ_1, ψ_2 and all coalitions $A \in \mathrm{Agt}$ define the satisfaction relation $\models$ by

$\mathcal{M}, s \models p$ if $p \in L(s)$

$\mathcal{M}, s \models \neg\varphi_1$ if $\mathcal{M}, s \not\models \varphi_1$

$\mathcal{M}, s \models \varphi_1 \vee \varphi_2$ if $\mathcal{M}, s \models \varphi_1$ or $\mathcal{M}, s \models \varphi_2$

$\mathcal{M}, s \models \langle\!\langle A \rangle\!\rangle \psi_1$ if there exist strategies $(\sigma_i)_{i \in A}$ so that

for all $\rho \in \mathrm{Play}_{\mathcal{M}}(s, (\sigma_i)_{i \in A})$, we have $\mathcal{M}, \rho \models \psi_1$

$\mathcal{M}, \rho \models \varphi_1$ if $\mathcal{M}, \rho \models \varphi_1$

$\mathcal{M}, \rho \models \neg\psi_1$ if $\mathcal{M}, \rho \not\models \psi_1$

$\mathcal{M}, \rho \models \psi_1 \vee \psi_2$ if $\mathcal{M}, \rho \models \psi_1$ or $\mathcal{M}, \rho \models \psi_2$

$\mathcal{M}, \rho \models \mathbf{X}\psi_1$ if $\mathcal{M}, \rho_{\geq 1} \models \psi_1$

$\mathcal{M}, \rho \models \psi_1 \mathbf{U} \psi_2$ if $\exists i \geq 0. \mathcal{M}, \rho_{\geq i} \models \psi_2$ and $\forall 0 \leq j < i. \rho_{\geq j} \models \psi_1$

As usual, we define the abbreviations $\psi_1 \wedge \psi_2 = \neg(\neg\psi_1 \vee \neg\psi_2)$, $\mathbf{F}\psi_1 = \top \mathbf{U} \psi_1$ and $\mathbf{G}\psi_1 = \neg\mathbf{F}\neg\psi_1$ where $\top$ is a special proposition that is true in all states. We say that a symmetry group G preserves the labelling function L if, for all $s, s' \in S$, we have $s \sim_G s' \Rightarrow L(s) = L(s')$. When G preserves L we define a labelling function L^G on the set of orbits by $L^G(t) = L(\mathrm{rep}(t))$ for all orbits t. By applying Theorem 1 we can now show that the symmetry reduction works for ATL*.

In order to prove this result, we rely on a characterization of ATL* equivalence in terms of alternating bisimulation [3].

Definition 6. *Let* AP *be a finite set of atomic propositions. Let* $\mathcal{M} = (S, R, S_I, S_{II})$ *be a game, with a labelling function* $L\colon S \to 2^{AP}$. *Two states* s *and* s' *of* S *are* alternating bisimilar *if there exists a binary relation* $\mathcal{B}$ *over* S *such that*

- $(s, s') \in \mathcal{B}$;
- *for every* $(t, t') \in \mathcal{B}$, *it holds that* $L(t) = L(t')$;
- *for every* $(t, t') \in \mathcal{B}$, *if it holds that* $t \in S_I$ *if and only if* $t' \in S_I$ *then*
  - *for every* u *s.t.* $(t, u) \in R$, *there exists* u' *such that* $(t', u') \in R$ *and* $(u, u') \in \mathcal{B}$;
  - *for every* u' *s.t.* $(t', u') \in R$, *there exists* u *such that* $(t, u) \in R$ *and* $(u, u') \in \mathcal{B}$;
- *for every* $(t, t') \in \mathcal{B}$, *if it holds that* $t \in S_I$ *if and only if* $t' \in S_{II}$ *then*
  - *for every* u, u' *s.t.* $(t, u) \in R$ *and* $(t', u') \in R$ *it holds that* $(u, u') \in \mathcal{B}$;

Proposition 2. *Let* AP *be a finite set of atomic propositions. Let* $\mathcal{M} = (S, R, S_I, S_{II})$ *be a game, with labelling function* $L\colon S \to 2^{AP}$. *Let* G *be a symmetry group that preserves* L, *and* L^G *be the quotient labelling function for* S^G. *Then for any* $s \in S$, s *and* $\theta(s)$ *are alternating bisimilar.*

Proof. Consider the disjoint union of $\mathcal{M}$ and $\mathcal{M}^G$, and the relation $\mathcal{B}$ defined by

$$(s, s') \in \mathcal{B} \quad \text{if, and only if,} \quad s' = \theta(s).$$

Then the first two conditions in the definition of alternating bisimilarity are fulfilled.

Now, pick $(t, t') \in \mathcal{B}$, assuming that t (hence also $t' = \theta(t)$) belongs to Player I. First, pick a successor u of t, i.e. $(t, u) \in R$. Then $(\theta(t), \theta(u)) \in R^G$ and since $(u, \theta(u)) \in \mathcal{B}$ the first condition is satisfied. Second, pick a successor u' of t', i.e. $(t', u') \in R^G$. Then there exists $v, w \in S$ such that $(v, w) \in R$, $v \in t'$ and $w \in u'$. Then there exists $\pi \in G$ such that $\pi(v) = t$. This means that $(\pi(v), \pi(w)) = (t, \pi(w)) \in R$. Since $\pi(w) \in u'$ we also have $(\pi(w), u') \in \mathcal{B}$ which means the second condition is satisfied. The proof is the same if t belongs to Player II.   □

Proposition 3. *Let $\mathcal{M} = (S, R, S_I, S_{II})$ be a game, $L: S \to 2^{AP}$ be a labelling function and G be a symmetry group that preserves L. Then for every $s \in S$, every $\rho \in \text{Play}_{\mathcal{M}}$, every ATL* state formula φ and every ATL* path formula ψ over AP we have*

- $\mathcal{M}, s \models \varphi$ *if, and only if,* $\mathcal{M}^G, \theta(s) \models \varphi$
- $\mathcal{M}, \rho \models \psi$ *if, and only if,* $\mathcal{M}^G, \theta(\rho) \models \psi$

where the satisfaction relation $\models$ in $\mathcal{M}^G$ is defined with respect to the labelling function L^G.

Proof. This is a consequence of the results of [3] for the case of finite state games since s and $\theta(s)$ are alternating bisimilar acccording to Prop. 2. This can also be proven directly by induction on the structure of the formula, using Lemma 3 for infinite games with finite branching.

The most interesting case is $\psi = \langle\!\langle \{P\} \rangle\!\rangle \psi_1$ with $P \in \{I, II\}$; define the objective $\Omega_{\psi_1} = \{\rho \in \text{Play}_{\mathcal{M}} \mid \mathcal{M}, \rho \models \psi_1\}$ as the set of plays in $\mathcal{M}$ satisfying ψ_1. We will first show that G preserves Ω_{ψ_1}. Suppose $\rho \in \Omega_{\psi_1}$ and $\rho' \in \text{Play}_{\mathcal{M}}$ is a play such that $\rho \sim_G \rho'$. According to the induction hypothesis, $\mathcal{M}, \rho \models \psi_1$ if and only if $\mathcal{M}^G, \theta(\rho) \models \psi_1$ but also that $\mathcal{M}, \rho' \models \psi_1$ if and only if $\mathcal{M}^G, \theta(\rho') \models \psi_1$. Since $\theta(\rho) = \theta(\rho')$ we have that ρ' satisfies ψ_1 since ρ does. Thus, $\rho' \in \Omega_{\psi_1}$ which means that G preserves Ω_{ψ_1}. Then by the induction hypothesis we have

$$\begin{aligned}
\Omega_{\psi_1}^G &= \{\theta(\rho) \in \text{Play}_{\mathcal{M}^G} \mid \rho \in \Omega_{\psi_1}\} \\
&= \{\theta(\rho) \in \text{Play}_{\mathcal{M}^G} \mid \mathcal{M}, \rho \models \psi_1\} \\
&= \{\theta(\rho) \in \text{Play}_{\mathcal{M}^G} \mid \mathcal{M}^G, \theta(\rho) \models \psi_1\}
\end{aligned}$$

Using this and Theorem 1 we have for all $s \in S$

$$\begin{aligned}
\mathcal{M}, s \models \langle\!\langle \{P\} \rangle\!\rangle \psi_1 \quad &\text{iff } s \in W_{\mathcal{M}}^P(\Omega_{\psi_1}) \\
&\text{iff } \theta(s) \in W_{\mathcal{M}^G}^P(\Omega_{\psi_1}^G) \\
&\text{iff } \mathcal{M}^G, \theta(s) \models \langle\!\langle \{P\} \rangle\!\rangle \psi_1 \qquad □
\end{aligned}$$

Remark 1. Even though the result for ATL* was only proved in two-player games above, this can easily be extended to handle n-player games for $n \geq 3$ as well. This is the case since formulas of the form $\langle\langle A \rangle\rangle \psi$ can be evaluated at a state by letting one player control the players in coalition A and let another player control the players in coalition Agt $\setminus A$.

Remark 2. Notice that the result of Prop. 3 does not extend to Strategy Logic [4, 14] or ATL with strategy contexts [7]. Considering the game depicted on Fig. 2, assume that s_2 and s_3 are labelled with p and s_5 is labelled with q. One can notice that there is a strategy of the circle player (namely, playing from s_2 to s_3 and from s_3 to s_5) under which the following two propositions hold in s_0:

− there is a strategy for the square player to end up in a p-state after two steps (namely, playing to s_2),
− there is a strategy for the square player to end up in a q-state after two steps (namely, playing to s_3).

This obviously fails in the reduced game.

Example 3. Consider the infinite game illustrated in Fig. 4 which is played on an infinite grid. Player I controls the circle states and player II controls the square states. The games starts in $(0,0)$ and in each state the player controlling the state can move up, down, left or right. The proposition p is true exactly when the first coordinate is odd. Formally, the game is defined by $\mathcal{M} = (S, R, S_\mathrm{I}, S_\mathrm{II})$ where

− $S = \mathbb{Z}^2$
− $R = \{((x_1, y_1), (x_2, y_2)) \in S \times S \mid |x_1 - x_2| + |y_1 - y_2| = 1\}$
− $S_\mathrm{I} = \{(x, y) \in S \mid y \text{ is even}\}$
− $S_\mathrm{II} = \{(x, y) \in S \mid y \text{ is odd}\}$

The labelling is defined by $L((x, y)) = \{p\}$ if x is odd and $L((x, y)) = \emptyset$ if x is even. Suppose we want to check if some ATL* formula φ over the set AP $= \{p\}$ is true in $(0,0)$. This is not necessarily easy to do in an automatic way since $\mathcal{M}$ is infinite. However, we can use symmetry reduction to obtain a finite quotient game as follows. Let us define

$$G = \{\pi \in \mathrm{Sym}_\mathcal{M} \mid \exists a, b \in \mathbb{Z}. \ \forall (x, y) \in S. \ \pi(x, y) = (x' + 2 \cdot a, y' + 2 \cdot b)\}.$$

It is simple to show that G is a group and also that it preserves the labelling L. Further, G induces four orbits $\theta((0, 0)), \theta((0, 1)), \theta((1, 0))$ and $\theta((1, 1))$. The corresponding quotient game can be seen in Fig. 5.

According to Prop. 3 we can just do model-checking in the quotient game since $\mathcal{M}, (0, 0) \models \varphi$ if and only if $\mathcal{M}^G, \theta((0, 0)) \models \varphi$. This shows how the original game can be infinite but still have a finite quotient game.

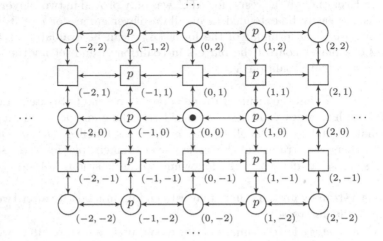

Fig. 4. Game on an infinite grid

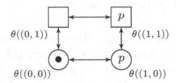

Fig. 5. Finite quotient game

5   Where Do the Symmetry Groups Come from?

Until now we have just assumed that a symmetry group G was known, but we have not mentioned how to obtain it. The short answer is that it is not tractable to find the symmetry group that gives the largest reduction in general. Indeed, even for the special case of finite-state transition systems, this problem is computationally hard. For a detailed discussion of this, see Section 6 in [6]. There it is shown that the orbit problem is as hard as the Graph Isomorphism problem when the transition system is finite: the orbit problem is to decide, for a given group G generated by a set $\{\pi_1, \ldots, \pi_n\}$ of permutations, whether two states s and s' belong to the same orbit. According to the knowledge of the authors, there is still no known polynomial time algorithm for the graph isomorphism problem. Unless the aim is to apply algorithms having high complexity in the size of the model, computing symmetries this way might not be so interesting.

While this may look quite negative, the approach has given very large speed-ups on practical verification instances. Here, it is typically the responsibility of the engineer designing the system to provide the symmetry groups as well as the orbits to the program. The main reason why this is possible is that many natural instances of embedded, concurrent and distributed systems have a number of identical components or processes. A simple example of this can be seen in Fig. 6.

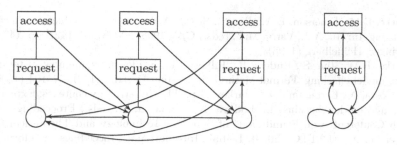

Fig. 6. A simple game $\mathcal{M}$ modeling a situation with a server and three clients is shown to the left. The smallest quotient game $\mathcal{M}^G$ such that G preserves the labelling of the propositions {request, access} is shown to the right.

This gives rise to symmetry in the model which is quite easy to detect for a human with some amount of experience. Another approach is to design modeling languages and data structures where certain forms of symmetry can be detected automatically. For discussions of this in different contexts, see [11,10,13]. We have no reason to believe that the symmetry reduction technique will be less applicable for model-checking properties of games.

6 Concluding Remarks

We have proved that the symmetry reduction technique can be generalized to infinite-state turn-based games with finite branching and provided particular applications of this result in the areas of parity games and model-checking of ATL*. The technique has not yet been implemented and tested on practical examples, but we expect that it should be as applicable as it has been in the context of model-checking of temporal logics, model-checking of real-time systems and probabilistic systems. It is still open whether the technique can be generalized to games with infinite branching since our application of König's Lemma requires that the games have finite branching.

References

1. Alur, R., Henzinger, T.A., Kupferman, O.: Alternating-time temporal logic. In: Proceedings of the 38th Annual Symposium on Foundations of Computer Science (FOCS 1997), pp. 100–109. IEEE Comp. Soc. Press (October 1997)
2. Alur, R., Henzinger, T.A., Kupferman, O.: Alternating-time temporal logic. Journal of the ACM 49(5), 672–713 (2002)
3. Alur, R., Henzinger, T.A., Kupferman, O., Vardi, M.Y.: Alternating refinement relations. In: Sangiorgi, D., de Simone, R. (eds.) CONCUR 1998. LNCS, vol. 1466, pp. 163–178. Springer, Heidelberg (1998)
4. Chatterjee, K., Henzinger, T.A., Piterman, N.: Strategy logic. In: Caires, L., Vasconcelos, V.T. (eds.) CONCUR 2007. LNCS, vol. 4703, pp. 59–73. Springer, Heidelberg (2007)

5. Clarke, E.M., Emerson, E.A., Jha, S., Sistla, A.P.: Symmetry reductions in model checking. In: Hu, A.J., Vardi, M.Y. (eds.) CAV 1998. LNCS, vol. 1427, pp. 147–158. Springer, Heidelberg (1998)

6. Clarke, E.M., Jha, S., Enders, R., Filkorn, T.: Exploiting symmetry in temporal logic model checking. Formal Methods in System Design 9(1/2), 77–104 (1996)

7. Da Costa, A., Laroussinie, F., Markey, N.: ATL with strategy contexts: Expressiveness and model checking. In: Lodaya, K., Mahajan, M. (eds.) Proceedings of the 30th Conferentce on Foundations of Software Technology and Theoretical Computer Science (FSTTCS 2010). Leibniz International Proceedings in Informatics, vol. 8, pp. 120–132. Leibniz-Zentrum für Informatik (December 2010)

8. Allen Emerson, E., Jutla, C.S.: Tree automata, mu-calculus and determinacy. In: Proceedings of the 32nd Annual Symposium on Foundations of Computer Science (FOCS 1991), pp. 368–377. IEEE Comp. Soc. Press (October 1991)

9. Allen Emerson, E., Prasad Sistla, A.: Symmetry and model checking. Formal Methods in System Design 9(1/2), 105–131 (1996)

10. Hendriks, M., Behrmann, G., Larsen, K., Niebert, P., Vaandrager, F.: Adding symmetry reduction to Uppaal. In: Larsen, K.G., Niebert, P. (eds.) FORMATS 2003. LNCS, vol. 2791, pp. 46–59. Springer, Heidelberg (2004)

11. Norris Ip, C., Dill, D.L.: Better verification through symmetry. Formal Methods in System Design 9(1/2), 41–75 (1996)

12. Kőnig, D.: Theorie der endlichen und unendlichen Graphen: kombinatorische Topologie der Streckenkomplexe. Akad. Verlag, Leipzig (1936)

13. Kwiatkowska, M., Norman, G., Parker, D.: Symmetry reduction for probabilistic model checking. In: Ball, T., Jones, R.B. (eds.) CAV 2006. LNCS, vol. 4144, pp. 234–248. Springer, Heidelberg (2006)

14. Mogavero, F., Murano, A., Vardi, M.Y.: Reasoning about strategies. In Kamal Lodaya and Meena Mahajan. In: Proceedings of the 30th Conferentce on Foundations of Software Technology and Theoretical Computer Science (FSTTCS 2010). Leibniz International Proceedings in Informatics, vol. 8, pp. 133–144. Leibniz-Zentrum für Informatik (December 2010)

15. Wahl, T., Blanc, N., Allen Emerson, E.: SVISS: Symbolic verification of symmetric systems. In: Ramakrishnan, C.R., Rehof, J. (eds.) TACAS 2008. LNCS, vol. 4963, pp. 459–462. Springer, Heidelberg (2008)

Incremental Encoding and Solving
of Cardinality Constraints*

Sven Reimer, Matthias Sauer, Tobias Schubert, and Bernd Becker

Institute of Computer Science, Albert-Ludwigs-Universität Freiburg
Georges-Köhler-Allee 051, D-79110 Freiburg, Germany
{reimer,sauerm,schubert,becker}@informatik.uni-freiburg.de

Abstract. Traditional SAT-based MaxSAT solvers encode cardinality
constraints directly as part of the CNF and solve the entire optimization problem by a sequence of iterative calls of the underlying SAT
solver. The main drawback of such approaches is their dependence on
the number of soft clauses: The more soft clauses the MaxSAT instance
contains, the larger is the CNF part encoding the cardinality constraints.
To counter this drawback, we introduce an innovative encoding of cardinality constraints: Instead of translating the entire and probably bloated
constraint network into CNF, a divide-and-conquer approach is used to
encode partial constraint networks successively. The resulting subproblems are solved and merged incrementally, reusing not only intermediate
local optima, but also additional constraints which are derived from solving the individual subproblems by the back-end SAT solver. Extensive
experimental results for the last MaxSAT evaluation benchmark suitew
demonstrate that our encoding is in general smaller compared to existing
methods using a monolithic encoding of the constraints and converges
faster to the global optimum.

1 Introduction

Recently, MaxSAT, a SAT-related optimization problem, gained large interest
due to a wide range of applications [1,2,3] which can be expressed with this
formalism. Many different variations and applicable techniques have been developed [4] leading not only to significant advances in terms of scalability but
also extending the problem formulations with variations like weighted and partial
MaxSAT.

One very popular approach to solve MaxSAT problems is the *iterative SAT-
based* [5] approach. This technique prunes the bounds for the number of satisfied
maximization constraints by iterative (and incremental) SAT solver calls. The
cardinality constraints are directly encoded into the SAT instance usually given
by a network of sorters, adders, counters, or networks explicitly designed for such
constraint systems. However, these data structures are growing with the number

---

* This work was partly supported by the German Research Council (DFG) as part
  of the Transregional Collaborative Research Center "Automatic Verification and
  Analysis of Complex Systems" (SFB/TR 14 AVACS).

F. Cassez and J.-F. Raskin (Eds.): ATVA 2014, LNCS 8837, pp. 297–313, 2014.

of maximization constraints – usually at least with $O(n \log^2 n)$ where n is the number of constraints [6] – and hence limit the applicability of such approaches.

In this paper we present an incremental divide-and-conquer approach for the construction of cardinality constraints using a partial encoding. Instead of building the entire supporting data structure at once we divide the construction into smaller steps to obtain locally optimal results that are merged together incrementally until the global optimal solution is found. This approach provides several advantages compared to the traditional method. Most notably, during the construction of each part, information gained from solving previous parts can be extracted and reused. This allows us not only to reduce the overall size of the encoding but also to improve the scalability of the approach.

Hence, our approach goes beyond standard incremental SAT solving and is able to yield early results which are close to the global optimum. While some presented optimizations are also applicable to classical approaches, our proposed method is in particular suitable for networks with divide-and-conquer approaches where parts of the network already fulfill the given sorter invariant, i. e. a network where firstly subsets are correctly sorted and afterwards merged together. In our implementation we use a bitonic sorting network [7] meeting these requirements.

Related work focuses on finding more efficient encodings for the cardinality constraints in CNF [6,8,9,10]. These approaches introduce new encodings, but in contrast to our approach do not consider a partial view. In [11] the authors formulate a synthesis problem in order to find an optimal sorting network with SAT for a small number of inputs. There is also some work on comparison of different existing encoding strategies [12,13]. The closest SAT-based approaches to our work are presented in [14,15]. In [14] a core-guided [16] MaxSAT approach is used, which does not use networks to encode cardinality constraints. Instead the solver seeks for unsatisfiability cores which are successively refined. The algorithm partitions the formula and starts with one subpart of the formula in order to find a local optimal solution. New parts are added incrementally refining the local solutions until all parts are added. [15] uses adders and/or BDDs for the encoding, partitions the instance and solves it incrementally by successive adding more subparts. As in our approach learnt information concerning the cardinality network and the original instance are shared and reused between the solver calls. However, in contrast to our work these approaches do not add additional information or utilize explicitly the partial composition of the cardinality network.

In our experiments we demonstrate the applicability of our method using recent benchmarks from the MaxSAT Evaluation [17]. Results show that our approach dominates the classical monolithic approach in all benchmark series not only in terms of the solved benchmarks, but also in quality of the (partial) results for not completely solved benchmarks. Additionally, the effectiveness of the individual optimizations is highlighted and evaluated.

The remaining paper is structured as follows: In Section 2 we briefly introduce the MaxSAT problem and its variations as well as the bitonic sorting network used in our approach. The basic algorithm computing partial optimal solutions and details on the encoding are presented in Section 3. In Section 4 we discuss several enhancements and optimizations of the implementation. Furthermore, we evaluate each extension using the MaxSAT evaluation benchmark set and compare our method with existing work. The paper is concluded in Section 5.

2 Preliminaries

In this section we introduce the main solving techniques for SAT and (partial) MaxSAT. For a deeper insight the reader is also referred to [18]. Furthermore, the bitonic sorting network [7] used in our approach is introduced.

2.1 SAT and MaxSAT

The *SAT problem* poses the question whether a propositional formula φ evaluates to 1 (or true). In this case we call φ *satisfiable* with an assignment $\mathcal{A} : V \to \{0,1\}$ (also referred to as model) of the Boolean variables V of φ. If there is no such model φ is *unsatisfiable*. We consider SAT formulae in *conjunctive normal form (CNF)*, which is a conjunction of *clauses*, whereas a clause is a disjunction of *literals*. A literal l is either a variable $v \in V$ or its negation $\bar{v}$. A clause containing only one literal is called a *unit clause*.

Algorithms for solving the SAT problem are predominated by the extensions of the DPLL algorithm [19], called Conflict Driven Clause Learning (CDCL), where reasons for unsatisfiable assginments are derived. These are added to φ in order to prevent the algorithm from choosing the same set of assignments again.

In recent years the concept of incremental SAT solving [20] became more and more popular, which is motivated by applications requiring repeated solving of similar instances. For instance, in SAT-based BMC [21] clauses are repeatedly added and deleted. Usually incremental solving is driven by assumptions, where additional constraints are added to the instance which are only valid for the current consideration of the instance. This allows to de-/activate clauses (properties) between different solver calls by relaxation variables.

MaxSAT is a SAT-related optimization problem which seeks for an assignment for a propositional formula φ in CNF *maximizing* the set of simultaneously satisfied clauses. In this paper, we focus on a variation of the MaxSAT problem called *partial MaxSAT*, where the formula is separated in *soft* and *hard clauses*. The objective is to satisfy all hard clauses (as in SAT) and to maximize the number of satisfied soft clauses (as in MaxSAT).

Iterative SAT-based approaches [22] use an incremental SAT solver as backend and encode the cardinality constraints via additional networks. In this paper we rely on such an approach using a bitonic sorting network [7] which is introduced in the following section.

2.2 Bitonic Sorting Networks

A Bitonic Sorting Network BSN is based on a divide-and-conquer principle. Formally $BSN(i_1, \ldots, i_m) = (o_1, \ldots, o_m)$ sorts the input $i = (i_1, \ldots, i_m)$ into

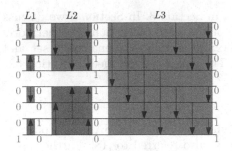

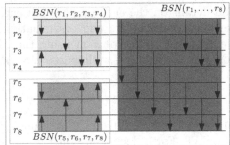

Fig. 1. *BSN* for eight inputs   **Fig. 2.** Partial encoding and solving

an output $o = (o_1, \ldots, o_m)$ with ascending order. Fig. 1 shows an example with eight inputs (left-hand side $i = (1, 0, 1, 0, 0, 0, 0, 1)$) returning eight lines sorted by a monotonically increasing sequence of 0 and 1 (right-hand side $o = (0, 0, 0, 0, 0, 1, 1, 1)$). Every arrow stands for a comparison between two lines, where the direction of the arrow indicates the direction of sorting. The colored boxes illustrate the divide-and-conquer principle. The outputs of the boxes are sorted according to the sorting direction indicated by green/red color. On the left-hand side at the first level ($L1$) the base case is shown, where only two lines have to be compared (i. e. there are four *BSN* with two inputs on this level). There are two *BSN* with four inputs each on $L2$ representing the first merge step, where two sorted base cases are merged to a combined block of four sorted lines. Finally, $L3$ merges these sorted four lines into one final *BSN* with eight output. Note, that the number of inputs does not necessarily has to be a power of two and moreover any arbitrary number of inputs can be handled.

Related implementations are odd-even sorting networks [7] and pairwise sorting networks [23]. The latter ones turn out to be one of the most effective sorting network encodings for SAT [9]. Unfortunately, the sorting invariant is lost, i. e., the intermediate subparts are not sorted anymore. Therefore this network type cannot be utilized as effective as the other types for our approach.

The comparison operator can be expressed in CNF using six clauses, or by the following relation: $comparator(a, b, c, d) \leftrightarrow ((c \leftrightarrow a \vee b) \wedge (d \leftrightarrow a \wedge b))$. The inputs a and b are sorted resulting in two outputs c and d.

2.3   Usage of Cardinality Networks in MaxSAT Solvers

Usually, network-based MaxSAT solvers introduce a new auxiliary relaxation literal r for each soft clause. If r is set to 0 the corresponding soft clause has to be satisfied, otherwise ($r = 1$) the clause is *relaxed*, i. e., it is satisfied by the relaxation literal and hence, the (original) soft clause does not have to be satisfied by the variables belonging to the original CNF. In the following we denote φ as the original MaxSAT instance including a unique relaxation literal $(r_1, \ldots, r_m)$ for each soft clause. Moreover we write $\beta(i_1, \ldots, i_m)$ for the CNF encoding of the bitonic sorting network with m inputs. In an iterative approach the relaxation literals are connected to the inputs of the sorting network and the instance

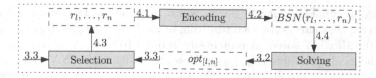

Fig. 3. Process overview

$\varphi \wedge \beta(r_1, \ldots, r_m) \wedge (\overline{o_i})$ is handed over to a SAT solver. If it is satisfiable there are at least i simultaneously satisfied soft clauses, otherwise there exists no solution with i satisfied soft clauses. The solution is narrowed by the incremental usage of the underlying SAT solver until a value k is identified with $\varphi \wedge \beta(r_1, \ldots, r_m) \wedge (\overline{o_k})$ being satisfiable and $\varphi \wedge \beta(r_1, \ldots, r_m) \wedge (\overline{o_{k+1}})$ being unsatisfiable. In the following we abbreviate the incremental search for k over m relaxation variables with $\sigma(r_1, \ldots, r_m)$ and denote $opt_{[1,m]}$ as the (locally) optimal result for the relaxation variables $r_1, \ldots, r_m$. There are several approaches for choosing and narrowing the values for i. In our approach we start with $i = 1$ and increase the value successively until $k + 1$. Between two incremental SAT solver calls we examine the returned model and count the number of relaxation literals j set to 0. Thus we narrow the solution interval by j (not by just incrementing i). In the following we call this procedure the *baseline approach*.

3 Incremental Encoding and Solving

In this section we present our approach based on partial sorter building for MaxSAT. At first the basic divide-and-conquer concept partitioning the entire sorting network into smaller subparts is presented (cf. Sec. 3.1). This technique has an increased number of incremental solver calls compared to the baseline approach, but allows new possibilities of information sharing over the subparts which is not possible in a traditional monolithic implementation of the network.

A schematic overview of the process is shown in Fig. 3. First, we select the next relaxation variables $r_l, \ldots, r_n$ (cf. Sec. 3.3), which are encoded locally into $BSN(r_l, \ldots, r_n)$. Finally the instance $\sigma(r_l, \ldots, r_n)$ is tackled by a MaxSAT solver returning the local optimum $opt[l, n]$. Afterwards local bounds are used to create additional information for the following computational steps (cf. Sec. 3.2) and the next relaxation variables are chosen until the global optimum $opt_{[1,m]}$ is found.

3.1 Concept

Given a MaxSAT instance φ the basic idea is to split the sorter into presorted subparts which are encoded and solved separately. In particular, the inputs of the network (i. e. the relaxation literals of the soft clauses) $r = (r_1, \ldots, r_m)$ are split into uniformly distributed subparts: $(r_1, \ldots, r_d), (r_{d+1}, \ldots, r_{d+d}), \ldots, r_{m-d}, \ldots,$ r_m where d denotes the number of considered relaxation variables per subpart. Instead of encoding the entire network, we only consider $\varphi \wedge \beta(r_1, \ldots, r_d)$ by solving the instance $\sigma(r_1, \ldots, r_d)$ (w.l.o.g. we always tackle the relaxation variables in ascending order). The MaxSAT solver will return the local optimum $opt_{[1,d]}$. Afterwards the next part is encoded resulting in $\varphi \wedge \beta(r_1, \ldots, r_d) \wedge \beta(r_{d+1}, \ldots, r_{d+d})$. We call the MaxSAT solver incrementally in order to solve $\sigma(r_{d+1}, \ldots, r_{d+d})$ and obtain the local optimum $opt_{[d+1,d+d]}$. Note, that although $BSN(r_1, \ldots, r_d)$ and $BSN(r_d, \ldots, r_{d+d})$ are encoded in the same instance, both parts are not connected. In order to merge these parts we have to encode $BSN(r_1, \ldots, r_{d+d})$, for which we reuse $BSN(r_1, \ldots, r_d)$ and $BSN(r_{d+1}, \ldots, r_{d+d})$ by encoding only the merge step ($L3$ in Fig. 1). A MaxSAT solver call for $\sigma(r_1, \ldots, r_{d+d})$ will return the local optimum $opt_{[1,d+d]}$. This partial composition is repeated until $BSN(r_1, \ldots, r_m)$ is encoded and we finally obtain $opt_{[1,m]}$ by solving $\sigma(r_1, \ldots, r_m)$. An example is given in Fig. 2 for eight relaxation variables and $d = 4$.

Splitting the instance into smaller parts, whose locally optimal solution is computed, eventually leads to the global optimum. However, as we will demonstrate in the following sections, this approach allows optimizations that are not possible otherwise leading to an increase in efficiency.

3.2   Reuse Local Bounds

We observed two main cases allowing to set global bounds derived from local partial bounds, which can be determined after solving a subpart.

Consider the example in Fig. 4 where at first $\sigma(r_1, \ldots, r_4)$ is tackled, followed by $\sigma(r_5, \ldots, r_8)$. The result for $\sigma(r_1, \ldots, r_4)$ can be reused for latter solving steps. In particular, the number of *non-satisfied* soft clauses of this part indicated by the red 1 in the example, can be fixed permanently by adding a corresponding unit clause ($o_{opt_{[1,d]}+1}$). Since we solved $\sigma(r_1, \ldots, r_4)$ without any further restrictions, there is no solution with more satisfied soft clauses possible. Generally, this observation applies to all MaxSAT instances $\sigma(r)$ where r contains $(r_1, \ldots, r_d)$ (i. e. the part which is encoded and solved at first). Hence, in the example in Fig. 4, also the number of non-satisfied clauses for $\sigma(r_1, \ldots, r_8)$ can be fixed for possible further computations. For all other parts we are not allowed to fix the result, but instead of the unit clause we add appropriate assumptions representing the same bounds. We do this in order to speed up calculations and dismiss the assumption whenever this subpart is tackled after a merge step. Note, that the number of *satisfied* soft clauses cannot be fixed, since in the global optimum the subpart may contain less satisfied clauses.

Furthermore, we analyze the number of soft clauses satisfied so far. Solving a partial instance also implies assignments among other relaxation variables whose BSN is not encoded so far. Before we tackle the instance $\sigma(r_l, \ldots, r_n)$, we count the number of *all* non-relaxed soft clauses nr, in particular, clauses for which the BSN is not encoded so far. This value nr represents a lower bound for the global optimum, and we use it in order to 1) provide early compelling global bounds and 2) fix an initial lower bound for solving the following subparts. Consider again the example in Fig. 4 with overall eight soft clauses. Assume, we have already obtained the result for $\sigma(r_1, \ldots, r_4)$ with $opt_{[1,4]} = 3$. In this example two additional soft clauses are satisfied by chance within the second part (whose cardinality constraints are not encoded so far) resulting in a lower bound $nr = 5$.

Before encoding $\beta(r_5, \ldots, r_8)$ and solving $\sigma(r_5, \ldots, r_8)$ we can fix a-priori a lower bound of one soft clause which has to be satisfied in the second part (indicated by the red 0 at the output). Generally, we evaluate whether we can set a lower bound of satisfied soft clauses for the current subpart using previous results. To do so, before solving $\sigma(r_l, \ldots, r_n)$, we check whether the term lb, defined as $lb = m - nr - sc$ evaluates to a value smaller than 0, where sc is the number of soft clauses in $\sigma(r_l, \ldots, r_n)$ and m is the overall number of soft clauses. In the example $lb = 8 - 5 - 4 = -1$ holds. If so, abs(lb) indicate a lower solution bound for the currently considered subpart, which is added by a suitable unit clause.

Setting unit clauses and assumptions for non-satisfied soft clauses is beneficial if the subpart containing $\sigma(r_1, \ldots, r_d)$ is considered as early as possible. In contrast, the second technique presented in this section benefits from early near optimal results which are close to the overall number of satisfiable soft clauses. By applying these techniques the subparts are not solved independently anymore, since local optima are reused for further steps. While the identified global optimum is not influenced, this will potentially decrease the quality of local optima, but may speed up later calculations due to additional constraints.

3.3 Size and Ordering

One further major aspect for the effectiveness of the encoding of partial constraint networks is the size of the subparts d. If the size is too large the advantages of considering easy to solve instances are reduced, whereas a too small splitting width will produce too much solving overhead (due to an unfavorable number of calls of the underlying SAT solver). Furthermore, a property of the BSN is that only parts of the same size (± 1) can be merged together. The latter issue can be solved in general by introducing *fake inputs* to the network, i.e., inputs which are not connected to the MaxSAT problem and assigned to a constant value. But an unbalanced choice of the subpart sizes will lead to a large overhead in fake inputs resulting in deeper and therefore inefficient network structures. Hence, we choose a splitting width which is balanced with respect to the number of sorter inputs as follows: If possible 1) all subparts have the same size of input lines and 2) merging all subparts adds up such that in all merging steps the number of fake lines is minimized. The splitting size is calculated a-priori and bounded by a user-defined width w. The value d is chosen as close as possible below w fulfilling the properties given above. In our experiments, we have identified $w = 64$ as a bound leading to the best trade-off between easy to solve instances and solver call overhead for the given benchmarks.

Another important aspect is the ordering in which the individual subparts should be processed. We implemented two approaches: 1) depth-first and 2) breadth-first ordering. The depth-first method tries to merge the deepest (according to the level in the BSN) two subparts whenever possible/available. Breadth-first always calculates a complete level of subparts first and if all subparts of a level have been processed the next level is tackled. The depth-first approach is mainly motivated in conjunction with the re-usage of local bounds as described in the previous section: After solving $\sigma(r_1, \ldots, r_d)$, we are allowed to set unit clauses to fix the found bound, which is not possible for the other subparts. By traversing the network in a depth-first manner this first part is always included as early as possible, whereas breadth-first method potentially allows to set early local lower bounds by unit clauses according to the second technique described in Sec. 3.2.

3.4 Experimental Evaluation

We implemented all of the methods described in this paper in our solver *antom* [24] which contains both, a SAT solver and MaxSAT solver. All measurements were performed on a machine using one core of a 3.3 GHz Intel Xeon, limiting the memory to 4 GB and the run time to 30 CPU minutes for each instance. We used the crafted and industrial partial MaxSAT instances from the MaxSAT Evaluation 2013 [17] with 1004 instances in total. All log files and further informations about the experiments can be found at [24].

All results are shown in Table 1. In the first four columns the benchmark family name, the number of instances per family and the average number of soft clauses and hard clauses are shown. The following columns indicate the results for the different approaches, where the average run time in CPU seconds ("time") and the number of solved instances ("#") is given for each method.

First, we discuss the effects of our newly introduced *incrementally encoded* and *solved* network ("ies") compared to the monolithic baseline approach ("baseline"). In the basic "ies" version we use a splitting width bound of $w = 64$ and breadth-first ordering. The results are a reference point for the optimizations in the following section, which could not be performed without the basic "ies". The "ies" method solves slightly more benchmarks than the "baseline" approach, mainly in the benchmark family "close_solutions" consisting of a huge number of soft clauses (up to over 1,000,000). In particular, in many cases "baseline" ran out of memory during the sorting network encoding (25 out of 50 instances). Thanks to the partial consideration, "ies" obtains early locally optimal results (see also Sec. 4.5) and solves eight more instances in this family (and overall 11).

Furthermore, we analyzed the number of comparators which have to be used. To do so, we measured the number of actually encoded comparators for those instances where both the baseline and the compared approach were able to build the complete cardinality network. Fig. 8 shows the average number of all these instances for different approaches in relation to "baseline". Due to the partition of the network there is a small overhead ($\sim 1\%$) in the encoding size for "ies". This overhead is dissolved by the techniques presented in the following section leading to an overall increasing of encoding and solving efficiency.

4 Optimizations

In this section we discuss several optimization which can be employed between the basic steps (cf. Fig. 3). Before the network encoding we first check whether some constraints are trivially contradicting (cf. Sec. 4.3) and during the construction we skip unnecessary comparators (cf. Sec. 4.1). When the network is

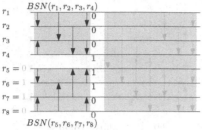
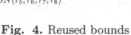

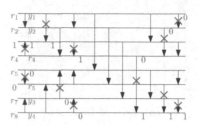

Fig. 4. Reused bounds   **Fig. 5.** Skipped comparisons

encoded we are able to add additional information into the network (cf. Sec. 4.2). Finally, before the instance is solved we set relaxation variables in advance in order to speed up calculations (cf. Sec. 4.4). For every optimization we present experimental results to show the implications and interactions of these methods.

In Sec. 4.5 we discuss related work and compare our MaxSAT solver with and without our presented approach against state-of-the-art MaxSAT solver.

4.1 Skip Comparisons

In many cases the encoding of the comparator between two lines within the sorting network can be skipped, as the result can be statically determined. This may appear due to the introduction of fake lines which are set to a constant or fixed values caused by the techniques described in Sec. 3.2, Sec. 3.3 and 4.3 or by conflict unit clauses derived by incremental SAT solver calls. In case of a constant line we do not have to encode the corresponding comparison operator, e. g. $comparator(a, 1, c, d) \leftrightarrow (c = 1 \land d = a)$.

In Fig. 5 an example is given where two lines (r_3 and r_6) are already fixed to values 1 and 0. The remaining six lines (r_i's) are not known so far. Furthermore, all (newly introduced) variables of the first level are shown (y_j's) – the remaining levels are left out for readability reasons. Standard encoding introduces an unnecessarily large network representation with 42 variables and 89 clauses for this small example. If the value of at least one line is already fixed (e. g., the third and forth input lines 1 and r_4) the comparison operation can be skipped (as indicated by the red cross in the figure). If the fixed value is 1 it will be set to c of $comparator(a, b, c, d)$, accordingly a fixed value 0 is always set to d (e. g., r_5 and 0 are swapped). In this small example where only two inputs are fixed, 11 out of 24 comparisons can be skipped leading to only 32 variables and 69 clauses for the representation of this network. Without this technique a modern SAT solver will keep one auxiliary variable and one encoded identity function per regular variable for each comparison with at least one fixed value. The remaining variables and clauses are removed by unit propagation of the fixed values, but in particular, the clauses representing the identity functions lead to longer implication chains.

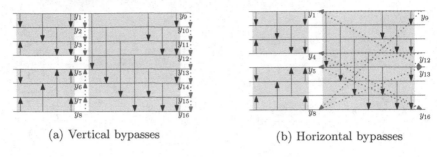

(a) Vertical bypasses   (b) Horizontal bypasses

Fig. 6. Bypass grid

By implementing and using this technique ("ies+skip") about 7% of used comparators could be saved compared to the "baseline" approach (cf. Fig. 8). Moreover three instances could be solved in addition to "ies" (cf. Table 1).

4.2 Bypass Grid

This technique introduces additional constraints, which we call *bypasses*, indicated by a red dotted arrow in Fig. 6. We distinguish between horizontal and vertical bypasses, building up together a *bypass grid*. Every bypass consists of just one additional binary clause. The basic idea is to add redundant information to the encoding in order to speed up the Boolean deduction within the sorting network and to improve the quality of learned conflicts due to shorter implication graphs.

Fig. 6a demonstrates vertical bypasses. In general these bypasses can be added after each merging step of the sorter (indicated by the light blue boxes). The output values of these subparts are already correctly sorted, and hence $y_1 \leq y_2 \leq y_3 \leq y_4$ as well as $y_5 \geq \ldots \geq y_8$ and $y_9 \leq \ldots \leq y_{16}$ hold. For *each* neighboring line of an output we add an appropriate binary bypass clause, e.g., $(\overline{y_1} \vee y_2)$ for the first two lines.

Horizontal bypasses are illustrated in Fig. 6b, where we distinguish between *forward horizontal bypasses* (indicated by arrows pointing from left to right) and *backward horizontal bypasses* (right to left). Like vertical bypasses they can be applied after each merging step and for each line – for the sake of readability the bypasses for the variables y_{10}, y_{11}, y_{14} and y_{15} are excluded in the figure. The forward bypasses for y_{16} are: $y_4 \leq y_{16}$ and $y_5 \leq y_{16}$, since there is at least one output equal to 1 in $BSN(r_1, \ldots r_8)$ if either one output of $BSN(r_1, \ldots, r_4)$ *or* $BSN(r_5, \ldots, r_8)$ is equal to 1. The corresponding bypasses are $(\overline{y_4} \vee y_{16})$ and $(\overline{y_5} \vee y_{16})$, and analogously for y_{13} (c.f. Fig. 6b). The backward bypasses for y_{12} are $y_{12} \leq y_4$ and $y_{12} \leq y_5$: if there are at least 5 outputs of $BSN(r_1, \ldots r_8)$ set to 1, there is also at least 1 output of $BSN(r_1, \ldots, r_4)$ *and* $BSN(r_5, \ldots, r_8)$ set to 1. This results in two clauses $(\overline{y_{12}} \vee y_4)$ and $(\overline{y_{12}} \vee y_5)$, and analogously for y_9.

Potentially, one could add more such bypasses, e.g., if $y_4 = y_5 = 1$, then $y_{15} = 1$ holds, but we omit this kind of bypasses since they require at least a ternary clause. Many modern SAT solvers treat binary clauses separately for even faster computation and therefore a binary clause is easier to handle for a SAT solver and also more constraining than ternary (or even larger) clauses.

In our experiments we apply both types of bypasses between each merge step: All possible vertical bypasses are considered, but we observed that there is too much overhead applying all horizontal bypasses. Instead we add both forward and backward horizontal bypasses only every four lines (as represented in Fig. 6b).

The results using the bypass grid ("ies+skip+grid") are shown in Tab. 1. The solver is now able to process faster the implications within the cardinality network and therefore also the soft clauses, such that pruning on hard clauses happens earlier within the solver. In classes with many hard clauses ("des", "Multiple path") more instances could be solved. The number of saved comparators increases by $\sim 2\%$ compared to "ies+skip", since the bypasses deduce more constant lines within the network.

4.3 Contradicting Soft Clauses

This method is a quick check whether two soft clauses are contradicting each other. To do so we check all soft clauses pairwise by activating both relaxation literals by according assumptions. Instead of solving the instance we force the solver only to deduce the resulting implications. If the result is already unsatisfiable we can ensure that these two soft clauses can never be satisfied simultaneously which is added as an additional constraint. Moreover, we collect for each soft clause the number of conflicting soft clauses, which is added to the output of a sorting network subpart. For example, suppose an overall number of m soft clauses and a particular soft clause c conflicting with n other soft clauses. By activating c we are never able to satisfy more than $m - n$ soft clauses simultaneously. This property is added as a binary constraint to the solver.

Like bypasses (cf. Sec. 4.2) this technique produces additional redundant information which aims at improving the deduction and conflict analysis routines. The checks are done for every partial and merged network. Additionally, we also check whether two soft clauses are always satisfied together or φ gets unsatisfiable activating a soft clause. Although these cases rarely take place, the corresponding checks are almost for free by checking the contradictions.

We use this method additionally to all techniques in the previous sections. The result are shown in Tab. 1 ("ies+skip+grid+csc"). Overall four instances more in different families could be solved due to the additional information.

4.4 Relaxing Soft Clauses

We additionally relax soft clauses a-priori that are not part of the current partial computation to a specific value in order to avoid unnecessary computational overhead. In contrast to Sec. 3.2 this technique is a heuristic method in order to speed up computations. We have established two kinds for relaxing those values, which are illustrated in Fig. 7.

The forward relaxation disables soft clauses which are not considered so far by setting the corresponding relaxation literals to 1. An example is given in Fig. 7a.

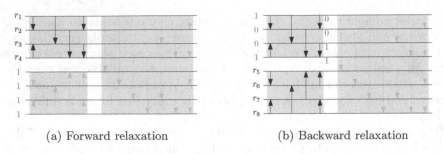

(a) Forward relaxation   (b) Backward relaxation

Fig. 7. Relaxation of soft clauses

Assume that we currently consider $\sigma(r_1, \ldots, r_4)$. As forward relaxation step r_5 to r_8 are set to 1, such that the corresponding soft clauses are already satisfied.

As backward relaxation step (cf. Fig. 7b) we set relaxation literals due to the model computed in an earlier step. In the example we assume that the result of $\sigma(r_1, \ldots, r_4)$ has deduced $r_2 = r_3 = 0$ and $r_1 = r_4 = 1$. When solving $\sigma(r_5, \ldots, r_8)$ we fix these values by assumptions, such that the solver does not have to compute the assignment of r_1 to r_4 again. Note that the relaxation variables r_l to r_n are never set when the instance $\sigma(r_l, \ldots, r_n)$ is solved. The solver is always free in setting the currently considered relaxation literals in order to obtain locally optimal results.

This technique allows to speed up the calculation of the partial sorter networks due to relaxed values. However, the solver is not able to recognize whether forward relaxed soft clauses may be satisfied by chance. The solver may also run into a local optimum when a backward relaxed literal is fixed 0, but needs to be 1 for the global optimum and vice versa. Both issues may decrease the effect of the method described in Sec. 3.2. To counter these side-effects of forward relaxation an additional *satisfied-by-chance examination* is employed. We check whether the soft clause is satisfied without the relaxation literal, if the relaxation literal is set to 1 (i. e., indicating that the soft clause is not satisfied). If this is the case we treat the soft clause as satisfied. We accept the drawback of backward muted relaxation variables, as experimental results show that the loss in quality is less than the benefit of the faster computation time.

We implemented the *r*elaxation of *s*oft *c*lauses and use it additionally to all techniques presented so far ("ies+skip+grid+csc+rsc" in Tab. 1). With this heuristic we could solve eight benchmarks in addition and one which could not be solved anymore compared to ("ies+skip+grid+csc"). In the family "des" (containing a large number of soft constraints) five instances more could be solved, due to the problem simplification. The number of encoded comparators slightly decreases compared to the previous version (cf. Fig. 8), since the quality of the local optima decreases – and therefore the number of skipped comparators due to Sec. 3.2 – as trade-off for the faster computation of the incremental steps.

Furthermore we used all techniques with a depth-first ordering as described in Sec. 3.3 ("ies_dfo+skip+grid+csc+rsc"). This approach is comparable to the breadth-first method. It dominates in the "haplotype" family needing only half of the run time as breadth-first ordering in average. More detailed result for the

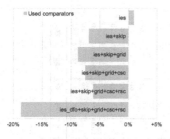

Fig. 8. Used comparators

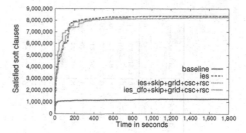

Fig. 9. Evolution of satisfied soft clauses

depth-first approach have to be excluded from the paper due to lack of space. The depth-first ordering variant leads to a large amount of skipped comparators ($\sim 18\%$ on average) in the networks which can be built completely (cf. Fig. 8). This is caused by the as-early-as-possible consideration of the first partition leading to more local bounds which can be fixed permanently than the breadth-first approach (cf. Sec. 3.2). Differently, the breadth-first ordering is able to provide early intermediate results considering all soft clauses, leading to overall two solved instances more than the depth-first approach.

Overall both variants clearly dominates the monolithic baseline approach in almost all benchmark families in terms of solved instances, average run time and encoding size of the cardinality network.

4.5 Related Work and Summary

In contrast to previous work on incremental solving of cardinality constraints [15] our approach is able to extract (Sec. 4.3) and set (Sec. 4.2) additional information going beyond standard reasoning on CNF. Furthermore, the cardinality network is optimized during the construction (Sec. 4.1), and we developed heuristics to speed up the incremental calculations (Sec. 4.4).

We compared our approach by using two available state-of-the-art MaxSAT solver: QMaxSAT0.21 [25] and MSUnCore [26] using bcd2, hardening and biased techniques (cf. Tab. 1). QMaxSAT0.21 is also an iterative method, but it uses a different SAT-solver as back-end as well as another type of cardinality network [8]. MSUnocre is an unsat-based MaxSAT solver, thus our approach cannot be adapted for this solver. Our best variant and the two competitors are quite close in the number of solved instances. As the results show our baseline implementation is already competitive, but including the proposed methods our solver performs on the same level as state-of-the-art solvers.

Finally, we logged whenever our solver was able to improve the current solution internally, i. e., the number of satisfied soft clauses. The results for "baseline", "ies", "ies+skip+grid+csc+rsc" and "ies_dfo+skip+grid+csc+rsc" are shown in Fig. 9. The plot represents the total number of satisfied soft clauses for all 1004 benchmarks on the y-axis over time in seconds on the x-axis. All incremental approaches were able to satisfy impressively more (almost an order of magnitude)

Table 1. Overview of all results

family	#	softclauses	hardclauses	baseline Sec. 2.3 time	#	ies Sec. 3.1 time	#	ies+skip Sec. 4.1 time	#	ies+skip+grid Sec. 4.2 time	#	ies+skip+grid+csc Sec. 4.3 time	#	ies+skip+grid+csc+rsc Sec. 4.4 time	#	ies.dfo+skip+grid+csc+rsc Sec. 3.3 time	#	QMaxSAT0.21 [25] time	#	MSUnCore [26] time	#
aes	7	166,206.86	55,988.43	1,800.00	0	1,800.00	0	1,800.00	0	1,800.00	0	1,800.00	0	1,800.00	0	1,800.00	0	1,800.00	0	1,583.72	1
bcp-fir	50	40,515.36	46,599.36	247.41	46	414.87	44	422.08	45	214.64	46	222.93	46	194.92	46	206.09	46	150.74	46	43.59	49
bcp-msp	50	14,507.76	24,757.56	1,160.34	18	1,160.32	18	1,160.06	18	1,158.67	18	1,163.24	18	1,163.72	18	1,162.53	18	1,155.79	18	813.23	29
bcp-mtg	40	489.30	11,851.15	0.20	40	0.20	40	0.15	40	0.14	40	0.19	40	0.17	40	0.17	40	0.09	40	0.92	40
bcp-syn	50	6405.96	756.00	1,190.05	17	1,172.58	18	1,155.65	19	1,193.34	17	1,182.62	18	1,180.04	18	1,162.92	18	1,143.29	19	855.71	27
ctc	4	165.00	550,234.00	24.28	4	23.71	4	23.90	4	36.56	4	29.24	4	24.32	4	28.48	4	32.34	4	67.28	4
close_solutions	50	865,248.12	2,153,275.38	1,725.06	4	1,443.34	12	1,446.10	12	1,437.97	12	1,438.86	12	1,432.30	12	1,408.14	12	1,421.67	8	958.62	26
des	50	31,735.20	329,559.86	986.70	29	1,123.29	23	1,111.35	23	962.50	27	1,032.30	27	947.13	32	975.91	31	705.57	38	848.76	32
frb	25	2,820.00	20,714.28	225.64	23	326.19	22	293.41	23	316.98	23	290.83	23	187.68	24	173.95	23	209.15	24	1,800	0
haplotype-*	6	57,798.00	38,532.00	1,800.00	0	1,747.19	1	1,800.00	0	1,465.59	2	1,462.75	3	1,477.94	3	723.31	5	420.25	5	619.67	4
job-shop	3	1,156.00	707,795.33	28.80	3	25.78	3	26.80	3	33.67	3	59.33	3	69.37	3	29.72	3	30.15	3	70.69	3
kbtree	42	5,383.00	300.50	1,596.68	6	1,632.16	6	1,609.10	6	1,570.17	6	1,586.38	6	1,571.02	6	1,585.31	6	1,567.49	6	1,573.79	6
maxclique-ran	96	900.00	5,587.50	429.45	76	425.18	76	422.68	77	425.80	76	411.42	77	411.88	77	411.97	77	346.28	80	516.45	71
maxclique-str	62	2,905.94	49,608.45	1,124.04	25	1,134.22	25	1,129.97	25	1,116.76	24	1,106.76	25	1,109.31	25	1,114.80	25	1,083.73	26	1,216.57	21
maxone-3sat	80	900.00	425.00	219.73	78	204.24	79	201.58	79	193.41	78	207.02	78	197.64	78	275.07	76	126.72	80	5.36	80
maxone-str	60	3,020.80	1,875.20	3.10	60	5.86	60	5.99	60	5.86	60	7.24	60	5.27	60	5.05	60	4.31	60	44.24	60
miplib	4	144.00	404.00	5.91	4	5.68	4	5.67	4	6.24	4	5.76	4	5.83	4	5.91	4	1.20	4	40.42	4
Multiple_path	48	7,141.50	289,883.96	799.86	32	864.56	31	855.57	31	772.67	34	773.68	34	787.82	34	708.95	34	553.68	41	674.75	39
nencdr	50	4,032.00	66,542.16	171.36	50	53.78	50	56.23	50	31.49	50	36.93	50	31.13	50	33.42	50	295.27	43	205.06	50
nlogencdr	50	4,032.00	37,578.88	64.11	50	19.34	50	17.90	50	12.04	50	13.12	50	10.85	50	12.12	50	241.97	45	57.11	50
One-path	50	2,178.00	37,956.56	339.81	50	301.50	50	276.63	50	194.11	50	191.60	50	169.71	50	231.52	50	202.24	50	30.30	50
packup-pms	40	44,263.65	49,480.65	984.93	29	196.09	40	185.13	40	138.08	40	163.98	40	151.40	40	226.09	40	13.64	40	196.79	40
pbo-routing	15	3,192.00	6,245.13	4.70	15	3.77	15	4.17	15	4.09	15	4.14	15	5.58	15	3.65	15	4.37	15	0.75	15
protein-ins	12	337.00	2,048,127.33	56.25	12	46.24	12	49.78	12	45.04	12	46.43	12	44.75	12	44.71	12	1,096.50	7	1,412.64	3
scheduling	5	8,773.20	444,063.80	1,800.00	0	1,800.00	0	1,800.00	0	1,800.00	0	1,800.00	0	1,800.00	0	1,800.00	0	1,800.00	0	1,800.00	0
simp	17	480.71	20,327.18	128.74	16	134.60	16	132.74	16	131.48	16	128.28	16	129.73	16	130.46	16	165.11	16	217.97	16
su	38	1,053.16	87,991.53	298.01	34	311.69	33	304.20	33	310.26	33	312.61	33	300.86	34	258.86	34	390.35	31	443.54	32
total	1,004	52,829.64	190,276.81	617.82	721	583.03	732	577.58	735	545.78	740	549.97	744	538.41	751	541.27	749	527.94	749	529.95	752

constraints than the baseline approach within the given time limit. Especially for instances with a large number of soft constraints the baseline approach is often not able to either build the network efficiently or provide applicable results.

One reason is that in 48 cases the "baseline" approach is not able to yield any intermediate result, which is comparable with the result of QMaxSAT0.21 (45 instances). This appears only for 12 instances considering "ies+skip+grid+csc+rsc". MSUnCore (which does not have to encode any cardinality network) is not able to return any intermediate result in 20 cases.

The number of satisfied soft clauses of the incremental approach is also higher than the bound of the reference solvers. MSUnCore was able to prove the satisfiability of overall $5,790,880$ soft clauses within the given time limit, i.e., about $2,500,000$ soft clauses less than the incremental methods. The result of QMaxSAT0.21 ($1,449,246$) is comparable with our "baseline" approach and therefore also almost an order of magnitude smaller than for the incremental approaches ($\sim 8,300,000$). I.e., the number of solved instances are comparable, but all incremental methods converge much faster to the global optimum in the long-term than the reference solvers (and the "baseline" approach).

5 Conclusions

We proposed an incremental approach for encoding and solving cardinality constraints based on divide-and-conquer networks. The method allows to profit from additional information learned during the search for partial results leading to a more efficient encoding of the network. This allows a fresh view on cardinality networks and its CNF encoding which would not be possible without the incremental view. Experiments using partial MaxSAT instances [17] show the applicability of the approach and demonstrate the effectiveness of the introduced optimizations compared to the standard encoding, especially for instances with a high number of soft clauses. The results also show that the incremental approach is able to prove lower bounds faster than the standard approach – even compared to unsat core based approaches, leading to a more robust method.

As future work we want to develop further heuristics for splitting the parts in terms of size and the order in which the individual parts get solved. Moreover, we like to extend the concept of incremental encoding to other sorting networks, since all presented methods are quite naturally adaptable to other divide-and-conquer-based networks. Hence, we also plan to use different networks like adders in [15] and counters, or even a mixture of those.

References

1. Lin, P.-C.K., Khatri, S.P.: Application of Max-SAT-based ATPG to optimal cancer therapy design. BMC Genomics 13(suppl. 6), S5 (2012)
2. Favier, A., Elsen, J.-M., De Givry, S., Legarra, A.: Optimal haplotype reconstruction in half-sib families. In: Proceedings of WCB 2010, p. 20 (2010)

3. Reimer, S., Sauer, M., Schubert, T., Becker, B.: Using MaxBMC for Pareto-optimal circuit initialization. In: DATE. IEEE (2014)
4. Menai, M., Al-Yahya, T.: A taxonomy of exact methods for partial Max-SAT. Journal of Computer Science and Technology 28(2), 232–246 (2013)
5. Zhang, H., Shen, H., Manya, F.: Exact algorithms for MAX-SAT. Electronic Notes in Theoretical Computer Science 86(1), 190–203 (2003)
6. Sinz, C.: Towards an optimal CNF encoding of boolean cardinality constraints. In: van Beek, P. (ed.) CP 2005. LNCS, vol. 3709, pp. 827–831. Springer, Heidelberg (2005)
7. Batcher, K.E.: Sorting networks and their applications. In: AFIPS Spring Joint Computing Conference, pp. 307–314. ACM (1968)
8. Bailleux, O., Boufkhad, Y.: Efficient CNF encoding of boolean cardinality constraints. In: Rossi, F. (ed.) CP 2003. LNCS, vol. 2833, pp. 108–122. Springer, Heidelberg (2003)
9. Codish, M., Zazon-Ivry, M.: Pairwise cardinality networks. In: Clarke, E.M., Voronkov, A. (eds.) LPAR-16 2010. LNCS, vol. 6355, pp. 154–172. Springer, Heidelberg (2010)
10. Asín, R., Nieuwenhuis, R., Oliveras, A., Rodríguez-Carbonell, E.: Cardinality networks: a theoretical and empirical study. Constraints 16(2), 195–221 (2011)
11. Morgenstern, A., Schneider, K.: Synthesis of parallel sorting networks using SAT solvers. In: MBMV, pp. 71–80 (2011)
12. Eén, N., Sörensson, N.: Translating pseudo-Boolean constraints into SAT. Journal on Satisfiability, Boolean Modeling and Computation 2, 1–26 (2006)
13. Martins, R., Manquinho, V., Lynce, I.: Exploiting cardinality encodings in parallel maximum satisfiability. In: 2011 23rd IEEE International Conference on Tools with Artificial Intelligence (ICTAI), pp. 313–320. IEEE (2011)
14. Martins, R., Manquinho, V., Lynce, I.: Community-based partitioning for maxSAT solving. In: Järvisalo, M., Van Gelder, A. (eds.) SAT 2013. LNCS, vol. 7962, pp. 182–191. Springer, Heidelberg (2013)
15. Manolios, P., Papavasileiou, V.: Pseudo-Boolean solving by incremental translation to SAT. In: Formal Methods in Computer-Aided Design (FMCAD), pp. 41–45. IEEE (2011)
16. Marques-Silva, J., Planes, J.: Algorithms for maximum satisfiability using unsatisfiable cores. In: Advanced Techniques in Logic Synthesis, Optimizations and Applications, pp. 171–182. Springer (2011)
17. Eighth MaxSAT evaluation (2013), http://maxsat.ia.udl.cat:81/13/
18. Biere, A., Heule, M., van Maaren, H., Walsh, T. (eds.): Handbook of Satisfiability. Frontiers in Artificial Intelligence and Applications, vol. 185. IOS Press (2009)
19. Davis, M., Logemann, G., Loveland, D.: A machine program for theorem-proving. Communications of the ACM 5(7), 394–397 (1962)
20. Eén, N., Sörensson, N.: Temporal induction by incremental SAT solving. Electronic Notes in Theoretical Computer Science 89(4), 543–560 (2003)
21. Biere, A., Cimatti, A., Clarke, E.M., Strichman, O., Zhu, Y.: Bounded model checking. Advances in Computers 58, 117–148 (2003)
22. Fu, Z., Malik, S.: On solving the partial MAX-SAT problem. In: Biere, A., Gomes, C.P. (eds.) SAT 2006. LNCS, vol. 4121, pp. 252–265. Springer, Heidelberg (2006)

23. Parberry, I.: The pairwise sorting network. Parallel Processing Letters 2(02n03), 205–211 (1992)
24. Schubert, T., Reimer, S.: Antom (2013), https://projects.informatik.uni-freiburg.de/projects/antom
25. Koshimura, M., Zhang, T., Fujita, H., Hasegawa, R.: QMaxSAT: A partial Max-SAT solver system description. Journal on Satisfiability, Boolean Modeling and Computation 8, 95–100 (2012), https://sites.google.com/site/qmaxsat/
26. Morgado, A., Heras, F., Marques-Silva, J.: Improvements to core-guided binary search for MaxSAT. In: Cimatti, A., Sebastiani, R. (eds.) SAT 2012. LNCS, vol. 7317, pp. 284–297. Springer, Heidelberg (2012), http://logos.ucd.ie/wiki/doku.php?id=msuncore

Formal Verification of Skiplists
with Arbitrary Many Levels*

Alejandro Sánchez[1] and César Sánchez[1,2]

[1] IMDEA Software Institute, Madrid, Spain
[2] Institute for Information Security, CSIC, Spain

Abstract. We present an effective method for the formal verification of skiplists, including skiplists with arbitrary length and unbounded size. The core of the method is a novel theory of skiplists with a decidable satisfiability problem, which up to now has been an open problem.

A skiplist is an imperative software data structure used to implement a set by maintaining several ordered singly-linked lists in memory. Skiplists are widely used in practice because they are simpler to implement than balanced trees and offer a comparable performance. To accomplish this efficiency most implementations dynamically increment the number of levels as more elements are inserted. Skiplists are difficult to reason about automatically because of the sharing between the different layers. Furthermore, dynamic height poses the extra challenge of dealing with arbitrarily many levels. Our theory allows to express the memory layout of a skiplist of arbitrary height, and has an efficient decision procedure. Using an implementation of our decision procedure, we formally verify shape preservation and a functional specification of two source code implementations of the skiplist datatype.

We also illustrate how our decision procedure can also improve the efficiency of the verification of skiplists with bounded levels. We show empirically that a decision procedure for bounded levels does not scale beyond 3 levels, while our decision procedure terminates quickly for any number of levels.

1 Introduction

A skiplist [13] is a data structure that implements a set, maintaining several sorted singly-linked lists in memory. Each node in a skiplist stores a value and at least the pointer corresponding to the list at the lowest level, called the *backbone list*. Some nodes also contain pointers at higher levels, pointing to the next node present at that level. The skiplist property establishes that: (a) the backbone list is ordered; (b) lists at all levels begin and terminate on special *sentinel* nodes called *head* and *tail* respectively; (c) *tail* points to *null* at all levels; (d) the list at level $i+1$ is a sublist of the list at level i. Search in skiplists is probabilistically logarithmic.

---

* This work was funded in part by Spanish MINECO Project "TIN2012-39391-C04-01 STRONGSOFT".

F. Cassez and J.-F. Raskin (Eds.): ATVA 2014, LNCS 8837, pp. 314–329, 2014.

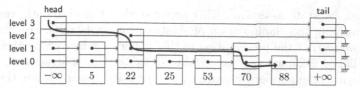

Fig. 1. A skiplist with 4 levels and the traversal searching 88 (heavy arrow)

Consider the skiplist layout in Fig. 1. Higher-level pointers allow to *skip* many elements during the search. A search is performed from left to right in a top down fashion, progressing as much as possible in a level before descending. For instance, in Fig. 1 a lookup for value 88 starts at level 3 of node *head*. The successor of *head* at level 3 is *tail*, which stores value $+\infty$, greater than 88. Consequently, the search continues at *head* by moving down to level 2. The expected logarithmic search follows from the probability of a node being present at a certain level decreasing by $1/2$ as the level increases.

Contributions. Most practical implementations of skiplists either can grow dynamically to any height or limit the maximum height of any node to a large value like 32. Both kinds of implementations use a variable to store the current highest level in use. In this paper we introduce TSL, a theory that captures skiplist memory layouts, and we show that the (quantifier-free) satisfiability problem for TSL is decidable, which has been up to now an open problem. This theory builds non-trivially from the family of theories $\mathsf{TSL_K}$ (see [17]) that allow to reason about skiplists of a *bounded* number of levels. TSL is a decidable theory which solves the following two *open problems*: (a) verification of skiplist implementations with an unbounded/growing number of levels; and (b) verification of skiplist implementations for any bounded number of levels, even beyond the practical limitation of 3 levels suffered by current verification techniques. With our implementation of the decision procedure for TSL, we verify two implementations of the skiplist datatype: one, part of the industrial open source project KDE [1,2], and a full implementation developed internally. In this paper we also show, empirically, that $\mathsf{TSL_K}$ does not scale beyond $K = 3$ levels but TSL allows to verify skiplist implementations of arbitrarily many levels (bounded by some value like 32 or not).

Related Work. Reasoning about skiplists requires to deal with unbounded mutable data stored in the heap. One popular approach to the verification of heap programs is Separation Logic [15]. Skiplists, however, are problematic for separation-like approaches due to the aliasing and memory sharing between nodes at different levels. Most of the work in formal verification of pointer programs are based on program logics in the Hoare tradition enriched to deal with the heap and pointer structures [4,9,20]. Our approach is complementary, consisting of the design of specialized decision procedures for memory layouts which can be incorporated into a reasoning system for proving temporal properties, in the style of Manna-Pnueli [10]. Proofs (of both safety and liveness properties) are ultimately decomposed into verification conditions (VCs) in the underlying theory used for state assertions. This paper studies the automatic verification of VCs involving the manipulation of skiplist memory layouts. For illustration purposes we restrict the presentation in this paper to safety properties.

Logics like [4,9,20] are very powerful to describe pointer structures, but they require the use of quantifiers to reach their expressive power. Hence, these logics preclude their combination with methods like Nelson-Oppen [12] or BAPA [8] for other aspects of the program state. Other alternatives based on shape analysis [19], like forest automata [3,7] can only handle skiplists only of a bounded height (empirical evaluation also suggest a current limit of 3). Unlike [7] our approach is not fully automatic in the sense that it requires some user provided annotations. On the other hand, our approach can handle skiplists of arbitrary and growing height. The burden of additional annotation can be alleviated with methods like invariant generation, but this is out of the scope of this paper.

Instead, we borrow from [14] a model-theoretic technique to deal with reachability to define the theory TSL and build its decision procedure. Our solution uses specific theories of memory layouts [16,17] that allow to express powerful properties in the quantifier-free fragment through the use of built-in predicates. For example, in [17] we presented a family of theories of skiplists of fixed height, based on a theory of ordered singly-linked lists [16]. However, handling dynamic height was still an open problem that precluded the verification of practical skiplist implementations. We solve this open problem here.

The rest of the paper is structured as follows. Section 2 presents a running example of two implementations of the skiplists datatype. Section 3 introduces TSL. Section 4 contains the decidability proof. Section 5 provides some examples of the use of TSL in the verification of skiplists. Finally, Section 6 concludes the paper.

2   An Implementation of Skiplists

Fig. 2 shows the pseudo-code of a sequential implementation of a skiplist, whose basic classes are *Node* and *SkipList*. Each *Node* object contains a *key* field for keeping the list ordered, a field *val* for the actual value stored, and a field *next*: an array of arbitrary length containing the addresses of the following nodes at each level. The program in Fig. 2 implements an unbounded skiplist. The local variables *lvl* in INSERT, *i* in SEARCH and *removeFrom* in REMOVE maintain the maximum level that these algorithms should consider.

An object *sl* of class *SkipList*, maintains fields *sl.head*, *sl.tail* and *sl.maxLevel* to keep the data members storing the addresses of the head and tail sentinel nodes, and the maximum level in use (resp). When the *SkipList* object *sl* is clear from the context, we use *head*, *tail* and *maxLevel* instead of *sl.head*, *sl.tail* and *sl.maxLevel*. The *head* node has $key = -\infty$ and *tail* has $key = +\infty$. These nodes are not removed during the execution and their *key* field is not modified.

```
class   Node      {  Value val;  Key key;  Array⟨Node*⟩ next;  Int @level;                    }
class   SkipList  {  Node* head;  Node* tail;  Int @maxLevel;  Set⟨Addr⟩ @reg;  Set⟨Value⟩ @elems;  }
```

```
 1: procedure MGC(SkipList sl)
 2:    while true do
 3:       v := NondetPickValue
 4:       nondet
          ⎡ call INSERT(sl, v)     ⎤
          ⎢ or                     ⎥
 5:       ⎢ call SEARCH(sl, v)     ⎥
          ⎢ or                     ⎥
          ⎣ call REMOVE(sl, v)     ⎦
 6:    end while
 7: end procedure


 8: procedure INSERT(SkipList sl, Value v)
 9:    Array⟨Node*⟩ [sl.maxLevel + 1]upd
10:    Bool valueWasIn := false
11:    Int lvl := randomLevel
12:    if lvl > sl.maxLevel then
13:       i := sl.maxLevel + 1
14:       while i ≤ lvl do
15:          sl.head.next[i] := sl.tail
16:          sl.tail.next[i] := null
17:          sl.maxLevel := i
18:          i := i + 1
19:       end while
20:    end if
21:    Node* pred := sl.head
22:    Node* curr := pred.next[sl.maxLevel]
23:    Int i := sl.maxLevel
24:    while 0 ≤ i ∧ ¬valueWasIn do
25:       curr := pred.next[i]
26:       while curr.val < v do
27:          pred := curr
28:          curr := pred.next[i]
29:       end while
30:       upd[i] := pred
31:       i := i − 1
32:       valueWasIn := (curr.val = v)
33:    end while
34:    if ¬valueWasIn then
35:       x := CreateNode(lvl, v)
36:       i := 0
37:       while i ≤ lvl do
38:          x.next[i] := upd[i].next[i]
39:          upd[i].next[i] := x
          ┌─────────────────────────────┐
          │ if i = 0 then                │
          │    sl.reg := sl.reg ∪ {x}    │
          │    sl.elems := sl.elems ∪ {v}│
          └─────────────────────────────┘
40:          i := i + 1
41:       end while
42:    end if
43:    return ¬valueWasIn
44: end procedure
```

```
45: procedure SEARCH(SkipList sl, Value v)
46:    Node* pred := sl.head
47:    Node* curr := pred.next[maxLevel]
48:    Int i := sl.maxLevel
49:    while 0 ≤ i do
50:       curr := pred.next[i]
51:       while curr.val < v do
52:          pred := curr
53:          curr := pred.next[i]
54:       end while
55:       i := i − 1
56:    end while
57:    return curr.val = v
58: end procedure


59: procedure REMOVE(SkipList sl, Value v)
60:    Array⟨Node*⟩[sl.maxLevel + 1] upd
61:    Int removeFrom := sl.maxLevel
62:    Node* pred := sl.head
63:    Node* curr := pred.next[sl.maxLevel]
64:    Int i := sl.maxLevel
65:    while i ≥ 0 do
66:       curr := pred.next[i]
67:       while curr.val < v do
68:          pred := curr
69:          curr := pred.next[i]
70:       end while
71:       if curr.val ≠ v then
72:          removeFrom := i − 1
73:       end if
74:       upd[i] := pred
75:       i := i − 1
76:    end while
77:    Bool valueWasIn := (curr.val = v)
78:    if valueWasIn then
79:       i := removeFrom
80:       while i ≥ 0 do
81:          upd[i].next[i] := curr.next[i]
          ┌─────────────────────────────┐
          │ if i = 0 then                │
          │    sl.reg := sl.reg \ {curr} │
          │    sl.elems := sl.elems \ {v}│
          └─────────────────────────────┘
82:          i := i − 1
83:       end while
84:       free (curr)
85:    end if
86:    return valueWasIn
87: end procedure
```

Fig. 2. On top, the classes *Node* and *SkipList*. Below, the most general client MGC, and the procedures INSERT, SEARCH and REMOVE.

Finally, *Node* objects also maintain a "ghost field" *level* for the highest relevant level of *next*. *SkipList* objects maintain two ghost fields: *reg* for the region (set of addresses) managed by the skiplist and *elems* for the set of values stored in the skiplist. We use the @ symbol to denote a ghost field, and boxes (see Fig. 2) to describe "ghost code". These small extra ghost annotations are only added for verification purposes and do not influence the execution of the real program.

Fig. 2 contains the algorithms for insertion (INSERT), search (SEARCH) and removal (REMOVE). Fig. 2 also shows the most general client MGC that non-deterministically performs calls to skiplist operations, and can exercise all possible sequences of calls. We use MGC to verify properties like skiplist preservation. The execution begins with an empty skiplist containing only *head* and *tail* nodes at level 0, that has already been created. New nodes are then added using INSERT. To maintain *reg* and *elems*: (a) a new node becomes part of the skiplist when it is connected at level 0 in INSERT; and (b) a node stops being part of the skiplist when it is disconnected at level 0 in REMOVE. For simplicity, we assume in this paper that *val* and *key* contain the same object. We wish to prove that in all reachable states of MGC the memory layout is that of a "skiplist". We will also show that this datatype implements a set.

3   TSL: The Theory of Skiplists of Arbitrary Height

We use many-sorted first order logic to define TSL, as a combination of theories. We begin with a brief overview of notation and concepts. A signature Σ is a triple (S, F, P) where S is a set of sorts, F a set of functions and P a set of predicates. If $\Sigma_1 = (S_1, F_1, P_1)$ and $\Sigma_2 = (S_2, F_2, P_2)$, we define $\Sigma_1 \cup \Sigma_2 = (S_1 \cup S_2, F_1 \cup F_2, P_1 \cup P_2)$. Similarly we say that $\Sigma_1 \subseteq \Sigma_2$ when $S_1 \subseteq S_2$, $F_1 \subseteq F_2$ and $P_1 \subseteq P_2$. Let t be a term and φ a formula. We denote with $V_\sigma(t)$ (resp. $V_\sigma(\varphi)$) the set of variables of sort σ occurring in t (resp. φ). Similarly, we denote with $C_\sigma(t)$ (resp. $C_\sigma(\varphi)$) the set of constants of sort σ occurring in t (resp. φ).

A Σ-interpretation is a map from symbols in Σ to values (see, e.g., [6]). A Σ-structure is a Σ-interpretation over an empty set of variables. A Σ-formula over a set X of variables is satisfiable whenever it is true in some Σ-interpretation over X. A Σ-theory is a pair $(\Sigma, \mathbf{A})$ where Σ is a signature and $\mathbf{A}$ is a class of Σ-structures. Given a theory $T = (\Sigma, \mathbf{A})$, a T-interpretation is a Σ-interpretation $\mathcal{A}$ such that $\mathcal{A}^\Sigma \in \mathbf{A}$, where $\mathcal{A}^\Sigma$ is $\mathcal{A}$ restricted to interpret no variables. Given a Σ-theory T, a Σ-formula φ over a set of variables X is T-satisfiable whenever it is true on a T-interpretation over X.

Formally, the theory of skiplists of arbitrary height is defined as TSL $= (\Sigma_{\mathsf{TSL}}, \mathbf{TSL})$, where Σ_{TSL} is the union of the following signatures, shown in Fig. 3 $\Sigma_{\mathsf{TSL}} = \Sigma_{\mathsf{level}} \cup \Sigma_{\mathsf{ord}} \cup \Sigma_{\mathsf{array}} \cup \Sigma_{\mathsf{cell}} \cup \Sigma_{\mathsf{mem}} \cup \Sigma_{\mathsf{reach}} \cup \Sigma_{\mathsf{set}} \cup \Sigma_{\mathsf{bridge}}$, and $\mathbf{TSL}$ is the class of Σ_{TSL}-structures satisfying the conditions listed in Fig. 4.

Informally, sort addr represents addresses; elem the universe of elements that can be stored in the skiplist; level the levels of a skiplist; ord the ordered keys used to preserve a strict order in the skiplist; array corresponds to arrays of addresses, indexed by levels; cell models *cells* representing objects of class *Node*;

mem models the heap, a map from addresses to cells; path describes finite sequences of non-repeating addresses to model non-cyclic list paths; finally, set models sets of addresses—also known as regions.

Σ_{set} is interpreted as finite sets of addresses. Σ_{level} as natural numbers with order and addition with constants. Σ_{ord} models the order between elements, and contains two special elements $-\infty$ and $+\infty$ for the lowest and highest values in the order $\preceq$. Σ_{array} is the theory of arrays [5, 11] with two operations: $A[i]$ to model that an element of sort addr is stored in array A at position i of sort level, and $A\{i \leftarrow a\}$ for an array update, which returns the array that results from A by replacing the element at position i with a. Σ_{cell} contains the constructors and selectors for building and inspecting cells, including $error$ for incorrect dereferences. Σ_{mem} is the signature of heaps, with the usual memory access and single memory mutation functions. The signature Σ_{reach} contains predicates to check reachability of addresses using paths at different levels. Finally, Σ_{bridge} contains auxiliary functions and predicates to manipulate and inspect paths as well as a

Signt	Sort	Functions	Predicates
Σ_{level}	level	$0 : \mathsf{level}$ $s : \mathsf{level} \to \mathsf{level}$	$< : \mathsf{level} \times \mathsf{level}$
Σ_{ord}	ord	$-\infty, +\infty : \mathsf{ord}$	$\preceq : \mathsf{ord} \times \mathsf{ord}$
Σ_{array}	array level addr	$\_[\_] \qquad : \mathsf{array} \times \mathsf{level} \to \mathsf{addr}$ $\_\{\_ \leftarrow \_\} : \mathsf{array} \times \mathsf{level} \times \mathsf{addr} \to \mathsf{array}$	
Σ_{cell}	cell elem ord array addr level	$error \quad : \mathsf{cell}$ $mkcell : \mathsf{elem} \times \mathsf{ord} \times \mathsf{array} \times \mathsf{level} \to \mathsf{cell}$ $\_.data \quad : \mathsf{cell} \to \mathsf{elem}$ $\_.key \quad : \mathsf{cell} \to \mathsf{ord}$ $\_.arr \quad : \mathsf{cell} \to \mathsf{array}$ $\_.max \quad : \mathsf{cell} \to \mathsf{level}$	
Σ_{mem}	mem addr cell	$null : \mathsf{addr}$ $rd \quad : \mathsf{mem} \times \mathsf{addr} \to \mathsf{cell}$ $upd : \mathsf{mem} \times \mathsf{addr} \times \mathsf{cell} \to \mathsf{mem}$	
Σ_{reach}	mem addr path	$\epsilon \ : \mathsf{path}$ $[\_] : \mathsf{addr} \to \mathsf{path}$	$append : \mathsf{path} \times \mathsf{path} \times \mathsf{path}$ $reach \quad : \mathsf{mem} \times \mathsf{addr} \times \mathsf{addr}$ $\times \mathsf{level} \times \mathsf{path}$
Σ_{set}	addr set	$\emptyset \qquad : \mathsf{set}$ $\{\_\} \qquad : \mathsf{addr} \to \mathsf{set}$ $\cup, \cap, \backslash : \mathsf{set} \times \mathsf{set} \to \mathsf{set}$	$\in : \mathsf{addr} \times \mathsf{set}$ $\subseteq : \mathsf{set} \times \mathsf{set}$
Σ_{bridge}	mem addr set path level	$path2set : \mathsf{path} \to \mathsf{set}$ $addr2set : \mathsf{mem} \times \mathsf{addr} \times \mathsf{level} \to \mathsf{set}$ $getp \qquad : \mathsf{mem} \times \mathsf{addr} \times \mathsf{addr} \times \mathsf{level} \to \mathsf{path}$	$ordList : \mathsf{mem} \times \mathsf{path}$ $skiplist : \mathsf{mem} \times \mathsf{set} \times \mathsf{level}$ $\times \mathsf{addr} \times \mathsf{addr}$

Fig. 3. The signature of the TSL theory

Each sort σ in Σ_{TSL} is mapped to a non-empty set $\mathcal{A}_\sigma$ such that:
(a) $\mathcal{A}_{\mathsf{addr}}$ and $\mathcal{A}_{\mathsf{elem}}$ are discrete sets   (b) $\mathcal{A}_{\mathsf{level}}$ is the naturals with order
(c) $\mathcal{A}_{\mathsf{ord}}$ is a total ordered set   (d) $\mathcal{A}_{\mathsf{array}} = \mathcal{A}_{\mathsf{addr}}^{\mathcal{A}_{\mathsf{level}}}$
(e) $\mathcal{A}_{\mathsf{cell}} = \mathcal{A}_{\mathsf{elem}} \times \mathcal{A}_{\mathsf{ord}} \times \mathcal{A}_{\mathsf{array}} \times \mathcal{A}_{\mathsf{level}}$ (f) $\mathcal{A}_{\mathsf{path}}$ is the set of all finite sequences of
(g) $\mathcal{A}_{\mathsf{mem}} = \mathcal{A}_{\mathsf{cell}}^{\mathcal{A}_{\mathsf{addr}}}$ (pairwise) distinct elements of $\mathcal{A}_{\mathsf{addr}}$
(h) $\mathcal{A}_{\mathsf{set}}$ is the power-set of $\mathcal{A}_{\mathsf{addr}}$

Signature	Interpretation
Σ_{level}	• $0^{\mathcal{A}} = 0$ • $s^{\mathcal{A}}(l) = s(l)$, for each $l \in \mathcal{A}_{\mathsf{level}}$
Σ_{ord}	• $x \preceq^{\mathcal{A}} y \wedge y \preceq^{\mathcal{A}} x \to x = y$ • $x \preceq^{\mathcal{A}} y \vee y \preceq^{\mathcal{A}} x$ • $x \preceq^{\mathcal{A}} y \wedge y \preceq^{\mathcal{A}} z \to x \preceq^{\mathcal{A}} z$ • $-\infty^{\mathcal{A}} \preceq^{\mathcal{A}} x \wedge x \preceq^{\mathcal{A}} +\infty^{\mathcal{A}}$ for any $x, y, z \in \mathcal{A}_{\mathsf{ord}}$
Σ_{array}	• $A[l]^{\mathcal{A}} = A(l)$ • $A\{l \leftarrow a\}^{\mathcal{A}} = B$, where $B(l) = a$ and $B(i) = A(i)$ for $i \neq l$ for each $A, B \in \mathcal{A}_{\mathsf{array}}$, $l \in \mathcal{A}_{\mathsf{level}}$ and $a \in \mathcal{A}_{\mathsf{addr}}$
Σ_{cell}	• $mkcell^{\mathcal{A}}(e, k, A, l) = \langle e, k, A, l \rangle$ • $error^{\mathcal{A}}.arr^{\mathcal{A}}(l) = null^{\mathcal{A}}$ • $\langle e, k, A, l \rangle.data^{\mathcal{A}} = e$ • $\langle e, k, A, l \rangle.key^{\mathcal{A}} = k$ • $\langle e, k, A, l \rangle.arr^{\mathcal{A}} = A$ • $\langle e, k, A, l \rangle.max^{\mathcal{A}} = l$ for each $e \in \mathcal{A}_{\mathsf{elem}}$, $k \in \mathcal{A}_{\mathsf{ord}}$, $A \in \mathcal{A}_{\mathsf{array}}$, and $l \in \mathcal{A}_{\mathsf{level}}$
Σ_{mem}	• $rd(m, a)^{\mathcal{A}} = m(a)$ • $upd^{\mathcal{A}}(m, a, c) = m_{a \mapsto c}$ • $m^{\mathcal{A}}(null^{\mathcal{A}}) = error^{\mathcal{A}}$ for each $m \in \mathcal{A}_{\mathsf{mem}}$, $a \in \mathcal{A}_{\mathsf{addr}}$ and $c \in \mathcal{A}_{\mathsf{cell}}$
Σ_{reach}	• $\epsilon^{\mathcal{A}}$ is the empty sequence • $[a]^{\mathcal{A}}$ is the sequence containing $a \in \mathcal{A}_{\mathsf{addr}}$ as the only element • $([a_1 .. a_n], [b_1 .. b_m], [a_1 .. a_n, b_1 .. b_m]) \in append^{\mathcal{A}}$ iff $a_k \neq b_l$. • $(m, a_{init}, a_{end}, l, p) \in reach^{\mathcal{A}}$ iff $a_{init} = a_{end}$ and $p = \epsilon$, or there exist addresses $a_1, \ldots, a_n \in \mathcal{A}_{\mathsf{addr}}$ such that: (a) $p = [a_1 .. a_n]$ (c) $m(a_r).arr^{\mathcal{A}}(l) = a_{r+1}$, for $r < n$ (b) $a_1 = a_{init}$ (d) $m(a_n).arr^{\mathcal{A}}(l) = a_{end}$
Σ_{bridge}	for each $m \in \mathcal{A}_{\mathsf{mem}}$, $p \in \mathcal{A}_{\mathsf{path}}$, $l \in \mathcal{A}_{\mathsf{level}}$, $a_i, a_e \in \mathcal{A}_{\mathsf{addr}}$, $r \in \mathcal{A}_{\mathsf{set}}$ • $path2set^{\mathcal{A}}(p) = \{a_1, \ldots, a_n\}$ for $p = [a_1, \ldots, a_n] \in \mathcal{A}_{\mathsf{path}}$ • $addr2set^{\mathcal{A}}(m, a, l) = \{a' \mid \exists p \in \mathcal{A}_{\mathsf{path}} \;.\; (m, a, a', l, p) \in reach^{\mathcal{A}}\}$ • $getp^{\mathcal{A}}(m, a_i, a_e, l) = p$ if $(m, a_i, a_e, l, p) \in reach^{\mathcal{A}}$, and ϵ otherwise • $ordList^{\mathcal{A}}(m, p)$ iff $p = \epsilon$ or $p = [a]$, or $p = [a_1, \ldots, a_n]$ with $n \geq 2$ and $m(a_j).key^{\mathcal{A}} \preceq m(a_{j+1}).key^{\mathcal{A}}$ for all $1 \leq j < n$, for any $m \in \mathcal{A}_{\mathsf{mem}}$ • $skiplist^{\mathcal{A}}(m, r, l, a_i, a_e)$ iff $\begin{bmatrix} ordList^{\mathcal{A}}(m, getp^{\mathcal{A}}(m, a_i, a_e, 0)) & \wedge \\ r = addr2set^{\mathcal{A}}(m, a_i, 0) & \wedge \\ 0 \leq l \wedge \forall a \in r \;.\; m(a).max^{\mathcal{A}} \leq l & \wedge \\ m(a_e).arr^{\mathcal{A}}(l) = null^{\mathcal{A}} & \wedge \\ (0 = l) \vee \\ (\exists l_p \;.\; s^{\mathcal{A}}(l_p) = l \wedge \forall i \in 0, \ldots, l_p \;. \\ m(a_e).arr^{\mathcal{A}}(i) = null^{\mathcal{A}} \wedge \\ path2set^{\mathcal{A}}(getp^{\mathcal{A}}(m, a_i, a_e, s^{\mathcal{A}}(i))) \subseteq \\ path2set^{\mathcal{A}}(getp^{\mathcal{A}}(m, a_i, a_e, i))) \end{bmatrix}$

Fig. 4. Characterization of a TSL-interpretation $\mathcal{A}$

native predicate for the skiplist memory shape. In the paper, for a variable l of sort level, we generally use $l + 1$ for $s(l)$.

4   Decidability of TSL

In this section we prove the decidability of the satisfiability problem of quantifier-free TSL formulas. We first start with some preliminaries.

Preliminaries. A flat literal is of the form $x = y$, $x \neq y$, $x = f(y_1, \ldots, y_n)$, $p(y_1, \ldots, y_n)$ or $\neg p(y_1, \ldots, y_n)$, where $x, y, y_1, \ldots, y_n$ are variables, f is a function symbol and p is a predicate symbol defined in the signature of TSL. We first identify a set of normalized literals. All other literals can be converted into normalized literals.

Lemma 1 (Normalized Literals). *Every TSL-formula is equivalent to a disjunction of conjunctions of literals of the following list, called* normalized TSL-literals*:*

$e_1 \neq e_2$	$a_1 \neq a_2$	$l_1 \neq l_2$
$a = null$	$c = error$	$c = rd(m, a)$
$k_1 \neq k_2$	$k_1 \preceq k_2$	$m_2 = upd(m_1, a, c)$
$c = mkcell(e, k, A, l)$	$l_1 < l_2$	$l = q$
$s = \{a\}$	$s_1 = s_2 \cup s_3$	$s_1 = s_2 \setminus s_3$
$a = A[l]$	$B = A\{l \leftarrow a\}$	
$p_1 \neq p_2$	$p = [a]$	$p_1 = rev(p_2)$
$s = path2set(p)$	$append(p_1, p_2, p_3)$	$\neg append(p_1, p_2, p_3)$
$s = addr2set(m, a, l)$	$p = getp(m, a_1, a_2, l)$	
$ordList(m, p)$		$skiplist(m, s, a_1, a_2)$

For instance, $e = c.data$ can be rewritten as $c = mkcell(e, k, A, l)$ for fresh variables k, A and l. The predicate $reach(m, a_1, a_2, l, p)$ can be similarly translated into $a_2 \in addr2set(m, a_1, l) \land p = getp(m, a_1, a_2, l)$. Similar translations can be defined for $\neg ordList(m, p)$, $\neg skiplist(m, r, l, a_i, a_e)$, etc.

We will use the following formula ψ as a running example:

$$\psi \quad : \quad i = 0 \land A = rd(heap, head).arr \land B = A\{i \leftarrow tail\} \land rd(heap, head).max = 3.$$

This formula establishes that B is the array obtained from the next pointers of node *head*, by replacing the pointer at the lower level by *tail*. To check the satisfiability of ψ we first normalize it, obtaining ψ_{norm}:

$$\psi_{\text{norm}} \quad : \quad i = 0 \land \begin{pmatrix} c = rd(heap, head) \land \\ c = mkcell(e, k, A, l) \land \\ l = 3 \end{pmatrix} \land B = A\{i \leftarrow tail\}.$$

4.1   A Decision Procedure for TSL

Fig. 5 sketches a decision procedure for the satisfiability problem of TSL formulas, by reducing it to the satisfiability of quantifier-free TSL_K formulas and

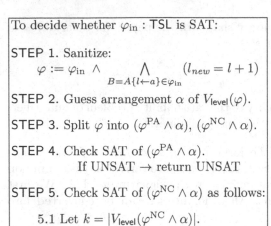

STEP 1. Sanitize:
$$\varphi := \varphi_{in} \wedge \bigwedge_{B=A\{l\leftarrow a\}\in\varphi_{in}} (l_{new} = l + 1)$$

STEP 2. Guess arrangement α of $V_{level}(\varphi)$.

STEP 3. Split φ into $(\varphi^{PA} \wedge \alpha)$, $(\varphi^{NC} \wedge \alpha)$.

STEP 4. Check SAT of $(\varphi^{PA} \wedge \alpha)$.
      If UNSAT → return UNSAT

STEP 5. Check SAT of $(\varphi^{NC} \wedge \alpha)$ as follows:

    5.1 Let $k = |V_{level}(\varphi^{NC} \wedge \alpha)|$.
    5.2 Check $\ulcorner\varphi^{NC} \wedge \alpha\urcorner : TSL_K(k)$:
          If SAT → return SAT
          else return UNSAT.

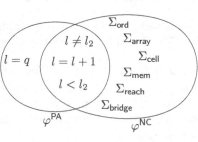

Fig. 5. A decision procedure for the satisfiability of TSL formulas (left). A split of φ obtained after STEP 1 into φ^{PA} and φ^{NC} (right).

quantifier-free Presburger arithmetic formulas. We start from a TSL formula φ expressed as a normalized conjunction of literals. The main idea is to guess a feasible arrangement between level variables, and then extract from φ the *relevant levels*, generating a TSL_K formula using only relevant levels. To show correctness, we will see that from the resulting model of the TSL_K formula we can create a model of the original TSL formula by replicating relevant levels into missing intermediate levels.

STEP 1: Sanitization. The decision procedure begins by sanitizing the normalized collection of literals received as input. A formula is sanitized when the level right above array updates is named explicitly by a level variable. Sanitization serves to infer the existence of large models from smaller models where only named levels are populated, in Theorem 1 below.

Definition 1 (Sanitized). *A conjunction of normalized literals is sanitized if for every literal $B = A\{l \leftarrow a\}$ there is a literal of the form $l_2 = l + 1$.*

A formula can be sanitized by adding a fresh variable l_{new} and a literal $l_{new} = l+1$ for every literal $B = A\{l \leftarrow a\}$ in case there is no literal $l_2 = l + 1$ already in the formula. Sanitizing a formula does not affect its satisfiability because it only adds an arithmetic constraint $(l_{new} = l + 1)$ for a fresh new variable l_{new}. For example, sanitizing ψ_{norm} we obtain $\psi_{sanit} : \psi_{norm} \wedge l_{new} = i + 1$.

STEP 2: Order Arrangements, and STEP 3: Split. A model of a formula assigns a natural number to every level variable. Hence, every two variables are either assigned the same value or are ordered by $<$. An *order arrangement* is an arithmetic formula that captures this relation between level variables.

Definition 2 (Order Arrangement). *Given a sanitized formula φ, an order arrangement is a collection of literals containing, for every pair of level variables $l_1, l_2 \in V_{\text{level}}(\varphi)$, exactly one of $(l_1 = l_2), (l_1 < l_2),$ or $(l_2 < l_1)$.*

For instance, an order arrangement of ψ_{sanit} is $\{i < l_{new}, i < l, l_{new} < l\}$. Since there is a finite number of level variables in a formula φ, there is a finite number of order arrangements. Note also that a formula φ is satisfiable if and only if there is an order arrangement α such that $\varphi \wedge \alpha$ is satisfiable. STEP 2 of the decision procedure consists of guessing an order arrangement α.

STEP 3 of the decision procedure first splits the sanitized formula φ into φ^{PA}, which contains precisely all those literals in the theory of arithmetic Σ_{level}, and φ^{NC} containing all literals from φ except those involving constants $(l = q)$. Clearly, φ is equivalent to $\varphi^{\text{NC}} \wedge \varphi^{\text{PA}}$. In our running example, ψ_{sanit} is split into ψ^{PA} and ψ^{NC}:

$$\psi^{\text{PA}} \quad : \quad i = 0 \wedge l = 3 \wedge l_{new} = i + 1$$

$$\psi^{\text{NC}} \quad : \quad \begin{pmatrix} c = rd(heap, head) \wedge \\ c = mkcell(e, k, A, l) \end{pmatrix} \wedge B = A\{i \leftarrow tail\} \wedge l_{new} = i + 1.$$

STEP 3 uses the order arrangement to reduce the satisfiability of a sanitized formula φ that follows an order arrangement α into the satisfiability of a Presburger Arithmetic formula $(\varphi^{\text{PA}} \wedge \alpha)$, checked in STEP 4, and the satisfiability of a sanitized formula without constants $(\varphi^{\text{NC}} \wedge \alpha)$, checked in STEP 5. An essential notion to show the correctness of this split is that of a *gap*, which is a level in a model that is not named by a level variable.

Definition 3 (Gap). *Let $\mathcal{A}$ be a model of φ. We say that a number n is a gap in $\mathcal{A}$ if there are variables l_1, l_2 in $V_{\text{level}}(\varphi)$ such that $l_1^{\mathcal{A}} < n < l_2^{\mathcal{A}}$, but there is no l in $V_{\text{level}}(\varphi)$ with $l^{\mathcal{A}} = n$.*

Consider ψ_{sanit} for which $V_{\text{level}}(\psi_{\text{sanit}}) = \{i, l_{new}, l\}$. A model $\mathcal{A}_\psi$ of ψ that interprets variables i, l_{new} and l as 0, 1 and 3 respectively has a gap at 2.

Definition 4 (Gap-less model). *A model $\mathcal{A}$ of φ is a gap-less model whenever it has no gaps, and for every array C in $\text{array}^{\mathcal{A}}$ and level $n > l^{\mathcal{A}}$ for all $l \in V_{\text{level}}(\varphi)$, $C(n) = null$.*

We will prove the existence of a gap-less model given that there is a model. But, before, we need one last auxiliary notion to ease the construction of similar models, by setting a condition under which reachability at different levels is preserved.

Definition 5. *Two interpretations $\mathcal{A}$ and $\mathcal{B}$ of φ agree on sorts σ whenever*
(i) $\mathcal{A}_\sigma = \mathcal{B}_\sigma$,

(ii) for every $v \in V_\sigma(\varphi)$, $v^A = v^B$,

(iii) for every function symbol f with domain and co-domain from sorts in σ, $f^A = f^B$ and for every predicate symbol P with domain in σ, P^A iff P^B.

Lemma 2. *Let A and B be two interpretations of a sanitized formula φ that agree on sorts $\{\text{addr}, \text{elem}, \text{ord}, \text{path}, \text{set}\}$, and s.t. for every $l \in V_{\text{level}}(\varphi)$, $m \in V_{\text{mem}}(\varphi)$, and $a \in \text{addr}^A$, the following holds: $m^A(a).\text{arr}^A(l^A) = m^B(a).\text{arr}^B(l^B)$ Then, $\left(\text{reach}^A(m^A, a^A_{init}, a^A_{end}, l^A, p^A)\right)$ iff $\left(\text{reach}^B(m^B, a^B_{init}, a^B_{end}, l^B, p^B)\right)$.*

Proof (Sketch). The proof follows an inductive argument on the length of the paths returned by reach.

We show now that if a sanitized formula without constants, as the one obtained after the split in STEP 3, has a model then it has a model without gaps.

Lemma 3 (Gap-reduction). *Let A be a model of a sanitized formula φ without constants, and let A have a gap at n. Then, there is a model B of φ such that, for every $l \in V_{\text{level}}(\varphi)$: $l^B = l^A - 1$ if $l^A > n$, and $l^B = l^A$ if $l^A < n$. The number of gaps in B is one less than in A.*

Proof. (Sketch) We only show here the construction of the model B. Let A be a model of φ with a gap at n. We build a model B with the condition in the lemma. B agrees with A on addr, elem, ord, path, set. In particular, $v^B = v^A$ for variables of these sorts. For the other sorts we let $B_\sigma = A_\sigma$ for $\sigma = \text{level}, \text{array}, \text{cell}, \text{mem}$. We define transformation maps for elements of the corresponding domains as follows:

$$\beta_{\text{level}}(j) = \begin{cases} j & \text{if } j < n \\ j - 1 & \text{otherwise} \end{cases} \qquad \beta_{\text{array}}(A)(i) = \begin{cases} A(i) & \text{if } i < n \\ A(i+1) & \text{if } i \geq n \end{cases}$$

$$\beta_{\text{cell}}((e, k, A, l)) = (e, k, \beta_{\text{array}}(A), \beta_{\text{level}}(l)) \qquad \beta_{\text{mem}}(m)(a) = \beta_{\text{cell}}(m(a))$$

Now, for variables l : level, A : array, c : cell and m : mem, we simply let $l^B = \beta_{\text{level}}(l^A)$, $A^B = \beta_{\text{array}}(A^A)$, $c^B = \beta_{\text{cell}}(c^A)$, and $m^B = \beta_{\text{mem}}(m^A)$.

The interpretation of all functions and predicates is preserved from A. An exhaustive case analysis on the normalized literals allows to show that B is indeed a model of φ. □

For instance, consider formula ψ_{sanit} and model A_ψ above. We can construct model B reducing one gap from A_ψ by stating that $i^B = i^{A_\psi}$, $l_{new}{}^B = l_{new}{}^{A_\psi}$ and $l^B = 2$, and completely ignore arrays in model A_ψ at level 2.

Similarly, by a simple case analysis of the literals of φ and Lemma 2 the following Lemma holds, and the corollary that shows the existence of gapless models.

Lemma 4 (Top-reduction). *Let A be a model of φ, and n a level such that $n > l^A$ for all $l \in V_{\text{level}}(\varphi)$ and $A \in \text{array}^A$ be such that $A(n) \neq \text{null}$. Then the interpretation B obtained from A by replacing $A(n) = \text{null}$ is also a model of φ.*

Corollary 1. *Let φ be a sanitized formula without constants. Then, φ has a model if and only if φ has a gapless model.*

We show now that STEP 2 and the split in STEP 3 preserve satisfiability.

Theorem 1. *A sanitized TSL formula φ is satisfiable if and only if for some order arrangement α, both $(\varphi^{PA} \wedge \alpha)$ and $(\varphi^{NC} \wedge \alpha)$ are satisfiable.*

Proof. (Sketch) The "$\Rightarrow$" direction follows immediately, since a model of φ contains a model of its subformulas φ^{PA} and φ^{NC}, and a model of φ^{PA} induces a satisfying order arrangement α.

For "$\Leftarrow$", let α be an order arrangement for which both $(\varphi^{PA} \wedge \alpha)$ and $(\varphi^{NC} \wedge \alpha)$ are satisfiable, and let $\mathcal{B}$ be a model of $(\varphi^{NC} \wedge \alpha)$ and $\mathcal{A}$ be a model of $(\varphi^{PA} \wedge \alpha)$. By Corollary 1, we assume that $\mathcal{B}$ is a gapless model. The obstacle in merging the models is that the values for levels in $\mathcal{A}$ and in $\mathcal{B}$ may differ. We will build a model $\mathcal{C}$ of φ using $\mathcal{B}$ and $\mathcal{A}$. In $\mathcal{C}$, all levels will receive $l^{\mathcal{C}} = l^{\mathcal{A}}$, but all other sorts will be filled according to $\mathcal{B}$, including the contents of cells at level l, which will be the corresponding cells of $\mathcal{B}$ at level $l^{\mathcal{B}}$. The remaining issue is how to fill intermediate levels, not existing in $\mathcal{B}$. Levels can be populated cloning existing levels from $\mathcal{B}$, illustrated in Fig. 6 (a) below. The two reasonable candidates to populate the levels between $l_1^{\mathcal{C}}$ and $l_2^{\mathcal{C}}$, are level $l_1^{\mathcal{B}}$ and level $l_2^{\mathcal{B}}$, but without sanitation both options can lead to a predicate changing its truth value between models $\mathcal{B}$ and $\mathcal{C}$, as illustrated in Fig. 6 (b) and (c). With sanitation, level l_{new} can be used to populate the intermediate levels, preserving the truth values of all predicates between models $\mathcal{B}$ and $\mathcal{C}$. $\square$

STEP 4: Presburger Constraints. The formula $(\varphi^{PA} \wedge \alpha)$ contains only literals of the form $l_1 = q$, $l_1 \neq l_2$, $l_1 = l_2 + 1$, and $l_1 < l_2$ for integer variables l_1 and l_2 and integer constant q, a simple fragment of Presburger Arithmetic.

STEP 5: Deciding Satisfiability of Formulas Without Constants. In STEP 5 we reduce a sanitized formula without constants ψ into an equisatisfiable formula $\ulcorner\psi\urcorner$ in the decidable theory $\mathsf{TSL_K}$, for a finite value $\mathsf{K} = |V_{\mathsf{level}}(\psi)|$ computed from the formula. This bound provides the number of levels required in necessary to reason about the satisfiability of ψ. We use $[\mathsf{K}]$ as a short for the set $0 \ldots \mathsf{K} - 1$. For ψ_{sanit}, we have $\mathsf{K} = 3$ and thus we construct a formula in $\mathsf{TSL_3}$.

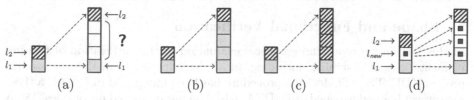

Fig. 6. Pumping a model of φ^{NC} to a model of φ is allowed thanks to the fresh level l_{new}. In (b) the truth value of $A = B\{l_1 \leftarrow e\}$ is not preserved. In (c) $A = B\{l_2 \leftarrow e\}$ is not preserved. In (d) all predicates are preserved.

The translation from ψ into $\ulcorner\psi\urcorner$ works as follows. For every variable A of sort array appearing in some literal in ψ we introduce K fresh new variables $v_{A[0]}, \ldots, v_{A[K-1]}$ of sort addr. These variables correspond to the addresses from A that the decision procedure for $\mathsf{TSL_K}$ needs to reason about. All literals from ψ are left unchanged in $\ulcorner\psi\urcorner$ except $(c = mkcell(e, k, A, l))$, $(a = A[l])$, $(B = A\{l \leftarrow a\})$, $B = A$ and $skiplist(m, s, a_1, a_2)$ that are changed as follows:

- $c = mkcell(e, k, A, l)$ is transformed into $c = (e, k, v_{A[0]}, \ldots, v_{A[K-1]})$.
- $a = A[l]$ gets translated into: $\bigwedge_{i\in[K]} l = i \rightarrow a = v_{A[i]}$.
- $B = A\{l \leftarrow a\}$ is translated into:

$$\left(\bigwedge_{i\in[K]} l = i \rightarrow a = v_{B[i]}\right) \wedge \left(\bigwedge_{j\in[K]} l \neq j \rightarrow v_{B[j]} = v_{A[j]}\right)$$

- $skiplist(m, r, a_1, a_2)$ gets translated into:

$$ordList(m, getp(m, a_1, a_2, 0)) \quad \wedge \quad r = path2set(getp(m, a_1, a_2, 0)) \wedge$$

$$\bigwedge_{i\in[K]} rd(m, a_2).arr[i] = null \qquad\qquad\qquad \wedge$$

$$\bigwedge_{i\in[K-1]} path2set(getp(m, a_1, a_2, i+1)) \subseteq path2set(getp(m, a_1, a_2, i))$$

Note that the formula $\ulcorner\varphi\urcorner$ obtained using this translation belongs to the theory $\mathsf{TSL_K}$. For instance, in our running example,

$$\ulcorner\psi^{NC}\urcorner : \begin{bmatrix} i = 0 \rightarrow tail = v_{B[0]} & \wedge\ i = 1 \rightarrow tail = v_{B[1]} & \wedge\ i = 2 \rightarrow tail = v_{B[2]} & \wedge \\ i \neq 0 \rightarrow v_{B[0]} = v_{A[0]} & \wedge\ i \neq 1 \rightarrow v_{B[1]} = v_{A[1]} & \wedge\ i \neq 2 \rightarrow v_{B[2]} = v_{A[2]} & \wedge \\ c = rd(heap, head) & \wedge\ c = mkcell(e, k, v_{A[0]}, v_{A[1]}, v_{A[2]}) & \wedge\ l_{new} = i+1 \end{bmatrix}$$

The following lemmas establishes the correctness of the translation.

Lemma 5. *Let ψ be a sanitized TSL formula with no constants. Then, ψ is satisfiable if and only if $\ulcorner\psi\urcorner$ is also satisfiable.*

The main result of this paper is the following decidability theorem, which follows from Lemma 5, Theorem 1 and the fact that every formula can be normalized and sanitized.

Theorem 2. *The satisfiability problem of QF TSL-formulas is decidable.*

5   Shape and Functional Verification

In this section we report an empirical evaluation of the verification of two implementations of a skiplist, including an implementation from the open-source project KDE. The TSL decision procedure has been integrated in LEAP[1], a theorem prover being developed at IMDEA, based on parametrized proof rules [18]. A TSL query is ultimately decomposed into simple Presburger arithmetic formulas

---

[1] LEAP and all examples can be downloaded from http://software.imdea.org/leap

and $\mathsf{TSL_K}$ formulas. We use the decidability theorem for $\mathsf{TSL_K}$ formulas, which essentially computes a cardinality bound on a small model. Then, the $\mathsf{TSL_K}$ procedure encodes in SMT the existence of one such small model by unrolling predicates (like e.g., *reach*) up to the computed bound.

We verified two kinds of properties: skiplist memory shape preservation and functional correctness. Memory preservation is stated using the predicate *skiplist* from TSL, and verified using the most general client from Fig. 2. For functional verification we use the simple spec in Fig. 7.

The proof of shape preservation requires some auxiliary invariants region, next and order (skiplist$_{KDE}$, nodes$_{KDE}$, pointers$_{KDE}$ and values$_{KDE}$ in the KDE implementation) that capture the separation between the skiplist region and new cells and the relation between the pointers used to traverse the skiplist. The precise definitions can be found in the web page of LEAP. Fig. 8 reports an evaluation of the performance of the decision procedure described in this paper for these two implementations with unbounded number of levels (first 8 rows of the table) compared with the performance of using only $\mathsf{TSL_K}$ on implementations with bounded levels (for bounds 1, 2, 3 and 4). The results for proving skiplist and its auxiliary invariants appear in the first four rows, and for skiplist$_{KDE}$ in the following four. The corresponding invariants for bounded levels are reported in rows labeled skiplist$_i$, region$_i$, next$_i$ and order$_i$ for $i = 1, 2, 3, 4$. Column #VC shows the number of VCs generated. Column #φ shows the number of formulas generated from these VCs (after normalization, etc). Column TSL shows the number of queries to the TSL decision procedure, and column TSL$_i$ the number of queries to $\mathsf{TSL_K}$ for K = i. A query to TSL can result in several queries to TSL$_i$. In some

```
1:  procedure FUNCSEARCH(SkipList sl)
2:     Set⟨Value⟩ elems_before := sl.elems
3:     v := NondetPickValue
4:     result := call SEARCH(sl, v)
5:     assert ( elems = elems_before   ∧
              result ↔ v ∈ elems        )
6:  end procedure

1:  procedure FUNCINSERT(SkipList sl)
2:     Set⟨Value⟩ elems_before := sl.elems
3:     v := NondetPickValue
4:     result := call INSERT(sl, v)
5:     assert (elems = elems_before ∪ {v})
6:  end procedure

1:  procedure FUNCREMOVE(SkipList sl)
2:     Set⟨Value⟩ elems_before := sl.elems
3:     v := NondetPickValue
4:     result := call REMOVE(sl, v)
5:     assert (elems = elems_before \ {v})
6:  end procedure
```

Fig. 7. Functional specification

cases there are fewer queries than formulas, because some formulas are trivially simplified. Finally, the columns labeled "avg" and "slowest" report the average and slowest running time to prove all VCs. The time reported in the column Leap corresponds to the total verification time excluding the invocation to the DPs. The column DP reports the total running time used in invoking all DPs.

This evaluation demonstrates that our decision procedure is practical to verify implementations with a variable number of levels, and allows to scale the verification of implementations with a fixed number of levels where previously known decision procedures time out. In the case of functional verification, Leap using the TSL decision procedure was capable of verifying all three specifications for the skiplist of unbounded height in less than one second.

	Formulas		#Calls to DPs					VC time (s.)		Total time (s.)	
	#VC	#φ	TSL	TSL_1	TSL_2	TSL_3	TSL_4	slowest	avg	Leap	DP
skiplist	80	560	28	45	92	38	14	5.40	0.24	0.15	19.64
region	80	1583	56	111	185	76	–	22.66	0.54	1.35	42.93
next	80	1899	30	39	55	22	–	0.32	0.02	1.59	1.60
order	80	2531	57	167	286	116	4	2.35	0.84	4.44	6.75
$skiplist_{KDE}$	54	214	14	37	61	32	12	5.93	0.24	0.05	13.14
$nodes_{KDE}$	54	585	32	99	174	76	–	3.10	0.17	0.31	9.36
$pointers_{KDE}$	54	1115	27	38	42	16	–	0.22	0.01	0.86	0.76
$values_{KDE}$	54	797	34	120	194	76	–	0.64	0.06	0.69	3.06
$skiplist_1$	77	119	–	32	–	–	–	0.10	0.01	0.20	0.32
$region_1$	77	119	–	27	–	–	–	0.14	0.01	0.37	0.28
$next_1$	77	79	–	19	–	–	–	0.02	0.01	0.15	0.14
$order_1$	77	79	–	25	–	–	–	0.02	0.01	0.58	0.11
$skiplist_2$	79	137	–	–	47	–	–	2.15	0.05	0.35	4.13
$region_2$	79	122	–	–	27	–	–	1.08	0.03	0.46	2.44
$next_2$	79	82	–	–	19	–	–	0.06	0.01	0.18	0.27
$order_2$	79	82	–	–	25	–	–	0.68	0.01	0.95	0.95
$skiplist_3$	80	154	–	–	–	62	–	776.45	15.27	0.45	1221.52
$region_3$	80	124	–	–	–	27	–	17.36	0.34	0.58	26.92
$next_3$	80	84	–	–	–	19	–	0.09	0.01	0.20	0.47
$order_3$	80	84	–	–	–	25	–	7.80	0.10	1.31	8.35
$skiplist_4$	81	171	–	–	–	–	77	**T.O.**	**T.O.**	0.80	**T.O.**
$region_4$	81	126	–	–	–	–	27	226.08	4.30	0.79	348.44
$next_4$	81	86	–	–	–	–	19	0.22	0.01	0.25	0.83
$order_4$	81	86	–	–	–	–	25	43.97	0.56	1.83	45.28

Fig. 8. Number of queries and running times for the verification of skiplist shape preservation. **T.O.** means time out, '–' means no calls to DP were required.

6   Conclusion and Future Work

We have presented TSL, a theory of skiplists of arbitrary many levels, useful to automatically prove the VCs generated during the verification of skiplist implementations. We showed that TSL is decidable by reducing its satisfiability problem to TSL_K, a decidable family of theories restricted to a bounded collection of levels. Our reduction illustrates that the decision procedure only needs to reason those levels explicitly mentioned in the (sanitized) formula. We have implemented our decision procedures on top of off-the-shelf SMT solvers (Yices and Z3), and integrated it into our prototype theorem prover. Our empirical evaluation demonstrates that our decision procedure is practical not only to verify unbounded skiplists but also to scale the verification of bounded implementations to realistic sizes.

Our main line of current and future work is the verification of liveness properties of concurrent skiplist implementations, as well as improving automation by generating and propagating invariants.

References

1. The KDE Platform, http://kde.org/
2. KDE Skiplist implementation,
   http://api.kde.org/4.1-api/kdeedu-apidocs/kstars/
   html/SkipList_8cpp_source.html
3. Abdulla, P.A., Holík, L., Jonsson, B., Lengál, O., Trinh, C.Q., Vojnar, T.: Verification of heap manipulating programs with ordered data by extended forest automata. In: Van Hung, D., Ogawa, M. (eds.) ATVA 2013. LNCS, vol. 8172, pp. 224–239. Springer, Heidelberg (2013)
4. Bouajjani, A., Drăgoi, C., Enea, C., Sighireanu, M.: A logic-based framework for reasoning about composite data structures. In: Bravetti, M., Zavattaro, G. (eds.) CONCUR 2009. LNCS, vol. 5710, pp. 178–195. Springer, Heidelberg (2009)
5. Bradley, A.R., Manna, Z., Sipma, H.B.: What's decidable about arrays? In: Emerson, E.A., Namjoshi, K.S. (eds.) VMCAI 2006. LNCS, vol. 3855, pp. 427–442. Springer, Heidelberg (2006)
6. Gallier, J.H.: Logic for Computer Science: Foundations of Automatic Theorem Proving. Harper & Row (1986)
7. Holík, L., Lengál, O., Rogalewicz, A., Šimáček, J., Vojnar, T.: Fully automated shape analysis based on forest automata. In: Sharygina, N., Veith, H. (eds.) CAV 2013. LNCS, vol. 8044, pp. 740–755. Springer, Heidelberg (2013)
8. Kuncak, V., Nguyen, H.H., Rinard, M.C.: An algorithm for deciding BAPA: Boolean Algebra with Presburger Arithmetic. In: Nieuwenhuis, R. (ed.) CADE 2005. LNCS (LNAI), vol. 3632, pp. 260–277. Springer, Heidelberg (2005)
9. Lahiri, S.K., Qadeer, S.: Back to the future: revisiting precise program verification using SMT solvers. In: Proc. of POPL 2008, pp. 171–182. ACM (2008)
10. Manna, Z., Pnueli, A.: Temporal Verif. of Reactive Systems. Springer (1995)
11. McCarthy, J.: Towards a mathematical science of computation. In: IFIP Congress, pp. 21–28 (1962)
12. Nelson, G., Oppen, D.C.: Simplification by cooperating decision procedures. ACM Trans. Program. Lang. Syst. 1(2), 245–257 (1979)
13. Pugh, W.: Skip lists: A probabilistic alternative to balanced trees. Commun. ACM 33(6), 668–676 (1990)
14. Ranise, S., Zarba, C.G.: A theory of singly-linked lists and its extensible decision procedure. In: Proc. of SEFM 2006. IEEE CS Press (2006)
15. Reynolds, J.C.: Separation logic: A logic for shared mutable data structures. In: Proc. of LICS 2002, pp. 55–74. IEEE CS Press (2002)
16. Sánchez, A., Sánchez, C.: Decision procedures for the temporal verification of concurrent lists. In: Dong, J.S., Zhu, H. (eds.) ICFEM 2010. LNCS, vol. 6447, pp. 74–89. Springer, Heidelberg (2010)
17. Sánchez, A., Sánchez, C.: A theory of skiplists with applications to the verification of concurrent datatypes. In: Bobaru, M., Havelund, K., Holzmann, G.J., Joshi, R. (eds.) NFM 2011. LNCS, vol. 6617, pp. 343–358. Springer, Heidelberg (2011)
18. Sánchez, A., Sánchez, C.: Parametrized invariance for infinite state processes. CoRR, abs/1312.4043 (2013)
19. Wies, T., Kuncak, V., Zee, K., Podelski, A., Rinard, M.: Verifying complex properties using symbolic shape analysis. In: Workshop on Heap Abstraction and Verification (collocated with ETAPS) (2007)
20. Yorsh, G., Rabinovich, A.M., Sagiv, M., Meyer, A., Bouajjani, A.: A logic of reachable patterns in linked data-structures. In: Aceto, L., Ingólfsdóttir, A. (eds.) FOSSACS 2006. LNCS, vol. 3921, pp. 94–110. Springer, Heidelberg (2006)

Using Flow Specifications of Parameterized Cache Coherence Protocols for Verifying Deadlock Freedom

Divjyot Sethi[1], Muralidhar Talupur[2], and Sharad Malik[1]

[1] Princeton University, Princeton, NJ, USA
[2] Strategic CAD Labs, Intel Corporation, Hillsboro, OR, USA

Abstract. We consider the problem of verifying deadlock freedom for symmetric cache coherence protocols. While there are multiple definitions of deadlock in the literature, we focus on a specific form of deadlock which is useful for the cache coherence protocol domain and is consistent with the internal definition of deadlock in the Murphi model checker: we refer to this deadlock as a *system-wide deadlock (s-deadlock)*. In s-deadlock, the entire system gets blocked and is unable to make any transition. Cache coherence protocols consist of N symmetric cache agents, where N is an unbounded parameter; thus the verification of s-deadlock freedom is naturally a parameterized verification problem.

Parametrized verification techniques work by using sound abstractions to reduce the unbounded model to a bounded model. Efficient abstractions which work well for industrial scale protocols typically bound the model by replacing the state of most of the agents by an abstract environment, while keeping just one or two agents as is. However, leveraging such efficient abstractions becomes a challenge for s-deadlock: a violation of s-deadlock is a state in which the transitions of all of the unbounded number of agents cannot occur and so a simple abstraction like the one above will not preserve this violation. Authors of a prior paper, in fact, proposed using a combination of over and under abstractions for verifying such properties. While quite promising for a large class of deadlock errors, simultaneously tuning over and under abstractions can become complex.

In this work we address this challenge by presenting a technique which leverages high-level information about the protocols, in the form of message sequence diagrams referred to as *flows*, for constructing invariants that are collectively stronger than s-deadlock. Further, violations of these invariants can involve only one or two interacting agents: thus they can be verified using efficient abstractions like the ones described above. We show how such invariants for the German and Flash protocols can be successfully derived using our technique and then be verified.

1 Introduction

We consider the problem of verifying deadlock freedom for symmetric cache coherence protocols. Consider a cache coherence protocol $\mathcal{P}$ (N) where the parameter N represents an unbounded number of cache agents. The protocol implements requests sent by the agents using messages exchanged in the protocol. For a protocol designer, the main property of interest is the request-response property, i.e., every request from an agent eventually gets a response. Since this property is a liveness property which is hard for

F. Cassez and J.-F. Raskin (Eds.): ATVA 2014, LNCS 8837, pp. 330–347, 2014.

existing model checking tools, designers resort to identifying causes for response property failure, such as deadlock-style failures, and verify against them.

The literature is abundant with various definitions of deadlock [8, 22]. We focus on deadlock errors in which the entire protocol gets blocked, i.e., no agent of the protocol can make any transition. We refer to such an error as a *system-wide deadlock* *(s-deadlock)*. If we model each transition τ of the protocol to have a guard $\tau.g$, which is $false$ if the transition is not enabled, the s-deadlock error occurs if the guards of all the transitions are *false*, i.e., $\bigwedge_\tau \neg(\tau.g)$ is *true*. This kind of failure, while weaker than other broader classes of deadlock failures, is commonly observed in industrial computer system designs and is consistent with the internal definition for deadlock used by the Murphi model checker as well [23]. This class of deadlocks is well motivated for parameterized cache coherence protocols as these use a centralized synchronization mechanism (e.g. a directory) and thus any deadlock results in the directory getting blocked. It is highly likely that such a deadlock in the shared directory will end up involving all of the agents of the protocol getting blocked, i.e., unable to make any transition.

Since an s-deadlock error involves all of the unbounded number of agents getting blocked and unable to make any transition, verification of s-deadlock freedom naturally is a parameterized verification problem. Parameterized verification techniques work by using sound abstractions to reduce the unbounded model to a finite bounded model that preserves the property of interest. These abstractions typically tend to be simple over-abstractions such as *data-type reduction* [30]. This abstraction keeps a small number of agents (1 or 2) as is and replaces all the other agents with an abstract environment. Such abstractions along with parameterized techniques like the CMP (CoMPositional) method [11] have had considerable success in verifying key safety properties like mutual exclusion and data integrity even for industrial scale protocols [11, 32, 38].

1.1 Challenge in Verifying S-deadlock

While parameterized techniques are successful for safety properties such as mutual exclusion and data integrity, the application of such abstractions for parameterized verification of properties such as s-deadlock is hard. The key challenge arises from the fact that an s-deadlock violation is a state in which all the guards are *false*, i.e., when $\bigwedge_\tau \neg(\tau.g)$ holds; simple over-abstractions such as data-type reduction will easily mask this violation due to the discarded state of agents other than 1 and 2 and the extra transitions of the environment.

One approach to address the above issue is to use a combination of over and under abstractions (i.e., a *mixed* abstraction) instead of data-type reduction, as described in a prior deadlock verification work [8]. While promising for verifying a large class of deadlock errors, the use of mixed abstraction requires reasoning about over and under abstraction simultaneously and easily becomes fairly complex.

In this paper we take a different approach. We show how high-level information about the protocols, in the form of message sequence diagrams referred to as *flows*, can be leveraged to construct invariants which are collectively stronger than the s-deadlock freedom property. These invariants are amenable to efficient abstractions like data-type reduction which have been used in the past for verifying industrial scale protocols.

1.2 Leveraging Flows for Deadlock Freedom

Cache coherence protocols implement high-level requests for read (termed *Shared*) or write (termed *Exclusive*) access from cache agents, or for invalidating access rights (termed *Invalidate*) of some agent from the central directory. The implementation of these requests is done by using a set of transitions which should occur in a specific protocol order. This ordering information is present in diagrams referred to as *message flows* (or *flows* for brevity). These flows are readily available in industrial documents in the form of message sequence charts and tables [38].

Fig. 1 shows two of the flows for the German cache coherence protocol describing the processing of the *Exclusive* and *Invalidate* requests. Each figure has a directory *Dir*, and two agents *i* and *j*. The downward vertical direction indicates the passage of time. The *Exclusive* request is sent by the cache agent *i* to the directory *Dir* to request a write access. The *Exclusive* flow in Fig. 1(a) describes the temporal sequence of transitions which occur in the implementation in order to process this request: each message is a transition of the protocol. The message $SendReqE(i)$ is sent by the agent *i* to *Dir* which receives this message by executing the transition $RecvReqE(i)$. Next, if the directory is able to grant *Exclusive* access, it sends the message $SendGntE(i)$ to agent *i* which receives this grant by executing $RecvGntE(i)$. However, in case the directory is unable to send the grant since another agent *j* has access to the cache line, the directory sends a request to invalidate the access rights of *j*. The temporal sequence of transitions which occurs in the implementation in this case is shown in the *Invalidate* flow in Fig. 1(b). This flow proceeds by the directory sending the $SendInv(j)$ message, the agent *j* sending the acknowledgment message $SendInvAck(j)$, and the directory receiving it by executing $RecvInvAck(j)$ transition.

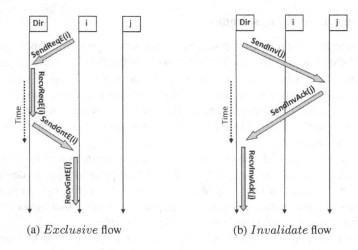

(a) *Exclusive* flow   (b) *Invalidate* flow

Fig. 1. Flows for the German protocol

Freedom from S-deadlock. At a high-level, our method tries to exploit the fact that if the protocol is s-deadlock free, when none of the transitions of an agent are enabled, another agent can be identified which must have a transition enabled. This identification leverages the key insight that in any state of the protocol, if all the transitions of some agent, say a_1, cannot occur, then, some flow of that agent must be blocked since it depends on another flow of another agent, say a_2, to finish. Then, there are two possibilities: (1) the agent a_2 is enabled, in which case the state is not an s-deadlock state, or (2) the agent a_2 is blocked as well, in which case it depends on another agent a_3. If this dependence chain is acyclic, with the final agent in the chain enabled, the protocol is s-deadlock free. However, if the final agent is not enabled, or if the dependence chain has a cycle, the protocol may either have an s-deadlock error or there may be an error in the flow diagrams used.

As an example, for the German protocol, if the $Exclusive$ flow of agent i is blocked since the transition $SendGntE(i)$ cannot occur, it is waiting for j to get invalidated. In the protocol, at least some transition of the $Invalidate$ flow on agent j can occur. This enables proving freedom from s-deadlock for the protocol.

Using the above insight, by analyzing the dependence between blocked agents, our method is able to point to an agent which must have at least one transition enabled in every reachable state of the protocol. Specifically, our method enables the derivation of a set of invariants $\mathcal{I}$ which collectively partition the reachable state of the protocol. Each invariant then points to the agents which must have at least one transition enabled when the protocol is in a state belonging to its partition. These invariants are derived in a loop by iteratively model checking them on a protocol model with c agents, where c is heuristically chosen as discussed in Section 3.

Verifying for an Unbounded Number of Agents. Once the invariants in $\mathcal{I}$ are derived, they hold for a model with c agents. These invariants use just one index (i.e., they are of the form $\forall i : \phi(i)$) and thus, they can be verified for an unbounded number of agents by using efficient parameterized verification techniques such as data-type reduction along with the CMP (CoMPositional) method [11]. This technique has previously been successful for verifying mutual exclusion for industrial protocols [32]. We note that our approach is not limited to the CMP method: the invariants derived may be verified by using any parameterized safety verification technique [15, 27, 34, 35].

1.3 Key Contributions
Our method proves s-deadlock freedom for parameterized protocols (formalized in Section 2). It takes a Murphi model of the protocol as input. As shown in Fig. 2, first, a set of invariants $\mathcal{I}$ which collectively imply s-deadlock freedom are derived on a model with c agents (Section 3). These invariants are verified for an unbounded number of agents by using state-of-the-art parameterized verification techniques (Section 4). We verified Murphi implementations of two challenging protocols, the German and Flash protocols using our method (Section 5).

Limitation: The key limitation of our approach is that the invariants have to be derived manually by inspecting counterexamples. This can be automated if additional information about conflicting flows is available in the flow diagram itself.

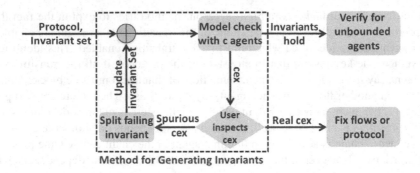

Fig. 2. Experimental Flow

1.4 Relevant Related Work

Deadlock Verification: The work closest to ours is by Bingham *et al.* [7, 8]. They formally verify deadlock as a safety property for protocols by specifying it using user-identified Quiescent states (*i.e.*, a state in which no resources are held): they specify a protocol state to be a deadlock state if no Quiescent state is reachable from it. They prove freedom from such a deadlock by using a combination of over and under abstractions (*i.e.*, a *mixed* abstraction [16]). Their approach is promising for verifying deadlock freedom and scales to the Flash protocol. However, the required tuning of both under and over abstractions simultaneously can be complex. In contrast, we take the flow-based alternative to enable simpler abstractions like data-type reduction.

Since the ultimate goal of any deadlock verification effort is to verify the response property (i.e. every high-level request eventually gets a response), we contrast our work with liveness verification efforts as well. Among techniques for parameterized verification of liveness, McMillan has verified liveness properties of the Flash protocol [28,29]. The proof is manual and works on the basis of user supplied lemmas and fairness assumptions. In contrast, our method reduces manual effort by leveraging information from flows along with the CMP method. Among automatic approaches for verifying liveness properties, Baukus *et al.* verified liveness properties of the German protocol [6] using a specialized logic called WSIS. Fang *et al.* used automatically deduced ranking functions [21] and, in a prior work, counter abstraction [35] to verify liveness properties. While fully automatic, these approaches tend to exhibit limited scalability for larger protocols such as Flash, due to the inherent complexity of the liveness verification problem. In contrast to these, our approach, while requiring some user guidance, achieves much greater scalability and enables us to verify the Flash protocol.

Parameterized Verification Techniques: We note that the invariants derived using our method can be verified for an unbounded number of caches by any parameterized safety verification technique, it is not dependent on the CMP method which we used. Our choice of using the CMP method was motivated by the fact that it is the only state-of-the-art method we are aware of which has been used successfully for verifying protocols like Flash and other industrial scale protocols. Among other techniques, an important technique by Conchon *et al.* [15] uses a backward reachability algorithm to automatically prove a simplified version of the Flash protocol. Next, there are numerous other prior approaches in literature for parameterized verification of safety properties. The CMP method falls in the broad category of approaches which use *compositional reasoning* [1, 2] and *abstraction* based techniques to verify parameterized systems; the literature is abundant with examples of these [13, 14, 17, 20, 27, 28, 34, 35]. Next, another category of approaches work by computing a *cutoff* bound k and showing that if the verification succeeds for k agents, then the protocol is correct for an arbitrary number of agents [3, 5, 12, 18, 19, 24]. Finally, there are approaches based on *regular model checking* which use automata-based algorithms to verify parameterized systems [4, 9, 10, 36]. To the best of our knowledge, the CMP method is the state-of-the-art for protocol verification in contrast to these methods and has been used to successfully verify larger protocols such as Flash with minimal manual effort. (Other key methods which verify Flash protocol in full complexity are by Park *et al.* [17, 33]. However, as described by Talupur *et al.* [38], these are significantly manual and take more time to finish verification of the Flash protocol compared to the CMP method.)

2 Protocols, Flows and S-deadlock Freedom: Background

2.1 Preliminaries

A protocol $\mathcal{P}$ (N) consists of N symmetric cache agents, with *ids* from the set $\mathbb{N}_N = \{1, 2, 3, \ldots, N\}$. We follow our prior approach [38] (which was inspired by the approach of Kristic [25]) in formalizing cache coherence protocols.

Index Variables: The protocol uses index variables quantified over the set of index values $\mathbb{N}_N$. Thus, if i is an index variable, then i takes values from the domain $\mathbb{N}_N$.

State Variables: The state of the protocol is encoded as local variables and global variables shared between the agents. These variables either are Boolean variables, or, are pointers which can hold agent *ids* and thus have values in $\mathbb{N}_N \cup \{null\}$ where *null* represents that the variable does not hold any index value. The global Boolean variables are denoted by G_B and pointers by G_P. The local Boolean variables of agent i are denoted by $L_B[i]$ and the local pointer variables by $L_P[i]$.

Expressions: An expression is a, possibly quantified, propositional formula with atoms G_B, $G_P = j$, $L_B[i]$ and $L_P[i] = j$, where, i and j are index variables.

Assignments: Assignments are of the form $G_B := b$, or $G_P := j$, $L_B[i] := b$ or $L_P[i] := j$, where, b is a variable with Boolean value and i, j are index variables.

Rules: Each agent i consists of a set of rules $rl_1(i), rl_2(i), rl_3(i), \ldots, rl_k(i)$. Each rule $rl_j(i)$ can be written as: $rl_j(i) : rl_j(i).\rho \rightarrow rl_j(i).a$, where, $rl_j(i)$ is the rule name, the guard $rl_j(i).\rho$ is an expression, and $rl_j(i).a$ is a list of assignments, such that these assignments are restricted to only update the global variables or the local variables of agent i. The local variables and rules for all agents i are symmetric.

Protocol: The above defined variables and rules naturally induce a state transition system. A *protocol*, then, is a state transition system (S, Θ, T), where S is the set of protocol states, $\Theta \subseteq S$ is the set of initial states, and $T \subseteq S \times S$ is the transition relation. Each protocol state $s \in S$ is a valuation of the variables G_B, G_P, and $L_B[i]$, $L_P[i]$ for each agent i. There exists a transition $\tau(i_v) = (s, s'), (s, s') \in T$ from state s to s' if there is a rule $rl_j(i)$ and value of index variable $i = i_v$, s.t. $rl_j(i_v).\rho$ holds in s, and s' is obtained by applying $rl_j(i_v).a$ to s. In state s, we say that the rule $rl_j(i)$

is *enabled* for agent with *id* i_v if the guard $rl_j(i_v).\rho$ is *true*. When the enabled rule is executed, its action is applied to update the state and we say that the rule $rl_j(i)$ has *fired* for agent i_v. The action is applied atomically to update the state, thus the transitions of the protocol have interleaving semantics. Finally, we define an execution *trace* of the protocol as a series of transitions where each transition is a fired rule. Thus, a trace can be represented by a series $(rl_a(i_0), rl_b(i_1), \ldots, rl_s(i_k))$, where the transition $rl_m(i_n)$ is the rule rl_m fired for the agent with *id* i_n.

S-deadlock Definition. We define a protocol state s to be an *s-deadlock state* if no rule in that state is enabled. Then, a protocol is s-deadlock free if in all states, there exists at least one rule which is enabled. This can be expressed as the invariant: $\bigvee_i \bigvee_j rl_j(i).\rho$, i.e., the protocol is s-deadlock free if the disjunction of the guards of all the rules of all the agents is *true* for all the reachable states.

Flows. Flows describe the basic organization of rules for implementing the high-level requests in a protocol (for example a request for *Exclusive* access or an *Invalidate*). We model a flow as a set of rules $\mathcal{F}(i)$ of the form $\{rl_a(i), rl_b(i), rl_c(i), \ldots, rl_n(i)\}$ which accomplish a high-level request of agent i.[1] The rules in a flow are partially ordered, with the partial order relation denoted as $\prec_{\mathcal{F}(i)}$. For example, in the *Exclusive* flow in Fig. 1(a), the rules (arrows) are totally ordered along the downward direction. Thus $SendReqE(i) \prec_{\mathcal{F}_E(i)} RecvReqE(i)$, where $\mathcal{F}_E$ denotes the set of rules for *Exclusive* flow. For every rule $rl_k(i)$ in the flow $\mathcal{F}(i)$, the partial order naturally induces the following *precondition*: for the rule $rl_k(i)$ to fire, all the rules preceding that rule in the partial order of the flow $\mathcal{F}(i)$ must have already been fired. This precondition is denoted by $rl_k(i).p_{\mathcal{F}(i)}$ and, formally, can be written as:

$$rl_k(i).p_{\mathcal{F}(i)} = \forall j : \big(\{(rl_j(i) \in \mathcal{F}(i)) \wedge (rl_j(i) \prec_{\mathcal{F}(i)} rl_k(i))\} \Rightarrow (rl_j(i).fired = true)\big),$$

where $rl_j(i).fired$ is an auxiliary variable which is initially set to *false* when the flow $\mathcal{F}(i)$ starts and is set to *true* when the rule $rl_j(i)$ has fired for that flow.

Designs of protocols are presented in industrial documents as a set of flows $\mathcal{F}_1(i)$, $\mathcal{F}_2(i)$, $\mathcal{F}_3(i)$, ..., $\mathcal{F}_k(i)$. In order to process a high-level request, a protocol may use a combination of these flows, e.g. in order to execute a request for *Exclusive* access the German protocol uses the *Exclusive* and *Invalidate* flows. Each flow in a protocol represents an execution scenario of the protocol for processing some high-level request. Thus many of the flows of a protocol tend to exhibit a lot of similarity as they are different execution scenarios of the same high-level request. This makes them fairly easy to understand. In Section 3, we show how a set of invariants collectively implying s-deadlock freedom can be derived from these flows.

Some Definitions: We define the union of all the flows of agent i by $\mathcal{R}(i)$, i.e., $\mathcal{R}(i) = \bigcup_k \mathcal{F}_k(i)$. Next, we define the operator $\widehat{en}$ which is *true* for a set of rules, if at least one rule in the set is enabled, else it is *false*. Thus, for example, $\widehat{en}(\mathcal{R}(i))$ holds if at

---

[1] For ease of exposition we assume that the guard and action of a rule are over the variables of a single agent. Thus, a flow containing such rules also involves a single agent. In general, a rule and thus a flow can involve a larger but fixed number of interacting agents as well. Our approach can be easily generalized to that case.

least one of the rules in $\mathcal{R}(i)$ is enabled. In this case, we say that the agent i is enabled. Similarly, we say that a flow $\mathcal{F}(i)$ is enabled if at least one of its rules is enabled, i.e., $\widehat{en}(\mathcal{F}(i))$ holds. In case a flow $\mathcal{F}(i)$ is not enabled, we say that it is *blocked* on some rule $rl_j(i) \in \mathcal{F}(i)$ if the precondition of the rule $rl_j(i).p_{\mathcal{F}(i)}$ holds but the guard of the rule $rl_j(i).\rho$ is *false*.

2.2 German Protocol Implementation

The German protocol consists of agents such that each agent can have *Exclusive* (E), *Shared* (S) or *Invalid* (I) access to a cache line, as stored in the variable $Cache[i].State$. An agent i requests these access rights by sending messages on a channel $ReqChannel[i]$ to a shared directory which sends corresponding grants along the channel $GntChannel[i]$. The directory is modeled as a set of global variables which serves one agent at a time: it stores the *id* of the agent being served in the variable $CurPtr$. It also stores the nature of the request in the variable $CurCmd$ with values in $\{ReqE, ReqS, Empty\}$, where $ReqE$ represents a request for *Exclusive* access, $ReqS$ for *Shared* and *Empty* for no request. Finally, the directory tracks if *Exclusive* access is granted to some agent or not using the variable $ExGntd$: it is *true* if access is granted and *false* otherwise. A simplified version of the code for the *Exclusive* request is shown in Fig. 3 (full version available in [11]).

In processing the *Exclusive* request, before sending the grant $SendGntE(i)$, the directory checks if there are any sharers of the cache line (by checking $ShrSet = \{\}$). If there are sharers, the *Invalidate* flow is invoked for each agent in $ShrSet$. Upon invalidation of all the agents in $ShrSet$, the $ShrSet$ becomes empty and so the $SendGntE(i)$ rule becomes enabled for execution. We show the code for the $SendInv(i)$ rule below.

```
∀ i : N_N; do Rule SendInv(i)
  InvChannel[i].cmd = Empty ∧ i ∈ ShrSet ∧
    ((CurCmd = ReqE) ∨ (CurCmd = ReqS ∧ ExGntd = true))
  →
  InvChannel[i].cmd := Invalidate;
End;
```

We note a condition Inv_Cond, which must be *true* for invoking the *Invalidate* flow and can be identified from the guard of $SendInv(i)$; Inv_Cond : $(((CurCmd = ReqE) \vee ((CurCmd = ReqS) \wedge (ExGntd = true))) \wedge (ShrSet \neq \{\}))$.

3 Deriving Invariants for Proving S-deadlock Freedom

In this section, we show how a set of invariants $\mathcal{I}$ can be derived from flows such that the invariants in $\mathcal{I}$ collectively imply s-deadlock freedom. At a high-level, our method tries to show s-deadlock freedom by partitioning the global state of the protocol using predicates, such that for each partition, some agent i has at least one transition enabled. Each invariant inv is of the form $inv.pred \Rightarrow (\forall i \in In^{inv} : \widehat{en}(\mathcal{R}(i)))$, where $inv.pred$ is a predicate on the global variables of the protocol, $In^{inv} \subseteq \mathbb{N}_N$ s.t. $\neg(In^{inv} = \{\})$ (this is discharged as a separate assertion for model checking) and

```
∀ i : ℕ_N; do Rule SendReqE(i)
  ReqChannel[i].cmd=Empty ∧
    (Cache[i].State=I ∨ Cache[i].State=S)
  →
  ReqChannel[i].cmd := ReqE;
End;

∀ i : ℕ_N; do Rule RecvReqE(i)
  ReqChannel[i].cmd=ReqE ∧ CurCmd=Empty
  →
  CurCmd := ReqE; CurPtr := i;
   ReqChannel[i].cmd := Empty;
End;

∀ i : ℕ_N; do Rule SendGntE(i)
  CurCmd=ReqE ∧ CurPtr=i ∧
    GntChannel[i]=Empty ∧ Exgntd=false
  ∧ ShrSet={}
  →
  GntChannel[i] := GntE; ShrSet := {i};
   ExGntd := true; CurCmd := Empty;
   CurPtr := NULL;
End;

∀ i : ℕ_N; do Rule RecvGntE(i)
  GntChannel[i]=GntE
  →
  Cache[i].State := E; GntChannel[i] := Empty;
End;
```

Fig. 3. Implementation of the $Exclusive$ Request

$\widehat{en}(\mathcal{R}(i))$ denotes a disjunction of the guards of the rules in $\mathcal{R}(i)$. *The key insight is that since $\widehat{en}(\mathcal{R}(i))$ has transitions from a single agent, the abstractions required for model checking inv for an unbounded number of agents are significantly simpler than those for checking the original s-deadlock property,*[2] *as discussed in Section 4.*

Our method iteratively model checks each invariant in $\mathcal{I}$ to refine it. Suppose, the invariant $inv \in \mathcal{I}$ fails on model checking with the state of the protocol at failure being s_f. Then, there exists some agent i_f such that when $inv.pred$ holds in s_f, $i_f \in In^{inv}$ is true and $\widehat{en}(\mathcal{R}(i_f))$ is *false* in s_f. This can happen due to two reasons: first, there may be a mismatch between the flow specification and the rule-based protocol description. Thus $\widehat{en}(\mathcal{R}(i_f))$ can be *false* due to a missing rule in some flow, a missing flow all together, or an implementation error: the cause for the mismatch can be discovered from the counterexample. As an example, the counterexample may show that all flows of the agent i_f are not enabled even when the agent has some rule $rl_e(i_f)$ enabled. This rule may be a part of a flow missing from the specification. Second, the invariant inv may

---

[2] In the case of rules involving more than one agent (say c), the corresponding invariants may involve transitions from c agents as well. Since c is small for practical protocols, the abstraction constructed for verifying such invariants will be simple as well.

fail as some flow $\mathcal{F}$ of the agent i_f is blocked (*i.e.*, it has a rule with precondition *true* but with guard *false*) as it is waiting for another flow $\mathcal{F}'$ of another agent i_s to complete. As an example, for the German protocol, the *Exclusive* flow may be blocked for agent i_f with the rule $SendGntE(i_f)$ having precondition *true* but guard *false* and waiting for an *Invalidate* request to complete for another agent i_s in the set *Sharers*. In this case, the set $\mathcal{I}$ is refined by splitting the invariant *inv*.

The invariant *inv* is split by, (1) splitting the predicate *inv.pred* to further partition the global state, and (2) updating the set In^{inv} for each partition. To accomplish this, the user identifies a pointer variable from G_P or $L_P[i]$ (or an auxiliary variable) $\hat{w}$, such that it has the value i_s in the failing state s_f (and so acts as a *witness* variable for i_s). The user also identifies a conflict condition *conf* on the global state which indicates when i_s is enabled and i_f fails. This is done by using the heuristic that if the rule $rl_f(i_f)$ of flow $\mathcal{F}$ of agent i_f is blocked, *conf* can be derived by inspecting the guard of $rl_f(i_f)$; the condition *conf* generally is the cause for the falsification of $rl_f(i_f).\rho$. For example, for the German protocol, *conf* is derived from the guard of $SendGntE$ and $\hat{w}$ points to some sharer which is being invalidated.

Using *conf* and $\hat{w}$, the invariant can be split into two invariants. (1) The first invariant excludes the case when conflict happens from the original invariant, i.e., $inv1$: $(inv.pred \wedge \neg conf) \Rightarrow (\forall i \in In^{inv1} : \widehat{en}(\mathcal{R}(i)))$, where $In^{inv1} = In^{inv}$. (2) The second invariant shows that when a conflict happens, the agent pointed to by $\hat{w}$ must be enabled and so the protocol is still s-deadlock-free, i.e., $inv2 : (inv.pred \wedge conf) \Rightarrow (\forall i \in In^{inv2} : \widehat{en}(\mathcal{R}(i)))$, where $In^{inv2} = \{i | (i \in \mathbb{N}_N) \wedge (i = \hat{w})\}$. For both the invariants, assertions which check that the corresponding set of indices are non-empty are also verified. For example, for $inv1$, this assertion is $(inv.pred \wedge \neg conf) \Rightarrow In^{inv1}$.

Our method derives these invariants by iteratively model checking with a small number c (3 for German protocol) of agents. (Once the invariants are derived for c agents, they are verified for an unbounded number of agents, as shown is Section 4.) This number c needs to be chosen to be large enough such that the proof of s-deadlock freedom is expected to generalize to an unbounded number of agents. For the protocols we verified, we found that as a heuristic, c should be one more than the maximum number of agents involved in processing a high-level request. For the German protocol, an *Exclusive* request may involve two agents, a requesting agent i and an agent j getting invalidated, so we chose c to be equal to 3.

Fig. 4 shows the details of the method. It starts with an initial broad guess invariant, $true \Rightarrow (\forall i \in \mathbb{N}_N : \widehat{en}(\mathcal{R}(i)))$ (line 1). This indicates that in all reachable states, every agent has at least one transition enabled. As this invariant is *false*, this broad guess invariant is refined into finer invariants, using the loop. On finishing, the user is able to derive a set of invariants, $\mathcal{I}$, which collectively imply s-deadlock freedom. Further, the user is also able to derive an assertion set, $\mathcal{A}$, such that for each invariant *inv* in $\mathcal{I}$, an assertion in $\mathcal{A}$ checks if the set of indices In^{inv} is non-empty when *inv.pred* holds.

Soundness of the Method. The following theorem (proof in the extended version [37]) shows that the invariants in $\mathcal{I}$ along with the assertions in $\mathcal{A}$ collectively imply s-deadlock freedom.

DERIVE_INVARIANTS($\mathcal{P}(c)$):
1: $\mathcal{I} = \{true \Rightarrow (\forall i \in \mathbb{N}_N : \widehat{en}(\mathcal{R}(i)))\}$
2: $\mathcal{A} = \{\}$
3: while $\mathcal{P}(c) \not\models \mathcal{I}$ do
4:    Let $inv \in \mathcal{I} : \mathcal{P}(c) \not\models inv$ and
        $inv : inv.pred \Rightarrow (\forall i \in In^{inv} : \widehat{en}(\mathcal{R}(i)))$, where, $In^{inv} \subseteq \mathbb{N}_N$
5:    Inspect counterexample cex and failing state s_f:
6:       Case 1: mismatch between flows and protocol
7:          Exit loop and fix flows or protocol
8:       Case 2: identify conflicting agents i_f and i_s s.t.
9:          (1) $i_f : ((i_f \in In^{inv}) \wedge (\neg\widehat{en}(\mathcal{R}(i_f))))$ holds in s_f.
10:          (2) $\exists rl_f \in \mathcal{F}(i_f)$ s.t. $(rl_f(i_f).p_{\mathcal{F}(i_f)} \wedge \neg(\widehat{en}(\mathcal{F}(i_f))))$ holds in s_f.
11:          (3) $\widehat{en}(\mathcal{R}(i_s))$ holds in s_f.
12:       Identify $conf$ and witness $\hat{w}$ from above information
13:       $inv1 : (\neg conf \wedge inv.pred) \Rightarrow (\forall i \in In^{inv} : \widehat{en}(\mathcal{R}(i)))$
14:       $inv2 : (conf \wedge inv.pred) \Rightarrow (\forall i \in In^{inv2} : \widehat{en}(\mathcal{R}(i)))$, where,
           $In^{inv2} = \{i| i = \hat{w}\}$
15:       $\mathcal{I} = \{\mathcal{I} \setminus inv\} \cup \{inv1, inv2\}$
16:       $\mathcal{A} = (\mathcal{A} \setminus (inv.pred \Rightarrow (In^{inv} \neq \{\}))) \cup$
           $\{(inv1.pred \Rightarrow (In^{inv1} \neq \{\})), (inv2.pred \Rightarrow (In^{inv2} \neq \{\}))\}$

Fig. 4. Method for Deriving Invariants from Flows

Theorem. *If the set of invariants $\mathcal{I}$ along with the set of assertions $\mathcal{A}$ hold, they collectively imply s-deadlock freedom, i.e.,* $((\bigwedge_{inv \in \mathcal{I}}(\mathcal{P} \models inv)) \wedge (\bigwedge_{asrt \in \mathcal{A}}(\mathcal{P} \models asrt))) \Rightarrow (\mathcal{P} \models (\bigvee_i \bigvee_j rl_j(i).\rho))$.

3.1   Specifying Invariants for the German Protocol

We derive the invariants for a model of the German protocol with 3 cache agents. We start with the initial invariant that for all agents, some flow is enabled, i.e., INV-1: $true \Rightarrow (\forall i \in \mathbb{N}_N : \widehat{en}(\mathcal{R}(i)))$.

Iteration 1: Model checking the invariant INV-1 returns a counterexample trace $(SendReqE(1), RecvReqE(1), SendReqE(2))$. Since the index of the last rule in the trace is 2, $\widehat{en}(\mathcal{R}(2))$ must be *false*. This is because the rule $RecvReqE(2)$ of the *Exclusive* flow of cache 2 is not fired and thus has precondition *true* but guard *false*. The user identifies the conflict condition $conf = \neg(CurCmd = Empty)$ from the guard of the blocked rule $RecvReqE(2)$. Since $CurPtr$ is the witness pointer in the protocol for the variable $CurCmd$, the witness $\hat{w}$ is set to $CurPtr$. Thus, the invariant is split as follows:

- INV-1.1: $(CurCmd = Empty) \Rightarrow (\forall i \in \mathbb{N}_N : \widehat{en}(\mathcal{R}(i)))$.
- INV-1.2: $\neg(CurCmd = Empty) \Rightarrow (\forall i \in In^{inv-1.2} : \widehat{en}(\mathcal{R}(i)))$, where $In^{inv-1.2} = \{i| (i \in \mathbb{N}_N) \wedge (i = CurPtr)\}$. The assertion $\neg(CurCmd = Empty) \Rightarrow \neg(In^{inv-1.2} = \{\})$ is also checked.

Iteration 2: Next, on model checking the invariants INV-1.1 and INV-1.2, the invariant INV-1.2 fails. The counterexample trace returned is $(SendReqE(1), RecvReqE(1),$

$SendGntE(1)$, $SendReqE(2)$, $RecvReqE(2)$, $SendReqE(2)$). Since the last rule of the counterexample is from cache 2, $\widehat{en}(\mathcal{R}(2))$ must be *false* even when $CurPtr = 2$. Further, there are two flows for two *Exclusive* requests by cache 2 active in the counterexample, the first with $SendReqE(2)$ fired and the second with $SendReqE(2)$, $RecvReqE(2)$ fired. Since the first flow is blocked on the rule $RecvReqE(2)$, the guard of this rule is inspected. The guard is *false* as $CurCmd$ is not empty. However, since the corresponding witness variable for $CurCmd$ is $CurPtr$ which is already 2 (due to the processing of the second flow), this is not a conflict with another cache. The conflict must then be for the second *Exclusive* flow. The second flow is blocked on the rule $SendGntE(2)$ with precondition *true* but guard *false*: the user identifies the conflict condition $conf$ from the guard of $SendGntE$ to be Inv_Cond. Now, if Inv_Cond is *true*, the *Invalidate* flow for some sharer cache (cache 1 in this trace) must be active. Thus, the user identifies $\hat{w}$ to point to a sharer which must be invalidated: this is done using the auxiliary variable $Sharer$, which points to the last sharer to be invalidated in $ShrSet$. Thus, the invariant INV-1.2 is split as follows:

- INV-1.2.1: $\big(\neg(CurCmd = Empty) \wedge (\neg Inv\_Cond)\big) \Rightarrow (\forall i \in In^{inv-1.2.1} : \widehat{en}(\mathcal{R}(i)))$, where, $In^{inv-1.2.1} = In^{inv-1.2}$. An assertion that the precondition implies the index set is non-empty is also checked.
- INV-1.2.2: $\big(\neg(CurCmd = Empty) \wedge (Inv\_Cond)\big) \Rightarrow (\forall i \in In^{inv-1.2.2} : \widehat{en}(\mathcal{R}(i)))$, where, $In^{inv-1.2.2} = \{i | (i \in \mathbb{N}_N) \wedge (i \in ShrSet)\}$. An assertion that the precondition implies the index set is non-empty is also checked.

Iteration 3: Next, on model checking, the invariants INV-1.1, INV-1.2.1, INV-1.2.2, along with the added assertions hold for a model with 3 caches. Then, to prove s-deadlock freedom, this set of invariants form a candidate set to verify a protocol model with an unbounded number of agents. The property is checked for unbounded agents using techniques described in Section 4.

4   Verifying Flow Properties for Unbounded Agents

We now show how to verify the invariants in $\mathcal{I}$ for an unbounded number of agents by leveraging the data-type reduction abstraction along with the CMP method.

Abstraction: Data-Type Reduction. Since the invariant is of the form $inv.pred \Rightarrow (\forall i \in In^{inv} : \widehat{en}(\mathcal{R}(i)))$, by symmetry, it is sufficient to check: $inv.pred \Rightarrow ((1 \in In^{inv}) \Rightarrow (\widehat{en}(\mathcal{R}(1))))$. In order to verify this invariant, just the variables of agent 1 are required. Then, our abstraction keeps just the agent 1, and discards the variables of all the other agents by replacing them with a state-less *environment* agent. We refer to agent 1 as a *concrete* agent and the environment as *Other* with *id o*.

In the original protocol, since all the agents other than agent 1 interact with it by updating the global variables, the actions of these agents on the global variables are over-approximated by the environment agent. This environment agent does not have any local state. The construction of this agent *Other* is automatic and accomplished syntactically: further details on the automatic construction are available in [38]. The final constructed abstraction then consists of: (1) a concrete agent 1, (2) an environment agent *Other* with *id o*, and (3) invariants specified on variables of agent 1 and global variables. This abstraction is referred to as *data-type reduction*. If the original protocol is $\mathcal{P}$, and invariant set $\mathcal{I}$, we denote this abstraction by *data_type* and thus the abstract model by *data_type*($\mathcal{P}$) and the abstracted invariants on agent 1 by *data_type*($\mathcal{I}$).

Abstraction for German Protocol. We now describe how the rule $SendGntE(i)$ gets abstracted in *data_type*($\mathcal{P}$). In the abstract model, there is one concrete agent 1, which has the rule $SendGntE(1)$. Next, $SendGntE(o)$ is constructed as follows. (1) The guard is abstracted by replacing all atoms consisting of local variables (e.g. $GntChannel[i] = Empty$) with *true* or *false* depending on which results in an over-abstraction and by replacing any usage of i in atoms with global variables (e.g. $CurPtr = i$) with o (i.e. $CurPtr = o$). (2) The action is abstracted by discarding any assignments to local variables. Further, assignments to global pointer variables are abstracted as well: any usage of i (e.g. $CurPtr := i$) is replaced by o (i.e. $CurPtr := o$). The rule for agent *Other* is shown below:

```
Rule SendGntE(o)
    CurCmd = ReqE ∧ CurPtr = o ∧ true ∧ Exgntd = false ∧
      ShrSet = {}
→
    no-op; ShrSet := {o}; ExGntd := true;
    CurCmd := Empty; CurPtr := NULL;
End;
```

The Abstraction-Refinement Loop of the CMP Method. The CMP method works as an abstraction-refinement loop, as shown in Fig. 5. In the loop, the protocol and invariants are abstracted using data-type reduction. If the proof does not succeed, the user inspects the returned counterexample *cex* and following possibilities arise. (1) Counterexample *cex* is real, in which case an error is found and so the loop exits. (2) Counterexample *cex* is spurious and so the user refines the protocol by adding a *non-interference lemma lem*. The function *strengthen* updates the guard $rl_j(i).\rho$ of every rule $rl_j(i)$ of the protocol to $rl_j(i).\rho \wedge lem(j)$; this way, on re-abstraction with *data_type* in line 1, the new abstract protocol model is refined. Additional details on the CMP method are available in [11,25].

$\text{CMP}(\mathcal{P}(N), \mathcal{I})$
1: $\mathcal{P}^{\#} = \mathcal{P}(N); \mathcal{I}^{\#} = \mathcal{I}$
2: *while data_type*($\mathcal{P}^{\#}$) $\not\models$ *data_type*($\mathcal{I}^{\#}$) *do*
3:     examine counterexample *cex*
4:     if *cex* is real, exit
5:     if spurious:
6:         find lemma $lem = \forall i.lem(i)$
7:         $\mathcal{P}^{\#} = strengthen(\mathcal{P}^{\#}, lem)$
8:         $\mathcal{I}^{\#} = \mathcal{I}^{\#} \cup lem$

Fig. 5. The CMP method

5 Experiments

Using our approach, we verified Murphi (CMurphi 5.4.6) implementations of the German and Flash protocols (available online [31]). Our experiments were done on a 2.40 GHz Intel Core 2 Quad processor, with 3.74 GB RAM, running Ubuntu 9.10.

German Protocol. We verified the invariants discussed in Section 3.1, in order to prove s-deadlock freedom. We chose to use an abstraction with 2 agents and an environment agent, so that the mutual exclusion property can also be checked.

The proof finished in 217s with 7M states explored. No non-interference lemmas were required to refine the model, in order to verify the invariants presented in Section 3.1. Since typically protocols are also verified for properties like data integrity (i.e. the data stored in the cache is consistent with what the processors intended to write) and mutual exclusion, we model checked the above invariants along with these properties. In this case, the abstract model was constrained and model checking this model was faster and took 0.1 sec with 1763 states explored.

Buggy Version. We injected a simple error in the German protocol in order to introduce an s-deadlock. In the bug, an agent being invalidated drops the acknowledgement *SendInvAck* it is supposed to send to the directory. This results in the entire protocol getting blocked, hence an s-deadlock situation. This was detected by the failing of the invariant INV-1.2.2, discussed in Section 3.1.

Flash Protocol. Next, we verified the Flash protocol [26] for deadlock freedom. The Flash protocol implements the same high-level requests as the German protocol. It also uses a directory which has a Boolean variable $Pending$ which is *true* if the directory is busy processing a request from an agent pointed to by another variable $CurSrc$ (name changed from original protocol for ease of presentation). However, the Flash protocol uses two key optimizations over the German protocol. First, the Flash protocol enables the cache agents to directly forward data between each other instead of via the directory, for added speed. This is accomplished by the directory by forwarding incoming requests from the agent i to the destination agent, $FwDst(i)$, with the relevant data. Second, the Flash protocol uses non-blocking invalidates, i.e, the $Exclusive$ flow does not have to wait for the $Invalidate$ flow to complete for the sharing agents in $ShrSet$. Due to these optimizations, the flows of the Flash protocol are significantly more complex than those of German protocol. Further, due to forwarding, some rules involve two agents instead of one for the German protocol: thus the flows involve two agents as well. Each flow then is of the form $\mathcal{F}_k(i, j)$, where i is the requesting agent for a flow and $j = FwDst(i)$ is the destination agent to which the request may be forwarded by the directory. Then, we define $\mathcal{R}(i)$ to be equal to $\bigcup_k \mathcal{F}_k(i, FwDst(i))$.

We derived the invariants from the flows by keeping c to be equal to 3, as each request encompasses a maximum of 2 agents (forwarding and invalidation do not happen simultaneously in a flow). The final invariants derived using our method are as follows:

Directory Not Busy: If the directory is not busy (i.e., $Pending$ is *false*), any agent i can send a request. Thus the invariant INVF-1: $\neg(Pending) \Rightarrow \left(\forall i \in \mathbb{N}_N : \widehat{en}(\mathcal{R}(i))\right)$.

However, if the directory is busy (i.e., $Pending$ is *true*), two possibilities arise. (1) It may be busy since it is processing a request from agent $CurSrc$. Or, (2) in case the request from $CurSrc$ requires an invalidate, the directory may remain busy with invalidation even after the request from $CurSrc$ has been served. This is because Flash allows the request from $CurSrc$ to complete before invalidation due to non-blocking invalidates. Hence the following invariants:

Directory Busy with Request: Invariant INVF-2: $((Pending) \land (ShrSet = \{\})) \Rightarrow (\forall i \in In^{invF-2}\widehat{en}(\mathcal{R}(i)))$, where $In^{invF-2} = \{i| (i \in \mathbb{N}_N) \land (i = CurSrc)\}$.

Directory Busy with Invalidate: Invariant INVF-3: $((Pending) \land \neg(ShrSet = \{\})) \Rightarrow (\forall i \in In^{invF-3}\widehat{en}(\mathcal{R}(i)))$, where $In^{invF-3} = \{i| (i \in \mathbb{N}_N) \land (i \in ShrSet)\}$.

Runtime: We verified the above invariants along with the mutual exclusion and the data integrity properties for an unbounded model abstracted by keeping 3 concrete agents (one agent behaves as a directory) and constructing an environment agent *Other*. The verification took 5127s with about 20.5M states and 152M rules fired. In this case we reused the lemmas used in prior work by Chou *et al.* [11] for verifying the mutual exclusion and data integrity properties in order to refine the agent *Other*.

Verifying Flash vs German Protocol: The flows of the Flash protocol involve two indices: we eliminated the second index by replacing it with the variable $FwDst(i)$ which stores information of the forwarded cache and thus made the verification similar to the German protocol case. Next, Flash protocol uses lazy invalidate: even if the original request has completed, the directory may still be busy with the invalidate. As explained above, this was in contrast to the German protocol and resulted in an additional invariant INVF-3.

Comparison with Other Techniques: The only technique we are aware of which handles Flash with a high degree of automation is by Bingham *et al.* [8]. While a direct comparison of the runtime between their approach and ours is infeasible for this paper, we note that the invariants generated using our approach only require an over-abstraction in contrast to theirs which requires a mixed-abstraction. This is an advantage since development of automatic and scalable over-abstraction based parameterized safety verification techniques is a promising area of ongoing research (e.g. [15]) which our approach directly benefits from.

6   Conclusions and Future Work

In this paper we have presented a method to prove freedom from a practically motivated deadlock error which spans the entire cache coherence protocol, an s-deadlock. Our method exploits high-level information in the form of message sequence diagrams—these are referred to as *flows* and are readily available in industrial documents as charts and tables. Using our method, a set of invariants can be derived which collectively imply s-deadlock freedom. These invariants enable the direct application of industrial scale techniques for parameterized verification.

As part of future work, we plan to take up verification of livelock freedom by exploiting flows. Verifying livelock requires formally defining a notion of the protocol doing useful work. This information is present in flows—efficiently exploiting this is part of our ongoing research.

Acknowledgment. This work was supported in part by C-FAR, one of the six SRC STARnet Centers, sponsored by MARCO and DARPA. The authors would also like to thank Sayak Ray for his comments which were very helpful in improving this paper.

References

1. Abadi, M., Lamport, L.: Composing specifications. ACM Trans. Program. Lang. Syst. 15(1), 73–132 (1993), http://doi.acm.org/10.1145/151646.151649
2. Abadi, M., Lamport, L.: Conjoining specifications. ACM Trans. Program. Lang. Syst. 17(3), 507–535 (1995), http://doi.acm.org/10.1145/203095.201069
3. Abdulla, P., Haziza, F., Holk, L.: A model-constructing satisfiability calculus. In: Giacobazzi, R., Berdine, J., Mastroeni, I. (eds.) VMCAI 2013. LNCS, vol. 7737, pp. 1–12. Springer, Heidelberg (2013), http://dx.doi.org/10.1007/978-3-642-35873-9_28
4. Abdulla, P.A., Jonsson, B., Nilsson, M., Saksena, M.: A survey of regular model checking. In: Gardner, P., Yoshida, N. (eds.) CONCUR 2004. LNCS, vol. 3170, pp. 35–48. Springer, Heidelberg (2004), http://dx.doi.org/10.1007/978-3-540-28644-8_3
5. Arons, T., Pnueli, A., Ruah, S., Xu, J., Zuck, L.D.: Parameterized verification with automatically computed inductive assertions. In: Berry, G., Comon, H., Finkel, A. (eds.) CAV 2001. LNCS, vol. 2102, pp. 221–234. Springer, Heidelberg (2001), http://dl.acm.org/citation.cfm?id=647770.734120
6. Baukus, K., Lakhnech, Y., Stahl, K.: Parameterized verification of a cache coherence protocol: Safety and liveness. In: Cortesi, A. (ed.) VMCAI 2002. LNCS, vol. 2294, pp. 317–330. Springer, Heidelberg (2002), http://dl.acm.org/citation.cfm?id=646541.696180
7. Bingham, B., Bingham, J., Erickson, J., Greenstreet, M.: Distributed explicit state model checking of deadlock freedom. In: Sharygina, N., Veith, H. (eds.) CAV 2013. LNCS, vol. 8044, pp. 235–241. Springer, Heidelberg (2013)
8. Bingham, B., Greenstreet, M., Bingham, J.: Parameterized verification of deadlock freedom in symmetric cache coherence protocols. In: Proceedings of the International Conference on Formal Methods in Computer-Aided Design, FMCAD 2011, pp. 186–195. FMCAD Inc, Austin (2011), http://dl.acm.org/citation.cfm?id=2157654.2157683
9. Boigelot, B., Legay, A., Wolper, P.: Iterating transducers in the large. In: Hunt Jr., W.A., Somenzi, F. (eds.) CAV 2003. LNCS, vol. 2725, pp. 223–235. Springer, Heidelberg (2003), http://dx.doi.org/10.1007/978-3-540-45069-6_24
10. Bouajjani, A., Jonsson, B., Nilsson, M., Touili, T.: Regular model checking. In: Emerson, E.A., Sistla, A.P. (eds.) CAV 2000. LNCS, vol. 1855, pp. 403–418. Springer, Heidelberg (2000), http://dl.acm.org/citation.cfm?id=647769.734106
11. Chou, C.-T., Mannava, P.K., Park, S.: A simple method for parameterized verification of cache coherence protocols. In: Hu, A.J., Martin, A.K. (eds.) FMCAD 2004. LNCS, vol. 3312, pp. 382–398. Springer, Heidelberg (2004)
12. Clarke, E.M., Grumberg, O., Browne, M.C.: Reasoning about networks with many identical finite-state processes. In: Proceedings of the Fifth Annual ACM Symposium on Principles of Distributed Computing, PODC 1986, pp. 240–248. ACM, New York (1986), http://doi.acm.org/10.1145/10590.10611
13. Clarke, E., Talupur, M., Veith, H.: Proving ptolemy right: the environment abstraction framework for model checking concurrent systems. In: Ramakrishnan, C.R., Rehof, J. (eds.) TACAS 2008. LNCS, vol. 4963, pp. 33–47. Springer, Heidelberg (2008), http://portal.acm.org/citation.cfm?id=1792734.1792740

14. Clarke, E., Talupur, M., Veith, H.: Environment abstraction for parameterized verification. In: Emerson, E.A., Namjoshi, K.S. (eds.) VMCAI 2006. LNCS, vol. 3855, pp. 126–141. Springer, Heidelberg (2006), http://dx.doi.org/10.1007/11609773_9
15. Conchon, S., Goel, A., Krstic, S., Mebsout, A., Zaidi, F.: Invariants for finite instances and beyond. In: Formal Methods in Computer-Aided Design (FMCAD), pp. 61–68 (October 2013)
16. Dams, D., Gerth, R., Grumberg, O.: Abstract interpretation of reactive systems. ACM Trans. Program. Lang. Syst. 19(2), 253–291 (1997), http://doi.acm.org/10.1145/244795.244800
17. Das, S., Dill, D., Park, S.: Experience with predicate abstraction. In: Halbwachs, N., Peled, D.A. (eds.) CAV 1999. LNCS, vol. 1633, pp. 160–171. Springer, Heidelberg (1999), http://dx.doi.org/10.1007/3-540-48683-6_16
18. Emerson, E.A., Kahlon, V.: Reducing model checking of the many to the few. In: McAllester, D. (ed.) CADE 2000. LNCS, vol. 1831, pp. 236–254. Springer, Heidelberg (2000), http://dl.acm.org/citation.cfm?id=648236.753642
19. Emerson, E.A., Kahlon, V.: Exact and efficient verification of parameterized cache coherence protocols. In: Geist, D., Tronci, E. (eds.) CHARME 2003. LNCS, vol. 2860, pp. 247–262. Springer, Heidelberg (2003)
20. Emerson, E.A., Namjoshi, K.S.: Automatic verification of parameterized synchronous systems (extended abstract). In: Alur, R., Henzinger, T.A. (eds.) CAV 1996. LNCS, vol. 1102, pp. 87–98. Springer, Heidelberg (1996), http://dl.acm.org/citation.cfm?id=647765.735841
21. Fang, Y., Piterman, N., Pnueli, A., Zuck, L.: Liveness with invisible ranking. Int. J. Softw. Tools Technol. Transf. 8(3), 261–279 (2006), http://dx.doi.org/10.1007/s10009-005-0193-x
22. Holt, R.C.: Some deadlock properties of computer systems. ACM Comput. Surv. 4(3), 179–196 (1972), http://doi.acm.org/10.1145/356603.356607
23. Ip, C.N., Dill, D.L.: Better verification through symmetry. In: Proc. Conf. on Computer Hardware Description Languages and their Applications, pp. 97–111 (1993)
24. Kaiser, A., Kroening, D., Wahl, T.: Dynamic cutoff detection in parameterized concurrent programs. In: Touili, T., Cook, B., Jackson, P. (eds.) CAV 2010. LNCS, vol. 6174, pp. 645–659. Springer, Heidelberg (2010), http://dx.doi.org/10.1007/978-3-642-14295-6_55
25. Kristic, S.: Parameterized system verification with guard strengthening and parameter abstraction. In: 4th Int. Workshop on Automatic Verification of Finite State Systems (2005)
26. Kuskin, J., Ofelt, D., Heinrich, M., Heinlein, J., Simoni, R., Gharachorloo, K., Chapin, J., Nakahira, D., Baxter, J., Horowitz, M., Gupta, A., Rosenblum, M., Hennessy, J.: The stanford flash multiprocessor. In: Proceedings the 21st Annual International Symposium on Computer Architecture, pp. 302–313 (1994)
27. Lahiri, S.K., Bryant, R.E.: Predicate abstraction with indexed predicates. ACM Trans. Comput. Logic 9(1) (2007), http://doi.acm.org/10.1145/1297658.1297662
28. Mcmillan, K.L.: Parameterized verification of the flash cache coherence protocol by compositional model checking. In: Margaria, T., Melham, T.F. (eds.) CHARME 2001. LNCS, vol. 2144, pp. 179–195. Springer, Heidelberg (2001)
29. McMillan, K.L.: Circular compositional reasoning about liveness. In: Pierre, L., Kropf, T. (eds.) CHARME 1999. LNCS, vol. 1703, pp. 342–346. Springer, Heidelberg (1999), http://dl.acm.org/citation.cfm?id=646704.701881
30. McMillan, K.L.: Verification of infinite state systems by compositional model checking. In: Pierre, L., Kropf, T. (eds.) CHARME 1999. LNCS, vol. 1703, pp. 219–237. Springer, Heidelberg (1999), http://dl.acm.org/citation.cfm?id=646704.702020
31. Murphi source code, https://github.com/dsethi/ProtocolDeadlockFiles

32. O'Leary, J., Talupur, M., Tuttle, M.R.: Protocol verification using flows: An industrial experience. In: Formal Methods in Computer-Aided Design, FMCAD 2009, pp. 172–179 (November 2009)
33. Park, S., Dill, D.L.: Verification of flash cache coherence protocol by aggregation of distributed transactions. In: SPAA '96: Proceedings of the eighth annual ACM symposium on Parallel algorithms and architectures, pp. 288–296. ACM Press (1996)
34. Pnueli, A., Ruah, S., Zuck, L.D.: Automatic deductive verification with invisible invariants. In: Margaria, T., Yi, W. (eds.) TACAS 2001. LNCS, vol. 2031, pp. 82–97. Springer, Heidelberg (2001), http://dl.acm.org/citation.cfm?id=646485.694452
35. Pnueli, A., Xu, J., Zuck, L.D.: Liveness with $(0, 1, \infty)$-counter abstraction. In: Brinksma, E., Larsen, K.G. (eds.) CAV 2002. LNCS, vol. 2404, pp. 107–122. Springer, Heidelberg (2002), http://dl.acm.org/citation.cfm?id=647771.734286
36. Resten, Y., Maler, O., Marcus, M., Pnueli, A., Shahar, E.: Symbolic model checking with rich assertional languages. In: Grumberg, O. (ed.) CAV 1997. LNCS, vol. 1254, pp. 424–435. Springer, Heidelberg (1997), http://dx.doi.org/10.1007/3-540-63166-6_41
37. Sethi, D., Talupur, M., Malik, S.: Using flow specifications of parameterized cache coherence protocols for verifying deadlock freedom. ArXiv:1407.7468
38. Talupur, M., Tuttle, M.R.: Going with the flow: Parameterized verification using message flows. In: Proceedings of the 2008 International Conference on Formal Methods in Computer-Aided Design, FMCAD 2008. FMCAD '08, pp. 1–10. IEEE Press, Piscataway (2008), http://dl.acm.org/citation.cfm?id=1517424.1517434

A Game-Theoretic Approach to Simulation of Data-Parameterized Systems

Orna Grumberg[1], Orna Kupferman[2], and Sarai Sheinvald[2]

[1] Department of Computer Science, The Technion, Haifa 32000, Israel
[2] School of Computer Science and Engineering, Hebrew University, Jerusalem 91904, Israel

Abstract. This work focuses on data-parameterized abstract systems that extend standard modelling by allowing atomic propositions to be parameterized by variables that range over some infinite domain. These variables may range over process ids, message numbers, etc. Thus, abstract systems enable simple modelling of infinite-state systems whose source of infinity is the data. We define and study a simulation pre-order between abstract systems. The definition extends the definition of standard simulation by referring also to variable assignments. We define VCTL* – an extension of CTL* by variables, which is capable of specifying properties of abstract systems. We show that VCTL* logically characterizes the simulation pre-order between abstract systems. That is, that satisfaction of VACTL*, namely the universal fragment of VCTL*, is preserved in simulating abstract systems. For the second direction, we show that if an abstract system $\mathcal{A}_2$ does not simulate an abstract system $\mathcal{A}_1$, then there exists a VACTL formula that distinguishes $\mathcal{A}_1$ from $\mathcal{A}_2$. Finally, we present a game-theoretic approach to simulation of abstract systems and show that the prover wins the game iff $\mathcal{A}_2$ simulates $\mathcal{A}_1$. Further, if $\mathcal{A}_2$ does not simulate $\mathcal{A}_1$, then the refuter wins the game and his winning strategy corresponds to a VACTL formula that distinguishes $\mathcal{A}_1$ from $\mathcal{A}_2$. Thus, the many appealing practical advantages of simulation are lifted to the setting of data-parameterized abstract systems.

1 Introduction

In system verification, we check that an implementation satisfies its specification. Both the implementation and the specification describe the possible behaviors of the system at different levels of abstraction. If we represent the implementation $\mathcal{I}$ and the specification $\mathcal{S}$ using Kripke structures, then the formal relation that captures satisfaction in the linear approach is *trace containment*: $\mathcal{S}$ trace-contains $\mathcal{I}$ iff it is possible to generate by $\mathcal{S}$ every (finite and infinite) sequence of observations that can be generated by $\mathcal{I}$. The notion of trace containment is logically characterized by linear temporal logics such as LTL in the sense that $\mathcal{S}$ trace-contains $\mathcal{I}$ iff every LTL formula that holds in $\mathcal{S}$ holds also in $\mathcal{I}$. Unfortunately, it is difficult to check trace containment (complete for PSPACE [29]). The formal relation that captures satisfaction in the branching approach is *tree containment*: $\mathcal{S}$ tree-contains $\mathcal{I}$ iff it is possible to embed in the unrolling of $\mathcal{S}$ every (finite and infinite) tree of observations that can be embedded in the unrolling of $\mathcal{I}$. The notion of tree containment is equivalent to the notion of simulation, as defined by Milner [24]: $\mathcal{S}$ tree-contains $\mathcal{I}$ iff $\mathcal{S}$ simulates $\mathcal{I}$; that is, we can relate each state of

F. Cassez and J.-F. Raskin (Eds.): ATVA 2014, LNCS 8837, pp. 348–363, 2014.
© Springer International Publishing Switzerland 2014

$\mathcal{I}$ to a state of $\mathcal{S}$ so that two related states i and s agree on their observations and every successor of i is related to some successor of s [26].

Simulation has several theoretical and practical appealing properties. First, like trace containment, simulation is robust: for universal branching temporal logics (where only universal path quantification is allowed) such as ACTL and ACTL* (the universal fragments of the computation tree logics CTL and CTL*), we have that $\mathcal{S}$ simulates $\mathcal{I}$ iff every formula that holds in $\mathcal{S}$ holds also in $\mathcal{I}$ [2,15]. Second, unlike trace containment, the definition of simulation is local, as the relation between two states is based only on their successor states. As a result, simulation can be checked in polynomial time [7,1]. The locality advantage is so compelling as to make simulation useful also to researchers that favor trace-based specification: in automatic verification, simulation is widely used as an efficiently computable sufficient condition for trace containment [19]; in manual verification, trace containment is most naturally proved by exhibiting local witnesses such as simulation relations or refinement mappings (a restricted form of simulation relations) [20,22,23,8].

In addition to the use of simulation in *step-wise refinement*, where a pre-order between an implementation and its specification is checked, simulation is helpful in coping with the state-explosion problem, as it enables the verification process to proceed with respect to an over-approximation of the implementation: instead of verifying $\mathcal{I}$, we abstract some of its details and generate a (typically much smaller) system $\mathcal{I}'$ that simulates $\mathcal{I}$. Verification then proceeds with respect to $\mathcal{I}'$, either proving that it satisfies the specification (in which case we can conclude that so does $\mathcal{I}$) or not, in which case the abstraction is refined [6].

Abstraction and simulation have turned out to be key methods in coping with the state-explosion problem. In particular, by abstracting elements of the system that have an infinite domain, one can verify infinite-state systems. Often, the source of infinity in a system is data that range over an unbounded or infinite domain, such as content of messages, process ids, etc. Traditional abstraction methods either hide the data or abstract its value by finite-domain predicates [27]. In [12,13], we introduced *abstract systems*, which finitely and naturally represent infinite-state systems in which the source of infinity is data that range over an infinite domain. Formally, an abstract system is a finite Kripke structure whose atomic propositions are parameterized by variables ranging over the infinite domain. A transition of the system may reset a subset of the variables, freeing them of their previous assignment. The different concrete computation trees, or *concretizations*, of an abstract system are obtained by legally assigning concrete domain values to the variables along an unwinding of the abstract system.

For example, consider the system presented in Figure 1. It represents a simple communication protocol, where the variable x represents the message id. The concretization presented in Figure 1 is obtained by assigning values to x in a way that agrees with the resets in the protocol: when the transition from the *timeout* state is taken, the message is resent with the same message id. When the transition from the *ack* state is taken, x is reset and may be reassigned, as reflected in the concretization.

Evidently, abstract systems are capable of describing communication protocols with unboundedly many processes, systems with interleaved transactions each carrying a unique id, buffers of messages with an infinite domain, and many more.

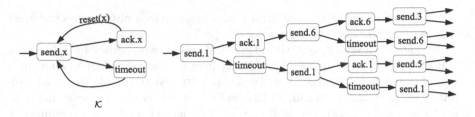

Fig. 1. A simple communication protocol and a possible concretization

In this paper we combine the clean treatment of data over infinite domain with the theoretical and practical advantages of simulation. We define simulation between abstract systems, study its properties, and describe a logical characterization for it.

The challenge of specifying behaviors with an infinite component has led to the development of various formalisms. One class of formalisms consists of variants of automata over infinite alphabets. Types of such automata include *register automata* [28], which have a finite set of registers, each of which may contain a letter from the infinite alphabet. Register automata have been extensively studied and may include features like alternation, two-wayness, a nondeterministic change of the content of registers, and further generalizations [25,18,13]. *Pebble automata* [25,30] place pebbles on the input word in a stack-like manner, and in *data automata* [4,3], the infinite alphabet consists of pairs – a letter from a finite alphabet and a data value from some infinite domain. The finite alphabet is accessed directly and the data is accessed indirectly via the equivalence relation it induces on the set of positions. Finally, closest to our abstract systems are nondeterministic finite automata with variables [11].

The second class of formalisms consists of extensions of temporal logics. An extension in which atomic propositions are parameterized by a variable that ranges over the set of processes ids was studied in [5,10]. These works are tailored for the setting of parameterized systems, and are also restricted to systems in which (almost) all components are identical. In Constraint LTL [9], atomic propositions may be constraints like $x < y$, and formulas are interpreted over sequences of assignments of variables to values in $\mathbb{N}$ or $\mathbb{Z}$. Unlike our approach, the focus is on reasoning about sequences of numerical values. In [21,16], LTL and CTL have been extended with a freeze quantifier, which is used for storing values from an infinite domain in a register.

In [12], we introduced *variable* LTL (VLTL), a first-order extension of LTL. Like abstract systems, VLTL uses atomic propositions parameterized with variables to describe the behaviors of computations that may carry infinitely many values. For example, the VLTL formula $\psi = \forall x; \mathrm{G}(send.x \rightarrow Freceive.x)$ states that for every value d in the domain, whenever a message with content d is sent, then a message with content d is eventually received. In this work, we define the logic VCTL*, a first-order extension of CTL*. Similarly to CTL*, the logic VCTL* has existential and universal path quantification. Similarly to VLTL, it also has existential and universal quantification over variables. While VLTL is interpreted over infinite computations of abstract systems, VCTL* is interpreted over their computation trees.

As an example, consider a variable x that ranges over process ids. The VCTL* formula $\varphi_1 = \exists x;$ AFAG$\neg idle.x$ states that there exists a process that is eventually not idle along all paths. The formula $\varphi_2 =$ AF$\exists x;$ AG$\neg idle.x$ states that every path eventually reaches a point where there exists a process that is never idle from that point on along all paths. The formula $\varphi_3 =$ AFA$\exists x;$ G$\neg idle.x$ states that along every path, from some point on, there exists a process that is never idle. Finally, $\varphi_4 =$ AFAG$\exists x;$ $\neg idle.x$ states that from some point on, in every step of every path, there exists a process that is never idle. Note that the formulas are not equivalent, and they demonstrate the power of the ability to nest the variable quantifiers within the formula.[1] In particular, in φ_3 (and not in φ_2) different paths may have different non-idle processes, and in φ_4 (and not in φ_3), this may be a different process at each step.

Our goal is to define a simulation relation for abstract systems in a way that preserves their behaviors. Preserving the behavior of the variables raises some challenges. Consider two states q_1 and q_2 of abstract systems $\mathcal{A}_1$ and $\mathcal{A}_2$. In standard simulation, q_1 and q_2 may be matched only if they agree on the labeling of the atomic propositions. In the abstract systems setting, we need, in addition, to make sure that the variables that parameterize these atomic propositions can be matched. For example, if q_1 is labeled by $a.x_1$ and q_2 is labeled by $a.x_2$, where a is an atomic proposition and x_1, x_2 are variables, then a simulation that matches q_1 with q_2 must make sure that every value that is assigned to x_1 can also be assigned to x_2. This latter condition is no longer local, as the value assigned to an occurrence of x_2 depends both on the history of the behavior before reaching q_2, and on the behavior of other states in which x_2 occures. Thus, a simulation relation between $\mathcal{A}_1$ and $\mathcal{A}_2$ must keep a memory component for the variables, and the challenge is to keep the definition of simulation as local as possible, with the global elements being restricted to the variables only.

We manage tracking the behavior of the variables locally by adding a function that maps the variables of $\mathcal{A}_2$ to the variables of $\mathcal{A}_1$ to each tuple in the simulation relation. Thus, our simulation relation consists of triplets: a state of $\mathcal{A}_1$, a state of $\mathcal{A}_2$, and a function over the variables. We present an algorithm for computing a maximal simulation from $\mathcal{A}_1$ to $\mathcal{A}_2$. The function component may create a simulation relation of size that is exponential in the number of variables. While this is worse than the polynomial size of standard simulation, one should bear in mind that trace containment for abstract systems is undecidable, as opposed to the PSPACE complexity of standard trace containment. We argue that our definition is indeed robust with respect to VACTL* – the universal fragment of VCTL*. First, if $\mathcal{A}_2$ simulates $\mathcal{A}_1$, denoted $\mathcal{A}_1 \preceq \mathcal{A}_2$, then every VACTL* formula that is satisfied in $\mathcal{A}_2$ is also satisfied in $\mathcal{A}_1$. The second direction is much harder, and we show that if $\mathcal{A}_1 \npreceq \mathcal{A}_2$, then we can construct a VACTL formula that $\mathcal{A}_2$ satisfies, and $\mathcal{A}_1$ does not.

A *simulation game* for (non-abstract) systems A_1 and A_2 is played between two players: a *prover*, who wishes to prove that A_2 simulates A_1, and a *refuter*, who wishes to prove the contrary. In each round of the game, the refuter advances along A_1 and the prover advances along A_2, aiming to match every move of the refuter by moving to a state with the same label. A simulation relation from A_1 to A_2 induces a winning strategy for the prover. Also, if A_2 does not simulate A_1, then a winning strategy for

---

[1] In VLTL, variable quantification is restricted to appear only at the head of the formula.

the refuter exists, and it induces an ACTL formula that holds only in A_2. We define a game-theoretic approach to simulation between abstract systems A_1 and A_2. As in the standard setting, the game proceeds in rounds along both abstract systems, where in every step the prover attempts to match the state it chooses in A_2 with the state in A_1 chosen by the refuter. Here, however, matching refers also to the variables, and the prover must make sure that the variables in the states it chooses can be assigned the same values that can be assigned to the variables in the states that the refuter chooses. As explained above, this property is not local, making the game more sophisticated: While in the traditional setting the game proceeds along a single path in each system, in our setting the refuter may split the game to continue temporarily along two different paths – those along which he plans to force the prover to use inconsistent assignments.

As in the traditional setting, a simulation relation induces a winning strategy for the prover. Also, if A_2 does not simulate A_1, then a winning strategy is induced by a VACTL formula that holds only in A_2. The need to refer to the variables makes the game and its correctness proof complicated. In particular, in case the refuter wins thanks to the inability of the prover to correctly handle the variables, the distinguishing formula captures this by requirements that refer to variable assignments. The construction of the formula relies on our algorithm for computing a simulation relation from A_1 to A_2. The time complexity of our algorithm is exponential in the number of variables, and accordingly, so is the depth of the formula. Still, the appealing properties of the game in the traditional setting are preserved, in particular the fact that the players have memoryless strategies.

In Section 7 we discuss directions for future research and the practical applications of defining the simulation pre-order in the setting of abstract systems.

2   Preliminaries

Kripke Structures and Simulation. Let AP be a finite set of atomic propositions. A *Kripke structure* is a tuple $A = \langle Q, q^0, AP, R, L \rangle$, where Q is a finite set of states, q^0 is an initial state, $R \subseteq Q \times Q$ is a total transition relation, and $L : Q \to 2^{AP}$ maps each state to the set of atomic propositions that hold in the state. We sometimes refer to Kripke structures as systems.

Let $A_1 = \langle Q_1, q_1^0, AP, R_1, L_1 \rangle$ and $A_2 = \langle Q_2, q_2^0, AP, R_2, L_2 \rangle$ be two Kripke structures over the same set of atomic propositions. A *simulation* [24] from A_1 to A_2 is a relation $H \subseteq Q_1 \times Q_2$ such that for every $\langle q_1, q_2 \rangle \in H$, we have that $L_1(q_1) = L_2(q_2)$, and for every $\langle q_1, q_1' \rangle \in R_1$ there exists $\langle q_2, q_2' \rangle \in R_2$ such that $\langle q_1', q_2' \rangle \in H$. If $\langle q_1^0, q_2^0 \rangle \in H$, then we say that A_2 *simulates* A_1, denoted $A_1 \preceq A_2$.

It is well known [14] that if $A_1 \preceq A_2$, then for every $\varphi \in$ ACTL*, if $A_2 \models \varphi$ then $A_1 \models \varphi$. If $A_1 \npreceq A_2$, then there exists an ACTL formula φ such that $A_2 \models \varphi$ and $A_1 \nvDash \varphi$. We call such a formula a *distinguishing formula for A_1 and A_2*.

A *simulation game* [17] for A_1 and A_2 is a protocol for two players: a prover $\mathcal{P}$, who wishes to prove that $A_1 \preceq A_2$, and a refuter $\mathcal{R}$, who wishes to prove that $A_1 \npreceq A_2$. A position in the game is a pair $\langle q_1, q_2 \rangle \in Q_1 \times Q_2$, where q_1 is the location of $\mathcal{R}$ and q_2 is the location of $\mathcal{P}$. A play in the game starts in $\langle q_1^0, q_2^0 \rangle$. If $L_1(q_0^1) \neq L_2(q_0^2)$, then $\mathcal{R}$ wins. Otherwise, the play continues as follows. Let $\langle q_1, q_2 \rangle$ be the current position.

In each round, $\mathcal{R}$ chooses a transition $\langle q_1, q_1' \rangle \in R_1$, and $\mathcal{P}$ responds by choosing a transition $\langle q_2, q_2' \rangle \in R_2$, such that $L_1(q_1') = L_2(q_2')$. The play then continues from position $\langle q_1', q_2' \rangle$. Hence, a play in the game induces two paths, one in A_1 and one in A_2. If at some point in the play, $\mathcal{P}$ is unable to respond with a suitable move, then $\mathcal{R}$ wins. Otherwise, the play continues forever and $\mathcal{P}$ wins.

It holds that $A_1 \preceq A_2$ iff $\mathcal{P}$ has a winning memoryless strategy in the game. Equivalently, $A_1 \npreceq A_2$ iff $\mathcal{R}$ has a winning strategy. The latter corresponds to a distinguishing formula for A_1 and A_2.

Abstract Systems. An *abstract system* is a tuple $\mathcal{A} = \langle Q, q^0, AP, X, R, L, S \rangle$, where Q, q^0, and R are as in Kripke structures, and

- X is a set of variables.
- AP is a set of atomic propositions that may be parameterized by variables from X.
- $L : Q \to 2^{AP \cup (AP \times X)}$ maps each state to the set of atomic propositions that hold in the state. We require that for every $q \in Q$ and $a \in AP$, the set $L(q)$ contains at most one occurrence of a.
- $S : R \to 2^X$ maps each transition to the set of variables that are reset along the transition.

A *concretization* of $\mathcal{A}$, which is a concrete computation tree of $\mathcal{A}$, is obtained by assigning values to the variables, as we explain next.

A Σ-labeled tree is a pair $\langle T, l \rangle$ where $T = \langle V, E \rangle$ is a directed tree with a set of nodes V and a set of edges E, and $l : V \to \Sigma$ is a function that labels each node in the tree by a letter from Σ.

Let $\langle T, l \rangle$ be the $2^{AP \cup (AP \times X)}$-labeled tree obtained by unwinding $\mathcal{A}$ from q^0. Formally, $T = \langle V, E \rangle$ is such that $V \subseteq Q^*$, where $q^0 \in V$ is the root of T, and $w \cdot q \cdot q'$ is in V, for $w \in Q^*$ and $q, q' \in Q$, iff $w \cdot q \in V$ and $\langle q, q' \rangle \in R$, in which case $\langle w \cdot q, w \cdot q \cdot q' \rangle \in E$. Also, $l(w \cdot q) = L(q)$. Note that we can associate with each edge in the tree the set of variables that are reset along it, namely these reset in the transition in $\mathcal{A}$ that induces the edge.

Let $\mathcal{D}$ be an infinite domain. A $\mathcal{D}$-*concretization of* $\mathcal{A}$ is an infinite $2^{AP \cup (AP \times \mathcal{D})}$-labeled tree $\langle T, l_f \rangle$ obtained from $\langle T, l \rangle$ by assigning values from $\mathcal{D}$ to the occurrences of the variables in every node in T in a way that agrees with the resets along the transitions of $\mathcal{A}$. That is, for every node s of T we assign a function $f_s : X \to \mathcal{D}$. The labeling $l_f(s)$ of s is obtained by replacing every variable x in $l(s)$ by $f_s(x)$. The functions f_s satisfy the following property. Let s be a node in T, let x be a variable, and let s' be a node in the subtree rooted in s. If x is not reset along the path from s to s', then $f_s(x) = f_{s'}(x)$. That is, all the occurrences of x in a subtree of T with root s that are not reset along the path in the abstract system that leads from s to them, are assigned the same $d \in \mathcal{D}$ in $\langle T, l_f \rangle$. Note that the tree $\langle T, l_f \rangle$ is in fact an infinite state system over $AP \cup (AP \times \mathcal{D})$.

3 VCTL*

In this section, we define *variable* CTL* (VCTL*, for short) – a first order extension of CTL* that handles infinite data. Like abstract systems, VCTL* uses atomic propositions that are parameterized with variables. In addition, VCTL* uses quantifiers over the variables that may be nested within the formula.

The syntax of VCTL* includes formulas of two types: state formulas and path formulas. Let X be a set of variables, and let AP be a set of atomic propositions that may be parameterized by variables from X. A VCTL* state formula is $p \in AP$, $a.x \in AP \times X$, $\neg\varphi_1$, $\varphi_1 \vee \varphi_2$, $\exists x; \varphi_1$, or $E\psi_1$, for VCTL* state formulas φ_1 and φ_2 and a VCTL* path formula ψ_1. A VCTL* path formula is φ_1, $\neg\psi_1$, $\psi_1 \vee \psi_2$, $X\psi_1$, $\psi_1 U\psi_2$, or $\exists x; \psi_1$, for a VCTL* state formula φ_1 and VCTL* path formulas ψ_1 and ψ_2. Finally, VCTL* is the set of all closed VCTL* state formulas.

We turn to define the semantics of VCTL*. Let $\mathcal{A}$ be an abstract system with a labeling function L, let φ be a VCTL* formula. We say that $\mathcal{A}$ satisfies φ (denoted $\mathcal{A} \models \varphi$) if for every infinite domain $\mathcal{D}$, every $\mathcal{D}$-concretization of $\mathcal{A}$ satisfies φ. Thus, it is left to define the semantics of VCTL* with respect to concretizations of abstract systems. As usual with first order logic, since we define the semantics inductively over open formulas, we define the semantics also w.r.t. an assignment $t : X \to \mathcal{D}$ over the variables. For closed formulas, the semantics is independent of an assignment to the variables.

Let $\langle T, I_f \rangle$ be a $\mathcal{D}$-concretization of $\mathcal{A}$, let s be a node in T, and let $\pi = s_0, s_1, s_2, \ldots$ be an infinite path in T. We assume that $\langle T, I_f \rangle$ is fixed and use $s \models_t \varphi$ and $\pi \models_t \psi$ to indicate that s satisfies φ under the assignment t, and similarly for π and ψ. The relation $\models_t$ is defined inductively as follows. Consider a state formula φ.

- If $\varphi \in AP$ or the outermost operator in φ is $\neg$, $\vee$, or E, then the definition is as in CTL*.
- If $\varphi = a.x \in AP \times X$, then $s \models_t \varphi$ iff $a.d \in l(s)$ and $t(x) = d$.
- If $\varphi = \exists x; \varphi_1$, then $s \models_t \varphi$ iff there exists $d \in \mathcal{D}$ such that $s \models_{t[x \leftarrow d]} \varphi_1$.

Consider a path formula ψ.

- If ψ is a state formula or the outermost operator in ψ is $\neg$, X, or U, then the definition is as in CTL*.
- If $\psi = \exists x; \psi_1$, then $\pi, i \models_t \psi$ iff there exists $d \in \mathcal{D}$ such that $\pi, i \models_{t[x \leftarrow d]} \psi$.

We use the usual abbreviations G ("always") and F ("eventually") for temporal operators, the path quantifier A ("for all paths"), and the $\forall$ quantifier over variables.

The logic VACTL* (*universal* VACTL*) is the fragment of VCTL* in which negation is restricted to atomic propositions and only the A path quantifier is allowed. The logic VACTL is the fragment of VACTL* in which temporal operators cannot be nested without a path quantifier between them. These fragments join the previously defined fragment VLTL [12], which is the set of all VCTL* formulas of the form $A\psi$, where ψ is a path formula that does not contain path quantifiers and all its variable quantifiers are at the head of the formula.

Remark 1. It is possible to augment the definition of abstract systems and VCTL* formulas to include inequalities over the set of variables, say $x_1 \neq x_2$. This restricts the set of legal concretizations and possible assignments, respectively. It is easy to extend our results to a setting with such an augmentation.

4 Simulation of Abstract Systems

In this section we define a simulation pre-order between abstract systems. Let $\mathcal{A}_1 = \langle Q_1, q_1^0, AP, X_1, R_1, L_1, S_1 \rangle$ and $\mathcal{A}_2 = \langle Q_2, q_2^0, AP, X_2, R_2, L_2, S_2 \rangle$ be abstract systems over the same set of atomic propositions.

We want to define simulation in such a way that if $\mathcal{A}_2$ simulates $\mathcal{A}_1$, then every behavior of $\mathcal{A}_1$ is exhibited in $\mathcal{A}_2$. In standard simulation, state q_1 of system A_1 may be matched with state q_2 of system A_2 only if q_1 and q_2 are equally labeled. In abstract systems, we need, in addition, to assure a match in the variables parameterizing the atomic propositions in q_1 and q_2. If, for example, $L_1(q_1)$ contains $a.x_1$ and $L_2(q_2)$ contains $a.x_2$, for $a \in AP$, $x_1 \in X_1$, and $x_2 \in X_2$, we want to match q_1 with q_2 only if every value that can be assigned to x_1 can also be assigned to x_2. Accordingly, a simulation relation H also indicates that when matching q_1 with q_2, the variable x_2 in q_2 is matched with the variable x_1 in q_1.

Formally, a simulation relation H from $\mathcal{A}_1$ to $\mathcal{A}_2$ consists of triplets of type $\langle q_1, q_2, f \rangle$, where q_1 is a state of $\mathcal{A}_1$, q_2 is a state of $\mathcal{A}_2$, and $f : X_2 \to X_1 \cup \{\top, \bot\}$ is a function that maps the variables that parameterize atomic propositions that hold in q_2 to the variables that parameterize atomic propositions that hold in q_1, and also contains information about previous and future matches. We elaborate, and explain the role of $\top$ and $\bot$, below.

We impose some restrictions on f that ensure that it matches the variables in a suitable way. We say that f is a *match for q_1 and q_2* if $L_1(q_1)$ is equal to the set obtained from $L_2(q_2)$ by replacing every x_2 in q_2 with $f(x_2)$. Note that in order for f to be a match for q_1 and q_2, for every variable $x_2 \in X_2$ that appear in q_2 it must hold that $f(x_2) \notin \{\top, \bot\}$. We require that if $\langle q_1, q_2, f \rangle \in H$, then f is a match for q_1 and q_2. That is, f must correctly match the variables locally.

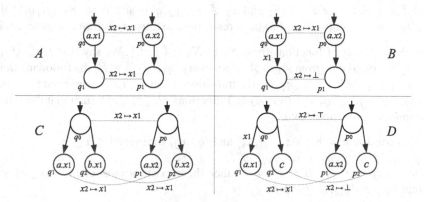

Fig. 2. Cases A, B, C and D

However, locally matching the variables is not enough. Consider Case A presented in Figure 2. The local match for q_0 and p_0 is $x_2 \mapsto x_1$. The variables x_1 and x_2 are not reset in the transitions $\langle q_0, q_1 \rangle$ and $\langle p_0, p_1 \rangle$. Then H remembers that the value of x_2 is bound to the value of x_1, by setting $x_2 \mapsto x_1$ also when matching q_1 with p_1.

Next, consider Case B. Again, the local match for q_0 and p_0 is $x_2 \mapsto x_1$. Since x_1 is reset in $\langle q_0, q_1 \rangle$ and x_2 is not reset in $\langle p_0, p_1 \rangle$, then x_2 cannot be matched with a variable in p_1, since it is still bound to the value x_1 was assigned. Then H remembers this when matching q_1 with p_1 by setting $x_2 \mapsto \bot$.

Now, consider Case C. Since x_2 is not reset along both $\langle p_0, p_1 \rangle$ and $\langle p_0, p_2 \rangle$, it must be mapped to the same variable both when matching q_1 with p_1, and when matching q_2 with p_2. The simulation sets $x_2 \mapsto x_1$ already when matching q_0 with p_0, even though x_1, x_2 do not appear in these states, and remembers this assignment when moving from p_0 to its two different subtrees. This forces both occurences of x_2 to be matched with the same (unreset) variable x_1.

Finally, consider Case D. The simulation must match x_2 with x_1 when matching q_1 with p_1. Unlike Case C, where both occurences of x_2 must be equally matched, here there is a single occurence of x_2, which can therefore be freely matched. x_1 is reset in $\langle q_0, q_1 \rangle$, and so x_2 cannot be mapped to x_1 when matching q_0 with p_0 (unlike Case C). On the other hand, x_2 is not reset in $\langle p_0, p_1 \rangle$, and so H must match x_2 with a non-$\bot$ value when matching q_0 with p_0. H solves this by allowing x_2 to remain "uncommitted" when matching q_0 with p_0, by setting $x_2 \mapsto \top$. To ensure that x_2 occurs only once, H sets $x_2 \mapsto \bot$ when matching q_2 with p_2, which means that x_2 cannot occur along the subtree from p_2, unless it is reset.

We now formalize these ideas. Let f be a match for q_1 and q_2, and let $\langle q_1, q_1' \rangle \in R_1$ and $\langle q_2, q_2' \rangle \in R_2$. We say that a function $f' : X_2 \to X_1 \cup \{\top, \bot\}$ is *consistent with f w.r.t $\langle q_1, q_1' \rangle$ and $\langle q_2, q_2' \rangle$* if f' is a match for q_1' and q_2', and

- If $f(x_2) \in X_1 \cup \{\bot\}$ and $x_2 \notin S_2(\langle q_2, q_2' \rangle)$ and $f(x_2) \notin S_1(\langle q_1, q_1' \rangle)$, then $f'(x_2) = f(x_2)$. In particular, since $\bot$ cannot be reset, if $f(x_2) = \bot$ and $x_2 \notin S_2(\langle q_2, q_2' \rangle)$, then also $f'(x_2) = \bot$. That is, if $x_2 \mapsto \bot$, then x_2 must be reset before it may be matched with a variable.
- If $f(x_2) = x_1$ for $x_1 \in X_1$ and $x_2 \notin S_2(\langle q_2, q_2' \rangle)$ and $x_1 \in S_1(\langle q_1, q_1' \rangle)$ then $f'(x_2) = \bot$. That is, if x_1 has been reset, then so must x_2 before it appears again.

Let F be the set of functions from X_2 to $X_1 \cup \{\top, \bot\}$. We say that $H \subseteq (Q_1 \times Q_2 \times F)$ is a *simulation from $\mathcal{A}_1$ to $\mathcal{A}_2$* if for every $\langle q_1, q_2, f \rangle \in H$, the following holds. Let $\langle q_1, q_1^1 \rangle, \langle q_1, q_1^2 \rangle, \ldots \langle q_1, q_1^k \rangle$ be the transitions from q_1. Then there exist transitions $\langle q_2, q_2^1 \rangle, \langle q_2, q_2^2 \rangle, \ldots \langle q_2, q_2^k \rangle$ from q_2 and functions $f^1, f^2, \ldots f^k$ such that the following *simulation conditions* hold.

1. f^i is consistent with f w.r.t $\langle q_1, q_1^i \rangle$ and $\langle q_2, q_2^i \rangle$ for every $1 \leq i \leq k$.
2. $\langle q_1^1, q_2^1, f^1 \rangle, \langle q_1^2, q_2^2, f^2 \rangle, \ldots \langle q_1^k, q_2^k, f^k \rangle \in H$.
3. For every $x_2 \in X_2$, if $f(x_2) = \top$, then there exists at most one $1 \leq i \leq k$ such that $x_2 \notin S_2(\langle q_2, q_2^i \rangle)$ and $f^i(x_2) \neq \bot$.

If there exists a function f^0 that is a match for q_1^0 and q_2^0 such that $\langle q_1^0, q_2^0, f^0 \rangle \in H$, then we say that $\mathcal{A}_2$ *simulates* $\mathcal{A}_1$, and denote $\mathcal{A}_1 \preceq \mathcal{A}_2$.

Example 1. Consider the abstract systems $\mathcal{A}_1$ and $\mathcal{A}_2$ presented in Figure 3. It holds that $\mathcal{A}_1 \preceq \mathcal{A}_2$ by a simulation relation $\{\langle q_0, p_0, x \mapsto x_1 \rangle, \langle q_1, p_1, x \mapsto x_2 \rangle, \langle q_2, p_0, x \mapsto x_2 \rangle, \langle q_3, p_1, x \mapsto x_1 \rangle\}$. Notice that $\mathcal{A}_2$ uses not only fewer states, but also fewer variables.

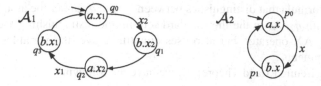

Fig. 3. The abstract systems $\mathcal{A}_1$ and $\mathcal{A}_2$

Computing a Simulation. We present an algorithm for computing a simulation relation from $\mathcal{A}_1$ to $\mathcal{A}_2$. The algorithm starts with the set of tuples that can be locally matched. Then, in every iteration, the tuples that violate one of the simulation conditions are omitted. The algorithm terminates when a fixed point is reached.

Let $H \subseteq Q_1 \times Q_2 \times F$ be a relation. Let $\langle q_1, q_2, f \rangle \in H$, and let $\langle q_1, q_1^1 \rangle, \langle q_1, q_1^2 \rangle, \ldots$ $\langle q_1, q_1^k \rangle$ be the transitions from q_1. We say that $\langle q_1, q_2, f \rangle$ is *good w.r.t.* H if there exist transitions $\langle q_2, q_2^1 \rangle, \langle q_2, q_2^2 \rangle, \ldots \langle q_2, q_2^k \rangle$ from q_2 and functions $f^1, f^2, \ldots f^k$ that meet the simulation conditions w.r.t. H.

We define a sequence of relations $H_0, H_1, \ldots$ as follows. First, H_0 is the set of all tuples $\langle q_1, q_2, f \rangle$ such that $q_1 \in Q_1$, $q_2 \in Q_2$, and f is a match for q_1, q_2. Then, for every $i > 0$, we define $H_i = \{\langle q_1, q_2, f \rangle | \langle q_1, q_2, f \rangle$ is good w.r.t. $H_{i-1}\}$. Notice that $H_0 \supseteq H_1 \supseteq H_2 \supseteq \ldots$, and since H_0 is finite, after finitely many i's a fixed point H^* is reached. Notice that H^* is a simulation from $\mathcal{A}_1$ to $\mathcal{A}_2$. In fact, H^* is a maximal simulation from $\mathcal{A}_1$ to $\mathcal{A}_2$. Indeed, every simulation G satisfies $G \subseteq H_0$, and it is easy to show by induction that for every i, the relation G is contained in H_i.

The complexity of this algorithm is exponential in the number of variables. This is not surprising, as there are pairs of abstract systems for which the size of a simulation relation is exponential in the number of variables (recall that $|F| = \mathcal{O}(|X_1|^{|X_2|})$).

5   A Logical Characterization of Simulation

In this section, we show that VACTL* logically characterizes the simulation pre-order for abstract systems. Formally, we prove the following.

Lemma 1. *If $\mathcal{A}_1 \preceq \mathcal{A}_2$, then for every $\varphi \in$ VACTL*, if $\mathcal{A}_2 \vDash \varphi$, then $\mathcal{A}_1 \vDash \varphi$.*

Lemma 1 follows from the following two properties. First, for an infinite domain $\mathcal{D}$, for every $\mathcal{D}$-concretization A_1 of $\mathcal{A}_1$ there exists a $\mathcal{D}$-concretization A_2 of $\mathcal{A}_2$, such that $A_1 \preceq A_2$ (by standard simulation). Second, standard simulation preserves VACTL*. Lemma 1 then follows from the semantics of VACTL* w.r.t. abstract systems.

Secondly, we prove that if $\mathcal{A}_1 \npreceq \mathcal{A}_2$, then there exists a *distinguishing* VACTL *formula for* $\mathcal{A}_1$ and $\mathcal{A}_2$: a formula that $\mathcal{A}_2$ satisfies, and $\mathcal{A}_1$ does not satisfy.

Theorem 1. *If $\mathcal{A}_1 \npreceq \mathcal{A}_2$, then there exists $\varphi \in$ VACTL, such that $\mathcal{A}_2 \vDash \varphi$ and $\mathcal{A}_1 \nvDash \varphi$.*

The proof of Theorem 1 is constructive: φ is induced by the algorithm for computing a simulation in Section 4. For every tuple $\langle q_1, q_2, f \rangle$ that is removed from H_i for some i, we construct a *semi-distinguishing formula*, which, roughly speaking, is an open VACTL formula that distinguishes between q_1 and q_2 under the assumption that f matches q_1 with q_2. As in the the standard setting, the distinguishing VACTL formula uses only the AX operator, but also uses quantifiers over the variables that refer to variable assignments.

Combining Lemma 1 and Theorem 1, we have the following.

Theorem 2. $\mathcal{A}_1 \preceq \mathcal{A}_2$ iff for every $\varphi \in$ VACTL*, it holds that if $\mathcal{A}_2 \models \varphi$, then $\mathcal{A}_1 \models \varphi$.

Thus, VACTL* offers a characterization of simulation of abstract systems, precisely as ACTL* offers a characterization of simulation of Kripke structures.

Example 2. Consider the abstract systems $\mathcal{A}_1$ and $\mathcal{A}_2$ presented in Figure 4. The relation H_0 is $\{\langle q_0, p_0, x_2 \mapsto x_1\rangle, \{\langle q_1, p_1, x_2 \mapsto x_1\rangle, \langle q_1, p_1, x_2 \mapsto \bot\rangle, \langle q_1, p_1, x_2 \mapsto \top\rangle, \langle q_2, p_2, x_2 \mapsto x_1\rangle\}$. When calculating H_1, the tuple $\langle q_1, p_1, x_2 \mapsto \bot\rangle$ is removed as it violates condition (2) of the simulation conditions. A semi-distinguishing formula AX$b.x_2$ for $\langle q_1, p_1, x_2 \mapsto \bot\rangle$ is calculated by the inconsistency of $x_2 \mapsto x_1$ in $\langle q_2, p_2, x_2 \mapsto x_1\rangle$ with $x_2 \mapsto \bot$. In H_2, the tuple $\langle q_0, p_0, x_2 \mapsto x_1\rangle$ violates condition (2), and a semi-distinguishing formula for it, which also distinguishes $\mathcal{A}_1$ from $\mathcal{A}_2$, is $\varphi = \exists x_2; a.x_2 \wedge$ AX$($AX$b.x_2)$. Indeed, $\mathcal{A}_2 \models \varphi$, whereas $\mathcal{A}_1 \nvDash \varphi$.

Next, consider the abstract systems $\mathcal{B}_1$ and $\mathcal{B}_2$. The states q_0 and p_0 appear in H_0 with the functions $x_2 \mapsto x_1, x_2 \mapsto x_1', x_2 \mapsto \bot, x_2 \mapsto \top$. The function $x_2 \mapsto x_1$ cannot match q_2 with p_2, and this contradiction ultimately creates the semi-distinguishing formula $\exists x_2;$ AX$(a.x_2 \vee$ AX$b.x_2)$ for $\langle q_0, p_0, x_2 \mapsto x_1\rangle$. Similarly, the functions $x_2 \mapsto x_1'$ and $x_2 \mapsto \bot$ contradict matching q_1 with p_1 and q_2 with p_2, respectively, ultimately creating the semi-distinguishing formulas $\exists x_2;$ AX$((\forall x_2 \neg a.x_2) \vee a.x_2)$ for $\langle q_0, q_2, x_2 \mapsto x_1'\rangle$, and $\exists x_2;$ AX$(a.x_2 \vee$ AX$b.x_2)$ for $\langle q_0, p_0, x_2 \mapsto \bot\rangle$.

Finally, the function $x_2 \mapsto \top$ succeeds in matching q_1 and p_1 by $x_2 \mapsto x_1$, and q_2 and p_2 by $x_2 \mapsto x_1'$ or $x_2 \mapsto \top$, but then condition (3) is violated. A semi-distinguishing formula for $\langle q_0, p_0, x_2 \mapsto \top\rangle$ is $\exists x_2;$ AX$(a.x_2 \vee$ AX$(b.x_2) \vee (\forall x_2 \neg a.x_2) \vee \exists x_2; a.x_2)$.

While $\mathcal{B}_2$ satisfies all these formulas, the abstract system $\mathcal{B}_1$ does not satisfy $\exists x_2;$ AX$(a.x_2 \vee$ AX$(b.x_2))$.

6   A Game-Theoretic Approach to Simulation

We present a game-theoretic approach to simulation of abstract systems. As usual, the game players are the prover $\mathcal{P}$, who wishes to prove that $\mathcal{A}_1 \preceq \mathcal{A}_2$, and the refuter $\mathcal{R}$, who wishes to prove that $\mathcal{A}_1 \npreceq \mathcal{A}_2$.

Recall that in the standard setting, in a game for systems A_1 and A_2, a game position is a pair of states $\langle q_1, q_2\rangle$ where q_1, q_2 are states of A_1 and A_2, respectively, and $\mathcal{R}$ is in location q_1 and $\mathcal{P}$ is in location q_2. A play continues along single paths in each system.

In abstract systems, the situation is a bit more complicated. First, in its every move, $\mathcal{P}$ must choose both a state q_2 and a function f that matches the variables of q_1 and q_2. Therefore, the game positions are tuples of the form $\langle q_1, q_2, f\rangle$. For $\mathcal{P}$ to prove the existence of simulation, f must be consistent w.r.t. the function it chose in its previous move, and with the transitions both players took from the previous position. Second, following a single path may not suffice for $\mathcal{R}$ to prove that there is no simulation. We demonstrate these points below.

Consider the systems $\mathcal{A}_1$ and $\mathcal{A}_2$ presented in Figure 4. It holds that $\mathcal{A}_1 \not\preceq \mathcal{A}_2$, since x_1 is reset and can be assigned different values in q_0 and q_2, whereas x_2 must be assigned the same value in p_0 and p_2. Consider a possible play between $\mathcal{P}$ and $\mathcal{R}$. The refuter $\mathcal{R}$ must start at q_0, and $\mathcal{P}$ must choose p_0 and $x_2 \mapsto x_1$ to match q_0 with p_0. Then, $\mathcal{R}$ continues to q_1, and $\mathcal{P}$ must move to p_1 and choose $x_2 \mapsto \bot$, since x_1 is reset along $\langle q_0, q_1 \rangle$, and x_2 is not reset along $\langle p_0, p_1 \rangle$. Finally, $\mathcal{R}$ moves to q_2, and $\mathcal{P}$ must move to p_2. To match q_2 with p_2, $\mathcal{P}$ must choose $x_2 \mapsto x_1$, but this is inconsistent with the function $x_2 \mapsto \bot$ that $\mathcal{P}$ chose in its previous move, and $\mathcal{R}$ wins.

Next, consider the systems $\mathcal{B}_1$ and $\mathcal{B}_2$. It holds that $\mathcal{B}_1 \not\preceq \mathcal{B}_2$, since x_1 and x_1' can be assigned different values in $\mathcal{B}_1$, whereas both occurences of x_2 in $\mathcal{B}_2$ must be equally assigned. In the first round, $\mathcal{P}$ chooses a function f_0 to match q_0 with p_0. Since the labeling of p_0, q_0 is empty, f_0 can match x_2 with either $x_1, x_1', \bot$ or $\top$. If $f_0(x_2) = x_1$ (or $f_0(x_2) = \bot$), then $\mathcal{R}$ can follow q_0, q_2, q_3, forcing $\mathcal{P}$ to follow p_0, p_2, p_3, and fail finding a match for q_3 and p_3 that is consistent with $x_2 \mapsto x_1$ (or with $x_2 \mapsto \bot$). Similarly, if $f_0(x_2) = x_1'$, then $\mathcal{R}$ follows q_0, q_1, and $\mathcal{P}$ must follow p_0, p_1, and fails to match q_1 and p_1.

However, if $f_0(x_2) = \top$, then if $\mathcal{R}$ follows either q_1 or q_2, q_3, then $\mathcal{P}$ can respond with suitable functions $x_2 \mapsto x_1$ to match p_1, or $x_2 \mapsto \top, x_2 \mapsto x_1'$ to match p_2, p_3 respectively. Thus, by following a single path, $\mathcal{P}$ may violate condition (3) of the simulation conditions, and (wrongly) win the game. We conclude that the game rules must enforce condition (3). In this case, this means that $\mathcal{P}$ may not assign x_2 non-$\bot$ values along both q_1 and q_2.

To enforce condition (3), we allow $\mathcal{R}$ to continue to both q_1 and q_2 in the same move. Then, to follow condition (3), $\mathcal{P}$ must choose $x_2 \mapsto \bot$ in either q_1 or q_2. Choosing $x_2 \mapsto \bot$ in q_1 causes $\mathcal{P}$ to fail in q_1. If $\mathcal{P}$ chooses $x_2 \mapsto \bot$ in q_2, then $\mathcal{R}$ can continue from q_2 to q_3, again causing $\mathcal{P}$ to get stuck.

The same holds also for the systems $\mathcal{C}_1$ and $\mathcal{C}_2$. Consider the first round in a play and the possible choices of $\mathcal{P}$ to match q_0 with p_0. The variable x_2 must be matched with x_1 when matching q_1 with p_1, and so $\mathcal{P}$ fails if it chooses $x_2 \mapsto \bot$. Also, since x_1 is reset in $\langle q_0, q_1 \rangle$, and x_2 is not reset in $\langle p_0, p_1 \rangle$, then $\mathcal{P}$ fails if it chooses $x_2 \mapsto x_1$. Finally, if $\mathcal{P}$ chooses $x_2 \mapsto \top$, then $\mathcal{R}$ can split as in the case of $\mathcal{B}_1$ and $\mathcal{B}_2$, and cause $\mathcal{P}$ to get stuck in either q_1 or q_3.

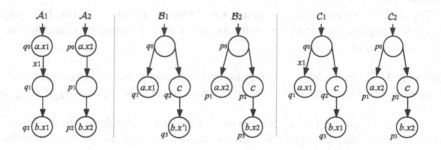

Fig. 4. The abstract systems $\mathcal{A}_1$ and $\mathcal{A}_2$, and $\mathcal{B}_1$ and $\mathcal{B}_2$, and $\mathcal{C}_1$ and $\mathcal{C}_2$

Thus, as opposed to the classical setting, when there is no simulation, the inability to locally match states is not enough to refute the existence of a simulation. Also, a single path may not suffice to properly refute, and two paths are needed, as in the case of the systems $\mathcal{B}_1$ and $\mathcal{B}_2$, and $\mathcal{C}_1$ and $\mathcal{C}_2$. Note that two paths suffice, since x_2 may only be assigned a non-$\perp$ value along one path, causing $\mathcal{P}$ to get stuck in the other, in case that x_2 appears in both paths without being reset.

Accordingly, we define the game such that $\mathcal{R}$ continues along a single path (mode (a) in the game), but may, at any point, choose two states on two different paths splitting from its current location (mode (b) in the game). $\mathcal{P}$ then chooses matching states and functions for both states. Then, $\mathcal{R}$ chooses along which of the two paths the play continues from, and switches back to mode (a). $\mathcal{P}$ then responds accordingly.

We formally define the game. A play begins as follows. $\mathcal{R}$ starts from q_1^0, and $\mathcal{P}$ starts from q_2^0 and chooses some function f_0 such that f_0 is a match for q_1^0 and q_2^0. Then, the game continues in mode (a) according to the following rules.

Let the current position be $\langle q_1, q_2, f \rangle$. If the game is in mode (a),

1. $\mathcal{R}$ chooses a transition $\langle q_1, q_1' \rangle \in R_1$ and moves to q_1', or switches to mode (b),
2. If $\mathcal{R}$ hasn't switched to mode (b), then $\mathcal{P}$ chooses a transition $\langle q_2, q_2' \rangle \in R_2$, and a function f' that is consistent with f w.r.t. $\langle q_1, q_1' \rangle$ and $\langle q_2, q_2' \rangle$, and moves to q_2'.

If the game is in mode (b),

1. $\mathcal{R}$ chooses two different transitions $\langle q_1, q_1' \rangle, \langle q_1, q_1'' \rangle \in R_1$.
2. $\mathcal{P}$ chooses a transition $\langle q_2, q_2' \rangle$ and a function f' such that f' is consistent with f w.r.t. $\langle q_1, q_1' \rangle$ and $\langle q_2, q_2' \rangle$, and dually a transition $\langle q_2, q_2'' \rangle$ and a function f'' for $\langle q_1, q_1'' \rangle$. Further, for every $x_2 \in X_2$ such that $f(x_2) = \top$, either $f'(x_2) = \perp$ or $f''(x_2) = \perp$.
3. $\mathcal{R}$ chooses between the game positions $\langle q_1', q_2', f' \rangle$ and $\langle q_1'', q_2'', f'' \rangle$, and switches to mode (a) from the chosen position.

Notice that a round does not exactly alternate between $\mathcal{R}$ and $\mathcal{P}$; from mode (a), $\mathcal{R}$ can switch to mode (b) and continue to choose two transitions as described. Also, after $\mathcal{R}$ chooses a single position at the last step of mode (b), it continues to choose a transition in the first step in mode (a), as described.

If at some point $\mathcal{P}$ cannot continue according to the game rules, then $\mathcal{R}$ wins. Otherwise, the play continues forever and $\mathcal{P}$ wins.

The simulation game indeed captures simulation of abstract systems: both players have a winning strategy, according to the existence or lack thereof of a suitable simulation from $\mathcal{A}_1$ to $\mathcal{A}_2$.

Theorem 3. $\mathcal{P}$ has a winning strategy in the simulation game for $\mathcal{A}_1$ and $\mathcal{A}_2$ iff $\mathcal{A}_1 \preceq \mathcal{A}_2$, and $\mathcal{R}$ has a winning strategy in the simulation game for $\mathcal{A}_1$ and $\mathcal{A}_2$ iff $\mathcal{A}_1 \npreceq \mathcal{A}_2$.

The winning strategy of $\mathcal{P}$ corresponds to a suitable simulation from $\mathcal{A}_1$ to $\mathcal{A}_2$, whereas the winning strategy of $\mathcal{R}$ corresponds to a distinguishing VACTL formula for $\mathcal{A}_1$ and $\mathcal{A}_2$. Despite the more complicated nature of the game, the winning strategies of both players, just like in the standard setting, are memoryless.

7 Discussion and Future Work

We have shown that the properties of standard simulation can be lifted to the setting of abstract systems. In this section we describe further theoretical challenges of abstract systems and simulation and their practical applications.

Consider a system S that describes the behavior of n processes. Typically, each process is associated with a set of atomic propositions, parameterized with its id. For example, it is common to see atomic propositions like $try_1, \ldots, try_n$ and $grant_1, \ldots, grant_n$. Consider now the system S' obtained by uniting all "underlying" atomic propositions, try and $grant$ in our example, and parameterizing them by a variable that ranges over the domain of processes ids. As another example, consider a system S in which messages from a list $L = \{l_1, \ldots, l_n\}$ of possible messages can be sent, and atomic propositions are parameterized by messages from L, say atomic propositions are $send_{l_1}, \ldots, send_{l_n}$ and $receive_{l_1}, \ldots, receive_{l_n}$. Again, we can obtain a system S' that abstracts the content of the messages and uses atomic propositions $send$ and $receive$, parameterized by variables that range over L. Note that the behavior of S with respect to the different values of processes ids or messages may be different. thus S' over-approximates S. Clearly, S' is also simpler than S.

It is straightforward to extend the definition of simulation to cases in which only the simulating system is abstract, and to do it in such a way that S' simulates S. Essentially, as noted above, S' includes all the behaviors with respect to all values of processes ids or messages, and also abstracts their number. We can thus use S' not only for the verification of S, but also, in case we abstract identical processes, for checking whether the specification is sensitive to their number, and for generalizing the reasoning to an arbitrary number of processes. We plan to formalize this method, namely define the simulation relation, a refinement procedure, and the connection to other methods of verification of parameterized systems.

The simulation pre-order defined here is the branching-time counterpart of trace containment, which is undecidable for abstract systems. In standard systems, the computational efficiency of the branching-time approach is carried over in the model-checking problem for CTL. In [12,13] we studied the model-checking problem for VLTL and abstract systems and pointed to useful fragments for which the complexity of the problem is in PSPACE – as is LTL model checking. We plan to study the model-checking problem for VCTL and abstract systems, and check whether the advantage of the branching approach is carried over also to this setting.

References

1. Paige, R., Bloom, B.: Transformational design and implementation of a new efficient solution to the ready simulation problem. Science of Computer Programming 24, 189–220 (1996)
2. Bensalem, S., Bouajjani, A., Loiseaux, C., Sifakis, J.: Property preserving simulations. In: Probst, D.K., von Bochmann, G. (eds.) CAV 1992. LNCS, vol. 663, pp. 260–273. Springer, Heidelberg (1993)
3. Bojańczyk, M., Muscholl, A., Schwentick, T., Segoufin, L.: Two-variable logic on data trees and XML reasoning. J. ACM 56(3), 1–48 (2009)

4. Bojanczyk, M., Muscholl, A., Schwentick, T., Segoufin, L., David, C.: Two-variable logic on words with data. In: LICS 2006, pp. 7–16 (2006)
5. Browne, M.C., Clarke, E.M., Grumberg, O.: Characterizing finite Kripke structures in propositional temporal logic. Theoretical Computer Science 59, 115–131 (1988)
6. Clarke, E.M., Grumberg, O., Jha, S., Lu, Y., Veith, H.: Counterexample-guided abstraction refinement. In: Emerson, E.A., Sistla, A.P. (eds.) CAV 2000. LNCS, vol. 1855, pp. 154–169. Springer, Heidelberg (2000)
7. Cleaveland, R., Parrow, J., Steffen, B.: The concurrency workbench: A semantics-based tool for the verification of concurrent systems. ACM TOPLAS 15, 36–72 (1993)
8. Damm, W., Pnueli, A.: Verifying out-of-order executions. In: Proc. 9th Conf. on Correct Hardware Design and Verification Methods, pp. 23–47. Chapman & Hall (1997)
9. Demri, S., D'Souza, D.: An automata-theoretic approach to constraint LTL. In: Agrawal, M., Seth, A.K. (eds.) FSTTCS 2002. LNCS, vol. 2556, pp. 121–132. Springer, Heidelberg (2002)
10. German, S., Prasad Sistla, A.: Reasoning about systems with many processes. Journal of the ACM 39, 675–735 (1992)
11. Grumberg, O., Kupferman, O., Sheinvald, S.: Variable automata over infinite alphabets. In: Dediu, A.-H., Fernau, H., Martín-Vide, C. (eds.) LATA 2010. LNCS, vol. 6031, pp. 561–572. Springer, Heidelberg (2010)
12. Grumberg, O., Kupferman, O., Sheinvald, S.: Model checking systems and specifications with parameterized atomic propositions. In: Chakraborty, S., Mukund, M. (eds.) ATVA 2012. LNCS, vol. 7561, pp. 122–136. Springer, Heidelberg (2012)
13. Grumberg, O., Kupferman, O., Sheinvald, S.: An automata-theoretic approach to reasoning about parameterized systems and specifications. In: Van Hung, D., Ogawa, M. (eds.) ATVA 2013. LNCS, vol. 8172, pp. 397–411. Springer, Heidelberg (2013)
14. Grumberg, O., Long, D.E.: Model checking and modular verification. In: Groote, J.F., Baeten, J.C.M. (eds.) CONCUR 1991. LNCS, vol. 527, pp. 250–265. Springer, Heidelberg (1991)
15. Grumberg, O., Long, D.E.: Model checking and modular verification. ACM Transactions on Programming Languages and Systems 16(3), 843–871 (1994)
16. Hallé, S., Villemaire, R., Cherkaoui, O.: Ctl model checking for labelled tree queries. In: TIME, pp. 27–35 (2006)
17. Henzinger, T.A., Kupferman, O., Rajamani, S.: Fair simulation. Information and Computation 173(1), 64–81 (2002)
18. Kaminski, M., Zeitlin, D.: Extending finite-memory automata with non-deterministic reassignment. In: Csuhaj-Varjú, Ézik, Z.E. (eds.) AFL, pp. 195–207 (2008)
19. Kesten, Y., Piterman, N., Pnueli, A.: Bridging the gap between fair simulation and trace inclusion. In: Hunt Jr., W.A., Somenzi, F. (eds.) CAV 2003. LNCS, vol. 2725, pp. 381–393. Springer, Heidelberg (2003)
20. Lamport, L.: Specifying concurrent program modules. ACM Transactions on Programming Languages and Systems 5, 190–222 (1983)
21. Lazić, R.S.: Safely freezing LTL. In: Arun-Kumar, S., Garg, N. (eds.) FSTTCS 2006. LNCS, vol. 4337, pp. 381–392. Springer, Heidelberg (2006)
22. Lynch, N.A., Tuttle, M.R.: Hierarchical correctness proofs for distributed algorithms. In: Proc. 6th ACM Symp. on Principles of Distributed Computing, pp. 137–151 (1987)
23. Lynch, N.A.: Distributed Algorithms. Morgan Kaufmann (1996)
24. Milner, R.: An algebraic definition of simulation between programs. In: Proc. 2nd Int. Joint Conf. on Artificial Intelligence, pp. 481–489. British Computer Society (1971)
25. Neven, F., Schwentick, T., Vianu, V.: Towards regular languages over infinite alphabets. In: Sgall, J., Pultr, A., Kolman, P. (eds.) MFCS 2001. LNCS, vol. 2136, pp. 560–572. Springer, Heidelberg (2001)

26. Pnueli, A.: Applications of temporal logic to the specification and verification of reactive systems: A survey of current trends. In: Rozenberg, G., de Bakker, J.W., de Roever, W.-P. (eds.) Current Trends in Concurrency. LNCS, vol. 224, pp. 510–584. Springer, Heidelberg (1986)
27. Graf, S., Saidi, H.: Construction of abstract state graphs with PVS. In: Grumberg, O. (ed.) CAV 1997. LNCS, vol. 1254, pp. 72–83. Springer, Heidelberg (1997)
28. Shemesh, Y., Francez, N.: Finite-state unification automata and relational languages. Information and Computation 114, 192–213 (1994)
29. Stockmeyer, L.J., Meyer, A.R.: Word problems requiring exponential time. In: Proc. 5th ACM Symp. on Theory of Computing, pp. 1–9 (1973)
30. Tan, T.: Pebble Automata for Data Languages: Separation, Decidability, and Undecidability. PhD thesis, Technion - Computer Science Department (2009)

Nested Reachability Approximation for Discrete-Time Markov Chains with Univariate Parameters*

Guoxin Su and David S. Rosenblum

Department of Computer Science, School of Computing
National University of Singapore
{sugx,david}@comp.nus.edu.sg

Abstract. As models of real-world stochastic systems usually contain inaccurate information, probabilistic model checking for models with open or undetermined parameters has recently aroused research attention. In this paper, we study a kind of parametric variant of Discrete-time Markov Chains with uncertain transition probabilities, namely *Parametric Markov Chains* (PMCs), and probabilistic reachability properties with nested PCTL probabilistic operators. Such properties for a PMC with a univariate parameter define univariate real functions, called *reachability functions*, that map the parameter to reachability probabilities. An interesting application of these functions is sensitivity and robustness analysis of probabilistic model checking. However, a pitfall of computing the closed-form expression of a reachability function is the possible dynamism of its constraint set and target set. We pursue interval approximations for reachability functions with high accuracy. In particular, for reachability functions involving only single-nested probabilistic operators, we provide an efficient algorithm to compute their approximations. We demonstrate the applicability of our approach with a case study on a NAND multiplexing unit.

1 Introduction

Probabilistic model checking, as a formal verification technology for stochastic systems, has matured over the past decade and has many successful applications, such as automatic analysis of communication protocols. In probabilistic model checking, discrete-time stochastic systems are formally represented by models such as Discrete-time Markov Chains (DTMCs) and Markov Decision Processes (MDPs). Because models of real-world stochastic systems usually contain inaccurate information, probabilistic model checking for discrete-time models with open or undetermined parameters has aroused much attention in the research community recently. Such parameters may be uncertain transition probabilities or initial distributions that are obtained via statistical experiments or are dependent on the dynamic environment, leading to *perturbations* of the model. In the state-of-the-art, one way to capture such systems is by setting the lower and upper bounds of the transition matrices, resulting in two groups of models: Uncertain Markov Chains [1], each of which is interpreted as a set of DTMCs, or Interval Markov Chains [2,3,4], each of which is variant of an MDP with an infinite set

---

* This work is partly supported by Grant R-252-000-458-133 from Singapore Ministry of Education Academic Research Fund.

F. Cassez and J.-F. Raskin (Eds.): ATVA 2014, LNCS 8837, pp. 364–379, 2014.

of actions. In this paper, we consider the UMC models, which can alternatively be formulated in the form of Parametric Markov Chains (PMCs) [5,6,7] with undetermined transition probabilities represented by variables.

Probabilistic Computation Tree Logic (PCTL) [8] is one of the most frequently used property languages for probabilistic model checking, and one essential PCTL syntactic construct is the nesting of probabilistic operators. Properties expressed by PCTL formulas with nested probabilistic operators are not able to be represented by common finite automata. However, model checking of a PMC against PCTL formulas with nested probabilistic operators can be very difficult in terms of computational cost. In particular, reachability model checking for UMCs is P-complete, while PCTL model checking for UMCs is NP-hard and Square-Root-Sum hard [9].

One important problem for probabilistic model checking is the sensitivity and robustness of the verification results. The informal idea is to study the effect of parameter perturbations on automata-based probabilistic model checking, and the outcome of the study is a group of *close-formed* perturbation bounds [10,11]. In this paper, we explore this problem for PMCs with *univariate* parameters and for reachability properties with *nested*, especially *single-nested*, PCTL probabilistic operators. Univariate PMCs account for a considerable proportion of discrete stochastic systems (such as those in the PRISM benchmark suite [12]), because the update of the system state contains at most two probabilistic choices in the high-level specification of those systems.

In the following, we further explain the motivation of our approach. For a DTMC $\mathcal{M}$ with state space S and predicate statements A, B over states, a (constrained) reachability model checking problem is the query of the probability of reaching states satisfying B via states satisfying A from a specific state $s \in S$. For a PMC $\mathcal{M}\langle x \rangle$ with state space S and a perturbed variable x, which is associated to some transition probabilities and ranges over a fixed small interval I such that $0 \in I$, the aforementioned reachability problem gives rise to a *reachability function* $Pr_{A,B} : I \times S \to [0,1]$. In words, given a value for the variable of the PMC and a starting state, a reachability function specifies a reachability probability. One application of $Pr_{A,B}$ is sensitivity analysis of the verification result against the perturbation of the model. A different, yet related application is the computation of the smallest or largest x such that $Pr_{A,B}(x, s)$ is not smaller or larger than some given probability. In theory, $Pr_{A,B}(x, s)$ for $\mathcal{M}\langle x \rangle$ is equivalent to the accepting regular expression of a finite automaton; therefore, the closed-form expression of $Pr_{A,B}(x, s)$ can be generated by a state-elimination algorithm [5]. Hence, the worst-case time-complexity of computing $Pr_{A,B}(x, s)$ is $\mathcal{O}(|S|^3)$, the same as that of the state-elimination algorithm [6].

Nested reachability functions are expressed by $Pr_{X,Y} : I \times S \to [0,1]$ where X and Y are PCTL formulas. Because of the perturbed variable x of $\mathcal{M}\langle x \rangle$, X and Y may be dynamic sets, namely mappings from I onto 2^S. Therefore, given $s \in S$, $Pr_{X,Y}(\cdot, s)$ may be a discontinuous function with possible "jumping" points caused by states moving into or off the satisfaction sets for X and Y. Those points are determined by rational equations of the form $Pr_{X,Y}(x, s') = p$ with $s' \in S$. To compute $Pr_{X,Y}$ with the automata-based and state-elimination method, we need to compute all involved non-nested reachability functions and then solve the corresponding rational equations to determine the "jumping" points. However, as the state space of the PMC gets larger, such a direct computation may become costly (for both generating the non-nested reachability functions and solving the rational equations). In the worst case, there can be as many as $|S|$ rational equations, each of which has up to $|S|$ roots. Hence, it can be deduced that the time complexity of computing $Pr_{X,Y}$ by that method is $\mathcal{O}(|S|^5)$.

In this paper, instead of directly computing reachability functions for PMCs with univariate parameters, we present an approximation alternative. Based on the fact that a non-nested reachability function $Pr_{A,B}(\cdot, s)$ (where $s \in S$) is a continuous rational function, we construct a pair of bounding polynomials of a relatively low order, called *interval approximations*, that rigorously bound and sufficiently approximate $Pr_{A,B}$. By repeating such constructions, we obtain interval approximations for a possibly discontinuous nested reachability function $Pr_{X,Y}$. In particular, for the case that $Pr_{X,Y}$ is *single-nested*, namely, neither the syntax of X nor Y contains nested PCTL probabilistic operators, we provide an efficient procedure to compute its interval approximations.

The pursuit of closed-from perturbation bounds in the setting of probabilistic model checking is initiated by the authors [10,11], but this paper contains two key aspects of novel contributions: First, the discontinuity arising from reachability functions with nested PCTL probabilistic operators is not addressed by the previous work, which explores non-nested reachability and ω-regular properties only. Second, in contrast to the asymptotic method developed in the previous work, the approximation characterization pursued in this paper rigorously bounds a reachability function and enjoys several elegant mathematical properties, such as monotonicity and convergency. To demonstrate the applicability of our approach, we conduct a case study based on a benchmark probabilistic system, namely a NAND multiplexing unit.

Note that we focus on the consequence of nested probabilistic operators on the cost of computing reachability functions, which is separated from the complexity of PCTL model checking. The P-hardness complexity of PCTL model checking for DTMCs (without parameters) is due to the embedding of propositional logic in the syntax of PCTL [9]. Because of involving solving polynomial equations, we foresee a pitfall to apply our technique to multi-variate PMCs.

The remainder of the paper is organized as follows. Section 2 defines the model of PMCs, a sublogic of PCTL and the definitions of non-nested and nested reachability functions. Section 3 provides our interval approximation characterization for non-nested and nested reachability functions. Section 4 develops a procedure for computing the interval approximations for single-nested reachability functions. Section 5 reports a case study on a NAND multiplexing unit. Section 6 discusses the related work. Section 7 concludes the paper and outlines directions for the future work.

2   Model and Reachability Function

In this section, we present the model of PMCs, a sublogic of PCTL that captures reachability formulas, and non-nested and nested reachability functions.

2.1   Parametric Markov Chain

A *Discrete-time Markov Chain* (DTMC) is a tuple $\mathcal{M} = (\iota, \mathbf{T})$ where ι is an initial probability distribution and $\mathbf{T}$ is a $k \times k$ *transition matrix* with $k = |\iota|$ (the length of ι)

that satisfies the following two properties: (i) $0 \leq \mathbf{T}[i, j] \leq 1$ for all $1 \leq i, j \leq k$ and (ii) $\sum_{j=1}^{k} \mathbf{T}[i, j] = 1$ for all $1 \leq i \leq k$.

A *parametric transition matrix* $\mathbf{T}\langle x \rangle$, based on the transition matrix $\mathbf{T}$ and with variable x, satisfies the following three properties: For each $1 \leq i, j \leq k$,

- if $\mathbf{T}[i, j] = 0$ then $\mathbf{T}\langle x \rangle[i, j] = 0$,
- $\mathbf{T}\langle x \rangle[i, j]$ is of the form $ax + \mathbf{T}[i, j]$ for some rational number $a \in \{-1, 1\}$, and
- $\sum_{j=1}^{k} \mathbf{T}\langle x \rangle[i, j] = 1$.

In the second clause above, if $a = +1$ (resp., $a = -1$), we say that x has a *positive* (resp., *negative*) occurrence at the (i, j)-entry of $\mathbf{T}\langle x \rangle$. Let $\mathbf{T}\langle c \rangle$ denote the matrix obtained by placing c into the positions of x in $\mathbf{T}\langle x \rangle$. Clearly, $\mathbf{T}\langle 0 \rangle$ and $\mathbf{T}$ are identical.

A *Parametric Markov Chain* (PMC) is a tuple $\mathcal{M}\langle x \rangle = (\iota, \mathbf{T}\langle x \rangle, I)$ where ι is an initial probability distribution, $\mathbf{T}\langle x \rangle$ is a parametric transition matrix, and I, called a *perturbation range*, is an (open or closed) interval such that $0 \in I$ and $|I| \ll 1$. As mentioned in the Introduction, throughout the paper, we restrict each PMC to have only one perturbed variable. The small interval I reflects the intuition of perturbations and allows us to assume the following two propositions: For each $c \in I$,

- $\mathbf{T}\langle c \rangle$ is a transition matrix, and
- if $\mathbf{T}\langle 0 \rangle[i, j] > 0$ then $\mathbf{T}\langle c \rangle[i, j] > 0$ for all $1 \leq i, j \leq k$.

The second condition above ensures that all matrices in the set $\{\mathbf{T}\langle c \rangle \mid c \in I\}$ share the same underlying graph. We let $\mathcal{M}\langle c \rangle$ for $c \in I$ be the DTMC $(\iota, \mathbf{T}\langle c \rangle)$, and identify $\mathcal{M}\langle 0 \rangle$ as $\mathcal{M}$. In our formulation of $\mathcal{M}$ and $\mathcal{M}\langle x \rangle$, the names of states are implicit. But normally we refer to the state space S of $\mathcal{M}$ and $\mathcal{M}\langle x \rangle$ as $\{1, \ldots, k\}$. We use s, s' to denote states in S. We use $rch(s)$ to denote a subset of S such that $s' \in rch(s)$ if and only if there is a path from s and passing by s' in the underlying graph of $\mathcal{M}$.

2.2 PCTL Sublogic

We assume an infinite set $\{A_i \mid i \in \mathbb{N}\}$ of atomic formulas. The syntax of $\mathcal{L}$, a sublogic of PCTL [8], is generated by the following syntactic rules:

$$X, Y ::= \mathbb{P}_{\sim p}[X \, \mathcal{U} Y] \mid \neg X \mid X \wedge Y \mid A \qquad \text{(formulas)}$$
$$A ::= \top \mid A_i \qquad \text{(basic formulas)}$$

where $\sim \in \{>, \geq, <, \leq\}$, $p \in [0, 1]$, $\mathbb{P}$ the PCTL probabilistic operator, $\mathcal{U}$ the "until" connective, $\neg$ the negation operator, and $\wedge$ the conjunction connective. The "next" operator and the "bounded until" connective in PCTL are excluded from $\mathcal{L}$. Throughout the paper, X, Y denote general formulas defined by the above syntactic rules, while A, B specifically denote basic formulas. Let $\mathcal{F}X$ denote $\top \, \mathcal{U} X$. Formal interpretation of formulas of $\mathcal{L}$ is provided later, but briefly, A, B are interpreted as "static" subsets of S, while X, Y are dynamic sets in 2^S that are dependent on x, the variable of $\mathcal{M}\langle x \rangle$.

For convenience, we also use $\mathcal{L}$ to denote the set of formulas generated by the syntactic rules of $\mathcal{L}$. The *depth* of $X \in \mathcal{L}$, denoted as $dep(X)$, is defined recursively as follows: (i) $dep(A) = 0$, (ii) $dep(\neg X) = dep(X)$, (iii) $dep(X \wedge Y) = dep(X, Y)$ and $dep(\mathbb{P}_{\sim p}[X \, \mathcal{U} Y]) = dep(X, Y) + 1$, where $dep(X, Y)$ denotes $\max\{dep(X), dep(Y)\}$. If X and Y are syntactically identical, we write $X \equiv Y$. We stress that, in spite of being a fragment of PCTL, the syntax of $\mathcal{L}$ allows the nesting of PCTL probabilistic operators.

2.3 Reachability Function

Given two subsets $S_?, S_!$ of S (the state space of $\mathcal{M}\langle x \rangle$), for convenience we define a fixed set

$$S_? \lceil S_! = \{s \in S_? \mid rch(s) \cap S_! \neq \varnothing\}$$

We define a parametric matrix $\mathbf{A}\langle x \rangle$ that is the restriction of $\mathbf{T}\langle x \rangle$ to $S_? \lceil S_!$, and a parametric column-vector $\mathbf{b}\langle x \rangle$ such that $\mathbf{b}\langle x \rangle[s] = \sum_{s' \in S_!} \mathbf{T}\langle x \rangle[s, s']$ for each $s \in S_? \lceil S_!$. The set $S_? \lceil S_!$ is called the *constraint* set of $\mathbf{A}\langle x \rangle$ and $\mathbf{b}\langle x \rangle$, and $S_!$ is called the *target* set of them.[1] Without loss of generality, we let $S_? \backslash S_!$ be a set of consecutive numbers from 1 to k', namely $S_? \lceil S_! = \{1, \ldots, k'\}$, for some $k' \leq k = |S|$. Before interpreting formulas of $\mathcal{L}$ and defining reachability functions, we set up an auxiliary definition. Let $f : 2^S \times 2^S \times S \times I \to [0, 1]$ be the function such that

$$f(S_?, S_!, s, x) = \left(\sum_{i=0}^{\infty} \mathbf{A}\langle x \rangle^i \cdot \mathbf{b}\langle x \rangle \right)[s]$$

The legitimacy of f is ensured by the fact that $\mathbf{I} - \mathbf{A}\langle x \rangle$ is invertible for each $x \in I$ and that the series $\sum_{i=0}^{\infty} \mathbf{A}\langle x \rangle^i = (\mathbf{I} - \mathbf{A}\langle x \rangle)^{-1}$ for any $x \in I$.

As stated, each basic formula $A \in \mathcal{L}$ is interpreted as a subset of S, denoted by sat_A and called a *non-nested satisfaction set*. In particular, $sat_\top = S$. Interpretation for the boolean operator and connective is standard: $sat_{\neg X} = S \backslash sat_X$ and $sat_{X \wedge Y} = sat_X \cap sat_Y$. It remains to deal with $\mathbb{P}_{\sim p}[X \mathcal{U} Y]$. Given basic formulas A and B, a *non-nested reachability function* $Pr_{A,B} : I \times S \to [0, 1]$ is a function such that

$$Pr_{A,B}(x, s) = \begin{cases} f(sat_A, sat_B, s, x) & \text{if } s \in sat_A \lceil sat_B \\ 1 & \text{if } s \in sat_B \\ 0 & \text{otherwise} \end{cases}$$

Intuitively, $Pr_{A,B}(x, s)$ captures the probability of reaching states in sat_B via states in sat_A from state s in the PMC $\mathcal{M}\langle x \rangle$ for any $x \in I$. A mathematical explanation of non-nested reachability functions based on the measurement theory for DTMCs can be found in standard texts on probabilistic model checking, such as Baier and Katoen [13]. The following theorem expresses an important property for non-nested reachability functions.

Theorem 1 *([14]). For each $s \in S$ and $A, B \in \mathcal{L}$, $Pr_{A,B}(\cdot, s)$ is a continuous rational function on I.*

A *reachability function* $Pr_{X,Y}$ and a *satisfaction set* sat_X for $X, Y \in \mathcal{L}$ are defined recursively as follows:

- $Pr_{X,Y} : I \times S \to [0, 1]$ such that

$$Pr_{X,Y}(x, s) = \begin{cases} f(sat_X(x), sat_Y(x), s, x) & \text{if } s \in sat_X(x) \lceil sat_Y(x) \\ 1 & \text{if } s \in sat_Y(x) \\ 0 & \text{otherwise} \end{cases}$$

---

[1] To avoid notation abuse, we do not explicitly indicate the association of $S_? \lceil S_!$ and $S_!$ to $\mathbf{A}\langle x \rangle$ and $\mathbf{b}\langle x \rangle$, as this association is clear from the context.

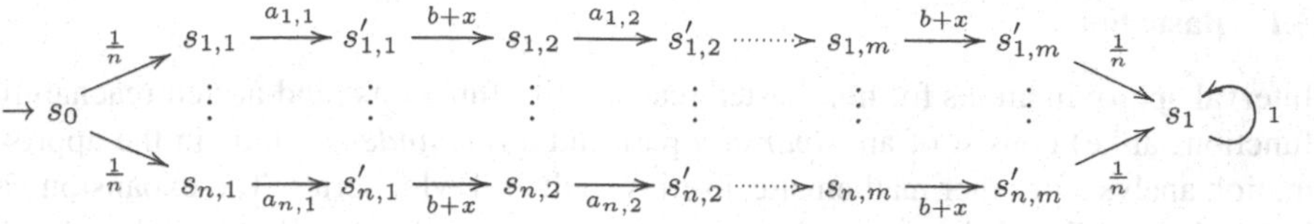

Fig. 1. Graphical model of $\mathcal{M}_0\langle x \rangle$

- $sat_{\mathbb{P}_{\sim p}[X\,\mathcal{U}Y]} : I \to 2^S$ with $\sim \in \{\geq, >, \leq, <\}$ such that

$$sat_{\mathbb{P}_{\sim p}[X\,\mathcal{U}Y]}(x) = \{s \in S \mid Pr_{X,Y}(x,s) \sim p\}, \quad x \in I$$

$Pr_{X,Y}$ is *nested* if $dep(X,Y) \geq 1$ and is *single-nested* if $dep(X,Y) = 1$. Although X with $dep(X) = 1$ contains only one occurrence of the $\mathbb{P}$-operator, for convenience, we also call a satisfaction set sat_X *nested* if $dep(X) \geq 1$ and *single-nested* if $dep(X) = 1$. As sat_A is a constant set, $sat_A(x) = sat_A$ for any $x \in I$. Given $s \in S$, unlike the non-nested reachability function $Pr_{A,B}(\cdot, s)$, a general-form reachability function $Pr_{X,Y}(\cdot, s)$ may be discontinuous because of the possible dynamism of sat_X and sat_Y.

Theorem 2. *For each* $s \in S$ *and* $X, Y \in \mathcal{L}$, *there is a (finite) partition* $\mathfrak{P}$ *on* I *such that* $Pr_{X,Y}(\cdot, s)$ *is a continuous rational function on each* $I' \in \mathfrak{P}(I)$.

Let Pr_X abbreviate $Pr_{\top,X}$. For illustrative purposes, the transition matrix of a PMC $\mathcal{M}_0\langle x \rangle$ is depicted in Figure 1. State s_0 of $\mathcal{M}_0\langle x \rangle$ is the initial state. All $a_{i,j}$'s and b are smaller than 1. (Hence, some of the states have transitions with positive probability to an implicit "failure" state.) Let A_1 and A_2 be formulas such that $sat_{A_1} = \{s_1\}$ and $sat_{A_2} = \{s_{1,1}, \ldots s_{n,1}\}$. It is easy to see that $Pr_{A_1}(\cdot, s_0)$ is a non-nested reachability function, while $Pr_{X_1}(\cdot, s_0)$ with $X_1 \equiv \mathbb{P}_{>p}[\mathcal{F}A_1] \wedge A_2$ is a single-nested reachability function.

The reachability function can be used for the prediction of maximally permitted perturbation distance of the perturbed variable in the PMC. For example, we let $X_2 \equiv \mathbb{P}_{>p'}[\mathcal{F}X_1]$ and suppose $s_0 \in sat_{X_2}(0)$ (namely, X_2 is satisfied by $\mathcal{M}_0\langle x \rangle$ at s_0 when $x = 0$); we want to know the smallest value c such that $s_0 \notin sat_{X_2}(c)$. This problem can be solved by optimizing the function $Pr_{X_2}(\cdot, s_0)$. However, a direct computation of $Pr_{X_2}(\cdot, s_0)$ involves solving the high-order polynomial $Pr_{X_1}(x, s_{i,1}) = p$ for each $1 \leq i \leq n$, which, as mentioned in the Introduction, may be costly. Hence, we are motivated to pursue interval approximations for reachability functions.

3 Interval Approximation

In this section, we present interval approximations for reachability functions and several key mathematical properties. Similar to reachability functions, the treatment of interval approximations is separated into basic and general forms.

3.1   Basic Form

Interval approximations for non-nested reachability functions (and nested reachability functions alike) consist of an *expansion* part and a *remainder* part, as in the approximation analysis of other mathematical series such as Taylor series. The expansion part is a polynomial and the remainder part is an estimated bound. We note that the decomposition of interval approximations into an expansion part and a remainder part (or something similar) is not unique. Our decomposition enjoys various mathematical properties presented below and facilitates the computation in practice (see Section 5).

Let $\mathbf{A} = \mathbf{A}\langle 0\rangle$, $\mathbf{A}^* = \sum_{i=0}^{\infty} \mathbf{A}^i$ and $\mathbf{A}'\langle x\rangle = \mathbf{A}\langle x\rangle - \mathbf{A}$. Let $\|\mathbf{A}\langle x\rangle\|$ be a parametric matrix such that $\|\mathbf{A}\langle x\rangle\|[s, s'] = |\mathbf{A}\langle x\rangle[s, s']|$, and $\|\mathbf{b}\langle x\rangle\|$ be a parametric column-vector such that $\|\mathbf{b}\|[s] = |\mathbf{b}[s]|$. In other words, for any $c \in I$, $\|\mathbf{A}\langle x\rangle\|$ and $\|\mathbf{b}\langle x\rangle\|$ are obtained from $\mathbf{A}\langle x\rangle$ and $\mathbf{b}\langle x\rangle$, respectively, by instantiating the negative (resp., positive) occurrences of x with $-c$ if $x \geq 0$ (resp., $x < 0$). Recall that $\mathbf{A}$ and $\mathbf{b}$ are based on the constraint set $S_? \lceil S_!$ and the target set $S_!$.

Let $\tau = \sup_{x \in I} |x|$. For $n \in \mathbb{N}$ and $n \geq 1$, we define the aforementioned expansion part and remainder part of f as functions f^n and $g^n : 2^S \times 2^S \times S \times I \to [0, 1]$ such that

$$f^n(S_?, S_!, s, x) = \left(\mathbf{A}^* \cdot \sum_{i=0}^{n-1}(\mathbf{A}'\langle x\rangle \cdot \mathbf{A}^*)^i \cdot \mathbf{b}\langle x\rangle\right)[s]$$

$$g^n(S_?, S_!, s, x) = \left(\mathbf{A}^* \cdot (\|\mathbf{A}'\langle x\rangle\| \cdot \mathbf{A}^*)^n \cdot (\mathbf{I} - \|\mathbf{A}'\langle \tau\rangle\| \cdot \mathbf{A}^*)^{-1} \cdot \|\mathbf{b}\langle \tau\rangle\|\right)[s]$$

The function f^n is an expansion up to the n order of x and the function g^n is a remainder, namely an estimated bound. Since $0 \in I$ and $|I| \ll 1$, $\mathbf{I} - \|\mathbf{A}'\langle x\rangle\| \cdot \mathbf{A}^*$ is invertible for any $x \in I$ and, thus, the definition of g^n is legitimate.

The *under-* and *over-approximations* for $Pr_{A,B}$ are $\underline{Pr}^n_{A,B}$ and $\overline{Pr}^n_{A,B} : I \times S \to [0, 1]$ such that

$$\underline{Pr}^n_{A,B}(x, s) = \begin{cases} f^n(sat_A, sat_B, s, x) - g^n(sat_A, sat_B, s, x) & \text{if } s \in sat_A \lceil sat_B \\ 1 & \text{if } s \in sat_B \\ 0 & \text{otherwise} \end{cases}$$

$$\overline{Pr}^n_{A,B}(x, s) = \begin{cases} f^n(sat_A, sat_B, s, x) + g^n(sat_A, sat_B, s, x) & \text{if } s \in sat_A \lceil sat_B \\ 1 & \text{if } s \in sat_B \\ 0 & \text{otherwise} \end{cases}$$

The number n is called the *order* of $\underline{Pr}^n_{A,B}$ and $\overline{Pr}^n_{A,B}$, which together are called *interval approximations* for $Pr_{A,B}$. The following lemmas are expected mathematical properties of interval approximations for non-nested reachability functions.

Lemma 3. $\underline{Pr}^n_{A,B}(x, s) \leq Pr_{A,B}(x, s) \leq \overline{Pr}^n_{A,B}(x, s)$ *for all basic formulas* $A, B \in \mathcal{L}, s \in S$, *any* $x \in I$ *and any* $n \in \mathbb{N}$.

Lemma 3 confirms that a non-nested reachability function is indeed bounded by its interval approximations from both below and above.

Lemma 4. *For all* $A, B \in \mathcal{L}, n_1, n_2 \in \mathbb{N}, x \in I$ *and* $s \in S$, *if* $n_1 < n_2$ *then*

- $\underline{Pr}^{n_1}_{A,B}(x,s) \leq \underline{Pr}^{n_2}_{A,B}(x,s)$
- $\overline{Pr}^{n_1}_{A,B}(x,s) \geq \overline{Pr}^{n_2}_{A,B}(x,s)$

Lemma 4 expresses a monotonicity property of interval approximations for non-nested reachability functions: As the order increases, the over-approximation is non-increasing and the under-approximation is non-decreasing.

Lemma 5. $\lim_{n\to\infty} \sup_{x\in I, s\in S} \overline{Pr}^n_{A,B}(x,s) - \underline{Pr}^n_{A,B}(x,s) = 0$ *for each basic formulas* $A, B \in \mathcal{L}$.

Lemma 5 states that, as the order gets large, the difference between the pair of interval approximations of a non-nested reachability function becomes small on the entire interval.

Lemma 6. *For* $s \in S$ *and* $A, B \in \mathcal{L}$, $\overline{Pr}^n_{A,B}(x,s) - \underline{Pr}^n_{A,B}(x,s)$ *is* $o(x^{n-1})$ *as* x *tends to* 0.

Lemma 6 states the rate of a non-nested reachability function being approximated by its interval approximations as the perturbed variable tends to 0.

3.2 General Form

Unlike their basic counterparts, reachability functions and satisfaction sets are mutually dependent on each other, and so are their interval approximations. For notation simplicity, we assume that all involved interval approximations share a *uniform* order. But as discussed at the end of the section, this assumption is not a theoretical restriction. Formally, the recursive definition of *interval approximations*, including *under-* and *over-approximations*, is as follows:

- $\underline{Pr}^n_{X,Y}$ and $\overline{Pr}^n_{X,Y} : I \times S \to [0,1]$ such that

$$\underline{Pr}^n_{X,Y}(x,s) = \begin{cases} f^n(\underline{sat}_X(x), \underline{sat}_Y(x), s, x) - \\ \quad g^n(\underline{sat}_X(x), \underline{sat}_Y(x), s, x) & \text{if } s \in \underline{sat}_X(x) \lceil \underline{sat}_Y(x) \\ 1 & \text{if } s \in \underline{sat}_Y(x) \\ 0 & \text{otherwise} \end{cases}$$

$$\overline{Pr}^n_{X,Y}(x,s) = \begin{cases} f^n(\overline{sat}_X(x), \overline{sat}_Y(x), s, x) + \\ \quad g^n(\overline{sat}_X(x), \overline{sat}_Y(x), s, x) & \text{if } s \in \overline{sat}_X(x) \lceil \overline{sat}_Y(x) \\ 1 & \text{if } s \in \overline{sat}_Y(x) \\ 0 & \text{otherwise} \end{cases}$$

- $\underline{sat}^n_Z$ and $\overline{sat}^n_Z : I \to 2^S$ with $Z \equiv \mathbb{P}_{\sim p}[X \, \mathcal{U} Y]$ such that (i) if $\sim \in \{<, \leq\}$ then

$$\begin{aligned} \underline{sat}^n_Z(x) &= \{s \in S \mid \overline{Pr}^n_{X,Y}(x,s) \sim p\} \\ \overline{sat}^n_Z(x) &= \{s \in S \mid \underline{Pr}^n_{X,Y}(x,s) \sim p\} \end{aligned} \tag{1}$$

and (ii) if $\sim \in \{>, \geq\}$ then $\underline{sat}^n_Z(x)$ and $\overline{sat}^n_Z(x)$ are defined by swapping their positions in Equation (1).

For consistency of notations, we let $\underline{sat}_A^n(x) = \overline{sat}_A^n(x) = sat_A$ for any $A \in \mathcal{L}$. As expected, the following conservation property holds for interval approximations of all reachability functions and satisfaction sets.

Theorem 7 (Conservation). *For all* $X, Y \in \mathcal{L}, n \in \mathbb{N}, x \in I$ *and* $s \in S$,

- $\underline{Pr}_{X,Y}^n(x, s) \le Pr_{X,Y}(x, s) \le \overline{Pr}_{X,Y}^n(x, s)$
- $\underline{sat}_X^n(x) \subseteq sat_X(x) \subseteq \overline{sat}_X^n(x)$

The monotonic property can also be generalized for interval approximations for all reachability functions and satisfaction sets, as below.

Theorem 8 (Monotonicity). *For all* $X, Y \in \mathcal{L}, n_1, n_2 \in \mathbb{N}, x \in I$ *and* $s \in S$, *if* $n_1 < n_2$ *then*

- $\underline{Pr}_{X,Y}^{n_1}(x, s) \le \underline{Pr}_{X,Y}^{n_2}(x, s), \underline{sat}_X^{n_1}(x) \subseteq \underline{sat}_X^{n_2}(x)$
- $\overline{Pr}_{X,Y}^{n_1}(x, s) \ge \overline{Pr}_{X,Y}^{n_2}(x, s), \overline{sat}_X^{n_1}(x) \supseteq \overline{sat}_X^{n_2}(x)$

The following theorem states that the integral of $Pr_{X,Y}(\cdot, s)$ on I is approximated by its interval approximations to an arbitrarily accurate degree as their order increases.

Theorem 9 (Convergency). *For each* $s \in S$,

$$\lim_{n \to \infty} \int_I (\overline{Pr}_{X,Y}^n - \underline{Pr}_{X,Y}^n)(x, s)\mathrm{d}x = 0$$

Theorems 7 and 9 imply the following corollary, which states that the difference between the integral of the over-approximation and that of the under-approximation on any sub-interval of I has a similar convergent property as their order increases.

Corollary 10. *Let* $a, b \in I$ *and* $a \le b$. *For each* $s \in S$,

$$\lim_{n \to \infty} \int_a^b (\overline{Pr}_{X,Y}^n - \underline{Pr}_{X,Y}^n)(x, s)\mathrm{d}x = 0$$

All above properties of the interval approximations for reachability functions and satisfaction sets are based on the assumption of a uniform order for the interval approximations. But this assumption is only for notation simplicity and we claim that for all these properties there are more general versions for interval approximations involving non-uniform orders.

4   Computational Procedure

In this section, we consider the computation of interval approximations for single-nested reachability functions, namely $Pr_{X,Y}$ with $dep(X, Y) = 1$. Because of the limitation of space, we only present a computational procedure for an over-approximation on the positive part of a perturbation range, while adopting the procedure for other cases, such as other forms of formulas in $\mathcal{L}$, an under-approximation and the negative part of a perturbation range, is straightforward. The pseudo-codes of the procedure

---

Algorithm 1. Over-approximation for single-nested satisfaction sets on a positive perturbation range

---

Input : $\mathcal{M}\langle x \rangle, X \equiv \mathbb{P}_{>p}[A \mathcal{U} B], n$
Output: $\overline{sat}_X$ of order n
$\overline{sat}_X(0) := sat_X(0);$
compute $\mathbf{A}\langle x \rangle$ and $\mathbf{b}\langle x \rangle$ based on sat_A and sat_B;
compute $\overline{Pr}_{A,B}(x, s)$ of order n for $s \in sat_A \upharpoonright sat_B$;
foreach $s \in sat_A \upharpoonright sat_B$ **do**
  $\quad$ let $J(X) = \{x \in I \mid x \geq 0, \overline{Pr}_{A,B}(x, s) = p\};$
  $\quad$ **foreach** $a \in J(X)$ **do**
    $\quad\quad$ **if** $\overline{Pr}_{A,B}(\cdot, s)$ *is increasing at* a **then**
      $\quad\quad\quad \lfloor\ \overline{sat}_X(a) := \overline{sat}_X(a) \cup \{s\};$
    $\quad\quad$ **if** $\overline{Pr}_{A,B}(\cdot, s)$ *is decreasing at* a **then**
      $\quad\quad\quad \lfloor\ \overline{sat}_X(a) := \overline{sat}_X(a) \backslash \{s\};$

---

are provided in Algorithms 1 and 2, which are for generating an over-approximations for a single-nested satisfaction set and that for a single-nested reachability function, respectively. The two algorithms are explained in greater detail in the following. For simplicity, we do not indicate the uniform order symbol n explicitly in the reachability functions and satisfactions sets throughout this section.

Algorithm 1 takes a PMC $\mathcal{M}\langle x \rangle$, an $\mathcal{L}$-formula $X \equiv \mathbb{P}_{>p}[A \mathcal{U} B]$ and an order number n as inputs and returns an over-approximation $\overline{sat}_X$ of order n for sat_X. In general terms, the algorithm computes $\overline{sat}_X$ by determining the "jumping" points of $\overline{sat}_X$ and the update operation of $\overline{sat}_X$ at those points, such as either putting a specific state into $\overline{sat}_X$ or removing a specific state from $\overline{sat}_X$. Initially, $sat_X(0)$ is assigned to $\overline{sat}_X(0)$. Then, $\mathbf{A}\langle x \rangle$ and $\mathbf{b}\langle x \rangle$ based on the constraint set $sat_A \upharpoonright sat_B$ and the target set sat_B is computed as in standard probabilistic model checking (except some entries involve symbolic operations). Next, in an essential step of the algorithm, the over-approximation $\overline{Pr}_{A,B}(\cdot, s)$ of order n for the non-nested reachability function $Pr_{A,B}(\cdot, s)$ for each $s \in sat_A \backslash sat_B$ is computed. We write $\overline{Pr}_{A,B}$ as the polynomial

$$\overline{Pr}_{A,B}(x, s) = \mathbf{b}_0[s] + \mathbf{b}_1[s]x + \ldots + \mathbf{b}_n[s]x^n$$

and aim to compute the column-vector coefficients $\mathbf{b}_i$'s, which are defined in the next lemma.

Lemma 11. *Let* $\mathbf{A}'\langle 1 \rangle = \mathbf{A}\langle 1 \rangle - \mathbf{A}$ *and* $\mathbf{b}'\langle 1 \rangle = \mathbf{b}\langle 1 \rangle - \mathbf{b}$. *It holds that*

$$\mathbf{b}_n = \mathbf{A}^* \cdot (\mathbf{A}'\langle 1 \rangle \cdot \mathbf{A}^*)^{n-1} \cdot \mathbf{b}'\langle 1 \rangle +$$

$$\mathbf{A}^* \cdot (\|\mathbf{A}'\langle 1 \rangle\| \cdot \mathbf{A}^*)^n \cdot \sum_{i=0}^{\infty} (\|\mathbf{A}'\langle \tau \rangle\| \cdot \mathbf{A}^*)^i \cdot \|\mathbf{b}\langle \tau \rangle\|$$

where $\tau = \sup_{x \in I} |x|$ *and for* $0 \leq i \leq n-1$

$$\mathbf{b}_i = \mathbf{A}^* \cdot (\mathbf{A}'\langle 1 \rangle \cdot \mathbf{A}^*)^i \cdot \mathbf{b} + \mathbf{A}^* \cdot (\mathbf{A}'\langle 1 \rangle \cdot \mathbf{A}^*)^{i-1} \cdot \mathbf{b}'\langle 1 \rangle$$

Algorithm 2. Over-approximation for single-nested reachability functions on a positive perturbation range

---

Input : $\mathcal{M}\langle x \rangle$, $\overline{sat}_X$, $\overline{sat}_Y$ with $dep(X, Y) = 1, n$
Output: $\overline{Pr}_{X,Y}$ of order n
let $a_0 < \ldots < a_m$ enumerate elements of $J(X) \cup J(Y) \cup \{0\}$;
for $1 \leq i \leq m$ **do**
  compute $\mathbf{A}\langle x \rangle$ and $\mathbf{b}\langle x \rangle$ based on $\overline{sat}_X(a_i)$, and $\overline{sat}_Y(a_i)$;
  compute $\overline{Pr}_{X,Y}(x, s)$ on each $[a_{i-1}, a_i)$ and $[a_m, \sup(I)]$ for each $s \in S$;

After computing $\overline{Pr}_{A,B}(\cdot, s)$ for each $s \in sat_A \backslash sat_B$, it computes a finite set $J(X) \subset \{x \in I \mid x \geq 0\}$ of "jumping" points for the equation $\overline{Pr}_{A,B}(x, s) = p$ where $X \equiv \mathbb{P}_{>p}[A \mathcal{U} B]$. Then, the algorithm determines the update of sat_X when the value of x locates at each "jumping" point $a \in J(X)$ in the following manner: If $\overline{Pr}_{A,B}(x, s)$ is increasing in some neighborhood of a, namely the interval $[a - \epsilon, a + \epsilon]$ for some small $\epsilon > 0$, then the element a is put into $\overline{sat}_X$; if the function is decreasing on that interval, a is removed from $\overline{sat}_X$.

Algorithm 2 takes a PMC $\mathcal{M}\langle x \rangle$, dynamic sets $\overline{sat}_X$ and $\overline{sat}_Y$ with $dep(X, Y)$ being 1 and an order number n as inputs, and returns an over-approximation $\overline{Pr}_{X,Y}$ for the reachability function $Pr_{X,Y}$. The algorithm first enumerates the "jumping" points of $\overline{sat}_X$ and $\overline{sat}_Y$. Note that if X (resp., Y) is a basic formula, then $J(X) = \varnothing$ (resp., $J(Y) = \varnothing$). Those "jumping" points form a sequence of sub-intervals of the non-negative part of I. Then, $\overline{Pr}_{X,Y}(\cdot, s)$ is iteratively computed for each of those sub-intervals using the same method as specified in Algorithm 1.

Theorem 12. *The time complexity for computing interval approximations for single-nested reachability functions is $\mathcal{O}(k^4 n^3)$ where k is the size of the state space of the PMC and n is the uniform order of the interval approximations.*

Proof. The generation of $\mathbf{A}\langle x \rangle$ and $\mathbf{b}\langle x \rangle$ is by a basic graph analysis algorithm (plus numerical and symbolic additions for the latter). The cost of the $k \times k$-matrix multiplications and computing $\mathbf{A}^*$ is $\mathcal{O}(k^3)$. The number of matrix multiplications of $\mathbf{b}^i$ for each $1 \leq i \leq n$ in Lemma 11 is bounded by mn^2 for some constant number m (note that $\mathbf{A}'\langle 1 \rangle \cdot \mathbf{A}^*$ is a recurrent component). The computational complexity of solving a polynomial is linear in the size of its order. The number of (real) roots of a polynomial is not larger than its order and hence there are no more than $2kn$ "jumping" points. Therefore, the overall complexity is $\mathcal{O}(k^4 n^3)$.

It should be noted that for perturbation analysis, we usually assume that the range I for the perturbed variable x is small [11]. Thus, we can anticipate a small n in practice and the time complexity for computing single-nested reachability functions is dominated by the quartic order of the size of the PMC state space. Also, one obvious way to boost the two algorithms is to combine states s and s' before solving the equations if $\overline{Pr}_{X,Y}(x, s)$ and $\overline{Pr}_{X,Y}(x, s')$ are equivalent. Also noteworthy is that, because large-size matrix multiplications are usually unstable and memory-consuming, matrix-vector

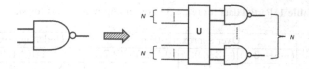

Fig. 2. NAND Multiplexing

multiplications are iteratively carried out and thus the recurrence of $\mathbf{A}'\langle 1 \rangle \cdot \mathbf{A}^*$ is broken apart in the actual numerical computation. As a final point, the properties of interval approximations presented in Section 3 are for general-form reachability functions, but algorithms in these section handle single-nested ones only. Although it is possible to construct a decision procedure for multiple-nested reachability functions, we do not foresee such a generalization without an overhead of computational complexity. The reason is that, for single-nested interval approximations, all satisfaction sets can be computed separately (c.f., Algorithm 1), but for multiple-nested ones, this "separation-of-concern" is no longer possible because some satisfaction sets may rely on others.

5 Case Study

In this section, we conduct a case study on NAND multiplexing to demonstrate the practicality of our approach. The purpose of NAND multiplexing is to enhance the reliability of imperfect NAND gates. Normally, a multiplexer consists of an executive stage and an even number of restorative stages, respectively for carrying out the basic function of the multiplexer and for reducing the degradation in the executive stage caused by the input error and the faulty device [15]. We consider a NAND multiplexing unit with the executive stage only.

The unit is built by replicating the NAND gate N times, as depicted in Figure 2. The inputs are two bundles of N logical values 1 (a stimulated result) or 0 (a non-stimulated result) as determined by a probability distribution. We refer each pair of bundles of logical values as *configurations*. The functionality of the "U" box is to randomly choose two input values as inputs for the NAND gates. Whether the overall output of the whole unit is stimulated or not depends on the number of stimulated outputs of the individual gates. More specifically, we specify some threshold number $K \leq N$. Then, the overall output is considered to be stimulated if at least $N - K$ outputs are stimulated and non-stimulated if no more than K outputs are stimulated. In case that neither of the conditions is met, the overall output is undecided. It is assumed that all gates have the *same* error rate and fail independently. Moreover, we let the error rate be *perturbed*.

The verification of the overall stimulated probability of the NAND multiplexing unit is a non-nested reachability problem [11]. With the more expressive syntax of $\mathcal{L}$, a more complicated analysis can be performed. We call a configuration non-stimulated if the probability of obtaining a non-stimulated overall output from it is not larger than some fixed probability p, and our analysis is to determine the probability of reaching some selected non-stimulated configurations. Because polynomials of order N are involved in a direct computation of the exact reachability probability, we aim to compute its interval approximations. Symbolically, let $X_1 \equiv \mathbb{P}_{\geq p}[\mathcal{F}A_{\text{non}}] \wedge A_{\text{sel}}$, where A_{non} is

Table 1. Partial data for order-3 interval approximations for sat_{X_1}

Configuration	Over approx. (E-03)				Under approx. (E-03)		
	$(-5, -3.9)$	$(-3.9, 0.1)$	$(0.1, 2.7)$	$(2.7, 5)$	$(-5, 0.1)$	$(0.1, 2.3)$	$(2.3, 5)$
$(18, 17)$	Y	Y	Y	N	Y	Y	N
$(19, 16)$	Y	Y	N	N	Y	N	N
$(20, 15)$	Y	N	N	N	N	N	N

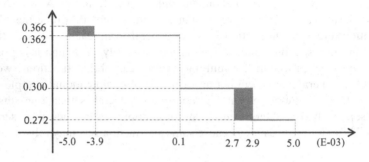

Fig. 3. Images of order-3 interval approximations for Pr_{X_2} at the initial state

the non-stimulated condition and A_{sel} is the selecting condition for configurations. Our goal is to compute a pair of interval approximations for Pr_{X_2} where $X_2 \equiv \mathcal{F}X_1$. The specification of the NAND multiplexing unit is provided in the modeling language of the probabilistic model checking tool PRISM [16]. The DTMC model underlying the specification has about 16,000 states and 24,000 transitions. We make use of the model export in PRISM to export the states and transition matrix of the DTMC in the Matlab language [17] and manipulated by our implementation of Algorithms 1 and 2.

In our experiment, the key parameters mentioned above are set as follows: The error rate of the NAND gates is 0.02 with a perturbation range being $[-0.005, 0.005]$; the rate of obtaining the logical value 1 in the inputs is 0.875; the size N of the two bundles is 20; the stimulated threshold number K for the overall output is 5; the non-stimulation threshold probability p for configurations is 0.80. The selecting condition for configurations is $(x_1 \geq 15) \wedge (x_2 \geq 15) \wedge (x_1 \geq x_2)$, where x_1, x_2 are the numbers of logical value 1 in the first and second bundles respectively. Instead of computing sat_{X_1} and Pr_{X_2} directly, our Matlab implementation computes their interval approximations. Table 1 summarizes experimental data for three different configurations and several intervals, which express which configurations belong to the order-3 interval approximations of sat_{X_1} at which intervals—"Y" (resp., "N") means "yes" (resp., "no"). Figure 3 depicts the function images of the interval approximations for Pr_{X_2}, in which the lower and upper ends of the boxes specify the under- and over-approximations of Pr_{X_2} respectively, while the lines are their overlapped part. The four "jumping" points of the functions, which are caused by the movement of three configurations $(18, 17)$, $(19, 16)$ and $(20, 15)$ into or off the interval approximations for sat_{X_1}, locate at $x = -0.0039, 0.0001, 0.0023$ and 0.0029.

The specification, implementation and all experiment data can be found in the first author's website http://www.comp.nus.edu.sg/~sugx/.

Overall, our experiment reflects that a small perturbation range of the error rate of the NAND gates in the multiplexing unit can cause obvious and singularly perturbed effects on the verification result, and that, even though the computation of the exact locations of the singularly perturbed points may be costly, these effects can be accurately and efficiently approximated with our approach.

6 Related Work

Our work is related to the approach of parametric DTMCs. Daws [5] pioneered the idea of representing a reachability problem in a DTMC or a parametric DTMC as a finite automaton, transforming the automaton into a regular expression using the state-elimination method, and evaluating the regular expression as a rational number or a rational reachability function. This language-theoretic and symbolic approach to the model checking of parametric DTMCs was advocated and further developed by Hahn *et al.* [6,18] and Jansen *et al.* [19] for non-nested reachability functions. A directed parameterization of the standard computational method of inversed matrices is used by Filieri *et al.* [20].

The other approach is the approach of interval-valued DTMCs, including Interval Markov Chains (IMCs) and Uncertain Markov Chains (UMCs). Each IMC is treated as a non-deterministic DTMC or, equivalently, a variant of an MDP with a possibly infinite set of actions [21]. According to the MDP semantics, the model checking problem for an IMC involves optimization problems [1,2,3,4]. Each UMC is interpreted as a set of DTMCs [22]. Although our PMCs are a special kind of UMCs, instead of computing function expressions like our approach does, the model checking problem for a UMC amounts to the search for a particular DTMC belonging to the UMC, which is NP-hard, as pointed out by Sen *et al.* [1]. Ghorbal *et al.* [23] proposed an approximation method for model checking UMCs based on affine arithmetic. Both our work and their work pursue rigorous bounds for verification results of DTMCs with open or undetermined quantities, but the scope of their method is UMCs (and thus broader than ours). However, they addressed neither non-linear approximations nor reachability problems with nested PCTL probabilistic operators.

Our work is also related to a separated line of research, the common goal of which is to find an inequality between the distance of stationary distributions of two DTMCs and the distance of their transition probability functions multiplied by some condition numbers [24,25,26,27]. Such an inequality holds universally for all DTMCs according to the mathematical definitions of the chosen condition numbers and distance metrics, instead of by numerical or symbolic computation.

7 Conclusions

To address the high cost of computing reachability functions with nested PCTL probabilistic operators, we presented an interval approximate characterization for such functions, which enjoys several elegant mathematical properties such as monotonicity and convergency, and developed an efficient procedure for computing interval approximations for single-nested reachability functions. We evaluate our approach with a case study on a NAND multiplexing unit.

We outline several directions for future work below. First, the logic that we defined is a sublogic of PCTL and thus it is natural to extend the approach to capturing the full-fledged PCTL syntax. Indeed, we believe that all properties in Section 3 would be preserved if formulas with the "next" operator and the "bounded until" connective were added to the syntax of the logic. A second interesting problem is to investigate the possibility of a similar technique, based on multi-variate mathematical analysis, for PMCs with multi-variate parameters. A third direction is the interval approximation analysis of other DTMC benchmarks in probabilistic model checking. Last but not the least, we want to investigate the convergence rate of interval approximations to the accurate result as the approximation order increases.

Acknowledgment. The authors are indebted to the anonymous reviewers for their comments on the earlier version of the paper.

References

1. Sen, K., Viswanathan, M., Agha, G.: Model-checking markov chains in the presence of uncertainties. In: Hermanns, H., Palsberg, J. (eds.) TACAS 2006. LNCS, vol. 3920, pp. 394–410. Springer, Heidelberg (2006)
2. Chatterjee, K., Sen, K., Henzinger, T.A.: Model-checking ω-regular properties of interval markov chains. In: Amadio, R.M. (ed.) FOSSACS 2008. LNCS, vol. 4962, pp. 302–317. Springer, Heidelberg (2008)
3. Puggelli, A., Li, W., Sangiovanni-Vincentelli, A.L., Seshia, S.A.: Polynomial-time verification of PCTL properties of mDPs with convex uncertainties. In: Sharygina, N., Veith, H. (eds.) CAV 2013. LNCS, vol. 8044, pp. 527–542. Springer, Heidelberg (2013)
4. Benedikt, M., Lenhardt, R., Worrell, J.: LTL model checking of interval markov chains. In: Piterman, N., Smolka, S.A. (eds.) TACAS 2013 (ETAPS 2013). LNCS, vol. 7795, pp. 32–46. Springer, Heidelberg (2013)
5. Daws, C.: Symbolic and parametric model checking of discrete-time markov chains. In: Liu, Z., Araki, K. (eds.) ICTAC 2004. LNCS, vol. 3407, pp. 280–294. Springer, Heidelberg (2005)
6. Hahn, E., Hermanns, H., Zhang, L.: Probabilistic reachability for parametric Markov models. International Journal on Software Tools for Technology Transfer 13(1), 3–19 (2011)
7. Lanotte, R., Maggiolo-Schettini, A., Troina, A.: Parametric probabilistic transition systems for system design and analysis. Formal Aspects of Computing 19(1), 93–109 (2007)
8. Hansson, H., Jonsson, B.: A logic for reasoning about time and reliability. Formal Aspects of Computing 6, 102–111 (1994)
9. Chen, T., Han, T., Kwiatkowska, M.Z.: On the complexity of model checking interval-valued discrete time markov chains. Inf. Process. Lett. 113(7), 210–216 (2013)
10. Su, G., Rosenblum, D.S.: Asymptotic bounds for quantitative verification of perturbed probabilistic systems. In: Groves, L., Sun, J. (eds.) ICFEM 2013. LNCS, vol. 8144, pp. 297–312. Springer, Heidelberg (2013)
11. Su, G., Rosenblum, D.S.: Perturbation analysis of stochastic systems with empirical distribution parameters. In: Proceeding of the 36th International Conference on Software Engineering, ICSE 2014 (2014)

12. Kwiatkowska, M., Norman, G., Parker, D.: The PRISM benchmark suite. In: Proc. 9th International Conference on Quantitative Evaluation of SysTems (QEST 2012), pp. 203–204. IEEE CS Press (2012)
13. Baier, C., Katoen, J.-P.: Principles of Model Checking. MIT Press (2008)
14. Chen, T., Feng, Y., Rosenblum, D.S., Su, G.: Perturbation analysis in verification of discrete-time markov chains. In: Baldan, P., Gorla, D. (eds.) CONCUR 2014. LNCS, vol. 8704, pp. 218–233. Springer, Heidelberg (2014)
15. Norman, G., Parker, D., Kwiatkowska, M., Shukla, S.: Evaluating the reliability of NAND multiplexing with PRISM. IEEE Transactions on Computer-Aided Design of Integrated Circuits and Systems 24(10), 1629–1637 (2005)
16. Kwiatkowska, M., Norman, G., Parker, D.: PRISM 4.0: Verification of probabilistic real-time systems. In: Gopalakrishnan, G., Qadeer, S. (eds.) CAV 2011. LNCS, vol. 6806, pp. 585–591. Springer, Heidelberg (2011)
17. MATLAB: version 8.0. The MathWorks Inc., Natick, Massachusetts (R2012b)
18. Hahn, E.M., Han, T., Zhang, L.: Synthesis for PCTL in parametric Markov decision processes. In: NASA Formal Methods, pp. 146–161 (2011)
19. Jansen, N., Corzilius, F., Volk, M., Wimmer, R., Ábrahám, E., Katoen, J.-P., Becker, B.: Accelerating parametric probabilistic verification. In: Norman, G., Sanders, W. (eds.) QEST 2014. LNCS, vol. 8657, pp. 404–420. Springer, Heidelberg (2014)
20. Filieri, A., Ghezzi, C., Tamburrelli, G.: Run-time efficient probabilistic model checking. In: Proceedings of the 33rd International Conference on Software Engineering, ICSE 2011, pp. 341–350. ACM, New York (2011)
21. Kozine, I., Utkin, L.V.: Interval-valued finite markov chains. Reliable Computing 8(2), 97–113 (2002)
22. Jonsson, B., Larsen, K.G.: Specification and refinement of probabilistic processes. In: International conference on Logics in Computer Science (LICS), pp. 266–277 (1991)
23. Ghorbal, K., Duggirala, P.S., Kahlon, V., Ivančić, F., Gupta, A.: Efficient probabilistic model checking of systems with ranged probabilities. In: Finkel, A., Leroux, J., Potapov, I. (eds.) RP 2012. LNCS, vol. 7550, pp. 107–120. Springer, Heidelberg (2012)
24. Schweitzer, P.J.: Perturbation theory and finite Markov chains. Journal of Applied Probability 5(2), 401–413 (1968)
25. Cho, G.E., Meyer, C.D.: Comparison of perturbation bounds for the stationary distribution of a Markov chain. Linear Algebra Appl. 335, 137–150 (2000)
26. Solan, E., Vieille, N.: Perturbed Markov chains. J. Applied Prob. 40(1), 107–122 (2003)
27. Heidergott, B.: Perturbation analysis of Markov chains. In: 9th International Workshop on Discrete Event Systems, WODES 2008, pp. 99–104 (2008)
28. Murdock, J.A.: Perturbation: Theory and Method. John Wiley & Sons, Inc. (1991)
29. Hopcroft, J.E., Motwani, R., Ullman, J.D.: Introduction to Automata Theory, Languages, and Computation, 3rd edn. Addison-Wesley Longman Publishing Co., Inc, Boston (2006)
30. Verification, Model Checking, and Abstract Interpretation (2004)
31. Agrawal, M., Akshay, S., Genest, B., Thiagarajan, P.S.: Approximate verification of the symbolic dynamics of markov chains. In: International conference on Logics in Computer Science (LICS), pp. 55–64 (2012)

Symbolic Memory with Pointers[*]

Marek Trtík[1],[**] and Jan Strejček[2]

[1] VERIMAG, Grenoble, France
Marek.Trtik@imag.fr
[2] Faculty of Informatics, Masaryk University, Brno, Czech Republic
strejcek@fi.muni.cz

Abstract. We introduce a segment-offset-plane memory model for symbolic execution that supports symbolic pointers, allocations of memory blocks of symbolic sizes, and multi-writes. We further describe our efficient implementation of the model in a free open-source project BUGST. Experimental results provide empirical evidence that the implemented memory model effectively tackles the variable storage-referencing problem of symbolic execution.

1 Introduction

Symbolic execution [9,2,7] is a classic automated program analysis technique based on a simple idea to execute a program on symbols representing arbitrary input data. It is nowadays used in many automatic test-generation and bug-finding tools including industrial ones. Some of the best known tools are EXE [4], KLEE [3], CUTE [10], SAGE [6], and PEX [15].

As symbolic execution runs a program on symbols instead of concrete input data, it has to manipulate expressions over these symbols instead of standard datatype values like integers or floats. However, reading and writing symbolic expressions is not the main problem associated with memory in symbolic execution. It is the *variable storage-referencing problem* originally presented by King [9]. The problem appears when one needs to read a value from (or write a value to) a memory location dependent on input symbols. For example, if we want to execute an assignment `A[i]:=0`, the memory location that should be set to 0 depends on the symbolic value stored in `i`. The issue becomes even more serious when we introduce pointers because a symbolic pointer may point literally to any memory location, not only to elements of one array.

King [9] proposed two possible solutions of the problem for symbolic execution (and he immediately mentioned that *'neither is very satisfactory'*):

1. Symbolic execution is forked for each memory location which is a potential concrete value of the symbolic pointer. This solution leads to an exhaustive case analysis. This approach is further improved in [8,5].

---

[*] The authors have been supported by The Czech Science Foundation, grant GBP202/12/G061.

[**] The paper has been written during M. Trtík's doctoral study at Faculty of Informatics, Masaryk University, Brno, Czech Republic.

F. Cassez and J.-F. Raskin (Eds.): ATVA 2014, LNCS 8837, pp. 380–395, 2014.

2. The second solution prevents intensive forking of symbolic execution by storing *conditional values* in the symbolic memory. For example, if array element A[3] has a value e and i has a value $\underline{i}$, then an assignment A[i]:=0 changes the value of A[3] to $\mathbf{ite}(\underline{i} = 3, 0, e)$ meaning that the value is 0 if $\underline{i} = 3$, and e otherwise. Note that each write can theoretically prolong all memory records by one application of $\mathbf{ite}$. Hence, this symbolic memory grows very quickly unless we use some reduction methods. Unfortunately, the reduction methods are typically expensive.

The presented symbolic memory elaborates on the second approach. Besides symbolic pointers, our approach also supports allocations of memory blocks of symbolic sizes and multi-writes, i.e. operations that write to symbolic number of memory locations at once. This is useful for example when one sets a block of allocated memory to 0, where the number of allocated bytes in the block is given by a symbolic expression.

Full description of our symbolic memory is divided into two parts: Section 2 explains our *segment-offset-plane memory model* and Section 3 then describes its implementation. Both the memory model and its implementation are designed to manipulate as simple expressions as possible, to make operations in symbolic memory efficient. The suggested symbolic memory provides just basic memory operations (i.e. allocation, read, write, deallocation, and test for memory initialisation). Handling of some advanced memory-related operations (e.g. manipulation with composed objects or unions) using our symbolic memory is discussed in Section 4. The high efficiency of our symbolic memory implementation is confirmed by measurements presented in Section 5.

2   Segment-Offset-Plane Memory Model

Our symbolic memory is not bound to any particular programming language or data types. For sake of accessibility, all examples use C statements and programs. Further, we assume that integers and pointers are 4 bytes long.

First we describe the structure of the memory model. The crucial memory operations (namely allocation, read, and write) are then illustrated on a simple example. Finally, we introduce extended versions of allocation and write operations called *multi-allocation* and *multi-write*. The remaining two operations provided by our symbolic memory interface (namely deallocation and test for memory initialisation) are described in the following section.

2.1   Structure of the Model

Structure of the model reflects needs of symbolic execution. A specific aspect of memory allocations in symbolic execution is that sizes of requested allocations can be given by symbolic expressions instead of concrete numbers. For example, if an integer variable n has a value represented by a symbol $\underline{n}$, then symbolic execution of `malloc(n * sizeof(int))` allocates $4\underline{n}$ bytes, which can represent

4 bytes as well as 4 megabytes. If we use a standard memory model where
memory cells are ordered into a linear sequence, it is very complicated to track
which cells are allocated and which are free. We rather represent every allocated
block as an isolated part of the memory called *segment*. Each segment is identified
by a unique integer number. Memory cells within the block are identified by a
nonnegative integer called *offset*. Hence, an address in our memory model is a
pair *segment:offset*.

Further, write and read operations know what type of data they manipulate.
Our memory model takes advantage of this fact and stores data of each basic
type into a separated part of the memory called *plane*. The separation increases
performance of our symbolic memory. For example, if we read an integer, we
do not have to deal with chars, floats, or any data of other types stored in
the memory. Pointers are composite datatypes and thus they are stored in two
planes: segments in the plane *Segments* and offsets in the plane *Offsets*.

The memory model is called *segment-offset-plane* as every read or write operation needs to know the address (i.e. its segment and its offset) and the plane
it should read from or write to.

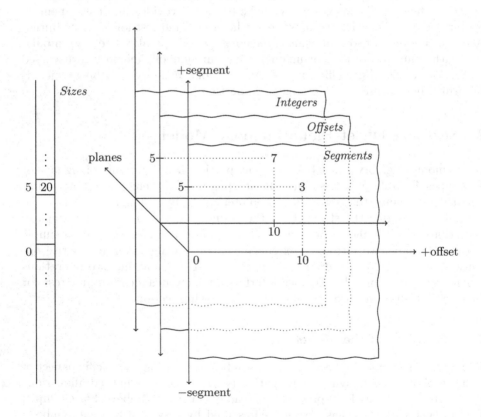

Fig. 1. A simple instance of the segment-offset-plane memory model

Figure 1 depicts a simple instance of the segment-offset-plane memory model. The segment axis (vertical) has two directions to positive and negative values. The offset axis (horizontal) has only one direction to positive values. On the planes axis there are depicted three parallel memory planes. They share the same address space. In the picture there is further depicted a pointer 3 : 7 which is stored at the address 5 : 10. We see that the segment 3 of the pointer is stored in the *Segments* memory plane, while the offset 7 is stored in the plane *Offsets*. Although both segment and offset are stored at the same address, they are stored into different planes. The figure also shows an array *Sizes* that stores the size of each allocated segment. In the figure, the size of segment 5 is 20 bytes. As we mentioned above, the size of a segment can be symbolic. Segments with size 0 are not allocated. The segment 0 is never used to store any data: addresses with segment 0 are interpreted as NULL pointers (assigning NULL sets a pointer to 0 : 0).

In our approach, memory operations do not automatically check whether addresses they work with are allocated or not. Instead, we provide an additional function that checks whether a given address points to an allocated memory or not. This function simply looks into the given address in the array *Sizes* and checks whether the value is greater then zero. We similarly do not implicitly test for memory initialisation in memory operations. We discuss details about the function providing memory initialisation test in the next section.

To unify the structures used in the model, we represent the array *Sizes* as another plane where we use only memory offsets 0, i.e. the size of a segment x is stored in plane *Sizes* at the address $x : 0$.

The content of a plane is represented by a list of write records, where each record has the form (*segment* : *offset*, *value*). In fact, the list reflects history of the plane content: a new record is always added at the end of the list. We use this representation just to explain principles of the model. An effective representation of a plane's content is described later in Section 3.

2.2   Basic Functionality of the Model

We explain the basic functionality of the memory model using a simple example. Let us consider the program depicted in Figure 2. The program contains a definition of a global pointer variable A and a function foo accepting two parameters

```
1    int* A = NULL;
2    int foo(int n, int i) {
3        A = (int*)malloc(n * sizeof(int));
4        A[3] = 777;
5        A[4] = 888;
6        A[3*i+1] = 999;
7        return A[3]+A[4];
8    }
```

Fig. 2. Running example with a global pointer variable A and a function foo

n and i. We symbolically execute the program with input values of variables n and i represented by symbols $\underline{n}$ and $\underline{i}$ respectively. As we are interested in an effect of statements forming the body of the function, we start by a description of the symbolic memory content just before execution of line 3. We especially need to know where program variables are stored in the memory and what are their values. Let the global variable A be stored at address $1 : 0$, and the stack variables n and i be stored at addresses $2 : 0$ and $2 : 4$ respectively. Note that we can consider the segment 1 as a memory block for the common 'data segment' of the program and we can consider the segment 2 as a memory block for the common 'stack segment' of the program. All other segments (except 0) then represent the program heap. As the program uses only pointers and integers, we will work with four planes: *Segments*, *Offsets*, *Integers*, *Sizes*. Before executing line 3, the planes have the following content:

$$Segments \equiv [(1 : 0, 0)] \qquad Integers \equiv [(2 : 0, \underline{n}), (2 : 4, \underline{i})]$$
$$Offsets \equiv [(1 : 0, 0)] \qquad Sizes \equiv [(1 : 0, 4), (2 : 0, 1024)]$$

Note that the record $(1 : 0, 4)$ in *Sizes* says that the data segment of the program consists of four bytes only. It is enough for storing the global pointer A (initialised to NULL, i.e. $0 : 0$) as we assume that a pointer is 4 bytes long. Further, the record $(2 : 0, 1024)$ says that we reserved 1024 bytes for the program stack. Currently, only variables n and i occupy their 8 bytes. Note that instead of a fixed size of the stack we can introduce a fresh symbol for its symbolic size.

Execution of line 3 of the program results in two modifications in the memory. First, we allocate $4\underline{n}$ bytes of memory in the first free segment which is the segment 3. We do so by a single write into the plane *Sizes* and we get

$$Sizes \equiv [(1 : 0, 4), (2 : 0, 1024), (3 : 0, 4\underline{n})].$$

Second, we assign the address $3 : 0$ of the first byte of the allocated memory to the pointer A. More precisely, the segment 3 and the offset 0 of the address are stored to the planes *Segments* and *Offsets* respectively, both to the address of A which is $1 : 0$. We have

$$Segments \equiv [(1 : 0, 0), (1 : 0, 3)] \quad \text{and} \quad Offsets \equiv [(1 : 0, 0), (1 : 0, 0)].$$

The statement at line 4 writes the value 777 to the address $3 : (0 + 4 \cdot 3)$ computed from the address $3 : 0$ (stored in the pointer A) by its increment by $4 \cdot 3$ bytes (which is the size of 3 four–byte integers). We obtain

$$Integers \equiv [(2 : 0, \underline{n}), (2 : 4, \underline{i}), (3 : 4 \cdot 3, 777)].$$

The statements at lines 5 and 6 are resolved similarly. The resulting content of the plane *Integers* is

$$Integers \equiv [(2 : 0, \underline{n}), (2 : 4, \underline{i}), (3 : 4 \cdot 3, 777), (3 : 4 \cdot 4, 888), (3 : 4 \cdot (3\underline{i} + 1), 999)].$$

Note that the last record refers to a symbolic offset. In fact, any part of a record is a symbolic expression (concrete number is a special kind of such expressions).

Now we execute line 7 with two read operations. The first operation reading A[3] is resolved in the plane *Integers* such that we compare the address where we read, i.e. the address $3 : 4 \cdot 3$, with addresses in all records in the list in the reverse order, and we build the composed **ite** expression

$$\mathbf{ite}(3 = 3 \ \wedge \ 4 \cdot 3 = 4 \cdot (3 \cdot \underline{i} + 1), 999,$$
$$\mathbf{ite}(3 = 3 \ \wedge \ 4 \cdot 3 = 4 \cdot 4, 888,$$
$$\mathbf{ite}(3 = 3 \ \wedge \ 4 \cdot 3 = 4 \cdot 3, 777,$$
$$\mathbf{ite}(3 = 2 \ \wedge \ 4 \cdot 3 = 4, \underline{i},$$
$$\mathbf{ite}(3 = 2 \ \wedge \ 4 \cdot 3 = 0, \underline{n},$$
$$\delta(3, 4 \cdot 3)))))),$$

where $\delta(3, 4 \cdot 3)$ denotes a symbolic default value stored initially at the address $3 : 4 \cdot 3$ in the memory plane *Integers*. This default value can be used for detection of read operations from uninitialised memory. After few trivial simplifications we reduce the **ite** expression to $\mathbf{ite}(2 = 3 \cdot \underline{i}, 999, 777)$. We can further see that the equation $2 = 3 \cdot \underline{i}$ does not have any solution, since $\underline{i}$ represents only integer values. With this knowledge we can simplify the expression even further to the final value 777.

Constraints like $2 = 3 \cdot \underline{i}$ can be resolved automatically by an SMT solver. Simplifications based on satisfiability checking of constraints have an important impact on size of expressions returned from the memory. As these expressions are often modified by the program and then stored back to the memory, the simplifications also reduce memory size and improve its performance. In Section 3 we present an actual implementation of the memory model, which substantially reduces the construction of compound **ite** expressions. In particular, the read of A[3] in our running example returns 777 without construction of any composed **ite** expressions.

The last memory operation of our running example reads A[4]. It proceeds in the same way as the previous one and results into the value $\mathbf{ite}(1 = \underline{i}, 999, 888)$.

2.3 Multi-Writes and Multi-Allocations

Our memory supports *multi-write* operations that can change content of more memory locations at once. This ability has some natural applications in symbolic execution. We only sketch the concept of multi-writes using the example code

```
char A[n];
memset(A,0,n);
```

that allocates an array A of n bytes and sets all its elements to 0. Let $\underline{n}$ represent the value of n. We need to write to $\underline{n}$ addresses. Use of one multi-write is definitely more efficient here than iterating over the array and writing to one address each time, especially when we do not know the concrete length of the array.

Let us assume that the array A is stored at an address $\sigma_A : \omega_A$. Then we need to write 0 to every address with segment σ_A and an offset ω satisfying the formula

$$\phi(\omega) = (\omega_A \leq \omega < \omega_A + \underline{n}).$$

We can describe the addresses using λ-notation as $\sigma_A : \lambda\omega.\,\phi(\omega)$.

Formally, we always work with λ-expressions of the form $\lambda\bar{\sigma}.\,\lambda\bar{\omega}.\,f(\bar{\sigma},\bar{\omega})$, i.e. functions of both, a segment $\bar{\sigma}$ and an offset $\bar{\omega}$. Thus, the arguments of the considered multi-write are

$$(\sigma_A : \lambda\bar{\sigma}.\,\lambda\bar{\omega}.\,\phi(\bar{\omega}), 0),$$

which is precisely the record that is added to the corresponding plane. In general, the values set by a multi-write operation do not have to be constant. They can also be given by a function of a segment and an offset. For example, the multi-write

$$(\sigma_A : \lambda\bar{\sigma}.\,\lambda\bar{\omega}.\,\phi(\bar{\omega}), \ \lambda\bar{\sigma}.\,\lambda\bar{\omega}.\,(\bar{\omega} - \omega_A)) \bmod 2)$$

sets all even elements of the array to 0 and all odd elements to 1.

Besides multi-writes, our model also supports a multi-allocation that allocates a number of segments given by a symbolic expression at once. A multi-allocation is basically a multi-write into the *Sizes* memory plane. Segments allocated in this way have negative numbers. We provide more information about multi-allocations in the next section.

3   Implementation of the Memory Model

This section describes data structures used for effective representation of planes' contents. Further, it describes the algorithms for basic memory operations.

The implementation distinguishes two types of addresses: *constant* and *symbolic*. An address is constant if its segment and offset are both concrete integer numbers. Non-constant addresses are called symbolic. Note that a segment or an offset of a symbolic address is either a symbolic expression not equivalent to a concrete integer number, or a boolean λ-function determining a set of integers.

In the previous section, plane contents are represented as lists of records. As most memory operations work with concrete addresses, we use a specific structure to quickly resolve operations on these addresses. More precisely, the content of a plane is held in two structures: *boostMap* and *iteList*. The *boostMap* contains only data stored at concrete addresses and not colliding with any newer record. For example, symbolic address $3 : 4 \cdot (3 \cdot i + 1)$ collides with concrete address $3 : 52$ as the two addresses are identical when $i = 4$. On the other hand, the symbolic address does not collide with $3 : 53$. The *boostMap* is implemented as a map assigning stored values to the corresponding constant addresses. All other records are stored in a doubly linked list called *iteList*, where the oldest record is at the beginning and the youngest at the end. An example of the two structures is depicted in Figure 3.

Write Operation. The write operation of a memory plane stores a passed symbolic expression ν at a given address $\sigma : \omega$. If the address is constant, the procedure is very simple: we remove the old value stored at the address from the *boostMap* (if any) and then we insert the pair $(\sigma : \omega, \nu)$ into the *boostMap*.

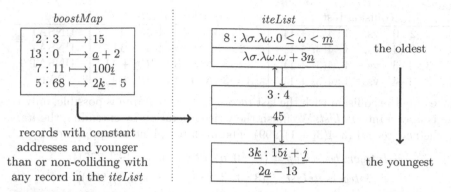

Fig. 3. An example of data structures *boostMap* and *iteList*. Each record in *iteList* is represented by an address (upper line) and the corresponding value (lower line).

If the passed address is symbolic, then there is a possibility that it collides with some constant addresses stored in the *boostMap*. To keep the *boostMap* correct, we must first detect all such collisions and move the colliding records from the *boostMap* to the *iteList*. Let $(\sigma' : \omega', \nu')$ be a record with a concrete address stored in the *boostMap*. There is a collision between the addresses $\sigma' : \omega'$ and $\sigma : \omega$ iff the *collision formula* $\Gamma(\sigma', \omega', \sigma, \omega)$ defined as $\sigma' = \sigma \wedge \omega' = \omega$ is satisfiable.[1] We ask an SMT solver to decide the satisfiability. To be on the safe side, we assume that the formula is satisfiable even if the SMT solver returns UNKNOWN (recall that SMT queries can refer to some undecidable theories). If the formula is satisfiable, we remove the record $(\sigma' : \omega', \nu')$ from the *boostMap* and we insert it at the end of the *iteList*. Otherwise, the record remains in the *boostMap*. When all records in the *boostMap* are examined, we finish the write operation by inserting a new record $(\sigma : \omega, \nu)$ at the end of the *iteList*.

We illustrate the write operation using the example of Figure 2. Let us assume that the first 5 lines of the program are already symbolically executed. Since these lines call writes to constant addresses only, all data are stored in *boostMap*s. We focus on the plane *Integers*, which has the following content:

$$Integers.boostMap = \{(2:0,\underline{n}), (2:4,\underline{i}), (3:4\cdot3,777), (3:4\cdot4,888)\}$$
$$Integers.iteList = []$$

Execution of line 6 of the program produces a write of the record $(3 : 4(3\underline{i} + 1), 999)$ to the plane *Integers*. As the address $3 : 4(3\underline{i}+1)$ is symbolic, the record will be added to the *iteList*. Before we do so, we have to detect collisions of the records in the *boostMap* with the new record:

---

[1] The structure of the collision formula is slightly different if some of its arguments are λ-expressions. For example, $\sigma' : \omega'$ collides with $\sigma : \lambda\bar{\sigma}. \lambda\bar{\omega}. \phi(\bar{\sigma}, \bar{\omega})$ iff $\Gamma(\sigma', \omega', \sigma, \lambda\bar{\sigma}. \lambda\bar{\omega}. \phi(\bar{\sigma}, \bar{\omega}))$ defined as $\sigma' = \sigma \wedge \phi(\sigma', \omega')$ is satisfiable.

collision test	collision formula	result
$2:0$ vs. $3:4(3\underline{i}+1)$	$2=3 \wedge 0 = 4(3\underline{i}+1)$	UNSAT
$2:4$ vs. $3:4(3\underline{i}+1)$	$2=3 \wedge 4 = 4(3\underline{i}+1)$	UNSAT
$3:4\cdot3$ vs. $3:4(3\underline{i}+1)$	$3=3 \wedge 4\cdot3 = 4(3\underline{i}+1)$	UNSAT
$3:4\cdot4$ vs. $3:4(3\underline{i}+1)$	$3=3 \wedge 4\cdot4 = 4(3\underline{i}+1)$	SAT

Since only the collision with the last record in the *boostMap* is possible, only this one is moved into *iteList*. We finish the write operation by extending the *iteList* by the new record $(3, 4(3\underline{i}+1), 999)$. The updated plane is represented by:

$$Integers.boostMap = \{(2:0,\underline{n}), (2:4,\underline{i}), (3:4\cdot3, 777)\}$$
$$Integers.iteList = [(3:4\cdot4, 888), (3, 4(3\underline{i}+1), 999)]$$

Read Operation. Given an address $\sigma : \omega$ and a memory plane, the read operation computes a single symbolic expression which determines the value stored in the memory plane at the passed address. If the address is constant, we check whether it lies in the domain of the *boostMap*. If so, we return the symbolic expression stored in the map for the address.

In all other cases, we construct a nested **ite** expression ψ holding the value. We initialise ψ to a symbol $\delta(\sigma, \omega)$ representing the default value stored in the plane at the passed address $\sigma : \omega$. This initialisation of ψ covers the case when no value has been written to the passed address so far. Now we enumerate records in the *iteList* from the oldest one to the youngest one. For each enumerated record $(\sigma' : \omega', \nu')$ we check whether its address collides with $\sigma : \omega$. That is, we build the collision formula $\Gamma(\sigma', \omega', \sigma, \omega)$ as described in the write operation. If the formula is satisfiable, we update ψ to

$$\mathbf{ite}(\Gamma(\sigma', \omega', \sigma, \omega), \rho, \psi), \text{ where } \rho = \begin{cases} \nu' & \text{iff } \nu' \text{ is not a } \lambda\text{-function,} \\ f(\sigma, \omega) & \text{iff } \nu' \equiv \lambda\bar{\sigma}.\lambda\bar{\omega}.\, f(\bar{\sigma}, \bar{\omega}). \end{cases}$$

After processing all records in the *iteList*, we do the same with the records stored in the *boostMap* (processed in an arbitrary order) unless $\sigma : \omega$ is a constant address. If it is a constant address, we already know that it does not collide with any record in the *boostMap* as this was already checked at the beginning.

We illustrate the read operation using the example of Figure 2. We describe two read operations, from the array of integers allocated at line 3, performed during symbolic execution of the line 7. The content of the plane *Integers* after symbolic execution of the first 6 lines is already shown right before the description of the read operation. Execution of A[3] invokes the read operation in the plane *Integers* at the address $3:4\cdot3$. Since there is a record in the *boostMap* for the address, we directly return its value 777. Execution of A[4] invokes the read operation in the plane *Integers* at the address $3:4\cdot4$. Since there is no record in the *boostMap* for this address, we construct the resulting expression ψ from all records in the *iteList* as depicted in the following table:

collision test	collision formula	result	ψ
$-$	$-$	$-$	$\delta(3, 4\cdot4)$
$3:4\cdot4$ vs. $3:4\cdot4$	$3=3 \wedge 4\cdot4 = 4\cdot4$	SAT	888
$3:4(3\underline{i}+1)$ vs. $3:4\cdot4$	$3=3 \wedge 4(3\underline{i}+1) = 4\cdot4$	SAT	$\mathbf{ite}(\underline{i}=1, 999, 888)$

In the first row there we initialise ψ to the default value $\delta(3, 4 \cdot 4)$. In the following lines we perform collision checks before we update ψ. Note that we automatically applied trivial simplification of ψ. In particular, in the second row we simplified ψ from $\mathbf{ite}(3 = 3 \wedge 4 \cdot 4 = 4 \cdot 4, 888, \delta(3, 4 \cdot 3))$ to 888 and in the third row we simplified the condition $3 = 3 \wedge 4(3\underline{i} + 1) = 4 \cdot 4$ to $\underline{i} = 1$.

Allocation and Deallocation. We distinguish allocations of a single segment and multi-allocations. We maintain an *allocation counter* initialised to 1 and a *multi-allocation counter* initialised to -1.

An allocation of a single segment of a symbolic length ψ proceeds in the following three steps. Let γ be a value of the allocation counter before the allocation. In the first step we write the passed size ψ into *Sizes* memory plane at the address $\gamma : 0$. Next, the counter is updated to the value $\gamma + 1$. Finally, we return the address $\gamma : 0$ as the result of the allocation.

Let φ and ψ be symbolic expressions. A *multi-allocation* of φ segments of the common size ψ proceeds in three steps as well. Let γ be a value of the multi-allocation counter before the allocation. In the first step we write the size ψ into the plane *Sizes* at addresses $(\lambda\bar{\sigma}. \lambda\bar{\omega}. \gamma \geq \bar{\sigma} > \gamma - \varphi) : 0$. In the next step the multi-allocation counter is updated to the value $\gamma - \varphi$. Finally, we return the address $(\gamma - \varphi + 1) : 0$ as the result of the allocation. Note that the returned address points to the memory block with the lowest segment identifier.

Segment deallocation works exactly the same way for all memory blocks, regardless of types of their allocation. We simply write the number 0 into the memory plane *Sizes* at the passed address. Note that the offset of the passed address must always be the number 0, since all memory blocks are allocated at that offset. We can also perform a multi-deallocation by the corresponding multi-write into the *Sizes* memory plane. Note that deallocations do not change allocation and multi-allocation counters.

Test for Memory Initialisation. Given an address $\sigma : \omega$ and a memory plane, test for memory initialisation returns a formula ψ over input symbols, which is valid for the concrete inputs for which the memory location $\sigma : \omega$ in the given plane is initialised. Computation of ψ proceeds as follows. If the address $\sigma : \omega$ is constant and it belongs to the domain of *boostMap* of the plane, then $\psi \equiv true$.

In all other cases, we construct ψ in form of disjunction. We first initialise ψ to *false*. Then we enumerate records in the *iteList* in any order. For each enumerated record $(\sigma' : \omega', \nu')$ we build the collision formula $\Gamma(\sigma', \omega', \sigma, \omega)$ as described in the write operation and then we update ψ to $\psi \vee \Gamma(\sigma', \omega', \sigma, \omega)$. After processing all records in the *iteList*, we do the same with the records stored in the *boostMap* (also processed in an arbitrary order) unless $\sigma : \omega$ is a constant address. If it is a constant address, we already know that it does not collide with any record in the *boostMap* as this was already checked at the beginning.

The passed address $\sigma : \omega$ can contain λ-expressions and thus it can represent a set of addresses. In this case, the returned formula ψ describes the concrete inputs for which *all* the represented locations are initialised. Hence, ψ is constructed in a slightly different way for addresses with λ-expressions. If $\sigma : \omega$ has the form

$\lambda\bar{\sigma}.\,\lambda\bar{\omega}.\,\phi(\bar{\sigma},\bar{\omega}) : \omega$, then ψ is defined as $\forall\bar{\sigma}.\,\phi(\bar{\sigma},\omega) \to \psi'$, where ψ' is constructed by the algorithm described above for the address $\bar{\sigma} : \omega$ (instead for the original address $\sigma : \omega$). The construction of ψ for addresses with a λ-expression in the offset is similar.

Caching Satisfiability Queries. During read or write operations not resolved by *boostMaps* we intensively construct collision formulae. We use an SMT solver to decide their satisfiability. Unfortunately, resolving SMT queries is usually very time consuming. Fortunately, the constructed collision formulae are often repeated. We thus implemented a cache in front of an SMT solver to improve amortised complexity of symbolic memory operations.

Remark. Our implementation of symbolic memory can be further improved. For example, it currently never removes any record from an *iteList* even if one can easily construct an example where such a record becomes useless. We left the removal of useless records for future work for two reasons: it does not seem to be a bottleneck in our evaluation, and it can be expensive to decide whether a record in *iteList* is useless or not.

4   Use of the Memory in Symbolic Execution Tool

Our symbolic memory defines language- and platform-independent low-level memory layout with basic operations only. However, symbolic executors often need to handle some higher-level features of supported language. For example, symbolic executors of C programs have to handle composed data types, unions, `void*`, implementation of type casting expressions, etc. In this section, we suggest possible implementation of the mentioned high-level features using our low-level symbolic memory.

Composed Data Types. A symbolic execution tool may create a plane for each basic data type of its instruction language and composed data (even nested) are treated simply as (nested) tuples of basic data types. So, individual attributes of an instance of a composed type are spread into the corresponding planes of basic types. Moreover, the tool can also introduce special separate planes for selected composed types of an analysed program.

Unions. Union is a special composed data type, which can easily be represented such that its attributes reside in different planes but all at the same address.

void*. Like other pointers, void pointers can be stored in the predefined planes *Segments* and *Offsets*. We do not define types for addresses, i.e. we treat all pointers the same way. It is responsibility of the tool to know which (pointer) variable has which type.

Type Casting. This feature of a programming language allows a programer to reinterpret meaning of referenced data. If the language also supports pointers and pointer arithmetic, then any sequence of bytes (starting basically at any address) can be reinterpreted according to programmer's will. This flexibility complicates designing of a symbolic executor. Here we show that our memory model provides a ground for efficient implementation of symbolic memory even for such flexible languages.

Let us consider the following C statement: `float f = *(float*)p;`, where p is of `int*` type. Obviously, the correct execution of this statement requires that the memory plane *Floats* contains at the address p such floating point number whose memory representation is equal to the memory representation of the integer stored at the same address in the plane *Integers*. This means that the last write into the plane *Integers* at the address p must have been extended by the corresponding write to the memory plane *Floats*.

With our memory model, a symbolic execution tool can optimise performance of the memory by implementing a data-flow analysis which detects all those write statements in the program whose extension is indeed necessary. Without any such analysis, the tool would have to extend each write such that it is performed to memory planes of all basic data types.

Note that in case of type-safe programming languages execution of type casting instructions is optimal in our memory model since no writes have to be extended. Therefore, performance of our memory scales according to properties of programming languages used in symbolic executors.

5 Experimental Results

We have implemented the symbolic memory as a library SEGY of an open-source project called BUGST [14]. The library is used by a symbolic execution tool RUDLA, which is another part of the project BUGST. The tool performs both classic [9] and compact [11] symbolic execution. We run RUDLA on a collection of benchmarks from the category 'Loops' of SV–COMP 2013 [1], revision 229. We have chosen this category for two reasons. First, the benchmarks manipulate with arrays. Reading from and writing to array elements with input-dependent indexes lead to memory operations on non-constant addresses. Second, compact symbolic execution of program loops is the source of multi-write operations. The category contains 79 benchmarks, but only 70 of them can be translated into RUDLA's internal program representation by the current version of BUGST. We symbolically executed each of the 70 benchmarks, both by classic and compact symbolic executions. Classic symbolic execution does not use multi-writes and thus the performed memory operations are relatively simple, while compact symbolic execution uses multi-writes which insert λ-expressions to the memory and make subsequent memory operations harder.

All experiments were performed on a laptop Acer Aspire 5920G (Intel® Core™ 2 Duo 2GHz, 2GB RAM) running Windows 7 Professional 64-bit. We used Z3 SMT Solver 4.3.0 [16] for deciding satisfiability queries. We apply a five minutes

Table 1. Comparison of efficient and naive implementation of the memory model

settings		visited nodes
classic	naive implementation	417627
SE	efficient implementation	8083024
compact	naive implementation	219285
SE	efficient implementation	3547706

Table 2. Usage of *BoostMap* structures and *iteList* structures. Numbers in brackets are counts of multi-writes and they are included in the numbers of write operations.

operation		boostMap				iteList			
		count		time		count		time	
		#	%	[s]	%	#	%	[s]	%
classic	write	7014327	99.98	15.50	69.01	1288(0)	0.02	6.959	30.99
SE	read	6765528	99.74	75.35	57.03	17748	0.26	56.77	42.97
compact	write	6365255	99.96	15.48	52.44	2698(236)	0.04	14.04	47.56
SE	read	3793442	98.38	65.81	26.48	62606	1.62	182.7	73.52
summary		23938552	99.65	172.1	39.78	84340	0.35	260.5	60.22

timeout for execution of each benchmark. In all experiments, we present cumulative data for classic symbolic execution of the 70 benchmarks and for compact symbolic execution of the 70 benchmarks.

The first experiment compares overall efficiency of our implementation with a naive implementation of the segment-offset-plane model. The naive implementation (also available in BUGST library SEGY) represents the content of a plane by a simple list of records. The naive read operation produces a nested **ite** expression containing all records of the list and asks an SMT solver to simplify it. Table 1 presents cumulative numbers of symbolic execution tree nodes visited during classic and compact symbolic executions of the 70 benchmarks (each with the five minutes timeout) using either the naive or the efficient symbolic memory implementation. The results show that classic symbolic execution runs more than 19 times faster when using our efficient implementation of the symbolic memory compared to the naive implementation. The compact symbolic execution with the efficient symbolic memory runs more than 16 times faster. The numbers of tree nodes visited by classic and compact symbolic executions should not be compared as nodes in compact trees have a slightly different semantics than nodes in classic symbolic execution trees.

The following experimental data provide more information about performance of our efficient implementation. We focus on read and write operations since they are essential for the memory. Note that memory allocations and deallocations are also considered as they are writes into the plane *Sizes* actually.

Table 2 shows total counts of read and write operations resolved purely by *boostMap* structures and the operations accessing *iteList* structures. The table also provides the total time (in seconds) of these operations. We always present

Table 3. Efficiency of our cache in front of Z3 SMT solver

operation		cache hits				cache misses			
		count		time		count		time	
		#	%	[s]	%	#	%	[s]	%
classic	write	3791	83.28	0.360	5.55	761	16.72	6.131	94.45
SE	read	27031	85.04	3.385	7.69	4756	14.96	40.65	92.31
compact	write	2471	67.74	1.700	12.69	1177	32.26	11.70	87.31
SE	read	69231	83.80	25.59	16.96	13382	16.20	125.3	83.04
summary		102524	83.62	31.04	14.45	20076	16.38	183.78	85.55

absolute as well as relative numbers. One can see that overwhelming majority of the memory operations are resolved in *boostMaps*. The table also shows that accesses to *boostMaps* are much faster than those to *iteLists*. So we have an empirical evidence that implementation of memory planes by the two structures *boostMap* and *iteList* is indeed very important.

Although memory operations accessing *iteLists* are relatively slow, we actually achieved an impressive speed up by introducing a cache in front of an SMT solver called by memory operations (note that operations resolved by *boostMaps* do not produce SMT queries). Table 3 shows the counts of cache hits and cache misses. Again, we show also total time needed to solve the cached and non-cached SMT queries. We can see that more than 80% of all SMT queries led to cache hits and thus to very fast responses.

Finally, the results also show that the performance of our symbolic memory scales according to complexity of expressions passed to the memory: the ratio of operations resolved by *boostMaps* is higher for classic symbolic execution than for compact symbolic execution, and the same holds for cache hits of SMT queries.

6   Other Approaches to Symbolic Memory

As far as we know, our symbolic memory is the only one that supports fully symbolic addresses. Other recognized tools based on symbolic execution including EXE [4], KLEE [3], CUTE [10], SAGE [6], PEX [12], and SIMC [13] solve the variable-storage referencing problem in different ways. For example, KLEE and SAGE support symbolic offsets, but only concrete segments. If a pointer can point to n memory segments, KLEE clones symbolic execution n times and fix the segment part of the pointer to one of the segments in each clone. Concolic executors like SAGE often take advantage of the fact that they perform both concrete and symbolic execution along the same path. Hence, if a symbolic pointer can point to more segments, SAGE fix the segment part of the pointer to the value of this pointer in the corresponding concrete execution. Another approach is used in CUTE: it supports only pointers that are either NULL, or they point to a concrete address, or they directly correspond to some input symbol.

None of the mentioned tools support allocation of memory blocks of symbolic size or multi-writes.

Different approaches and abilities of our symbolic memory and symbolic memories of the above tools prevent their reasonable performance comparison. Indeed, other tools solve dereference of fully symbolic pointers outside symbolic memory. This allows them to use simpler structures and faster algorithms implementing symbolic memory, but for the price of more symbolic executions (due to cloning in KLEE) or loss of information (like in SAGE where a symbolic value is replaced by the corresponding value in a concrete execution).

7   Conclusion

We presented a symbolic memory supporting symbolic pointers, allocations of memory blocks of symbolic sizes, and multi-writes. The memory is based on storing conditional values. It uses the introduced segment-offset-plane memory model where addresses are *segment : offset* pairs. Data stored in the memory are distributed into memory planes according to their semantic information, e.g. data type. The model leads to a natural fragmentation of the memory, which makes memory operations faster. We also describe our implementation of the memory model that uses specific data structures and a cache for SMT queries to improve efficiency of the symbolic memory. Experimental results give us an empirical evidence that the implemented symbolic memory successfully tackles the variable storage-referencing problem.

References

1. Beyer, D.: Second competition on software verification. In: Piterman, N., Smolka, S.A. (eds.) TACAS 2013 (ETAPS 2013). LNCS, vol. 7795, pp. 594–609. Springer, Heidelberg (2013)
2. Boyer, R.S., Elspas, B., Levitt, K.N.: SELECT – A formal system for testing and debugging programs by symbolic execution. In: ICRS, pp. 234–245. ACM (1975)
3. Cadar, C., Dunbar, D., Engler, D.: KLEE: Unassisted and automatic generation of high-coverage tests for complex systems programs. In: OSDI, pp. 209–224. USENIX Association (2008)
4. Cadar, C., Ganesh, V., Pawlowski, P.M., Dill, D.L., Engler, D.R.: EXE: Automatically generating inputs of death. In: CCS, pp. 322–335. ACM (2006)
5. Deng, X., Lee, J.: Robby. Efficient and formal generalized symbolic execution. Autom. Softw. Eng. 19(3), 233–301 (2012)
6. Elkarablieh, B., Godefroid, P., Levin, M.Y.: Precise pointer reasoning for dynamic test generation. In: ISSTA, pp. 129–140. ACM (2009)
7. Howden, W.E.: Symbolic testing and the DISSECT symbolic evaluation system. IEEE Trans. Software Eng. 3, 266–278 (1977)
8. Khurshid, S., Păsăreanu, C.S., Visser, W.: Generalized symbolic execution for model checking and testing. In: Garavel, H., Hatcliff, J. (eds.) TACAS 2003. LNCS, vol. 2619, pp. 553–568. Springer, Heidelberg (2003)
9. King, J.C.: Symbolic execution and program testing. Commun. ACM 19(7), 385–394 (1976)
10. Sen, K., Marinov, D., Agha, G.: CUTE: A concolic unit testing engine for C. In: ESEC/FSE, pp. 263–272. ACM (2005)

11. Slaby, J., Strejček, J., Trtík, M.: Compact symbolic execution. In: Van Hung, D., Ogawa, M. (eds.) ATVA 2013. LNCS, vol. 8172, pp. 193–207. Springer, Heidelberg (2013)
12. Vanoverberghe, D., Tillmann, N., Piessens, F.: Test input generation for programs with pointers. In: Kowalewski, S., Philippou, A. (eds.) TACAS 2009. LNCS, vol. 5505, pp. 277–291. Springer, Heidelberg (2009)
13. Xu, Z., Zhang, J.: A test data generation tool for unit testing of C programs. In: QSIC, pp. 107–116. IEEE (2006)
14. Bugst, http://sourceforge.net/projects/bugst
15. Pex, http://research.microsoft.com/Pex
16. Z3, http://z3.codeplex.com

Trace Abstraction Refinement for Timed Automata

Weifeng Wang[1,2] and Li Jiao[1]

[1] State Key Laboratory of Computer Science, Institute of Software,
Chinese Academy of Sciences, Beijing 100190, China
{wangwf,ljiao}@ios.ac.cn
[2] University of Chinese Academy of Sciences, Beijing 100049, China

Abstract. Timed automata are a well known formalism for modeling real-time systems. Model checking of timed automata is important for ensuring that the systems satisfy certain properties. Safety is one of the most important properties for timed automata. In this paper we propose a method for the safety checking of timed automata, which is an adaptation of the general trace abstraction refinement framework to timed automata. The feature of our work is that we use zone-based LU-abstraction instead of interpolation techniques. This method performs zone computation only when necessary, and the abstraction on zones is coarser because only part of the control structure is considered when computing LU-bounds. We give an example to show when this method could perform more efficiently than the traditional zone-based search algorithm.

Keywords: Timed Automata, Trace Abstraction Refinement, Safety.

1 Introduction

Timed automata are a well-known model for real-time systems. Since it was proposed [1], many works have been focused on model checking of timed automata. Model checking of timed automata is non trivial due to the dense state space. This problem was initially solved by the construction of region graph [1], which results from partitioning the state space into a finite number of bisimulation equivalence classes. However, this method is impractical because it induces severe state explosion.

The zone-based method has been extensively investigated for symbolically represent the region graph. In zone-based timed automata model checking, difference bound inequalities are used to symbolically represent a convex set of regions [6]. Abstraction techniques are used to reduce the number of zones, and consequently improve performance. Efforts have been made to obtain coarser abstractions through inventing new abstraction techniques [4], or by static analysis [3] and dynamic analysis [14] of the timed automata model. The zone based method is used in tools such as UPPAAL [5] and KRONOS [24].

Traditional symbolic model checking techniques can also be used on region graphs. Both BDD structures [2,7,20] and SAT formulas [23,25] have been used

F. Cassez and J.-F. Raskin (Eds.): ATVA 2014, LNCS 8837, pp. 396–410, 2014.
© Springer International Publishing Switzerland 2014

to encode region graphs. Several works try to develop extensions of BDDs in order to represent dense valuation space fully symbolically. Examples of this kind of extensions include Clock Difference Diagrams (CDD) [18], Difference Decision Diagrams DDD [19], Clock Restriction Diagrams (CRD) [22], Constraint Matrix Diagrams (CMD) [10] and so on. The basic idea is to develop a data structure that combines clock difference constraints into BDD, making it efficient to perform zone operations. Some researchers use SMT-based method for timed automata model checking [17], which exploit the ability of SMT-solvers in handling linear inequations to directly encode the dense semantics of timed automata.

Abstraction refinement techniques [8,13] have been invented for software and hardware verification, and have received much attention in recent years. Abstraction refinement techniques start by model checking a simpler model which is a coarse abstraction of the original model. In each iteration, model checking is performed on a new abstract model which is obtained by refining the one in the previous iteration. Abstraction refinement techniques fight the state explosion by automatically extracting the information related to the correctness of the system, and abstracting away those that are not relevant. Various works have been devoted on adapting abstraction refinement techniques to the verification of timed automata [9,15,16,21].

Recently, the trace abstraction refinement scheme has been proposed for software model checking [11,12]. Trace abstraction refinement views the system to be verified as a finite automaton accepting sequences of statements as words, and performs the refinement by iteratively constructing finite automata (which the author call *interpolant automata*) to remove infeasible traces.

In this paper, we adapt the trace abstraction refinement method to the model checking of timed automata. We see the set of timed transitions in timed automata as the alphabet, and perform a zone-based automata construction in each iteration. While in the original trace abstraction refinement framework automata construction depends on SMT interpolation, in our work we use zone-based abstraction instead. This is because zones are very suitable and efficient for the analysis of timed automata.

Organization of the Paper. In Section 2 we will give the basic definitions related to timed automata, and recall the zone-based symbolic semantics and LU-extrapolation. Then in Section 3 we will introduce the trace abstraction refinement framework, and in Section 4, we show how to adapt it to timed automata verification. In Section 5 we present an example to show how our method behaves in comparison with zone based search algorithm. Last, in Section 6, we give the conclusion and possible future works.

2   Preliminaries

2.1   Timed Automata and the Safety Property

A set of *clock variables* X is a set of non-negative real-valued variables. A *clock constraint* is a conjunction of inequations of the form $x \sim c$, where $x \in X$, $c \in \mathbb{N}$, and $\sim \in \{<, \leq, >, \geq\}$. A *clock valuation* is a function $\nu : X \mapsto \mathbb{R}_{\geq 0}$, which assigns to each clock variable a nonnegative real value. We denote $\mathbf{0}$ the special clock valuation that assigns 0 to every clock variable. For a formula φ on X, we denote by $[\![\varphi]\!]$ the set of all clock valuations satisfying φ, i.e., $[\![\varphi]\!] = \{\nu | \nu \models \varphi\}$.

Definition 1 (Timed automata). *A* timed automaton *is a tuple* $\langle L, l_{init}, X, E \rangle$, *where L is the set of locations, l_{init} is the initial location, X is the set of clocks, and E is the set of transitions of the form $l \xrightarrow{a,g,r} l'$, where a is an action label, g is a clock constraint, which we call* guard, *and $r \subseteq X$ is the set of clocks to be reset.*

Definition 2 (Semantics of timed automata). *A* configuration *of a timed automaton $\mathcal{A} = \langle L, l_{init}, X, E \rangle$ is a pair (l, ν), where $l \in L$ is a location, and ν is a clock valuation. The initial configuration is $(l_{init}, \mathbf{0})$. There are two kinds of transitions*

- **Action.** *For each pair of states (l, ν) and (l', ν'), $(l, \nu) \xrightarrow{a,g,r} (l', \nu')$ iff there is a transition $l \xrightarrow{a,g,r} l' \in E$, and*
  - $\nu \models g$, *and*
  - $\nu'(x) = \nu(x)$ *for each $x \notin r$, and*
  - $\nu'(x) = 0$ *for each $x \in r$.*
- **Delay.** *For each pair of configurations (l, ν) and (l', ν'), and an arbitrary $\delta \in \mathbb{R}_{\geq 0}$, $(l, \nu) \xrightarrow{\delta} (l', \nu')$, iff $l = l'$ and $\nu'(x) = \nu(x) + \delta$ for each clock $x \in X$.*

A run *of a timed automaton is a (possibly infinite) sequence of configurations $\rho = (l_0, \nu_0)(l_1, \nu_1) \cdots$, where $(l_0, \nu_0) = (l_{init}, \mathbf{0})$, and for each $i \geq 0$, either $(l_i, \nu_i) \xrightarrow{a,g,r} (l_{i+1}, \nu_{i+1})$ or $(l_i, \nu_i) \xrightarrow{\delta} (l_{i+1}, \nu_{i+1})$ for some $\delta \in \mathbb{R}_{\geq 0}$.*

The definition of timed automata is usually extended to parallel composition of timed automata (networks of timed automata). The parallel composition of a set of timed automata is the product of these timed automata [6]. So the verification of networks of timed automata can be reduced to the verification of the product timed automaton.

In this paper we will consider the *safety* property. Basically, a timed automaton is safe iff the given *error location* can not be reached.

Definition 3 (Safety property). *A timed automaton $\mathcal{A}$ with an error location l_{err} is safe iff there does not exist a run $\rho = (l_0, \nu_0)(l_1, \nu_1) \cdots$, and an index i such that $l_i = l_{err}$.*

The reachability problem of timed automata, which asks whether a given configuration is reachable, can be easily reduced to the safety checking problem.

2.2 Zone Based Symbolic Semantics

The symbolic semantics of timed automata has been proposed to fight state explosion. Basically, the idea is to represent a set of clock valuations using difference constraints on the clock variables.

Zones are used in timed automata model checking to symbolically represent the sets of clock valuations. A *zone* is a set of difference inequalities over the set of clock variables. A zone represents all clock valuations satisfying its constraints.

For a zone D and a clock constraint g, we define $D \wedge g$ as $\{\nu | \nu \in D \wedge \nu \models g\}$, $D[r := 0]$ as $\{\nu | \exists \nu' \in D \cdot (\forall x \in r \cdot \nu(x) = 0 \wedge \forall x \notin r \cdot \nu(x) = \nu'(x))\}$, and $D \uparrow$ as $\{\nu | \exists \nu' \in D, \delta \in \mathbb{R}_{0+} \cdot \nu = \nu' + \delta\}$. Zones are closed under the above operations [6].

Definition 4 (Symbolic Semantics of Timed Automata). *The symbolic semantics of a timed automaton* $\mathcal{A} = \langle L, l_{init}, X, E \rangle$ *is a labeled transition system* $(S, \rightarrow, s_0)$, *and each state* $s \in S$ *is a pair* (l, D), *where* l *is a location, and* D *is a zone. The initial state is* $s_0 = (l_{init}, [\![0 \leq x_1 = x_2 = \cdots = x_n]\!])$. *For each pair of states* $s = (l, D)$ *and* $s' = (l', D')$, $s \xrightarrow{a,g,r} s'$ *iff there exists a transition* $l \xrightarrow{a,g,r} l' \in E$ *such that* $D' = (D \wedge g)[r := 0] \uparrow$. *A symbolic run is a sequence* $(l_0, D_0)(l_1, D_1) \cdots$, *where* $(l_0, D_0) = (l_{init}, [\![0 \leq x_1 = x_2 = \cdots = x_n]\!])$, *and for each* $i \geq 0$, $(l_i, D_i) \xrightarrow{a,g,r} (l_{i+1}, D_{i+1})$ *for some* $l_i \xrightarrow{a,g,r} l_{i+1} \in E$.

The safety property can be expressed in terms of symbolic semantics. The given timed automaton is safe iff there is no symbolic run reaching the error location and a non-empty zone.

Zones can be represented as Difference Bound Matrices (DBMs), and efficient algorithms for manipulating DBMs have already been proposed [6]. The DBM representation of a zone on the clock set X is a $(|X|+1) \times (|X|+1)$ matrix, each element of which is a tuple $(\prec, c)$, where $\prec \in \{<, \leq\}$ and $c \in \mathbb{N}$. In the DBM, $D_{0i} = (\prec, c)$ means $0 - x_i \prec c$, i.e., $x_i \succ -c$, $D_{i0} = (\prec, c)$ means $x_i - 0 \prec c$, i.e., $x_i \prec c$. For $i, j \neq 0$, $D_{ij} = (\prec, c)$ represents the constraint $x_i - x_j \prec c$. Two different DBMs might correspond to the same zone. In order to tackle this problem, *canonical forms* of DBMs can be computed by the Floyd-Warshall algorithm [6].

2.3   LU-Extrapolation

Abstraction techniques are used to reduce the symbolic state space, while still preserving the properties that we care about. Among the various Max-bound and LU-bounds based abstraction techniques, we choose to use the LU-extrapolation technique $Extra_{LU}^+$ [4], which is the coarsest among the existing convex-preserving extrapolations. The LU-extrapolation of a zone is still a zone, which makes it suitable to use in timed automata model checking.

An LU-bound is a pair of functions LU, where $L : X \to \mathbb{N} \cup \{-\infty\}$ is called a lower bound function and $U : X \to \mathbb{N} \cup \{-\infty\}$ an upper bound function. $L(x)$ (respectively, $U(x)$) is the maximum constant c that appeared in the guards of the timed automaton of the form $x > c$ or $x \geq c$ (respectively, $x < c$ or $x \leq c$).

Definition 5 (LU-preorder [4]). *For two clock valuations* ν *and* ν', *and an LU-bound LU, we say that* $\nu' \preceq_{LU} \nu$ *iff the following conditions are satisfied*

- If $\nu'(x) < \nu(x)$, then $\nu'(x) > L(x)$, and
- if $\nu'(x) > \nu(x)$, then $\nu(x) > U(x)$.

It has been proved in [4] that the relation $\{((l,\nu),(l,\nu'))|\nu' \preceq_{LU} \nu\}$ is a simulation relation. Intuitively, for a zone D, and an LU-bound LU, an abstraction operator based on LU-preorder can be defined: $\mathfrak{a}_{\preceq_{LU}}(D) \equiv \{\nu|\exists\nu' \in D \cdot \nu \preceq_{LU} \nu'\}$. Unfortunately, $\mathfrak{a}_{\preceq_{LU}}$ is not convex-preserving, i.e., the $\mathfrak{a}_{\preceq_{LU}}(D)$ for an arbitrary zone D is not necessarily a zone. However, some slightly finer abstractions based on LU-preorder that are convex-preserving exist, among which is $Extra_{LU}^+$.

Definition 6 (LU-extrapolation [4]). *Let D be a zone whose canonical DBM is $\langle c_{i,j}, \prec_{i,j}\rangle_{i,j=0,1,\ldots,|X|}$. Given an LU-bound LU , the LU-extrapolation $Extra_{LU}^+(D)$ of D is a zone D' which can be represented by a DBM $\langle c'_{i,j}, \prec'_{i,j}\rangle_{i,j=0,1,\ldots,|X|}$, where*

$$\langle c'_{i,j}, \prec'_{i,j}\rangle = \begin{cases} \infty & if\ c_{i,j} > L(x_i) \\ \infty & if\ -c_{0,i} > L(x_i) \\ \infty & if\ -c_{0,j} > U(x_j), i \neq 0 \\ (-U(x_j), <) & if\ -c_{0,j} > U(x_j), i = 0 \\ (c_{i,j}, \prec_{i,j}) & otherwise \end{cases}$$

The following properties hold for LU-extrapolation. These properties are important for the LU-bound computation in Section 4.

Since the LU-extrapolation can only relax constraints, the original zone must be included in the resulting zone. Thus we have:

Property 1. For each zone D, and the LU-bound LU: $D \subseteq Extra_{LU}^+(D)$.

The second property comes from [4]. It clarifies the relation between LU-extrapolation and LU-preorder:

Property 2. For each zone D, and the LU-bound LU: $Extra_{LU}^+(D) \subseteq \mathfrak{a}_{\preceq_{LU}}(D)$.

3 Trace Abstraction Refinement Framework

Trace abstraction refinement was originally proposed in [11] for software model checking. In this section, we will introduce the trace abstraction refinement framework in terms of timed automata.

3.1 Timed Automata as Finite Automata

We could view a timed automaton as a finite automaton by ignoring the semantics of guards and resets in the transitions. Formally, the finite automaton view of a timed automaton can be described as follows:

Given a timed automaton $\mathcal{A} = \langle L, l_{init}, X, E\rangle$ and the error location $l_{err} \in L$, we define a finite automaton $\mathcal{F_A} = \langle \Sigma, Q, \delta, \{q_{init}\}, \{q_{fin}\}\rangle$ over the alphabet $\{\langle a, g, r\rangle|\exists l, l' \in L \cdot l \xrightarrow{a,g,r} l' \in E\}$ as follows:

- $\Sigma = \{\langle a, g, r\rangle | \exists l, l' \in L \cdot l \xrightarrow{a,g,r} l' \in E\}$
- $Q = L$, i.e., the set of states of $\mathcal{F}_A$ is exactly the set of locations of $\mathcal{A}$.
- $q_{init} = l_{init}$, the initial state is the initial location.
- $q_{fin} = l_{err}$, the accepting state is the error location.
- $\delta = \{q \xrightarrow{\langle a,g,r\rangle} q' | \exists l \xrightarrow{a,g,r} l' \in E \cdot q = l \wedge q' = l'\}$.

We use $\Sigma(\mathcal{F})$ to denote the alphabet of the finite automaton $\mathcal{F}$. For a label $t = \langle a, g, r\rangle \in \Sigma(\mathcal{F})$, we use $t.a, t.g, t.r$ respectively to denote the three components of t.

Example 1. For the timed automaton $\mathcal{A}_1$ shown in Figure 1 with the error location $L2$, the alphabet of the corresponding finite automaton is $\{\langle a, true, \{x\}\rangle,$ $\langle b, y > 2 \wedge x \leq 2, \{\}\rangle, \langle c, true, \{x\}\rangle, \langle d, true, \{y\}\rangle, \langle e, x > 3 \wedge y \leq 3, \{\}\rangle\}$. If we use a, b, c, d, e as the abbreviations of the above five elements of the alphabet, the language that the finite automaton recognizes can be expressed by the regular expression $(a|((b|c)d))^*(b|c)e$. One of the words in the language is:

$$\langle a, true, \{x\}\rangle\langle b, y > 2 \wedge x \leq 2, \{\}\rangle\langle e, x > 3 \wedge y \leq 3, \{\}\rangle$$

which induces the sequence of states $L0, L0, L1, L2$ in the finite automaton.

Notice that, although this path is recognized by the finite automaton, it is not possible to execute along this path for the corresponding timed automaton.

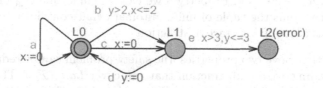

Fig. 1. The timed automaton $\mathcal{A}_1$

A word of $\mathcal{F}_A$ might induce an unsafe symbolic run $(l_0, D_0), (l_1, D_1), \ldots, (l_n(= l_{err}), D_n)$ in the symbolic semantics of $\mathcal{A}$, or it might be *infeasible*. Let's denote by $Lang(\mathcal{F}_A)$ the language of $\mathcal{F}_A$. $Lang(\mathcal{F}_A)$ is an over-approximation of the set of unsafe paths of $\mathcal{A}$. Thus proving that $\mathcal{A}$ is safe is just equal to proving that all words in $Lang(\mathcal{F}_A)$ are infeasible. So we get the following property:

Property 3. A timed automaton $\mathcal{A}$ is safe iff every sequence $\pi \in Lang(\mathcal{F}_A)$ is infeasible.

Consequently, we could check the safety property of $\mathcal{A}$ by checking that all traces in $Lang(\mathcal{F}_A)$ are infeasible.

3.2   Trace Abstraction Refinement

In this subsection we will introduce the concept of trace abstraction, followed by a brief description of the trace abstraction refinement procedure proposed in [11]. We describe them based on the timed automata model.

In order to check that all traces in $Lang(\mathcal{F}_A)$ are infeasible, we can build a trace abstraction that abstracts the set of traces in $Lang(\mathcal{F}_A)$. A *trace abstraction* is a tuple of finite automata $(\mathcal{F}_1, \mathcal{F}_2, \ldots, \mathcal{F}_n)$, each of which having the same alphabet as $\mathcal{F}_A$, and accepting a subset of infeasible traces. For an arbitrary finite automaton $\mathcal{F}$, let $\overline{\mathcal{F}}$ be its complement. $Lang(\mathcal{F}_A) \cap Lang(\overline{\mathcal{F}_1}) \cap \cdots \cap Lang(\overline{\mathcal{F}_n})$ is an over-approximation of the set of unsafe traces of A. Moreover, this over-approximation is refined incrementally as new finite automata are added to the tuple. If the trace abstraction satisfies the condition $Lang(\mathcal{F}_A) \subseteq Lang(\mathcal{F}_1 \cup \mathcal{F}_2 \cup \cdots \cup \mathcal{F}_n)$, we can conclude that all traces in $Lang(\mathcal{F}_A)$ are infeasible, and consequently A is safe. Formally:

Property 4. If there exists a trace abstraction $(\mathcal{F}_1, \mathcal{F}_2, \ldots, \mathcal{F}_n)$ such that $Lang(\mathcal{F}_A) \subseteq Lang(\mathcal{F}_1 \cup \mathcal{F}_2 \cup \cdots \cup \mathcal{F}_n)$, then A is safe.

In fact, if A is safe, then there is always a trace abstraction satisfying the above condition.

Theorem 1. *If A is safe, then there exists a trace abstraction $(\mathcal{F}_1, \mathcal{F}_2, \ldots, \mathcal{F}_n)$ such that $Lang(\mathcal{F}_A) \subseteq Lang(\mathcal{F}_1 \cup \mathcal{F}_2 \cup \cdots \cup \mathcal{F}_n)$.*

Proof. When A is safe, from Property 3 we can conclude that $\mathcal{F}_A$ only accepts infeasible traces, thus the tuple of finite automata that contains only one component $(\mathcal{F}_A)$ is a qualifying trace abstraction.   □

According to the above two properties, the safety problem can be reduced to the problem of finding a trace abstraction that can cover $Lang(\mathcal{F}_A)$. This task can be done incrementally, following a counterexample guided abstraction refinement (CEGAR) [8] paradigm. Initially $\mathcal{F}_A$ is constructed as the over-approximation of A. In the ith iteration a word $\pi \in Lang(\mathcal{F}_A) \cap Lang(\overline{\mathcal{F}_1}) \cap \cdots \cap Lang(\overline{\mathcal{F}_{i-1}})$ is found and checked whether it is feasible according to the semantics of A. If π is feasible, then a real counterexample is found, and the timed automaton A is unsafe, otherwise a finite automaton $\mathcal{F}_i$ such that $\pi \in Lang(\mathcal{F}_i)$ and for all $\pi' \in Lang(\mathcal{F}_i)$, π' is infeasible, is constructed and added to the trace abstraction. The iteration continues until we find a real counterexample, which means the system is unsafe, or $Lang(\mathcal{F}_A) \cap Lang(\overline{\mathcal{F}_1}) \cap \cdots \cap Lang(\overline{\mathcal{F}_{i-1}}) = \emptyset$, which means there is no feasible counterexample, and the system is safe. In the latter case, we can conclude that $Lang(A) \subseteq Lang(\mathcal{F}_1 \cup \cdots \cup \mathcal{F}_{i-1})$, so that $(\mathcal{F}_1, \mathcal{F}_2, \ldots, \mathcal{F}_{i-1})$ is the final trace abstraction. This procedure is called trace abstraction refinement because in each iteration a finite automaton is added to the trace abstraction to refine it. The overall procedure is illustrated in Figure 2.

In the procedure shown in Figure 2, there are three modules that need to be implemented: the language emptiness checking, the path-infeasibility checking, and the construction of finite automata. The first task can be accomplished using

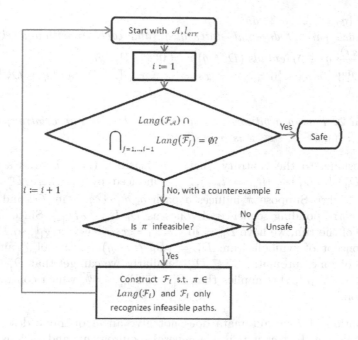

Fig. 2. Trace abstraction refinement framework

existing algorithms on finite automata, and the second task can be performed using existing algorithms in timed automata verification. What remains to be explained is the construction of the finite automata that recognize the given infeasible paths, which we will address in the next section.

4 Zone Automata Construction

In this section we describe how to construct the finite automaton according to the infeasible path in each iteration. In the original literature [11], an interpolant automaton was constructed based on a sequence of interpolants. In this paper, we propose to use zones instead of interpolants to construct the finite automata.

4.1 Zone Automata

We use a sequence of zones to construct the finite automaton that recognizes a set of infeasible traces, thus we call it a *zone automaton*, which corresponds to *interpolant automata* in [11].

Definition 7 (Zone automata). *Given a sequence of zones $D_0, D_1, \ldots, D_n$, where $[\![0 <= x_1 = x_2 = \cdots = x_{|X|}]\!] \subseteq D_0$ and $D_n = \emptyset$, a zone automaton $\mathcal{F}_I = (Q_I, \delta_I, Q_I^{init}, Q_I^{fin})$ is a finite automaton, where*

- $Q_I = \{q_0, q_1, \ldots, q_n\}$, and
- For each pair of different states q_i, q_j and each transition label (a, g, r),
  $q_i \xrightarrow{(a,g,r)} q_j \in \delta_I$ entails $(D_i \wedge g)[r := 0] \uparrow \subseteq D_j$, and
- $q_i \in Q_I^{init}$ implies $[\![0 <= x_1 = x_2 = \cdots = x_{|X|}]\!] \subseteq D_i$, and $q_i \in Q_I^{fin}$ implies $D_i = \emptyset$.

Theorem 2. *For an arbitrary zone automaton $\mathcal{F}_Z$, and an arbitrary word $\pi \in Lang(\mathcal{F}_Z)$: $(l_0, \mathbf{0}) \overset{\pi}{\nrightarrow}$, i.e., π is infeasible.*

Proof. Assume, to the contrary, that π is feasible, then there is a symbolic run $(l_0^\pi, D_0^\pi)(l_1^\pi, D_1^\pi) \cdots (l_{|\pi|}^\pi (= l_{err}), D_{|\pi|}^\pi)$ induced by π, where $D_j^\pi \neq \emptyset$ for $j = 0, 1, \ldots, |\pi|$. Suppose π induces a path $q_{i_0} q_{i_1} \cdots q_{i_{|\pi|}}$ in $\mathcal{F}_I$, and let's denote the corresponding sequence of zones as $D_{i_0} D_{i_1} \cdots D_{i_{|\pi|}}$. Since D_0^π is the first zone of the run, we have $D_0^\pi = [\![0 <= x_1 = x_2 = \cdots = x_{|X|}]\!]$, so $D_0^\pi \subseteq D_{i_0}$, by the concept of symbolic run, $D_1^\pi = (D_0^\pi \wedge \pi_1.g)[\pi_1.r := 0] \uparrow$, and by the definition of zone automata, $D_1^\pi \subseteq D_{i_1}$. Similarly, we can get that $D_j^\pi \subseteq D_{i_j}$ for all $j = 0, 1, \ldots, |\pi|$, this implies that $D_{|\pi|}^\pi \subseteq D_{i_{|\pi|}} = \emptyset$, which contradicts the assumption. $\qquad \square$

The definition of zone automata does not give an algorithmic description to the construction. In fact it is just a general requirement, and various different schemes exist. In the following subsection, we will show, given a spurious counterexample trace, how to construct a zone automaton that recognizes this trace (and possibly other infeasible traces).

4.2 Inductive Sequence of Zones

In this subsection, we will describe how an inductive sequence of zones is constructed from an infeasible path. Basically, it is built by performing abstractions to the sequence of zones that the infeasible trace induces in the timed automaton. Formally, a word $\pi \in Lang(\mathcal{F}_A)$ is *infeasible*, iff for the corresponding symbolic run $(l_0^\pi, D_0^\pi), \ldots, (l_{|\pi|}^\pi, D_{|\pi|}^\pi)$, we have $D_{|\pi|}^\pi = \emptyset$.

In order to generate a zone automaton that accepts π, we define the *inductive sequence of zones*.

Definition 8 (Inductive sequence of zones). *Given an infeasible path π, an inductive sequence of zones is a sequence $D_0, D_1, \ldots, D_{|\pi|}$ of zones satisfying:*

- $[\![0 \leq x_1 = x_2 = \cdots = x_{|X|}]\!] \subseteq D_0$,
- $D_{|\pi|} = \emptyset$,
- $((D_{i-1} \wedge \pi_i.g)[\pi_i.r := 0]) \uparrow \subseteq D_i$, for $i = 1, 2, \ldots, |\pi|$.

For each trace $\pi \in Lang(\mathcal{F}_A)$, we can calculate the corresponding zones induced by the path according to the symbolic semantics of timed automata.

Although this sequence of zones is a qualified candidate of inductive sequence of zones for π, it contains redundant information. If we can "grasp" the "real reason" why the path is infeasible, reducing away unrelated information, it would be possible to construct a zone automaton that recognizes more paths that share the same reason of infeasibility. This is achieved by abstraction on zones.

For a guard g and a clock x, we denote $L_g(x)$ the largest constant c such that $x > c$ or $x \geq c$ appeared in g. If there is no such constant, then $L_g(x) = -\infty$. Similarly, we denote $U_g(x)$ the largest constant c such that $x < c$ or $x \leq c$ appeared in g. For two LU-bounds LU and $L'U'$, and a clock variable x, we define the max operator $L''U''(x) = \max\{LU(x), L'U'(x)\}$ as $L''(x) = \max\{L(x), L'(x)\}$, and $U''(x) = \max\{U(x), U'(x)\}$.

For an infeasible path π, we compute the corresponding sequence of LU-bounds $(L_0U_0, L_1U_1, \ldots, L_{|\pi|}U_{|\pi|})$ as follows:

- $L_{|\pi|}(x) = U_{|\pi|}(x) = -\infty$
- For $i = 0, 1, \ldots, |\pi| - 1$,

$$L_iU_i(x) = \begin{cases} L_{\pi_{i+1}.g}U_{\pi_{i+1}.g}(x) & \text{if } x \in \pi_{i+1}.r \\ \max\{L_{i+1}U_{i+1}(x), L_{\pi_{i+1}.g}U_{\pi_{i+1}.g}(x)\} & \text{otherwise} \end{cases}$$

This computation procedure is in fact a static guard analysis procedure [3]. Using these LU-bounds, the inductive sequence of zones $D_0, D_1, \ldots, D_{|\pi|}$ can be computed as follows:

- $D_0 = Extra^+_{L_0U_0}(\llbracket 0 \leq x_1 = x_2 = \cdots = x_{|X|} \rrbracket)$, and
- $D_i = Extra^+_{L_iU_i}(((D_{i-1} \wedge \pi_i.g)[\pi_i.r := 0]) \uparrow)$ for $i = 1, 2, \ldots, |\pi|$.

In order to prove that this sequence of zones is indeed an inductive sequence of zones for π, it suffices to prove that $D_{|\pi|} = \emptyset$, since the other two conditions can be easily observed.

Property 5. For the sequence of zones $D_0, D_1, \ldots, D_{|\pi|}$ computed as described above: $D_{|\pi|} = \emptyset$.

Proof. Suppose the sequence of zones in the symbolic run of π is $D_0^\pi, D_1^\pi, \ldots, D_{|\pi|}^\pi$. We can prove that, for each $i = 0, 1, \ldots, |\pi| - 1$, if $D_i \subseteq \mathfrak{a}_{\preceq_{L_iU_i}}(D_i^\pi)$, then $D_{i+1} \subseteq \mathfrak{a}_{\preceq_{L_{i+1}U_{i+1}}}(D_{i+1}^\pi)$.

For any valuation $\nu \in D_{i+1}$, there is a valuation $\nu' \in (D_i \wedge \pi_{i+1}.g)[\pi_{i+1}.r := 0] \uparrow$ such that $\nu \preceq_{L_{i+1}U_{i+1}} \nu'$, and consequently there is a valuation $\nu'_1 \in D_i$ such that $\nu'_1 \models \pi_{i+1}.g$ and $\nu'_1[\pi_{i+1}.r := 0] + \delta = \nu'$. Since $D_i \subseteq \mathfrak{a}_{\preceq_{L_iU_i}}(D_i^\pi)$, there is a valuation $\nu''_1 \in D_i^\pi$ such that $\nu'_1 \preceq_{L_iU_i} \nu''_1$. From the definition of LU-preorder and the computation of LU-bounds we know that $\nu''_1 \models \pi_{i+1}.g$. It can be easily proved that $\nu'_1[\pi_{i+1}.r := 0] + \delta \preceq_{L_{i+1}U_{i+1}} \nu''_1[\pi_{i+1}.r := 0] + \delta$, which implies that $\nu \preceq_{L_{i+1}U_{i+1}} \nu''_1[\pi_{i+1}.r := 0] + \delta$. By the definition of symbolic semantics, $\nu''_1[\pi_{i+1}.r := 0] + \delta \in D_{i+1}^\pi$, so $\nu \in \mathfrak{a}_{\preceq_{L_{i+1}U_{i+1}}}(D_{i+1}^\pi)$. Since ν is taken arbitrarily from D_{i+1}, we can conclude that $D_{i+1} \subseteq \mathfrak{a}_{\preceq_{L_{i+1}U_{i+1}}}(D_{i+1}^\pi)$.

From the symbolic semantics of timed automata we know that $D_0^\pi = \llbracket 0 \leq x_1 = x_2 = \cdots = x_{|X|} \rrbracket$, so $D_0 = Extra^+_{L_0U_0}(D_0^\pi) \subseteq \mathfrak{a}_{L_0U_0}(D_0^\pi)$, from which $D_1 \subseteq \mathfrak{a}_{L_1U_1}(D_1^\pi), \ldots, D_{|\pi|} \subseteq \mathfrak{a}_{L_{|\pi|}U_{|\pi|}}(D_{|\pi|}^\pi)$ can be obtained. Since $D_{|\pi|}^\pi = \emptyset$, we have $\mathfrak{a}_{L_{|\pi|}U_{|\pi|}}(D_{|\pi|}^\pi) = \emptyset$, and consequently $D_{|\pi|} = \emptyset$. □

Example 2. For the sequence of zones in Example 1, the corresponding sequence of LU-bounds is given in Table 1. Consequently, we get the sequence of abstract zones:

$$[\![y \geq 0]\!], \ [\![0 \leq x \leq y]\!], \ [\![x < y \wedge y > 2]\!], \ \emptyset.$$

Table 1. LU-bounds for the sequence of zones in Example 1

Location	$L(x)$	$U(x)$	$L(y)$	$U(y)$
L_0	$-\infty$	$-\infty$	2	3
L_1	3	2	2	3
L_2	3	$-\infty$	$-\infty$	3
L_3	$-\infty$	$-\infty$	$-\infty$	$-\infty$

4.3 Canonical Zone Automata

Based on the infeasible path and the corresponding inductive sequence of zones that can be constructed following the previous subsection, we can now give a candidate scheme that constructs a zone automaton, which recognizes the infeasible path.

Definition 9 (Canonical zone automata). *Given an infeasible path π and the corresponding inductive sequence of zones $D_0, D_1, \ldots, D_{|\pi|}$, a canonical zone automaton is a zone automaton $\mathcal{F}_Z = (Q_Z, \delta_Z, Q_Z^{init}, Q_Z^{fin})$, where:*

- $Q_Z = \{q_0, q_1, \ldots, q_{|\pi|}\}$, *and*
- $\delta_Z = \{q_i \xrightarrow{\pi_j} q_{j+1} | i, j = 0, \ldots, |\pi| - 1, (D_i \wedge \pi_j.g)[\pi_j.r := 0] \uparrow \subseteq D_{j+1}\} \cup$
  $\{q_{|\pi|} \xrightarrow{\langle a, g, r \rangle} q_{|\pi|} | \langle a, g, r \rangle \in \Sigma(\mathcal{F}_A)\}$, *and*
- $Q_Z^{init} = \{q_0\}$, $Q_Z^{fin} = \{q_{|\pi|}\}$.

From the construction described above we can see that the resulting finite automaton recognizes the trace π. Moreover, it recognizes all infeasible paths that contain π as a prefix.

Example 3. Following Example 2, now we have the infeasible trace π:

$$\langle a, true, \{x\} \rangle \langle b, y > 2 \wedge x \leq 2, \{\} \rangle \langle e, x > 3 \wedge y \leq 3, \{\} \rangle$$

and the corresponding inductive sequence of zones

$$[\![y \geq 0]\!], \ [\![0 \leq x \leq y]\!], \ [\![0 \leq x < y \wedge y > 2]\!], \ \emptyset.$$

Using the candidate construction scheme, we can construct a zone automaton as shown in Figure 3, in which a, b, c, d, e are abbreviations for $\langle a, true, \{x\} \rangle, \langle b, y > 2 \wedge x \leq 2, \{\} \rangle, \langle c, true, \{x\} \rangle, \langle d, true, \{y\} \rangle, \langle e, x > 3 \wedge y \leq 3, \{\} \rangle$, respectively. We can see that this finite automaton recognizes the trace π and many other infeasible traces – in fact all traces with a prefix of the form aa^*be in $\mathcal{F}_A$ are recognized by this automaton.

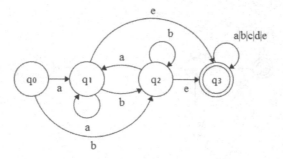

Fig. 3. The zone automaton for Example 3

Theorem 3. *For each timed automaton safety problem, the trace abstraction refinement procedure with the canonical zone automata construction scheme will terminate.*

Proof. From the construction we know that, if $D_i = D_j$ for $i, j \in \{0, 1, \ldots, |\pi| - 1\}$, then q_i and q_j are bisimulation equivalent. Consequently, if there are N different zones in a canonical construction, the resulting finite automaton would be bisimulation equivalent to a finite automaton with no more than $N+1$ states. By the properties of $Extra^+_{LU}$, there exists a number B such that the number of different zones in each canonical construction is no more than B. This entails that for each finite automaton $\mathcal{F}_Z$ obtained by the canonical construction, there is a finite automaton $\mathcal{F}'_Z$ with no more than $B+1$ states, such that $Lang(\mathcal{F}_Z) = Lang(\mathcal{F}'_Z)$. Since the alphabet $\Sigma(\mathcal{F}_A)$ is finite and our construction ensures that $\Sigma(\mathcal{F}_Z) = \Sigma(\mathcal{F}_A)$, the number of finite automata with this alphabet and no more than $B + 1$ states is finite.

Assume the trace abstraction refinement procedure does not terminate, then an infinite number of finite automata $\mathcal{F}_1, \mathcal{F}_2, \ldots$ are constructed for counterexample traces $\pi^1, \pi^2, \ldots$, there must be two finite automata $\mathcal{F}_i$ and $\mathcal{F}_j$ with $i < j$ and a finite automaton $\mathcal{F}'$ with no more than $B + 1$ states, such that $Lang(\mathcal{F}_i) = Lang(\mathcal{F}') = Lang(\mathcal{F}_j)$, and thus $\pi^j \in Lang(\mathcal{F}_i)$. However, by the trace abstraction refinement procedure π^j will never be found as a counterexample, which leads to a contradiction.   □

5   An Example

Now let's consider the timed automaton shown in Figure 4, with $L3$ as the error location. We can easily see that this timed automaton is safe. If we adopt the traditional zone based search algorithm with static guard analysis, the following zones will be explored on the location $L1$:

$$[\![0 \le z \le x = y]\!],$$
$$[\![x - y = 1 \wedge y \ge 0 \wedge z \ge 0 \wedge z \le x]\!],$$
$$[\![x - y = 2 \wedge y \ge 0 \wedge z \ge 0 \wedge z \le x]\!],$$

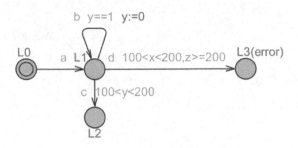

Fig. 4. A timed automaton

$$\cdots,$$
$$[\![x - y = 100 \wedge y \geq 0 \wedge z \geq 0 \wedge z \leq x]\!],$$
$$[\![x - y \geq 101 \wedge y \geq 0 \wedge z \geq 0 \wedge z \leq x]\!].$$

We can see that in this example the number of states explored highly depends on the constants in the guards, which might be very large. However, if we use the method proposed in this paper, only exploring the path

$$\langle a, true, \{\}\rangle\langle b, y = 1, \{y\}\rangle\langle d, 100 < x < 200 \wedge z \geq 200, \{\}\rangle$$

would be enough to remove all error traces and arrive to the result that the timed automaton is safe. The inductive sequence of zones is

$$[\![0 \leq z \leq x = y]\!], [\![0 \leq z \leq x = y]\!], [\![0 \leq z \leq x \wedge y \geq 0]\!], \emptyset$$

The canonical zone automaton corresponding to this trace is shown in Figure 5.

In this example, the efficiency of our method comes from the fact that the algorithm only focuses on those parts of the timed automaton related to the properties we want to check. When constructing zone automata, LU bounds are obtained from the part of control structure that is related with the counterexample trace, which leads to smaller bounds, and consequently coarser abstraction.

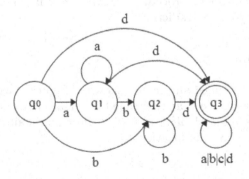

Fig. 5. The zone automaton for the path *abd*

6 Conclusion

In this paper we proposed a method to adapt trace abstraction refinement to the safety checking of timed automata. In some cases, this method might have better performance due to delayed computation of zones, and potential reuse of infeasibility proofs.

In the future, we will implement our method and perform experiments to investigate its efficiency. Moreover, we may consider the possibility of extending our method to verify more expressive properties such as Metric Interval Temporal Logic. For the zone automata construction procedure, we could explore the use of other zone based abstraction techniques. Furthermore, in some cases the timing information is not the only source of state explosion: for networks of timed automata, the state explosion might also come from the composition of control structures. It would be interesting if we tackle the state explosion caused by parallel composition of timed automata in addition.

Acknowledgement. We thank the anonymous reviewers for their helpful comments.

References

1. Alur, R., Dill, D.L.: Automata for modeling real-time systems. In: Paterson, M. (ed.) ICALP 1990. LNCS, vol. 443, pp. 322–335. Springer, Heidelberg (1990)
2. Asarin, E., Bozga, M., Kerbrat, A., Maler, O., Pnueli, A., Rasse, A.: Data-structures for the verification of timed automata. In: Maler, O. (ed.) HART 1997. LNCS, vol. 1201, pp. 346–360. Springer, Heidelberg (1997)
3. Behrmann, G., Bouyer, P., Fleury, E., Larsen, K.G.: Static guard analysis in timed automata verification. In: Garavel, H., Hatcliff, J. (eds.) TACAS 2003. LNCS, vol. 2619, pp. 254–270. Springer, Heidelberg (2003)
4. Behrmann, G., Bouyer, P., Larsen, K.G., Pelánek, R.: Lower and upper bounds in zone based abstractions of timed automata. In: Jensen, K., Podelski, A. (eds.) TACAS 2004. LNCS, vol. 2988, pp. 312–326. Springer, Heidelberg (2004)
5. Bengtsson, J., Larsen, K.G., Larsson, F., Pettersson, P., Yi, W.: Uppaal - a tool suite for automatic verification of real-time systems. In: Alur, R., Sontag, E.D., Henzinger, T.A. (eds.) HS 1995. LNCS, vol. 1066, pp. 232–243. Springer, Heidelberg (1996)
6. Bengtsson, J., Yi, W.: Timed automata: Semantics, algorithms and tools. In: Desel, J., Reisig, W., Rozenberg, G. (eds.) Lectures on Concurrency and Petri Nets. LNCS, vol. 3098, pp. 87–124. Springer, Heidelberg (2004)
7. Beyer, D.: Improvements in bdd-based reachability analysis of timed automata. In: Oliveira, J.N., Zave, P. (eds.) FME 2001. LNCS, vol. 2021, pp. 318–343. Springer, Heidelberg (2001)
8. Clarke, E.M., Grumberg, O., Jha, S., Lu, Y., Veith, H.: Counterexample-guided abstraction refinement. In: Emerson, E.A., Sistla, A.P. (eds.) CAV 2000. LNCS, vol. 1855, pp. 154–169. Springer, Heidelberg (2000)
9. Dierks, H., Kupferschmid, S., Larsen, K.G.: Automatic abstraction refinement for timed automata. In: Raskin, J.-F., Thiagarajan, P.S. (eds.) FORMATS 2007. LNCS, vol. 4763, pp. 114–129. Springer, Heidelberg (2007)

10. Ehlers, R., Fass, D., Gerke, M., Peter, H.-J.: Fully symbolic timed model checking using constraint matrix diagrams. In: RTSS, pp. 360–371. IEEE Computer Society (2010)
11. Heizmann, M., Hoenicke, J., Podelski, A.: Refinement of trace abstraction. In: Palsberg, J., Su, Z. (eds.) SAS 2009. LNCS, vol. 5673, pp. 69–85. Springer, Heidelberg (2009)
12. Heizmann, M., Hoenicke, J., Podelski, A.: Software model checking for people who love automata. In: Sharygina, N., Veith, H. (eds.) CAV 2013. LNCS, vol. 8044, pp. 36–52. Springer, Heidelberg (2013)
13. Henzinger, T.A., Jhala, R., Majumdar, R., Sutre, G.: Lazy abstraction. In: Launchbury, J., Mitchell, J.C. (eds.) POPL, pp. 58–70. ACM (2002)
14. Herbreteau, F., Srivathsan, B., Walukiewicz, I.: Better abstractions for timed automata. In: LICS, pp. 375–384. IEEE (2012)
15. Herbreteau, F., Srivathsan, B., Walukiewicz, I.: Lazy abstractions for timed automata. CoRR abs/1301.3127 (2013)
16. Kemper, S., Platzer, A.: Sat-based abstraction refinement for real-time systems. Electr. Notes Theor. Comput. Sci. 182, 107–122 (2007)
17. Kindermann, R., Junttila, T.A., Niemelä, I.: Beyond lassos: Complete smt-based bounded model checking for timed automata. In: Giese, H., Rosu, G. (eds.) FORTE/FMOODS 2012. LNCS, vol. 7273, pp. 84–100. Springer, Heidelberg (2012)
18. Larsen, K.G., Pearson, J., Weise, C., Yi, W.: Clock difference diagrams. Nord. J. Comput. 6(3), 271–298 (1999)
19. Møller, J.B., Lichtenberg, J., Andersen, H.R., Hulgaard, H.: Fully symbolic model checking of timed systems using difference decision diagrams. Electr. Notes Theor. Comput. Sci. 23(2), 88–107 (1999)
20. Nguyen, T.K., Sun, J., Liu, Y., Dong, J.S., Liu, Y.: Improved bdd-based discrete analysis of timed systems. In: Giannakopoulou, D., Méry, D. (eds.) FM 2012. LNCS, vol. 7436, pp. 326–340. Springer, Heidelberg (2012)
21. Sorea, M.: Lazy approximation for dense real-time systems. In: Lakhnech, Y., Yovine, S. (eds.) FORMATS/FTRTFT 2004. LNCS, vol. 3253, pp. 363–378. Springer, Heidelberg (2004)
22. Wang, F.: Efficient verification of timed automata with bdd-like data-structures. In: Zuck, L.D., Attie, P.C., Cortesi, A., Mukhopadhyay, S. (eds.) VMCAI 2003. LNCS, vol. 2575, pp. 189–205. Springer, Heidelberg (2002)
23. Wozna, B., Zbrzezny, A., Penczek, W.: Checking reachability properties for timed automata via sat. Fundam. Inform. 55(2), 223–241 (2003)
24. Yovine, S.: Kronos: A verification tool for real-time systems. STTT 1(1-2), 123–133 (1997)
25. Zbrzezny, A.: Improvements in sat-based reachability analysis for timed automata. Fundam. Inf. 60(1-4), 417–434 (2003)

Statistically Sound Verification and Optimization for Complex Systems*

Yan Zhang, Sriram Sankaranarayanan, and Fabio Somenzi

University of Colorado, Boulder, CO 80309, USA
{yan.zhang,srirams,fabio}@colorado.edu

Abstract. This paper discusses verification and optimization of complex systems with respect to a set of specifications under stochastic parameter variations. We introduce a simulation-based statistically sound model inference approach that considers systems whose responses depend on a few design parameters and many stochastic parameters. The technique iteratively searches over the space of design parameters by alternating between verification and optimization phases. The verification phase uses statistical model checking to check if the model using the current design parameters satisfies the specifications. Failing this, we seek new values of the design parameters for which statistical verification could potentially succeed. This is achieved through repeated simulations for various values of the design and stochastic parameters, and quantile regression to construct a model that predicts the spread of the responses as a function of the design parameters. The resulting model is used to select a new set of values for the design parameters. We evaluate this approach over several benchmark examples. In each case, the performance is improved significantly compared to the nominal design.

1 Introduction

We address the problem of selecting design parameter values for complex systems that are "robust" with respect to varying stochastic parameters. For instance, a control designer often faces the problem of selecting gain values of a controller so that the design is robust under stochastic disturbances and variations in the plant model parameters. Elsewhere, the problem of designing "robust" analog circuits that can function correctly under stochastic process variations is also well known. Thus, the problem of finding appropriate design parameter values for a complex system whose output responses depend on a few controllable (tunable) design parameters, and numerous uncontrollable stochastic parameters with known probability distributions, is quite common. In this work, we present an automatic search method that seeks to adjust the design parameters so that the resulting system satisfies the specifications with a given probability bound.

We introduce an approach that combines simulation, quantile regression [12] and a generalization procedure. The approach iterates between two phases: *verification* and *optimization*. The verification phase determines whether the system is safe given the

---

* This work was supported by the US National Science Foundation (NSF) through grants CNS 1016994 and CCF 1320069. All opinions expressed are those of the authors, and not necessarily of the NSF.

F. Cassez and J.-F. Raskin (Eds.): ATVA 2014, LNCS 8837, pp. 411–427, 2014.

currently chosen design parameters. If not, we search for a new set of values for the design parameters (design point) that can potentially yield a safe system. The new design point is chosen by constructing a relational model that captures the spread of the responses as a function of the design parameters using simulations and *quantile regression*. This relational model is then constructed to search for new design points that potentially satisfy the specifications with the given probability bound. Repeated iterations of this process checks correctness over a sequence of design points, while iteratively refining the relational model, converging to optimal values for the design parameters.

The relational model effectively marginalizes the effects of the stochastic parameters. It is constructed using *quantile regression* to fit through the upper and lower quantiles of the responses as a function of the design parameters, followed by a *generalization* procedure that relaxes the model into a statistical over-approximation of the response. The procedure iterates until it successfully finds a design point that satisfies the specifications, or stops when a new design point cannot be found. In the latter case, we report that we cannot find a safe design point and suggest that the specifications may be too stringent.

The main contribution of this paper is the introduction of a simulation-based statistically sound model inference approach that combines verification and optimization. This problem is hard for formal verification techniques that reason symbolically about the distribution of an output response. In recent years, statistical verification techniques have received increasing attention [24,19,10,22,27,17,13]. They are simulation-based, requiring just the ability to simulate the model efficiently for various values of design and stochastic parameters. Such a technique can be used to place "high confidence" bounds on the probability that a response satisfies a given specification. Statistical model checking (SMC) [24,10] is a family of statistical verification techniques that relies on sequential hypothesis testing [21,11]. An SMC technique checks whether a time-bounded LTL property is satisfied with a certain probability bound by deciding between two mutually exclusive hypotheses through simulation.

SMC provides a "likely yes/no" answer for a system and its specifications. In contrast, we wish to find design points for which the system is likely to satisfy the specifications. A straightforward, but impractical, approach iterates through individual design points, and runs SMC for each of them. Hence, it is desirable to build a model that characterizes the relationship between design parameters and responses. For this purpose, regression-based performance modeling techniques are natural candidates and have been studied extensively [20,15,14,3,26,6]. They use simulation data to fit functions that approximate the true response. However, since the outcome of a regression-based approach is an approximation, rather than a sound model of the response function, few guarantees can be provided. Our previous work attempts to combine regression and hypothesis testing techniques to provide a *statistically sound model inference* approach [25]. A statistically sound model provides an envelope of a response that is guaranteed to contain the corresponding response with a high probability. Such a model is useful when dealing with complex systems, in which case a formally sound model cannot be obtained.

In the control community, similar problems have been considered, such as robust convex optimization [2] and chance-constrained optimization [16]. A classic technique to solve for these problems is known as the scenario approach [4], which provides solutions that guaranteed to be optimal with a desired probability. The similarity between the scenario approach and our approach lies in that both of them deal with uncertainties in a system and provide statistical guarantees on the solutions. However, the scenario approach assumes that the system dynamics are available in a closed form, while our approach only relies on the ability to simulate the system.

To our knowledge, the idea of this paper, which combines quantile regression with SMC is unique. Nevertheless, the use of SMC for tuning model parameters has received some attention in the past. Jha *et al.* present the use of SMC to tune parameters for closed loop controller models in order to satisfy a given set of temporal logic specifications [9]. Their approach uses Monte-Carlo sampling over the design parameter values, wherein the number of simulation runs required to resolve the hypothesis testing problem is used as the fitness function for each design parameter. A similar idea is used by Palaniappan *et al.* to fit parameter values for biological models based on experimental observations as well as model specifications [17]. In their work, SMC is used to derive a fitness function that seeks to measure the fraction of the specifications satisfied by a particular choice of model parameters. Our approach builds a more sophisticated "global" model of how the properties depend on the design parameters using quantile regression, and is expected to use fewer number of simulations.

While our approach considers controllable design parameters, a significant body of work treats problems involving uncontrollable, non-deterministic parameters along with stochastic parameters using SMC. We refer the reader to recent papers by Zuliani *et al.* [8] and Ellen *et al.* [7] that use reinforcement learning techniques to verify the correctness properties under the worst case values of non-deterministic parameters.

The paper is organized as follows. Section 2 presents an overview of the proposed approach. Section 3 formulates the use of quantile regression. Section 4 discusses how to manipulate the model from quantile regression to achieve statistical soundness. Section 5 introduces a method to find new design points that are potentially safe. Section 6 shows applications of the proposed approach.

2 Overview

Consider a system with design parameters $\mathbf{u} \in \mathbb{U}$ and stochastic parameters $\mathbf{x} \in \mathbb{X}$, where $\mathbb{U}$ and $\mathbb{X}$ are the domains of the parameters. Assume that the design parameters are controllable, i.e., we can choose values for them, and the stochastic parameters, following a joint distribution $F(\mathbf{x})$, are uncontrollable. We also assume give nominal design parameters $\mathbf{u}_{nom}$. A response ϕ is defined by a function $r(\mathbf{u}, \mathbf{x})$ where r is computable as a *black-box*, but has an complex analytic form. A specification of such a system has the form $\phi \in [a, b]$, with $a, b \in \mathbb{R}$. We wish to find a design parameter $\mathbf{u}$ that satisfies the specification with probability at least θ_0 (a given probability threshold):

$$\Pr_{\mathbf{x} \sim F(\mathbf{x})} (r(\mathbf{u}, \mathbf{x}) \in [a, b]) \geq \theta_0 , \tag{1}$$

First, we statistically verify whether the system with the nominal parameters $\mathbf{u}_{nom}$ satisfies (1). If the verification fails, we search for new design point $\mathbf{u}_{new} \in \mathbb{U}$.

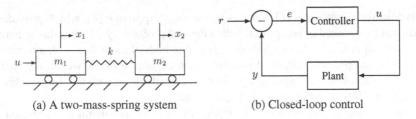

(a) A two-mass-spring system   (b) Closed-loop control

Fig. 1. A two-mass-spring system and the closed-loop system with a controller

Example 1 (A Two-Mass-Spring System). A two-mass-spring system [23] is shown in Figure 1a. It consists of two rigid bodies and a spring. The model is uncertain in which $m_1 = 1.0 \pm 20\%$, $m_2 = 1.0 \pm 20\%$ and $k = 1.0 \pm 20\%$ with appropriate units. We apply force u to m_1 and measure $y = x_2$, the position of m_2. In Figure 1b, a controller is used to track y with r, the reference position.

A lead compensator controls the plant. It has two tunable parameters, the pole $p \in [-1200, -800]$ and the zero $z \in [-1.2, -0.8]$. Nominally, $p = -1000$ and $z = -1$. The goal is to design a controller so that the step response of the system satisfies: (1) the settling time $t \leq 2.5$ and (2) the overshoot $r \leq 15\%$ of the steady state value.

The key idea of the proposed approach is to fit a *relational model* for the response $r(\mathbf{u}, \mathbf{x})$. Let $\mathbb{I}$ be the set of real-valued intervals. A relational model g maps design parameters $\mathbf{u} \in \mathbb{U}$ to intervals $g(\mathbf{u}) \in \mathbb{I}$. In effect, $g(\mathbf{u})$ marginalizes the effects of the stochastic parameters. Such a model attempts to over-approximate the spread of $r(\mathbf{u}, \mathbf{x})$ over $\mathbf{x} \sim F(\mathbf{x})$. The key notion that we seek to satisfy is called *statistical soundness*.

Definition 1 (Statistical Soundness). *Given a probability* $\theta_0 \in (0, 1)$*, a relational model* $g : \mathbb{U} \to \mathbb{I}$ *is* θ_0*-statistically sound if for all* $\mathbf{u} \in \mathbb{U}$

$$\Pr_{\mathbf{x} \sim F(\mathbf{x})} (r(\mathbf{u}, \mathbf{x}) \in g(\mathbf{u})) \geq \theta_0. \tag{2}$$

While constructing an accurate but fully sound relational model is often expensive, if not impossible, a statistically sound model can be used instead with guarantees that are probabilistic rather than absolute.

In Definition 1 there is a universal quantifier over $\mathbf{u}$. Since the response function r is assumed to be a black-box, finding a model that satisfies (2) is not possible. In the proposed approach, we will restrict ourselves to show that (2) is true for some finite subset of design points. Furthermore, checking if a model $g(\mathbf{u})$ is statistically sound at a given design point $\mathbf{u}$ requires detailed knowledge of the function $r(\mathbf{u}, \mathbf{x})$, which is not available. To address this, we will use hypothesis testing techniques such as the sequential Bayesian test to conclude statistical soundness *with high confidence* at a given design point $\mathbf{u}$.

Figure 2 shows the basic flow of the proposed approach. First, using quantile regression, we compute a relational model $\hat{g}(\mathbf{u}) = [\hat{g}_\ell(\mathbf{u}), \hat{g}_u(\mathbf{u})]$ with affine functions $\hat{g}_\ell$ and $\hat{g}_u$, to approximate the response function $r(\mathbf{u}, \mathbf{x})$ with $\mathbf{u} \in \mathbb{U}$ and $\mathbf{x} \in \mathbb{X}$. Quantile regression is carried out using randomly sampled design and stochastic parameters, and the corresponding values of the response. However, $\hat{g}$ is not guaranteed

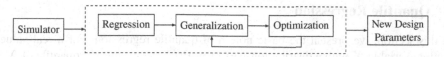

Fig. 2. Basic working flow of the proposed approach

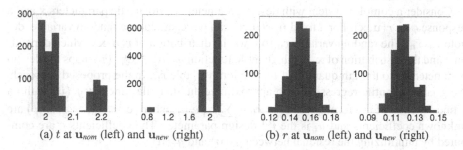

(a) t at $\mathbf{u}_{nom}$ (left) and $\mathbf{u}_{new}$ (right)   (b) r at $\mathbf{u}_{nom}$ (left) and $\mathbf{u}_{new}$ (right)

Fig. 3. Histogram of t (in seconds) and r (percentage) in the two-mass-spring example

to be statistically sound. Next, we check whether the nominal design point $\mathbf{u}_{nom}$ satisfy the specifications under stochastic parameter variations. This is achieved by a generalization technique [25], which derives a relational model $g(\mathbf{u})$ that is θ_0-statistically sound for $\mathbf{u} = \mathbf{u}_{nom}$ with high confidence. Intuitively, the procedure fixes the design parameters to $\mathbf{u}_{nom}$ and samples the stochastic parameters sequentially. A tolerance interval $I : [\ell, u]$ is computed so that a long enough sequence of the observed responses fall in the interval $[\hat{g}_\ell(\mathbf{u}_{nom}) + \ell, \hat{g}_u(\mathbf{u}_{nom}) + u]$. This procedure is guaranteed to yield $g(\mathbf{u}) \equiv [\hat{g}_\ell(\mathbf{u}) + \ell, \hat{g}_u(\mathbf{u}) + u]$ that is statistically sound at $\mathbf{u} = \mathbf{u}_{nom}$, with high confidence. For a specification $\phi \in [a, b]$, if $g(\mathbf{u}_{nom})$ is contained in $[a, b]$, we conclude that with a high probability (which depends on θ_0) the system is safe at $\mathbf{u}_{nom}$. Otherwise, we search for new design point that yields a safe system.

To carry out the search, the response $r(\mathbf{u}, \mathbf{x})$ is modeled by $g(\mathbf{u})$. We then look for a point $\mathbf{u}_1 \in \mathbb{U}$ that has the largest margin from violating the specifications. Since g is statistically sound only at $\mathbf{u}_{nom}$, generalization is applied again so that g becomes statistically sound at $\{\mathbf{u}_{nom}, \mathbf{u}_1\}$. Then we check whether the specifications hold. The procedure continues until either the system is safe at some $\mathbf{u}_i$ at the ith iteration, or a limit on the number of iterations is exceeded, in which case, a failure is returned.

Example 2. Let us continue with Example 1. First, we simulate the system with randomly sampled design and stochastic parameters

$$p \in [-1200, -800], \ z \in [-1.2, -0.8], \ m_1 \in [0.8, 1.2], \ m_2 \in [0.8, 1.2], \ k \in [0.8, 1.2].$$

We use quantile regression to fit a lower and an upper bound function for the responses t and r. For instance, $1.157 + 0.03966p + 0.7071z$ is the lower bound of t, with p and z normalized to $[-1, 1]$. Figure 3 shows the histograms of t and r at $\mathbf{u}_{nom}$ and $\mathbf{u}_{new}$. Apparently, the system violates the specification $r \leq 15\%$ at $\mathbf{u}_{nom}$ ($p = -1000$ and $z = -1$). After optimization, we have $p = -1200$ and $z = -0.928$. The histograms show that both specifications are satisfied.

3 Quantile Regression

In this section, we present the basic notion of quantile regression. For a real-valued random variable X with a distribution $F_X(x) = \Pr(X \leq x)$, the τth quantile of X is defined as $Q_X(\tau) = \inf\{x : F_X(x) \geq \tau\}$. Informally, it is the smallest x such that $\Pr(X \geq x)$ is at most $1 - \tau$.

Consider a complex system with design parameters $\mathbf{u}$, stochastic parameters $\mathbf{x}$ and a response $\phi = r(\mathbf{u}, \mathbf{x})$. For a fixed $\mathbf{u}$, $r(\mathbf{u}, \mathbf{x})$ can be regarded as a random variable, denoted as $\tilde{r}_{\mathbf{u}}$. The random variable $\tilde{r}_{\mathbf{u}}$ follows the distribution of $r(\mathbf{u}, \mathbf{x})$, which depends on r and the distribution of $\mathbf{x}$. A τth quantile function $g_\tau(\mathbf{u}) = Q_{\tilde{r}_{\mathbf{u}}}(\tau)$ maps the design parameters onto the τth quantile of the random variable $\tilde{r}_{\mathbf{u}}$. In the proposed approach, the goal of quantile regression is to approximate the quantile function $g_\tau(\mathbf{u})$ with an affine function of the form $\hat{g}_\tau(\mathbf{u}; \mathbf{c}) = c_0 + \sum_{i=1}^{k} c_i u_i$, where $\mathbf{c} = (c_0, c_1, \ldots, c_k)$ are unknown coefficients and u_i is the ith design parameter. The coefficients $\mathbf{c}$ are computed by minimizing the residual between $g_\tau(\mathbf{u})$ and $\hat{g}_\tau(\mathbf{u})$,

$$\min_{\mathbf{c}=(c_0,c_1,\ldots,c_k)} \|g_\tau(\mathbf{u}) - \hat{g}_\tau(\mathbf{u}; \mathbf{c})\| . \tag{3}$$

Since $g_\tau(\mathbf{u})$ is often not available, (3) is merely conceptually useful. We show a general approach to solve for $\hat{g}_\tau(\mathbf{u}; \mathbf{c})$. For a given set of simulation data with m data points, quantile regression relies on the following penalty function,

$$\rho_\tau(\mathbf{e}) = \sum_{\substack{i=1 \\ e_i \geq 0}}^{m} \tau e_i + \sum_{\substack{i=1 \\ e_i \leq 0}}^{m} (\tau - 1)e_i , \tag{4}$$

where $e_i = r(\mathbf{u}^{(i)}, \mathbf{x}^{(i)}) - \hat{g}_\tau(\mathbf{u}^{(i)})$ are the residuals between the response function and the approximation, evaluated at $(\mathbf{u}^{(i)}, \mathbf{x}^{(i)})$. Here $\mathbf{u}^{(i)}$ and $\mathbf{x}^{(i)}$ refers to the ith observations of the design and the stochastic parameters, respectively. For a fixed τ (except for 0.5), (4) incurs an asymmetric penalty on the positive and the negative side of the residual $\mathbf{e}$. For $\tau > 0.5$ ($\tau < 0.5$), a positive (negative) residual incurs more penalty and thus is minimized. The penalty function (4) leads to the following optimization problem.

$$\min_{\mathbf{c}=(c_0,c_1,\ldots,c_k)} \rho_\tau\left(r(\mathbf{u}, \mathbf{x}) - \hat{g}_\tau(\mathbf{u}; \mathbf{c})\right) . \tag{5}$$

Since (4) is piecewise linear, it has a unique minimum.

The problem in (5) is solved as a linear program [12]. The penalty function in (4) is encoded by adding auxiliary variables $\mathbf{s} = (s_1, \ldots, s_m)$ and $\mathbf{t} = (t_1, \ldots, t_m)$. The auxiliary variables $\mathbf{s}$ and $\mathbf{t}$ correspond to the cases that the response ϕ is greater and less than the approximation $\hat{g}_\tau$, respectively. With them, we write (5) as

$$\min_{\mathbf{c}=(c_0,c_1,\ldots,c_k)} \sum_{i=1}^{m} \tau s_i + \sum_{i=1}^{m} (1 - \tau)t_i$$

subject to $\tag{6}$

$$r\left(\mathbf{u}^{(i)}, \mathbf{x}^{(i)}\right) - \hat{g}_\tau\left(\mathbf{u}^{(i)}; \mathbf{c}\right) = s_i - t_i, \quad i = 1, 2, \ldots, m,$$

$$\mathbf{s} \geq 0, \ \mathbf{t} \geq 0.$$

To minimize the objective function, at most one of s_i and t_i should be non-zero. The first constraint forces that either **s** or **t** equals to the residuals. The last two constraints ensures **s** and **t** to be non-negative (notice the sign change in the second sum of the objective function in (4) and (6)).

It is important to understand that the formulation in (6) only solves for $\tau \in (0, 1)$. For $\tau = 0$ and $\tau = 1$, (6) fails to find the maximum lower bound and the minimum upper bound. This is because in the two cases, (4) penalizes only one side of the residuals and thus allows the approximation to behave arbitrarily on the opposite side. Such a solution is meaningless in practice. For instance, for $\tau = 0$, the lower bound function of t in Example 2 can be either $0 + 0p + 0z$ or $-100 + 0p + 0z$, with the same objective value of 0. To obtain a meaningful lower (upper) bound approximation from quantile regression, we set τ close to 0 (1). Note that $\hat{g}_\tau$ is not necessarily close to the true lower (upper) bound. In the case that there are outliers in the simulation data, $\hat{g}_\tau$ can be distant from the true bound. In contrast, $\hat{g}_\tau$ tends to leave out the outliers and only concerns with the normal data. Such a property is often desirable when dealing with data from practical settings. In the following, we write $\hat{g}_\ell$ and $\hat{g}_u$ to indicate the estimated lower and the upper bound, respectively. By default, we assume that $\hat{g}_\ell$ is computed with $\tau = 0.01$ and $\hat{g}_u$ with $\tau = 0.99$.

4 Generalization and Verification

As mentioned in Section 2, $\hat{g}_\ell$ and $\hat{g}_u$ form a relational model $\hat{g}(\mathbf{u}) \equiv [\hat{g}_\ell(\mathbf{u}), \hat{g}_u(\mathbf{u})]$. Clearly, $\hat{g}$ is not necessarily statistically sound (see Definition 1) and thus does not provide guarantees on the behavior of the underlying system. We now present a generalization technique that converts $\hat{g}$ into a statistically sound model with high likelihood, and statistically verifies whether specifications of the form $\phi \in [a, b]$ are satisfied.

Generalization. Recall that Definition 1 defines statistical soundness for all $\mathbf{u} \in \mathbb{U}$. Such a condition is too strong since our goal is to (1) learn whether the specifications hold at $\mathbf{u}_{nom}$ and if not, (2) find a new point $\mathbf{u}_{new}$ that satisfies them. Hence we are only concerned with statistical soundness at these two design points.

Once the design parameters are fixed, $\hat{g}$ becomes an interval. We derive a tolerance interval $[\ell, u]$ so that the interval $[\hat{g}_\ell(\mathbf{u}) + \ell, \hat{g}_u(\mathbf{u}) + u]$ is a statistically sound bound for the response ϕ under stochastic parameter variations. The procedure is based on sequential Bayesian test which is briefly reviewed here.[1] Sequential Bayesian test investigates statistical hypotheses through a sequence of observations and determine which one should be accepted. It computes Bayes factor

$$B = \frac{\Pr(z_1, \dots, z_N \mid \mathcal{H}_1)}{\Pr(z_1, \dots, z_N \mid \mathcal{H}_2)}, \quad z_i = \begin{cases} 1, & \mathcal{H}_1 \vdash s_i \\ 0, & \mathcal{H}_2 \vdash s_i \end{cases},$$

where $\mathcal{H}_1$ and $\mathcal{H}_2$ are mutually exclusive hypotheses, each z_i is a random variate of a Bernoulli random variable Z, and $\mathcal{H} \vdash s$ is interpreted as s is in favor of $\mathcal{H}$. A large Bayes factor indicates that the observed data support $\mathcal{H}_1$ over $\mathcal{H}_2$. Thus we specify a

---

[1] The interested readers are referred to Kass and Raftery [11] and Zhang *et al.* [25].

Data: Model $\hat{g}(\mathbf{u}) = [\hat{g}_\ell, \hat{g}_u]$, Design Parameters $\mathbf{u}$, Probability θ_0, Threshold T
Result: Tolerance Interval $[\ell, u]$, Model $g(\mathbf{u})$
$K = -\log(T+1)/\log\theta_0 - 1$;
$\ell, u, count = 0$;
while $count < K$ **do**
$\quad$ $\mathbf{x}$ = Sample the stochastic parameter space ;
$\quad$ ϕ = Simulate the system at design parameters $\mathbf{u}$ and measure response ;
$\quad$ **if** $\hat{g}_\ell(\mathbf{u}) + \ell \le \phi \le \hat{g}_u(\mathbf{u}) + u$ **then**
$\quad\quad$ $count = count + 1$;
$\quad\quad$ continue ;
$\quad$ **else**
$\quad\quad$ $count = 0$;
$\quad\quad$ $\ell, u = \min(\phi - \hat{g}_\ell(\mathbf{u}), \ell)$, $\max(\phi - \hat{g}_u(\mathbf{u}), u)$;
$\quad$ **end**
end
Return $[\ell, u]$, $[\hat{g}_\ell(\mathbf{u}) + \ell, \hat{g}_u(\mathbf{u}) + u]$;

Algorithm 1. Generalization that achieves statistical soundness at fixed $\mathbf{u}$

threshold T such that we accept $\mathcal{H}_1$ when B grows beyond T, and accept $\mathcal{H}_2$ when it falls below $1/T$. Usually $\mathcal{H}_1$ and $\mathcal{H}_2$ have the form $\Pr(\Psi) \ge \theta_0$ and $\Pr(\Psi) < \theta_0$, where θ_0 is a specified probability and Ψ denotes the assertion

$$r(\mathbf{u}, \mathbf{x}) \in [\hat{g}_\ell(\mathbf{u}) + \ell, \hat{g}_u(\mathbf{u}) + u], \text{ for fixed } \mathbf{u} \text{ and } \mathbf{x} \sim F(\mathbf{x}), \qquad (7)$$

The goal is to derive proper ℓ and u for given θ_0 and T such that $\mathcal{H}_1$ is accepted.

Algorithm 1 shows the generalization procedure to derive a tolerance interval to achieve statistical soundness at fixed design parameters. The inputs are the model $\hat{g}(\mathbf{u}) = [\hat{g}_\ell(\mathbf{u}), \hat{g}_u(\mathbf{u})]$, fixed design parameters $\mathbf{u}$, a probability θ_0 which indicates the desired probability that (7) should happen, and a Bayes factor threshold T. The algorithm first computes a sequence length K with the specified θ_0 and T. Intuitively, it is the minimum number of consecutive supportive observations required to accept $\mathcal{H}_1$ for the given θ_0 and T. Then the tolerance interval $[\ell, u]$, as well as a *count* variable, is initialized to 0. The *count* variable records the number of consecutive supportive observations. Next, we sample the stochastic parameters $\mathbf{x}$ according to the distribution $F(\mathbf{x})$ and simulate the system to obtain the response ϕ. The observation supports $\mathcal{H}_1$ if (7) holds. In this case, the variable *count* is incremented, terminating when it reaches K. Otherwise, *count* is reset to 0, and ℓ and u are updated to satisfy (7).

One may have noticed that Algorithm 1 did not employ the comparison between the Bayes factor B and its threshold T. Instead, it derives a sequence length K and lets a *count* variable grows towards K. In fact, there is a natural correspondence between *count* and B, as well as K and T (see Zhang et al. [25] for details). An important observation is that *count* is only incremented when we find a supportive observation. Therefore, for fixed θ_0 and T, that *count* reaches K is equivalent to that the Bayes factor B grows to at least T.

Theorem 1. *Algorithm 1 terminates and when it terminates, we have $B \ge T$.*

Verification. Algorithm 1 yields a tolerance interval $[\ell, u]$ and a model

$$g(\mathbf{u}) = [\hat{g}_\ell(\mathbf{u}) + \ell, \hat{g}_u(\mathbf{u}) + u] \tag{8}$$

that is θ_0 statistically sound at the fixed design parameters. It means that for a fixed $\mathbf{u}$, we have a high level of confidence to claim that the response ϕ has a probability of at least θ_0 to lie in the interval (8). It has been shown that the level of confidence is linked to the Bayes factor threshold T such that the type I/II error is bounded by $\frac{1}{T+1}$ [10,27]. Hence with large θ_0 and T, the interval (8) is almost an over-approximation of the response ϕ under stochastic parameter variations. To verify whether specifications $\phi \in [a, b]$ hold at some $\mathbf{u}$, we simply check whether (8) is contained in $[a, b]$. If yes, we conclude that with a confidence level of at least $1 - \frac{1}{T+1}$, the system is safe with a probability of at least θ_0 at $\mathbf{u}$. Otherwise, we continue to search for new design point.

5   Optimization

To find a new design point, we introduce an iterative procedure. At the ith iteration, we try to find a candidate $\mathbf{u}_{new}^{(i)}$ that is safe *with respect to the model in* (8). We may fail if either the specifications are too stringent or our approximation is too excessive. In these cases, we stop and report that for $\mathbf{u} \in \mathbb{U}$ and $\mathbf{x} \in \mathbb{X}$, we cannot find a design point which satisfies all the specifications. Suppose $\mathbf{u}_{new}^{(i)}$ is found. Since (8) is not guaranteed to be statistically sound at $\mathbf{u}_{new}^{(i)}$, we apply generalization so that (8) becomes statistically sound at $\mathbf{u}_{new}^{(i)}$, and check whether the system is safe there. If yes, $\mathbf{u}_{new}^{(i)}$ is the final design point. Otherwise, we try again with the updated model in (8). After the ith iteration, $\mathbf{u}_{new}^{(i)}$ is included in the set of points at which (8) is statistically sound.

It is easy to pick up a candidate point from (8) that satisfies the specifications. However, an arbitrary choice can easily lead to a failed attempt in verification. As a consequence, more iterations and thus more simulations would be required. Therefore, the candidate should be the one that is most likely to satisfy the specifications. Our solution is to search for the point that has the largest margin from violating the specifications using the following linear program:

$$\max_{\mathbf{u}_{new} \in \mathbb{U}} (b - \hat{g}_u(\mathbf{u}_{new}) - u) + (\hat{g}_\ell(\mathbf{u}_{new}) + \ell - a)$$

subject to $\hspace{8cm}$ (9)

$$a \le \hat{g}_\ell(\mathbf{u}_{new}) + \ell \le \hat{g}_u(\mathbf{u}_{new}) + u \le b.$$

In the case of multiple specifications, (9) consists of multiple constraints, each corresponding to a specification. Also, the objective function of becomes the sum of the margin for each specification. Clearly, (9) is infeasible if and only if we cannot find any candidate.

6   Experimental Evaluation

We present four applications: (1) a motor with a rigid arm controlled by a PI controller, (2) a ring oscillator circuit modeled at the transistor-level, (3) an insulin pump that controls the blood glucose level of diabetic patients, and (4) an aircraft flight control model.

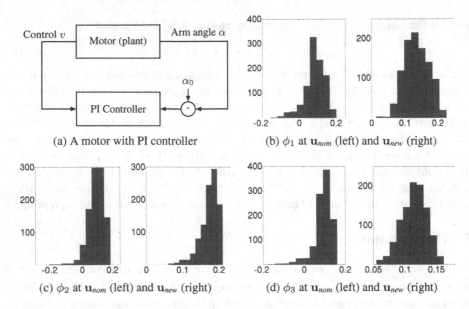

(a) A motor with PI controller   (b) ϕ_1 at $\mathbf{u}_{nom}$ (left) and $\mathbf{u}_{new}$ (right)

(c) ϕ_2 at $\mathbf{u}_{nom}$ (left) and $\mathbf{u}_{new}$ (right)   (d) ϕ_3 at $\mathbf{u}_{nom}$ (left) and $\mathbf{u}_{new}$ (right)

Fig. 4. A motor with a rigid arm controlled by a PI controller is shown in (a). Figure (b), (c) and (d) shows the histograms of ϕ_1, ϕ_2 and ϕ_3.

All models have stochastic parameter variations. We use our approach to search for a design point that maximizes the empirical probability of satisfying the given specifications. The experiments are performed on a AMD Athlon II quad-core 2.8 GHz CPU with 4 G RAM. The proposed approach is implemented in Python-2.7.

6.1   Motor with PI Controller

Figure 4a shows a DC motor with an attached rigid arm controller by a PI controller. We control the input voltage v of the motor which determines the angle α of the rigid arm. The goal is to set α to a reference α_0, thus holding the arm at a constant angle. The design parameters are the proportional gain K_p and the integral gain K_i. There are 5 stochastic parameters, such as the resistance and the inductance in the motor model.

The step response $\alpha(t)$ should satisfy the following specifications. Over $t \in [0, 2]$, $\alpha(t) \leq 1.5$. The specification is $\phi_1 \geq 0$ where

$$(1)\ \phi_1 = \min(1.5 - \alpha(t)),\ t \in [0, 2];$$

Over $t \in [2, T]$ where T is the total simulation time, $\alpha(t) \in [0.8, 1.2]$. The specifications are $\phi_2 \geq 0$ and $\phi_3 \geq 0$ where

$$(2)\ \phi_2 = \min(\alpha(t) - 0.8),\ (3)\ \phi_3 = \min(1.2 - \alpha(t)),\ t \in [2, T].$$

The nominal design point $\mathbf{u}_{nom}$ is $K_p = -2.5$ and $K_i = -1$. Our goal is to verify whether the specifications hold at $\mathbf{u}_{nom}$ and if not, find a new design point $\mathbf{u}_{new}$ from $K_p \in [-3, -2]$ and $K_i \in [-1.2, -0.8]$ to satisfy the specifications.

Table 1. Results for the motor example ($\theta_0 = 0.95$ and $T = 100$)

Spec	MC-1000		Proposed Approach							
	u_{nom}	u_{new}	I_{nom}	Sim_R	T_R	Iters	Sim_W	T_W	T_O	I_{new}
1	93.1%	100%	$[-0.08, 0.19]$				307			$[0.06, 0.22]$
2	95.8%	100%	$[-0.13, 0.17]$	500	189 s	1	247	148 s	1 s	$[0.06, 0.22]$
3	95.5%	100%	$[-0.13, 0.16]$				398			$[0.06, 0.17]$
all	92.1%	100%	-				-			-

The system is designed in Matlab® with Simulink®. Table 1 shows the results of this example. The column "MC-1000" shows the yields of each specification at u_{nom} and u_{new} estimated through 1000 Monte-Carlo simulations. Sim_R and T_R are the number of simulations and time spent, respectively, for quantile regression; Sim_W, T_W represent the same for generalization and Sim_O, T_O for optimization. "Iters" is the number of iterations of our search. Finally, I_{nom} and I_{new} are the statistically sound performance bounds at u_{nom} and u_{new}.

First, notice that the the system fails to satisfy all the three specifications at u_{nom} as shown by the Monte-Carlo simulations. The proposed approach makes the same conclusion by showing that the performance bounds I_{nom} are not contained in the specifications. The bounds are derived from a relational model g that is statistically sound at u_{nom}. Next, we pick up a new design point u_{new} from the model g according to the linear program (9), and check whether it satisfies the specifications. In fact it does, as shown by the performance bounds I_{new}. Having yields of 100%, the conclusion is also confirmed by the Monte-Carlo simulations at u_{new}. The new design parameters for this application is $K_p = -2$ and $K_i = -0.8$. To obtain this result, 500 simulations are spent in quantile regression and 398 simulations in generalization.[2]

Figure 4b, 4c and 4d present the histograms of the responses ϕ_1, ϕ_2 and ϕ_3 at u_{nom} and u_{new}. We choose $\theta_0 = 0.95$ and $T = 100$ in generalization. This means that the probability that the intervals under I_{nom} and I_{new} are the true performance bounds is at least 95%. Given that, we have at least $100\% - \frac{1}{T+1} \times 100\% \approx 99\%$ confidence that u_{new} satisfies the specifications. Yield estimation from the Monte-Carlo simulations is a strong support to our conclusion.

6.2   Ring Oscillator

Figure 5 shows a ring oscillator. It is is designed to oscillate at a frequency f of 2.1 GHz with a power consumption w of 5 mW. However, a real circuit suffers from process variations, such as the doping concentration and oxide layer thickness, resulting in deviation from the ideal performance. The performance specifications are

$$(1)\; f \in [2.0, 2.2]\text{GHz}\,, \quad (2)\; w \leq 5.5\,\text{mW}\,.$$

We choose 12 design parameters. They are the channel widths and lengths of each transistor. Also, 54 stochastic parameters are considered, arising from process variations

---

[2] Simulation data are reusable with respect to different specifications.

Table 2. Results for the 3-stage ring oscillator ($\theta_0 = 0.95$ and $T = 100$)

Spec	MC-1000			Proposed Approach						
	$\mathbf{u}_{nom}$	$\mathbf{u}_{new}$	I_{nom}	Sim_R	T_R	Iters	Sim_W	T_W	T_O	I_{new}
1	95.8%	98.9%	[2.05, 2.23]GHz				309			[2.04, 2.19]GHz
2	60.1%	100%	[5.18, 5.85]mW	500	307 s	1	332	233 s	1 s	[4.75, 5.41]mW
all	60.0%	98.9%	-				-			-

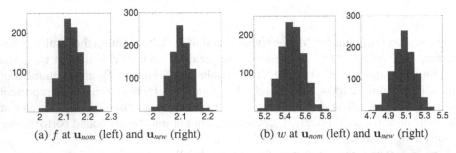

(a) f at $\mathbf{u}_{nom}$ (left) and $\mathbf{u}_{new}$ (right)   (b) w at $\mathbf{u}_{nom}$ (left) and $\mathbf{u}_{new}$ (right)

Fig. 6. Histograms of f (left, GHz) and w (right, mW) at in the ring oscillator

in the transistor parameters. The goal is to verify whether the two specifications can be satisfied under the nominal design point and if not, choose new values for the width and length of each transistor.

We use LTSpice® [1], a freely available SPICE simulator, to simulate the circuit. The results are shown in Table 2. The columns have the same meanings as in Table 1. The circuit at the nominal widths and lengths has a poor performance in the power consumption w, which has a yield of only 60.1%. The upper bound of I_{nom} violates the specification (2) excessively. Our approach finds a new design point that has performance bounds

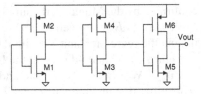

Fig. 5. A 3-stage ring oscillator

that satisfies both specifications, which is confirmed by the Monte-Carlo simulations. The yield is boosted from 60% to almost 100%. Figure 6 shows the histograms of the two responses, f and w, at $\mathbf{u}_{nom}$ and $\mathbf{u}_{new}$. Obviously, we have a significant performance improvement.

6.3 Insulin Pump

We study a previously published model of an insulin pump used by type-1 diabetic patients [18,5]. Our model incorporates a physiological model of the human insulin-glucose response from Dalla-Man *et al.* [5], models of sensor errors and a typical pump usage by type-1 diabetic patients [18]. A type-1 diabetic patient uses their insulin pump with at least three "design parameters" that include (a) the *basal rate* (basal) that represents the rate at which background insulin is delivered, (b) the insulin-to-carbohydrates

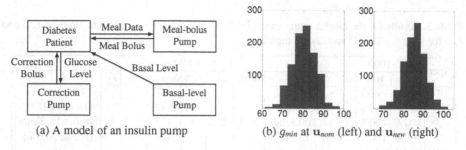

(a) A model of an insulin pump   (b) g_{min} at $\mathbf{u}_{nom}$ (left) and $\mathbf{u}_{new}$ (right)

Fig. 7. A model of an insulin pump (left) and the histograms of $\min(g(t))$, the minimum glucose level during simulation (right)

ratio (icRatio) that controls how much bolus insulin is to be administered to the patient for each gram of carbohydrate to be consumed, and (c) a *correction factor* (cor) to correct blood glucose levels that are higher than normal. Clinically, these values are tuned manually by a physician upon close observation of the patient's blood glucose levels, meal and sleep patterns over time. Our study attempts to automate this choice assuming that personalized models are available for patients.

The stochastic parameters include the time of the meal, the amount of carbohydrates in each meal, sensor noise and the discrepancies between the planned and actual meals [18]. Overall, the model has 3 design parameters and 10 stochastic parameters. We used virtual patient parameters published for 30 patients by Dalla Man et al. [5]. Our study here focuses on a single model patient. The total simulation time is 1400 min.

There are many important correctness properties. Ideally, the human blood glucose level should be between 70 mg/dl and 180 mg/dl. A level lower than 70 mg/dl is called *hypoglycemia*, and a level higher than 180 mg/dl is called *hyperglycemia*. In practice, hypoglycemia is usually much more critical than hyperglycemia since it can cause seizures, unconsciousness and even death. Therefore, our goal is to control the blood glucose level higher than 70 mg/dl at all time time and reduce the time that the patient stays in hyperglycemia as much as possible.

The above description yields the following specifications. The blood glucose level $g(t)$ should be between 70 mg/dl and 240 mg/dl over $t \in [0, T]$ where T is the total simulation time.

$$(1) \ \min(g(t)) \geq 70 \, \text{mg/dl}, \ (2) \ \max(g(t)) \leq 240 \, \text{mg/dl};$$

The maximum period p_h for hyperglycemia is at most 240 min, and the total time in hyperglycemia is at most 20% of the total simulation time.

$$(3) \ p_h \leq 240 \, \text{min}, \ (4) \ r_h \leq 20\%.$$

Table 3 shows the results of applying our approach to the data for model that pertains to a single patient, whose insulin pump is tuned to a nominal design point basal $= 0.3$, icRatio $= 0.06$ and cor $= 0.06$. Observe that the pump works well except that it has a 3.8% chance of dangerous hypoglycemia. *Our approach lowers this chance to 0.4%*, a significant lowering of a risk. Another observation comes from the number

Table 3. Results for the insulin pump example ($\theta_0 = 0.95$ and $T = 100$). The units of I_{nom} and I_{new} for specification (1) and (2) are mg/dl.

Spec	MC-1000			Proposed Approach						
	u_{nom}	u_{new}	I_{nom}	Sim_R	T_R	Iters	Sim_W	T_W	T_O	I_{new}
1	96.2%	99.6%	[68.12, 95.28]				567			[70.0, 102.1]
2	100%	100%	[186.6, 219.3]				549			[189.2, 227.0]
3	100%	100%	[41.44, 209.8]min	500	624s	3	423	701s	4s	[48.6, 213.3]min
4	100%	100%	[6.0%, 18.8%]				420			[6.2%, 20.0%]
all	96.2%	99.6%					-			-

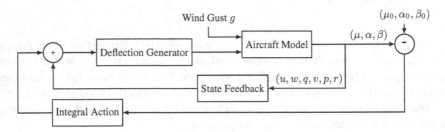

Fig. 8. An aircraft flight control model

of iterations. Unlike the other examples, our approach takes 3 iterations to find a new design point. It indicates that the system has a relatively small margin from violating the specifications, as shown by I_{new}. The new design point basal = 0.225, icRatio = 0.080 and cor = 0.049. Histograms of $\min(g(t))$ at u_{nom} and u_{new} are shown in Figure 7b.

6.4   Aircraft Flight Control System

Figure 8 shows a model of the flight control system in an aircraft. This model is available in Matlab® R2014a Robust Control Toolbox™. The aircraft is modeled as a 6th-order state-space system. The state variables include the velocity on x, y and z-body axis (u, v, w), the pitch rate q, the roll rate p and the yaw rate r. These variables together with three responses, the flight-path bank angle μ, the angle of attack α and the sideslip angle β, are available to the controller. The controller, which consists of a state feedback control and an integral control, is designed to generate the deflections of the elevators, the ailerons and the rudder so that a good tracking performance is maintained on the responses with respect to the reference μ_0, α_0 and β_0.

The controller has two gain matrices, K_x and K_i, that maps the controller inputs to deflections. K_x is a 3×6 state-feedback matrix, and K_i is a 3×3 matrix for integrating the three tracking errors. In all, we have 27 design parameters. The stochastic parameters arise from uncertainties in the state matrix and the input matrices along with the stochastic wind disturbance. In all, we have 73 stochastic parameters. The following specifications concern the step response of $\mu(t)$, $\alpha(t)$ and $\beta(t)$. First, the settling time of each trajectory should be smaller than 7.5 s.

$$(1)\ t_\mu \leq 7.5\,\text{s}, \quad (2)\ t_\alpha \leq 7.5\,\text{s}, \quad (3)\ t_\beta \leq 7.5\,\text{s};$$

Table 4. Results for the aircraft flight control example ($\theta_0 = 0.95$ and $T = 100$)

Spec	MC-1000		I_{nom}	Proposed Approach						
	$\mathbf{u}_{nom}$	$\mathbf{u}_{new}$		Sim_R	T_R	Iters	Sim_W	T_W	T_O	I_{new}
1	100%	100%	$[1.40, 6.47]$s				326			$[1.98, 6.42]$s
2	76.7%	99.9%	$[5.00, 7.79]$s				332			$[5.86, 7.48]$s
3	100%	100%	$[3.82, 6.23]$s				479			$[3.80, 6.34]$s
4	100%	100%	$[3.8\%, 9.5\%]$	500	307s	1	399	341s	2s	$[0, 11.7\%]$
5	82.5%	99.5%	$[0, 26\%]$				402			$[0, 19.5\%]$
6	100%	100%	$[5.3\%, 9.4\%]$				507			$[7.7\%, 12.7\%]$
all	74.1%	99.5%	-							-

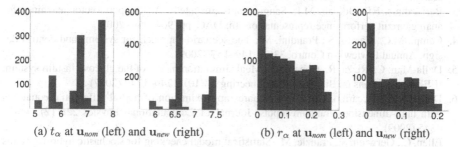

(a) t_α at $\mathbf{u}_{nom}$ (left) and $\mathbf{u}_{new}$ (right)   (b) r_α at $\mathbf{u}_{nom}$ (left) and $\mathbf{u}_{new}$ (right)

Fig. 9. Histograms of t_α (left, in seconds) and r_α (right, as percentage) in the aircraft flight control model

Also, the overshoot should be less than 20% of the steady state value.

$$(4)\ r_\mu \leq 20\%,\ (5)\ r_\alpha \leq 20\%,\ (6)\ r_\beta \leq 20\%.$$

Table 4 presents the results of applying our approach. Observe that the specification (2) and (5) are not satisfies at $\mathbf{u}_{nom}$, confirmed by both the Monte-Carlo simulations and the performance bounds I_{nom}. We use 500 simulations in quantile regression and 507 in generalization, and find a new design point in one iteration. The new point leads to better performance on t_α and r_α and thus a boost of the overall yield from 74.1% to 99.5%. Figure 9 shows the histograms of t_α and r_α at $\mathbf{u}_{nom}$ and $\mathbf{u}_{new}$, which clearly shows the performance improvement.

Now let us compare I_{nom} with I_{new}. Note that except for t_α and r_α in specification (2) and (5), all the other responses have larger performance bounds at $\mathbf{u}_{new}$ but still satisfy the specifications. It indicates that the proposed approach trades off the performance of the other responses so that (2) and (5) can be satisfied.

7 Conclusion

In this paper, we have introduced a statistically sound model inference approach for the verification and optimization of complex systems. First, using quantile regression, a relational model is computed to approximate the marginalized response function. Then a generalization procedure is employed to relax the model so that it becomes statistically sound at the nominal design point. The resulting model is used to verify the specifications. If fail, the model is then used to search for a new design point. We show several interesting examples that through the application of our approach, the yield of these systems are improved significantly.

References

1. LTSpice: A high performance SPICE simulator, schematic capture and waveform viewer, `http://www.linear.com/designtools/software/`
2. Ben-Tal, A., Nemirovski, A.: Robust convex optimization. Mathematics of Operations Research 23(4), 769–805 (1998)
3. Bernardinis, F.D., Jordan, M.I., Sangiovanni-Vincentelli, A.: Support vector machines for analog circuit performance representation. In: DAC, pp. 964–969 (2003)
4. Campi, M.C., Garatti, S., Prandini, M.: The scenario approach for systems and control design. Annual Reviews in Control 33(2), 149–157 (2009)
5. Dalla-Man, C., Rizza, R., Cobelli, C.: Meal simulation model of the glucose-insulin system. IEEE Transactions on Biomedical Engineering 54(10), 1740–1749 (2007)
6. Doostan, A., Iaccarino, G.: A least-squares approximation of partial differential equations with high-dimensional random inputs. Journal of Computational Physics 228(12), 4332–4345 (2009)
7. Ellen, C., Gerwinn, S., Fränzle, M.: Statistical model checking for stochastic hybrid systems involving nondeterminism over continuous domains (2014), to appear in a special issue on Statistical Model Checking
8. Henriques, D., Martins, J., Zuliani, P., Platzer, A., Clarke, E.: Statistical model checking for markov decision processes. In: QEST 2012 (2012)
9. Jha, S.K., Datta, R., Langmead, C., Jha, S., Sassano, E.: Synthesis of insulin pump controllers from safety specifications using bayesian model validation. In: Proceedings of 10th Asia Pacific Bioinformatics Conference, APBC (2012)
10. Jha, S.K., Clarke, E.M., Langmead, C.J., Legay, A., Platzer, A., Zuliani, P.: A bayesian approach to model checking biological systems. In: Degano, P., Gorrieri, R. (eds.) CMSB 2009. LNCS, vol. 5688, pp. 218–234. Springer, Heidelberg (2009)
11. Kass, R.E., Raftery, A.E.: Bayes factors. Journal of the American Statistical Association 90(430), 774–795 (1995)
12. Koenker, R.: Quantile regression, vol. 38. Cambridge University Press (2005)
13. Lagoa, C.M., Dabbene, F., Tempo, R.: Hard bounds on the probability of performance with application to circuit analysis. IEEE Transactions on Circuits and Systems 55(10), 3178–3187 (2008)
14. Li, X.: Finding deterministic solution from underdetermined equation: large-scale performance variability modeling of analog/RF circuits. IEEE Transactions on Computer-Aided Design of Integrated Circuits and Systems 29(11), 1661–1668 (2010)
15. Mitev, A., Marefat, M., Ma, D., Wang, J.M.: Principle Hessian direction-based parameter reduction for interconnect networks with process variation. IEEE Transactions on VLSI Systems 18(9), 1337–1347 (2010)
16. Nemirovski, A., Shapiro, A.: Convex approximations of chance constrained programs. SIAM Journal on Optimization 17(4), 969–996 (2006)
17. Palaniappan, S.K., Gyori, B.M., Liu, B., Hsu, D., Thiagarajan, P.S.: Statistical model checking based calibration and analysis of bio-pathway models. In: Gupta, A., Henzinger, T.A. (eds.) CMSB 2013. LNCS, vol. 8130, pp. 120–134. Springer, Heidelberg (2013)

18. Sankaranarayanan, S., Miller, C., Raghunathan, R., Ravanbakhsh, H., Fainekos, G.: A model-based approach to synthesizing insulin infusion pump usage parameters for diabetic patients. In: 2012 50th Annual Allerton Conference on Communication, Control, and Computing (Allerton), pp. 1610–1617 (2012)

19. Sen, K., Viswanathan, M., Agha, G.: Statistical model checking of black-box probabilistic systems. In: Alur, R., Peled, D.A. (eds.) CAV 2004. LNCS, vol. 3114, pp. 202–215. Springer, Heidelberg (2004)

20. Singhee, A., Rutenbar, R.A.: Beyond low-order statistical response surfaces: latent variable regression for efficient, highly nonlinear fitting. In: DAC, pp. 256–261 (2007)

21. Wald, A.: Sequential tests of statistical hypotheses. The Annals of Mathematical Statistics 16(2), 117–186 (1945)

22. Wang, Y.C., Komuravelli, A., Zuliani, P., Clarke, E.M.: Analog circuit verification by statistical model checking. In: ASP-DAC, pp. 1–6 (2011)

23. Wie, B., Bernstein, D.S.: A benchmark problem for robust control design. In: American Control Conference, pp. 961–962 (May 1990)

24. Younes, H.L.S., Simmons, R.G.: Probabilistic verification of discrete event systems using acceptance sampling. In: Brinksma, E., Larsen, K.G. (eds.) CAV 2002. LNCS, vol. 2404, pp. 223–235. Springer, Heidelberg (2002)

25. Zhang, Y., Sankaranarayanan, S., Somenzi, F., Chen, X., Ábraham, E.: From statistical model checking to statistical model inference: Characterizing the effect of process variations in analog circuits. In: ICCAD (2013)

26. Zhang, Y., Sankaranarayanan, S., Somenzi, F., Chen, X., Ábraham, E.: Sparse statistical model inference for analog circuits under process variations. In: ASP-DAC, pp. 449–454 (2014)

27. Zuliani, P., Platzer, A., Clarke, E.M.: Bayesian statistical model checking with application to stateflow/simulink verification. Formal Methods in System Design 43(2), 338–367 (2013)

Author Index

Ábrahám, Erika   146
Aiswarya, C.   1
Alberti, Francesco   18
André, Étienne   242

Becker, Bernd   297
Belo Lourenço, Cláudio   24
Boigelot, Bernard   31
Bourke, Timothy   47
Bouyer, Patricia   64
Bozzano, Marco   81
Brázdil, Tomáš   98

Chatterjee, Krishnendu   98
Chmelík, Martin   98
Cimatti, Alessandro   81

Dang, Thao   115
David, Alexandre   129
Dehnert, Christian   146

Fan, Dongrui   264
Fijalkow, Nathanaël   163
Forejt, Vojtěch   98
Frade, Maria João   24

Gardy, Patrick   64
Gastin, Paul   1
Ghilardi, Silvio   18
Grumberg, Orna   348
Guck, Dennis   168
Guldstrand Larsen, Kim   129
Gupta, Ashutosh   185

Hatefi, Hassan   168
Herbreteau, Frédéric   31
Höfner, Peter   47

Iosif, Radu   201

Jansen, Nils   146
Jensen, Peter G.   129
Jiao, Li   396

Katoen, Joost-Pieter   146
Keiren, Jeroen J.A.   219
Komárková, Zuzana   235
Kovács, Laura   185
Kragl, Bernhard   185
Křetínský, Jan   98, 235
Kuperberg, Denis   163
Kupferman, Orna   348
Kwiatkowska, Marta   98

Le, Dinh-Thuan   242
Legay, Axel   129
Leroux, Jérôme   248
Lime, Didier   129
Liu, Yang   242
Lv, Yi   264

Mai, Phuong-Nam   242
Mainz, Isabelle   31
Malik, Sharad   330
Markey, Nicolas   64, 281
Mattarei, Cristian   81

Narayan Kumar, K.   1
Nguyen, Huu-Vu   242
Nguyen, Van-Tinh   242

Parker, David   98
Penelle, Vincent   248
Petrucci, Laure   242
Pham-Duy, Bao-Trung   242

Quan, Thanh-Tho   242

Reimer, Sven   297
Rogalewicz, Adam   201
Rosenblum, David S.   364
Ruijters, Enno   168

Sánchez, Alejandro   314
Sánchez, César   314
Sankaranarayanan, Sriram   411
Sauer, Matthias   297
Schubert, Tobias   297
Sethi, Divjyot   330

Shalev, Noa   115
Sharygina, Natasha   18
Sheinvald, Sarai   348
Sørensen, Mathias Grund   129
Somenzi, Fabio   411
Sousa Pinto, Jorge   24
Stoelinga, Mariëlle   168
Strejček, Jan   380
Su, Guoxin   364
Sun, Luming   264
Sutre, Grégoire   248

Taankvist, Jakob H.   129
Talupur, Muralidhar   330
Timmer, Mark   168
Tonetta, Stefano   81
Trtík, Marek   380

Ujma, Mateusz   98

van Glabbeek, Rob   47
Vester, Steen   281
Vojnar, Tomáš   201
Voronkov, Andrei   185

Wang, Weifeng   396
Wesselink, Wieger   219
Willemse, Tim A.C.   219
Wimmer, Ralf   146
Wu, Peng   264

Ye, Xiaochun   264

Zhang, Yan   411